D0390891

Time Out

San Francisco

timeout.com/sanfrancisco

Penguin Books

PENGUIN BOOKS

Published by the Penguin Group
Penguin Books Ltd, 80 Strand, London WC2R ORL, England
Penguin Books USA Inc., 375 Hudson Street, New York, New York 10014, USA
Penguin Books Australia Ltd, 250 Camberwell Road, Camberwell, Victoria 3124, Australia
Penguin Books Canada Ltd, 10 Alcorn Avenue, Toronto, Ontario, Canada M4V 3B2
Penguin Books (NZ) Ltd, 182-190 Wairau Road, Auckland 10, New Zealand

Penguin Books Ltd, Registered Offices: Harmondsworth, Middlesex, England

First published 1996
Second edition 1998
Third edition 2000
Fourth edition 2002
10 9 8 7 6 5 4 3 2 1

Copyright © Time Out Group Ltd, 1996, 1998, 2000, 2002
All rights reserved

Colour reprographics by Icon, Crown House, 56-58 Southwark Street, London SE1
and Precise Litho, 34-35 Great Sutton Street, London EC1
Printed and bound by Cayfosa-Quebecor, Ctra. de Caldes, Km 3 08 130 Sta, Perpètua de Mogoda, Barcelona, Spain

Except in the United States of America, this book is sold subject to the condition that it shall not, by way of trade or otherwise, be lent, re-sold, hired out, or otherwise circulated without the publisher's prior consent in any form of binding or cover other than that in which it is published and without a similar condition including this condition being imposed on the subsequent purchaser.

Edited and designed by
Time Out Guides Limited
Universal House
251 Tottenham Court Road
London W1T 7AB
Tel + 44 (0) 20 7813 3000
Fax + 44 (0) 20 7813 6001
Email guides@timeout.com
www.timeout.com

Editorial

Editor Cath Phillips
Deputy Editor Christi Daugherty
Consultant Editor Bonnie Wach
Listings Editors Jake Bumgardner, Tamar Love, Sharron Wood
Proofreader Marion Moisy
Indexer Selena Cox

Editorial Director Peter Fiennes
Series Editor Ruth Jarvis
Deputy Series Editor Jonathan Cox
Guides Co-ordinator Jenny Noden

Design

Group Art Director John Oakey
Art Director Mandy Martin
Art Editor Scott Moore
Designers Benjamin de Lotz, Lucy Grant
Picture Editor Kerri Littlefield
Deputy Picture Editor Olivia Duncan-Jones
Scanning & Imaging Dan Conway
Ad make-up Glen Impey

Advertising

Group Commercial Director Lesley Gill
Sales Director Mark Phillips
International Sales Co-ordinator Ross Canadé
Advertising Director, North American Guides Liz Howell (1-808 732 4661/1-888 333 5776 US only)
Advertising in the US co-ordinated by *Time Out New York* Alison Tocci (Publisher), Tom Oesau (Advertising Production Manager), Maggie Puddu (Assistant to the Publisher)

Administration

Publisher Tony Elliott
Managing Director Mike Hardwick
Group Financial Director Kevin Ellis
Marketing Director Christine Cort
Marketing Manager Mandy Martinez
Group General Manager Nichola Coulthard
Production Manager Mark Lamond
Production Controller Samantha Furniss
Accountant Sarah Bostock

Features in this guide were written and updated by:
Introduction Bonnie Wach. **History** Daniel Bacon. **San Francisco Today** Bonnie Wach. **Architecture** Rob Farmer. **Literary San Francisco** Zoë Francesca. **Accommodation** Victoria Maitland. **Sightseeing** Kristan Lawson, Anneli Rufus. **Museums** Julie Jares. **Restaurants & Cafés** Rob Farmer, GraceAnn Walden (consultant). **Bars** William Friar, Teresa Tulipano. **Shops & Services** Deborah Bishop. **By Season** Catherine Guthrie. **Children** Jacqueline Frost. **Film** Kristan Lawson, Anneli Rufus. **Galleries** Chiori Santiago. **Nightlife** William Friar, Teresa Tulipano. **Performing Arts** Patrick Craig. **Queer San Francisco** Catherine Guthrie. **Sport & Fitness** Julie Jares. **Trips Out of Town** Victoria Maitland (Heading North, Heading South, Heading East, *Mud, mud, glorious mud*). Rob Farmer (Wine Country). Christi Daugherty (*Gentle giants*). **Directory** Clare Gross. Christi Daugherty (Further Reference).

The Editor would like to thank:
Kelly Chamberlin of the San Francisco Convention & Visitors Bureau, Celeste Wilson of Alamo, Angela Jackson of the Ritz-Carlton, Diane Shields, Harriet Swift, Ella Milroy of Departure Lounge, Karen Hales of Yosemite Concession Services Corporation, Caro Taverne, Shirley Fong-Torres, Kath Stanton, Mike Harrison, and all contributors (especially Colin Berry) from previous editions, whose work formed the basis for parts of this book.

Car hire was provided by Alamo Rent-a-Car (US 1-800 327 9633/UK 08705 994000/www.goalamo.com).

Maps by Mapworld, 71 Blandy Road, Henley on Thames, Oxon RG9 1QB and JS Graphics, 17 Beadles Lane, Old Oxted, Surrey RH8 9JG.

Photography by Amanda Edwards except: pages 6, 8, 11, 25 left, 25 right, 59, 188, 250, 251, 252, 254, 255, 263, 265, 268 Corbis; pages 13, 14, 25 middle, 190, 193, 194, 239 Associated Press; page 232 Gaze International; page 267 Tony Stone Images.

The following images were supplied by the featured artists/establishments: 34, 198, 199, 221, 225.

© Copyright Time Out Group Ltd
All rights reserved

Contents

Introduction 2

In Context

History 6
San Francisco Today 17
Architecture 21
Literary San Francisco 25

Accommodation

Accommodation 30

Sightseeing

Introduction 52
Downtown & Around 56
North Beach & Around 71
The Mission & the Castro 83
The Haight & Around 87
The Marina & Around 93
Ocean Beach & Around 99
The East Bay 103
Museums 105

Eat, Drink, Shop

Restaurants & Cafés 114
Bars 148
Shops & Services 159

Arts & Entertainment

By Season 188
Children 195
Film 199
Galleries 203
Nightlife 209
Performing Arts 221
Queer San Francisco 228
Sport & Fitness 238

Trips Out of Town

Introduction 250
Heading North 251
Wine Country 256
Heading South 262
Heading East 267

Directory

Getting Around 272
Resources A-Z 277
Further Reference 289
Index 291
Advertisers' Index 298

Maps

BART & Muni map 300
Bay Area 302
City Overview 303
San Francisco by Area 304
San Francisco street maps 306
Berkeley street map 315
Street Index 316

Introduction

San Francisco is one of the loveliest cities in the United States. Perched on the top of a peninsula, surrounded on three sides by the blue waters of San Francisco Bay and the Pacific Ocean, and bookended by the majestic sweeps of the Golden Gate and Bay Bridges, it's a charming jumble of distinctly different neighbourhoods, all squeezed up against one another and against the ridiculously up-and-down streets. The views are endless and everywhere. Catch a ferry across the bay to Sausalito or Tiburon – on a sunny day if possible – and catch your breath looking in one direction at the orange spires of the Golden Gate bridge and in the other at the city's glistening ribbons of streets and the unmistakable point of the Transamerica Pyramid poking out of the Financial District skyscrapers. Even on one of summer's notoriously chilly, foggy days, the city retains its particular charm.

Its relatively small size and lack of sprawl – certainly in comparison to its monolithic Californian cousin, Los Angeles, further down the coast – makes it easily accessible to the visitor. You don't need a car to explore San Francisco; in fact, it's a positive hindrance, what with the crowded streets and impossible parking. Instead, take advantage of the comprehensive public transport system – buses, streetcars, BART trains and the absurdly romantic cable cars – or strike out on foot. Despite the heart attack-inducing inclines, this is a city made for walking. Europeans feel at home, while Americans from car-dependent towns find it a refreshing change.

Despite its fantastic dining scene – one of the best in the world – acclaimed theatre, opera and ballet companies, designer fashion shops, sky-high housing prices and state-of-the-art techno businesses, it still has the air of a small town. High-rises are few and far between; pretty, pastel-coloured Victorian houses are the predominant building type. And the relatively safe streets, well-manicured parks, friendly shopkeepers and the city's reputation as a centre for liberal, alternative lifestyles add to its appeal.

Enjoy. It won't be hard.

ABOUT THE TIME OUT CITY GUIDES

The *Time Out San Francisco Guide* is one of an expanding series of *Time Out* City Guides, now numbering over 35, produced by the people behind London and New York's successful listings magazines. Our guides are all written and updated by resident experts who have striven to provide you with all the most up-to-date information you'll need to explore the city or read up on its background, whether you're a local or a first-time visitor.

THE LOWDOWN ON THE LISTINGS

Above all, we've tried to make this book as useful as possible. Addresses, telephone numbers, websites, transport information, opening times, admission prices and credit card details have all been included in the listings. And, as far as possible, we've given details of facilities, services and events, all checked and correct as we went to press. However, owners and managers can change their arrangements at any time, and they often do. Before you go out of your way, we'd advise you to telephone and check opening times, ticket prices and other particulars. While every effort has been made to ensure the accuracy of the information contained in this guide, the publishers cannot accept responsibility for any errors it may contain.

PRICES AND PAYMENT

We have noted where venues such as shops, hotels, restaurants, museums, attractions and the like accept the following credit cards: American Express (AmEx), Diners Club (DC), Discover (Disc), MasterCard (MC) and Visa (V). Many will also accept travellers' cheques, along with other credit cards (Carte Blanche, for example).

The prices we've supplied should be treated as guidelines, not gospel. If you find that prices vary wildly from those we've quoted, please write and let us know. We aim to give the best and most up-to-date advice, so we always want to know if you've been badly treated or overcharged.

THE LIE OF THE LAND

San Francisco is made up a series of distinct neighbourhoods, each with its own quirks and characteristics (and often its own climate). Although the names of these neighbourhoods are pretty much fixed – North Beach, Pacific Heights, Russian Hill, Civic Center, the

Tenderloin and so on – the boundaries that separate them are occasionally fuzzy. We have used the commonly accepted boundaries – see page 304 for a map of the various areas – but you may find slightly different limits in other tourist literature or maps. See the Introduction to the Sightseeing section – on page 52 – for a more detailed breakdown of San Francisco's neighbourhoods.

Most of the city's street layout is fairly easy to understand, based as it is on the grid system common to so many US towns. When listing an address for a venue, we have given the street address plus the nearest cross street or streets, to make it easier to identify. The public transport system is comprehensive and efficient and will take you pretty much wherever you want to go within San Francisco; for more details, see page 273. You will only need a car if you are planning a journey outside the city to places ill-served by public transport, such as the wineries of Napa and Sonoma Valleys. Our Trips Out of Town section starts on page 250. For information on driving and car rental, see page 275.

There is an online version of this guide, as well as weekly events listings for over 30 international cities, at www.timeout.com.

TELEPHONE NUMBERS

There are various telephone area codes that serve the Bay Area: 415 for San Francisco and Marin County, 510 for Berkeley and Oakland, 650 for the peninsula cities and 707 for Napa and Sonoma Counties. Phone numbers throughout the guide are listed as if you're dialling from within San Francisco. All 1-800 and 1-888 numbers can be dialled free of charge within the US; most are also free from the UK. For more on telephones and codes, see page 286.

ESSENTIAL INFORMATION

For all the practical information you might need for visiting San Francisco, including visa and customs information, advice on facilities and access for the disabled, emergency telephone numbers and local transport, turn to the Directory chapter at the back of the guide. It starts on page 272.

MAPS

Wherever possible, a map reference is provided for every venue listed in the guide, indicating the page and grid reference at which it can be found on our detailed street maps of San Francisco and downtown Berkeley. There is also a map showing the different neighbourhoods within San Francisco, overview maps of the city and the wider Bay Area, and a transport map showing the BART and Muni system in downtown San Francisco. The maps section starts on page 304.

LET US KNOW WHAT YOU THINK

We hope you enjoy the *Time Out San Francisco Guide*, and we'd like to know what you think of it. We welcome tips for places that you consider we should include in future editions and take note of your criticism of our choices. There's a reader's reply card at the back of this book for your feedback, or you can email us at sanfranciscoguide@timeout.com.

Advertisers

We would like to stress that no establishment has been included in this guide because it has advertised in any of our publications and no payment of any kind has influenced any review. The opinions given in this book are those of *Time Out* writers and entirely independent.

timeout.com

The World's Living Guide

In Context

History 6
San Francisco Today 17
Architecture 21
Literary San Francisco 25

Features

The city on foot: Barbary Coast Trail 12
Key events 16
Home truths 18
Slam funk 26

The ruins of City Hall after the **Great Quake** of 1906.

History

How Babylon by the Bay came into being.

THE OHLONE AGE

San Francisco Bay is actually an estuary, mixing the cold Pacific Ocean with the San Joaquin and Sacramento rivers, whose flows originate from the fresh snowmelt of the Sierra Nevada. The bay reached its present size about 100,000 years ago when melting glaciers flooded the world's oceans and rising sea water flowed inland through the Golden Gate. Prominent coastal hills jostle around two sandy peninsulas that almost meet at either end of the Golden Gate, like a forefinger and thumb hooked towards each other. This natural estuary protects three islands – Alcatraz, Angel and Yerba Buena.

Fifteen thousand years ago, during the last Ice Age, nomadic tribes migrated across the Bering Strait from Asia and eventually settled along the shores of the bay. Ringed by tule reeds and hilly banks covered with grassy pastures, the Bay Area sustained more than 10,000 Northern Californian Indians of different tribes, collectively known as the Costanoans – or 'coast dwellers' – as they were later dubbed by the Spanish.

The people who inhabited the site of the future San Francisco were the Ohlone. They apparently lived in harmony both with their Miwok neighbours and the land, which provided them with rich pickings of game, fish, shellfish, fruit and nuts – a land of 'inexpressible fertility' in the words of a later French explorer. The Ohlone and their neighbours lived a successful hunter-gatherer existence – 'dancing on the brink of the world,' as an Ohlone song went – until their disastrous introduction to 'civilisation' with the arrival of Spanish missionaries. Their previous rare contacts with Europeans had been friendly and travellers had been impressed by the welcome the Costanoans gave them. But the Spanish brought with them the dubious gifts of Christianity, hard labour in the fields and diseases like smallpox, which would annihilate half the native population of California in a matter of 75 years.

The destruction of their culture has been largely ignored because the Ohlone and other tribes had no tradition of recording their history, orally or otherwise. *The Ohlone Way* (Heyday Books) by Malcolm Margolin is an attempt to trace the lost culture of Northern Californian Indians; today, the only surviving traces of the Costanoans is found in the records of their destroyers.

COLONISING CALIFORNIA

Looking at the Golden Gate today, it's not hard to imagine how early navigators missed the mile-wide opening. The bay and its Indians were hidden from view by 'stynkinge fogges' (as Drake later complained), which prevented numerous explorers over a period of 200 years from discovering the harbour entrance.

An early series of Spanish missions – sent up the coast by Hernán Cortés, notorious conqueror of Mexico and the Aztecs – never got as far as Upper California. In 1542, under the flag of Cortés's successor, Antonio de Mendoza, Portuguese explorer Juan Cabrillo became the first European to visit the area. The Spanish named their new-found land California, after a mythical island described in a popular 16th-century Spanish novel. The island was said to be inhabited by Amazon-like women warriors who wore gold armour and were ruled by the great Queen Calafia. Though Cabrillo passed the bay's entrance, both on his way north and back again, he failed to discover its large natural harbour.

An Englishman got even closer, yet still managed to miss it. In 1579, during a foraging and spoiling mission in the name of the Virgin Queen, Elizabeth I, the then-unknighted Francis Drake landed in Miwok Indian territory just north of the Bay. With one ship, the *Golden Hind*, and a crew in dire need of rest and recreation, he put in for a six-week berth somewhere along the Marin coastline, probably near Point Reyes. Long before the Pilgrims landed at Plymouth Rock or the English settled Cupid's Cove at Newfoundland, Drake claimed California for Elizabeth I, naming it 'Nova Albion' or 'New Britain'.

It would take another 190 years for a white man to set eyes on the Bay. Spurred on by the pressure of British colonial ambitions in America, the Spanish sent northbound missions to stake out their own territories, intent upon converting the *bestias* and claiming land for the Spanish crown. In 1595, Portuguese explorer Sabestian Cermeno, sailing under the Spanish flag, shipwrecked just north of the Golden Gate at what is now known as Drake's Bay. Before he made his way back to Mexico in a small boat saved from the ship, he named the protected cove Bahia de San Francisco.

In 1769, the 'sacred expedition' of Gaspar de Pórtola, a Spanish aristocrat who would later become the first governor of California, and the Franciscan priest Father Junípero Serra, set off with 60 men on a gruelling march across the Mexican desert to establish a mission at San Diego. The expedition then worked its way north to Monterey, to claim it for Spain, building missions and baptising Indians as they went. During the expedition, an advance party discovered the unexpectedly long bay 100 miles (160 kilometres) further up the coast. Mistaking it for Cermeno's cove, they called it Bahia de San Francisco. But since the expedition's brief was only to claim Monterey, the party returned to San Diego.

'Over time, favouritism, authoritarianism and religious fervour sowed the seeds of resistance in all the Spanish territories.'

It was not until August 1775 that the *San Carlos*, a Spanish supply vessel, became the first ship to sail into the bay. Meanwhile, a mission set off to establish a safer land route to what would eventually become San Francisco. Roughly concurrent with the signing of the American Declaration of Independence, Captain Juan Bautista de Anza led an advance party to the southern point of the Golden Gate, which he declared a perfect location for a Spanish military garrison, or *presidio*, to strengthen Spain's western claims. Three miles inland to the south-east, the party found a site suitable for a mission. Before the year was out, the presidio was erected and the mission – named Mission San Francisco de Asis after the holy order operating in Upper California, but popularly known as Mission Dolores – was established by Father Junípero Serra.

YERBA BUENA AND THE BEAR FLAG REVOLT

Over time, a combination of favouritism, authoritarianism and religious fervour helped sow the seeds of resentment and resistance in all the territories colonised by Spain. The country's hold on its American empires first began to crumble in Mexico, which declared itself a republic in 1821. The Mexican annexation of California in the same year opened up the area to foreign settlers, among them American pioneers such as fur trapper Jedediah Smith, who in 1828 became the first white American to reach California over the Sierra Nevada mountain range. His feat might have been the more impressive, but the sedate arrival by whaler ship of an Englishman had a more lasting impact. Captain William Richardson, who built the first dwelling on the site of the future San Francisco in 1835, is credited with giving San Francisco its first name: Yerba Buena, named after the sweet mint the Spanish used to make tea.

That same year, the United States tried unsuccessfully to buy the whole of the Bay Area from the Mexicans. In the long run, however, they got California for free: the declaration of independence of the territory of Texas, and its subsequent annexation by the US, triggered the Mexican-American war in June 1846. The resulting Guadalupe-Hidalgo Treaty of 1848 officially granted the Union all the land from Texas to California and the Rio Grande to Oregon. But before the treaty could be nailed down, a few hotheads decided to 'liberate' the territory from Mexico themselves.

The short-lived Mexican rule of California coincided with the era of idealistic frontiersmen like Captain John Fremont and Kit Carson. In June 1846, Fremont convinced a motley crew to take over the abandoned presidio to the north of Yerba Buena in Sonoma, proclaiming his new state the 'Bear Flag Republic' after the ragged banner he raised over Sonoma's square (the design was eventually adopted as California's state flag). Fremont also christened the mouth of San Francisco Bay the 'Golden Gate', after Istanbul's Golden Horn. A few weeks after the Bear Flaggers annexed Sonoma, the US Navy captured Yerba Buena without a struggle and the whole of California became US territory.

At this point, the infant Yerba Buena was just a sleepy trading post of 500 people. On 30 January 1847, the newly appointed mayor, Lieutenant Washington A Bartlett, officially renamed it 'San Francisco'. Unbeknown to its residents, the tiny settlement was about to change beyond all recognition: something was glittering in the hills…

THE GOLD RUSH

In the early 1840s, the Swiss-born John Sutter was running New Helvetia, a large ranch in California's Central Valley, where he encouraged American citizens to settle the land. One of his homesteaders was James Marshall, who built a sawmill for his landlord on the American River, near Sacramento. While putting the finishing touches on the water-powered mill, Marshall discovered gold in a sawmill ditch. 'Boys,' Marshall told the group of labourers who were helping him build the sawmill, 'by God, I believe I have found a gold mine.' Sutter and Marshall attempted to keep their findings secret, but when newspaper publisher Sam Brannan dramatically waved a bottle of gold dust in San Francisco's town square, gold fever quickly spread around the world, and the 1849 Gold Rush was on.

The news of riches sent droves of drifters and fortune-seekers to California. Some sailed around Cape Horn in windjammers, sloops and steamships, some trekked across Panama, others crossed prairies from the east in covered wagons. Their fever was fanned by people like Brannan, whose *California Star* newspaper told of men digging up a fortune in an hour. Many potential prospectors never made it: by land, the journey meant months of exposure to blizzards, mountains, deserts and hostile Indians; by sea, they faced disease, starvation or brutal weather. Still, many made it through. More than 90,000 Forty-Niners travelled to California in the first two years after gold was discovered. More than 300,000 had arrived in

Idealistic frontiersman **John Fremont.**

the state by 1854 – or one of about every 90 people then living in the US. Though they called themselves the Argonauts, after the sailors who accompanied the mythical Jason in search of the Golden Fleece, locals named them after the year the Rush began, and they will forever be known as Forty-Niners.

'San Francisco at the time of the Gold Rush was not a place for the faint-hearted. Guns, violence, gambling and prostitution were the norm.'

In many ways, they besieged San Francisco. The port town they arrived in was one without structure, government or even a distinct name – to many it was still 'Yerba Buena'. They found hardship more than gold: on their way through San Francisco to the mines, predatory merchants fleeced them; when they returned, broke, they were left to grub mean existences from the city streets, seeking refuge in brothels, gambling dens and bars. Within two years of the Sutter discovery, nearly 100,000 men had passed through the city, swelling the tiny community into a giant, muddy campsite. A huge fire levelled the settlement on Christmas Eve in 1849, but a new town quickly rose up to take its place. The permanent population leapt from 800 to 25,000.

San Francisco at the time of the Gold Rush was not a place for the faint-hearted. Lawlessness and arson ruled; frontier justice was commonplace. Writers Mark Twain and Bret Harte and, later, Robert Louis Stevenson, Oscar Wilde and Anthony Trollope all travelled to the area to report about its exciting, lurid reputation, describing an anarchic boom town where guns, violence, gambling and prostitution were the norm.

The opening of a post office marked the city's first optimistic stab at improving communications with the rest of the continent and the world. John White Geary, appointed postmaster by President James Knox Polk, rented a room at the corner of Montgomery and Washington Streets, where he marked out a series of squares for each letter of the alphabet and began filing letters. This crude set-up was the first postal system for San Francisco's 10,000 residents. Then, in April 1850 – the same year that California became the Union's 31st state – San Francisco's city charter was approved and the city elected Geary its first mayor. In order to furnish the city with proper streets, Geary established a council, which later bought the ship *Euphemia* and turned it into San Francisco's first jail. It proved a sound investment.

The council's first concern was to impose law and order on San Francisco's massive squatter town. Gangs of hoodlums controlled certain districts: the Ducks, led by Australian convicts, lived at a spot known as Sydney Town. Together with New York toughs the Hounds, they roamed Telegraph Hill, raping and pillaging those among the more orderly community of Chilean merchants who occupied 'Little Chile'. Eventually, their crimes incurred the wrath of right-minded citizens who decided to take the law into their own hands. Whipped into a fury by rabble-rousing Sam Brannan, vigilantes lynched their first victim, John Jenkins, at a Portsmouth Square 'necktie party' in June 1851. They strung up three more thieves during the following weeks by way of warning to the other Ducks and Hounds – who wisely cut out for the Sierras.

Though their frontier justice temporarily curbed the area's excesses, Mayor Geary understandably viewed the vigilantes as part of the problem, not the solution. His crusade against lawlessness was hardly helped when riverbed gold started running dry. By 1853, boom had turned to bust and the resulting depression set a cyclical pattern oft-repeated through the city's history. By the mid-1860s, San Francisco was bankrupt.

NOBS AND IMMIGRANTS

But then came the Silver Rush. Henry Comstock's 1859 discovery of a rich blue vein of silver (the 'Comstock Lode') in western Nevada triggered a second invasion by fortune-seekers. This time, though, the ore's nature demanded more elaborate methods of extraction, with high yields going to a small number of companies and tycoons rather than individual prospectors. Before the supply had been exhausted, silver barons had made enough money to transform San Francisco, establishing a neighbourhood of *nouveaux riches* mansions atop Nob (a name adapted from the word 'nabob') Hill. By 1870, the city was no longer just a raucous boom-and-bust town.

If the nabobs on the hill took the moral and geographical high ground, those on the waterfront at the bottom of Telegraph Hill were busy legitimising their reputation as occupants of the 'Barbary Coast'. Naïve newcomers and drunken sailors were viewed as fair game by the gamblers and hoods waiting to 'shanghai' them (like 'hoodlum', shanghai is a San Francisco expression), as were immigrant women who found themselves trapped into a life of prostitution or slavery. At one low point, the female population numbered just 22; many a brothel madam made fortune enough to buy her way on to Nob Hill.

The seeds of San Francisco's present-day multiculturalism were sown during this period, when a deluge of immigrants providing food, goods and services poured in from all over the world. French immigrants vying with Italians for the 'best bread' vote in North Beach started baking sourdough. A young German garment maker named Levi Strauss started using rivets to strengthen the jeans he made for miners.

In Chinatown, criminal *tongs*, mafia-like gangs, controlled the opium dens and other rackets; a Chinese immigrant, Wah Lee, opened the city's first laundry. Chinatown expanded in the 1860s with the building of the transcontinental railroad, which employed thousands of Chinese labourers at low pay rates. Despite their usefulness as a cheap source of labour, however, the Chinese became the targets of racist anti-immigrant activity. Proscriptive anti-Chinese legislation would persist until 1938.

But it wasn't all work: entertainment was always high on the agenda for San Franciscans. In 1853, the city boasted five theatres and some 600 saloons and taverns serving 42,000 customers. Locals downed seven bottles of champagne for every bottle swallowed in Boston. When Lola Montez, entertainer to European monarchs and thieves, arrived on a paddle-steamer from Panama in 1853, her 'spider dance' became an instant hit at the American Theater.

San Francisco's relative isolation from the rest of the continent meant the city was hardly affected by the Civil War that devastated the American South in the early 1860s. The rest of the country seemed remote; sometimes mail took six months to arrive. Communications were slowly improving, however. Telegraph wires were gradually being strung across the continent and where the telegraph poles ran out, the Pony Express would pick up messages, relaying up to 75 dispatch riders across the West to the Pacific coast. By the mid-1860s, the telegraph had all but rendered the Pony Express obsolete and the transcontinental railroad provided its *coup de grâce*.

The completion of the Central Pacific Railroad in 1869 was the signal for runaway consumption in the city. The biggest spenders were the 'Big Four', Charles Crocker, Collis P Huntington, Mark Hopkins and Leland Stanford, a quartet of millionaires who were the powerful and influential principal investors behind the Central Pacific. Their eagerness to impress the West with their flamboyantly successful business practices manifested itself in the mansions they built up on Nob Hill.

The Big Four were highly adept at making money for themselves and their favoured partners. They were brutally competitive, too. By 1871, 121 businessmen controlled $146 million, according to one newspaper – but others got in on their act. In particular, four Irishmen – James Flood, William O'Brien, James Fair and John Mackay – rough-hewn miners and bartenders who'd chipped their fortunes from the Comstock Lode, became known as the 'Bonanza Kings', after they made money enough to buy their way on to Nob Hill.

'The 1906 quake generated more energy than all the explosives used in World War II combined.'

A Scottish-Irish banker, William Ralston, opened the Bank of California on Sansome Street in 1864. Partnered by a Prussian engineer called Adolph Sutro (later famous for building the first Cliff House and the Sutro Baths), Ralston was determined to extract every last ounce of silver from the Comstock's Sun Mountain. Unfortunately, he did so too quickly, and the ore ran out before he recouped his investment. Ralston's bank collapsed. Smiling to the last in an effort to calm his investors, Ralston drowned himself. He left behind the luxurious Palace Hotel and a lasting contribution towards San Francisco's new civic pride: Golden Gate Park. Ralston's company provided the water for designer William Hammon Hall's audacious project, which transformed 1,013 acres of city sand dunes into a magnificent expanse of trees, plants, flowers and lakes.

THE GREAT QUAKE

The city continued to grow, and by 1900 its population had reached more than a third of a million, making it the ninth-largest city in the Union. But on 18 April 1906, shortly after 5am, dogs began howling and horses whinnying – noises, along with glasses tinkling and windows rattling, that marked the unnerving moments before an earthquake.

The quake hit: a rending in the tectonic plates 25 miles (40 kilometres) beneath the ocean bed that triggered the shifting of billions of tons of rock, generating more energy than all the explosives used in World War II. The rip snaked inland, tearing a gash now known as the San Andreas Fault down the coastline. Cliffs appeared from nowhere, cracks yawned, ancient redwoods toppled and part of the newly built City Hall collapsed like a deck of cards. Streets began to undulate and church bells pealed crazily. A second tremor struck, ripping the walls out of buildings. A ghastly pause followed, then people ran into the streets in their nightclothes.

Tragically, one of the earthquake's many victims was a man the city badly needed just then: Fire Chief Dennis Sullivan, who was not long back from fighting a blaze at a cannery when the earthquake struck. He was found in the rubble of the fire-house and died some days later. The fire brigade seemed lost without him. The second tremor had destroyed the city alarms and disrupted the water pipes feeding the fire hydrants, leaving the famous firefighters of the West absolutely helpless.

The fire that followed compounded the disaster of the earthquake. It spread until Mayor Eugene Schmitz and General Frederick Funston were forced to carry out a desperate plan to blow up the houses along Van Ness Avenue and create a fire-break. The mansions belonged to rich folk that any politician would be loathe to alienate; in this instance, however, necessity spoke louder than money.

The earthquake and 74-hour inferno was initially thought to have accounted for some 700 dead, though military records now reveal that the figure probably ran into several thousand. Those suspected of looting were shot dead in the chaos that followed the quake and fire. A quarter of a million people were left homeless and 3,000 acres of buildings were destroyed. On the third day of the catastrophe the wind changed direction and brought rain, and by 21 April the fire was out.

Even before the ashes cooled, the citizens set about rebuilding their city, and within ten years San Francisco had risen, phoenix-like, from the ruins. Some claimed that in the rush to rebuild, city planners passed up the chance to replace its grid street system with a more sensible one that followed the area's natural contours. But there's no doubt that San Francisco was reborn as a cleaner, more attractive city – one that, within three years of the fire, could boast half of the nation's concrete and steel buildings. Such statistical pride was not out of keeping with the 'boosterism' that accelerated its post-Gold Rush growth from tiny settlement to large, modern city ready to meet the 20th century.

BUILDING BRIDGES

The most potent symbol of the city's restored civic pride was the new City Hall, whose construction was secured by an $8-million city bond. By the time it was completed in 1915, City Hall rose some 16 feet (five metres) higher than its model – the Capitol building in Washington, DC.

Between 1913 and 1915, two new waterways were opened that would prove critical to California's economic vitality. In 1913, the Los Angeles aqueduct was completed, beginning the transformation of a sleepy Southern California cowtown into the urban sprawl of modern LA. And, in 1915, the Panama Canal's opening considerably shortened shipping times between the Atlantic and Pacific coasts; San Francisco celebrated this achievement by hosting the Panama-Pacific Exposition.

Not even the outbreak of World War I in Europe could dampen the city's spirits. On the contrary, the war provided a boost to

Alcatraz became a high-security prison for 'incorrigible' convicts in 1933.

California's mining and manufacturing industries. But, as elsewhere in America, the good times were quickly swallowed up in the world depression signalled by the Wall Street Crash of 1929.

The Great Depression brought to an end the economic well-being of the 1920s. It hit San Francisco port especially badly – half the workforce was laid off. On 9 May 1934, under the leadership of Harry Bridges, the International Longshoremen's Association declared a coastwide strike. Other unions, including the powerful Teamsters, came out in sympathy, shutting down West Coast ports for three months. A crew of blackleg workers managed to break through the picket on 5 July – Bloody Thursday – but with disastrous results. As violence escalated, police opened fire, killing two strikers and wounding 30. A general strike was called for 14 July, when 150,000 people stopped work and brought San Francisco to a standstill for three days. The strike fizzled out when its leaders couldn't agree on how to end the stalemate, but the action wasn't completely futile: the longshoremen won a wage increase and control of the hiring halls.

Despite this black chapter in the city's labour relations, San Francisco managed an extraordinary amount of construction. In 1932, the Opera House was completed; in 1933, the island of Alcatraz was transferred from the army to the Federal Bureau of Prisons, which set about building a high-security lock-up for 'incorrigible' convicts. The decade's two other landmark constructions were the San Francisco Oakland Bay and Golden Gate bridges. The former, completed in 1936, constituted two

The city on foot: Barbary Coast Trail

Walking along San Francisco's Barbary Coast Trail, you arrive at a weathered brick building. Below your feet, a Gold Rush-era ship lays entombed underground. But even more interesting is a sign painted over the brick. It reads 'Old Ship Saloon – Henry Klee prop'. Klee owned the place from 1897 to 1912. He was one of the last 'shanghaiers' (men who kidnapped sailors to serve on ships) to operate on San Francisco's notorious Barbary Coast waterfront.

Most cities are strewn with tantalising clues to their heritage, but often these details are tucked away in obscure alleys and little-known nooks. The challenge is to ferret them out. To this end, in 1998 the San Francisco Historical Society created a 3.8-mile (six-kilometre) self-guided walking trail (almost entirely flat or gently sloping) and a 20-minute cable car ride through the heart of historic San Francisco. The walk is called the Barbary Coast Trail, after the 19th-century maritime district famous for its bustling port and infamous for its brothels, opium dens and bawdy music halls.

A series of bronze medallions (emblazoned with a miner and a clipper ship – *pictured*) embedded in the pavement mark the path at every street corner. Down Gold Rush-era streets and Chinatown alleys, past Beat poet hangouts and Bonanza King mansions, the trail traces the city's colourful history from its days as a Mexican village to the 1906 earthquake and fire. It connects 20 of San Francisco's most important historic sites,

including the oldest Asian temple in America, the Pony Express, a Barbary Coast saloon and the largest collection of historic ships in the United States. Five local history museums – all free of charge – dot the trail.

If you want to explore the whole trail properly, allow the better part of a day, though it's easy to join at any point and walk for as long as you like. Two guides are available: *Walking San Francisco on the Barbary Coast Trail* ($14.95) – a detailed anecdotal history of SF and trail guide in one – and the *Barbary Coast Trail Official Guide* ($5.95), a more concise trail guide only. Both are available at the Visitor Information Center at Hallidie Plaza and various bookshops around town.

bridges, one a suspension bridge from San Francisco to Yerba Buena Island, the other a cantilever span from Yerba Buena to Oakland. Six months after the Bay Bridge was finished, the Golden Gate Bridge began to rise from the bay with its revolutionary suspension design. The bridges' impact on the ferries that had served the city and its suburbs so well was devastating, and commuter trains also suffered.

In 1939, the city hosted another fair on man-made Treasure Island. The Golden Gate International Exposition was described as a 'pageant of the Pacific'; those who went were dubbed 'the Thirty-Niners' by local wits. Nobody knew at the time, but this was to be San Francisco's last big celebration for a while: in 1941 the Japanese attacked Pearl Harbor and America entered World War II.

World War II changed the city almost as much as the Gold Rush or the Great Quake. More than a million and a half men and thousands of tons of material were shipped out to the Pacific from the Presidio, Travis Air Force Base and Treasure Island. Between 1941 and 1945, almost the entire Pacific war effort passed under the Golden Gate. The massed ranks of troops and some half a million civilian workers flooding San Francisco turned the city into a milling party town hell-bent on sending its boys into battle with smiles on their faces.

Towards the end of the war in Europe, in April 1945, representatives of 50 nations met at the San Francisco Opera House to draft the United Nations Charter. It was signed on 26 June 1945 and formally ratified in October at the General Organisation of the United Nations in London. Many people felt that San Francisco was the ideal location for its headquarters, but the British and French thought it was too far to travel and – much to the city's disappointment – the UN moved to New York.

THE BEATS AND THE SUMMER OF LOVE

The immediate post-war period was coloured by the return of the demobilised GIs. One was poet Lawrence Ferlinghetti, who, while studying at the Sorbonne in the early 1950s, discovered Penguin paperbacks and was inspired to open his tiny, wedge-shaped bookshop at 261 Columbus Avenue. Called City Lights, it became a mecca for the bohemians later dubbed the Beat Generation, many of whose works he published in the City Lights Pocket Poets series.

The Beat Generation, so named by novelist Jack Kerouac, reflected the angst and ambition of a post-war generation attempting to escape both the shadow of the Bomb and the rampant consumerism of ultra-conformist 1950s America.

Happy hippies in 1967's **Summer of Love**.

In Kerouac's definition, Beat could stand for beatific or being beat – exhausted. The condition is best explained in his novel *On the Road*, which charts the coast-to-coast odysseys of San Francisco-based Beat saint Neal Cassady (thinly disguised as Dean Moriarty), poet Allen Ginsberg and Kerouac himself (named Sal Paradise).

'The emergence of the Beat Generation made North Beach the literary centre of San Francisco and nurtured a new vision that would spread far beyond its bounds,' reflected Lawrence Ferlinghetti, 40 years on. 'The Beats prefigured the New Left evolution and the impulse for change that swept eastward from San Francisco.' The attention of the world might have been on the beret-clad artists and poets populating North Beach cafés, but an event in Anaheim, 500 miles (800 kilometres) to the south, was perhaps more truly reflective of mainstream America: Disney's first theme park, Disneyland, opened in 1955.

Despite the imaginary perfect world portrayed by Disney, the media exposure received by Kerouac and Ginsberg established the Bay Area as a centre for the burgeoning counter-culture, generating mainstream American suspicions that San Francisco was the fruit and nut capital of the US. Their fears were about to be confirmed by the hippie explosion of the 1960s. The Beats and the hippies might have shared a love of marijuana and a common distaste for 'the system', but the Beats sometimes mocked their juniors as part-time bohemians. For his part, Kerouac – by now an embittered alcoholic – abhorred what he saw as the hippies' anti-Americanism. His distaste for these new bohemians was shared by John Steinbeck, winner of the Nobel Prize for Literature in 1962, who shied away from the recognition he was receiving in the streets.

Where the original Beats were never interested in political action, the newer generation were prepared to embrace it full on. A sit-in protest against a closed session of the House of Representatives Un-American Activities Committee (HUAC) at the City Hall in 1961 drew ranks of protesters from San Francisco State University and the University of California's Berkeley campus. It quickly degenerated into a riot, establishing a pattern of protest and police response to come. In the following years, the civil rights movement and America's involvement in the Vietnam War added urgency to the voices of dissent; Berkeley students were at the forefront of protests on campuses around the country. By the mid-1960s, the counterculture was split between the politically conscious students behind the free speech movement and the hippies who'd chosen to opt out of the system altogether.

The availability of LSD, its popularity boosted in San Francisco by such events as the Human Be-in organised by Allen Ginsberg in 1967 and the Acid Tests overseen by Owsley Stanley and the Grateful Dead, drew an estimated 8,000 hippies from across America. Some 5,000 stayed, occupying the cheap Victorian houses around the Haight-Ashbury district (dubbed 'the Hashbury') not far from Golden Gate Park. The combination of San Francisco's *laissez-faire* attitude, sun, drugs and the acid-induced psychedelic music explosion gave rise to the famous Summer of Love that same year. By 1968, however, the spread of hard drugs, notably heroin, had taken much of the shine off the hippie movement.

Like its drugs, the city's politics were getting harder, too. Members of the Black Panther movement, a radical black organisation founded across the bay in Oakland by Huey Newton and Bobby Seale, asked themselves why they should ship out to shoot the Vietnamese when the real enemy was at home. Around Oakland, the Panthers took to exercising the American right to bear arms; gunfights inevitably followed. In April 1968, Panther leader Eldridge Cleaver was wounded and 17-year-old Bobby Hutton was killed in a shoot-out with Oakland police. By the early 1970s, the Black Panther movement had petered out, its leaders either dead, imprisoned or, like Cleaver, on the run.

The kidnapping of Patty Hearst, heir to the Hearst newspaper fortune, by the Symbionese Liberation Army in 1974, was perhaps the point at which the 1960s revolution turned into deadly farce. When she was eventually captured along with the other members of the tiny radical outfit, Hearst had apparently been brainwashed into joining its cause.

Despite the violence that characterised the student and anti-war protests, black radicalism and failed revolutions, the enduring memory of 1960s' San Francisco is as the host city to the Summer of Love. The psychedelic blasts of the Grateful Dead, Big Brother and the Holding Company, Janis Joplin, Country Joe and the Fish, Jefferson Airplane and Quicksilver Messenger Service defined both the San Francisco sound and countercultural attitude. Jann Wenner founded *Rolling Stone* magazine in 1967 to explain and advance the cause, and later document its growth into a multimillion-dollar mass entertainment industry, helping to invent New Journalism in the process.

THE RISE OF GAY RADICALISM

San Francisco's radical baton was taken up in the 1970s by the gay liberation movement. Local activists insisted that gay traditions had always existed in San Francisco, first among the Ohlone Indians and later during the 1849 Gold Rush, when women in the West were more scarce than gold. Early homophile groups like the Daughters of Billets, the Matching Society and the Society for Individual Rights (SIR) had paved the way for more radical political movements in the 1970s. In 1977, gay activists made successful forays into mainstream

Kidnap victim-turned-terrorist **Patty Hearst.**

politics: SIR's Jim Foster became the first openly gay delegate at a Democratic Convention and Harvey Milk was elected on to the city's Board of Supervisors.

Then, on 28 November 1978, Dan White entered City Hall and shot and killed Milk and Mayor George Moscone. White was a former policeman from a working-class background, who had run for supervisor as an angry, young, blue-collar populist – and won. But he suffered poor mental health and had to resign under the strain of office. He quickly changed his mind and asked Mayor Moscow to reinstate him. Milk, who held the deciding vote, persuaded the mayor not to let the unstable White back in – with catastrophic consequences. White turned himself in after the killings; in the poorly prosecuted court case, the jury returned two verdicts of voluntary manslaughter and White was sentenced to seven years.

'Gay life and politics changed radically and irrevocably with the onset of the HIV virus.'

Just as the killings had stunned San Francisco, so the verdict outraged its gay populace, who responded by storming City Hall and hurling rocks through the windows. The disturbance escalated into a full-blown battle, known as the White Night Riot. White's sentence prompted one journalist to wonder why the jury had not posthumously convicted Harvey Milk of 'unlawful interference with a bullet fired from the gun of a former police officer'. Dan White committed suicide not long after his release from prison.

Gay life and politics changed radically and irrevocably with the onset of the HIV virus, which tore the gay community apart and caused controversy when the bath houses (long a symbol of gay liberation and promiscuity) were closed in panic over the disease's spread. Gay radicals branded writer Randy Shilts a 'fascist Nazi, traitor and homophobe' when he ran a story in the *San Francisco Chronicle* criticising bath house owners who refused to post safe sex warnings.

Since its identification, some 18,000 San Franciscans have died of AIDS. Although the levelling in the numbers of new cases in the gay community and the dangerous misperception that the epidemic is ebbing have endangered fundraising efforts of late, the city remains home to the most efficient volunteers in the country. Medical preventionists continue to make inroads into all sexually active communities; caretakers have taken charge of housing, food and legal problems for the many thousands of people – about two per cent of the city – diagnosed as HIV-positive. Hospices, support agencies, hotlines, even pet services are available to those living with HIV. As sufferers are living longer thanks to new drug treatments, the city continues to need more resources and money to assist them.

STRIKE TWO

Because of its location on the San Andreas Fault, San Francisco has always lived in anticipation of a major earthquake to rival the 1906 disaster. One came in October 1989, interrupting the first game of the World Series between the Oakland Athletics and the San Francisco Giants baseball teams. The Loma Prieta earthquake (named after the ridge of mountains at its epicentre) registered 7.1 on the Richter scale. Damage was extensive: part of the West Oakland Freeway collapsed, crushing drivers; the Marina district and Bay Bridge were hit hard; and buildings in the area suffered billions of dollars worth of damage.

At the start of the 21st century, San Francisco reflects many of the social problems that plague major US cities. Homelessness is particularly severe, with up to 14,000 destitute men and women sleeping without nightly shelter, overwhelming the underfunded agencies set up to help them. Those who have shelter are doubly lucky: available housing is at one per cent – an all-time low – and rents have risen sky-high. Traditionally ethnic neighbourhoods are being gentrified, and Bay Area freeway traffic grows ever more congested.

But San Francisco also experienced a remarkable renaissance in the 1990s. Its proximity to Silicon Valley's economic boom rejuvenated the city's business structure and reshaped the skyline. In the wake of the Loma Preita earthquake, the Embarcadero Freeway was torn down and the city's historic bayside boulevard transformed into a palm tree-lined haven for walkers, joggers, inline skaters and bicyclists. Numerous major projects were opened in the decade, including the highly rated San Francisco Museum of Modern Art; the Yerba Beuna Gardens arts and culture complex; Zeum children's museum; the Pacific Bell Park baseball stadium; and the refurbished City Hall.

San Francisco remains a magnet for the world's migrants, especially Asians, who now comprise over 30 per cent of the population. And the city maintains its best-of-the-West-Coast reputation for magnificent food, stylish design, charming architecture and a multicultural, idea-driven population.

Key events

c10,000 BC The Ohlone and Miwok Indians begin to settle the Bay Area.
1542 Juan Cabrillo sails up the California coastline.
1579 Francis Drake lands north of San Francisco Bay, claiming the land he finds for Elizabeth I as New Albion.
1769 Gaspar de Pórtola and Father Junípero Serra lead an overland expedition to establish a mission at San Diego. An advance party is sent to scout out the coast and they become the first white men to see San Francisco Bay.
1775 The *San Carlos* is the first ship to sail into the bay.
1776 On 4 July, 13 American colonies declare their independence from Great Britain. In the autumn, a Spanish military fort is founded near Fort Point and Father Junípero establishes the Mission Dolores.
1821 Mexico declares its independence from Spain and annexes California.
1828 Fur trapper Jedediah Smith becomes the first white man to reach California across the Sierra Nevada mountain range.
1835 English-born sailor William Richardson sets up a trading post, calling it 'Yerba Buena'.
1846 The 'Bear Flag Revolt' takes place against Mexican rule in California. Captain John B Montgomery takes possession of Yerba Buena and claims it for the US.
1847 Yerba Buena is renamed San Francisco. It has 800 inhabitants.
1848 A US-Mexican treaty confirms American dominion over California. Gold is discovered in the low Sierras near Sacramento.
1849 The Gold Rush swells the city's population from 800 to 25,000 in less than a year. A fire levels the city on Christmas Eve.
1850 California becomes the 31st State of the Union.
1859 The Comstock Lode is discovered in western Nevada, triggering the Silver Rush.
1861 Civil War breaks out between the Union and the Confederacy. California, being so far west, remains largely untouched by hostilities.
1868 The University of California is established at Berkeley.
1869 The transcontinental railroad connects San Francisco with the rest of the US.
1873 Andrew Hallidie builds the first cable car.
1906 The Great Earthquake strikes and the fire that follows razes the city. Several thousand die, and more than 28,000 buildings are destroyed.
1915 San Francisco celebrates the opening of the Panama Canal with the Panama-Pacific Exposition.
1932 San Francisco Opera House opens.
1934 On 'Bloody Thursday', police open fire on striking longshoremen, leaving two dead, and prompting a three-day general strike that brings the Bay Area to a standstill.
1936 The Bay Bridge is completed.
1937 The Golden Gate Bridge is completed.
1941 The Japanese attack Pearl Harbour and the US enters World War II.
1945 Fifty nations meet at the Opera House to sign the United Nations Charter.
1955 Allen Ginsberg reads *Howl* at the Six Gallery, with other members of the Beat Generation cheering him on.
1961 UC Berkeley students stage a sit-in protest against a closed session of the House of Representatives Un-American Activities Committee at City Hall.
1964 Student sit-ins and mass arrests grow as the civil rights, free speech and anti-Vietnam War movements gain momentum.
1967 The Human Be-in marks the start of the Summer of Love.
1968 Teenager Bobby Hutton is killed in a Black Panther shoot-out with Oakland police.
1972 The Bay Area Rapid Transit (BART) transport system opens.
1978 Gay supervisor Harvey Milk and Mayor George Moscone are shot and killed by former supervisor Dan White.
1981 The first cases of AIDS are recorded.
1989 An earthquake measuring 7.1 on the Richter scale strikes San Francisco.
1992 Fire sweeps through the Oakland hills, killing dozens and destroying 3,000 homes.
1995 Jerry Garcia, icon of the Grateful Dead, dies. Willie Brown Jr becomes the city's first African-American mayor. The San Francisco 49ers win their fifth Super Bowl.
1996 Engineers announce the Bay Bridge needs a $1.3-billion seismic retrofit.
1997 Herb Caen, long-time *Chronicle* columnist, dies aged 80.
1998 The War Memorial Opera House in the Civic Center, damaged in the 1989 quake, reopens.
1999 San Francisco City Hall reopens after a $300-million retrofit.
2000 Pacific Bell Park, the San Francisco Giants' new baseball stadium, opens to great acclaim.

San Francisco Today

The effects of the dotcom bust, and what lies ahead.

If you'd picked up a copy of our San Francisco guide two years ago and looked around the city today, you might wonder if we'd got it mixed up with some other place. The biggest problems facing San Francisco at that time were how developers were going to squeeze one more luxury loft on to a peninsula where houses were already stacked cheek by jowl, and how to snag a table at a restaurant such as Jardiniere or Rose Pistola, so that you could impress your 22-year-old CEO with your knowledge of '93 Cabernets.

Then, in what amounts to a click of a mouse on the urban evolutionary scale, the wild exuberance of the Internet boom turned into the biggest bust the city had seen since the Great Depression. Dotcoms shuttered their windows and abandoned their astronomically priced South of Market offices in droves – some before the paint had even dried on their 'Grand Opening' signs. Names that had made Wall Street headlines just two years earlier – WebVan, Excite, eToys, Pets.com and so on – were suddenly filing for bankruptcy, and with their demise, all of the dizzying extravagance of San Francisco's second gold rush came to a screeching halt.

These days, the most obvious signs of decline are in SoMa, once the bustling hub of Multimedia Gulch. At press time, some 40 websites were going out of business every month, and office vacancies in the neighbourhood were up to an estimated 20 per cent – even as workers put the finishing touches on half a dozen major new construction projects. The largest – the first phase of the 6,000-unit Mission Bay mixed-use complex across from Pacific Bell Park – is still on target for completion in 2003. The $4-billion redevelopment effort, which is funded with

Home truths

As constant as the fog and the cable cars, San Francisco's homeless population remains the perennial tarnish on the city's polished image, and the Achilles heel of every mayoral candidate for the past two decades. Everywhere you look in downtown – in doorways, on street corners, in alleyways and (most inconveniently for city officials) at the entrance to the Visitor Information Center on Powell and Market Streets and in the plaza in front of City Hall – sad-looking, bedraggled, drug-addicted and often mentally ill men and women lie on dirty sleeping bags, push shopping carts filled with possessions and sit cross-legged with their cats on the pavement begging for spare change.

If it seems as if there are more people living on the streets here than in other cities, it's probably because there are – a conservative estimate of 6,000 to 10,000 in San Francisco alone, with thousands more in surrounding Bay Area counties. Why that is, and how to address the problem, appears as elusive to local politicians as it is to homeless advocates. In one camp, there's the Coalition on Homelessness, which insists that more affordable housing, drug treatment and mental healthcare centres, and better paying blue-collar jobs are the answer; in the other, there are the politicos, whose solutions over the years have ranged from police issuing 'quality of life' tickets for public urination and drunkenness to arresting people under the city's public nuisance laws and sweeping them out of encampments.

As to the why, certainly San Francisco's legacy of tolerance and its live-and-let-live

attitude have something to do with it. This is, after all, the place that spawned the Diggers, a group of 1960s thespian-activists who believed food, shelter, clothing et al should be handed out free to whoever needed it. The homeless have at their call a slew of social services, ranging from welfare and food stamps to free health clinics and soup kitchens. The local street newspaper, the *Street Sheet*, is sold by homeless vendors for $1. San Francisco's benign climate doesn't hurt either: it would be a lot harder to live on the mean streets if it was 40-below for four straight months.

Though traditionally a sympathetic bunch, San Franciscans have been harangued with sob stories and outstretched hands for so long that they barely blink an eye any more. These days, locals donate when the mood strikes, and accept homelessness as just another of the city's social ills. With housing costs at an all-time high and homeless shelters overflowing, it's likely the problem will only get worse before it gets better.

a combination of tax revenue and private bonds, will ultimately take 28 years to finish. When complete it will fill 300 acres of prime waterfront property with housing, a university campus and elementary school, recreation and research facilities, shops, offices, parks and a 500-room hotel. Likewise, the restoration of the historic Ferry Building and plaza – the terminus for the Sausalito, Larkspur and Tiburon ferries, expected to be a waterfront showpiece – is proceeding as scheduled.

The future is more murky for others. The expansive new headquarters for the Gap, which will eventually include a waterfront park, a Claes Oldenberg sculpture garden and two upmarket restaurants, has been scaled back: the hip clothing company is already looking to sublease 130,000 square feet (1,209 square metres) of the not-yet-finished building. Boutique hotel king Chip Conley's plans for a hotel on the Embarcadero at the foot of Mission Street have been put on hold. And with only 17 of the 136 condominiums sold by the time of its opening in October 2001, layoffs loomed at the lavish new Four Seasons combination hotel and condominium high-rise on Mission Street. Finally, a proposed new football stadium for the San Francisco 49ers, already on shaky ground before the slump, was expected to be the first big construction casualty of the 21st century.

It's not all bleak news, however, especially for tourists, homeowners and those in the market for a cheap computer. Many of the city's swank restaurants, where waiting lists had been only slightly longer than the number of zeros on their entrée prices, had become more accessible and considerably less expensive. Low occupancy, combined with a rash of recently approved large hotel projects (including the St Regis Museum Tower and the Omni San Francisco), should translate to continued rate drops at many high-end hotels. Best of all, housing prices, although still among the highest in the nation, have started to settle down.

'Today, the most common words in the real estate market, are "Just Reduced" and "Now Available".'

At the peak of the boom, renters were trampling each other to pay $2,000 for a room the size of a closet in neighbourhoods where the homeless population outnumbered those with beds to sleep in. Homebuyers were forced to overbid – often by tens of thousands of dollars – to get in the door of a tiny, ramshackle cottage. Today, the most common words in the real estate market, particularly in reference to the scads of unoccupied live-work lofts, are 'Just Reduced' and 'Now Available'.

San Francisco's other big headaches, parking and traffic, have also been somewhat alleviated by the economic downturn, though you're still likely to sit in bumper-to-bumper gridlock at almost any time of day on the Golden Gate and Bay Bridges. The best news for commuters and travellers alike is the scheduled opening in 2002 of a BART station at San Francisco International Airport, making it accessible to public transport for the first time in the airport's history. Muni, the city's bus and streetcar system, has made several major improvements in the past year that should help quell San Franciscans' incessant whining about mass transit. Some key routes have been extended and several new streetcar lines added, including a new fleet that now travels along the Embarcadero from Pacific Bell Park down to Fisherman's Wharf, making access to those top tourist destinations infinitely less frustrating. For all its shortcomings – rude drivers, ruder passengers, delays, overcrowding – Muni is still one of the best transport bargains around. Where else in the free world can you go from one end of the city to the other at practically any time of day for only $1?

THE CUP'S HALF FULL

San Francisco may be down on its luck at the moment, but it's never down and out. In true Bay Area fashion, gallows humour abounds: as dotcoms continue to bomb by the dozen, the website www.fuckedcompany.com has taken up a game of corporate deadpool, awarding points to people who can predict which company will go under next. The site's enormous popularity has been one more ironic footnote to the city's financial fallout.

Despite all the dismal news – the job losses, soaring petrol and electricity prices, and the terrorist attacks on the World Trade Center and the Pentagon – San Franciscans remain an upbeat, optimistic lot. In the weeks following the tragic events of 11 September 2001, locals nursed their wounds by attending Bay Area museums in record numbers, and cheering with wild abandon as Giants' superstar left-fielder Barry Bonds made baseball history by hitting 73 home runs in a single season. (Glorious Pac Bell Park is certainly one of the shining lights in the gloomy economic picture; the bayside baseball stadium has sold out virtually every game since its opening in April 2000, not to mention the piles of revenue generated from the sale of all those garlic fries.)

San Franciscans have always been strong champions of the arts, so it's no surprise that, even in hard times, the city would find money in its coffers for visual and performing arts. Barring unforeseen stumbling blocks, the Mexican, Jewish, African-American, Asian Art and MH de Young fine arts museums, and the

After the bust, empty offices abound.

California Academy of Sciences natural history museum, will all have new or renovated homes within the next few years – a number of them designed by world-famous architects. The San Francisco Opera, the second-largest opera company in the US, was to embark in 2001 on an ambitious five-year programme under new director Pamela Rosenberg. In addition, both the American Conservatory Theater (ACT) and the Magic Theatre, two of San Francisco's most acclaimed repertory houses, continue to commission and stage US and world-première works by playwrights such as Harold Pinter, Sam Shepard and Charles Mee.

As for the legions of out-of-work young technocrats, there are still plenty of low-budget diversions in the City by the Bay: summers full of free concerts and street festivals; farmers' markets and good, cheap eateries that cater to every ethnic colour and stripe; and, thanks to the past few years of untamed cash flow, a slew of newly revitalised (some would say yuppified) neighbourhoods in which to play.

'The frenzied pace of gentrification seems to have slowed to a crawl.'

Signs of gentrification, the operative buzzword of the dotcom age, are everywhere, but perhaps most evident – and least welcome – in the Mission District, where Latinos, starving artists and non-profit groups have always staked a claim. At the height of the dotcom boom, it seemed that there was a story in the local media almost daily about this dance troupe being evicted or that Mexican bakery being replaced by a pricey sushi restaurant. Neighbourhood resentment ran so high at one point that a small coalition known as the Yuppie Eradication Project formed to drive out the interlopers. Their modus operandi was to scratch expensive new Land Rovers and to throw dog poo on the front steps of WASP residences. Needless to say, they didn't succeed, but in the post-boom era, the Mission has settled back into a more laconic state of mind, and the frenzied pace of gentrification seems to have slowed to a crawl.

The hard truth of the matter is that all of the grassroots protests, loft moratoriums and ballot petitions in the world won't stop San Francisco's demographic evolution. The high cost of living, the influx of Asian immigrants and wuppies (white urban professionals) and the prohibitive price of owning a home continue to take a toll on the city's minority groups – in particular, on African-Americans. In fact, recent

The counter-culture spirit lives on.

census figures show that the city's black population has dwindled in the past decade from 79,039 to 60,515 – indeed, there are many neighbourhoods in San Francisco where you rarely see a black face these days.

Still, the flesh may be weak, but at least the spirit of diversity is willing. Immediately after the start of the war in Afghanistan, public radio stations such as KALW, KQED and KPFA all maintained an open forum for alternative and controversial viewpoints, keeping alive the Bay Area's reputation as a place of tolerance, acceptance and counter-culture values – even if the tone was a bit restrained. With baby boomers rapidly becoming grandparents, it seems inevitable that their wild-eyed idealism would give way to a more moderate approach. Heck, even anti-establishment heroes such as Wavy Gravy and Country Joe McDonald have websites nowadays.

But that's the beauty of San Francisco. A small peninsula of quirkiness in an ocean of contradictions; a place where an African-American mayor presides over a city that is nearly devoid of African-Americans, where treehuggers drive polluting, gas-guzzling Jeeps, and where dreamers and schemers, the needy and the greedy, gay and straight, and everything in between, all agree to disagree.

San Francisco's famous 'Painted Ladies' in **Alamo Square**. *See p22.*

Architecture

San Francisco's best buildings, from palaces to pyramids.

Rather than being a handicap, San Francisco's spectacular topography – a series of dramatic hills framed by the bay's surrounding waterscape – poses challenges that entice architects and inspire some of their best designs. San Francisco's built environment – particularly its colourful, 19th-century terraced houses – are one of its features that visitors find most appealing. And the city's resolute avoidance of 'Manhattanisation' – the unwillingness to build concrete boxes a mile high – has been helped by the threat of earthquakes and the diligence of the city's conservation lobbies.

EARLY ARCHITECTURE

The oldest building in the city is the Mission Dolores (*see p85*) in the Mission district, whose thick adobe walls and painted hammer beams represent the early European settlement of Yerba Buena. Founded in 1776, the simple chapel sits north of a cemetery where Indians, outlaws and the city's first Irish and Hispanic mayors are buried. Mission Dolores was one of 21 missions built in California by the Spanish; only two others, at Carmel and Monterey, rival it for authentic atmosphere. Along with a portion of the original walls of the Officers' Club in the Presidio, the mission is the only piece of colonial architecture to have outlived the city's steep progress from hamlet to metropolis.

The town inhabited by the Forty-Niners or 'Argonauts', as the Gold Rush immigrants were called, suffered a series of fires. Tiny Portsmouth Square (in present-day Chinatown) marked the heart of the early outpost, but was razed by two blazes; the surrounding streets all perished in the fire that followed the 1906 earthquake. The best examples of buildings surviving from the Gold Rush era are preserved in the Jackson Square Historical District (best viewed on Jackson between Montgomery and Sansome Streets) and now serve as design showrooms, law offices and antique shops.

THE PAINTED LADIES

A sudden burst of 19th-century prosperity quickly filled San Francisco's once-empty sloping streets with what have become its signature Victorian terraced houses. Built by middle-class tradesmen in the Mission and Lower Haight districts and by rich merchants in Presidio Heights and around Alamo Square, these famous 'Painted Ladies' provide the city's most characteristic architectural face. One of the most popular views of the city framed by a row of six painted Victorians is along Steiner Street between Hayes and Grove Streets; although these are the most-photographed examples, there are more than 14,000 other, equally charming versions of the city's architectural vernacular to rival (and, in many cases, surpass) them in ornamentation.

'San Francisco's Victorians come in four styles: Gothic Revival, Italianate, Stick-Eastlake and Queen Anne.'

Built of wooden frames decorated with mass-produced ornamentation, San Francisco's Victorians come in four distinct styles. The earliest Gothic Revival houses have pointed arches over their windows and were often painted white, rather than the bright colours of the later styles. The Italianate style, with tall cornices, neo-classical elements and add-on porches, are best exemplified in the Lower Haight, notably on Grove Street near Webster Street. Other examples can be found at 1900 Sacramento Street (near Lafayette Park) and at the Lilienthal-Pratt House, built in 1876 at 1818 California Street.

The Italianate was succeeded by the Stick-Eastlake style, named after furniture designer Charles Eastlake and characterised by square bay windows framed with angular, carved ornamentation. The 'Sticks' are the most common among Victorian houses left in the city; a shining example is the over-the-top extravaganza at 1057 Steiner Street, on the corner of Golden Gate Avenue. Finally, with its turrets, towers and curvaceous corner bay windows, the so-called Queen Anne style is amply demonstrated by the Wormser-Coleman House in Pacific Heights (1834 California Street, at Franklin Street). The most extravagant example is the Haas-Lilienthal House (*see p93*), built in 1886 by Bavarian grocer William Haas. He treated himself to a home with 28 rooms and six bathrooms – one of which has a bidet, a Victorian Gothic showerhead and a gas jet used for heating curling tongs. The house has been turned into a museum and is one of the few Victorians open to the public.

HOTELS AND MANSIONS

Another example of the ostentation that was part and parcel of San Francisco's booming late 19th-century lifestyle can be seen at the Palace Hotel (*see p41*), whose guests have included everyone from Rudyard Kipling to visiting European royalty. Opened in 1875, it epitomised local entrepreneur Billy Ralston's dreams – and his inability to resist Italian marble and solid gold dinner services, still on display in the lobby. Locals mourned the original building after it burned down in the 1906 fire, but the city rebuilt it, glassing in the atrium for elegant dining and adding fashionable art deco murals in the bar. It remains a wonderful time-tunnel to the past, combining echoes of Old Vienna and a Prohibition-era speakeasy.

Engineer Adolph Sutro was Ralston's friend and equal in ambition, buying a sandy wasteland on San Francisco's westernmost edge in 1881 for his Sutro Baths. Annexed by the new Golden Gate Park, Sutro's therapeutic baths were the most elaborate in the western world. Much in need of repair by the 1960s and badly burned in a fire, the baths were sold to developers for high-rise apartments that were never built. They are now the city's unofficial ruins. For its part, the adjoining Cliff House hotel and saloon (*see p101*) burned to the ground twice: the rebuilt eight-storey 'castle' destroyed in 1907 is now open to the public as a bar and restaurant.

Closer to the downtown area, San Francisco's 'Big Four' businessmen – Mark Hopkins, Leland Stanford, Collis P Huntington and Charles Crocker – made their architectural mark in the late 19th century by building substantial edifices. Their mining investments funded railroads and public transport, banks and businesses, and their baronial mansions on Nob Hill, victims of the 1906 fire, now mark the sites of some of the city's best luxury hotels. These include the Mark Hopkins Inter-Continental Hotel (1 Nob Hill, at California and Mason Streets) and the Stouffer Stanford Court Hotel (905 California Street).

The Crocker Mansion, a Queen Anne manor built in 1888, filled half the block now occupied by Grace Cathedral (*see p82*). Directly across from the cathedral is the Flood Mansion, a brilliant example of the size and grandeur of the homes that were once perched on Nob Hill. The 42-room sandstone marvel was built in 1886 by silver baron James C Flood. It now houses a private club. Another surviving house that has not been turned into a hotel is the Spreckels Mansion (2080 Washington Street), an impressive Beaux Arts building occupying an entire block. It was built in 1912

The 1886 **Haas-Lilienthal House**. *See p22.*

for sugar baron Adolph Spreckels and is now owned by mega-selling novelist Danielle Steel. It is not open to the public.

The city also has more than its share of architectural curiosities, among them the Columbarium (*see p102*) in the Richmond District. Built in 1898, this neo-classical temple holds the ashes of thousands of San Franciscans and is decorated with mosaic tiling and elaborate urns in imaginatively bedecked niches – a china football and photograph of Candlestick Stadium fill one, doll's furniture another.

Oriental promise meets occidental vulgarity at the Vedanta Temple (2963 Webster Street), an eccentricity built in 1905 for the Hindu Vedanta Society. Its bizarre mix of architectural styles includes a Russian Orthodox onion-shaped dome, a Hindu cupola, castle-like crenellations and Moorish arches. It is open to the public for Friday night services. You can also visit the Octagon House in Pacific Heights (*see p93*). Built in 1861, when the latest craze dictated that an eight-sided building was better for one's health, the house is one of just two octagon-shaped buildings left in the city. Furnished in early colonial style with Chippendale and Hepplewhite furniture, the upper floors have been restored to their original state, with a central staircase leading to a domed skylight.

CIVIC STRUCTURES

When the growing city began to burst at its peninsula seams, a ferry network evolved to carry passengers to and from the Bay Area cities. In 1896, the Ferry Building on the Embarcadero was built as a centrepiece, its clock-tower inspired by the Moorish campanile of Seville Cathedral. After the 1906 earthquake, a passion for engineering spurred an interest in Chicago architect Daniel Burnham's 'City Beautiful' project. This proposed a heroic new Civic Center planted below a terraced Telegraph Hill, enlaced with tree-lined boulevards that traced the city's contours. The plan was the result of Burnham's two-year consultations with leading city architects Bernard Maybeck and Willis Polk, and countered the city's impractical grid street pattern – but it never came to fruition.

Under Mayor 'Sunny Jim' Rolph, the main thrust of the 1915 Civic Center complex came from public contests, many won by Arthur Brown, architect of the mighty-domed City Hall (*see p67*). Other Civic Center buildings erected at this time include the former main library (soon to be the Asian Art Museum, at Larkin and McAllister Streets), the War Memorial Opera House (*see p226*) and the Bill Graham Civic Auditorium (*see p210*). All reflect the imperial style named after the Ecole des Beaux Arts in Paris and sometimes described as French Renaissance or classical baroque. The buildings were distinguished by their grandiose proportions and their ornamentation, as well as their theatrical halls and stairways.

It was largely Rolph's idea to host the huge Panama-Pacific Exposition in 1915, for which he commissioned Bernard Maybeck to build the Palace of Fine Arts and its myriad pavilions. Originally made of wood and plaster, the Palace (*see p95*) is the only building that remains from the Exposition (it was rebuilt of reinforced concrete in the 1960s). At around the same time, Julia Morgan, another Arts and Crafts architect, was at work on much of the East Bay and on the extravagant Hearst Castle – home of San Francisco newspaper magnate William Randolph Hearst – located down the coast at San Simeon.

Passionate rebuilding continued during the Depression, resulting in the opening of the San Francisco-Oakland Bay Bridge (1936), Golden Gate Bridge (1937) and a slew of Works Progress Administration buildings, such as Coit Tower (*see p82*) and Alcatraz island prison. The WPA, introduced as part of President Roosevelt's New Deal job-creation scheme, had a hand in everything from murals by Mexican artist Diego Rivera to the organisation of community archives. The best examples of projects from this period include the 1932 Herbst Theatre (*see p222*) with its murals by Frank Brangwyn, the 1930 Pacific Coast Stock Exchange (*see p61*) with its Rivera mural, and the Rincon Annex Post Office Building (now part of the Rincon Center – *see p63*). The Rincon, built in 1940 to include Anton Refregier's murals of Californian history, is a wonderful example of steel-trimmed marble.

The only Frank Lloyd Wright building in the city is the oval-entranced, red-brick Folk Art International at 140 Maiden Lane, near Union Square. Designed in 1948, this prototype Guggenheim now houses a tribal and folk art gallery, open to the public.

RECENT ARCHITECTURE

Pietro Belluschi's St Mary's Cathedral (*see p89*), a 200-foot (61-metre) high concrete structure supporting a cross-shaped, stained-glass ceiling, is a 1970s symbol of anti-quake defiance (its nickname is St Maytag, because it resembles a giant washing machine agitator). The 853-foot (260-metre) Transamerica Pyramid (*see p61*), built in 1972, is another example of architectural defiance. One of San Francisco's best-known buildings, the $34-million, seismic-proofed structure boasts an internal suspension system to protect it against tremors. Successfully, it would seem: the 48 storeys and 212-foot (65-metre) spire did not suffer in the 1989 quake. At first unpopular, the tower now has few detractors – indeed, it has come to symbolise the city and even features prominently in the *Beach Blanket Babylon* revue – a sure sign of civic affection.

Frank Lloyd Wright's **Folk Art International**.

The new Main Library (*see p68*), designed by Cathy Simon of architects Pei Cobb Freed, is a marriage of Beaux Arts and newer modern forms. One side links the building to the more contemporary Marshall Plaza, while the other echoes the old library to the north with grandiose, neo-classical columns. The dramatic interior centres around a five-storey atrium beneath a domed skylight designed to let natural light filter throughout the building.

Recent architectural activity has centred around the Moscone Convention Center and nearby SFMOMA (*see p107*), both part of the Yerba Buena complex. SFMOMA, designed by Mario Botta and opened in 1995, features a series of stepped boxes and a signature squared circle facing west. West of SFMOMA, Yerba Buena's Esplanade Gardens is one of the city's most beautiful urban parks, framed by museums, theatres and shops, and replete with lush greenery, fountains, sculptures, cafés and the Metreon (*see p161*), a hyper-modern urban mall owned by Sony and not without its own architectural significances. Across Mission Street from the Metreon, the new Jewish Museum (scheduled to open in 2003) is architect Daniel Libeskind's strikingly contemporary update of a former substation originally created by Willis Polk in 1907. The city's beloved MH de Young Museum is also scheduled to move into a new home on its current site in Golden Gate Park. The controversial ultra-modern design is by Herzog & de Meuron (creators of London's Tate Modern) and should be completed in 2005.

San Francisco has been courting architectural controversy quite a bit lately (nothing new, really). Among several pending projects making waves in the community and among the stuffy members of the city's planning department are the Rem Koolhaas-designed Prada emporium under construction near Union Square, and Thom Mayne's radical proposal for the new Federal Building at Seventh and Mission Streets. Meanwhile, such far less interesting and garishly large structures as the new Four Seasons Hotel on Market Street get built with little scrutiny. But such is the life of buildings in San Francisco, where temperament, design and ideas change as frequently as the hills go up and down.

San Francisco Beats **Jack Kerouac**, **Lawrence Ferlinghetti** and **Allen Ginsberg**.

Literary San Francisco

From Twain to Tan, the Bay has its say.

Perhaps it's the hills that unfold like the plot of a good story or the rolling fog that seems to foreshadow mystery, but San Francisco has always drawn writers to its streets – poets, novelists and essayists who eke out their living by crafting words. In the mid 19th century, Mark Twain and Bret Harte arrived to report on the Gold Rush; 100 years later, Tom Wolfe came to write about hippies in his *Electric Kool-Aid Acid Test*. From Dashiell Hammett and Jack London to Gertrude Stein, William Saroyan and Danielle Steel – some of the country's best-known writers have called the city home. And while a few big names have marked the city on the book lover's map, a number of lesser-known authors are intent on guaranteeing the city's future as a literary port of call.

FROM TOM SAWYER TO MCTEAGUE

Journalist and budding fiction writer Mark Twain worked in the city in the 1860s, constructing his literary persona and leaving for New York once *The Celebrated Jumping Frog of Calaveras County* hit the big time in 1867. Legend has it he took the name Tom Sawyer from a man who owned a bar on Montgomery Street. Twain, Bret Harte and Ambrose Bierce built on a foundation of journalistic irony and muckraking that gave the West an independent literary culture in the 1860s and 1870s – something that didn't happen again in San Francisco until after the end of World War II.

An ailing Robert Louis Stevenson arrived in 1879 in pursuit of the strong-willed (but already married) Fanny Osbourne. He lived at 868 Bush Street while Osbourne was in Oakland awaiting her divorce. Despite Stevenson's ill health, the two married in 1880. He then wrote about San Francisco in *The Wrecker* and about their Napa Valley honeymoon in *The Silverado Squatters*. Stevenson's house is in St Helena in Napa Valley and Robert Louis Stevenson State Park is nearby (*see p259*).

Jack London, one of San Francisco's few native sons to make it as a writer, was born at Third and Brannan Streets, the illegitimate son of a wandering astrologer and a medium. As an adolescent, Jack held seafaring jobs including a stint as an oyster pirate in the San Francisco Bay. He headed north in 1897 for the Yukon Gold Rush and began publishing stories in 1899. London became famous with *The Call of the Wild* and *The Sea Wolf* and spent his later years in the part of northern Sonoma Valley known as the Valley of the Moon, also the name of a Jack London novel. The museum there is worth a visit, if only to get a chilling sense of the connection between turn-of-the-century US Nietzscheanism and Nazi philosophy. The Jack London Museum, Wolf House and the writer's grave can all be found in the Jack London State Historic Park in Glen Ellen, north of the town of Sonoma (*see p257*).

Like London, Gertrude Stein was raised in Oakland. Her partner Alice B Toklas was born in San Francisco on O'Farrell Street and raised at 2300 California, among the Jewish bourgeoisie. In her autobiography *What is Remembered*, Toklas wrote about it – and about the 1906 earthquake: 'My father was apparently asleep,' Toklas wrote of the quake. Do get up, I said to him. The city is on fire. That, said he with his usual calm, will give us a black eye in the East.' Jack London wrote a much more dramatic account of the quake for the *Argonaut*. Both remembrances are published in the excellent collection *San Francisco Stories*, edited by John Miller (Chronicle Books, 1990).

Frank Norris, Jack London's contemporary, represents the left-wing version of the early 20th-century mixture of romanticism and naturalism. Norris was one of the first American disciples of Zola and a forerunner of the progressive era. His most famous novel, *The Octopus*, is about the railroad barons; his book *McTeague*, is set on Polk Gulch where Norris grew up.

THE CITY OF SAM SPADE

Dashiell Hammett came to San Francisco in 1921, at the tail-end of his career as a Pinkerton operative. Beginning in 1923, Hammett wrote and published 11 of his 'Continental Op' stories in *Black Mask*, stories set in the city and written while the tubercular Hammett was living at 620 Eddy Street. In 1926 he went to work for the Albert Samuels jewellery company at 985 Market (the Samuels clock is still standing). Shortly afterwards, he collapsed. He went on full disability pay, shipped his family to the countryside and became a full-time writer. Living at 891 Post Street, he wrote the series of novels that established the hard-boiled detective novel as the American genre, including *Red Harvest* and *The Dain Curse* (1929), *The Maltese Falcon* (1930) and *The Glass Key* (1931).

The Maltese Falcon sent Hammett to Hollywood, where he wrote *The Thin Man* and a string of movie sequels; he was saved from drinking himself to death by the onset of World War II. Blacklisted in the 1950s as a Communist, Hammett was jailed for refusing to testify during the McCarthy trials and disappeared from public life until the playwright Lillian Hellman found and rehabilitated him.

America is still uncomfortable with Hammett, which may be why his commemorative plaque (on Burrit Alley, off Bush Street) acknowledges Sam Spade and *The Maltese Falcon*, not his creator. 'On approximately this spot', it reads,

Slam funk

No longer the property of academic institutions and publishers, poetry has returned to its rightful place in popular culture – thanks to poetry slams. In San Francisco, slams happen regularly and garner an attendance of 100 to 500 people. Although Chicago, Boston and New York were among the first cities to catch on to the slam scene, SF's style has proved to be somewhat more creative than its eastern counterparts; poets have even staged an 'underwater' slam on a BART train as it sped under the San Francisco Bay to Berkeley.

Slams as we know them today originated in Chicago in the late 1980s and started as mock boxing matches, hence the name 'slam'. To emphasise artistic responsibility, the slams focused on the community and the audience. The performance aspect, with poets memorising and dramatising their poems, also helped rescue slams from becoming stuffy or boring.

The rules of all slams are basically the same. They include the random choice of five judges from the audience, a time limit of three minutes or less for each poem, and the prohibition of any props or costumes. Most slams feature a host and several well loved poets, as well as an open-mic session – meaning that anyone can sign up to perform his or her poetry (sign-up is usually half an hour before the show starts). The crowd tends to be young, but is often surprisingly diverse in age, gender and ethnicity. The poets are outspoken, outrageous and full of bravado. They speak of love, hate and the loss of innocence, always with an edge of comedy and political savvy to their rants.

To get a flavour of what happens at a slam, check out David Huang's pictures at www.poeticdream.com. Below we've listed regular poetry slams in the Bay Area; Second Sundays is the biggest and probably the best.

'Miles Archer, partner of Sam Spade, was done in by Brigid O'Shaughnessy'. The plaque's author, Warren Hinckle (a San Francisco journalist famous for bankrupting magazines), published a Dashiell Hammett issue of his *City* magazine in 1975. It lists every known Hammett and Sam Spade location and is required reading for enthusiasts. Both Hammett's and Spade's intertwined lives are detailed in *The Literary World of San Francisco* (City Lights, 1985) by Don Herron and Nancy Peters. Herron's *The Dashiell Hammett Tour* (City Lights, 1991) is a companion guide to the walking tour he conducts in May and June (*see p55*). Both books are out of print, but you may be able to find copies in a second-hand bookshop. John's Grill (63 Ellis Street, between Market and Powell Streets; 986 0069), which appeared in *The Maltese Falcon*, is another Hammett shrine.

'Allen Ginsberg read the first part of his famous poem *Howl*, with Kerouac and the 150-strong crowd shouting 'Go! Go! Go!''

THE BEAT GENERATION

Jack Kerouac came to the city in 1947, at the end of the cross-country trip that was to make him famous a decade later with the publication of *On the Road*. Because Neal Cassady was in San Francisco, the city became the western terminus of Kerouac's restless cross-country swings. He turned the original teletype-roll manuscript of *On the Road* into paragraphs in Cassady's flat on Russian Hill in 1952 (in May 2001, the manuscript was sold to a private collector, causing some public outrage, for a record-breaking $2.4 million). *San Francisco Blues* was written in the Cameo Hotel in what was then skid row on Third Street, an area later bulldozed to make way for the Moscone Center. *The Subterraneans*, written in 1953, is set in North Beach, but is actually a New York story transposed to protect the characters.

Another Kerouac novel, *The Dharma Bums*, chronicles the impact of the Beat movement on the West Coast. It also vividly reports the poetry reading of 13 October 1955 at the old Six Gallery on Fillmore Street, when Allen Ginsberg read the first part of his famous poem *Howl*, with Kerouac and the 150-strong crowd shouting 'Go! Go! Go!' That night, other notable poets Philip Whalen, surrealist Philip Lamantia, Michael McClure and Gary Snyder were also introduced to the wildly enthusiastic audience by literary guru Kenneth Rexroth, then the leading figure of post-World War II literary San Francisco. An irascible literary pacifist and orientalist, whose salon at 250 Scott Street was the centre of the post-war poetry renaissance, Rexroth's main contribution to San Francisco

Northern California Poetry Slam's website – www.norcalslam.org – includes a calendar of poetry slam events.

Bezerkely Open Slam

Starry Plough, 3101 Shattuck Avenue, between Prince & Woolsey Streets, Berkeley (1-510 841 2082). BART Ashby. **Show** 8.30-11pm Wed. **Admission** $5. No under-21s after 9pm. **Credit** MC, V.
This place has a friendly, enthusiastic crowd in an Irish pub-type atmosphere.

Java on Ocean

1700 Ocean Avenue, between Faxon & Capitol Avenues, Ingleside (333 6075). Muni Metro K. **Show** 4pm Sat. **Admission** free. **Credit** MC, V.

Poetry Above Paradise

Paradise Lounge, 308 11th Street, at Folsom Street, SoMa (861 6906). Bus 9, 12, 42. **Show** 9pm Sun. No under-21s. **Admission** free. **Credit** MC, V. **Map** p310 G5.
Local independent publisher Manic D Press hosts this weekly event, which includes music, poetry, slam and spoken word. Featured readers are followed by a raucous open-mic session.

Second Sundays

The Justice League, 628 Divisadero Street, between Grove & Hayes Streets, Western Addition (440 0409). Bus 21, 24. **Show** 8-11pm 2nd Sun of the month. **Admission** $5 before 9pm; $8 after 9pm. No under-21s. **Credit** AmEx, MC, V. **Map** p313 D5.

Tongue Tuesdays

Eli's Mile High Club, 3629 Martin Luther King Jr Way, at 37th Street, Oakland (1-510 655 6661). BART MacArthur/AC Transit bus CB. **Show** 9pm Tue. **Admission** $5-$10. No under-21s. **No credit cards**.

literary history – much to his own disgust – is his role as godfather to the Beats. He believed he should have been remembered for his work.

Ginsberg himself had come to San Francisco to (in his own words) 'find the Whitman self-reliance to indulge a celebration of self'. Here he came to terms with his homosexuality, met his lover Peter Orlovsky, moved into the Hotel Wentley and began writing the poem that would turn into *Howl*. The central image of the poem is the Moloch-face of the Drake Hotel on Powell Street as observed by Ginsberg high on peyote. Lawrence Ferlinghetti, owner of City Lights Booksellers & Publishers at 261 Columbus Avenue (*see p165*), later wrote to Ginsberg: 'I greet you at the beginning of a great career. Where's the manuscript?' *Howl*'s subsequent obscenity charges and the resulting trial catapulted the Beats to public attention and opened the way for the breakdown of the American obscenity laws in the 1960s.

The Beat scene was centred on North Beach – the Coexistence Bagel Store at Grant Avenue and Green Street, the Cellar on Green, the Coffee Gallery and the Place on Upper Grant (home of the 'blabbermouth nights', predecessors of today's poetry slams). Gino and Carlo's bar still stands at 548 Green Street (between Columbus and Grant Avenues; 421 0896). Vesuvio (*see p152*) is where Kerouac drank away his chance of meeting Henry Miller. It is located across Jack Kerouac Alley from City Lights, the scene's epicentre and still the best literary bookshop in San Francisco. 'So here comes Snyder with a bottle of wine,' Kerouac wrote, 'and here comes Whalen, and here comes what's-his-name… Rexroth and everybody… and we had the Poetry Renaissance of San Francisco.'

FROM THE HASHBURY TO BARBARY LANE

Compared to North Beach, the Haight-Ashbury scene doesn't seem to have much of a literary monument – though this is perhaps because (to quote Tom Wolfe) if you can remember it, you weren't really there. Ken Kesey and the reborn Neal Cassady began their trips festivals at the Longshoreman's Hall on Fisherman's Wharf, and the scene moved through the Avalon Ballroom on Polk Street and the Fillmore on Geary, to the Haight itself. Wolfe's *Electric Kool-Aid Acid Test* is the best account of the literary and psychological voyage, along with Emmet Grogan's memoir of the Diggers, *Ringolevio*. Kesey and Robert Stone, who was part of the scene and wrote about the era's psychic fallout in *Dog Soldiers*, were both products of Wallace Stegner's writing programme at Stanford University. Stegner, a long-respected Western writer and conservationist, was the author of the well-known 1960 'Wilderness Letter', a call for the preservation of wild places, and the 1972 Pulitzer Prize-winning novel *Angle of Repose*.

The Castro hasn't produced its literary testament yet, although A Different Light bookstore (*see p165*) is one of the best sources for gay, lesbian and bisexual fiction. Before his death, Randy Shilts produced an account of the coming of AIDS in *And The Band Played On*, a treatise on gays and lesbians in the US military, and also wrote a biography of Harvey Milk. Frances Fitzgerald gives a cooler view in *Cities on a Hill*. Armistead Maupin's very popular *Tales of the City* series is, in fact, set in Macondray Lane on Russian Hill.

CONTEMPORARY CURRENTS

The number of well-known writers living in the Bay Area seems to be growing, despite the rising cost of living and the bust of the dotcom market. Michael Chabon, winner of the 2001 Pulitzer Prize for fiction (*The Amazing Adventures of Kavalier & Clay*), lives in Berkeley, with his wife and writer Ayelet Waldman, whose latest mystery novel is *The Big Nap*. There's also Amy Tan (author of *The Bonesetter's Daughter* and *The Joy Luck Club*), Alice Walker (who wrote *The Color Purple* from her Alamo Square Victorian) and Isabelle Allende, whose 2000 novel *Daughter of Fortune* takes 19th-century San Francisco as one of its settings. Danielle Steel divides her time between her Pacific Heights mansion and Napa Valley.

Ethan Canin's latest is *Carry Me Across the Water* and Terry McMillan has come out with *A Day Late and a Dollar Short*. Armistead Maupin wrote *The Night Listener* in 2000, and Chitra Banerjee Divakaruni's newest is *The Unknown Errors of Our Lives*. Keep an eye out for new titles from Matthew Iribarne, James Houston, Dorothy Allison, Thomas Sanchez and Molly Giles. Other popular Bay Area writers are children's author Lemony Snicket, mystery writers Joe Gores and Cara Black, lesbian writers Pat Califia and Mabel Maney, and science fiction/fantasy writers Robert Silverberg, Tad Williams and Rudy Rucker.

Readings and book signings are a popular SF pastime. The top three independent shops that hold the most frequent readings and events are **A Clean Well Lighted Place For Books**, the **BookSmith** (for both, *see p165*) and **Stacey's Bookstore** (581 Market Street, at Second Street; 421 4687) and the **Books by the Bay** festival in July (*see p191*).

► For San Francisco's best **bookshops**, *see p164*.

Accommodation

Accommodation 30

Features

The best hotels 33
Reservation agencies 38
Chain gang 43

Accommodation

From high-rise hotels to charming B&Bs, there's no shortage of lodging options.

It sometimes seems as if San Francisco offers anything and everything to anyone and everyone. Its hotel scene is no different. When it comes to finding somewhere to stay, the choice is vast – from down-and-dirty hostels to flower-power boarding houses, gaudy Victorian mansions and modern five-star suites.

You'll find most of the city's hotels in and around touristy **Union Square** and the nearby **Tenderloin.** While this means there are many centrally located rooms close to transport and shopping areas, unfortunately many of them are lookalike spaces in cloned national chains. Still, there are some exceptions. It's certainly not the most attractive area in San Francisco, but if a convenient location is important, this is probably the place to head.

Those looking for a little more soul and originality in their hotel should head out to the less crowded and more charming surrounding neighbourhoods. **North Beach**, **Nob Hill**, **Pacific Heights**, the **Haight** and **Cow Hollow** all are home to one-of-a-kind boutique hotels and self-consciously quaint B&Bs. Some of these unusual inns date back to Victorian times, with four-poster beds, claw-footed bathtubs and working fireplaces.

Wherever you choose to stay, book well in advance because the city's hotels fill quickly, especially during the high season – from May to October – and during conventions, which are unpredictable and can make things crowded at the most unexpected times.

PRICES & SERVICES

For a basic double room with a private bath, phone and TV (and often continental breakfast), expect to pay at least $100 to $120 a night. For anything more luxurious you'll fork out considerably more. This price doesn't include a 14 per cent room tax. When making a hotel reservation, be prepared to pay for at least one night in advance. Most hotels hold reservations until about 6pm, unless you've notified them that you will be arriving later. Be warned that most hotels add a surcharge for every phone call, whatever the number may be; even 'toll-free' numbers can incur hefty hotel fees. Parking fees range from negligible to around $20 per night, sometimes a lot more.

All hotels are required by law to provide accommodation for disabled visitors, and, thanks to California's strict anti-smoking policies, all hotels have no-smoking rooms or floors; many are no-smoking throughout. Unless otherwise stated, all rooms listed below have a telephone.

Union Square

There is also a clutch of hotels, including some of San Francisco's most idiosyncratic and swanky, in the northern edge of the **Tenderloin** – *see p37* – which is also very close to the shopping and transport hub of Union Square.

First-class

Campton Place Hotel

340 Stockton Street, CA 94108, at Post Street (1-800 235 4300/781 5555/fax 955 5536/ www.camptonplace.com). BART Powell Street/ Muni Metro F, J, K, L, M, N/bus 2, 3, 4, 30, 38, 45, 76/cable car Powell-Hyde or Powell-Mason. **Rates** rooms $325-$450; suites $550-$2,100. **Credit** AmEx, DC, MC, V. **Map** p309 G3.

It's been 20 years since the former Drake-Wiltshire Hotel gave itself a hefty $18-million retrofit and reopened as the Campton Place, and ever since it has attracted a very discreet (and wealthy) following. The hotel neatly packs 110 rooms into a small space. Service is exceptional and includes valet-assisted packing and unpacking, as well as 24-hour room service and concierge. In true olde worlde style, it is the only hotel in the area that allows guests to bring small dogs with them; staff will even walk the pets of those too busy to do so themselves. The elegant Campton Place Restaurant is an excellent place to pass a romantic evening.

Hotel services *Air-conditioning. Babysitting. Bar. Business services. Concierge. Conference facilities. Garden (roof). Gym. Laundry. Limousine service. Parking ($15). Restaurant. Safe.* **Room services** *Dataport. Fax. Iron. Minibar. Room service (24hr). Turndown. TV: cable.*

Four Seasons Hotel & Residences

757 Market Street, CA 94103, between Third & Fourth Streets (633 3000/www.fourseasons.com). BART Powell Street/Muni Metro F, J, K, L, M, N/ bus 30, 38, 45, 76/cable car Powell-Hyde or Powell-Mason. **Rates** rooms $469-$600; suites $800-$3,900. **Credit** AmEx, DC, Disc, MC, V. **Map** p311 G/H4.

Scheduled for completion in autumn 2001, this long-anticipated, 36-storey hotel will contain 277 rooms and suites, 142 residential condos, high-end shops, an upscale restaurant (everyone in town is gossiping

Grand is a good description of the **Grand Hyatt**. *See p33.*

Travel to a different place.

hotel nikko san francisco

www.nikkohotels.com | 415.394.1111 | 1.800.NIKKO.US

off union square | 222 Mason St. | San Francisco, CA 94102

about who the chef will be) and a two-storey health club. It's ideally situated in the middle of Market Street, two blocks from both SFMOMA and Union Square. You'll never be bored while brushing your teeth here, as the large bathroom windows offer glorious views of the city and bay. As you might expect, the hotel understands the needs of business travellers: staff at the in-house tech centre can help you and your computer understand one another. Once guests are through working, they can enjoy the health club, indoor pool and jacuzzi.
Hotel services *Air-conditioning. Babysitting. Bar. Beauty salon. Business services. Concierge. Conference facilities. Gym. Laundry. Limousine service. Outdoor verandah. Parking ($34-$40). Pool. Restaurant. Safe. Spa.* **Room services** *CD player. Dataport. Minibar. Room service (24hr). Turndown. TV: cable.*

Grand Hyatt

345 Stockton Street, CA 94108, between Post & Sutter Streets (1-800 233 1234/398 1234/fax 391 1780/http://sanfrancisco.hyatt.com). BART Powell Street/Muni Metro F, J, K, L, M, N/bus 2, 3, 4, 30, 38, 45, 76/cable car Powell-Hyde or Powell-Mason. **Rates** rooms $189-$280; suites $450-$1,500. **Credit** AmEx, DC, Disc, MC, V. **Map** p309 G3.
The 684-room Grand Hyatt offers just about everything the business or pleasure traveller would expect from a four-star hotel. Its location at the north-east corner of Union Square couldn't be better, nor could the view from most of its 36 floors (especially from the rooftop Club 36 jazz club). Decor-wise, the rooms are rather corporate, but perks include a spacious health club, car service to the Financial District, a fully equipped business centre and good (and surprisingly reasonably priced) food at the handsome top-floor Grandviews Restaurant. Request a larger-than-average Regency Room, which includes continental breakfast and evening hors d'oeuvres.
Hotel services *Air-conditioning. Babysitting. Bar. Business services. Concierge. Conference facilities. Garden. Gym. Laundry. Parking ($38). Restaurant. Safe.* **Room services** *Dataport. Iron. Minibar. Room service (6am-midnight). Turndown. TV: cable.*

Hotel Nikko

222 Mason Street, CA 94102, at O'Farrell Street (1-800 645 5687/394 1111/fax 394 1106/ www.nikko hotels.com/americas/sanfran.html). BART Powell Street/Muni Metro F, J, K, L, M, N/bus 27, 38/cable car Powell-Hyde or Powell-Mason. **Rates** rooms $215-$425; suites $500-$2,500. **Credit** AmEx, DC, Disc, MC, V. **Map** p310 G4.
The minute you walk into the Nikko's vast, white marble lobby, with its soothing flow of cascading water and the hushed voices of the gracious hotel staff, you begin to relax. Part of the Japan Airlines hotel chain, the 25-storey hotel is, as you might expect, very popular with Japanese visitors. Recently refurbished, the 533 rooms and 22 suites are large and bright, furnished with luxurious fabrics, light wood furniture and lush green plants. The design is clean, tranquil and elegant – modern but with Asian touches – very different from the old-fashioned fussiness of San Fran's more traditional hotels. Suites on the Nikko Club floors offer stunning views and use of a private lounge with laptops and refreshments. Amenities include an indoor swimming pool, gym and sauna, and the acclaimed Anzu restaurant off the lobby.
Hotel services *Air-conditioning. Bars (2). Beauty salon. Business services. Concierge. Conference facilities. Gym. Laundry. Limousine service. Parking ($30). Pool. Restaurant. Safe. Spa.* **Room services** *CD player. Dataport. Fax. Iron. Minibar. Room service (24hr). Turndown. TV: cable.*

Pan Pacific

500 Post Street, CA 94102, at Mason Street (1-800 533 6465/771 8600/fax 398 0267/ www.panpacific.com). Bus 2, 3, 4, 30, 38, 45, 76/cable car Powell-Hyde or Powell-Mason. **Rates** rooms $390-$490; suites $545-$2,500. **Credit** AmEx, DC, Disc, MC, V. **Map** p308 G3.
Located one block from Union Square, the 330-room Pan Pacific is near perfection: the rooms are immaculate, the service outstanding, the architecture breathtaking and the East-meets-West ambience exudes tranquillity. Rooms are costly, but you get

The best Hotels

To be ridiculously trendy
At this nanosecond, the **W Hotel** is *the* place (*see p42*). Of course, a few hours ago the *only* place was the chic **Clift Hotel** (*see p37*).

For a room with a view
The **Grand Hyatt** (*see left*) on Union Square, the **Sherman House** (*see p48*) in Cow Hollow and the **Fisherman's Wharf Youth Hostel** (*see p50*) all offer gasp-worthy views.

To have a bath
In a claw-footed tub at the **Archbishop's Mansion** (*see p47*) or a glass bath-with-a-view at the **Mandarin Oriental** (*see p35*).

To pretend you're a high roller
Let's be honest; no place will do but the **Ritz-Carlton San Francisco**. *See p45.*

To behave like a rock star
Most rock types like the **Commodore** (*see p45*), but Johnny Depp prefers the **Phoenix** (*see p38*).

To explore your inner self
Where else but the Flower Power suite at **The Red Victorian** in the Haight. *See p47.*

something for your money: guests are treated like royalty, there are lavish marble bathrooms, personal valets and even a complimentary Rolls Royce service, for heaven's sake. If you're not staying here, the hotel is worth a visit to have dinner at the excellent Pan Asian Restaurant, or to sneak a ride in one of the glass lifts in the 18-storey atrium lobby.
Hotel services *Air-conditioning. Babysitting. Bar. Butler service (24hr). Business services. Concierge. Conference facilities. Gym. Laundry. Limousine service. No-smoking rooms. Parking ($34). Restaurant. Safe.* **Room services** *Dataport. Fax. Iron. Minibar. Room service (24hr). Turndown. TV: cable.*

Mid-range

Hotel Diva

440 Geary Street, CA 94102, at Mason Street (1-800 553 1900/885 0200/fax 346 6613/ www.hoteldiva. com). BART Powell Street/Muni Metro F, J, K, L, M, N/bus 2, 3, 4, 38, 76/cable car Powell-Hyde or Powell-Mason. **Rates** rooms $140-$259; suites $289-$700. **Credit** AmEx, DC, Disc, MC, V. **Map** p310 G4.
Conveniently located a block from Union Square in the heart of the city's theatre district, the Diva is stylish if a bit sterile. Its owners – who also run the Metropolis (*see below*) – have given the 114 rooms and suites a modern maritime feel, with white walls, pools of cobalt carpet and sculptured steel headboards fashioned into waves. Some rooms are rather dark and poky; those ending 08 and 12 are the biggest. For late-night cravings, a California Pizza Kitchen and Starbucks are bang next door.
Hotel services *Air-conditioning. Business services. Concierge. Conference facilities. Gym. Laundry. Parking ($22). Safe.* **Room services** *CD player. Dataport. Fax. Iron. Minibar. Room service (10am-midnight). Turndown. TV: cable/Nintendo/ Web TV. VCR.*

Hotel Metropolis

25 Mason Street, CA 94102, at Turk Street (1-800 553 1900/775 4600/fax 775 4606/ www.hotel metropolis.com). BART Powell Street/ Muni Metro F, J, K, L, M, N/bus 27, 31/cable car Powell-Hyde or Powell-Mason. **Rates** rooms $110-$225; suites $295-$365. **Credit** AmEx, DC, Disc, MC, V. **Map** p310 G4.
With its four elements decorating scheme, this hotel is all eco-friendly ying meets mid-priced yang. Each floor is colour-coded in shades of olive green (earth), taupe (wind), yellow (fire) and aquamarine (water), and the 105 rooms and five suites have nicely understated furnishings, with wave-shaped headboards and porthole-like windows. There's a small library and a lovely painted ceiling in the lobby. Nintendo and cable TV and better-than-average toiletries complete the comfortable picture. The pitfall of its less-than-salubrious location on the edge of the Tenderloin is skilfully overcome. The management participates in projects to help local homeless people,

Lavish living at **Hotel Nikko**. *See p33.*

while carefully directing guests to turn left, not right, out of the front door, to avoid them. There are splendid views over Potrero Hill and the Oakland hills beyond from the tenth floor, where some rooms also have balconies.
Hotel services *Business services. Concierge. Gym. Laundry. Parking ($19). Safe. Rooftop deck.* **Room services** *Dataport. Fax. Iron. Minibar. TV: cable/ Nintendo.*

Hotel Triton

342 Grant Avenue, CA 94108, at Bush Street (1-800 433 6611/394 0500/fax 394 0555/ www.hoteltriton. com). Bus 2, 3, 4, 15, 30, 45, 76. **Rates** rooms $239-$389; suites $329-$359. **Credit** AmEx, DC, Disc, MC, V. **Map** p309 G3.
This avant-garde hotel and local artists' showcase is right next to the ornate Chinatown gateway. The decor is a wonderland of dreamlike eccentricities, with mythological murals, glimmering dervish chairs and inverted-pyramid podiums. There is really no telling who you'll bump into at the Triton – the likes of Courtney Love, Cher and Bono have all pitched tent here. Of the 140 rooms, there is an Eco Floor for the environmentally sensitive, along with Zen Dens for those looking for inner meaning. If you feel like splashing out, choose between suites that pay homage to rock icons Jerry Garcia, Carlos Santana and Graham Nash.
Hotel services *Air-conditioning. Business services. Concierge. Conference facilities. Gym. Laundry. Parking ($28). Restaurant. Safe.* **Room services** *Dataport. Fax. Iron. Minibar. Room service (7am-10pm). TV: cable. VCR.*

The Maxwell

386 Geary Street, CA 94102, between Mason & Powell Streets (1-888 734 6299/986 2000/fax 397 2447/www.maxwellhotel.com). BART Powell Street/Muni Metro F, J, K, L, M, N/bus 2, 3, 4, 38, 76/cable car Powell-Hyde or Powell-Mason. **Rates** rooms $185-$205; suites $495-$595. **Credit** AmEx, DC, Disc, MC, V. **Map** p310/311 G4.
Call it chic boutique, or masterfully moody, but don't liken this boldly designed new hotel to the Rafael, its quirky predecessor. After reopening in 1997 in its current incarnation, all that's left of the old version is its convenient location on Geary Street. After the 12-storey, 153-room hotel's metamorphosis, rooms blend colour, texture, patterns and eclectic extras to create a deco-Victorian look. If you have the dough, book one of the suites, which are like personalised penthouses.
Hotel services *Air-conditioning. Babysitting. Bar. Business services. Conference facilities. Laundry. Limousine service. Parking ($22). Restaurant. Safe.* **Room services** *Dataport. Iron. Room service (8am-10pm). Turndown. TV: cable/ Nintendo.*

Orchard Hotel

665 Bush Street, CA 94108, at Powell Street (1-888 717 2881/362 8878/fax 362 8088/www.theorchard hotel.com). Bus 2, 3, 4, 76/cable car Powell-Hyde or Powell-Mason. **Rates** rooms $209-$299; suites $319-$499. **Credit** AmEx, DC, Disc, MC, V. **Map** p309 G4.
San Francisco's newest boutique hotel, the brand-new, ten-storey Orchard opened in November 2000. Its 96 rooms and nine suites are rather bland in design, but pristine and very comfortable. Perks include cotton bathrobes, Aveda toiletries, a free newspaper and continental breakfast. The smart V restaurant is an oenophile's delight, with a stupendous wine list and fine French-influenced California cuisine. It's a bit of a steep hike up to Bush Street, but the Powell cable car line is a few steps away. The hotel is no-smoking throughout.
Hotel services *Air-conditioning. Babysitting. Bar. Business services. Concierge. Conference facilities. Gym. Laundry. Limousine service. Parking ($30). Restaurant. Safe.* **Room services** *CD player. Dataport. Fax. Iron. Minibar. Room service (6.30am-10pm). Turndown. TV: cable.*

Also recommended

Hotel Rex *562 Sutter Street, CA 94102, between Powell & Mason Streets (1-800 433 4434/433 4434/ fax 433 3695/www.thehotelrex.com).* **Rates** rooms $215-$245; suites from $475.

Hotel Union Square *114 Powell Street, CA 94102, between Ellis & O'Farrell Streets (1-800 553 1900/ 397 3000/fax 399 1874/www.hotelunionsquare. com).* **Rates** rooms $139-$189; suites $325-$425.

Kensington Park Hotel *450 Post Street, CA 94102, between Powell & Mason Streets (1-800 433 4434/788 6400/fax 399 9484/www.kensingtonpark hotel.com).* **Rates** rooms $189-$249; suites $550.

Stratford Hotel *242 Powell Street, CA 94102, at Geary Street (1-888 554 6835/397 7080/ fax 397 7087/www.stratfordhotel.com).* **Rates** rooms $119-$189.

The Financial District

First-class

Mandarin Oriental

222 Sansome Street, CA 94104, between Pine & California Streets (1-800 622 0404/276 9888/fax 433 0289/www.mandarinoriental.com). BART Embarcadero or Montgomery Street/Muni Metro F, J, K, L, M, N/bus 12, 15, 41, 42/cable car California. **Rates** rooms $500-$725; suites $1,400-$3,000. **Credit** AmEx, DC, Disc, MC, V. **Map** p309 H3.
Few hotels in the world can boast such an extraordinary view as the Mandarin Oriental. Its lobby is on the ground floor of the 48-storey First Interstate Building and all of its 158 rooms, including four suites, are on the top 11 floors. The view is simply phenomenal, particularly when the fog settles below you – it's like being in heaven. (Note for secret exhibitionists: you can feel like you're sharing your body with the world in the glass bathtubs-with-a-view.) In keeping with the Japanese theme, the rooms contain a sparse selection of blond-wood furnishings and Asian artwork. Rumour has it that the staff to guest ratio is 1:1. Adjoining the lobby is the hotel's restaurant, Silks.

Best Bay Views in San Francisco

Best Locations

- Short walk to Fisherman's Warf, Ghirardelli Square, the "Crookedest" Street, Historic Cable Cars & Union Street Boutiques and Restaurants.

Best Facilities

- 2001 *Choice Hotels International* Silver Award for excellence in hospitality.
- 138 Renovated Guest Rooms; many with Views of the Golden Gate Bridge and the Bay.
- Daily Deluxe Complimentary Continental Breakfast.
- Guest room amenities including coffee makers, Hairdryer, Iron, and Satellite TV.
- Special Group Rates Available

Comfort Inn By the Bay 2775 Van Ness Avenue at Lombard St. San Francisco, CA 94109
For reservations call 415-928-5000 Fax 415-441-3990 • LTOUT-Mention this code to get 15% off your room rates, subject to availability. • Choice Hotels Internaional 800-228-5150 http:/www.choicehotel.com

GRANT PLAZA
HOTEL

$59 & UP

465 GRANT AVENUE • SAN FRANCISCO • CA 94108
(415) 434-3883 • FAX (415) 434-3886 • 800-472-6899
http://www.grantplaza.com

Great Location:
Chinatown Gateway and Union Square, walk to cable cars and great restaurants.

Modern rooms with:
Electronic locks (key cards), private baths with hair dryers, direct dial phones and satellite color TV.

"Best Buy" Consumer's Travel Letter

Recommended by: Mobil Travel Guide, Access, Fodor's, Frommer's, Time Out City Guides, Lonely Planet and many others.

PRESENT this ad at check-in for $10. CREDIT

The avant-garde **Hotel Triton**: popular with pop stars. *See p35.*

Hotel services *Air-conditioning. Bar. Business services. Concierge. Conference facilities. Gym. Laundry. Limousine service. Parking ($34). Restaurants (2).* **Room services** *Dataport. Iron. Minibar. Room service (24hr). Turndown. TV: cable/Nintendo.*

Also recommended

Hyatt Regency *5 Embarcadero Center, CA 94111, at California Street (1-800 233 1234/788 1234/ fax 398 2567/http://sanfrancisco.hyatt.com/).*
Rates rooms $189-$474; suites $379-$1,100.

Park Hyatt *333 Battery Street, CA 94111, at Clay Street (1-800 492 8822/392 1234/fax 421 2433/http://sanfrancisco.hyatt.com/).*
Rates rooms $225-$404; suites $390-$529.

The Tenderloin

First-class

Clift Hotel

495 Geary Street, CA 94102, at Taylor Street (1-800 652 5438/775 4700/fax 931 7417/ www.clifthotel.com). Bus 2, 3, 4, 27, 38, 76.
Rates rooms $325-$400; suites $950-$2,025.
Credit AmEx, DC, Disc, MC, V. **Map** p310 G4.

The Clift reopened its doors in July 2001 after a massive renovation – and it was well worth the wait. Designed by international hotel maestro Philippe Starck, its fantastical decor surpasses even that of New York's Royalton and LA's Mondrian hotels. The Italian Renaissance façade does battle with a postmodern, Daliesque interior, but don't worry – the 373 rooms and suites are not as self-consciously eclectic as the lobby, with its oversized furniture and vivid colours. In fact, most rooms are decorated in soft, relaxing tones, with comfortable sleigh beds and elegant floor-to-ceiling mirrors that endlessly reflect one another. The popular Redwood Room bar (*see p150*) and Asia de Cuba restaurant (*see p114*) both share the same enthusiastic decor.
Hotel services *Air-conditioning. Bar. Business services. Concierge. Conference facilities. Garden. Gym. Laundry. Limousine service. Parking ($40). Restaurant. Safe. Spa.* **Room services** *Dataport. Iron. Minibar. Room service (24hr). Turndown. TV: cable/Web TV.*

Hotel Monaco

501 Geary Street, CA 94102, at Taylor Street (1-800 214 4220/292 0100/fax 292 0111/ www.monaco-sf.com). Bus 2, 3, 4, 27, 38, 76.
Rates rooms $269-$399; suites $349-$599.
Credit AmEx, DC, Disc, MC, V. **Map** p310 G4.

Few hotels offer the romantic, larger-than-life ambience of the Monaco. The remodelled Beaux Arts building, built in 1910, underwent a $24-million facelift in 1995. Everything about the place is big: from the hand-painted ceiling domes and grandiose, art nouveau-style common areas, where antique knick-knacks contrast with local contemporary art, to the 201 rooms (including 35 suites),

with canopy-draped beds surrounded by a jumble of vibrant patterns (though the cheaper rooms are a tad too small). The sumptuous Grand Café next door has the feel of a 1920s Paris train station, accented by more local art – including a three-storey bunny sculpture. Rates include free coffee (mornings), tea (afternoons) and wine and cheese receptions with neck massages and tarot card readings (evenings). Welcome to California.
Hotel services *Air-conditioning. Bar. Business services. Concierge. Conference facilities. Gym. Laundry. Limousine service. Parking ($30). Restaurant. Safe. Spa.* **Room services** *Dataport. Fax. Iron. Room service (24hr). Turndown. TV: cable/Nintendo/Web TV.*

The Prescott

545 Post Street, CA 94102, at Taylor Street (1-800 283 7322/563 0303/fax 563 6831/ www.prescotthotel.com). Bus 2, 3, 4, 27, 38, 76. **Rates** rooms $290-$320; suites $315-$1,200. **Credit** AmEx, DC, Disc, MC, V. **Map** p310 G3/4.
There was a time when guests would check in here solely to get preferential seating at the adjoining Postrio restaurant (*see p114*). While the restaurant has lost some of its almighty status since then, this remains one of San Francisco's finer small hotels. The 164 rooms, including 40 suites, are decorated with custom-made cherry-wood furnishings, silk wallpaper and comfy beds. The penthouse is a lavish affair complete with roof-top jacuzzi, grand piano and twin fireplaces. Highly recommended is the Club Level, a private floor where perks includes free drinks, hors d'oeuvres, continental breakfast and a host of amenities.
Hotel services *Air-conditioning. Babysitting. Bars (2). Concierge. Gym. Laundry. Limousine service. Parking ($30). Restaurant. Safe.* **Room services** *Dataport. Fax. Iron. Minibar. Room service (7am-midnight). Turndown. TV: cable.*

Mid-range

Phoenix Hotel

601 Eddy Street, CA 94109, at Larkin Street (1-800 248 9466/776 1380/fax 885 3109/ www.sftrips.com/hotels/phoenix.html). Bus 19, 31. **Rates** rooms $119-$155; suites $195-$205. **Credit** AmEx, DC, Disc, MC, V. **Map** p310 F4.
What do Ziggy Marley, Johnny Depp, the late John F Kennedy Jr and Pearl Jam have in common? They've all stayed at the funky Phoenix, one of San Francisco's glam pads – located, oddly enough, in one of the city's least glamorous neighbourhoods. The 44 bungalow-style rooms equipped with bamboo furniture and tropical plants help to create the feel of an oasis, particularly when guests bask by the pool on a sunny day. The adjoining Backflip restaurant and cocktail lounge (*see p217*) provides funky food and music in perfect Phoenix style.
Hotel services *Bar. Concierge. Garden. Parking (free). Pool. Safe.* **Room services** *Dataport. TV: cable.*

Savoy Hotel

580 Geary Street, CA 94102, between Jones & Taylor Streets (1-800 227 4223/441 2700/ fax 441 0124/http://thesavoyhotel.com). Bus 2, 3, 4, 27, 38. **Rates** rooms $129-$265; suites $209-$279. **Credit** AmEx, DC, Disc, MC, V. **Map** p310 G4.
A slice of Paris, the Savoy was built in 1913 for the Panama-Pacific Exposition. Today, it still overflows with luxury: sumptuous fabrics, marble floors and billowy feather beds in each of the 83 small but individually decorated rooms distinguish it from the rest. Centrally located in the Theatre District, the Savoy is just a few blocks from Union Square, but is also near enough to the Tenderloin to keep its prices low.

Reservation agencies

If you would rather hand over the booking process to a reservation service, a number of reputable companies will do the work for you. You can also contact the **Visitor Information Center** (24-hour hotline 1-888 782 9673/www.sfvisitor.org), operated by the San Francisco Convention & Visitors Bureau. This provides a citywide hotel reservation service with no booking fee. It also offers online reservations.

Bed & Breakfast California

1-800 872 4500/1-408 867 9662/ fax 1-408 867 0907/www.bbintl.com.
Open 9am-4pm Mon-Fri.
This Saratoga-based agency offers a selection of B&Bs, ranging from budget to moderately priced, with a two-night minimum stay. Options are as varied as the prices, ranging from simple rooms in private houses to luxurious Victorian homes, carriage houses and houseboats. There is a $10 non-refundable booking fee.

San Francisco Reservations

1-800 677 1500/1-510 628 4450/ fax 1-510 628 9025/www.hotelres.com.
This company offers reservations at more than 300 of San Francisco's hotels, often at discounted rates. It's worth enquiring about their events and hotel packages, which include VIP or discount admissions to various San Francisco museums. There is no booking fee.

Phoenix Hotel: downright funky. *See p38.*

Hotel services *Business services. Concierge. Conference facilities. Laundry. Limo service. Parking ($18). Restaurant (breakfast only). Safe.* **Room services** *Dataport. Iron. Minibar. Room service (breakfast only). Turndown. TV: cable/Nintendo.*

Budget

Adelaide Inn

5 Isadora Duncan Court, CA 94102, off Taylor Street, between Post & Geary Streets (441 2261/ fax 441 0161). Bus 2, 3, 4, 27, 38. **Rates** rooms $42-$80. **Credit** AmEx, MC, V. **Map** p310 G4.

It's mostly European tourists who reap the benefits of this old-fashioned *pension* tucked into a quiet downtown cul-de-sac. All three levels are bright and cheery, adorned with the sort of unintentionally funky furniture that reminds you just how old this place is. If you don't mind sharing a bathroom and sleeping on a spongy mattress, the place is cheap and cheerful. The 18 rooms have TVs, but no phones, and breakfast is not included.

Hotel services *Payphone. Safe.* **Room services** *Dataport. Iron. No phone. TV.*

The Andrews

624 Post Street, CA 94109, between Jones & Taylor Streets (1-800 926 3739/563 6877/fax 928 6919/ www.andrewshotel.com). Bus 2, 3, 4, 27, 38, 76. **Rates** rooms $99-$165; suites $149-$175. **Credit** AmEx, DC, MC, V. **Map** p310 G3/4.

It's not that easy to find a decent room for $100 within walking distance from Union Square – but this place comes close. With 48 small, comfortable rooms, this seven-storey hotel is cosy and affordable. And there are charming, thoughtful extra touches: every morning guests find a tray at their door, with a continental breakfast of freshly baked croissants and muffins, tea and coffee. The adjoining Fino Bar & Restaurant serves moderately priced Italian dishes with complimentary wine for hotel guests.

Hotel services *Bar. Concierge. Parking ($20). Restaurant. Safe.* **Room services** *Dataport. Iron. Minibar. Room service (evenings only). Telephone. TV: cable.*

The Gaylord

620 Jones Street, CA 94102, between Geary & Post Streets (1-800 336 8445/673 8445/fax 673 8476/ www.sirius.com/~gaylord/). Bus 2, 3, 4, 27, 38, 76. **Rates** per week $400-$475; per month $1,200-$1,600. **Credit** AmEx, Disc, MC, V. **Map** p310 G3/4.

If you want to live like a local and enjoy the benefits of cooking your own meals, this hotel-apartment hybrid might be for you. Located in the heart of the Theatre District, the Gaylord has a distinctive ornate exterior and a large lobby with a glorious painted ceiling. Although the 172 apartments are not elegant by any means, they come equipped with refrigerators and microwaves – but no phone. The staff are rather quirky, but you can't beat the convenience. Note that the minimum stay is one week.

1 800 USA HOTELS .com

The fastest and easiest way to save on hotel reservations worldwide!

- Savings of up to 70% at 46,000 hotels!
- Expert Agents 24-hour service
- Free Frequent Flyer Miles with every stay!

1800usahotels.com/timeout

1.800.872.4683

Please mention the *Time Out* City Guides when you call!

Get treated like royalty at the sumptuous **Palace Hotel**.

Hotel services *Cooking facilities. Payphone.*
Room services *Dataport. Iron. Kitchenette. No phone. TV: cable.*

Also recommended

Halcyon Hotel *649 Jones Street, CA 94102, between Post & Geary Streets (1-800 627 2396/929 8033/fax 441 8033/www.bradyacres.com).*
Rates rooms $89-$129.

Touchstone Tulip Inn *480 Geary Street, CA 94102, between Mason & Taylor Streets (1-800 524 1888/771 1600/fax 931 5442.*
Rates rooms $109-$169.

Civic Center

Mid-range

The Abigail

246 McAllister Street, CA 94102, between Hyde & Larkin Streets (1-800 243 6510/626 6500/fax 626 6580/www.abigailhotel.com). BART Civic Center/Muni Metro F, J, K, L, M, N/bus 5, 19.
Rates rooms $109-$169; suites $300. **Credit** AmEx, DC, Disc, MC, V. **Map** p310 F/G4.

Near the Opera House, Davies Symphony Hall and the San Francisco Ballet, the Abigail is a safe bet for culture-hungry visitors seeking clean, comfortable rooms at a reasonable price. The 60 rooms are individually decorated with antiques, imported quilts and 19th-century English lithographs and paintings. A free continental breakfast is provided, and the hotel's Millennium restaurant (*see p121*) offers gourmet vegetarian cuisine in a romantic setting.
Hotel services *Business services. Concierge. Laundry. Parking ($20). Restaurant. Safe.*
Room services *Dataport. Iron. Turndown. TV: cable.*

SoMa

First-class

Palace Hotel

2 New Montgomery Street, CA 94105, at Market Street (1-800 325 3589/512 1111/fax 543 0671). BART Montgomery/Muni Metro F, J, K, L, M, N/bus 2, 3, 4, 5, 9, 10, 15, 21, 30, 31, 38, 45, 71.
Rates single $300-$330; suites $800-$2,900.
Credit AmEx, DC, Disc, MC, V. **Map** p309 H3.

Built in 1875, this place has long been one of the world's grandest hotels; famous guests have included Winston Churchill, Thomas Edison and Franklin D Roosevelt. A $160-million restoration in 1991 kept the dignitaries coming. Today, its dining rooms are absolutely breathtaking, while the spectacular Garden Court has 80,000 panes of stained glass in its ceiling dome. The hotel's glass-domed swimming pool is by far the finest in the city. By comparison, the 553 rooms are rather modest but even if you don't stay here, it's worth a look or – even better – a visit for afternoon tea.
Hotel services *Air-conditioning. Babysitting. Bar. Business services. Concierge. Conference facilities. Gym. Laundry. Limousine service. Parking ($30). Pool. Restaurants (3). Safe. Sauna.* **Room services** *Dataport. Iron. Minibar. Room service (24hr). Turndown. TV: cable/Web TV.*

W Hotel

181 Third Street, CA 94103, at Howard Street (1-800 946 8357/777 5300/fax 817 7823/ www.whotels.com). BART Montgomery/Muni Metro F, J, K, L, M, N/bus 2, 3, 4, 5, 9, 10, 15, 21, 30, 31, 38, 45, 71. **Rates** rooms $179-$369; suites from $1,300. **Credit** AmEx, DC, Disc, MC, V. **Map** p311 H4.
This is the trendiest hotel in town, bar none, and it's not difficult to see why. The sparse elegance of its minimalist decor, the hip dance music playing throughout and the stylish after-work crowd sauntering through for cocktails all scream: cool place *du jour*. The 423 rooms are as artistically modern as the lobby, and are loaded with all the latest gizmos: CD players, 27-inch TVs, high-speed Internet access and cosy, goose-down duvets. Black-and-white photos of San Francisco line the walls. Some rooms have great views over Yerba Buena Gardens. Located next door to SFMOMA, the W is ideally placed for downtown and SoMa. If you don't stay here, you can always slap on some Prada and head to the bars (*see p150*) or XYZ restaurant (*see p125*). Just make sure you're carrying your platinum AmEx card.
Hotel services *Air-conditioning. Bars (2). Business services. Concierge. Conference facilities. Gym. Laundry. Parking ($36). Pool. Restaurants (2). Safe.* **Room services** *CD player. Dataport. Fax. Iron. Minibar. Room service (24hr). TV: cable/Web TV. VCR.*

Budget

Bay Bridge Inn

966 Harrison Street, CA 94107, between Fifth & Sixth Streets (397 0657/fax 495 5117/www.bay bridgeinn.com). Bus 27, 42. **Rates** rooms $69-$135. **Credit** AmEx, DC, Disc, MC, V. **Map** p311 H5.
There's absolutely no reason why you would want to spend a lot of time in this place's 22 plain, motel-style rooms; however, they're cheap and clean, and convenient for the Moscone Convention Center and the city's nightclub scene. Those are, it's fair to say, the only reasons to stay here.
Hotel services *Air-conditioning. Limousine service. Parking (free). Jacuzzi. Restaurant. Safe.* **Room services** *Dataport. Iron. TV: cable.*

Chinatown

Budget

Grant Plaza Hotel

465 Grant Avenue, CA 94108, at Pine Street (1-800 472 6899/434 3883/fax 434 3886/ www.grantplaza. com). Bus 15, 30, 45/cable car California. **Rates** rooms $55-$129. **Credit** AmEx, DC, Disc, MC, V. **Map** p309 G3.
As long as you don't have a car – the Grant Plaza is located in the middle of crowded Chinatown – you'd be hard-pressed to find a better deal anywhere in the city. As little as $55 buys you a night in one of 72 immaculately clean (albeit small) rooms complete with contemporary furnishings, private bath, TV and phone. If you split one of the larger rooms four ways, you'll pay less than hostel rates. Note that the corner rooms on the higher floors are the largest and brightest.
Hotel services *Concierge. Parking ($17.50). Safe.* **Room services** *Dataport. TV: cable.*

North Beach

Mid-range

Hotel Bohème

444 Columbus Avenue, CA 94133, between Vallejo & Green Streets (433 9111/fax 362 6292/www. hotelboheme.com). Bus 15, 30, 39, 41, 45. **Rates** rooms $154-$194. **Credit** AmEx, DC, Disc, MC, V. **Map** p309 G2.
If you can't deal with the monster hotel chains and prefer a smaller, sophisticated inn, you may like the Bohème. Its 16 rooms are charming, if tiny, and its location on Columbus Avenue – the lifeline of North Beach – is hard to beat. It's surrounded by small cafés and boutiques, and is within walking distance of Chinatown and Fisherman's Wharf. Light sleepers should request a room that doesn't face the hustle and bustle of Columbus Avenue.
Hotel services *Concierge. Parking ($27.50). Safe.* **Room services** *Dataport. Turndown. TV: cable.*

Washington Square Inn

1660 Stockton Street, CA 94133, at Filbert Street (1-800 388 0220/981 4220/fax 397 7242). Bus 15, 30, 39, 41, 45/cable car Powell-Mason. **Rates** rooms $155-$245. **Credit** AmEx, DC, Disc, MC, V. **Map** p308 G2.
Location is key to the charm of this hotel in the heart of North Beach, but it's not the only attraction. While it's within easy strolling distance of the area's many boutiques and Italian restaurants, the hotel is also worthwhile for its lovely decor, with large gilt mirrors and pots of exotic orchids. Each of the 15 rooms is decorated with French antiques

and lush fabrics, with loads of fresh flowers. The service is also excellent: guests are offered tea, wine and hors d'oeuvres every afternoon. A continental breakfast is included in the room price.
Hotel services *Laundry. Parking ($25). Safe.* **Room services** *Dataport. Room service (7.30am-11pm). Turndown. TV: cable.*

Budget

San Remo Hotel

2337 Mason Street, CA 94133, at Chestnut Street (1-800 352 7366/776 8688/fax 776 2811/ www.sanremohotel.com). Bus 15, 30, 39/ cable car Powell-Mason. **Rates** rooms $65-$90; penthouse $150. **Credit** AmEx, DC, MC, V. **Map** p308 G2.
Originally a boarding-house for dock workers displaced in the Great Fire of 1906, this meticulously restored Italianate Victorian is now home to one of the city's best bargains. Though the rooms are small and the spotless bathrooms (showers, actually) shared, you'd be hard-pressed to find finer accommodation at this price elsewhere. Aping a European pension, the 63 rooms have brass or cast-iron beds, wicker furniture and antique armoires – they do not have a telephone or TV. Ask for a room on the upper floor facing Mason Street or, if the penthouse is free, book it – you'll never want to leave. The hotel's 1947 Ford 'Woody' is always parked out front.
Hotel services *Bar. Business services. Concierge. Conference facilities. Laundry (self-service). No-smoking rooms. Parking ($10-$14). Payphone. Restaurant. Safe.* **Room services** *No phone or TV.*

Chain gang

High-season vacancy is a bitch. When the city's packed, it may be time to try a hotel from the corporate cookie cutter. All those listed below are either in the city or nearby.

First-class ($200 up)

Crowne Plaza 1-888 218 0808
www.crowneplaza.com
Hyatt 1-866 333 8881
www.hyatt.com
Marriott 1-800 932 2198
www.marriott.com
Starwood (Sheraton) 1-888 625 5144
www.starwood.com/sheraton

Mid-range ($100-$200)

Best Western 1-800 528 1234
www.bestwestern.com
Hilton 1-800 774 1500
www.hilton.com
Holiday Inn 1-800 465 4329
www.holiday-inn.com
Travelodge 1-800 255 3050
www.travelodge.com

Budget (under $100)

Howard Johnson 1-800 654 2000
www.hojo.com
Ramada 1-800 272 6232
www.ramada.com
Super 8 1-800 800 8000
www.super8.com

Fisherman's Wharf

Mid-range

Tuscan Inn

425 North Point Street, CA 94133, at Mason Street (1-800 648 4626/561 1100/fax 561 1199/www.tuscaninn.com). Muni Metro F/bus 39, 42/cable car Powell-Mason. **Rates** rooms $149-$299; suites $339. **Credit** AmEx, DC, Disc, MC, V. **Map** p308 G1.
Part of the Best Western motel chain, but still a classy hotel, the 221-room Tuscan Inn is located in the heart of Fisherman's Wharf. The rooms are handsome, spacious and comfortable; the staff are exceedingly helpful and the adjoining Café Pescatore – a gleaming Italian trattoria – is as good as it looks for breakfast, lunch or dinner. If you tire of the touristy Wharf, escape is at hand: the Inn is a block away from the cable car turnaround.
Hotel services *Air-conditioning. Concierge. Conference facilities. Garden. Laundry. Parking ($28). Restaurant. Safe.* **Room services** *Dataport. Iron. Minibar. Room service (7am-9.30pm). Turndown. TV: cable/Nintendo.*

The Wharf Inn

2601 Mason Street, CA 94133, at Beach Street (1-800 548 9918/673 7411/fax 776 2181/ www.wharfinn.com). Muni Metro F/bus 39, 42/ cable car Powell-Mason. **Rates** rooms $99-$399. **Credit** AmEx, DC, Disc, MC, V. **Map** p308 G1.
For those who can't resist the lure of Fisherman's Wharf, this hotel is a reasonable option. It's essentially a motel, but the owners have done an admirable job of refurbishing the rooms in handsome tones of forest green, burgundy and pale yellow. The 51 rooms and three suites have all the standard amenities – TV, telephone, private bath. The hotel is central to the Wharf, and is a two-block walk from Pier 39 and the cable car turnaround.
Hotel services *Business services. Concierge. Limousine service. Parking (free). Safe.* **Room services** *Dataport. Iron. Turndown. TV: satellite.*

Nob Hill

First-class

Huntington Hotel

1075 California Street, CA 94108, at Taylor Street (1-800 227 4683/474 5400/fax 474 6227/ www.huntingtonhotel.com). Bus 1/cable car California. **Rates** rooms $300-$350; suites $445-$825. **Credit** AmEx, DC, Disc, MC, V. **Map** p308 G3.

Hipper than hip: the **W Hotel**, next to SFMOMA. *See p42.*

Perched high on Nob Hill next to Grace Cathedral, this family-owned and operated hotel exemplifies understated luxury. One of the city's *grandes dames*, its 137 charming, well-appointed rooms and 32 suites offer incredible views of the city. A stay at the Huntington would be wasted without a swim in the pool overlooking Union Square. Or you could indulge in a treatment at the lush Nob Hill Spa (345 2888); you might pass Bruce Willis, Jerry Seinfeld or Keanu Reeves in an adjoining treatment room enjoying a reflexology massage and green tea salt scrub. The California cable car line goes past the door.
Hotel services *Air-conditioning. Bar. Concierge. Conference facilities. Gym. Laundry. Limousine service. No-smoking rooms. Parking ($19.50). Pool. Restaurant. Safe. Spa.* **Room services** *Dataport. Fax. Minibar. Room service (6am-11pm). Turndown. TV: cable.*

Nob Hill Lambourne

725 Pine Street, CA 94108, between Powell & Stockton Streets (1-800 274 8466/433 2287/ fax 433 0975/www.nobhilllambourne.com). Bus 30, 45/cable car Powell-Hyde or Powell-Mason. **Rates** rooms $210-$230; suites $275-$350. **Credit** AmEx, DC, Disc, MC, V. **Map** p309 G3.
Billed as a 'business-boutique' hotel, the 20-room Lambourne has found its niche as a haven for well-paid, health-obsessed business execs. Apparently they do exist. Mints on the pillow? Hardly. Extras here include beta-carotene tablets, yoga lessons and an in-room massage service, as well as your own fax machine, voicemail and laptop computer with Internet access. Instead of a minibar, guests will find a 'balancing basket' of workout essentials: dumbells, bottled water, energy bars and a yoga mat. But there are no futons here: the expensive hand-sewn bedcovers show the Lambourne's hidden indulgence (even the nearby Ritz-Carlton – *see below* – sends guests here when it's overbooked). The hotel provides a free 'healthy' breakfast, and wine and cheese receptions in the evening. Sweetly, they offer parents one free daily phone call home (in the US).
Hotel services *Concierge. Conference facilities. Laundry. Parking ($28). Safe. Spa.* **Room services** *Dataport. Fax. Iron. Kitchenette. Turndown. TV: cable.*

Ritz-Carlton San Francisco

600 Stockton Street, CA 94108, at California Street (1-800 241 3333/296 7465/fax 291 0288/ www.ritzcarlton.com). Bus 1, 30, 45/cable car California. **Rates** rooms $375-$475; club level rooms $475-$595; junior suites $600-$720; executive suites $675-$675; presidential suites $3,600-$4,800. **Credit** AmEx, DC, Disc, MC, V. **Map** p309 G3.
Among the fine hotels on Nob Hill, it's the Ritz that gets all the attention, and deservedly so. After a four-year, multi-million dollar renovation, the 1909 neo-classical landmark first opened its doors as the Ritz-Carlton in 1991, and has wowed its affluent guests ever since. Amenities at the 336-room hotel include an indoor spa with gym, swimming pool, whirlpool and sauna; the award-winning French restaurant, the Dining Room (*see p121*); daily piano performances in the Lobby Lounge; and an armada of valets to fill your every need. The rooms, while sumptuously appointed, are rather staid compared with the grandiose façade and lobby, but include all the luxury items you would expect from the Ritz. Club level guests get use of the elegant Club Lounge, with continuous food and drinks and other services. If you can't afford to stay here, come for the lavish Sunday Jazz Brunch in the terrace courtyard surrounded by roses and bougainvillea.
Hotel services *Air-conditioning. Babysitting. Bar. Business services. Concierge. Conference facilities. Garden. Gym. Laundry. Limousine service. Parking ($45). Pool. Restaurants (2). Safe. Spa.* **Room services** *Dataport. Iron. Minibar. Room service (24hr). Turndown. TV: cable/ Nintendo.*

Also recommended

Fairmont Hotel & Tower *950 Mason Street, CA 94108, at California Street (1-800 527 4727/ 772 5000/fax 772 5013/www.fairmont.com).* **Rates** rooms $249-$580; suites $630-$8,000.

Mark Hopkins Inter-Continental *1 Nob Hill, CA 94108, at Mason Street (1-800 662 4455/ 392 3434/fax 421 3302).* **Rates** rooms $185-$360; suites $299-$1,600.

Mid-range

Commodore International Hotel

825 Sutter Street, CA 94109, between Jones & Leavenworth Streets (1-800 338 6848/923 6800/ fax 923 6804/www.thecommodorehotel.com). Bus 2, 3, 4, 27. **Rates** rooms $149-$225. **Credit** AmEx, DC, Disc, MC, V. **Map** p308 G3.
Are you an internationally travelled hipster? Do you secretly envy the 'it' crowd? Well, this is where they stay when in town. From the company that raised the legendary Phoenix Hotel (*see p38*) from its ashes, this neo-deco hotel is one of the grooviest rent-a-pads in town. Of the 110 spacious rooms – all with large bath-tubs and closets – request one of the post-modern deco rooms with custom furnishings fashioned by local artists. The Red Room bar (*see p150*) is very popular; drenched in hypnotic red, it has the decadence of a past era.
Hotel services *Bar. Concierge. Conference facilities. Laundry. Limousine service. Parking ($22). Restaurant (breakfast & lunch only). Safe.* **Room services** *Dataport. Iron. TV: cable.*

White Swan Inn

845 Bush Street, CA 94108, between Taylor & Mason Streets (1-800 999 9570/775 1755/fax 775 5717/www.foursisters.com/inns/whiteswanninn.html). Bus 2, 3, 4, 76/cable car Powell-Hyde or Powell-Mason. **Rates** rooms $180-$210; suites $225-$285. **Credit** AmEx, DC, MC, V. **Map** p308 G3.
If you like the idea of a hotel that is decorated with teddy bears and offers guests platters of fresh-baked cookies, read on. The 26-room White Swan Inn likes to think of itself as a cosy 'English inn', right down

Where the nobs stay: the grandiose **Ritz-Carlton San Francisco** on Nob Hill. *See p45.*

to the wallpaper, working fireplaces and fresh flower arrangements in each room. Guests are treated to a full complimentary breakfast each morning and a wine reception each evening. Afternoon tea is served in a large parlour decorated with old teapots and yet more teddy bears. Just as sweet as can be, though not to everyone's taste.
Hotel services *Concierge. Conference facilities. Garden. Gym. Laundry. Parking ($30). Safe.*
Room services *Dataport. Iron. Room service (breakfast only). Turndown. TV: cable. VCR.*

Also recommended

Nob Hill Inn *1000 Pine Street, CA 94102, at Taylor Street (1-888 982 2632/673 6080/fax 673 6098).* **Rates** rooms $125-$165; suites $195-$275.

Renaissance Stanford Court Hotel *905 California Street, CA 94108, at Powell Street (1-800 227 4736/989 3500/fax 391 0513/www.marriott.com).* **Rates** rooms $169-$289; suites $409.

Budget

Golden Gate Hotel

775 Bush Street, CA 94108, between Powell & Mason Streets (1-800 835 1118/392 3702/fax 392 6202/www.goldengatehotel.com). Bus 2, 3, 4, 76/ cable car Powell-Hyde or Powell-Mason. **Rates** rooms with shared bath $85; rooms with private bath $130. **Credit** AmEx, DC, MC, V. **Map** p308/309 G3.

The 1913 Edwardian hotel is one of San Francisco's best small hotels, with an excellent location, reasonable rates and 25 clean rooms furnished with 19th-century antiques. Innkeepers John and Renate Kenaston take pride in maintaining the olde worlde feel here, with historical photos lining the walls on all four levels. Even the original birdcage lift is perfectly maintained. Request a room with a claw-foot tub if you enjoy a good soak, and don't be alarmed if hotel cat Captain Nemo wants to share your pillow at night – it's that kind of a place. Free afternoon tea and cookies are served in the parlour. The hotel is no-smoking throughout.
Hotel services *Parking ($15). Safe.*
Room services *Dataport. TV: cable.*

The Mission & the Castro

For accommodation in the Castro catering for a queer clientele, *see p229.*

Mid-range

Dolores Park Inn

3641 17th Street, CA 94114, between Church & Dolores Streets (phone/fax 621 0482). Muni Metro J/ bus 22, 33. **Rates** rooms $109-$249; suites $259. **Credit** MC, V. **Map** p314 Y1.
Rumour has it that Tom Cruise and Robert Downey Jr, among other celebrities, have stayed at this small, discreet Victorian inn – one of the best lodgings in

the Mission District – where the three rooms and one suite are exquisitely decorated with antiques. The Carriage House room has a jacuzzi, kitchen with washer/dryer, heated marble floor, fireplace and surround-sound TV, while the suite has a four-poster bed and a large sundeck with a view of Twin Peaks. There are no phones in the room, but a communal phone is available. A full breakfast is included in the price, as is afternoon tea and wine. A two-night minimum stay is required, and no under-14s are allowed. The property is no-smoking.
Hotel services *Business services. Concierge. Garden. Laundry (self-service). Parking (free). Phone. Safe.* **Room services** *Iron. No phone. Turndown. TV: cable.*

Also recommended

Castillo Inn *48 Henry Street, CA 94114, at Sanchez Street (1-800 865 5112/864 5111/ fax 641 1321).* **Rates** rooms $60-$80.
Credit MC, V.

The Haight-Ashbury

Mid-range

Stanyan Park Hotel

750 Stanyan Street, CA 94117, at Waller Street (751 1000/fax 668 5454/www.stanyanpark.com). Muni Metro N/bus 7, 33, 43, 66, 71. **Rates** rooms $125-$180; suites $259-$309. **Credit** AmEx, DC, Disc, MC, V. **Map** p313 C6.

Funky decor at **The Red Victorian**.

This stately, three-storey Victorian building on the edge of Golden Gate Park has been accommodating travellers in style since 1904 and is on the National Register of Historic Places. Its 30 rooms are filled with authentic Victorian antiques, right down to the drapes and quilts. Large groups may be attracted to the six large suites with full kitchens, dining rooms and living spaces. Rates include free breakfast and afternoon tea. No-smoking throughout.
Hotel services *Concierge. Parking ($12). Safe.*
Room services *Dataport. Iron. TV: cable.*

Budget

The Red Victorian

1665 Haight Street, CA 94117, between Clayton & Cole Streets (864 1978/fax 863 3293/www.redvic.com). Muni Metro N/bus 7, 33, 37, 43, 66, 71.
Rates rooms $86-$120; suite $200. **Credit** AmEx, Disc, DC, MC, V. **Map** p313 C6.
Nothing comes as close to offering the quintessential Haight-Ashbury experience as a night at the unique Red Vic. Haight Street's only hotel offers 18 wildly decorated rooms, each with its own thematic twist – such as the rainbow-coloured Flower Child room and the tie-dyed Summer of Love room. Spend some time in the Peace & Arts Gallery and Meditation Room to really find yourself. Is it cheesy or a flashback? You'll have to decide for yourself. Six of the rooms have private baths; the others have shared baths. Rooms do have a phone but do not have a TV, although you can request one. A continental breakfast is included in the room price. Mr Mouser, the hotel cat, stays downstairs. The hotel is no-smoking throughout.
Hotel services *Concierge. Parking ($12). Safe.*
Room services *Dataport. Iron.*

Also recommended

Metro Hotel *319 Divisadero Street, CA 94117, between Oak & Page Streets (861 5364/fax 863 1970).* **Rates** rooms $59-$109.

The Western Addition

First-class

Archbishop's Mansion

1000 Fulton Street, CA 94117, at Steiner Street (1-800 543 5820/563 7872/fax 885 3193). Bus 5, 22. **Rates** rooms $145-$165; suites $235-$425.
Credit AmEx, DC, Disc, MC, V. **Map** p313 E5.
Built for the Archbishop of San Francisco in 1904, this opulent French château mansion is centrally located on historic Alamo Square Park facing the historic row of 'Painted Ladies'. With its Belle Epoque style – chandeliers, antiques and canopy beds – this luxury hotel offers history, elegance and friendly staff at surprisingly affordable prices. Indulge in splendour in one of the ten rooms and five suites, all named after an opera – such as the Don Giovanni suite with its hand-carved, cherub-laden,

four-poster bed, two fireplaces and seven-headed shower. Breakfast is included in the room price, as is afternoon wine and cheese.
Hotel services *Business services. Concierge. Conference facilities. Laundry. No-smoking rooms. Parking (free). Safe.* **Room services** *CD player. Dataport. Iron. Room service (24hr). TV: cable. VCR.*

Pacific Heights

Mid-range

Hotel Drisco

2901 Pacific Avenue, CA 94115, at Broderick Street (1-800 634 7277/346 2880/fax 567 5537/www.eldriscohotel.com). Bus 3, 24. **Rates** rooms $195-$245; suites $395-$600. **Credit** AmEx, DC, Disc, MC, V. **Map** p307 D3.
Built as a luxury hotel in 1903, this place has been receiving famous and intellectual guests ever since; former president Dwight Eisenhower was a regular. These days, most of the guests are business travellers, so the atmosphere is a bit stiff, but the service is excellent and the rooms are very comfortable. Remodelled a few years ago, it has 24 rooms and 19 suites, some with spectacular panoramic views. It's a residential area, so parking is usually easy.
Hotel services *Concierge. Conference facilities. Gym. Laundry. Limousine service. Safe.* **Room services** *CD player. Dataport. Iron. Minibar. Room service (7am-10.30pm). Turndown. TV: cable. VCR.*

Hotel Majestic

1500 Sutter Street, CA 94109, at Gough Street (1-800 869 8966/441 1100/fax 673 7331/www.thehotelmajestic.com). Bus 2, 3, 4, 38, 42, 47, 49, 76. **Rates** rooms $170-$285; suites from $375. **Credit** AmEx, DC, Disc, MC, V. **Map** p310 F4.
Built in 1902 as a private residence, the Majestic has long been regarded as one of the city's most romantic hotels. Each of its 58 rooms and nine suites were renovated in 1999; they feature canopied, four-poster beds with quilts, a host of French Empire and English antiques, and tons of Crabtree & Evelyn goodies. Many rooms also have fireplaces. Free wine and hors d'oeuvres are served in the evening. Perlot, the hotel's restaurant, is known for its seasonal regional American cuisine; after dinner, you can adjourn to the Mahogany Bar for a cognac.
Hotel services *Air-conditioning. Babysitting. Bar. Concierge. Conference facilities. Laundry. Limousine service. Parking ($23). Restaurant. Safe.* **Room services** *Dataport. Iron. Minibar. Room service (24hr). Turndown. TV: cable.*

Jackson Court

2198 Jackson Street, CA 94115, at Buchanan Street (929 7670/fax 929 1405/www.jacksoncourt.com). Bus 12, 22, 24. **Rates** rooms $150-$175; suites $205-$215. **Credit** AmEx, MC, V. **Map** p308 E3.
Not many people have discovered this 19th-century brownstone mansion, and that's a shame, as it is a superb B&B. Located on a quiet residential stretch of Pacific Heights, it's as quiet as a church. Each of the ten rooms has a private bath and is furnished with a soothing combination of antiques and tasteful contemporary pieces. It's worth requesting the Library room, with its brass bed and working fireplace. Room rates include free continental breakfast and afternoon tea service.
Hotel services *Concierge. Kitchen. Laundry.* **Room services** *Iron. Turndown. TV: cable. VCR.*

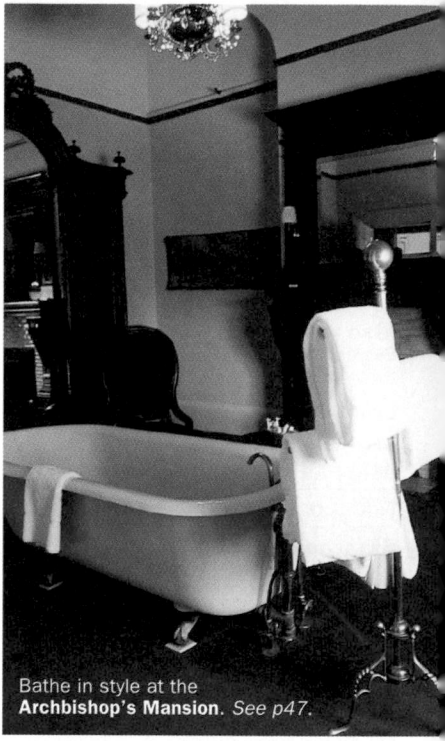

Bathe in style at the **Archbishop's Mansion**. *See p47.*

Cow Hollow

First-class

Sherman House

2160 Green Street, CA 94123, between Webster & Fillmore Streets (1-800 424 5777/563 3600/fax 563 1882/www.theshermanhouse.com). Bus 22, 41, 45. **Rates** rooms $460-$545; suites $775-$1,200. **Credit** AmEx, DC, MC, V. **Map** p307 E3.
A mansion-turned-hotel and designated landmark, the Sherman House is located in one of the city's most exclusive neighbourhoods. Its 14 rooms are decorated with European tapestries and brocaded bed hangings. If it's good enough for Shirley MacLaine, Ted Kennedy and Bill Cosby, it's probably good enough for you – as long as you have a bank balance

to match. The gardens are beautiful, the service impeccable and the view of sailing boats on the bay almost compensates for the steep prices. You get a free breakfast, plus champagne and hors d'oeuvres in the afternoon. You can smoke only in the garden.
Hotel services *Concierge. Garden. Parking (free). Restaurant. Safe.* **Room services** *Dataport. Iron. Room service (24hr). Turndown. TV: cable.*

Mid-range

Bed and Breakfast Inn

4 Charlton Court, CA 94123, off Union Street, between Laguna & Buchanan Streeets (921 9784/ fax 921 0544/www.thebandb.com). Bus 41, 45.
Rates rooms with shared bath $90-$135; rooms with private bath $175-$185; suites $280-$420.
Credit MC, V. **Map** p308 E2.
This place is a real charmer. A classic B&B, this ten-room inn is awash with fresh flowers and antiques. Tucked into a tiny cul-de-sac off Union Street, the Inn consists of three Victorian houses and one large garden – a good place to enjoy the complimentary breakfast on sunny mornings. Those travelling in groups might consider the Garden Suite, which has two queen beds, two twin beds, kitchen, a jacuzzi bath and its own private garden.
Hotel services *Garden. Parking ($16). Safe.* **Room services** *Dataport. Iron. Room service (breakfast only). Turndown. TV.*

Hotel Del Sol

3100 Webster Street, CA 94123, at Greenwich Street (1-800 738 7477/921 5520/931 4137/ www.thehoteldelsol.com). Bus 22, 43, 76. **Rates** rooms $125-$175; suites $215-$285. **Credit** AmEx, DC, Disc, MC, V. **Map** p307 E2.
This funky 1950s motor hotel has been transformed to reflect a playful West Coast spirit. External appearances to the contrary, this is not your typical motel: each of the 47 rooms and 11 suites is decorated with bright colours, and even the clock radios wake guests to the sound of rain or waves. The family suite has bunk beds, toys and games. Guests can go to the quirky Pillow Library to choose their own luxury pillows. Complimentary coffee, tea and muffins are served by the outdoor heated pool each morning. Added bonuses are free parking (a valuable commodity in this crowded neighbourhood) and the location, a few blocks from Chestnut and Union Streets. No smoking throughout.
Hotel services *Air-conditioning. Business services. Garden. Laundry. Parking (free). Pool. Safe. Sauna.* **Room services** *Dataport. Iron. TV: cable. VCR.*

Union Street Inn

2229 Union Street, CA 94123, between Fillmore & Steiner Streets (346 0424/fax 922 8046/ www. unionstreetinn.com). Bus 22, 41, 45.
Rates rooms $159-$289. **Credit** AmEx, MC, V. **Map** p307 E2/3.
Based in a two-storey Edwardian house, this B&B is a haven from bustling Union Street. The seven rooms are furnished in traditional style, with canopied or brass beds, feather duvets and fresh flowers. All have private bathrooms (some with jacuzzi tubs). Alternatively, you could opt for the private Carriage House behind the inn with its own garden. An extended continental breakfast is served in the parlour, in your room or on a terrace overlooking the garden. Evening hors d'oeuvres and cocktails are included in the room price.
Hotel services *Concierge. Garden. Parking ($15). Safe.* **Room services** *Dataport. Iron. Turndown. TV: cable. VCR.*

Also recommended

Art Center Bed & Breakfast *1902 Filbert Street, CA 94123, at Laguna Street (567 1526).* **Rates** rooms $125-$215.

The Marina

Budget

Edward II Inn & Pub

3155 Scott Street, CA 94123, at Lombard Street (1-800 473 2846/922 3000/fax 931 5784/ www.edwardii.com). Bus 28, 30, 43, 76. **Rates** rooms with shared bath $82.50-$87.50; rooms with private bath $115-$120; suites $185-$235.
Credit AmEx, MC, V. **Map** p307 D2.
While the Edward II may style itself as an 'English country inn' it actually has a wide array of room styles catering to almost every whim and budget. You can choose from 25 rooms – some with shared baths – or seven suites and cottages, with kitchens, living rooms and whirlpool baths. All the rooms contain antique furnishings and fresh flowers. A free breakfast and evening drinks are served in the adjoining pub. The inn's location is a little traffic-heavy, but it's near the shops and restaurants of Chestnut and Union Streets.
Hotel services *Bar. Concierge. Parking ($11). Safe.* **Room services** *Dataport. Iron. TV: cable. VCR.*

Marina Inn

3110 Octavia Street, CA 94123, at Lombard Street (1-800 274 1420/928 1000/fax 928 5909/ www.marinainn.com). Bus 28, 30, 76. **Rates** rooms $85-$125. **Credit** AmEx, DC, MC, V. **Map** p308 E2.
Although this 1924, four-storey, Victorian-style inn is located on one of the city's busiest streets, the 40 rooms are surprisingly quiet and stylishly furnished in soothing tones of yellow, green and rose, with pine fittings and four-poster beds. Nice touches include a nightly turndown service. A continental breakfast is included in the room price, as is afternoon sherry.
Hotel services *Beauty salon. Concierge. Cooking facilities. Safe.* **Room services** *Iron. Turndown. TV: cable. VCR.*

Also recommended

Marina Motel *2576 Lombard Street, CA 94123, at Divisadero Street (1-800 346 6118/921 9406/ fax 921 0364/www.marinamotel.com).* **Rates** rooms $75-$129.

The colourful **Hotel Del Sol**. *See p49.*

The Richmond District

Budget

Seal Rock Inn

545 Point Lobos Avenue, CA 94121, at 48th Avenue (1-888 732 5762/752 8000/fax 752 6034/ www.sealrockinn.com). Bus 18, 38.
Rates rooms $100-$129; suite $132-$158.
Credit AmEx, DC, MC, V.

One might be forgiven for assuming that San Francisco, surrounded on three sides by shimmering water, would have a wide selection of seaside hotels. Not the case. In fact, this inn, the only plausible contender, isn't even on the beach. Located at the western edge of the Richmond District, next to Sutro Heights Park, it's ideal for anyone who wants to stay in San Francisco, but doesn't want the bustling big-city scene or steep room rates. Most of the 27 rooms in the boxy brown building have at least partial ocean views. They're also large and spotless, though the ageing furnishings in hues of beige, brown and grey won't win any interior design awards. You can upgrade to a two-room suite with a wood-burning fireplace. There's free covered parking and a patio and heated outdoor pool. When things quieten down at night, you can fall asleep to the sound of distant foghorns.
Hotel services *Parking (free). Patio. Pool. Restaurant.* **Room services** *Dataport. Iron. Refrigerator. TV: cable.*

Hostels

Hostelling International publishes a useful free brochure, *California Hostels*, with details of affordable accommodation throughout the state, often in spectacular locations. Get a copy from either of the hostels listed below, or email hiayh@norcalhostels.org. Better still, go to www.hostels.com/us.ca.sf.html for a full listing of all San Francisco's hostels.

Fisherman's Wharf Youth Hostel

Building 240, Fort Mason, CA 94123, at Bay & Franklin Streets, Marina (771 7277/fax 771 1468/ www.norcalhostels.org). Bus 28, 30, 42, 47, 49.
Rates $22.50. **Credit** MC, V. **Map** p308 E1.

Many San Franciscans would kill for the bay view offered at this humble hostel. It's one of the most desirable locations in the city, and it's yours for less than $25 per night, if you book at least 24 hours in advance. Located in a historic Civil War building on National Park property, the hostel's dorm-style accommodation sleeps 170 in rooms of three to 24 people. Unlike some hostels, where, if you're not asleep, you'd prefer to be anywhere else, here you'll want to hang out and enjoy the pool table, dining room, coffee bar, complimentary movies and the rarest of San Francisco amenities – free parking. There's no curfew, and the café has free breakfast and $3 dinner several nights a week. There's no smoking inside the building.
Services *Café. Internet access. Kitchen. Laundry. Lockers. Payphone. Parking (free).*

Hostelling International Downtown

312 Mason Street, CA 94102, between Geary & O'Farrell Streets, Union Square (1-800 909 4776 access code 02/788 5604/fax 788 3023/ www.hiayh.org). BART Powell Street/Muni Metro F, J, K, L, M, N/bus 27, 38/cable car Powell-Hyde or Powell-Mason. **Rates** $22-$25. **Credit** MC, V. **Map** p310 G4.

Make your reservation at least five weeks in advance during the high season (June-September) to stay at this popular 260-bed hostel in downtown, which prides itself on its privacy and security. Guests are accommodated in small two-, three-, four- or five-person rooms, with their own lock and key (the larger rooms also have their own bathroom). Beds for walk-ins are available on a first come, first served basis: bring ID or you'll be turned away at the door. Smoking is not allowed on the premises.
Services *Internet access. Kitchen. Lockers. Payphone. Safe. TV room.*

Sightseeing

Introduction 52
Downtown & Around 56
North Beach & Around 71
The Mission & the Castro 83
The Haight & Around 87
The Marina & Around 93
Ocean Beach & Around 99
The East Bay 103
Museums 105

Features

Top ten sights 53
The city on foot: Walking tours 54
The end of Fatty 59
Cable cars 60
Sun, wind and fog 66
Fantasy islands 74
The city on foot: Stairways 78
On a clear day, you can see for ever 80
Coit Tower 82
Golden Gate Park 90
The city on foot: Along the waterfront 94
Bridging the gap 96
On the beach 100
CityPass 105
Top five museums 106
Out of town 111

Introduction

There's a thousand and one things to see and do. Get your bearings here.

Sightseeing

Bounded by the wild Pacific Ocean on one side and one of the world's most beautiful bays on two more, San Francisco benefits from a geography as unique as its history. Squeezed by the limitations of the land into a relatively small area – a square seven by seven miles – the city is a sightseer's dream, with all of its neighbourhoods and their eclectic attractions close at hand, many within walking distance of each other. And unlike many US cities, the public transport system is comprehensive and efficient; if the steep slopes daunt you, hop on a bus, BART train or cable car.

Rather than having one true centre, San Francisco is instead a thriving network of individualistic neighbourhoods, each with its own character and style, its own distinctive cuisine and, in many cases, even its own climate (*see p66* **Sun, wind and fog**). A few rambles around town will reveal which parts best suit your soul. Most visitors make forays to Fisherman's Wharf and the shopping mecca of Union Square, but both are touristy, crowded and rather unappealing; savvy travellers will quickly realise that they offer but the barest introductory glimpses of a complex, intensely colourful city. Our advice? Go where the locals go, take your leisure where they live: in the Castro, the Haight, the Mission and other only-in-San Francisco areas. Savour splendid views from atop Russian Hill or the palm-fringed Embarcadero. Start walking, and see where the streets lead you.

THE NEIGHBOURHOODS

Arranged by area, our sightseeing chapters start at **Union Square**, where visitors are most likely to have procured a hotel or emerged from BART. From here, we explore the rest of downtown: the high-rise **Financial District**, the **Embarcadero**, the perpetually run-down **Tenderloin**, **Civic Center** and **South of Market**, centre of the city's nightlife and the recent dotcom boom – districts that make up San Francisco's north-eastern corner.

From downtown, we move north towards the water, to espresso-scented **North Beach**, vibrant **Chinatown**, **Fisherman's Wharf** and swanky **Russian Hill** and **Nob Hill**. We then jump south to the **Mission**, San Francisco's Latino stronghold, neighbouring **Potrero Hill**, the city's queer heartland of the **Castro**, and pretty **Noe Valley**. The central neighhourhoods come next: hippyish **Haight-Ashbury**, the sprawling **Western Addition** (including the sub-neighbourhoods of **Japantown** and the **Fillmore District**) and up-and-coming **Hayes Valley**, as well as the bucolic delights of **Golden Gate Park**.

North from the Western Addition lie the palatial mansions of **Pacific Heights**, upmarket **Cow Hollow**, the waterfront yuppy enclave of the **Marina** and the **Presidio**, a former military site. Below the Presidio are the areas tucked up against the Pacific: the outlying residential neighbourhoods of the **Richmond** and **Sunset Districts**. Finally, we cross the Bay Bridge to the East Bay – a 20-minute ride by BART – to the People's Republic of **Berkeley** and ethnically diverse **Oakland**. The city's bridges (Golden Gate and Bay), beaches and the islands within San Francisco Bay are covered in separate sections.

A few things about San Francisco never change: its relative safety, compared with other large US cities (for danger zones, *see chapter* **Directory: Safety & security**), and its topographical challenges, namely, hills. So stretch those quads and calves, lace up your walking shoes and hit the streets.

► We include some restaurants, bars, nightspots and shops in our Sightseeing chapters, but for the full lowdown on the best options in each area, *see chapters* **Restaurants & Cafes**, **Bars**, **Nightlife** and **Shops & Services**.

► For information on the **public transport system**, *see p272* **Getting Around**. **Street maps** of the city start on *p306*.

Tours

To get city-savvy in a short time span, it's always a good idea to take a tour. If you fancy exploring the city without mechanical aids, *see p54* **The city on foot: Walking tours**.

Bus tours

Shamelessly touristy **Gray Line** (558 7300/www.graylinesanfrancisco.com) offers several daily bus tours, most of which pick up passengers at central hotels. Its Cable Car Tours send motorised cable cars from Union Square to Fisherman's Wharf, or to the Golden Gate Bridge, the Presidio and Japantown. Prices start at $15. Other tour companies include **Golden Gate Tours** (788 5775/www.ggtours.com) and **Super Sightseeing Tours** (362 7808/www.caohwy.com/s/superst.htm).

49-Mile Scenic Drive

San Francisco's all-in-one driving tour, signposted by blue-and-white seagull markers, is designed to lead car drivers through the most picturesque and historic parts of the city. If you've never been to San Francisco before – and if you have a car – the 49-Mile Scenic Drive is an enjoyable introduction to the city's charms – though it can be traffic-snarled and difficult to follow. Get a map of the drive from the Visitor Information Center on Market and Powell Streets (*see p287*).

San Francisco Fire Engine Tours & Adventures

333 7077/www.fireenginetours.com. **Tours** 1pm Mon, Wed-Sun (also 11am, 3pm, 5pm on some days; call for details). **Cost** $25; $15 under-13s. **Credit** MC, V.

Climb aboard a shiny red 1955 Mack fire engine and join eccentric husband-and-wife team Robert and Marilyn Katzman for the most entertaining trip in town. The 75-minute tour departs from outside the Cannery on Beach Street, and heads through the Presidio to Fort Point, across the Golden Gate Bridge to Sausalito, Fort Baker and then back. Marilyn provides an informative non-stop commentary, you get to wear a fireman's coat (essential when crossing the very windy bridge) and there's plenty of singing and bell-clanging. Kids love it. The fire truck seats only 13, so make sure you book ahead.

San Francisco Seaplane Tours

332 4843/www.seaplane.com. **Open** 9am-5pm daily. **Cost** $119; $99 2-12s; $139 sunset Champagne tour. **Credit** AmEx, MC, V.

Fly the old-fashioned way on an eight-seater de Havilland Beaver seaplane, taking off from the water just outside Pier 39 for a 30-minute trip over the Bay, the Golden Gate Bridge and downtown. There are also flights from Sausalito. Tours run roughly every hour; call for more details.

Spinnaker Sailing

543 7333/www.spinnaker-sailing.com. **Tours** *Sunset cruise* from 2hrs before sunset Wed, Fri, Sat. *Brunch cruise* 11am-2pm Sun. *Afternoon sail* 3-5pm Sun. **Cost** $25 sunset & afternoon; $40 brunch. **Credit** AmEx, MC, V.

This seafaring outfit takes up to 49 passengers for sailing cruises on the bay aboard its classic 78ft (24m) square-rigged brigantine, built in 1933. It's a bit like travelling on a grand, 19th-century sailing ship. Trips leave from Pier 40 in South Beach Harbor; food is provided, but drinks must be purchased aboard. Dress warmly; it can get chilly out on the water. Advance reservations are required.

Top ten Sights

Golden Gate Bridge

The city's bright red welcome mat, it's one of the Seven Engineering Wonders of the World. *See p96* **Bridging the gap**.

Cable cars

Thumbing their noses at progress, the endearing cable cars continue to climb halfway to the stars up San Francisco's steep slopes. *See p60.*

Alcatraz

The ghosts of Al Capone and 'Machine Gun' Kelly haunt this notorious island prison in the middle of the bay. *See p74* **Fantasy islands**.

Golden Gate Park

Winding footpaths, museums, lakes, meadows, windmills and 101 secret gardens make up this glorious greenbelt – San Francisco's collective backyard. *See p90.*

SFMOMA

Mario Botta's bold, striped, cylindrical skylight towers over the second largest museum in the US devoted to modern art. *See p107.*

North Beach cafés

Sit at a sidewalk table, order a cappuccino, listen to Italian opera and take a sip of history. *See p71.*

City Hall

The centre of San Francisco political life, the magnificent gilded dome of this Beaux Arts building can be seen from almost all points west. *See p67.*

Coit Tower

The fluted observation tower at the top of Telegraph Hill offers one of the city's most romantic views. *See p82.*

Sunset at Ocean Beach

Join in the applause as a fiery orange sun sets on the Pacific to the accompaniment of barking sea lions, raucous seagulls and surf crashing on the ruins of Sutro Baths. *See p100.*

Grace Cathedral

A grand neo-Gothic ecclesiastical landmark at the top of Nob Hill. *See p82.*

The city on foot: Walking tours

San Francisco is an eminently walkable city, so, not surprisingly, there's a booming business in walking tours. Most are independently organised and often led by scholars, historians, actors and aspiring comedians. There are excursions that cover specific neighbourhoods, and those that focus on themes, such as architecture, literature and history. For more options, stop by the Visitor Information Center at the corner of Market and Powell Streets (*see p287*) or consult the pink 'Datebook' section of the Sunday *San Francisco Chronicle*. Most tours require advance reservations.

Neighbourhood walks

City Guides

557 4266/www.walking-tours.com/cityguides/. **Tours** schedule varies; call for details. **Cost** free.
The San Francisco Public Library sponsors this walking tour series in which volunteer guides steer visitors around North Beach, Victorian San Francisco, Pacific Heights, the Mission and Japantown. Other tours cover Beaux Arts buildings and City Hall, Chinatown and Roof Gardens. City Guides tours provide for free the same service for which other companies can charge $20 or more.

The Castro

Crusin' the Castro

550 8110/www.webcastro.com/castrotour/. **Tours** 10am Tue-Sat. **Cost** $40; $35 concessions, 14-18s; $30 4-14s. **No credit cards**.
Famed lesbian raconteur Trevor Hailey runs the Castro's most entertaining tour, pointing out historic homosexual landmarks and tracing the origins of San Francisco's gay community. The tour lasts four hours, including brunch.

Chinatown

Wok Wiz Chinatown Tour

981 8989/1-650 355 9657/www.wokwiz.com. **Tours** 10am daily. **Cost** *Walk only* $28; under-11s $23. *Walk & lunch* $40; $35 under-11s. **Credit** MC, V.
This outfit, run by TV chef and writer Shirley Fong-Torres, offers various tours, including the 2½-hour Wok Wiz tour, which explores the culinary heritage of Chinatown through visits to Chinese herbalists and groceries, dim sum restaurants, fortune cookie factories and back-alley surprises. The walk includes a seven-course dim sum lunch.

Glorious Food Culinary Walktours: Chinatown

441 5637. **Tours** 9.30am daily. **Cost** $40. **No credit cards**.
This daily four-hour tour focuses on food, food and more food, stopping at a noodle factory, seafood shops, Chinese markets and a tea tasting. It ends with an eight-course lunch. The same outfit also runs a tour of North Beach.

Golden Gate Park

Friends of Recreation & Parks

263 0991/www.frp.org. **Tours** schedule varies; call for details. **Cost** free.
Several free walking tours led by a park-loving non-profit group reveal some of the many secrets of the Japanese Tea Garden, Stow Lake, Conservatory of Flowers, hidden statues, bison, windmills and so much more.

The Haight-Ashbury

Flower Power Walking Tour

863 1621. **Tours** 9.30am Tue, Sat. **Cost** $15. **No credit cards**.
This 2½-hour walk relives the Summer of Love, with pointers to the history and locations of the Haight's world-changing 1960s cultural experiment. Follow the trail of the Dead, Janis and the Diggers, and sites where the spirit of the hippies will live forever.

Nob Hill

Hobnob Tours

1-650 851 1123/www.hobnobtours.com. **Tours** 9.30am, 1.30pm Mon-Fri (Sat on request). **Cost** $30. **Credit** AmEx, MC, V.
The profligate lifestyle of the wealthy 'nabobs', after whom Nob Hill is named, serves as the basis for a lighthearted two-hour tour, which also dips into the Financial District to trace the riches of the city's high-society robber barons. Meet at the Fairmont Hotel, on California and Mason Streets.

North Beach

Mangia! North Beach Tour

397 8530/www.graceannwalden.com. **Tours** 10am Sat; group tours by arrangement Mon-Fri. **Cost** $50. **No credit cards.**
San Francisco restaurant writer and history buff GraceAnn Walden leads an entertaining and informative five-hour tour about the food, history and culture of North Beach, with visits to bakeries, churches, a deli and lunch. There are also occasional tours of Chinatown and the Mission.

Pacific Heights

Pacific Heights Walking Tour

441 3000/www.sfheritage.org/events+tours.html. **Tours** 12.30pm Sun. **Cost** $5; $3 concessions, under-12s. **No credit cards.**
Preservation group San Francisco Architectural Heritage offers a weekly two-hour tour of Pacific Heights' eastern edge, stopping to admire mansions, Victorian homes and classic San Francisco row houses. It starts at the Haas-Lilienthal House, 2007 Franklin Street.

Themed walks

For details of mural walks, *see p204* **The city on foot: Murals**. For a self-guided historical walk around downtown, *see p12* **The city on foot: Barbary Coast Trail**.

Dashiell Hammett Walking Tour

1-510 287 9540/www.donherron.com. **Tours** *May, June* noon Sat; call for details of other times. **Cost** $10. **No credit cards.**
Follow Hammettologist Don Herron around the Tenderloin and Union Square in the footsteps of the city's most famous mystery writer. This comprehensive four-hour tour covers Hammett's real-life homes and hangouts, and locations used in *The Maltese Falcon* and other stories. Meet at the north-west corner of the Main Library, at Fulton and Larkin Streets. No reservations needed.

History Walkabouts

357 1848/www.calhist.org/frost1/calchron-v10no3/walkabouts.html. **Tours** schedule varies; call for details. **Cost** $20. **Credit** MC, V.
The California Historical Society sponsors an irregular series of walking tours for the serious historian. The topics are ever-changing but always esoteric, such as the gardens of Golden Gate Park or the Inner Sunset district, and the guides have a depth of knowledge that can't be matched. Tours last about two hours, or three if they include a stop for tea.

Javawalk

673 9255/www.javawalk.com. **Tours** 10am Sat. **Cost** $20; $10 under-18s. **No credit cards.**
San Francisco has always been a coffee town – mass-market coffee producer MJB, Folgers and Hills Brothers all got their starts in Gold Rush San Francisco – as is amply demonstrated on this coffee-themed walking tour that extends from Union Square to North Beach.

San Francisco Ghost Hunt

922 5590/www.sfghosthunt.com. **Tours** 8pm Mon, Wed, Fri-Sun. **Cost** $20; $10 under-16s. **No credit cards.**
This frightful two-hour evening tour not only drifts past the haunted houses of Pacific Heights, it also serves as an introductory course in spook-tracking techniques for novice ghost hunters. Meet in the lobby of the Queen Anne Hotel (1590 Sutter Street). The tour is sometimes held on Tuesdays and Thursdays, too.

San Francisco Then... and Now

317 8687/www.sfhistorytour.com. **Tours** daily; call for details. **Cost** $25; $20 concessions; free under-17s. **No credit cards.**
The vast sweep of San Francisco's convoluted history is crammed into an exhaustive two-hour tour that starts on Market Street and ends up in North Beach, leaving no detail unexplained in between. At the end of the walk, you get a souvenir photograph album.

Victorian Home Walk

252 9485/www.victorianwalk.com. **Tours** 11am daily. **Cost** $20. **No credit cards.**
This 2½-hour tour combines walking with bus rides to view the most outstanding Victorian architecture in Cow Hollow and Pacific Heights. The meeting place is by the clock in the lobby of the Westin St Francis Hotel on Union Square.

Downtown & Around

The financial, political and shopping heart of the city, this is San Francisco at its buzziest best.

The loosely defined area that is San Francisco's downtown is a humming hive of urban intensity, where smartly suited stockbrokers mix with rubbernecking tourists and homeless people cadging spare change. This area, a demographic Babel that relies on always-jammed Market Street as its main axis, sports the city's busiest sidewalks and most significant buildings. Camera-toting out-of-towners queuing for cable cars rub elbows with street-corner evangelists; kids on skateboards whizz past foreign diplomats; and everyone seems to be carrying a shopping bag or a briefcase, or both. From **Union Square**'s glittering department stores to the **Financial District**'s bustle; from **Civic Center**'s stately white opulence to the **Tenderloin**'s forlorn grit; from the booming arts scene in **SoMa** to the **Embarcadero**'s stunning vistas, this is the city at its most vital.

Around Union Square

With Post and Geary Streets to the north and south, and Stockton and Powell to the east and west, **Union Square** (*see p57*) is Northern California's premier shopping nexus. A phalanx of upscale department stores surrounding the square offers miles and miles of clothing, jewellery, gifts and more, tempting window-shoppers to max out their credit cards.

These days, the name Union Square refers more to the surrounding neighbourhood than the square itself, which is generally used merely as a route from one shop to the next, not as a destination. In the past, panhandlers, mad ranters and chilly winds made the square less than inviting. It currently looks rather pitiful, with its grass and palm trees removed, as the entire block undergoes major relandscaping. Scheduled for completion in 2002, this promises to make the square more user-friendly, though its new design is being kept under wraps, so only time will tell whether this prime piece of real estate will finally emerge as the convenient gathering place it deserves to be.

The square takes its name from pro-Union rallies held here on the eve of the Civil War. But the 97-foot (30-metre) Corinthian column soaring upwards from its centre celebrates yet another conflict, Admiral Dewey's 1898 victory at Manila during the Spanish-American War – a monument to imperialism that might irk plenty of locals if they actually knew what the column commemorated. Following the great 1906 earthquake, the square became a sort of high-class tent city for VIPs suddenly dislodged from surrounding hotels. And the key scene in Francis Ford Coppola's 1974 paranoiac masterwork *The Conversation* was shot here.

Overlooking the square's western flank is the glamorous **Westin St Francis Hotel**, where silent-era film star Fatty Arbuckle's lethal libido ignited Hollywood's first sex scandal in 1921 (*see p59* **The end of Fatty**), Al Jolson died in 1950 and President Gerald Ford dodged bullets in a failed 1975 assassination attempt. Soak up history in the hotel's lavish and labyrinthine lobby. Outside, embracing the square, are Macy's, Saks Fifth Avenue, Tiffany, Neiman-Marcus, the Disney Store, Louis Vuitton and Baccarat, to name but a few; if your feet get tired, shoe chain Niketown will fix you right up. On the easternmost side of the square, the **Tix Bay Area booth** sells half-price day-of-show tickets to theatre and other performances.

A two-block walk south on Powell Street from Union Square delivers you to Market Street, where you'll find the **Powell Street cable car turnaround**, usually heaving with a lemming-like queue of tourists waiting to board the next car (*see p60* **Cable cars**). Also here is the entrance to the lower level of Hallidie Plaza, site of the very useful **Visitor Information Center** (*see p287*) and the BART station. (Don't be deterred by the gaggles of homeless people, who tend to congregate around this spot.)

On the opposite side of Market Street is the uninspiringly titled **San Francisco Shopping Centre** – a nine-storey complex that includes Nordstrom and other fashion emporia, a basement food court and a graceful spiral escalator leading directly to the Powell Street BART station. Also nearby are Diesel, Urban Outfitters and scores of other fashion arsenals. But the true essence of Union Square consumerism – a cool elegance that turns this district into a jam-packed wonderland in the weeks before Christmas – lies in its older, streetside shops rather than prefab centres.

The unmistakeable **Transamerica Pyramid**.

For example, Gump's has been accessorising posh Bay Area homes for more than a century, and the toys at huge FAO Schwarz are hard to pass up if you have a child in tow, and, frankly, even if you don't. A few blocks east, Crocker Galleria has more top-notch stores competing for tourist dollars. For more details on how to spend yourself into bankruptcy around Union Square, *see chapter* **Shops & Services**. The area around Union Square is also thick with commercial art galleries: *see chapter* **Galleries**.

Architectural landmarks in the vicinity include Market Street's triangular **Phelan Building**, built in 1908 by Mayor James Phelan as part of his famous post-quake reconstruction programme. The largest of San Francisco's 'flat iron' structures (so-called because of their shape), it's on the north side of Market between Stockton and O'Farrell Streets. A more modern counterpart lies further up the street at 388 Market, erected in 1986.

Linking Stockton and Kearny Streets just east of the square, **Maiden Lane** was once a sinister alleyway, where, 100 years ago, randy San Franciscans patronised the city's cheapest prostitutes. It's now a chic shopping artery (gated to keep out cars by day); the exquisite **Folk Art International** at No.140 (392 9999), designed by Frank Lloyd Wright in 1948, sports a swooping circular interior. Pricey cafés along the lane set up tables outside on sunny days. Just north of Union Square, atop the Stockton Tunnel, brass wall plaques (on Burritt Alley, off Bush Street, west of Stockton) mark the fictional location of the murder that launched the *The Maltese Falcon*'s byzantine plot and the real-life location of Scotsman Robert Louis Stevenson's San Francisco rooming house (across the street at 608 Bush). Gumshoes and literary pilgrims also congregate at **John's Grill** (63 Ellis Street, between Market and Powell Streets; 986 0069), an old-fashioned eatery frequented by both author Dashiell Hammett and his *Maltese Falcon* alter-ego Sam Spade; Hammettiana adorns the walls.

Union Square

Bounded by Geary, Powell, Post & Stockton Streets. BART Powell Street/Muni Metro F, J, K, L, M, N/ bus 2, 3, 4, 30, 38, 45, 76/cable car Powell-Hyde or Powell-Mason. **Map** p309 G3/4.

The Financial District

East of Union Square, the Financial District fills to bursting the area that is bounded by Market, Kearny and Jackson Streets and the Embarcadero, and has been the business and banking hub of San Francisco and the American West for over a century and a half, as far back as the Gold Rush. Nowadays, it's a forest of steel-and-glass skyscrapers that soar above the old brick banks, as briefcase-wielding crowds stream in on weekday mornings and out after work, leaving it silent as a graveyard at night and on weekends.

Its northern edge is guarded by the **Transamerica Pyramid** (*see p61*) on Montgomery Street. This striking triangular structure is San Francisco's tallest building. On its east side, tiny **Redwood Park** is a cool refuge, and just about the only spot in San Francisco where you can still see California's famous redwood trees – albeit rather small ones. A long-gone building formerly on this spot is where Samuel Clemens, aka Mark Twain, met a former firefighter named Tom Sawyer, whose childhood memories Twain turned into classic American literature.

The **Bank of America** building (555 California Street, at Kearny Street) towers over the Financial District, both physically and psychologically; though just a bit shorter than the Transamerica Pyramid, it is much more massive, its deep red zigzag walls often disappearing into the clouds above. First as the Bank of Italy and then in its current incarnation after a name change and corporate merger, the Bank of America has long been the West Coast's major financial dynamo. Unlike most

"A ROARING GOOD TIME!"

-San Francisco Chronicle

STOMP™

THE BEAT GOES ON FOR 8 PERFORMANCES A WEEK

Tues-Fri 8PM • Sat 5 & 9PM • Sun 3 & 7PM

MARINES MEMORIAL THEATRE

609 Sutter at Mason 2 blocks West of Union Square

Tues - Fri 8pm • Sat 5 & 9pm • Sun 3 & 7pm

CALL TOLL-FREE

877-771-6900

TicketWeb (415) 478-2277

stomponline.com

PHOTO © OLEG MICHEETEV

Val Diamond

San Francisco's longest running musical revue.

STEVE SILVER'S

BEACH BLANKET BABYLON®

CLUB FUGAZI • 678 BEACH BLANKET BABYLON BLVD

(GREEN STREET) • SAN FRANCISCO

WED & THURS AT 8 PM • FRI & SAT AT 7 & 10 PM • SUN AT 3 & 7 PM

415-421-4222

PHOTO ID REQUIRED EVENINGS • PERSONS UNDER 21 WELCOME TO MATINEES

www.beachblanketbabylon.com • www.ticketweb.com

©SSPI 2002

Photo: David Allen

other San Francisco skyscapers, its top floor is open to the public: take the thrill-ride elevator to the dizzying **Carnelian Room** (433 7500) on the 52nd floor (open 3-11pm daily). In private use during the day, in the evenings the room metamorphoses into a cocktail lounge and upscale restaurant where the price of a drink earns you the right to hover above the city as evening falls. The building was also the setting for the 1974 disaster epic *The Towering Inferno* (though special effects added more storeys to make it even more towering).

Other buildings nearby shelter not only fortunes but also artistic and architectural surprises. The **Merchant's Exchange** (*see p61*) is filled with extraordinary art, while the high-rise at **456 Montgomery** makes interesting use of two quaint turn-of-the-20th-century banks as its foundation, both literally and figuratively. To stoke your gold fever, step next door to the free **Wells Fargo History Museum** (*see p112*) and fawn over gold nuggets, Wild West paintings, unique historical photographs and two real century-old stagecoaches (you can climb aboard and 'ride' the one upstairs). Nearby, in the basement of the Union Bank of California, is the **Museum of the Money of the American West** (*see p61*), containing a handful of small pieces of California's Wild West heritage.

The impressive art deco granite sculptures in front of the **Pacific Coast Stock Exchange** (*see p61*) are impressive, but not as impressive as the vibrant Diego Rivera mural inside. Sadly, access to the building is only available on a once-monthly guided tour. Tucked away nearby, in the city's original mint on Commercial Street, the modest **Pacific Heritage Museum** (*see p111*) holds a small art collection, but one that is worth discovering. Another artistic marvel – a huge Maxfield Parrish original – can be found behind the bar at the historic and lavishly Victorian **Palace Hotel** (*see p41*) on Market Street, at New Montgomery Street.

Every year, on 18 April at 5am, a select few centenarians who survived the 1906 earthquake gather around **Lotta's Fountain** at the

The end of Fatty

These days, when superstars are quite often supermodels as well, or at least look like them, it's hard to imagine how popular the early Hollywood comedian Fatty Arbuckle was. The 300lb (136kg) actor was more famous than Charlie Chaplin and, say many, funnier. Between 1913 and 1921, he starred in scores of slapstick comedies with names like *Fatty's Magic Pants* and *A Reckless Romeo*, which American audiences adored, and he savoured the high life and all that came with it. (Rumours persist that one of his expensive novelties was a car with its own built-in toilet.)

Arbuckle's wild parties were legendary – other rumours tell of elaborate backyard weddings he staged between pet dogs – but the one he threw on Labor Day weekend of 1921 at San Francisco's elegant St Francis Hotel ended in tragedy. With some Hollywood chums, he rented a suite on the 12th floor. As the carousing in rooms 1219 and 1220 spilled over from one day into the next, room 1221 was set aside for quick assignations. It was there on 5 September that Arbuckle, whose girth made him no less a lure for groupies, had a fateful encounter with a slightly built and very inebriated starlet named Virginia Rappe. Exactly what happened between them is anyone's guess – some say he crushed her; some say he raped her

with a champagne bottle. In any case, Rappe was rushed to hospital with a ruptured bladder and died soon afterward of peritonitis.

Arbuckle's career was promptly over: he was pilloried in the national press and charged with manslaughter. It was Hollywood's first real scandal, and would forever taint the film industry's image in American popular consciousness, even though he was eventually acquitted. The actor subsequently directed a few movies using the wistfully clever pseudonym Will B Good, but he would never appear on the other side of the camera again. And in one of fate's inexplicable coincidences, 29 years later, singing star Al Jolson died of a heart attack while playing cards in the same hotel room.

Cable cars

It's not often you'll find a city willing to let its most valuable, most delicate antiques hurtle daily through rush-hour traffic and plunge down streets so steep they might be more properly called cliffs. But San Francisco's world-famous cable cars were designed to do just that, and they've been doing it so well for over a century that there's no reason to stop them now.

First installed in 1873 by wily Scotsman Andrew Hallidie, the cable cars were an ingenious solution to San Francisco's eternal problem: how to get up those unforgiving hills. Nob Hill and Russian Hill, in particular, were tempting morsels of real estate, yet they remained mostly undeveloped. Horse-drawn carriages could barely make the climb, and Victorian gentlefolk were hardly willing to exhaust themselves clambering up and down on a daily basis. Enter Hallidie and his ideas for cable-drawn transport, which he had first used hauling ore carts in California's gold mines. When, to everyone's amazement, the first cars worked flawlessly, imitators sprang up overnight and soon more than 100 miles (160 kilometres) of tracks criss-crossed the city, operated by seven cable car companies.

But it was not to last. Earthquakes, fires and the advent of automobiles and electric trolleys spelled doom for most of the cable car lines, so much so that by 1947 the city even proposed tearing up the remaining lines and replacing them with diesel buses. An outraged citizenry nixed the idea. The federal government declared the system a National Historic Landmark, and now the beloved cars are here to stay.

Only three lines survive, covering a total of eight miles (13 kilometres): the **Powell-Mason** and **Powell-Hyde** lines, both of which depart from the Powell Street turnaround (at the bottom of Powell, at Market Street) and end up at Fisherman's Wharf; and the **California** line, which runs between Market Street and Van Ness Avenue in a long, straight path up and down California Street.

Visitors are often surprised to learn that cable cars have no engine or other means of propulsion. All they need is a 'grip', a steel clamp that grabs on to a subterranean cable, which runs under the streets at a constant 9.5mph (15kmph). (You can hear it humming even when there are no cars in sight, because the cable never stops moving.)

Every car has two operators: a gripman, who works the cranks and levers that grab on to and release the underground cable; and a conductor, who takes fares and somehow manages to cram 90 or more passengers on to the vehicle, many of them hanging off the running boards.

Visit the **Cable Car Museum** (*see p109*) to inspect the system's inner workings. You'll find Hallidie's original 1873 car and roomloads of unique cable car paraphernalia, but the real draw are the immense winding turbines that power the cables. Stand on the balcony and look down into the powerhouse to see the ten-foot (three-metre) wheels spin amid an incessant whir of gears and pulleys.

TIPS AND TRICKS

If cable cars are a legendary part of San Francisco, so is the hassle of waiting to board one at the Powell Street turnaround. Don't be tempted, lemming-like, to join the long queue of tourists. Instead, do what the locals do – walk up Powell a few blocks and board the car at O'Farrell or Union Square. If you just want the experience of riding a cable car and aren't using it to go anywhere in particular, the California Street line is rarely crowded. The views aren't quite as good as on the Powell lines, but it's still a cable car, and when the trip is over you can hop right back on and do it all again – or step off at Grant Avenue and visit Chinatown.

Tired of forking over the $2 fare? Cable cars are free to holders of most transit passes, including Muni passports, Fast Passes, BART Plus tickets and the CityPass (*see p105*). For more information on travelling by cable car, *see p273*.

intersection of Market, Kearny and Geary Streets. Recently restored, the ornate, lion-headed fountain served as a message centre for families separated by the quake, an 8.0 temblor that destroyed most of the city and led to a four-day fire, killing hundreds – some say thousands.

On the northern fringe of the Financial District, tiny **Jackson Square Historical District** (bounded by Washington, Kearny and Sansome Streets and Pacific Avenue) is a last vestige of San Francisco's Barbary Coast, once a seething mass of low-life bars and 19th-century sex clubs whose floor shows were shocking even by postmodern standards. Though today they're far from the waterfront, these few blocks of 1850s-era brick buildings – now housing upmarket antique shops and lovingly restored offices – mark the city's one-time shoreline, having been built on foundations made from the hulls of ships abandoned by eager gold-seekers. Stroll Jackson Street (between Sansome and Montgomery) and Hotaling Street to see the only pre-Victorian-style neighbourhood left in San Francisco, inexplicably spared during the 1906 quake and fire. In the 1930s, Jackson Square became popular with artists and writers, including John Steinbeck and William Saroyan, who used to drink at the long-vanished Black Cat Café.

Local establishments popular with after-work drinkers today include **Bix** (*see p148*), which enjoys a well-founded reputation for brilliant Martinis and authentic late-1930s decor; and the **Cypress Club** restaurant (*see p117*), where a bizarre, bulbous Minoanesque interior might make you wonder if your appetisers have been spiked with hallucinogens. If its prices make you blanch, step across Jackson to **Clown Alley** (42 Columbus Avenue; 421 2540), a kitschy burger joint that has for decades been a favourite with cash-strapped locals.

Financial District sidestreets occasionally sprout cafés with outdoor seating: a good example is **Belden Place**, just east of Kearny Street between Pine and Bush. It's a short alley containing no fewer than four chi-chi bistros (including **Plouf** – *see p118*) with big umbrellas and Mediterranean flair. On the corner of Belden and Bush is the historic **Sam's Grill** (421 0594), a staple for the three-Martini, surf 'n' turf crowd since 1867.

Merchant's Exchange

465 California Street, between Montgomery & Sansome Streets (421 7730). Bus 1, 12, 15, 42/cable car California. **Open** by appointment 8am-6pm daily. **Admission** free. **Map** p309 H3.

This building is no longer used to trade shares, but its historic spaces show the important role it once played. An impressive collection of William Coulter seascapes highlights its lavish, Julia Morgan-designed trading hall, now occupied by a bank that welcomes the curious.

Museum of the Money of the American West

Basement, Union Bank of California, 400 California Street, at Sansome Street (705 7000). Bus 12, 15, 42/cable car California. **Open** 9am-5pm Mon-Fri. **Admission** free. **Map** p309 H3.

The small Wild West collection includes rare gold coins, three-dollar bills, plenty of gold nuggets and a notorious pair of pistols used in a fateful 1859 duel between two California politicians.

Pacific Coast Stock Exchange

301 Pine Street, at Sansome Street (tours 285 0495/Mzakheim@earthlink.net). Bus 12, 15, 42/cable car California. **Tours** 3pm 1st Wed of the month; booking essential. **Map** p309 H3.

While the Stock Exchange building is closed to the public, those lucky enough to be in town on the first Wednesday of the month can join a unique free tour of sections of the classic art deco structure. It was modernised in 1928 by architect Timothy Pflueger. Pflueger believed art should be an integral part of architecture, so he commissioned sculptor Ralph Stackpole to create the two granite statues outside, which represent agriculture and industry (the twin sources of wealth). Above the entrance is a figure with arms outstretched, called 'Progress of Man'. On the tenth floor, within the private City Club, is more art, including the building's main attraction, Diego Rivera's 1930 mural 'Allegory of California'. It is one of art's ironies that Rivera, a well-known communist, would create a piece within the very heart of capitalism. But Stackpole and Rivera were old friends, and he recommended Rivera for the job. The mural shows Bay Area industries, with Mother Earth in the centre, and the emphasis on the workers rather than the bosses.

Transamerica Pyramid

600 Montgomery Street, between Clay & Washington Streets (983 4100). Bus 1, 15, 41, 42. **Open** *Lobby* 8.30am-4.30pm Mon-Fri. **Map** p309 H3.

William Pereira's 853ft (260m) 1972 building – the city's tallest – provoked public outrage when its design was unveiled, but has since become an iconic spike in the city's skyline. Built to be earthquake-proof, the pyramid sits on giant rollers that allow it to rock safely – it must work, since the building wasn't damaged by the 1989 Loma Prieta quake. It was once a public attraction, but the current owners do not offer public access to the 27th-floor observation deck. However, you can see the deck and accompanying view through cameras in the lobby.

The Embarcadero

Before San Francisco's bridges were built in the 1930s, the Embarcadero – which stretches along the waterfront from China Basin all the

Take a stroll by the bay along the tree-lined **Embarcadero**. *See p61.*

way up to Fisherman's Wharf – used to be the landing point for more than 50,000 daily commuters from Marin County and the East Bay. Later, when a hideous freeway was erected that ran all the way from the Bay Bridge to North Beach, overshadowing the Embarcadero, the area turned from one of the city's busiest into one of its emptiest. The 1989 Loma Prieta earthquake may have destroyed some other neighbourhoods, but it proved to be a blessing in disguise for the Embarcadero: the freeway, damaged beyond repair, had to be demolished. The waterfront strip has since re-emerged as a graceful, palm-lined boulevard with a distinctive personality all its own.

At its centre is the stately **Ferry Building** (at the foot of Market Street), which divides even-numbered piers (to the south) from odd (to the north). Before the construction of the Golden Gate Bridge and, later, the Transamerica Pyramid, the Ferry Building was the nationally recognised symbol of San Francisco. It is currently undergoing a long-term restoration, but you can still catch ferries to Marin and the East Bay.

Opposite the Ferry Building stands **Justin Herman Plaza** and a controversial sculpture/fountain by French-Canadian artist Armand Vaillancourt. Eyesore or modern art? You decide. A half-block walk up Market brings you to the terminus of the California Street cable car line. The phalanx of wafer-thin towers behind the plaza comprises the **Embarcadero Center** (at the foot of Sacramento Street – *see p161*), a maze-like shopping/dining complex popular with Financial District workers.

A perfect place for a long walk on a balmy autumn evening, the Embarcadero has been refurbished, dotted with costly Canary Island palm trees and outdoor art, fortified with historical markers and benches, and highlighted with a path of glass bricks that glow at night. Heading south from Market Street, marvel at stupendous views of the **San Francisco-Oakland Bay Bridge** (*see p96* **Bridging the gap**) before taking a worthwhile detour one block inland to **Rincon Center** (*see p62*), at the intersection of Mission and Spear Streets. The former main post office, containing a number of impressive art pieces and historic murals, it also has an enormous glass atrium with more than a dozen ethnic food stalls.

In the other direction, north from the Ferry Building, the Embarcadero becomes a long, gently curving promenade extending all the way along the waterfront to Fisherman's Wharf. This stretch is favoured by cyclists, skateboarders and rollerbladers because it has no street intersections. Along the way, Pier 7 – a wide-open public pier with old-fashioned streetlamps and friendly benches – juts out into the bay, with lovely views of **Treasure Island** (*see p74* **Fantasy islands**). Thanks to a declining shipping industry, many of the remaining covered piers are one by one being converted to other uses, such as film soundstages and exhibition spaces.

Note for history buffs: two blocks inland at the intersection of Green and Sansome Streets, the offices of **Philo TV** occupy the former laboratory of boy-genius Philo T Farnsworth, who, in 1927, invented the current system of TV transmission on this very spot (commemorated by a plaque). At Pier 29 is an establishment that dates back to the days before Philo invented the tube: the unusual **Teatro ZinZanni** (438 2668) offers lavishly staged dinner shows of cabaret acts, illusionists and circus acrobats. You never know quite what to expect, but it's pricey ($99-$125).

Rincon Center

101 Spear Street, at Mission Street (243 0473). BART Embarcadero/Muni Metro F/bus 1, 14.
Open 24hrs daily. **Map** p309 J3.
This art deco post office and residential tower has (in the lobby facing Mission Street) intriguing WPA-style murals by Anton Refrigier, an incorrigible Russian artist whose luscious historical panorama includes many dark moments from California's past, such as lynchings and other executions. The central atrium has a unique all-water sculpture dubbed 'Rain Column', a sort of free-floating waterfall cascading four stories to a central pool.

The Tenderloin

West of Union Square, the atmosphere changes abruptly; within the space of a few blocks, downtown's swanky shopping scene rapidly gives way to an impoverished red-light district known as the Tenderloin. This nickname is variously attributed to the flesh boldly on offer here (it's been a hotbed of prostitution since the 19th century) and (less likely) to the district's long, narrow shape on maps. A large community of Southeast Asian immigrants – Vietnamese, Cambodian and Hmong refugees of the Vietnam War – moved into the area in the 1980s and revived it somewhat, establishing grocery stores and coffee-shops, but in truth the Tenderloin remains rather unsightly during the day and not particularly safe at night. Several major hotels are situated on the cusp between Union Square and the Tenderloin – among them the **Clift Hotel**, **Hotel Monaco** and the **Prescott** (for all, *see p37*) – and many a tourist has emerged for the first time to stroll around famously beautiful San Francisco, only to take a wrong turn and head west, directly into the city's least savoury neighbourhood.

City Hall looms over downtown. *See p65.*

The main lure is the city's theatre district, which runs along the Tenderloin's slightly gentrified northern edge. Here you'll find some of the city's best and grandest theatres; for details, *see chapter* **Performing Arts**. Another attraction – for the brave and trendy – is the nightclub scene that rocks around the edges of the Tenderloin. Some of the city's most famous and happening live music venues, bars and dance clubs are here; *see chapters* **Nightlife** and **Bars** for details.

Unfortunately, aside from the nightlife, there's little to lure you here. When the sun comes up, Hmong grandmothers forage the markets while Vietnamese street-toughs patrol their turf, and the down-and-out drug dealers and the homeless struggle to make it through another day. At night, hookers and hustlers take to the streets and the aroma of Asian cooking mixes with the smell of cheap perfume and forbidden fruit.

In keeping with this theme, the neighbourhood also holds a porn tourist attraction of a sort, the **Mitchell Brothers O'Farrell Theatre** (*see p65*). This is the city's largest pornographic theatre, and the tragic story of its mercurial fraternal owners is unique enough to bring in perfectly moral folks toting cameras. Apropos of nothing, the outside wall of the building sports a huge, photo-realistic mural of marine life that has been featured as a backdrop in many films and advertisements.

The large number of impoverished and homeless people in the Tenderloin are cared for in various soup kitchens in the area, including a pair of churches that share a long and compassionate history. **St Boniface Catholic Church** (*see p65*) offers Mass in English, Spanish, Tagalog and Vietnamese, hosts dozens of benefit programmes and has a dining room that serves more than 2,000 daily meals to the needy, while **Glide Memorial Church** (*see below*) serves food to some 3,000 homeless a day.

Glide Memorial United Methodist Church

330 Ellis Street, at Taylor Street (674 6000/ www.glide.org). BART Powell Street/Muni Metro F, J, K, L, M, N/bus 27, 31, 38. **Map** p310 G4.
Glide and the Reverend Cecil Williams are icons in San Francisco, and the church's Sunday services are legendary. Transvestite prostitutes wave arms and sing gospel next to Pacific Heights socialites and the likes of Oprah Winfrey.

One Low Price, 5 Famous Attractions, Unlimited Cable Car Rides!

It's a great New Way to Enjoy San Francisco!

CityPass Includes:

7 day unlimited use Cable Car & MUNI Transportation Pass

Plus admission to:

Blue & Gold Fleet Bay Cruise • California Palace of the Legion of Honor • Exploratorium Academy of Sciences and Steinhart Aquarium • San Francisco Museum of Modern Art

Only $35.75 a $71.50 Value!

CityPass is **on sale at all** of the above attractions. Ask for it at the first one you visit!
Good for 9 days! For more information visit **www.citypass.com** or call (707) 256-0490.

New York City Boston Philadelphia Seattle Chicago Hollywood

It's very San Francisco.

Ghirardelli Square showcases intriguing shops, outstanding restaurants, fascinating galleries, and incredible views. Any of which could hold the key to an unforgettable day. And to top it off, we've got world-famous chocolate.

Ghirardelli Square

(415) 775-5500 www.GhirardelliSq.com
Discounted parking with validation. At the corner of Beach and Larkin.

The United Nations was born at the **War Memorial Opera House** in 1945. *See p66.*

Mitchell Brothers O'Farrell Theatre

895 O'Farrell Street, at Polk Street (776 6686). Bus 38. **Map** p310 F4.

This porn palace was founded by sex pioneers and brothers Artie and Jim Mitchell, who were as famous for introducing professional business savvy to the 'adult entertainment' industry as for their fratricidal relationship. They founded the theatre on Independence Day 1969 and spent decades fighting US morality laws, but it all went wrong in 1991, when Jim shot Artie to death. Jim's lawyers claimed he accidentally killed his brother in an attempt to get him off drugs and alcohol. The jury didn't buy it, and Jim went to San Quentin prison. He was released in 1997. The theatre they founded still thrives, and remains SF's biggest venue for sex shows.

St Boniface Catholic Church

133 Golden Gate Avenue, at Leavenworth Street (863 7515). Bus 5. **Map** p310 G4.

Fairly unremarkable from the street, St Boniface's Romanesque interior, restored in the 1980s, includes some impeccable stencilling and a beautifully gilded apse topped by a four-storey cupola painted with Latin text and scenes from the life of St Francis. The church was undergoing renovation in 2001, with a hopeful completion date of mid 2002.

Civic Center

Built on a more grandiose scale than the rest of town, the Civic Center is an orderly complex of imposing government buildings and immense performance halls. In the centre of it all is **Civic Center Plaza**, an expansive and well-tended lawn that's a good place to relax and get your bearings. Facing the plaza is the stunning Beaux Arts **City Hall** (*see p67*), which was recently retrofitted to repair damage from the 1989 earthquake and to protect the structure against future seismic shocks. City planners took advantage of the retrofitting work to spend four years and $300 million completely restoring the building to its original grandeur. It was finally finished in 1999, so it still looks all shiny and new. In 1954, Joe DiMaggio and Marilyn Monroe got hitched in a third-floor office (no one's quite sure which one), and it was here in 1978 that Dan White assassinated Mayor George Moscone and gay Supervisor Harvey Milk. Equal parts history lesson and architectural masterpiece, City Hall remains the guiding force that shepherds the town through good times and bad. The soul of San Francisco may lie elsewhere, but its brain is here.

On the south side of Civic Center Plaza, the **Bill Graham Civic Auditorium** (*see p210*) is named after the beloved late concert promoter who was the driving force behind San Francisco's rock 'n' roll explosion in the 1960s, and who dominated the city's music scene for 30 years. Continuing around the plaza, you'll see the new **Main Library** (*see p68*) at Grove and Larkin Streets, a gorgeous six-storey

1996 structure that combines the Beaux Arts style with a healthy dash of modernism. On the north side of the Main Library across Hyde Street is **United Nations Plaza**, which hosts a farmers' market each Wednesday and Sunday morning, where scores of local growers sell fresh produce. On other days, the grandly named plaza is a political battleground between the city government and homeless advocates in a never-ending argument over what to do about the many streetpeople who congregate here. The site of the former library building at Larkin and McAllister Streets will eventually contain the **Asian Art Museum** (*see p106*), currently in Golden Gate Park, but due to move in 2002 after the building has undergone a formidable interior redesign and seismic retrofit.

The area's parade of grand edifices continues on the west side of City Hall, lined up along Van Ness Avenue. The **Louise M Davies Symphony Hall** (*see p226*), at Grove Street, is the headquarters of the San Francisco Symphony Orchestra, and regularly hosts lectures and other special events, too. Its multistorey, curving glass street façade is easily recognisable. North across Grove Street, the **War Memorial Opera House** (*see p226*) sits directly behind City Hall and is in many ways its companion, designed by the same architect (Arthur Brown) in the same style. Like its older sibling, the Opera House also underwent major retrofitting and renovation after the Loma Prieta quake and now sports newly gilded trim on the doors and walls, re-upholstered seats and new curtains. In June 1945, 51 nations signed the United Nations charter here and so gave birth to the UN.

North of the Opera House is the **Veterans' Memorial Building** (Van Ness Avenue, at McAllister Street), a venerable workhorse of an edifice used for everything from city offices and chamber music performances to museum exhibits and lectures. It also contains the petite **San Francisco Arts Commission Gallery** (*see p205*), a free exhibition space on the main floor that specialises in politically – or sociologically – driven art. Take the lift to the fourth floor for the unique collection of performing arts memorabilia at the **San Francisco Performing Arts Library &**

Sun, wind and fog

Mark Twain once famously remarked that the coldest winter he had ever endured was a summer in San Francisco. But that was only because he didn't properly understand the city's microclimates. True, there are days in summer when clouds blanket the entire city uniformly, and others when the sun shines beatifically over the whole region. But often as not, San Francisco's bewildering weather is determined by an epic, unending battle between fog and terrain.

Along the California coastline, weather generally flows from west to east: breezes blow in off the Pacific Ocean, often bringing ocean fog inland. Just how far inland is determined by the height of the coastal hills, which serve as a barrier to the heavy, earth-clinging clouds.

The Golden Gate is one of the few gaps in the state's coastal mountain range, and the fog takes advantage of this by spilling over the bridge and into the bay. It swallows Alcatraz, sluices across the bay, swirls around the base of Albany Hill, turns left across the city of Richmond and – if it's really got momentum – oozes through the Carquinez Strait toward the Delta. But San Francisco has its own struggles.

The city's western third is comparatively flat, so there is little to prevent the fog from covering the Richmond and Sunset Districts and Golden Gate Park; as a result, those areas are notoriously gloomy and were the last to be settled. But the fog is often too heavy to climb the hills in the centre – Twin Peaks, Mount Davidson and Mount Sutro – so the areas east of this barrier, including the Mission, the Castro, Noe Valley and Potrero Hill, are often warm and sunny when the rest of town is shivering.

Instead, the fog squeezes through low points in the topography, cascading up Geary Boulevard and the Panhandle, and pouring into the Western Addition, where it often settles for a bit before drifting through the Tenderloin into the Financial District, wending its way among the skyscrapers out into the bay. North Beach is nicely protected by Russian Hill, though Fisherman's Wharf, just a few blocks away, often endures dank fog (on calm days) or freezing gusts (on windy days).

But locals are not always as climate-savvy as they ought to be: planners foolishly built San Francisco Airport at the mouth of the San Bruno Gap, a low pass in the Peninsula range

Museum (*see p112*). The building also houses the comfy **Herbst Theatre** (*see p222*) for intimate classical music performances.

You'll have problems finding many shopping opportunities in the area, aside from the wonderfully named **A Clean Well-Lighted Place For Books** (*see p165*), which offers a broad selection of reading material and weekly authors' readings. **Stars** restaurant (*see p121*) is the local place for celebrity-spotting. More offbeat is **Ananda Fuara** (1298 Market Street, at Larkin Street; 621 1994), operated by devotees of guru Sri Chinmoy, which serves eye-opening vegetarian world cuisine with a dollop of religious propaganda.

City Hall

1 Carlton B Goodlett Place (Polk Street), between McAllister & Grove Streets (554 4000/tours 554 6023). BART Civic Center/Muni Metro F, J, K, L, M, N/bus 5, 19, 21, 42, 47, 49. **Open** 8am-5pm Mon-Fri. **Admission** free. **Map** p310 F4/5.

Built in 1915 and designed by Arthur Brown and John Bakewell, City Hall is the epitome of the Beaux Arts style seen in the rest of Civic Center, with lots of ornamental ironwork, elaborate plasterwork and a giant dome modelled on the one at St Peter's in Rome. San Francisco's version is, in fact, bigger than the state capitol dome in Sacramento and even stands 16ft (5m) higher than the dome of the nation's capitol in Washington, DC. Facts and figures, however, cannot convey the experience of seeing it for yourself. Step through the doors on Polk Street (or rather, as Polk is called for this one block, Carlton B Goodlett Place) and into the central rotunda, a breathtaking space with a sweeping staircase. Above, the magnificent dome overlooks a five-storey colonnade, limestone and granite masonry, regal lighting and majestic marble floors. Dubbed 'the most significant interior space in the United States' by a New York architecture critic when it opened, the two-block-long, one-block-wide City Hall inspires a sense of municipal awe.

Beneath its neo-classical exterior, the building hums with modern technology. A system of rubber-and-steel 'base isolators' allows the structure to move a metre in any direction, thus protecting it from quakes to come. The building contains 600 rooms, each allowing natural light, and houses both the legislative and executive branches of San Francisco's city and county branches of government. Free tours are available daily (call for details

that funnels fog straight over the runways, often leading to low visibility and flight delays. Similarly, the city's old sports stadium, Candlestick Park, was built smack in the middle of a natural wind tunnel, making it a miserable place to play baseball.

On any given day, the sun is most likely to break through between noon and 4pm, though it is often a brief victory. Summer – plagued by a daily invasion of fog – is not the warmest season in San Francisco. If you want warmth and sunshine, try coming in September and the first half of October, or even in February, which sometimes has inexplicable heat waves.

It is best to dress in layers, so that as you pass from one neighbourhood and one microclimate to the next, you can add or remove bits. The weather can change block by block – often several times an hour.

Although there are no hard and fast rules, here's a quick guide to the typical summer weather patterns in different neighbourhoods:

- **Sunny** The Mission, Potrero Hill, the Castro, Noe Valley, North Beach
- **Windy** Fisherman's Wharf, Financial District, Twin Peaks, Hunter's Point
- **Foggy** Richmond District, Sunset District, Golden Gate Park, Western Addition

of the weekly schedule), offering behind-the-scenes views of the Board of Supervisors' chambers (panelled in hand-carved Manchurian oak) and the mayor's office (only open on weekdays). The view of the rotunda from the fourth floor is superb. **The Museum of the City of San Francisco** (*see p110*) is also located here.

San Francisco Main Library

Grove Street, between Larkin & Hyde Streets (Library 557 4400/History Room 557 4567). BART Civic Center/Muni Metro F, J, K, L, M, N/bus 5, 6, 7, 9, 19, 21, 66, 71. **Open** *Library* 10am-6pm Mon, Sat; 9am-8pm Tue-Thur; noon-6pm Fri; noon-5pm Sun. *History Room* 10am-6pm Tue-Thur, Sat; noon-6pm Fri; noon-5pm Sun. **Admission** free; 3-month visitor's card $10. **Map** p310 F/G4/5.

Built in 1996 by architect Pei Cobb Freed, the library is beautifully designed in a traditional style. From the main entrance, descend the stairway into the atrium-like lobby, where vaulted floors rise in tiers above you. The San Francisco History Room occupies the top floor and has changing exhibitions, a large photo archive and knowledgeable, friendly staff. The café in the basement sells mediocre food, recommended only if you're desperate.

SoMa

Known in days of yore as South-of-the-Slot (for the 'slots' or narrow gaps in the street used by cable cars), the area south of Market Street got a much niftier nickname in the 1990s when it became SoMa. Like New York's SoHo, from which it swiped the moniker, this neighbourhood was, for most of its existence, a gritty industrial wasteland occupied mainly by warehouses and sweatshops. A flurry of new residents – mostly dotcommers – thought the old name was just a bit too gritty, and worried it might hurt their steadily increasing property value. Whether it was the new name or their money, the plan to revitalise the area worked, and trendy nightspots sprouted like domain names as the streets filled with the young and overpaid. Economic woes have since tarnished the area's short-lived gloss, and how much of what sprang up in those optimistic times will survive remains to be seen. World-weary San Franciscans over 35 have started to drop the once-trendy term SoMa and reverted, with a bit of *schadenfreude*, to calling it South of Market.

SoMa's showpiece is its **Yerba Buena Gardens Complex**, bounded by Mission, Third, Folsom and Fourth Streets. If you can't find something to occupy yourself here, well, there's no hope for you. This section of SoMa was renovated as part of a city-funded neighbourhood revitalisation project in the 1980s and '90s. Once a blighted area littered

The many faces of **Yerba Buena Gardens.**

with abandoned and condemned properties, it's a warren of attractions, gardens and businesses in a purpose-built complex that's half above ground and half below. **Esplanade Gardens** is an urban park with sculpture walks, shady trees and a waterfall in commemoration of Martin Luther King Jr. Surrounding them are the **Yerba Buena Center for the Arts** (*see p107*) and, at the corner of Third and Howard Streets, the **Yerba Buena Center for the Arts Theater** (*see p224*), an architectural beauty of an auditorium.

Filling the other half of the block (Fourth Street, from Howard to Mission Streets), huge **Sony Metreon** (*see p161*) is a four-storey, futuristic entertainment mall with no fewer than 15 cinemas augmented by gadget shops, restaurants, video game rooms and a 270-foot (86-metre) lobby that exits into the Esplanade Gardens. Though parking in the area is a problem, the centre became one of the city's most popular attractions as soon as it opened.

Across Third Street from Yerba Buena Gardens, the **San Francisco Museum of Modern Art** (*see p107*), designed by Mario Botta and opened in 1995, is the second-largest modern art museum in the country. A $60-million red-brick landmark with a huge slanted cylindrical skylight, SFMOMA houses an important permanent collection, including works by Jasper Johns, Imogen Cunningham, Roy Lichtenstein and many more. It also has a renowned museum shop (*see p179*) and a pleasant café, handy for sustenance after you've been tramping the museum.

Two huge works of public art flank the museum: a two-part mural, *SKY/GROUND*, by local artist Rigo 99, is painted on two sides of a building at Third and Mission (which is currently being turned into a new hotel); and a dramatic, 30-foot (nine-metre) figure by sculptor MD Stutz reclines on the upper atrium of the swanky **W Hotel** (*see p42*) at Third and Howard Streets. The W is also home to trendy restaurant **XYZ** (*see p125*) and a swinging bar (*see p150*).

Vast **Moscone Convention Center**, a two-block hive of exhibition halls on either side of (and under) Howard Street, named after assassinated Mayor George Moscone, has entertained millions of conventioneers since it was erected in 1978. Moscone North is largely hidden beneath the Esplanade Gardens; Moscone South is more of the same, of no interest to casual visitors not attending a conference. Moscone West is currently under construction at Fourth and Howard Streets.

Ingeniously covering the top of Moscone Center on the south side of Howard Street, the **Rooftop at Yerba Buena Gardens** sports various child-friendly attractions: a high-tech, hands-on museum called **Zeum** (*see p197*) that has been struggling to stay afloat despite the popularity of nearby activities; **Yerba Buena Bowling Center** (*see p242*); **Yerba Buena Ice Skating Center** (1750 Folsom Street; 777 3727); and a lovely, refurbished carousel.

Contrasting all this modernity is high-ceilinged **St Patrick's Church** (756 Mission Street; 421 3730), built in 1851; noon concerts are staged regularly amid its stained glass and marble. Also on Mission Street, the **Friends of Photography/Ansel Adams Center** (*see p109*), named after the San Franciscan hailed as the 20th-century's greatest photographer, exhibits the work of photographic masters, old and new, and has its own bookshop. Across the street, the free **California Historical Society** (*see below*) offers changing displays about the history of the Golden State, while the nearby **Society of California Pioneers** (*see p70*) offers more historical art and artefacts.

Several blocks south-west of Yerba Buena, Folsom Street savours its gloriously kinky reputation each autumn during the annual **Folsom Street Fair** (*see p192*), where leather fetishists turn out in a display of leashes and bondage gear that makes even the Gay Pride Parade seem tame. To get in the spirit, check out historic gay bar the **Stud** (*see p234*) on Ninth Street. One of the city's cleanest bars, **Brainwash** (*see p143*) is a real-life *My Beautiful Laundrette,* with a full-service bar and café in a laundromat; it has both a fine selection of beers on tap and shiny, front-loading dryers.

SoMa is also awash with live music venues and dance clubs – for the pick of the best, *see chapter* **Nightlife**. This part of SoMa may swing at night, but it tends to doze by day, though the non-profit **New Langton Arts** and **San Francisco Camerawork** (*see p205*) share an exhibition space at 1246 Folsom Street, where edgy new art is always on display. Taking an afternoon stroll around the rest of SoMa, you might wonder what all the fuss is about; it still looks as industrial as it ever did, and certain zones (such as parts of Sixth Street) are as grotty as San Francisco gets.

California Historical Society

678 Mission Street, between Third & New Montgomery Streets (357 1848/www.californiahistoricalsociety.org). BART Montgomery Street/ bus 12, 14, 30, 45, 76. **Open** 11am-5pm Tue-Sat. **Admission** $3. Free 1st Tue of the month. **No credit cards. Map** p311 H4.

This is the state's official historical group, and it focuses all its efforts on assembling this impressive collection of Californiana. Its vaults hold half

San Francisco's snazzy new baseball stadium, **Pacific Bell Park.**

a million photographs and thousands of books, magazines and paintings, as well as an extensive Gold Rush collection. All its short-term exhibitions are connected in some way to historic California.

Society of California Pioneers

Seymour Pioneer Museum, 300 Fourth Street, at Folsom Street (957 1849/www.californiapioneers.org). Bus 12, 15, 30, 45, 76. **Open** 10am-4pm Tue-Fri, 1st Sat of the month. **Admission** $3; $1 concessions. **No credit cards**. **Map** p311 H4. Operated by descendants of the state's first settlers, this small museum occasionally features intriguing displays on California history. There is also a small permanent exhibition of 19th-century paintings, sculpture and furniture.

South Park & South Beach

The oval green known as South Park started life in pre-quake San Francisco as one of the ritziest neighbourhoods in the city. San Francisco's first gated community, the original was modelled on London's Berkeley Square; the developer even had sparrows flown in to give it an authentic atmosphere. It burned down in the early part of the 20th century. With the invention of the cable car, the millionaires absconded to Nob Hill, and the area was given over to industry. Still later, after World War II, it became an African-American enclave. Largely neglected for decades, the neighbourhood soared to a rather sudden prominence as a dotcom paradise in the 1990s, when well-paid, young techno-things flocked to offices and condos here. The district was promptly dubbed 'Multimedia Gulch' – but that moment in the sun turned out to be more brief than anyone expected, and many of the local Internet and design businesses that once basked in its glow have closed shop, leaving South Park once again feeling abandoned.

The first restaurant to move in and milk the cash cow was **South Park Café** (*see p125*). It is still serving French bistro food, albeit to a smaller and less cocky crowd. **Caffè Centro** (102 South Park), another early arrival, is home to a hip breakfast-and-lunch scene, while newcomer **The Butler & the Chef Café** (*see p143*) doubles as a shop. Fashionistas in search of designer bargains should head to second-hand emporium **Jeremy's** (*see p171*).

South-east of South Park, South Beach also saw a short spurt of gentrification and now waits with bated breath to see what harder times will bring. Its jewel is the brand-new baseball stadium **Pacific Bell Park** – known locally as Pac Bell Park – near Pier 40 (*see p241* **Home run**). Home to the SF Giants, it's a beautifully designed structure and well liked by locals. In the shade of the ballpark, **MoMo's San Franciscan Grill** (760 Second Street; 989 8660) has hearty, rustic fare.

The area also contains an intriguing architectural gem: the **Francis 'Lefty' O'Doul Bridge** (Third Street, near Berry Street) is the city's only working drawbridge. A charming antique, it was designed by JB Strauss, who is better known for a much bigger span: the Golden Gate Bridge.

North Beach & Around

Fisherman's Wharf may be overrated, but many of San Francisco's best sights are in this part of town – and the views are breathtaking.

Whoever it was who sang about leaving his heart in San Francisco undoubtedly left a large chunk of it in this part of town, which abounds with all the qualities that make the city one of the world's best-loved. From clanging cable cars to **Chinatown**'s colourful Grant Avenue, Italian cafés in **North Beach**, swanky hotels on **Nob Hill** and **Russian Hill**'s breezy, breathtaking views, romance could hardly find a better place on earth to bloom. At the northern edge of the district, **Fisherman's Wharf** and Ghirardelli Square remain tourist hubs, largely for no other reason than their reputation as, well, tourist hubs. (Fisherman's Wharf is also the departure point for trips to popular **Alcatraz Island** and **Angel Island**.) This region is dense and compact, especially well suited to walkers who like to pack a lot into a single outing. And make that cappuccino a double: extra caffeine comes in handy with so many steep slopes at hand.

Chinatown

Its souvenir shops stocked with teakwood buddhas and its steamy tea houses smelling of oolong tread the fine line between tourist trash and authenticity, but that's nothing new. Chinatown has been one of America's most-visited attractions for more than 100 years, yet throughout that time it's always been a living and working neighbourhood. The 1849 Gold Rush drew shiploads of Cantonese to California; famine and wars across China in the ensuing decades gave little incentive for the immigrants to return home. After the gold fields had played out, many Chinese got decent jobs building the transcontinental railway. Like most new arrivals, they dreamed of striking it rich, despite severe anti-Chinese laws and overeager racist vigilantes in the late 19th century. The Chinese neighbourhood that arose in San Francisco had a well deserved reputation for cheap whores, opium dens and all-hours gambling – activities that lured throngs of curious Caucasians. The 1906 earthquake and fire devastated the district, though the vice continued well into the 1920s.

In the aftermath of the quake, city fathers strove to appropriate what had become prime real estate, but the Chinese held fast and rebuilt Chinatown on the same ground. Today, its crowded streets and dark alleys, with laundry fluttering from fire escapes overhead, have the feel of an earlier era. Nearly 100 restaurants serve specialities ranging from duck's feet to taro-root dumplings; herbalists weigh out portions of medicinal plant and animal matter just as they have for more than a century; and on special occasions lion-dancers swerve and reel to the sound of drums and firecrackers. Some 10,000 Chinese still live in the neighbourhood, which is one of the country's most densely populated. While many of their wealthier counterparts now live in the Richmond and Sunset Districts, Chinatown is the historic heart of one of the largest Asian populations outside Asia.

A few blocks from Union Square, at Grant Avenue and Bush Street, the dragon-topped **Chinatown Gate** marks Chinatown's southern entrance. A gift from Taiwan in 1970, the green-tiled gate is fashioned after traditional village designs, with a quotation from Confucius in Chinese characters urging us to work for the common good. Through the gate is **Grant Avenue**, Chinatown's main thoroughfare.

In the 1870s and '80s, when Grant was called Dupont Street, it was patrolled and controlled by *tongs*, mutual-protection societies whose Mafia-style dealings sparked bitter, bloody battles over gambling and prostitution rackets. Today, the mood is wholly commercial, with shops as far as the eye can see selling countless T-shirts, toys, ceramics, souvenirs and jewellery, the genuine mixed with junk.

Most of the buildings along Grant sport undistinguished American-style architecture, although the **Ying On Labor Association** building (745-7 Grant Avenue) is a gaudy study in chinoiserie, while directly across the street the **Sai Gai Yat Bo Company** building (736 Grant Avenue) has antiquated ornate balconies and a pagoda-style roof. With its circular gold entrance, **Li Po Bar** (*see p151*), named after the great drunken poet, is drenched in kitsch. Across the street, **Kowloon Vegetarian Café** serves full meals and takeaway vegan dim-sum snacks at outrageously low prices. **Ten Ren Tea Company** (*see p177*), the city's largest tea retailer, offers free samples to help patrons

Chinatown has been a thriving community since the days of the Gold Rush.

choose from 40 varieties – it's a favourite stop on most Chinatown guided tours. On the corner of California Street and Grant is the Roman Catholic **Old St Mary's Cathedral** (*see p73*), a sturdy 1854 edifice made of granite imported from China.

A half-block east of Grant Avenue, bounded by Washington Street to the north and Clay Street to the south, **Portsmouth Square** is historic yet unprepossessing. The village then called Yerba Buena (the name was later changed to San Francisco) was first claimed for the United States from Mexico on this very spot in 1846. Two years later, Sam Brannan, owner of the city's first newspaper, the *California Star*, announced in this square that gold had been discovered at Sutter's Mill in the Sierra foothills. For these two reasons, Portsmouth Square is considered by many as the true birthplace of the city. Within a few years of Brannan's announcement, Chinese immigrants settled in the area for good. Today, the elderly congregate here to practise t'ai chi, argue politics and kibbitz over games of Chinese chess. Monuments include a copy of the Goddess of Liberty that figured in 1989's Tiananmen Square incident, and another, shaped like the galleon *Hispaniola*, dedicated to Robert Louis Stevenson. The writer used to sit in the park during his stint as a San Franciscan in 1879.

Linked to the square by a concrete footbridge, the **Chinese Culture Center** (*see p73*) is on the third floor of the Holiday Inn. At 743 Washington Street, the pagoda-like **Bank of Canton** is one of Chinatown's most photographed buildings. The *California Star*'s offices originally occupied the site, but the present creation was built in 1909 for the Chinese American Telephone Exchange, where for four decades multilingual phone operators routed calls throughout Chinatown by sheer memory, as there was no phone book or directory of numbers for Chinese residents.

Cameron House (920 Sacramento Street, at Joice Street) is named after Donaldina Cameron, the determined New Zealand crusader who devoted her life to saving San Francisco's Chinese girls from prostitution and sexual slavery. It's just about the only place in the whole city where you can still see physical traces of the great 1906 fire: misshapen 'clinker' bricks, melted by the intense heat, protrude from the walls of the still-thriving shelter. Trace your finger over the twisted bricks and touch history.

To the west of Grant Avenue, running the length of Chinatown, **Stockton Street** is where the locals shop. Loud with diverse Chinese dialects, its grocery stores attract throngs of customers but few tourists; its fish markets and butcher's shops sport tanks swarming with live fish, turtles and crabs. Restaurants on Stockton have a more authentic feel, for better or worse, than their Grant Avenue counterparts. If you want to experience what many consider the 'real' Chinatown, head up to Stockton.

Nearly 150 years old, the **Kong Chow Temple** (855 Stockton Street, on the fourth floor) is thick with incense smoke. Divination sticks, red satin banners, flowers and pyramids of oranges flank a fabulous altar from which the god Kuan Ti's statue has a keen view of the bay. (Another ancient shrine, the **Tien Hau Temple**, can be found at 125 Waverly Place. At both locations, act as you would in a cathedral: quiet and respectful.) The façade of the photogenic **Chinese Six Companies Building** (843 Stockton Street) sports ceramic carp, stone lions and auspiciously coloured tiles.

Chinatown is at its most Chinese in its alleys. Follow your nose to the **Golden Gate Fortune Cookie Factory** (56 Ross Alley; 781 3956) where you can watch cookies being made by hand. South of Washington Street, between Grant and Stockton, is picturesque **Waverly Place**, scene in 1879 of a famous fight between two *tongs* over the ownership of an especially beautiful prostitute. **Duncombe Alley** is no longer home to the famous opium resorts that once filled it and nearby Jackson Street. Another kind of history was made in quiet **Spofford Alley**, where Sun Yat-sen launched an overthrow of the Manchu Dynasty between 1904 and 1910 in the **Ghee Kung Tong Building** (36 Spofford). **Wentworth Alley**, east of Grant Avenue between Jackson and Washington Streets, is another untouristed backstreet catering exclusively to locals.

Chinese Culture Center

Third floor, Holiday Inn, 750 Kearny Street, at Portsmouth Square (986 1822). Bus 1, 15, 30, 45/cable car California. **Open** 10am-4pm Tue-Sun. **Admission** free. **Credit** MC, V. **Map** p309 H3.

Changing Asian-themed exhibitions at this small centre are augmented by a gift shop. The centre is also host to various musical and dance performances, as well as numerous classes, and organises occasional walking tours.

Old St Mary's Cathedral

660 California Street, at Grant Avenue (288 3800). Bus 1, 15, 30, 45/cable car California. **Open** 7am-5pm Mon-Fri; 10am-6.30pm Sat; 7am-5pm Sun. **Map** p309 G3.

Much early missionising and the city's first English lessons for Chinese immigrants went on under this 19th-century building's forbidding clock tower, which warns: 'Son, observe the time and fly from evil'. Lunchtime concerts are staged in its daintily glorious interior.

Washington Square, the green heart of North Beach. *See p75.*

Fantasy islands

Though San Francisco Bay is sprinkled with 14 islands, only a few are accessible to visitors. The most famous, of course, is **Alcatraz**, but a ramble or bicycle ride around **Angel Island** is only a 40-minute ferry ride away, while man-made **Treasure Island** offers stunning views of the city.

Alcatraz

Alcatraz: www.nps.gov/alcatraz/. Blue & Gold Ferry: recorded information 773 1188/tickets 705 5555/www.blueandgoldfleet.com/. Blue & Gold ferry from Pier 41, Embarcadero. **Tickets** *With audio tour* $13.25; $8-$11.50 concessions. *Without audio tour* $9.25; $6-$7.50 concessions. *After dark tours* (6.20pm, 7pm Thur-Sun) $20.75; $11-$18 concessions. **Credit** AmEx, Disc, MC, V.

Alcatraz is Spanish for pelican, but to Al Capone, 'Machine Gun' Kelly and Robert 'the Birdman' Stroud, this tiny but forbidding penal island (*pictured*) was simply 'the Rock'. The West Coast's first lighthouse was built here in 1854, but it was soon decided that its escape-proof setting in the middle of the bay made it a perfect site for a prison. The island became a military jail in the 1870s, though it wasn't until it was converted into a high-security federal penitentiary in 1934 that the name Alcatraz became an international symbol of punishment. Despite only being in operation for 30 years, Alcatraz remains fixed in the imagination as the ultimate penal colony, an American Devil's Island.

The island made headlines in 1969 when a group of Native Americans claimed it under the terms of an old treaty granting surplus federal lands to Indian tribes; the temporary occupation is still commemorated in a ritual on the island every November.

Filmmakers love the prison's atmospheric setting – 1979's *Escape From Alcatraz* was made here with Clint Eastwood, as was 1996's *The Rock*. The island also boasts one of the Bay Area's last deep-pitched foghorns. Today, its ominous prison buildings are no longer used, and the craggy outcrop lures so many voluntary visitors – well over a million each year – that it has become one of San Francisco's top tourist attractions. The admission price includes a ferry ride from Pier 41 in Fisherman's Wharf (ferries leave every half hour from 9.30am to 4.15pm daily), and a walking tour of the facility with audio narration by former inmates. There are also evening tours, and one-day combined tours of Alcatraz and Angel Island. The semi-derelict concrete cellblocks are chilling, both figuratively and literally – dress warmly. Book your visit in advance and come prepared for crowds.

Angel Island

Angel Island: 897 0715/www.angelisland.org. Blue & Gold Ferry: recorded information 773 1188/tickets 705 5555/www.blueandgoldfleet.com/. Blue & Gold ferry from Pier 41, Embarcadero. **Open** 8am-sunset daily. **Tickets** $10.50; $5.50-$9 concessions. **Credit** AmEx, Disc, MC, V.

Now a state park, this delightfully wild isle – by far the bay's largest – was the site of a US government immigration station built in 1910. Boatloads of new arrivals from China were detained for weeks and even months here at 'the Ellis Island of the West', while officials decided their fate. Many were sent home without ever touching the mainland. During World War II, the 740-acre island housed a POW camp and, later, a missile base.

There are three ferry departures daily on weekends (9.45am, 11.30am, 2pm), two on weekdays (10am, 11.30am). Boats arrive at Ayala Cove, where you can pick up maps at the visitor centre, rent bikes and claim a picnic table. The five-mile (eight-kilometre) Perimeter Trail brings you past immigration quarantine buildings, picturesque Civil War barracks and other military remnants among the trees, and Quarry Beach – a sheltered, sandy sunbathing strip popular with kayakers. For those who can't deal with the walk, a tram tour encircles the island. The top of Mount Livermore (781 feet/238 metres) affords a lovely panoramic view of the bay. The island also has nine campsites with still more vistas of the bay and city skyline.

Treasure Island

Flat-as-a-griddle **Treasure Island**, built on the shoals of neighbouring Yerba Buena Island, was man-made from boulders and sand as a site for 1939's Golden Gate International Exposition. After the fair closed, the plan was to turn the island into the Bay Area's airport, but with the outbreak of World War II, it instead became a US Naval station. Largely off-limits to visitors for decades, Treasure Island was recently deeded back to the city and is now a sort of mid-bay suburb, with some lucky San Franciscans moving into the former military housing. Though it's open to the public, there's little to do on the island aside from admiring spectacular views of San Francisco from the western shoreline.

Adjoining **Yerba Buena Island** remains an important Coast Guard station mostly closed to tourism, despite its exquisite location. It's legal to drive on the island's one road but there's nowhere to stop.

North Beach

North and east of Columbus Avenue, North Beach nursed much of what made San Francisco famous: food, literature, espresso and sex. Originally home to the city's Italian community and thus to many family-style restaurants, North Beach in the 1950s attracted Beat writers led by the likes of Allen Ginsberg, who is said to have written his epic poem 'Howl' upstairs at 1010 Montgomery Street. Legendary comedy clubs and, later, punk venues gave North Beach the indelible stamp of hipness.

Today, the mellow streets of North Beach with their famously lambent light on sunny days are still home to elderly Italians who play *bocce* ball, read Neapolitan newspapers and nibble cannoli in a dazzling array of coffee-houses. And the big, brash strip joints along Broadway remain a tourist draw, whether locals like it or not. Now North Beach is as well known for its literary heritage and sex shows as for its lasagne; its blend of sleaze, bohemiana and the city's best espresso gives you plenty of good reasons to stay up late.

Much of North Beach's history and many of its treasures lie along **Columbus Avenue**. Francis Ford Coppola has an office in **Columbus Tower**, the turreted green building on the corner of Columbus and Kearny. On its ground floor is elegant **Café Niebaum-Coppola** (291 1700), which sells its own brand of pasta alongside wines from the film director's Napa Valley vineyard. The epicentre of the Beat movement, **City Lights** bookshop (*see p165*) is still owned by poet Lawrence Ferlinghetti and stays open until midnight daily. Adorned with over-the-top murals, **Vesuvio** bar (*see p152*) was a favourite of literary drunks Dylan Thomas and Jack Kerouac; the alley separating the bar from City Lights has been officially renamed Jack Kerouac Street. The liquor's been flowing even longer at **Spec's** (William Saroyan Place, directly across Columbus Avenue from City Lights – *see p151*), one of the city's oldest saloons, outfitted museum-style with Native American artefacts and sailors' souvenirs.

Operatic arias erupt on Saturday afternoons at **Caffè Trieste** on Vallejo Street (*see p143*); native son Coppola allegedly worked on his script for *The Godfather* here. On a sunny day, its outside tables are a lovely spot to soak up the late-afternoon rays. **Molinari Delicatessen** (*see p176*) sells olives, cheeses, salads, cold cuts and house-made tortellini for *la dolce vita* and picnics in **Washington Square**. Marking the heart of North Beach, this grassy rectangle is overlooked by the white stucco Romanesque **Church of Saints Peter**

Nowadays, the fishermen are few and far between at bustling **Fisherman's Wharf**, where

and Paul, where Marilyn Monroe and local-guy Joe DiMaggio had their wedding photos taken. (Since both were divorced and Joe was a Catholic, they had to get married at City Hall.) An 1879 statue of Benjamin Franklin stands in the park atop a granite-encased time capsule scheduled for reopening in 2079. The park is a lovely place to watch people walk their dogs, play frisbee and kiss. At **Caffé Roma** (526 Columbus; 296 7942), coffee is roasted fragrantly on the premises, while atmospheric **Mario's Bohemian Cigar Store** (*see p144*) sells delicious focaccia sandwiches and great cappuccinos – but no cigars.

Home to lap dancers and their fans, **Broadway** between Columbus Avenue and Montgomery Street is lined with ridiculous nightclubs offering sexy floor shows, though there are far fewer now than in the swinging sixties. History was made at the Condor Club (300 Columbus Avenue, at Broadway – now a sports bar), where, in 1964, buxom waitress Carol Doda dropped her bikini top and initiated the topless dancing era. And 443 Broadway is the site of the former Mabuhay Gardens, a world-famous punk mecca where local acts like the Dead Kennedys and the Avengers got their start and out-of-towners Devo, the Ramones and Madness made a name for themselves.

Two hotels sum up the different sides of North Beach. The aptly named **Hotel Bohème** (*see p42*) celebrates its Beat heritage with framed photographs of bohemian North Beach scenes from the 1950s and '60s, while the *pension*-like **San Remo Hotel** (*see p43*), a pretty Italianate Victorian, is the ideal spot for soaking up the area's Italian ambience. **Telegraph Hill**, bordered by Grant Avenue, Green, Bay and Sansome Streets, was the site of the West Coast's first telegraph, which tapped out bulletins of ships arriving from across the Pacific. Its most noticeable feature is **Coit Tower**, which looks like the nozzle of a firehose, has some fabulous WPA murals at the bottom and great views from the top (*see p82* **Coit Tower**).

Fisherman's Wharf

San Francisco's port was once the soul of the city, but as most commercial shipping and fishing moved elsewhere, **Fisherman's Wharf** – roughly bounded by Jefferson, North Point and Kearny Streets and the edge of Fort Mason – became a garish and inexplicably popular tourist purgatory. Day-trippers descend in their hundreds from the terminus of the Powell-Hyde cable car line, at Victorian Park. Except as a departure point (from Pier 41) for day trips by ferry to Alcatraz and Angel Island (*see p74* **Fantasy islands**), the area is best avoided – unless you're an unrepentant tourist or masochist who enjoys pointless souvenirs, pricey seafood and lacklustre crowds wondering why they came.

Jefferson Street, the wharf's main drag, is the ultimate in tourist traps; the **Wax Museum** (145 Jefferson Street; 1-800 439 4305) and **Ripley's Believe It Or Not! Museum** (175 Jefferson Street; 771 6188) are clichéd seafront diversions. Sidewalk crab stalls and

tourists throng among the sea lions, street performers and crab stalls.

seafood restaurants do a booming business amid a dizzying panoply of gimcrackery. For the only remaining glimpse of an authentic Fisherman's Wharf as it was meant to be, turn north (toward the water) on Leavenworth Street, off Jefferson, then slip right into **Fish Alley**, where real fishing boats are docked and real fishermen still go about their salty business. Within shouting distance of thronged Jefferson, it might as well be miles away – there's nary a tourist to be seen.

At the eastern end of the area, **Pier 39** is a sprawling prefab array of seafront shops, attractions and arcade games patently designed to separate you from your money. Luckily, crowds of sea lions barking and belching on nearby pontoons on the west side of the pier provide a nice natural respite (their population varies with the seasons). Offshore from H Dock on Pier 39, **Forbes Island** (951 4900) is a man-made, engine-propelled, 700-ton floating isle with its own lighthouse and a restaurant. Further west along the waterfront at Pier 45, a World War II submarine, the **USS Pampanito** (*see p79*), has ended its ship-sinking days and is now open to the public, for a fee.

A reminder of the area's former industrial life is the **Cannery** (enter on Jefferson or Beach Streets, next to Leavenworth Street; *see p161*). Built in 1907 as a fruit-canning factory, it's now yet another twee shopping mall modelled along the lines of London's Covent Garden, complete with street performers. The Cannery also houses **Cobb's Comedy Club** (928 4320), which showcases the top comedians in the country. Nineteenth-century red-brick **Ghirardelli Square** (at Beach and Larkin Streets; *see p161*) housed a famous chocolate factory until the 1960s, when it was turned into a complex of shops and restaurants. You can sort through your swag in the central plaza, with its lovely Mermaid Fountain designed by local artist Ruth Asawa.

The shores of **Aquatic Park** (between Hyde Street and Van Ness Avenue) offer one of the best strolls in the city, with a panorama of the Golden Gate Bridge, Alcatraz, windsurfers, sailing boats, wildly coloured kites and dogs catching frisbees. Along the **Municipal Pier** (accessible from the northern end of Van Ness Avenue), fishermen try their luck, while a fleet of carefully restored historic ships, all of them National Historic Landmarks, are docked permanently at the **Hyde Street Pier** (*see p79*). The pier is under the same administration as the **San Francisco Maritime National Historical Park Museum Building** (*see p111*), opposite Ghirardelli Square. A white art deco building that looks like an ocean liner, it recaptures West Coast whaling, steamboating and perilous journeys 'around the Horn'.

The **Golden Gate Promenade** begins from here, continuing for three miles (five kilometres) along the shoreline all the way to **Fort Point** (*see p98*). The entire waterfront from Aquatic Park to Ocean Beach was incorporated into the Golden Gate National Recreation Area in 1972, when the authorities successfully stopped the infection of Fisherman's Wharf-style tourist kitsch from spreading further.

The city on foot: Stairways

Although many are unmarked and overgrown with foliage, San Francisco's public stairways provide an intimate glimpse of city life and an exhilarating alternative to the gym. The city's treacherous topography made stairway paths a necessity in some areas: urban street builders, faced with precipitous slopes on the city's 42 hills, often found themselves needing to build steps in places where normal, smooth thoroughfares would be suicidally steep. The result is a far-flung network of 400 public stairways, many blessed with quaint crannies and secret vistas. Stairway-walking is not for the faint-hearted or cardiac-challenged, but for those who persevere, there is usually a parapet or seat at the top to rest on while admiring the usually stunning view.

Novice stairway spotters should look for the yellow diamond-shaped signs on hilly routes that say 'Not a Through Street' and assume that a staircase lies beyond. You won't walk many before you become a stairway snob; soon you'll be discriminating between those that are just a small set of stairs ending a street, those that are normal roads with stairs next to them (Filbert Street, between Leavenworth and Hyde Streets, on Russian Hill) and those that offer architect-designed steps, breathtaking views and arum lilies growing in the adjacent flower beds (Vallejo Street Stairway – *pictured* – between Jones and Mason Streets, also on Russian Hill).

For more detailed guidance, consult Adah Bakalinsky's comprehensive book *Stairway Walks in San Francisco* (Wilderness Press), which offers 27 graded and tested self-guided stairway tours throughout the city.

Culebra Terrace

Chestnut Street, between Larkin & Polk Streets, Russian Hill. Bus 19/cable car Powell-Hyde. **Map** p308 F2.

This Russian Hill climb is shaded by Monterey pines, and offers a great view of the Golden Gate Bridge.

Lyon Street Steps

Between Green Street & Broadway, Cow Hollow/ Pacific Heights. Bus 41, 45. **Map** p307 D3.

Begin at Green Street, where you'll climb the edge of the Presidio into Pacific Heights. There are great views of Alcatraz, the Palace of Fine Arts and the Golden Gate Bridge. At the top you're just a stone's throw from the entrance to the Presidio.

Macondray Lane

North of Green Street, between Taylor & Jones Streets, Russian Hill. Bus 41, 45. **Map** p308 G2.

The best stairways are those that replaced road or pavement altogether, such as leafy Macondray Lane, legendary inspiration for Barbary Lane in Armistead Maupin's postmodern soap opera *Tales of the City*. It's miraculously secluded: idiosyncratic houses line one side, through which you catch tantalising glimpses of the bay beyond. As with many of the better stairways, its signpost is hard to spot (look for the name imprinted in the concrete of the kerb).

Ord Court Feline Appreciation Walk

Off Ord Street, between States & Lower Stairway Terrace Streets, Buena Vista. Bus 37. **Map** p313 D6.

A shady, intimate walk in the heart of Buena Vista overlooking the Haight-Ashbury. More cats than people will be visible on your descent.

23rd Street Urban Hike

Begin at 23rd & Diamond Streets, Noe Valley. Bus 24, 35, 48. **Map** p314 X2.

Climb west up 23rd Street. At Grand View, take the pedestrian overpass across Upper Market, then follow the series of stairways that climb to the base of Twin Peaks. A trail to the right will lead you to the top of the southernmost peak, a full 910 feet (278 metres) above the city's skyline.

Hyde Street Pier

At the foot of Hyde Street (561 7100/www.maritime.org). Muni Metro F/bus 19, 30, 42/cable car Powell-Hyde. **Open** 9.30am-5pm daily. **Admission** $6; concessions $2. **No credit cards**. **Map** p308 F1.

Maritime fans, students of history and children will love the eight historic vessels permanently docked here. Typical of the ships that would have been common in the area in the 19th and early 20th centuries, they include the 1886 full-rigged *Balclutha*, built to carry grain from California to Europe; the *CA Thayer*, an 1895 sailing ship that carried timber along the West Coast; the *Wapama*, a 1915 steam schooner that replaced the sailing timber ships; *Hercules*, a 1907 ocean tugboat; and the 1890 San Francisco commuter ferry *Eureka*.

USS Pampanito

Pier 45 (775 1943/www.maritime.org). Muni Metro F/bus 19, 30, 42/cable car Powell-Hyde. **Open** 9am-6pm Mon-Thur, Sun; 9am-8pm Fri, Sat. **Admission** $7; concessions $4. **Credit** AmEx, MC, V. **Map** p308 F1.

The *Pampanito* is a World War II Balao class Fleet submarine with an impressive record: it made six patrols in the Pacific at the height of the war, sinking six Japanese ships and damaging four others. The vessel was recently restored to look much as it would have in its prime in 1945. The sub is still seaworthy, too: in 1995, it sailed under the Golden Gate Bridge for the first time in 50 years.

Russian Hill

Named after a group of wayward Russian sailors whose graves were discovered here in the 1840s, Russian Hill is a quiet, residential and very pricey neighbourhood roughly bordered by Larkin and North Point Streets, Columbus Avenue, Powell Street and Pacific Avenue. Its name is deceptive: it bears not the slightest trace of anything Russian today. Its most notorious landmark is the world's 'crookedest' (and perhaps most photographed) thoroughfare, **Lombard Street**, which snakes steeply down from Hyde Street to Leavenworth, packing nine hairpin bends into one brick-paved and over-landscaped block. In summer, tourists queue up for the thrill of driving down its hazardous 27 per cent gradient at 5mph (much to the annoyance of local residents) – arrive early or late if you want to avoid them and their cameras. For further thrills, test your skills behind the wheel on the steepest street in the city: **Filbert Street** between Hyde and Leavenworth descends at a whopping 31.5 per cent gradient.

Lombard Street: it's very, very crooked.

Rivera's mural in the **SF Art Institute**.

Also on Russian Hill is the **San Francisco Art Institute** (*see p81*), housed in an attractive 1920s Spanish Revival building on Chestnut Street and containing a wonderful Diego Rivera mural. Struggle up Vallejo Street to take in the views from **Ina Coolbrith Park** at Taylor Street – it's less a park than a narrow ledge outfitted with benches; arrive early in the morning and you'll catch elderly Chinese practising t'ai chi here. Up from the park, the top of the **Vallejo Street Stairway**, designed by Willis Polk and surrounded on each side by landscaped gardens, is the apex of Russian Hill, where *Little House on the Prairie* author Laura Ingalls Wilder once lived at 1019 Vallejo – far from the long grass of the prairie. Russian Hill is riven with quaint stairs

On a clear day, you can see for ever

San Francisco is a city of views: nearly every neighbourhood has a view of at least one other neighbourhood looking pretty in the distance. Here's your guide to the best of the vistas; the places with the kind of grand panoramas that will make you want to never leave.

Coit Tower

Unbeatable 360° vistas of North Beach, Fisherman's Wharf and the Financial District, with the entire San Francisco Bay spreading out before you. The best views are from the top of the tower, though they're not half bad from ground level, too. *See also p82.*

The Carnelian Room

After 3pm, an exclusive club on the top (52nd) floor of the Bank of America building opens its doors to the public. The cocktails are pricey, but from up here all those other Financial District skyscrapers look downright puny. *See also p59.*

Top of the Mark

A classic bar on the 19th floor of the Mark Hopkins Hotel at the crest of Nob Hill, with sparkling night-time views over the city. *See also p152.*

North side of Russian Hill

Almost any intersection along the northern flank of Russian Hill – try the intersections of Green and Leavenworth Streets, and Hyde and Chestnut Streets – provides lordly vistas of Fisherman's Wharf, the bay and Alcatraz.

Twin Peaks

It's often windy at the top and not easy to reach without a car, but Twin Peaks has an unobstructed view of Market Street, the Financial District, Civic Center, the Mission, the Bay Bridge and the East Bay (*pictured*). The giant TV and radio aerial Sutro Tower looms to the north-west. If you're driving, take Twin Peaks Boulevard off Portola Drive or Clarendon Avenue. To get there by public transport, take Muni Metro K, L or M to Forest Hill station, then bus 52 south. Ask the driver to let you off at the stop nearest Portola Drive and Twin Peaks Boulevard, then follow the boulevard to the top.

Grand View Park

This little-known park above the Inner Sunset lives up to its name, with a truly jaw-dropping panorama encompassing the Pacific on one side and most of San Francisco and the bay on the other. Enter from 14th Avenue and Moraga Street.

Golden Gate Promenade

The bridgescapes along this three-mile (five-kilometre) coastal path, which runs all the way from Aquatic Park to Fort Point, are stunning, especially when gargantuan tankers – having just crossed the vast

Pacific – steam in through the Golden Gate. Note the unique underbelly view of the bridge from Fort Point. *See also p94* **The city on foot: Along the waterfront**.

San Francisco-Oakland Bay Bridge

Approaching San Francisco by bus or car across the top deck of the Bay Bridge provides a brief but soul-stirring view of the Financial District and Telegraph Hill, with subtle variations of light and colour at different times of day and evening. If you want to enjoy the scene at less than 65mph, pull off at Treasure Island and park on Avenue of the Palms.

Conzelman Road

Though most tourists, when crossing the Golden Gate Bridge, stop at Vista Point to gaze back at the city, professional photographers don't rest until they reach Conzelman Road with its fabled views of San Francisco seen through the cables and towers of the bridge. To get there, take the bridge north to Marin, exit at Vista Point and cross under the bridge to the Marin Headlands. Kirby Cove, the beach below Conzelman, has a similarly splendid perspective.

Lawrence Hall of Science

The plaza in front of this educational science museum in Berkeley is justifiably famous for having the best view of the entire Bay Area; from here atop the Berkeley Hills, scan all of the East Bay, the Peninsula, San Francisco and the Golden Gate, Marin County and points north. A slightly attenuated version of the same view can be had from the top of the Campanile in the middle of the UC campus. *See also p198.*

Mount Diablo

The peak of this solitary East Bay mountain (access is via North Gate Road in Walnut Creek) has what some call the most expansive view in the entire world. If the air quality is good enough (and it rarely is), you could see west to the Farallon Islands in the Pacific, east all the way to the Sierra Nevada mountains, north to Lake Shasta and south practically to Bakersfield – with binoculars, at least.

and alleyways: if you don't mind climbing up and down hills, it's fun to prowl the neighbourhood searching for secret passages (*see p78* **The city on foot: Stairways**).

Landmark addresses in the district include **29 Russell Street**, off Hyde Street, where Jack Kerouac lived with Neal and Carolyn Cassady during his most creative period in the 1950s; and the **Feusier Octagon House**, one of San Francisco's oldest dwellings, at 1067 Green Street near Leavenworth. Best viewed from across the street to appreciate its odd shape, the pastel structure is one of two survivors from San Francisco's 19th-century octagonal-house craze.

San Francisco Art Institute

800 Chestnut Street, between Leavenworth & Jones Streets (749 4545/www.sanfranciscoart.edu/institute.htm). Bus 30/cable car Powell-Hyde or Powell-Mason. **Open** *Diego Rivera Gallery* 10am-5pm daily. *Cafeteria* 9am-9pm Mon-Thur; 8am-4pm Fri; 9am-2pm Sat. **Admission** free. **Map** p308 F2.

This hip and prestigious art school offers the spectrum in fine arts, including painting, film, photography, sculpture and new media. Its student shows are legendary. Most people visit to see Diego Rivera's mural *The Making of a Fresco*, one of various works he completed in San Francisco in the 1930s (for more information on the city's mural scene, *see p204* **The city on foot: Murals**). If you're worn out from climbing all those hills, have a rest in the pretty open-air courtyard, where plants and benches surround a fountain, or grab a cheap snack in the cafeteria.

Nob Hill

South of Russian Hill and overlooking the Tenderloin and Union Square, Nob Hill was named after the wealthy 'nabobs' who built their mansions in the area; it was described by Robert Louis Stevenson – who lived briefly on its lower flank – as 'the hill of palaces'. A short but incredibly steep jaunt up from Union Square, the summit stands 338 feet (103 metres) above the bay. After a cable car line started operating here in the 1870s, the once-barren hill began to attract wealthy residents, namely the 'Big Four' boom-era railroad tycoons: Charles Crocker, Leland Stanford, Mark Hopkins and Collis P Huntington. Their 'palaces' perished in the fire that swept through Nob Hill after the 1906 earthquake, and only the 1886 home belonging to James C Flood survived. Later remodelled by Willis Polk, the brownstone mansion is now the site of the private **Pacific-Union Club** (1000 California Street, at Mason Street). Next to it, at California and Taylor Streets, is the public but prissy **Huntington Park**, with its landscaped greenery and a fountain modelled on Rome's Tartarughe Fountain. Across the park, **Grace Cathedral** (*see below*) is another lovely landmark that was once a private home. Midnight mass here, intoned by the celebrated boys' choir, is a Christmas tradition.

Surrounding the park and club are Nob Hill's elegant hotels. The **Fairmont Hotel** (950 Mason Street, at California Street) has a plush marble lobby and the basement **Tonga Room** (*see p152*), an ersatz-South Seas bar complete with simulated tropical rainstorm. The quieter **Huntington Hotel** (*see p43*) is known as a royals' hideaway, but you don't have to stay there to use its luxurious Nob Hill Spa (345 2888). Nearby, the **Top of the Mark** bar (*see p152*), on the 19th floor of the Mark Hopkins Inter-Continental Hotel, offers fabulous views of the city. Moving down from the peak of the hill, the free **Cable Car Museum** (*see p109*) on Mason Street displays antique cable cars and the mighty turbines that power the cables running under the city's streets.

At the base of Nob Hill's western slopes, Polk Street between Geary and Union Streets comprises a one-block-wide, mile-long neighbourhood known locally as **Polk Gulch**. Before the middle-class Castro came into its own, Polk was San Francisco's gay mecca: home to bold bars, adult bookshops and streetcorner encounters. In the mid-1970s, the area fell on hard times, as the exodus to the Castro left Polk Gulch with the unsavoury reputation as a last resort for runaway teenage boys resorting to selling sexual favours. While it has rebounded considerably and its ambience has mellowed – shops and restaurants crowd every block – the teenage boys have grown up into sad-eyed transvestites, and the area still seems to be searching for a new identity.

Grace Cathedral

1100 California Street, at Taylor Street (749 6300/www.gracecathedral.org). Bus 1, 27/cable car California. **Open** *Cathedral* 7am-6pm Mon-Fri, Sun; 8am-6pm Sat. *Tours* 1-3pm Mon-Fri; 11.30am-1.30pm Sat; 12.30-2pm Sun. **Map** p308 G3.

Begun in 1928, this Episcopalian house of worship was once a private mansion. It was later taken over by the church and is, by US-cathedral standards, an architectural extravaganza, with a façade modelled on Paris's Notre Dame, a fine rose window, gilded bronze portals made from casts of the Doors of Paradise in Florence's Baptistery, and a magnificent organ. Murals depict the founding of the UN and the burning of Grace's predecessor; an AIDS Interfaith Chapel has an altarpiece by Keith Haring. Indoor and outdoor Labyrinth Walks are based on the one at Chartres. Free guided tours are also available, and there are regular concerts and other events.

Coit Tower

This 210-foot (64-metre) concrete turret, built by City Hall architect Arthur Brown in 1933, was a gift to the city from the eccentric Lillie Hitchcock Coit, who as a child was snatched from a blaze and subsequently became a lifelong fan of firemen. Before you take the lift to the top of the tower (which provides spectacular vistas of the city and bay – *see p80* **On a clear day, you can see for ever**), inspect the murals inside the base of the building, which were supervised by Diego Rivera for the WPA. The socialist realist images of muscle-bound California workers were deemed subversive at the time of their completion in 1934; a hammer and sickle were erased from one and nervous authorities delayed the tower's opening, though much Marxist symbolism remains. Outside, the views from the parking lot are wonderful, too, though partially obscured by encroaching hedges. Also look out for the wild parrots (one of two flocks in San Francisco) that fly around Telegraph Hill; more details on www.wildparrots.com.

Descend the hill east from Coit Tower via the steep wooden **Filbert Street Steps**, which run from Montgomery Street down to Sansome Street, past flower-bedecked paths and cottages and the eccentric Julius Castle restaurant perched at the crest of Montgomery. Along the way, note **Napier Lane**, the last woodplank street in the city (they were common in the Gold Rush). At the bottom, head a block east to **Levi Plaza**, where you can follow a path through a fountain designed by Lawrence Halprin.

Coit Tower

Peak of Telegraph Hill, at the end of Telegraph Hill Boulevard (362 0808). Bus 39. **Open** 10am-7pm daily. **Admission** *Lift to top of tower* $3.75. **Map** p309 G2.

The Mission & the Castro

Come to the sunny centre of the city for Latino landmarks and queer culture.

Experience the Mission: loud, colourful and multicultural.

Few regions summarise the diverse character of San Francisco as well as this one. Clustered together in the perpetually sunny geographic centre of town, the **Mission**, the **Castro** and **Noe Valley** are each charmingly unique, epitomising (respectively) the city's Hispanic, gay and yuppie cultures. Want to see where the real San Franciscans live and shop? You've come to the right place.

The Mission

The city's oldest neighbourhood is still one of its most vibrant, and relatively free of the chain store onslaught that homogenises other, wealthier, more tourist-oriented districts. Bargains and local colour are everywhere in this loud, sunny phalanx of second-hand shops and avant-garde nightspots. Even the smells are different: a mix of chilli, garlic, tomatoes, coriander and seared meat permeates the air, punctuated by the occasional whiff of urine and cheap beer in the dodgy alleys around 16th Street. First settled by the Spanish in the 1770s and later by Irish, German, Italian and Asian immigrants, the Mission today is again the centre of Latino culture in the city, thanks to a steady influx of families and workers from Mexico and Central America. It also includes the nouveau riche and many musicians and artists, though the invasion by cash-rich dotcommers in the past few years forced many artists to find cheaper quarters.

The Mission's history is one of tolerance. It is home to a dazzling array of political and spiritual art: there are more than 200 murals in the district alone, many celebrating the struggles and achievements of its Latino residents (*see p204* **The city on foot: Murals**). In autumn, shops and art galleries are filled with traditional items for **Día de los Muertos** (*see p190* **The Day of the Dead**). Though the barrio also has more than its fair share of prostitutes, drug addicts and gangs, it definitely invites exploration beyond Mission Dolores, the only stop on the tourist bus routes.

Fab views from **Mission Dolores Park**.

Until the recent economic bust, locals feared that an invasion of Internet millionaires along the Mission's residential eastern flank would change the area's face from brown to lily-white, gentrifying the place beyond recognition – though many of those very doomsayers savoured the hip clubs and restaurants this dreaded invasion spawned.

Mission Street is the district's throbbing artery. Palm trees tower over cheque-cashing operations, cut-rate shops, taquerias and groceries selling sugar cane and prickly-pear cactus, as Mexican pop music pulses out of open doors and windows. Near 24th Street, the narrow, crowded pavements look as though they've been transported directly from Guadalajara; near 16th Street, doorway drug-deals scare the timid away.

Spots not to miss along this unabashedly authentic thoroughfare include **Ritmo Latino** (*see p182*), Latin music's answer to a Virgin Megastore – it even has handprints of Ricky Martin, Celia Cruz and other stars in the wall outside – and the one-off **Foreign Cinema** (*see p135*), a restaurant/cinema/cocktail lounge.

(Tip: confusingly, the addresses along Mission and Valencia do not match the intersecting numbered streets; thus, the 2400 block of Mission is at 20th Street, not 24th.)

The other main thoroughfare is **Valencia Street**. The nearby Castro's lesser-known lesbian counterpart, it has been steadily building on its feminist heritage for 30 years. Browsers can lose themselves for hours in the progressive **Modern Times Bookstore** (*see p166*) – one of many bookshops in this literary neighbourhood – or offbeat **Paxton Gate** (*see p179*), a cabinet of curiosities offering stuffed animals, pinned insects and exotic plants amid a pot-pourri of Victoriana. The **Women's Building** (3543 18th Street, at Valencia; 431 1180/www.womensbuilding.org) houses a women's refuge, a performance space and the headquarters of a dozen feminist non-profit groups. The riot of colour on the building's exterior is dubbed *Maestrapeace*, a larger-than-life mural retelling the history of women in the New World.

Botanica Yoruba (998 Valencia Street, at 21st; 826 4967) stocks herbs, candles and other tools for magic and spell-casting from Cuba, Brazil and beyond. The pioneering (and women-owned) **Good Vibrations** sex shop (*see p183*) prides itself on forthright customer service and even has its own mini vibrator museum. Test the district's culinary reputation at popular nouveau-Vietnamese **Slanted Door** (*see p134*), tapas-happy **Esperpento** (3295 22nd Street; 282 8867), or **Bombay Ice Creamery** (*see p176*), whose scoops include cardamom, saffron, rose and fig. Well over a dozen cafés decorate both sides of Valencia between 16th and 24th Streets, each with its own unique ambience.

A favourite destination for budget-conscious students and artists, the three-block stretch of **16th Street** between Mission and Dolores Streets is chockfull of colourful and inexpensive hangouts. **City Blend Café** (3087 16th Street, at Valencia; 522 1223), itself a boldly painted work of art, has a huge menu of smoothies and coffees. At always-packed **Pancho Villa Taqueria** (3071 16th Street; *see p126*), the machine-gun rat-tat-tat of cleavers bouncing on butcher's blocks accompanies the perfume of coriander and roast pork. Fill up there or at the authentically Breton **Ti Couz Crêperie** (*see p135*) before a screening at the avant-garde **Roxie** cinema (*see p201*). Afterwards, round out your 16th Street adventure at the sleek **Skylark** bar (*see p154*).

A short walk west to Dolores Street reveals the building which gave its name to the city, the 225-year-old Misión San Francisco de Asis, better known as **Mission Dolores** (*see p85*). Founded at the end of June 1776 – just a week before a rather more famous founding on the other side of the continent – the structure was completed on 2 August 1791, one of 21 missions built in California by Franciscan monks.

A couple of blocks south is **Mission Dolores Park** (bordered by 18th, 20th, Church and Dolores Streets), worth visiting during daylight hours for great people-watching and for views of downtown and the bay from the park's apex near 20th and Church Streets. At the same intersection, notice the bronze-painted fire hydrant near the trolley tracks. During the fire after the 1906 earthquake, all the city's water mains were broken, leaving the hydrants dry while the city burned. Inexplicably, this single hydrant kept working, and because of it firefighters saved most of the Mission District and beyond. To this day it holds a place of honour as the city's 'miraculous hydrant'.

At the neighbourhood's southern end, **24th Street** is where the Mission's Latin American cultures flourish in their greatest variety. **El Nuevo Frutilandia** (*see p135*) tempts with Puerto Rican and Cuban delicacies. **La Palma Mexica-Tessen** (2884 24th Street, at Florida; 647 1500) sells the only authentic, hand-made, extra-thick corn tortillas in the district. **Taqueria Vallarta** (No.3033, at Treat; 826 8116) is a quintessential Mission District restaurant, with traditional Mexican specialities at rock-bottom prices. Nearby, the fruit-juice-and-garlic-marinated chicken of **El Pollo Supremo** (2801 Folsom Street, at 25th; 550 1193) draws Financial District business types as well as local families. If you just want a snack, the intersection of 24th and Alabama is a hub of *tipico* Mexican bakeries and quick-bite grills. And floating in a delicious universe of its own, **St Francis Fountain Ice Cream Parlor** (2801 24th Street, at York; 826 4200) is a nearly 100-year-old, pink-and-chrome anachronism, complete with an old-fashioned soda fountain. It's also rumoured to be the birthplace of the 49ers football team.

Near the intersection of 18th and Bryant Streets, a media community started flourishing a few years ago. Headed by local public radio and TV station KQED-FM and KQED-TV and the offices of alternative newspaper the *San Francisco Bay Guardian*, tiny multimedia start-ups, including animation studios, publishers, Internet companies and game developers, leapt into the largely industrial area while rents were still cheap. Economic woes have since taken their toll, but the hardy still hang out at the **Slow Club** (*see p134*) on Mariposa Street, and sunny **Universal Café** (*see p134*) on 19th Street. And edgy **Blowfish Sushi** (2170 Bryant Street; 285 3848) and **Gordon's House of Fine Eats** (*see p133*) on Florida Street attract hungry gourmands.

Mission Dolores

3321 16th Street, at Dolores Street (621 8203/ www.missiondolores.citysearch.com). BART 16th Street/Muni Metro J/bus 22. **Open** 8am-4pm daily. **Admission** $3; $1 concessions. **Credit** (groups only) AmEx, MC, V. **Map** p310 E6.

The mission's depressing nickname (*dolores* means 'sorrows' in Spanish) is merely an accident of fate: it was built on the shores of a marsh (Laguna de los Dolores) that had been named, following tradition, after the day in the Catholic calendar on which it was discovered. The oldest standing structure in the city, the mission's thick adobe walls have withstood the test of time (and earthquakes). Small wonder that the cool, dim interior looks and feels authentic – almost everything about it is unreconstructed and original, from the redwood logs holding up the roof to the ornate altars brought from Mexico centuries ago. (The flashy church next door, with its two imposing towers, is a 20th-century basilica with little architectural significance, though it does handle most of the mission's religious services.) There is a small historical museum at the back and a flower-filled cemetery containing California's first governor and the city's first mayor, as well as Spanish settlers and the mass grave of thousands of Indians who died in their service. Hitchcock fans may recognise this as the very cemetery where an entranced Kim Novak leads *Vertigo*'s Jimmy Stewart on a wild goose chase to the gravestone of the mysterious Carlotta Valdes (don't bother looking for it; it was a prop removed after filming).

Potrero Hill

To the east of the Mission, isolated Potrero Hill is nearly always sunny, even when the rest of the city is shrouded in fog. It's a lovely place to live, but its charms aren't really geared to attract visitors. Newspaper and magazine outlet **Farley's Café** (1315 18th Street; 648 1545) is a dessert and strong coffee favourite, while **Klein's Delicatessen** (510 Connecticut Street; 821 9149) stacks succulent sandwiches. **Circadia** (2727 Mariposa Street; 552 2649),

The one-and-only **Castro Theatre**. *See p86.*

a cosy café by day and a wine bar with live music by night, provides laptop hook-ups, while the **Bottom of the Hill** (*see p212*) has good local bands and an outdoor patio, where barbecues are held on Sunday afternoons. (History note: Potrero Hill's most famous native son, for better or worse, is OJ Simpson.)

The Castro

Bordered by Market, Church, 20th and Diamond Streets, and festooned with rainbow flags, the Castro is an international gay mecca. Along this stretch of trendy shops and see-and-be-seen cafés, most of them gay-owned, a predominantly male populace basks in an ambience that was hard-won, but is here to stay. A steadfastly Irish-Catholic working-class stronghold for nearly a century, the neighbourhood changed rapidly and drastically in the 1970s after **Twin Peaks Bar** (401 Castro Street, at 17th Street; 864 9470) shattered taboos by attracting an ever-increasing crowd of upfront gay men who chatted and socialised unashamedly in the bar's big, pavement-facing windows. Conservative old-timers fled to the suburbs in a mass exodus; gays moved in, buying businesses and battered Victorians at rock-bottom prices and renovating them, turning this real estate into what is now some of the city's priciest – and prettiest.

A dignified sense of style and pride pervades in a district where the AIDS crisis has wrought immeasurable pain, but where community spirit is among the strongest in the world. Cowboy boots and buffed biceps, long blond hair and stiletto heels on size 13 shoes are as comfortably at home here as Armani suits. The Castro is one of the few places in the world where being gay is the norm; and while straights are accepted happily, they do get to experience that unusual and intriguing sensation of – for once – being in the minority.

Beneath a huge rainbow flag, **Harvey Milk Plaza** – the Muni stop at the corner of Market and Castro Streets – is named after the camera-shop owner and activist who in 1977 became the nation's first openly gay elected official. The dazzlingly art deco **Castro Theatre** (*see p200*) is the architectural flagship of a block where **RoCocoa's Faerie Queene Chocolates** (415 Castro; 252 5814) has unforgettable home-made fudge. Crowds fill **Cliff's Variety** (479 Castro, at 18th Street; 431 5365) to pick out costumes for the district's uproarious outdoor **Halloween** extravaganza (*see p193*). During the rest of the year, Cliff's is an old-fashioned five-and-dime that functions as the local general/hardware store. **A Different Light** (*see p165*) sells books by, for and about queers.

On the next block down, **Skin Zone** (575 Castro; 626 7933) occupies Harvey Milk's former camera shop (and campaign headquarters), considered by many as significant as New York's Stonewall bar in the history of gay politics; the martyred Milk – he was assassinated by a rival politician – is now commemorated by a small plaque in the pavement and a modest mural high on the outside wall. Forks and gossip fly at the immensely popular garden patio of **Café Flore** (*see p235*) on Market Street, which locals dub 'Café Hairdo'. **Fuzio** (*see p236*) serves a stylish mix of Asian and Italian dishes at affordable prices, while, deeper into the neighbourhood, **Firewood Café** (*see p236*) dishes up Italian classics with a California touch.

► For a more detailed look at the queer scene, *see chapter* **Queer San Francisco**.

Noe Valley

Quaint Noe Valley, roughly bordered by 20th, Dolores, 30th and Douglass Streets, is a self-contained mountain village cut off from the rest of the city by steep hills on every side. In the 1970s, it was a fairly bohemian mix of straight, gay, working-class and white-collar residents; it became more family-oriented in the 1980s and '90s, a place where well-paid young couples could retreat to raise a family away from the chaos of the rest of the city. But now Noe Valley is happy to fade back into obscurity, a crime-free enclave with little need for the outside world. The bustle of Mission Street feels a million miles away, though it's only ten blocks. Twin Peaks overlooks the area from the west and its flanks offer nice views of the East Bay.

24th Street is Noe Valley's high street, outfitted with all the amenities you might expect in a country resort: gourmet groceries, romantic restaurants and boutiques where the owners welcome regulars by their first names. Stroll it for the ambience, and when hunger strikes there's always **Legume** (4042 24th Street; 401 7668), which takes vegetarian world cuisine to the next level, while **Firefly** (4288 24th Street; 821 7652) serves satisfying portions in intimate surroundings. A few blocks off the main drag, **Lovejoy's English Tea Room** (1351 Church Street, at Clipper Street; 648 5895) is a Lake District mirage, serving Victorian high tea and ploughman's lunch to an afternoon crowd; its antique cups and saucers are for sale, too. The **San Francisco Mystery Bookstore** (*see p166*) stocks mysteries and nothing but, specialising in whodunnits set in San Francisco.

The Haight & Around

Hippy history in the Haight and gorgeous green acres in Golden Gate Park.

The past few years' economic excesses may have left their mark elsewhere in the city, but the **Haight** and the **Western Addition** remain so rooted in their own history, community and sense of self that to see them you'd never know a boom had come… and gone. A changing cast of characters may call Haight-Ashbury home, and the Western Addition may withstand good times and bad, but the intrinsic spirit of these places – be it hip, gritty or posh – endures. If you want a change from urban exploration, myriad natural wonders await amid the green and luscious acres of **Golden Gate Park**.

The Haight-Ashbury

The Haight's fabulous Victorians, their soaring columns and gingerbread trim painted in acid-trip colours by later residents, are clues to the neighbourhood's 19th-century incarnation as a resort where wealthy San Franciscans had weekend homes and crowds came to play in Golden Gate Park. But it was 1967's warm, delirious Summer of Love, when local acts Jefferson Airplane and Janis Joplin reigned, that put this district on the map forever. And in its hash-scented wake neither rock 'n' roll nor a turned-on, tuned-in America would ever be the same again. Two generations on, hippies have long since given way to lavishly tattooed teens loitering in record shops and on street corners angling for spare change. Cool boutiques and smoothie shops lining the main drag, **Haight Street**, have replaced a bygone era's altruistic restaurants and stores, some of which went of out of business because it was just too unhip to charge for their wares.

Wandering the length of Haight Street from Stanyan Street (the entrance to Golden Gate Park) to around Central Avenue will give you a true feel for the area, but must-sees on any pilgrimage here include former homes of the Grateful Dead (710 Ashbury Street), Janis Joplin (124 Lyon Street) and Jefferson Airplane (a few blocks north at 2400 Fulton Street, at Willard North). The 'Red House' in the Jimi Hendrix song of the same name is now the Ashbury Tobacco Center at 1524 Haight Street. A more ominous landmark is the house at 636 Cole Street, where Charles Manson lived with his harem before moving to Los Angeles and launching his reign of terror. Take the Flower Power Tour (*see p54* **The city on foot: Walking tours**) for the full lowdown.

Stroll the main drag, **Haight Street**…

For nostalgic lodgings, the **Red Victorian** (*see chapter* **Accommodation**) has rooms with hippie decor and serves companionable breakfasts in the morning; you can work the meal off cycling or rollerblading in Golden Gate Park. **The Booksmith** (*see p165*) carries international newspapers and magazines and organises readings, but for more colourful entertainment, the **Red Vic** cinema (*see p200*) has church-pew seating (with cushions) and serves home-made snacks and popcorn in big wooden bowls while screening indie films. **Cha Cha Cha** (1801 Haight Street, at Shrader Street; 386 5758) is a hotspot for Caribbean food and atmosphere; the tapas are cheap and the sangria is excellent. Other highlights include the tiny and legendary bar **Persian Aub Zam Zam** (*see p157*) and **Amoeba Music** (*see p181*), located in a converted bowling alley and offering a huge range of music in every format.

If you want to adopt the Haight lifestyle permanently, **Anubis Warpus** (1525 Haight Street; 431 2218) will pierce any part of your body, insert the ornament of your choice, then cover you head to toe in exhibitionistic tattoos. Then all you need to do is squat on the sidewalk, adopt a mangy puppy and you're an authentic Haight-Ashbury street denizen.

Lower Haight

A mile east, the Lower Haight – from Divisadero Street to around Octavia Street – lacks the Haight-Ashbury's cachet and historical cred, and is comparatively seedy. Down-and-outers sell dubious goods from rugs on the pavement, and unsavoury characters make the neighbourhood feel less than warmly welcoming. However, there are places on this section of Haight Street worth visiting.

Mad Dog in the Fog (*see p156*) turns Noel Coward on his ear by cultivating a lively pub atmosphere with British and American beers, darts and ploughman's lunch. A contrast is the self-consciously hip and deliberately trashy **Noc Noc** bar (*see p157*). **Nickie's BBQ** (*see p220*) is a popular and often overcrowded dance club, offering an eclectic array of sounds, while **Kate's Kitchen** (471 Haight Street; 626 3984) serves fine pancake breakfasts for those who stay on the dancefloor till dawn. A few blocks away, the **Justice League** (*see p211*) has sought to keep a good club scene thriving on Divisadero, drawing local and international DJs to its huge space and excellent sound system.

Cole Valley

If the panhandlers and scruffy kids get too much for you, walk south on Cole Street from Haight Street to the comparatively charming confines of Cole Valley. Nicely situated between UC San Francisco Medical Center, Buena Vista Park and Twin Peaks, the tiny neighbourhood centres on the intersection of Cole and Carl Streets. Tiny, stylish French-owned **Zazie** (941 Cole Street; 564 5332) is a café by day and a bistro by night, while the friendly **Kezar Bar & Restaurant** (900 Cole Street; 681 7678) is a local pub that also serves food. For some peace and quiet, walk south up Cole to Tank Hill. Overlooking the district, this secluded and usually deserted slope offers a romantic view of San Francisco at night.

The Western Addition

Bounded approximately by Fell, Gough and Bush Streets and Masonic Avenue, the sprawling region called the Western Addition – once a huge barren sweep of fog-bound sand dunes – is one of the city's most diverse. A Jewish community thrived here in the 1920s and '30s, as did a large number of Japanese – though the latter were uprooted and lost their homes and businesses when the US government sent all West Coast-dwelling Japanese Americans to internment camps after the attack on Pearl Harbor. The region – long considered undesirable because of its perpetual chill – subsequently became African American when thousands of black Southerners came west for work during World War II and moved into the homes left vacant by the Japanese and Jews. For a short while it then reigned as one of the country's biggest jazz and blues meccas, before being extensively razed during the 1960s under the guise of urban renewal.

Today, the Western Addition wears its scars boldly alongside earnest but often unattractive efforts to remedy them. Elements of its hep heyday prevail in its soul food and barbecue restaurants, barbershops and nightspots, and a new Japantown hums with a sense of community the war couldn't kill. Businesses throughout the Western Addition cater mostly to locals, not tourists, with a high concentration of cheque-cashing places and churches. But for the most part, the region is residential, with low-income housing projects and senior citizens' homes stretching for blocks on end. Luckily, even though thousands of Victorian homes perished under the wrecking ball, many thousands more survived, making parts of the Western Addition prime territory for architectural sightseeing.

Grassy **Alamo Square** park (bounded by Steiner, Scott, Hayes and Fulton Streets) provides San Francisco's most frequently photographed image: six pretty Victorian houses (aka 'Postcard Row') flanking its eastern side. They aren't the city's most marvellous Victorians by a long shot, but the sweeping downtown vistas behind them clinch the deal. At the opposite corner of Alamo Square is a much more intriguing Victorian, an Italianate mansion called **Westerfield House** (1998 Fulton Street, at Scott Street). Now a private home, it saw previous adventures as Guglielmo Marconi's early radio transmission tower, then as a Russian social centre boiling with political intrigue, and finally as a legendary 1960s commune with members that included filmmaker Kenneth Anger, Satanist Anton LaVey, author Ken Kesey and many other wild San Francisco characters.

At the neighbourhood's eastern end, the vast white concrete structure of **St Mary's Cathedral** (*see p89*) was designed by Pietro Belluschi and completed in 1971.

Fillmore District

Once the epicentre of San Francisco's now-dwindling African-American community, the Fillmore District radiates from the intersection of Fillmore Street and wide, ugly Geary Boulevard. High hopes circulated for years about bringing back the so-called Fillmore Historic Jazz District, aimed at revitalising the area, but little has materialised so far. Even so, the area is still a destination for live music. Blues king John Lee Hooker was a part-owner of the **Boom Boom Room** (*see p216*) and performed there right up until his death in 2001; it still books major blues acts. With seats for 200, sleek **Rasselas** (*see p216*) stages nightly jazz and blues shows and serves Ethiopian meals. The nearby **Fillmore Auditorium** (*see p210*) on Geary Boulevard – where in the 1960s legendary promoter Bill Graham booked the likes of Jimi Hendrix and the Velvet Underground – upholds its reputation by showcasing the latest major rock headliners.

Speaking of history: the punk era came to a crashing, disastrous end in 1978 when the Sex Pistols gave their notorious final concert ('Ever get the feeling you've been cheated?' was how Johnny Rotten summed up their 20-minute set, if not their entire career) at Winterland, just a block away at the north-west corner of Post and Steiner Streets. The building is long gone, but the condominiums built on the site have a small photo exhibit (in the Post Street lobby) about the history of the concert hall.

Cathedral of St Mary of the Assumption

1111 Gough Street, at Geary Boulevard (567 2020). Bus 2, 3, 4, 38. **Open** 7am-4.30pm Mon-Fri; 7am-6.30pm Sat; 7am-4.45pm Sun. **Map** p310 F4.

Dominating the skyline for miles around, the exterior of St Mary's Cathedral resembles the blades of a gigantic washing-machine. Its unapologetically modern interior sports towering stained-glass windows of forgettable design, but magnificent views through its ordinary clear panes. The hyperbolic curves of the lofty 'ceiling' present a very unusual redefinition of inner space.

Japantown

East of Fillmore Street and north of Geary Boulevard lies a prefab shopping complex known as Japantown. This labyrinthine cement mall is all that's left of the Western Addition's once-thriving Japanese community, displaced and disenfranchised by government fiat in World War II. Erected in 1968 with an eye towards reparation, **Japan Center** (its official name) suffers from that era's charmless concrete aesthetic, as epitomised by its chunky, uninspiring Peace Pagoda. Yet the centre's restaurants and shops do a booming trade to both San Francisco's resurgent Japanese population and its many Japanophiles.

The mall itself is a vast retail, dining and entertainment complex that occupies three entire city blocks bounded by Fillmore, Post and Laguna Streets and Geary Boulevard. Japantown has kimonos and silk fans aplenty, for sure, but it's much more than that: the shops are throbbing with young people of all races nabbing the latest manga (Japanese graphic novels), anime (animation) videos, jpop (bubbly Japanese pop music) CDs and even cutting-edge electronic gadgets made only for the domestic Japanese market and unavailable anywhere else in the States. The restaurants cater to the demanding

... for the sights and sounds of times past.

Golden Gate Park

One of the world's largest urban green havens – spanning 1,017 acres – Golden Gate Park is an oasis of lakes, landscaped vistas, flowerbeds and soaring eucalyptus and pine trees, the city almost completely out of sight. Over the past hundred-plus years, the park has hosted everything from earthquake victims' encampments to the hippies' historic Human Be-In, rock concerts and plays to a funeral for Grateful Dead icon Jerry Garcia. Fully enjoying all the park's possibilities could take days.

In 1871, landscape architect William Hammond Hall took up the challenge of turning a barren stretch of sand dunes into a park respecting the land's natural contours. A million trees were planted under the tutelage of eccentric gardener John McLaren; as the park's fame spread, horticulturists from all over the world sent in seeds and cuttings. Today, a rose garden, a Shakespeare garden, a rhododendron dell and a tulip garden are among hundreds of living delights whose colours dazzle on a sunny day and console on a foggy one.

It's quite a trek from end to end of the long, narrow park, but bicycles and rollerblades can be rented from various locations (*see p244* **On your bike** and *p243* **Rollerblading**) to speed the time between sights. In any case, John F Kennedy Drive runs right through the park from east to west and is the best route for sightseeing. The most convenient introduction to the park is to enter from Stanyan Street along the park's eastern edge, either from the Haight-Ashbury or the park's 'Panhandle'; then work your way west, ending at the Great Highway, with the Pacific Ocean across the street. But, of course, it's entirely possible to make a beeline straight to your favourite spot.

On an east–west jaunt, your first stop should be **McLaren Lodge** (John F Kennedy Drive, at Stanyan Street; 831 2700), original residence of the park's famed gardener, a Scotsman who so loved plants and hated people that he 'hid' the park's statuary amid foliage, so that folks wouldn't have to see the human form. His home now houses the park's offices and a small visitor centre (open 8am-5pm weekdays), where you can pick up a park map.

Not shown on that map, but a favourite hangout nonetheless, **Hippie Hill** (south of John F Kennedy Drive and west of Kezar

Drive, near Sharon Meadow) has been a meeting place and hotspot for hippie culture since the 1960s, and remains so today. If you can't find it, follow the sound of drums.

Currently closed for repairs, the **Conservatory of Flowers** (a short way behind McLaren Lodge) is modelled on the Palm House in London's Kew Gardens. South, past the tennis courts, a children's playground and carousel off Kezar Drive are especially popular with young kids. The sombre but serene **National AIDS Memorial Grove**, inaugurated in 1991, has names of the dead engraved in stone amid redwoods, oaks and maples; for guided tours, call 750 8340.

Further west, the **California Academy of Sciences** (*pictured above – see p106*) encompasses a natural history museum, the **Morrison Planetarium** and the **Steinhart Aquarium** (*see p196*) – all are especially good on rainy days. Dinosaur bones and an 'earthquake theatre' are among the thousands of exhibits that make the natural history museum one of America's best. The aquarium contains 150 tanks swarming with watery creatures, while the planetarium, with its specially designed, one-of-a-kind star projector, offers spectacular shows that reveal how minuscule we really are. Below the Music Concourse is **Strybing Arboretum & Botanical Gardens** (661 1316), where 70 leafy acres are home to some 7,000 species from diverse climates, arranged by country. Special attractions include a moon-viewing pavilion and a fragrant garden for the visually impaired.

The **MH de Young Memorial Museum** is currently closed and will reopen in 2005, while the nearby **Asian Art Museum**, housing the largest collection of Asian art outside

Asia, is due to move to the Civic Center in autumn 2002 (for details, *see p106*). Directly west, the **Japanese Tea Garden** (open 9am-6pm daily; 752 1171), built in 1893, is an oasis of peace with delightful bridges, flowering trees, relaxing paths, waterways, a huge bronze Buddha and an outdoor tearoom with kimono-clad servers. Admission is $3.50, $1.25 concessions (half-price on the first Wednesday of every month). Further along, the **Pioneer Log Cabin** gives the flavour of an earlier American West.

Near the park's centre, **Stow Lake** offers one of the most pleasant activities in the city: renting paddle-boats or canoes for a dreamy circuit around **Strawberry Hill** (the lake's large central island) in the company of ducks, turtles and smiling couples adrift. Or cross the bridge to the peak of the island for a view of the entire park. The boathouse is on Stow Lake Drive (open summer 10am-5pm Mon-Fri; 9am-5pm Sat, Sun; winter 9am-4pm daily).

Lloyd Lake, Mallard Lake, Elk Glen Lake and Metson Lake dot the park as you approach its **Polo Field**, site of the storied Human Be-In, a 1967 gathering of dreamers, drop-outs and counterculture visionaries that is credited with launching the hippie revolution. Not that you could tell, looking at this unremarkable oval lawn. You can go horse riding at the adjacent **Golden Gate Park Stables** (*see p243*).

Continuing west, **Spreckels Lake** at the northern edge of the park is a haven for model yacht racers, while the Bison Paddock's hefty, bearded beasts are true American icons, grazing as if this was the wild prairie. A fly-casting pool and North Lake, South Lake and Middle Lake offer further aqueous pleasures before you reach the archery field, golf course (*see p242*) and then, near 48th Avenue, the **Wilhelmina Tulip Garden** that surrounds the rather startling **Dutch Windmill**. Both garden and mill were gifts from the Dutch queen in 1902.

Overlooking the Pacific Ocean at the park's western edge, the **Beach Chalet** (*see p101*) originally opened in 1925 as a restaurant and bathhouse. Designed by Willis Polk, the building houses a magnificent 1936 mural depicting San Francisco life. Below you, Ocean Beach and the wide Pacific spread out to infinity.

Golden Gate Park

Bounded by Fulton & Stanyan Streets, Lincoln Way & the Great Highway. Muni Metro N/ bus 5, 7, 18, 21, 28, 29, 33, 44, 66, 71. **Open** dawn-dusk daily. **Admission** free. **Map** p312 A-C/5/6.

Park highlights include the **Conservatory of Flowers** and the **Japanese Tea Garden** (*right*).

palates of many native Japanese customers as well, so the sushi and udon are among the best you'll find in the city.

Running north from the centre along Buchanan Street, block-long **Buchanan Mall** is a refreshing change in ambience: paved in cobblestones, this pedestrian-only outdoor mall is designed to resemble a Japanese mountain village, dotted with quaint businesses. During Japantown's two annual celebrations – the Cherry Blossom Festival in April (*see p189*) and the Nihonmachi Street Fair in the first weekend in August – Buchanan Street is so expertly decked out you'd swear you were in Japan.

For a literal immersion into the Japanese experience, try the recently renovated **Kabuki Springs & Spa** (*see p200*), a traditional bathhouse with communal pools, private tubs, saunas, steam rooms and masseurs. The eight-screen **Kabuki 8** cinema complex (*see p200*) is the main venue for the annual San Francisco International Film Festival (*see p202*) in April and May, and is a favourite for viewing new releases the rest of the year.

Hayes Valley

Just west of the Civic Center, SF's most recently developed shopping district used to be one of its least salubrious. Despite Hayes Valley's proximity to the Opera House, for years its sole lures for the outside world were prostitutes and drug dealers. But now gentrification has taken firm hold, helped by the removal of an ugly raised freeway following the 1989 earthquake and then the dismantling of a nearby housing project. Today, Hayes Street is home to fashion and furniture designers and is trying to turn itself into a chic destination. Block parties are held twice a year (midsummer and Christmas), when shops serve wine and hold fashion shows, bands play, fire-eaters perform and the streets are packed with revellers.

The strolling is best along **Hayes Street** between Franklin and Laguna Streets, with clothing, gift and antique shops cheek by jowl. **San Francisco Women Artists** (370 Hayes Street; 552 7392), a proto-feminist non-profit gallery, has been showing off works by female painters, sculptors and jewellers since the 19th century. For the best of the area's shops, *see p175* **The city on foot: Hayes Valley crawl**.

There's plenty to eat here, too. **Frjtz** (579 Hayes Street, at Laguna Street; 864 7654) has moved into the space once occupied by the beloved Mad Magda's; now it's a hub of Flemish culture, serving Belgian chips and beer and nouveau crêpes; after-hours DJs turn the space into a dance club. Across the border – er, street – sparsely furnished **Suppenküche** (No.601 Hayes; 252 9289) is a jolly German inn complete with spätzle and sauerbraten. An ever-changing Asian-fusion menu at the **Hayes Street Grill** (324 Hayes; 863 5545) spotlights seafood. And a refreshingly low-priced reminder of the neighbourhood's past is **Powell's Place** (511 Hayes; 863 1404), a down-home Southern-cookin' roadhouse with fried chicken and sweet potato pie – definitely worth a try if you've never had real soul food.

Welcome to **Japantown**. *See p89.*

Internationally touted **Zuni Café** (1658 Market Street; 552 2522) anchors a mini-neighbourhood of its own along Market Street just south of Hayes Valley. The surrounding blocks have in the past few years become a hub for antique and upmarket home-decor shopping, though the economic downturn might just squelch all that. Characteristic of the area are **New Deal** (1632B Market Street; 552 6208) with fine *objets d'art* and sleek furnishings; **Yum** (1750 Market; 626 9866), where imported chocolates and exotic olives augment a California-cuisine takeaway menu; and the seasonal menu at **Carta** (1772 Market Street; 863 3516). Nearby at 66 Page Street, the city's oldest Harley Davidson dealership, **Dudley Perkins Co** (703 9494), has been selling the noisy beauties since 1914; its showroom is a veritable museum with gleaming hogs, vintage artefacts and rare photographs.

The Marina & Around

Money and ex-military strongholds mark the city's northern waterfront.

The northern neighbourhoods from Bush Street to the bay and from Van Ness Avenue to the Presidio – **Pacific Heights**, **Cow Hollow** and the **Marina** – are strongholds of WASP wealth, both old and nouveau. Dazzling antiques and artworks can be glimpsed through the windows of sprawling Italianate villas and exclusive apartment towers with seagull's-eye views. Upscale beauty salons, restaurants, nightspots and boutiques cater to urbanites who zip in and out with mobile phones in one hand, babies or briefcases in the other, and no money troubles visible to the naked eye.

And then there is the **Presidio** itself – the vast, former military area that occupies the north-western corner of San Francisco.

Pacific Heights

True to its name twice over, Pacific Heights is perched high over the water and its mansions are home to the cream of San Francisco's high society. Billionaire socialites Gordon and Ann Getty, scions of one of the US's richest families, have a house here, as does novelist Danielle Steel, who lives in the ornate **Spreckels Mansion** spanning the entire block between Jackson, Gough, Washington and Octavia Streets. (The address is 2080 Washington, but don't attempt a personal visit.) Thousands of lesser-known millionaires pass unnoticed, shopping for cartons of milk and tins of caviar in their neighbourhood corner markets.

A Pacific Heights stroll is optimal for either marvelling at opulent real estate or trying to make rich new friends. Any block in the area offers a sobering look at how the other half lives, but the stretch of **Broadway** between Divisadero Street and the Presidio affords some of the best architecture. On the other side of the hill, the blue-and-white **Octagon House** (*see below*) on Gough Street is open for viewing a few days a month. The **Haas-Lilienthal House** (*see below*) is the city's only Queen Anne Victorian open to the public, a rare chance to see the inside of one of the city's grand residences, in pristine condition.

A rest stop at nearby **Lafayette Park** (Washington and Gough Streets) or **Alta Plaza Park** (Jackson and Steiner Streets) commands views of the nearby homes and the city beyond, and of pedigreed dogs out walking their pedigreed owners.

Upper Fillmore Street between Bush and Jackson Streets comprises the region's central shopping hub, with plenty of smart shops and restaurants. With a cornucopia of mouth-watering regional Italian delicacies to eat in or take away, **Vivande Porta Via** (2125 Fillmore Street; 346 4430) made a name for itself as cookery queen Elizabeth David's favourite San Francisco lunch spot – quite a recommendation, considering that she had several thousand others to choose from. A few blocks west, antique shops, ateliers and boutiques on **Sacramento Street** between Presidio Avenue and Spruce Street are pricey and elegant, while nearby charity shops such as the **San Francisco Symphony Repeat Performance Thrift Store** (2436 Fillmore Street; 563 3123) and **Next-to-New** (2226 Fillmore Street; 567 1628) stock the cast-offs of the rich and famous for a fraction of the cost. For the ultimate in canine decadence, **George** pet shop (*see p178*) on California Street proffers rawhide shish kebabs, gourmet home-baked dog confections and couture canine sweaters.

Poet Allen Ginsberg launched a literary renaissance in 1955 when he gave his first public reading of 'Howl' at the (long vanished) Six Gallery, the site now occupied by the **Silkroute International Oriental** rug shop (3119 Fillmore Street).

Haas-Lilienthal House

2007 Franklin Street, between Washington & Jackson Streets (441 3000/www.sfheritage.org/house.html). Bus 1, 12, 42, 47, 49, 83. **Open** noon-3pm Wed; 11am-4pm Sun. **Admission** $5; $3 concessions. **Credit** AmEx, MC, V. **Map** p308 F3.

Built in 1886 by Bavarian William Haas, this Stick-style house with elaborate wooden gables, a circular tower and 28 rooms has been fully restored and filled with period furniture. A display of photos documents the history of the house and the family that lived in it until 1972. It's maintained by San Francisco Architectural Heritage, which also organises walking tours.

Octagon House

2645 Gough Street, between Union & Green Streets (441 7512). Bus 41, 45. **Open** noon-3pm 2nd & 4th Thur & 2nd Sun of the month. **Admission** free. **Map** p308 E2.

The 1861 Octagon House houses the small Museum of Colonial & Federal Decorative Arts, but is most notable as one of two surviving examples of San

Francisco's brief craze for eight-sided homes; the other is the Feusier Octagon House on Russian Hill, which is not open to the public.

Cow Hollow

From Pacific Heights, it's a few blocks downhill toward the bay to Cow Hollow. Once a dairy pasture, as its name reveals, the area centred on **Union Street** between Broderick and Buchanan Streets is still serene, but its browsers are now of the well-heeled, two-legged kind. Chic bars and restaurants occupy carefully restored Victorians; the neighbourhood's standout restaurants include Shanghai-in-the-'30s-style **Betelnut** on Union Street, with ceiling fans, a bold pan-Asian menu, rice ale and Vietnamese beer; and **PlumpJack Cafe** on Fillmore Street, where wine connoisseurs dine on California classics (for both, *see chapter* **Restaurants & Cafes**). Cow Hollow was one of the city's trendiest neighbourhoods in the 1970s, but has now mellowed into a transitional borderland between the established wealth above and the jetsetters below.

The Marina

In a city justifiably famous for its gay scene, the pastel-painted Marina district, between Fort Mason and the Presidio, is noticeably straight. It's also one big pick-up joint. By night, its bars fill with bare-midriffed twentysomethings sipping cocktails and making eye contact, and for decades even the Safeway supermarket at 15 Marina Boulevard was a famous pick-up joint. Built on soft rubble from the 1906 earthquake, the Marina shook harder than any other part of San Francisco in 1989's Loma Prieta quake, when the seismic waves caused the underlying soil to liquefy. Buildings collapsed hither and thither, yet today the only reminders of that terrifying evening are renovated pavements and some suspiciously new-looking structures among the staid townhouses.

The main drag, **Chestnut Street** between Fillmore and Divisadero Streets, is a shrine to self-indulgence. Clothing boutiques and beauty salons seem to occupy fully half the shopfronts, although the **House of Magic**

The city on foot: Along the waterfront

The Golden Gate Promenade is a three-mile (five-kilometre) paved pathway that runs along the northern bay shore from Aquatic Park to Fort Point. Part of the Golden Gate National Recreation Area, it's popular with joggers, cyclists, dog-walkers, kite-flyers and families. It's a beautiful if bracing walk (the winds are strong next to the water), with staggering views of the city behind (or ahead – if you do it in the opposite direction), Alcatraz and scudding sailboats in the bay, and the fiery orange flanks of the Golden Gate Bridge.

The beach near the Marina end is one of the city's best windsurfing spots and always busy with wetsuited enthusiasts. Further along is Crissy Field, originally a marshy dunelands, later a dump and staging ground for the army before it was paved over and converted to a military airfield after World War II. Years of restoration work paid off in 2001, when a newly revamped Crissy Field opened to the public. Some of the original marshland and coastal dunes have been restored and the airfield is now an endless, beautiful lawn, edged by historic buildings. It's the traditional place to watch the municipal Fourth of July fireworks (*see p190*) and October's spectacular Fleet Week military air show (*see p192*), when the daredevil Blue Angels fly *under* the Golden Gate Bridge.

Further on there's a historic coastguard station (now a visitor centre for the Gulf of Farallones National Marine Sanctuary), a pier where Chinese fishermen try their luck, picnic tables and barbecue grills and – at the end – the looming red-brick mass of Fort Point. Backtrack from the fort to the Warming Hut (now a bookshop and café) and take the trail opposite; it leads up through eucalyptus and wild flower groves and past old gun batteries to the bridge. From there, you can catch a bus back into town.

(2025 Chestnut Street, at Fillmore Street; 346 2218) makes a change with fright wigs, trick cards, fake dog-doo and other unforgivable practical jokes. The lovely **Presidio** cinema (No.2340, at Scott Street; 922 1318) shows new releases; **Lucca Deli** (No.2120; 921 7873) has been dishing up old-fashioned Italian takeaway delectables since 1929; and the woodsy **Grove** café (No.2250; 474 4843) serves fresh-brewed coffee and filling sandwiches.

The vast sloping lawns of the **Marina Green** (Marina Boulevard, between Scott and Webster Streets) are San Franciscans' favourite place to fly kites, jog or picnic, with dizzying views of the Golden Gate Bridge and the bay. At the end of the yacht harbour jetty to the west of the Marina Green is the amazing **Wave Organ** – an underwater artwork whose pipes and benches, built from the remains of San Francisco's dismantled cemeteries, make music with the ebb and flow of the bay's currents.

At the eastern edge of the Marina waterfront, **Fort Mason** (*see below*) started as a US Army command post in the 1850s. Today, this complex of reconditioned military buildings has a forbidding, windswept mien, but it houses several eclectic museums, exhibition spaces and non-profit organisations. The Marina is also the starting point for the **Golden Gate Promenade**, the name given to the coastal walk along the shore to Fort Point – *see p94* **The city on foot: Along the waterfront**.

For the 1915 Panama-Pacific Exposition, a mile-long swath of fanciful structures was erected from Fort Mason to Fort Point. All were meant to be temporary, and when the fair was over the fantastic city-within-a-city was torn down to make way for the houses we see today. Yet a small part of the fantasyscape survived: the **Palace of Fine Arts** (*see below*), set in a little park at the western edge of the Marina. The original plaster edifice was expensively converted to concrete just in time for the 1969 opening of the adjacent **Exploratorium** (*see p196*), one of the world's first hands-on science museums, extremely – and deservedly – popular with children.

Fort Mason

Marina Boulevard, at Buchanan Street. Bus 28.
Map p308 E1.

This collection of ex-military buildings houses a bevy of cultural institutions. Across the hall from each other in Building C are the African American Historical & Cultural Society Museum (*see p109*) and the Museo ItaloAmericano (*see p110*), both of which have changing exhibitions on their respective ethnic themes. Shows at the Museum of Craft & Folk Art (*see p110*) in Building A range from bookbinding to handmade furniture. (The small Mexican Museum is currently closed; it's due to relocate to the Yerba Buena Center in 2003.) Other outlets include the airy SFMOMA Artists' Gallery (Building A; 441 4777), which sells contemporary works by Northern Californians, while the Book Bay Bookstore (Building C; 771 1076) sells second-hand volumes as well as LPs and art at rock-bottom prices. Fort Mason also houses the Magic Theatre (*see p222*) and other small performance spaces. Greens (inside Building A) is one of the city's favourite vegetarian restaurants, with high ceilings framing a wide marina and bay view. A constant array of changing displays is on view at two waterside pavilions (actually reconstituted shipbuilding bays); concerts, gardening competitions and even the Spiral Dance, the local pagan community's major Halloween fête, are held here. Note that all the museums are closed on Mondays.

The atmospheric **Palace of Fine Arts**.

Palace of Fine Arts

3301 Lyon Street, at Bay Street (563 6504/ www.palaceoffinearts.org). Bus 28, 30, 76.
Map p307 C2.

This is local architect Bernard Maybeck's *pièce de résistance*, a neo-classical domed rotunda supported by a curved colonnade topped with friezes and statues of weeping women, and flanked by a pond alive with ducks, swans and lily pads. You can see the brown-coloured dome from many parts of the city, and it remains one of the most atmospheric spots in San Francisco. As you wander around, look out for a street artist who balances rocks in astounding, gravity-defying arrangements.

Bridging the gap

Few cities need bridges as much as San Francisco does. Without the Golden Gate Bridge connecting it to the northern half of the state and the Bay Bridge connecting it to the rest of the country, San Francisco would be isolated at the tip of a mountainous peninsula. Yes, it thrived that way for almost a century, but the rise of the automobile meant the city could no longer survive with only ferries and ocean liners – it was a choice of building bridges or becoming irrelevant. So bridges were built. And San Francisco being San Francisco, they were built with a bang. Within a few years, the city's spans were the most famous in the United States.

Golden Gate Bridge

Linking the Toll Plaza near the Presidio with Marin County (921 5858/www.goldengate bridge.com). Bus 28, 29, 76 to the bridge. Golden Gate Transit bus 10, 20, 30, 50, 60, 70, 80, 90 across the bridge. **Bridge vehicle toll** $3 southbound. **Map** p306 A1.

Luminous symbol of San Francisco and of the Golden State itself, the Golden Gate Bridge remains the city's ultimate icon. It may not be the longest bridge in the world, but nearly everyone agrees it is the most beautiful. And certainly the most recognisable.

Statistics, for the record: the towers are 746 feet (227 metres) high; the roadway is 1¾ miles (2.75 kilometres) long; enough cable was used in its construction to encircle the globe three times; it was completed in 1937 after nearly five years of construction; and since then more than 1,000 people have committed suicide by plunging more than 250 feet (76 metres) to the water below.

But statistics can't convey the sense of grandeur and awe the bridge inspires, especially from close up. No trip to San Francisco would be complete without a walk across. Drive, walk or catch a bus to the Toll Plaza, and head out on foot along the pedestrian walkway. Once you feel it thrumming beneath your feet, as if alive, you'll understand even more why people feel such a strong connection to the span. There's no need to hike all the way across – if the 3½-mile (5.5-kilometre) round-trip is a bit much for you, just go out to the midway point and return.

The one person most responsible for making the bridge a reality was a pugnacious Chicago engineer named Joseph Strauss who spent over a decade lobbying to promote the idea and circumventing innumerable financial and legal hurdles. For that he deserves credit. But it was a little-known freelance architect named Irwin F Morrow who actually designed the bridge we see today; his brilliantly simple plan was selected over a hideous and complicated cantilever design championed by Strauss. The result was a shape, a curve, an unforgettable swoop that places the Golden Gate Bridge among the world's pantheon of architectural masterpieces, alongside the Pyramids and the Eiffel Tower.

Although it's not apparent to the naked eye, the bridge is also a magnum opus of over-engineering, and is reputedly five times stronger than it needs to be. Because of this, it has survived hundreds of earthquakes, hurricane-force winds and 65 years of abuse without the slightest defect or sign of damage.

The bridge was not named after its colour, but rather after the official title of the narrow strait it spans: the Golden Gate, which connects the bay with the ocean. And in a strange twist of history, the strait itself was not named (as logic might seem to dictate) after the city's historical association with the Gold Rush. Rather, Captain John Fremont dubbed this passage 'the Golden Gate' in 1846, two years before gold was discovered in the California foothills; he borrowed the name from 'the Golden Horn', the geologically similar channel that links the Black Sea to the Mediterranean.

The bridge's stroke-of-genius orange colour was also an accident of fate; San Franciscans were so delighted by the reddish tint of the primer paint used to temporarily cover the newly completed span that the builders decided to stick with it, rather than paint the whole bridge the traditional grey or silver. Ever since, it's been continuously repainted with rust-proof paint (innumerable gallons of 'International Orange' each year), rendering it fiery at sunset and contrasting surreally with the blue sky or white fog during the day.

San Francisco–Oakland Bay Bridge

Linking downtown San Francisco with the East Bay (1-510 286 1148). Muni Metro N/bus 15, 42 to the bridge. Bus 108 to Treasure Island.

AC Transit bus A-Z across the bridge. **Bridge vehicle toll** $2 westbound. **Map** p309 J3.

Heading east from Downtown, the San Francisco-Oakland Bay Bridge – better known simply as the Bay Bridge – is much less famous than its sister span, but more useful on a day-to-day basis, linking San Francisco not just to the East Bay, but also to the nationwide network of highways and railroads. Divided into two by dramatic Yerba Buena Island, the Bay Bridge is actually three separate bridges, all linked together: two suspension spans placed end to end of the west side of Yerba Buena, and a cantilever span on the east side. Combined, they make one of the world's longest bridges, nearly 8½ miles (13.7 kilometres) across.

Completed a year before the Golden Gate Bridge in 1936, the Bay Bridge was even more of an engineering challenge, as the distance to be spanned was much greater. The solution was to build a concrete pylon of inconceivably massive proportions in the middle of the bay, and use it as an anchor point for two different suspension spans. Because much of it is hidden underwater, this central pylon draws little notice from the thousands who cross it and see it every day, even though it remains one of the largest structures ever built in California – a solid concrete tower nearly as tall as the Transamerica Pyramid.

Designed by Charles H Purcell, the Bay Bridge has two levels, each with five lanes of traffic that cruise straight through Yerba Buena Island inside the largest vehicular tunnel on earth. When you emerge on the top deck heading west, the bridge offers by far the most dramatic entrance to the city (*see p80* **On a clear day, you can see for ever**). Sadly, unlike the Golden Gate Bridge, this one has no pedestrian walkway – though you can get a good view of the Bay Bridge from the Embarcadero, south of the Ferry Building.

For a brief moment in October 1989, the Bay Bridge was more famous than the Golden Gate Bridge, when part of its eastern upper level collapsed during the Loma Prieta quake. Engineers warned that the next big one could take out the entire eastern half of the Bay Bridge, as the cantilever section was built on unstable sediment. Bureaucrats have been bickering ever since over the details of an updated span, though many see it as a once-in-a-lifetime opportunity to replace the uninspired cantilever design with something more majestic.

Just as long as they remember to paint it orange.

The Presidio

It's been called 'the prettiest piece of real estate in America'. And it certainly ranks among the most valuable. San Francisco's Presidio is situated perfectly at the northern tip of the city, overlooking San Francisco Bay, the Pacific Ocean and the Golden Gate Bridge. It was a location fit for the gods, yet for centuries it endured the workaday drudgery of life as a military base. But in 1994, a miracle happened: after 220 years in the hands of soldiers, the Presidio was reborn as a public commons when the US Army handed the property over to the Park Service, claiming it could no longer afford the expensive upkeep.

Though now technically a National Park (along the lines of Yosemite or Yellowstone), the Presidio is managed by a confusing welter of agencies, including the Golden Gate National Recreation Area, the National Park Service and a controversial board of directors called the Presidio Trust, whose mission is to make the Presidio 'self-sustaining' by building resorts and business parks on the 1,500-acre property while maintaining its historic character. Conservationists howl in protest, and the battle over development is likely to continue for quite some time. For now, luckily, the Presidio remains in a state of arrested decay, artful and picturesque.

The tip of the San Francisco Peninsula was first established as a military outpost in 1776 when a group led by Captain Juan Bautista de Anza planted the Spanish flag here to protect the newly discovered San Francisco Bay. First claimed as a garrison for Spain (*presidio* means fortress in Spanish) and then Mexico, the property was taken (along with the rest of the state) by the United States in 1848.

The base grew rapidly under US rule as the Presidio played a significant role in a century's worth of wars and conflicts. During this time, the military embarked on a massive landscaping project, converting hundreds of acres of sandy, windswept moors into a tree-lined garden that now includes some 11 miles (18 kilometres) of hiking trails, 14 miles (22.5 kilometres) of bicycle routes and three miles (five kilometres) of beaches.

The gate from Pacific Heights on Presidio Avenue and Jackson Street leads into fairytale woods, often shrouded in mist for an extra melancholic dash. Without a map (which you can pick up for free at the Presidio's various visitor centres), you're likely to get lost on the many trails and meandering roads – a pleasant experience, actually – so here in no particular order are the main points of interest you may come across while wandering.

The centre of the Presidio is the **Main Post**, a complex of old buildings arrayed along parallel streets on the site of the original Spanish fort. Here you'll find the **visitor centre** (Building 102, Montgomery Street; 561 4323; open 9am-5pm daily), two 17th-century Spanish cannons on Pershing Square near the luxuriant Officers' Club, and rows of military homes from the Victorian era along Funston Avenue. **San Francisco National Cemetery** (Lincoln Boulevard, at Sheridan Avenue), full of war heroes, is sombre and inspiring, while, at the other end of the spectrum, the beloved, ramshackle **Pet Cemetery** (McDowell Avenue under the freeway) is quirky and sentimental.

Along the Presidio's western edge, **Baker Beach** is a favourite getaway spot (*see p100* **On the beach**), while **Mountain Lake Park** (access from Lake Street and Funston Avenue, at the southern end of the Presidio) is a relaxing idyll. Golfers nationwide were ecstatic when the ultra-exclusive **Presidio Golf Course** (*see p242*), formerly a private, officers-only club favoured by presidents and generals, opened its manicured fairways to the public.

But most of all, San Franciscans love to wander the miles and miles of hiking trails and little-used roads that criss-cross the park, stopping to admire the remarkable hillside vistas and beautifully restored officers' homes. All in all, about 500 structures from the former military base remain, ranging from Civil War mansions to simple turn-of-the-century barracks. There are also many decommissioned batteries (gun emplacements) that invite exploration. At the northernmost tip of the Presidio, underneath the Golden Gate Bridge, is **Fort Point**, which is open to the public.

Fort Point

Marine Drive, beneath the Golden Gate Bridge (556 1693/www.nps.gov/fopo). Bus 28, 29. **Open** 10am-5pm Mon, Thur-Sun. **Admission** free. **Map** p306 A1.

A spectacular brick citadel perched breathtakingly beneath the southern end of the Golden Gate Bridge, Fort Point was built between 1853 and 1861 to protect San Francisco from a sea attack that never came. Its 126 cannons remained idle, and the fort was closed in 1900. Today, the four-storey, open-roofed building houses various military exhibitions; children love to scamper among the battlements and passageways. You can climb on to the roof for a fabulous view of the underbelly of the bridge; outside, watch daredevil surfers brave the waves and the rocks next to the fort, and windsurfers dart in and out beneath the bridge. The fort's pier is famous as the spot where Kim Novak's character attempts suicide (or, at least, pretends to) in Alfred Hitchcock's *Vertigo*. Above the fort is the toll plaza for the Golden Gate Bridge and the starting point for walks across the span.

Ocean Beach & Around

Residential streets and windswept beaches nestle against the wild Pacific.

Relaxing on the sand at **Ocean Beach**.

The city's outermost districts, though lesser-known to outsiders, are just as saturated in personality as the better-known – and more crowded – inner ones. The **Richmond** and **Sunset Districts** are what many call the true San Fran: neighbourhoods that were made to be lived in. In this comparatively quiet and usually fog-swathed section of town, you can dine on dim sum, rollerblade down a wooded road or savour the ocean spray alongside locals who are that much friendlier and more relaxed for not having to combat a daily onslaught of tourists.

The Richmond District

Bordering the northern edge of Golden Gate Park, from Arguello Boulevard to the ocean and from Fulton Street to Clement Street, the largely residential Richmond has in its restaurants, shops and other businesses all the flavours of its predominantly Russian, Chinese and Irish population. Once a sandy waterfront wasteland, the region was developed for housing after the Geary Boulevard tramway was constructed in 1906. Eastern European Jews formed a strong community here after World War I, and their synagogues and delicatessens still thrive in a serenely multicultural landscape.

Clement Street is the district's primary commercial centre. While between 20th and 25th Avenues its flavour is mainly Russian, the stretch from Fourth to 11th Avenues is arguably a more authentic Chinatown than the more famous one downtown. Scattered among no-nonsense emporia selling Asian groceries, shrine accoutrements, cheap kitchenware and ginseng, are dozens of restaurants. Notable spots include big, busy, Shanghai-style **Fountain Court** (354 Clement Street, between Fourth and Fifth Avenues; 668 1100); humble Vietnamese **Minh's Garden** (208 Clement, at Third; 751 8211); **Le Soleil** (133 Clement, between Second and Third; 668 4848); and real-deal **D&A Café** (407 Clement, at Fifth; 668 7883) where late-afternoon Chinese specials cost only $2 and tapioca teas are the best around. **Chung Chou City** (324 Clement, at Fourth; 666 3668) is a well-appointed herbalist's shop with exotic teas.

Further west on your way to the beach, the ethnic character of the neighbourhood changes; signs change from Roman to Cyrillic, ginger gives way to poppy seed. Scores of Russian and Jewish bakeries and delis line both sides of Clement Street, tempting passers-by with Slavic delicacies. The food may be mediocre at **Tommy's Mexican Restaurant** (5929 Geary Boulevard, between 23rd and 24th Avenues; 387 4747), but tequila fans will be in heaven. With about 100 varieties in stock, it claims to have the widest selection of 100 per cent agave tequila outside Mexico.

At 34th Avenue, turn north into Lincoln Park to find the **California Palace of the Legion of Honor** (*see p106*), architect George Applegarth's homage to the Palais de la Légion d'Honneur in Paris. Built in the 1920s on a promontory that now overlooks the Golden Gate Bridge, it was donated to the city as a memorial to Californians who died in World War I. The museum originally displayed only French works of art, but today contains a wide-ranging permanent array of works by the likes of El Greco, Rembrandt and Monet. Its Rodin collection is the second-finest outside the Musée Rodin in Paris (the Stanford Art Museum now has more works by the sculptor) and it includes some fine works by Camille Claudel. Just north of the Palace's car park is the haunting **Jewish Holocaust Memorial** by George Segal. The surrounding wooded and hilly park houses the 18-hole **Lincoln Park Golf Course** (*see p242*) and offers picturesque glimpses of the Golden

On the beach

Don't look for surfers and sandcastles in North Beach or South Beach: not only are the titular beaches long gone, but even the shoreline where those beaches used to be is but a distant memory. In fact, none of the beaches along the bay, east of the Golden Gate, are much to speak of – they're mostly just feeble waves lapping narrow crescents of trucked-in sand; if you're absolutely desperate, you'll find family-friendly strands at Aquatic Park and Crissy Field. The city's best beaches – though a Southern Californian wouldn't be very impressed – lie to the west of the Golden Gate.

Beach swimming is a relatively rare activity, mostly because of the coast's prevailing onshore winds, which often chill even the loveliest day and draw the accursed fog off the Pacific. Most San Franciscans go to the beach, if at all, only a few times a year, usually during the rare spate of hot days that come in late spring or autumn. And thanks to rip tides, treacherous currents and the occasional great white shark sighting, it's only the wetsuited few who find a way to 'enjoy' the water, paddling into the freezing waves to surf.

But San Francisco's beaches do have their charms, and as long as you dress for the occasion (bring an extra layer, just in case) they make a refreshing break from the urban frenzy.

Baker Beach

Gibson Road, off Bowley Street. Bus 29.

Running for almost a mile along the craggy Presidio shoreline, Baker Beach (*pictured*) is a city favourite. Picnicking, sunbathing and fishing are the real lures here, since the usual suspects – cold water and strong currents – deter swimmers. The northern half of the beach is predominantly (though not exclusively) nudist, a popular place for gay bodybuilders to strut their stuff. Even so, don't be surprised if you see film crews or photographers fiddling with equipment in the sand at the beach's northern tip: they're snapping not the bums and biceps (a definite no-no), but rather the afternoon sun illuminating the orange flanks of the Golden Gate Bridge soaring into the distance, seen best from this angle. Baker Beach was once the hiding place of a huge 95,000lb cannon, camouflaged here by the army in 1905 to protect the bay from naval invasions (it was never used). A replica of the original has been installed for the curious.

China Beach

Seacliff Avenue, off 26th Avenue. Bus 1, 18, 29.

Hidden between Baker Beach and Lincoln Park in the exclusive Sea Cliff neighborhood, exquisitely sheltered James D Phelan Beach – better known as China Beach – takes its nickname from the settlement of Chinese fishermen who camped here in the 19th century. It's the nicest of all the beaches, small and protected from the wind, and neighbourhood residents would prefer to keep it for themselves, though by law it remains open to the public. Pacific Heights nannies, rich kids and avoiders of the hoi polloi all favour China Beach, which has plenty of parking and a pleasant hike down to the sand, and then a free sundeck, showers and changing rooms once you get there. The stunning mansions of Sea Cliff cling to precipices nearby.

Ocean Beach

Great Highway, between Balboa Street & Sloat Boulevard. Muni Metro N, L/bus 5, 18, 31, 38, 48, 71.

Extending from Cliff House south past the city limits, Ocean Beach is by far San Francisco's biggest beach: a three-mile (five-kilometre) sandy strip along the city's Pacific coast. Widening into dunes and plateaus at the end of the fog-bound Sunset District, Ocean Beach is a fine place for strolling, sunbathing (if you're lucky), dog-walking and the odd illicit midnight ritual. What it's not good for is a casual dip: tremendous waves often come thundering ashore, and even on seemingly calm days the tides and currents can be lethal. Experienced surfers have been known to drown here, and every year an unsuspecting tourist or two gets whisked away to the briny deep.

If nature had its way, the sand dunes would advance inland as far as Twin Peaks (as they did until the 1920s), but now the natural movement of the beach is halted by a large retaining wall that runs parallel to the Great Highway. A bicycle and pedestrian path runs along Ocean Beach as far as Sloat Boulevard and the San Francisco Zoo, from where you can stroll to Fort Funston to watch daredevil hang-gliders in action.

Further afield

North and south of the San Francisco is where the beaches are best. A glorious string of them dot the coastline, all accessible via Highway 1, California's shore-hugging coastal road. Heading south, the San Mateo County beaches extend all the way to Santa Cruz, each an unspoiled gem: a few standouts include **Gray Whale Cove**, **James V Fitzgerald Marine Reserve** (great tidal pools), **San Gregorio** and **Año Nuevo** (with elephant seals on view in season). To the north, Marin County has several isolated coves just across the Golden Gate in the Marin Headlands, but **Muir Beach** and especially ever-popular **Stinson Beach** are impossibly crowded on warm weekends, and this often results in maddening traffic jams along the narrow winding roads. Beach heaven continues further north, as **Point Reyes National Seashore** sports miles and miles of surf-pounded shoreline. And perhaps nicest of all, the **Sonoma coast state beaches**, north of Point Reyes, are crowd-free and picture-perfect.

Gate Bridge and Marin Headlands. A winding, hilly coastal trail leads from Lincoln Park to the Golden Gate Bridge.

At the Ocean Beach end of the Richmond, **Sutro Heights Park** is a tiny idyll, virtually empty except for a few Russians walking their dogs or playing chess. Near the park entrance a statue of the goddess Diana is often decorated with flowers by local pagans. In the nearby walled garden you can enjoy a secluded picnic and marvel at the spectacular panoramic view of the Pacific – fog permitting.

Perched on the very verge of the city and also overlooking the ocean is the **Cliff House** (*see below*), the brainchild of tobacco magnate Adolph Sutro. Below the Cliff House to the north are the ruins of **Sutro Baths**. Built by Sutro in 1896, these were once the world's biggest swimming baths, with seven heated pools under a magnificent glass roof. All were destroyed by fire in 1966. Ugly apartment buildings slated to replace them were, luckily, never built. The pool ruins are strangely photogenic, famously used in a scene in the movie *Harold and Maude*. A windswept three-mile (five-kilometre) coastal path winds all the way from here to the Golden Gate Bridge. Shrubbery alongside the path is a notorious rendezvous site for lovers with no place else to go, so it can be scenic in more ways than one. South from the Cliff House, on the edge of Golden Gate Park, is the **Beach Chalet** (*see below*). Closed for many years, it finally reopened in 1996. The main floor is now a visitor centre for the park, with a good restaurant upstairs.

Don't leave the Richmond without visiting the unusual **Columbarium** (*see p102*), set amid two acres of gardens.

Beach Chalet

1000 Great Highway, in Golden Gate Park (visitor centre 751 2766/restaurant 386 8439/ www.beach chalet.com). Bus 18. **Open** *Visitor centre* 9am-6pm daily. *Restaurant* 8am-10pm Mon-Fri; 8am-11pm Sat, Sun.

A stylish, quality restaurant and ale house in a historic Willis Polk-designed building. The walls on the bottom floor are awash in WPA frescos by Lucien Labaudt that depict notable San Franciscans, among them sculptor Benny Bufano and Golden Gate Park's famous gardener, John McLaren. The views of the ocean from upstairs are stupendous.

Cliff House

1090 Point Lobos Avenue, at the Great Highway (386 3330/www.cliffhouse.com). Bus 18, 38. **Open** *Bar* 11am-2am daily. *Restaurant* 9am-10.30pm Mon-Fri; 8.30am-10.30pm Sat, Sun. *Walkways* 24hrs daily.

The first house was built on this spot in the 1860s; after a fire in 1894, tobacco magnate Adolph Sutro replaced it with a magnificent, eight-storey Victorian turreted palace. When that also burned down, a year

Take in the view and a round or two at **Lincoln Park Golf Course**. *See p99.*

after surviving the great quake of 1906, it was replaced by today's nominally neo-classical architectural muddle. It's now a rather touristy spot – with a bar, gift shop and restaurant – whose superb views almost compensate for the crowds. The Cliff House is due to undergo a major restoration, which might displace the complex's Musée Mécanique (*see p110*), an arcade stocked with antique coin-operated games, and Camera Obscura (*see p109*), a 19th-century optical marvel. The National Park Service maintains a visitor centre (556 8642) for the Golden Gate National Recreation Area on the premises.

Columbarium

1 Loraine Court, off Anza Street (752 7891). Bus 31, 33, 38. **Open** 10am-4pm Mon-Fri; 10am-2pm Sat, Sun. **Admission** free.

This round, domed neo-classical rotunda is honeycombed with hundreds of niches. Its cremation urns are lavishly and individualistically decorated, alternately dignified and flamboyantly whimsical. The niches house the remains of many of the city's first families – the Folgers (of coffee fame), Magnins, Kaisers and others whose names appear on street signs all around town. It's the only active funereal resting place in the city and is the sole remnant of what was once a vast burial ground.

The Sunset District

South of Golden Gate Park, the large southern twin to the Richmond District usually belies its own name. Habitually swathed in fog from June to September (and often other months as well), the residential Sunset District only experiences spectacular sunsets on rare fair days. **Irving Street**, between Fifth and Tenth Avenues, is the main shopping area. The neighbourhood (like most in SF) is a haven for interesting restaurants, including seafood specialist **PJ's Oyster Bed**; **Ebisu**, which serves some of San Francisco's best sushi; and the Asian-flavoured **House** (for all, *see chapter* **Restaurants & Cafés**). **Le Video** (1231 Ninth Avenue; 566 3606) is arguably the best video shop in San Francisco, with more than 30,000 titles in all genres. Anyone with photo ID, a credit card and a San Francisco address is welcome to rent a film. At the edge of Golden Gate Park, the **Canvas Cafe Gallery** (*see p158*) is a combined café, wine bar, gallery and performance space.

Along the western edge of the Sunset, **Ocean Beach** is a good spot for a blustery walk and for watching surfers, but not, thanks to strong rip tides and chilly water, for a swim. (For more information on San Francisco's beaches, *see p100* **On the beach**.) Take a break at the **Java Beach Café** (1396 La Playa Boulevard; 665 5282), where the coffee is famously good, or at Vietnamese restaurant **Thanh Long** (4101 Judah Street, at 46th Avenue; 665 1146), loved for its garlic crab.

At the south-west corner of the district, the **San Francisco Zoo** (*see p196*) has all the Sumatran tigers, gorillas, African wart hogs, otters and penguins you might expect, as well as a hands-on 'family farm'. It is one of few zoos in the world to house koalas (two of which were stolen recently as pets for the teenage thieves' less-than-thrilled girlfriends, and subsequently returned). Beyond the zoo is the municipal **Harding Park & Golf Course** (*see p242*), cradled by the picturesque **Lake Merced**, and its biking and jogging trails. North of the lake, **Stern Grove**, a 63-acre oasis of eucalyptus and redwood trees, is the summer home of the **Stern Grove Festival** (*see p191*).

Finally, **Fort Funston Reservation** is a large, natural area at the city's south-west corner, an acreage criss-crossed with hiking trails, dramatic promontories and jagged beaches. Many Sunset residents steal a few hours here to run, stroll or meditate.

The East Bay

More delights await across the Bay Bridge.

Often undersung, the East Bay has much that San Francisco lacks, including sunnier weather, a world-class university, a unique heritage as the birthplace of California cuisine – and a lot more places to park. As prices soar in San Francisco, many young professionals have migrated to the East Bay, a region that ranges from intimidatingly rich to shockingly poor, with much in the middle, and extends from the Carquinez Strait in the north down to San Jose in the south. The best-known East Bay cities – and the ones closest to San Francisco and easily accessible via a 20- to 30-minute train ride on BART or a half-hour drive across the Bay Bridge – are **Oakland** and **Berkeley**.

The telephone area code for both Berkeley and Oakland is 1-510, which you'll need to use if calling from San Francisco. For tourist offices in both cities, *see p287*.

Oakland

Named after its now-vanished oak forests, San Francisco's image-challenged stepsister made headlines in the 1960s as the headquarters of both the radical Black Panthers and the rowdy Hell's Angels. Earlier still, the completion of America's transcontinental railroad in 1869 made Oakland a household name when it was fortunate enough be chosen as the terminus; the promised land at the end of a 3,000-mile (4,800-kilometre) journey. After the 1906 earthquake, thousands of suddenly homeless San Franciscans established themselves here.

Today, many residents commute to and from San Francisco by BART (eight stations serve Oakland – the City Center/12th Street and 19th Street ones are in the heart of downtown) or across the Bay Bridge (follow signs for I-580 Downtown Oakland). Ferries also run to the waterfront area from Pier 41 in Fisherman's Wharf.

While Oakland's ramshackle downtown and various other districts are not overly inviting, despite the best efforts of famous mayor (and former California governor) Jerry Brown, one of the nation's most ethnically diverse populations ensures a dizzying array of cultural and culinary surprises that you just can't find anywhere else. Burmese food, Ethiopian, Peruvian, African-American, Caribbean – it's hard to decide in a city with a restaurant selection second only to San Francisco's. Restaurants are scattered all over, but you'll find that there are many in Oakland's Chinatown and in the Rockridge area.

On the waterfront, **Jack London Square** (at Broadway and the Embarcadero) is named for the noted local author, who used to carouse at the **First & Last Chance Saloon** (*see p156* **East Bay drinking**); his rustic cabin shipped down from the Yukon rests nearby. Art and artefacts at the strikingly designed **Oakland Museum of California** (*see p111* **Out of town**) showcase the Golden State; many rank it as the best California-themed museum. For a picnic or a hike, head to **Lake Merritt Park**, where waterfowl pose in the sun and where the children's park **Children's Fairyland** (*see p198* **Out of town**) is filled with scenarios based on classic nursery rhymes – Walt Disney was so impressed by the place that legend claims it inspired him to create Disneyland.

Oakland also hosts an eclectic range of theatre, dance, ballet and classical music events. For jazz and Japanese food, **Yoshi's at Jack London Square** (*see p214* **East Bay sounds**) is a popular nightspot.

Berkeley

Fuelled by a continuous river of coffee, Berkeley works hard to live up to its reputation as a hotbed of avant-garde arts, left-leaning politics and revolutionary food. It has three BART stations: Berkeley, North Berkeley and Ashby; the first is in the middle of downtown and thus most convenient to all attractions. By car, head across the Bay Bridge and turn north on I-80, following signs for Berkeley exits.

Near the BART Berkeley station, bustling restaurants and coffee-houses include the highly unusual **Capoeira Arts Café** (2026 Addison Street; 1-510 666 1349/0289), in which students practising acrobatic Brazilian martial arts share a room with nonchalant caffeine addicts. A short walk east brings you to the town's hub, the campus of the **University of**

► For info on the **music** and **nightclub scene**, *see p214* **East Bay sounds**. For the area's best **bars**, *see p156* **East Bay drinking**. For the pick of Berkeley's **shops**, see *p185* **Buying Berkeley**.

California (known locally as just Cal). Thirty years ago, this was the birthplace of America's youth revolution: students protesting campus rules and the Vietnam war in the 1960s radicalised and rose up against society at large, and a nation of disgruntled youths followed their lead. These days, the sprawling, park-like campus, with its creeks and redwood groves, is comparatively placid. Studious undergraduates and Nobel laureates absentmindedly stroll the paths between historic buildings. An elevator ride to the top of **Sather Tower** (better known simply as the Campanile) offers stunning views and a 61-bell carillon, while several museums dedicated to art, anthropology, palaeontology and other disciplines dot the property. Pick up a map at the **Visitors' Center** (at the corner of University Avenue and Oxford Street; 1-510 642 5215). It's open 8.30am to 4.30pm weekdays. The **Lawrence Hall of Science** (*see p198*), above the campus on Centennial Drive, is a fascinating science museum and commands vistas over the entire Bay Area (*see p80* **On a clear day, you can see for ever**).

Spiking southwards from campus, **Telegraph Avenue** still vibrates with the energy that gave birth to the Free Speech Movement. A string of outstanding bookshops on the street includes **Cody's** (No.2454, at Haste Street; 1-510 845 7852) and **Moe's** (No.2476; 1-510 849 2087), while jewellers and other craftspeople sell their wares in open-air streetside stalls, lending a carnival atmosphere to this Haight-Ashbury East.

North-west of campus, the culinary hot zone known as the 'Gourmet Ghetto' runs along **Shattuck Avenue** between Delaware and Rose Streets. Chef/owner Alice Waters kickstarted the California cuisine revolution in the 1970s at **Chez Panisse** restaurant (1517 Shattuck, between Cedar and Vine; 1-510 548 5049), and you'll find what might just be the world's strongest and best coffee at the original (opened 1966) **Peet's Coffee** (2124 Vine Street, at Walnut; 1-510 841 0564).

UC Berkeley: historical hotbed of protest.

For hardcore capitalists, the trendy new **Fourth Street** district near the waterfront (between Hearst Avenue and Virginia Street) has exclusive upmarket shops by the dozens, while traditionalists turn to century-old fish house **Spenger's** (No.1919; 1-510 845 7771) and **Brennan's** (Fourth Street and University Avenue; 1-510 841 0960), a cavernous, old-fashioned Irish pub and cafeteria.

A decadent vacation getaway straddling the Berkeley-Oakland border, the sprawling hillside palace known as the **Claremont Resort & Spa** (41 Tunnel Road, at Claremont Avenue; 1-510 843 3000) is as much an architectural landmark as a famously pampering splurge. And in the hills above the city, the lovely and magnificently wild **Tilden Regional Park** offers miles and miles of hiking trails.

Don't stop to think, just go to the **California Palace of the Legion of Honor**. *See p106.*

Museums

From the Gold Rush to Rodin to Gary Larson, San Francisco has it all – but stay alert, the city's museums are on the move.

Although San Francisco may not rival the great museum cities of the world such as London and New York, it has a number of dynamic smaller museums that offer innovative, often high-tech, contemporary exhibitions, as well as museums like the beautiful **California Palace of the Legion of Honor**, where the setting of the museum is a work of art itself. And unlike visiting the British Museum, you won't need a compass and the stamina of a sherpa to pay a visit to San Francisco's museums.

Unfortunately for those who want to check every museum off their 'to see' list, this is not the best of times, as many are undergoing renovation or relocation. San Francisco's oldest public museum, the **MH de Young Memorial Museum**, closed in January 2001 for renovations and seismic retrofitting; it will reopen in 2005 in the same location in Golden Gate Park. The small **Mexican Museum** formerly at Fort Mason has also closed temporarily; it is slated to reopen in the Yerba Buena arts district in 2003, in a new, expansive home designed by famed Mexican architect Ricardo Legorreta. Check its website – www.mexicanmuseum.org – or call 202 9700 for more details. The very popular **Cartoon Art Museum** also closed in 2001; at press time it hoped to reopen by the end of the year in a larger space; you can check out www.cartoonart.org for the latest news on how it's coming along.

If you're looking for museums of special interest to kids, including Zeum and the Exploratorium, *see chapter* **Children**. For art galleries, *see chapter* **Galleries**.

CityPass

If you're in town for a week or even a bit less, consider getting a CityPass booklet. Valid for seven days, it gives you free transport on Muni buses, streetcars and cable cars (but not BART) and one Blue & Gold ferry cruise, plus free admission to **SFMOMA**, the **California Palace of the Legion of Honor**, the **California Academy of Sciences** and **Steinhart Aquarium**, and the **Exploratorium**. CityPass costs $33.75 ($26.75 seniors, $24.75 5-17s) – a substantial saving on normal prices. You can buy a booklet at any of the attractions, the **Visitor Information Center** (*see p287*) or online at www.citypass.com.

Major museums

Asian Art Museum

200 Larkin Street, at Fulton Street, Civic Center (668 8921/www.asianart.org). BART Civic Center/ Muni Metro F, J, K, L, M, N/bus 5, 9, 21, 47, 49. **Map** p310 F4.

The Asian Art Museum left its long-time home in Golden Gate Park in October 2001, in preparation for moving its precious cargo to a new and bigger residence in the Civic Center area. The new museum will open in autumn 2002 (so call for details of opening hours and admission prices). Its vast collection will then again be open to its many admirers. Within its vaults are more than 12,000 objects (only a fraction are displayed at any one time), including jade pieces, bronzes, ceramics, fans, albums, scrolls, sculptures and painting. In addition to Chinese works, such as embroidered silk gauze garments from the Ming dynasty, you'll also find many pieces from India, Tibet, Japan and the Middle East. The museum's new home will be the 1917 Beaux Arts former Main Library, redesigned by superstar architect Gae Aulenti (who was also responsible for turning a former railway station into the very popular Musée d'Orsay in Paris). The move is part of an extensive $1.3-billion revitalisation scheme for the whole Civic Center area.

Top five Museums

Cable Car Museum

Discover how these San Francisco landmarks actually work. Great for kids. *See p109.*

California Palace of the Legion of Honor

The city's most regal museum: fabulous setting, Rodin sculptures and Sunday concerts. *See right.*

Friends of Photography/ Ansel Adams Center

Work by Adams and other major snappers enjoy a bigger and better home in SoMa. *See p109.*

SFMOMA

The stunning building by Mario Botta is as much a work of art as the paintings within. *See p107.*

Yerba Buena Center for the Arts

Where to see the most innovative contemporary work – before it ends up in SFMOMA across the street. *See p107.*

California Academy of Sciences

55 Concourse Drive, Golden Gate Park (recorded information 750 7145/Morrison Planetarium 750 7127/www.calacademy.org). Bus 5, 21, 44, 71. **Open** *Summer* 9am-6pm daily; 9am-8.45pm 1st Wed of the month. *Winter* 10am-5pm daily; 10am-8.45pm 1st Wed of the month. **Admission** $8.50; $5.50 concessions, 12-17s; $2 4-11s; free under-4s. Free 1st Wed of the month. *Planetarium shows* $2.50; $1.25 concessions, 6-17s. **Credit** (museum only) MC, V. **Map** p312 B6.

More than 1.5 million visitors visit this science museum in Golden Gate Park each year to see the displays mounted by the oldest scientific institution in the western US. It's a perennial favourite of school groups and families, though curious grown-ups will find plenty to keep them occupied, too. The big attraction is the Steinhart Aquarium (*see p196*) with its floating crowd of more than 14,000 sea creatures, but there's much more here, including a simulated earthquake exhibit that re-creates the seismic lurches of the 1906 and 1989 temblors, old-fashioned dioramas and a brilliant display of the flora and fauna of California's numerous climates and varied terrain. The Academy has a permanent exhibition of works by 'Far Side' cartoonist/science freak Gary Larson, while changing displays have included everything from dinosaurs to venomous animals. Also within the complex is the Morrison Planetarium, which presents educational and amusing sky shows, including some geared toward kids. Visitors with a public transport ticket get $2.50 off the admission price.

California Palace of the Legion of Honor

Lincoln Park, at 34th Avenue & Clement Street, Richmond District (863 3330/www.thinker.org). Bus 1, 2, 18, 38. **Open** 9.30am-5pm Tue-Sun. **Admission** $8; $6 concessions; $5 12-17s; free under-12s. **Credit** AmEx, MC, V.

Located in a wooded spot overlooking the Pacific Ocean, the Palace of the Legion of Honor is San Francisco's prettiest museum, its neo-classical façade virtually unchanged since it was completed in 1924. A cast of Rodin's 'Le Penseur' still dominates the entrance, which has now been enhanced by a glass pyramid. The Legion's collections include more than 87,000 paintings, sculptures, decorative arts, works on paper, tapestries and other objects, spanning 4,000 years – though the emphasis is on European paintings and decorative arts, and extensive holdings of Rodin sculptures, the personal passion of the museum's founder, Alma Spreckels.

The entrance level is dedicated to the permanent collection; while an expanded garden level houses temporary exhibition galleries, as well as the Achenbach Foundation for Graphic Arts and the Bowles Collection of porcelain from France and England. Travelling exhibitions here can be wonderful: in 2001, the museum curated an impressive exhibit of Henry Moore sculptures. Bus 18 goes directly to the museum, and visitors with a Muni ticket get $2 off admission.

SFMOMA, where the building is as much a work of art as its contents.

San Francisco Museum of Modern Art (SFMOMA)

151 Third Street, between Mission & Howard Streets, SoMa (357 4000/www.sfmoma.org). BART Powell or Montgomery Streets/Muni Metro F, J, K, L, M, N/bus 9, 15, 30, 45, 76. **Open** *Memorial Day-Labor Day* 10am-6pm Mon, Tue, Fri-Sun; 10am-9pm Thur. *Labor Day-Memorial Day* 11am-6pm Mon, Tue, Fri-Sun; 11am-9pm Thur. **Admission** $10; $6-$7 concessions; free under-12s. Half-price 6-9pm Thur; free 1st Tue of the month. **Credit** (café & shop only) AmEx, MC, V. **Map** p311 H4.

The second-largest museum in the US devoted to modern art (after MOMA in New York), SFMOMA opened with a flourish in 1995, reaping enthusiastic approval as much for its modernist design as for any improvement over its predecessor. Swiss architect Mario Botta was widely celebrated for his design of the distinctive brick building, which is topped with a huge, circular skylight that's as dramatic from the outside as within. It still feels brand new. Four floors of galleries rise above the stark and stunning black marble reception area, which also holds a café and splendid gift shop (*see p179*). The permanent collection of more than 15,000 works includes paintings, sculptures and works on paper, as well as thousands of photographs and a growing collection of works related to the media arts. Its range is formidable – from Jeff Koons to Anselm Kiefer, Magritte to Man Ray, there's a smattering of everything, though not in any number. Recent acquisitions include a characteristic geometric painting by Piet Mondrian, a lighthearted 'ready-made' by Marcel Duchamp, and one of Mark Rothko's luminous canvases of rectangular swathes of colour. With an evident fondness for electronic and digital works, SFMOMA director David Ross has made efforts to include Bay Area artists in most group shows. Don't miss the spectacular catwalk just beneath the skylight, accessible from the top-floor galleries. Though not recommended for those who suffer from vertigo, it offers a stunning view of the striped marble below. Note that the museum is closed on Wednesdays.

Yerba Buena Center for the Arts

701 Mission Street, at Third Street, SoMa (978 2787/www.yerbabuenaarts.org). BART Powell or Montgomery Streets/Muni Metro F, J, K, L, M, N/bus 9, 15, 30, 45, 76. **Open** 11am-6pm Tue, Wed, Sat, Sun; 11am-8pm Thur, Fri. **Admission** $6; $4 concessions. Free 1st Tue of the month. **Credit** AmEx, MC, V. **Map** p311 H4.

Last in the alphabet but first in the hearts of many, Yerba Buena Center for the Arts is located opposite SFMOMA and lurks in its shadow, yet seems unintimidated, tugging at the modern art scene's shirttails with a scrappy itinerary and a great attitude. Housed in a futuristic-looking building designed by Fumihiko Maki, it contains four changing galleries and a 96-seat theatre. The museum's focus is on the new and innovative – installation and video art, outsider art, art that challenges the existing canon – and has included such diverse names as Henry Darger, Fred Thomaselli and Kumi Yamashita.

www.111minnagallery.com 111 Minna Gallery ph. 415 974 1719

Specialist museums

African American Historical & Cultural Society

Building C, Fort Mason Center, at Buchanan Street, Marina (441 0640). Bus 10, 28, 49. **Open** noon-5pm Wed-Sun; noon-7pm 1st Wed of the month. **Admission** $2. Free 1st Wed of the month. **Credit** (shop only) AmEx, MC, V. **Map** p308 E1.

This museum and gallery combines a permanent collection with changing exhibitions. Its archival materials relate to African-American life and culture from the 19th century to the present day, including photos and related items that shed light on little-known aspects of American history, while the gallery's emphasis is on new and master artists of African descent. The gift shop sells African and African-American arts and crafts.

Cable Car Museum

1201 Mason Street, at Washington Street, Nob Hill (474 1887/www.sfcablecar.com). Bus 1, 12, 30, 45, 83/cable car Powell-Hyde or Powell-Mason. **Open** *Apr-Sept* 10am-6pm daily. *Oct-Mar* 10am-5pm daily. **Admission** free. **Map** p308 G3.

After the mooing foghorn, the sound most often associated with San Francisco is the clanging bells of the cable cars. The best way to study them is, of course, to ride one of the three lines that operate nowadays; second best is to tour the Cable Car Museum, where you can view the actual cable winding machinery that powers the cars, as well as find out how these unusual vehicles work. You'll also learn about emergency procedures, bell-ringing competitions and the workmanship that goes into each cable car. Vintage cable cars, associated artefacts and dozens of old photos complete the display. *See also p60* **Cable cars**.

Chinese American National Museum & Learning Center

965 Clay Street, between Stockton & Powell Streets, Chinatown (391 1188/www.chsa.org). Bus 1, 30, 45/cable car Powell-Hyde or Powell-Mason. **Open** 11am-4pm Tue-Fri; noon-4pm Sat, Sun. **Admission** $3. Free 1st Thur of the month. **Credit** MC, V. **Map** p309 G3.

At the time of writing, the museum (formerly the Chinese Historical Society Museum) was closed but scheduled to reopen in autumn 2001 in improved digs in the historic Chinese YWCA building, designed by renowned local architect Julia Morgan (who also built Hearst Castle). The museum will continue its mission of promoting an understanding of Chinese history, with bilingual displays tracing the contributions of California's Chinese population, from the frontier years to the Gold Rush, the building of the railroads, and the days of the opium dens on the Barbary Coast. Displays include a small 19th-century Chinese Buddhist altar, a Californian sampan (fishing boat), and a Chinese dragon head made in 1911 for use in ceremonies and parades – and one of the first to incorporate electric lights. The expanded centre is intended to also serve as a learning resource for students of Chinese history, providing access to books, videos and CD-Roms.

Friends of Photography/ Ansel Adams Center

655 Mission Street, between Third & New Montgomery Streets, SoMa (495 7000/www.friendsofphotography.org). BART Montgomery Street/ Muni Metro F, J, K, L, M, N/bus 9, 14, 15, 30, 45, 76. **Open** 11am-5pm Mon-Wed, Fri-Sun; 11am-9pm Thur. **Admission** $7; $4 concessions. **Credit** AmEx, Disc, MC, V. **Map** p311 H4.

In 1989, 22 years after Ansel Adams founded the Friends of Photography, along with other prominent photographers, the group relocated its headquarters from Carmel to San Francisco. Now the museum has sleek, brand-new digs near SFMOMA and Yerba Buena Center for the Arts. One room is dedicated to the work of Ansel Adams himself, while the other four present rotating exhibitions. Among the recent, high-profile shows here have been the works of Annie Leibovitz, and Alfred Stieglitz, the early master of photogravure. The book shop is a great source of souvenirs, with Ansel Adams reproductions and a wide variety of photography-related books.

Holographic Museum & Camera Obscura

Cliff House, 1090 Point Lobos Avenue, at the Great Highway, Ocean Beach (750 0415). Bus 18, 38. **Open** 11am-sunset daily. **Admission** $2. **No credit cards**.

Next door to the Musée Mécanique (*see p110*), this museum is the only one of its kind: several dozen holographs are displayed at eye level around the tiny chamber that houses the camera obscura, a Victorian creation that projects an image of the outside world (including a large stretch of Ocean Beach) on to a giant parabolic screen. Because the camera uses sunlight, the museum is only open until sunset. The museum joined the National Registry of Historic Places in May 2001.

Jewish Museum of San Francisco

121 Steuart Street, between Mission & Howard Streets, SoMa (788 9990/www.jmsf.org). BART Embarcadero/Muni Metro F, J, K, L, M, N/bus 7, 9, 14, 21, 31, 66, 71. **Open** noon-5pm Mon-Thur, Sun. **Admission** $4. **Credit** MC, V. **Map** p309 J3.

This museum is devoted to linking the art of the Jewish community with the community at large. It offers educational programmes and shows works by students and established artists, many of which are political or controversial in nature. It is moving (like so many museums in San Francisco at the moment) in early 2004 to a site across the street from Yerba Buena Gardens. The new home, originally designed as a power substation by Willis Polk in 1907, is being transformed by superstar architect Daniel Libeskind, in his first US commission. The museum is also joining forces (and collections) with the Judah Magnes Museum in Berkeley (1-510 549 6950).

Musée Mécanique

Cliff House, 1090 Point Lobos Avenue, at the Great Highway, Ocean Beach (386 1170/www.musee mecanique.citysearch.com). Bus 18, 38. **Open** *June-Oct* 10am-8pm daily. *Nov-May* 11am-7pm Mon-Fri; 10am-8pm Sat, Sun. **Admission** free.

Pack a pocketful of quarters and visit this wonderful cliffside museum, actually an arcade housing dozens of old-fashioned mechanical gizmos ranging from fortune-telling machines to player pianos. Best of all is Laughing Sal, a relic from Playland at the Beach, San Francisco's long-defunct coastside amusement park. She's an enormous mechanical figure with a crazy laugh that sends little kids running for their parents. Don't miss the camera obscura next door (*see p109*).

Museo ItaloAmericano

Building C, Fort Mason Center, at Buchanan Street, Marina (673 2200/www.museoitaloamericano.org). Bus 10, 28, 49. **Open** by appointment Mon, Tue; noon-5pm Wed-Sun; noon-7pm 1st Wed of the month. **Admission** $3; $2 concessions; free under-12s. Free 1st Wed of the month. **Credit** MC, V. **Map** p308 E1.

One of two ethnic museums housed in the unprepossessing Fort Mason complex (the other is the African American Historical & Cultural Society – *see p109*), the Museo ItaloAmericano functions as a combination gallery and community centre, offering classes in Italian language, art, architecture and related subjects to anyone who is interested to learn. Along with a few historical exhibits, the museum also shows works by Italian and Italian-American artists. It also has a nice little gift shop.

Museum of Craft & Folk Art

Building A, Fort Mason Center, at Buchanan Street, Marina (775 0991/www.mocfa.org). Bus 10, 28, 49. **Open** *Jan-Nov* 11am-5pm Tue-Fri, Sun; 10am-5pm Sat; *Dec* 11am-5pm Mon, Sun; 11am-6pm Tue-Fri; 10am-6pm Sat. *All year* 11am-7pm 1st Wed of the month. **Admission** $3; $1 concessions, 12-17s; $5 family; free under-12s. Free 10am-noon Sat; 11am-7pm 1st Wed of the month. **Credit** MC, V. **Map** p308 E1.

The quirky exhibits here prove that not all art has to involve canvas and oil paint, marble and chisel. It might be created with tattoo needles and human flesh, or out of ordinary paper bags. The Museum of Craft & Folk Art celebrates the infinite variety of artistic expression with rotating exhibitions and educational programmes. Recent shows include the work of Moses, who fashions elaborate headgear out of paper bags, and examples of shibori, a Japanese method of shaping and dyeing fabric.

The Museum of the City of San Francisco

South Light Court, City Hall, Van Ness Avenue & Grove Street, Civic Center (928 0289/www.sf museum.org). Muni Metro F, J, K, L, M, N/bus 5, 21, 47, 49. **Open** 8am-8pm Mon-Fri; noon-4pm Sat. **Admission** free. **Map** p310 F5.

City archivist Gladys Hansen maintains this room of exhibits tracing the city's history, from Spanish settlement to Gold Rush den of iniquity to modern metropolis. Photographs document San Francisco's big 20th-century earthquakes, in 1906 and 1989, and you can also see the head of the 'Goddess of Progress' statue, which topped City Hall before it toppled in the 1906 quake.

Explore the colourful and creepy world of carnivals and arcades at the **Musée Mécanique**.

Out of town

Berkeley Art Museum & Pacific Film Archive Galleries

2626 Bancroft Way, at Bowditch Street, Berkeley (1-510 642 0808/www.bampfa.berkeley.edu). BART Berkeley/bus AC Transit 7, 8, 40, 51, 52, 65. **Open** 11am-5pm Wed, Fri-Sun; 11am-9pm Thur. **Admission** $6; $4 concessions; free under-12s. Free 11am-noon, 5-9pm Thur. **Credit** DC, MC, V. **Map** p315 N4.

Modernist printer Hans Hofmann provided the impetus for an art museum on the UC Berkeley campus. Opened in 1970, the dramatic exhibition space is arranged in terraces so visitors can see the works from various vantage points. The collection's strength is in 20th-century painting, sculpture, photography and conceptual art, as well as Asian art. Ten galleries and a book store occupy the upper level, while a sculpture garden and café share the lower level. At press time, the museum was closed for seismic improvements, and expected to reopen in autumn 2001 with an exhibit of Buddha sculptures from throughout Asia, which will remain until 2003. The Pacific Film Archive, one of the country's most comprehensive academic film collections, is across the street and half a block away (at 2575 Bancroft Way). *See also p200.*

Oakland Museum of California

1000 Oak Street, at Tenth Street, Oakland (1-510 238 2200/www.museumca.org). BART Lake Merritt. **Open** 10am-5pm Wed-Sat; noon-5pm Sun; 10am-9pm 1st Fri of the month. **Admission** $6; $4 concessions; free under-5s. Free 2nd Sun of the month. **Credit** AmEx, DC, MC, V.

The only museum in California devoted exclusively to the state's art, history and environment, the Oakland Museum was first established in 1969. The Gallery of California Art displays paintings, sculpture, prints, illustrations, photos and decorative arts by Californian artists, or by artists addressing related themes and subjects. The collection includes sketches by early explorers and genre pictures from the Gold Rush, along wtih massive panoramic landscapes and Bay Area figurative, pop and funk works. The Hall of California Ecology is devoted to the variegated Californian landscape, while the Cowell Hall of California History has furniture, machines, tools, costumes, craftwork, decorations and vehicles prominent in the state's development.

San Francisco Bay Model Visitor Center

2100 Bridgeway, at Olive Street, Sausalito (332 3870/www.spn.usace.army.mil/bmvc). Ferry Golden Gate Transit from Ferry Building or Red and White Fleet from Fisherman's Wharf, Pier 43/bus Golden Gate Transit 3, 10, 50. **Open** *June-Sept* 9am-4pm Tue-Fri; 10am-5pm Sat, Sun. *Oct-May* 9am-4pm Tue-Sat. **Admission** free.

A 1½-acre, 3-D, hydraulic model of San Francisco Bay and beyond, built (for some reason) by the US Army Corps of Engineers, shows how navigation, recreation and ecology all interact in this complex water system. The best part of it all, can be found in the walkways that are strung above the model so that visitors can, figuratively at least, walk on water. When the model is in operation, a lunar day is simulated in under 15 minutes, complete with tidal action. Hands-on displays include video games and an introduction to indigenous birds and fish, and there are videos about the Corps' work in hydroelectric power, flood control and construction. The model is an actual engineering tool, so avail yourself of one of the self-guided audio tours to make sense of it all.

Pacific Heritage Museum

608 Commercial Street, at Montgomery Street, Financial District (399 1124). Bus 1, 5, 41, 42. **Open** 10am-4pm Tue-Sat. **Admission** free. **Map** p309 H3.

Once the city's mint, this structure is now a bank (the Bank of Canton) and also home, oddly, to a museum. With an emphasis on the city's connections to the Pacific Rim, the museum features changing exhibits of contemporary Asian artists from countries such as China, Taiwan, Japan and Thailand. Much of the art is rarely seen elsewhere and is on loan from private collections.

San Francisco Maritime National Historical Park Museum Building

Beach Street, at Polk Street, Fisherman's Wharf (556 3002/www.maritime.org). Bus 19, 30, 32, 42, 47, 49/cable car Powell-Hyde. **Open** 10am-5pm daily. **Admission** free. **Map** p308 F1.

Based in a curvaceous 1930s building that looks like an ocean liner, this museum documents maritime history with the aid of photographs and ship models, including miniatures of passenger liners and US Navy ships. It's a little dated, and might not be thrilling for adults, but it still offers interactive exhibits that most

It's pen-and-ink drawing with a twist at the **Tattoo Art Museum**.

children will likely enjoy and enough sea lore to fill a few hours. It's just across the street from the tourist-oriented Ghirardelli Square shopping centre. Three blocks away and under the same administration is Hyde Street Pier, where historical ships such as the 1890 ferry *Eureka* and 1886 full-rigged sailing ship *Balclutha* are open for viewing on self-guided tours.

San Francisco Performing Arts Library & Museum

Fourth floor, Veterans' Memorial Building, 401 Van Ness Avenue, at McAllister Street, Civic Center (255 4800/www.sfpalm.org). Muni Metro F, J, K, L, M, N/bus 5, 21, 42, 47, 49. **Open** 11am-5pm Tue, Thur-Sat; 11am-7pm Wed. **Admission** free. **Map** p310 F5.
With exhibitions relating to the performing arts – be it a puppet show or an opera – this museum is worth a visit if you're in the Civic Center area. Of most interest to fine arts scholars is the prodigious amount of resource material: thousands of books on design, fashion, music, theatre, opera and other art forms augment a focus on local arts groups.

Tattoo Art Museum

841 Columbus Avenue, at Lombard Street, North Beach (775 4991). Bus 15, 30/cable car Powell-Mason. **Open** noon-9pm daily. **Admission** free. **Map** p308 G2.
The arrival of tattoos in the Western world supposedly occurred after English privateer William Dampier returned from the South Pacific to shock and titillate London with the sight of Giolo, a native 'painted prince'. Now, it seems, everyone has one – especially in San Francisco. Master tattoo artist Lyle Tuttle has gathered a varied assortment of skin art paraphernalia, from photos of dramatically inked men and women to tattoo needles from Sarawak that look more like torture instruments than artists' tools. Though Tuttle himself is rarely at the adjoining shop, the talented Tanja Nicklish, who, for those who want to add a little plumage to their skin, specialises in bright colours, is usually available, if you're ready to take the plunge yourself (*see also p181*).

Wells Fargo History Museum

420 Montgomery Street, between California & Sacramento Streets, Financial District (396 2619/www.wellsfargohistory.com/museums/index.html). Muni Metro F, J, K, L, M, N/bus 1, 12, 15, 41, 42. **Open** 9am-5pm Mon-Fri. **Admission** free. **Map** p309 H3.
If you're in the Financial District during business hours, it's worth a quick stop to see this collection of memorabilia relating to the history of the Gold Rush and banking in California, and a smattering of Western art. You'll also find gold nuggets, an old telegraph machine and a Concord stagecoach, built in 1867. The museum is inside the headquarters of Wells Fargo, California's oldest bank.

Eat, Drink, Shop

Restaurants & Cafés 114
Bars 148
Shops & Services 159

Features

The best restaurants 118
Tasty taquerias 126
Bay Area dining 132
Best brunches 144
Booze, smoking and the law 151
Don't miss bars 152
East Bay drinking 156
Top five bookshops 164
Don't miss Fashion 168
The city on foot: Hayes Valley crawl 175
Buying Berkeley 185
Shopping by area 186

Restaurants & Cafés

Welcome to one of the world's best dining scenes.

Restaurants

Fusion? Fresh focaccia? Fish and chips? Whatever you want, you'll find it here. For all of the city's obvious attractions, for many, San Francisco's top draw may be its restaurants. The city is home to some 3,500 dining establishments; it doesn't take a statistician to figure out that locals like to eat out. Hence, the dining scene has the competitive nature of an Olympic sport.

Since the 1970s, when Alice Waters of Chez Panisse in Berkeley (still going strong – *see p132* **Bay Area dining**) gained global fame for her 'California cuisine' (the infusing of local seasonal ingredients and traditional recipes with cross-cultural influences), the Bay Area has gradually evolved into a food mecca. While California cuisine hasn't eased its grip on kitchens throughout the region, it also hasn't ceased being a source of inspiration for chefs whose ideas are further flung.

For its relatively compact size, San Francisco has a culinary scene that is as diverse as its citizenry; a virtual world of flavour. Locals delight in their ability to dine on fare from all points of the globe, from Afghan to Asian-fusion and Vietnamese to vegetarian. With taquerias in the Mission, Italian bakeries in North Beach, an endless array of Thai, Chinese, Vietnamese and Korean restaurants in the Sunset district, and in-and-out noodle shops in Japantown, it's possible to take an around-the-world culinary trip during a single San Francisco weekend.

There was a time, not long ago, when the dining scene here grew exponentially along with a stock market that seemed to be without a ceiling. More recently, the downturned market has chilled the once fevered pace at which new and grandiose places open, but it hasn't kept foodies from their favourite dining spots. If nothing else, at least it's easier to get a table at the city's most coveted high-end spots. Yet good food isn't just found in high-priced restaurants. Great ethnic cooking can be had in any number of small, hole-in-the-wall eateries, where reservations are neither accepted nor needed. Whatever you fancy, you're sure to be amazed by the number, variety and quality of restaurants San Francisco has to offer.

We've divided restaurants by the area of the city into which they fall and the type of cuisine they offer. Note that the cuisine categories are quite broad; 'American', for example, includes both new-wave Californian and old-fashioned grills, while 'Asian' covers such options as Japanese, Chinese, Thai, Vietnamese, Korean and Asian-fusion restaurants.

Don't forget to tip. The exact amount you tip is up to you, but 15-20 per cent of the bill is standard. A handy rule of thumb is to double the sales tax (currently 8.5 per cent).

Union Square & the Tenderloin

American

Postrio

545 Post Street, between Taylor & Mason Streets, Union Square (776 7825/www.postrio.com). Bus 2, 3, 4, 76/cable car Powell-Hyde or Powell-Mason. **Open** 11.30am-2pm, 5.30-10pm Mon-Wed; 11.30am-2pm, 5.30-10.30pm Thur-Sat; 11am-2pm, 5.30-10pm Sun. **Main courses** lunch $15-$20; dinner $27-$38. **Credit** AmEx, DC, Disc, MC, V. **Map** p308 G3/4.

Large, sleek and oozing a sort of Hollywood panache, Postrio is celebrity chef Wolfgang Puck's mooring in Northern California. The kitchen executes his signature dishes with seasonal interpretations. The famed salmon pizza is the popular draw, and one of the best places to enjoy it is at the bar, where you can watch from a distance the drama unfold in the bustling dining room.

Asian

Asia de Cuba

Clift Hotel, 495 Geary Street, at Taylor Street, Tenderloin (929 2300/www.clifthotel.com). Bus 2, 3, 4, 27, 38, 76. **Open** 6.30am-1am daily. **Main courses** $15-$60. **Credit** AmEx, DC, MC, V. **Map** p310 G4.

Much anticipated and, prior to its opening, much maligned, swanky Asia de Cuba opens on to the similarly decorated – and venerable – Redwood Room bar (*see p150*) inside Ian Schrager's recently opened Clift Hotel (*see p37*). It takes its cue from the Asia de Cuba restaurants at two other Schrager hotels, in LA and New York. The restaurant is so dimly lit you'll need a flashlight to read the menu. The hit-and-miss food is a *mélange* of Asian and Cuban techniques and spices, characterised by rich, sweet sauces. Although the prices are as high as the soaring 40ft (12m) redwood ceiling, this is likely to be an in-spot for a long while.

European

Fifth Floor

Hotel Palomar, 12 Fourth Street, at Market Street, Union Square (348 1555/http://fifthfloor.citysearch.com). BART Powell Street/Muni Metro F, J, K, L, M, N/bus 5, 6, 7, 9, 21, 31, 66, 71/cable car Powell-Mason. **Open** 7-10am, 5.30-10pm Mon-Thur; 7-10am, 5.30-11pm Fri; 8-11am, 5.30-11pm Sat; 8-11am Sun. **Main courses** $30-$41. **Credit** AmEx, DC, Disc, MC, V. **Map** p311 G4.

Set as it is in the Hotel Palomar, the Fifth Floor seems like an exclusive club for the tragically hip and perennially shopping. The room is fabulous: an idyllic blend of romance and chic. A zebra-print rug lies beneath your feet as you stroll to your table. Chef George Morrone was lured from a high-profile post in New York to run the kitchen, but has announced his departure at the end of October 2001; so keep your eyes peeled for his replacement. Rather than have diners puzzle over what kind of duck to order, it is made four ways here – confit, foie gras, smoked and honey-lavender – on a single plate. Undoubtedly, dining here is an experience.

Fleur de Lys

777 Sutter Street, between Jones & Taylor Streets, Tenderloin (673 7779/http://fleurdelys.citysearch.com). Bus 2, 3, 4, 27, 76. **Open** 6-9.30pm Mon-Thur; 5.30-9.30pm Fri, Sat. **Main courses** $30-$38; prix fixe menu $70 (vegetarian $58). **Credit** AmEx, DC, MC, V. **Map** p308 G3.

To many, the grand, tent-draped interior here is synonymous with fine dining in San Francisco, and a recent remodel did much to invigorate this local staple. Over the years, chef Hubert Keller's cuisine hasn't missed a step. He has a vast culinary repertoire and his menu is lush – and extraordinarily expensive – but the quality of the French food and the splendid wine list go a long way towards helping you forget you're about to spend a fortune. Service is attentive without being overbearing. Splash out on the prix-fixe, five-course tasting menu; there's also one for vegetarians.

Masa's

648 Bush Street, between Stockton & Powell Streets, Union Square (989 7154/http://masas.citysearch.com) Bus 2, 3, 4, 76/cable car California. **Open** 5.30-9.30pm Tue-Sat. **Prix fixe menus** $60 for 3 courses; $75 for 6 courses; $105 for 9 courses. **Credit** AmEx, DC, Disc, MC, V. **Map** p309 G3.

Masa's helped create fine dining in San Francisco. It was the first notable restaurant to combine haute cuisine with the French dining aesthetic. It staved off the threat of irrelevance recently with a brilliant remodel and 're-introduction' to the community, and also snared local culinary legend Ron Siegel to run the kitchen. Diver scallops, veal tenderloin; it's all just so sumptuous. It's also worth the splurge to go with the sommelier's wine pairings.

Scala's Bistro

Sir Francis Drake Hotel, 432 Powell Street, between Post & Sutter Streets (395 8555/www.scalasbistro.com). BART Powell Street/Muni Metro F, J, K, L, M, N/bus 2, 3, 4, 76/cable car Powell-Hyde or Powell-Mason. **Open** 8am-midnight Mon-Sat; 9am-midnight Sun. **Main courses** $12-$21. **Credit** AmEx, DC, Disc, MC, V. **Map** p309 G3.

Jellyfish light fixtures adorn seafood specialist **Farallon**. *See p117.*

HARRIS' RESTAURANT 2100 VAN NESS AVENUE, SF, CA 94109
DINNER PRIVATE DINING BANQUETS (415) 673-1888

Ooh la la, c'est **Plouf**. *See p118.*

Located within the Sir Francis Drake Hotel, this bustling bistro is frequented by tourists staying in Union Square and locals attracted by the reasonably priced Italian food. Salads always feature the season's freshest produce, and the sweetbreads are worth every calorie. Enjoy a plate of house-made ravioli with basil and ricotta in a lemon-cream sauce, or seared salmon with mashed potatoes.

Seafood

Farallon

450 Post Street, between Powell & Mason Streets (956 6969/www.farallonrestaurant.com). Bus 2, 3, 4, 38, 76/cable car Powell-Hyde or Powell-Mason. **Open** 5.30-10.30pm Mon; 11.30am-10.30pm Tue, Wed; 11.30am-11pm Thur-Sat; 5-10pm Sun. **Main courses** $14-$33. **Credit** AmEx, Disc, DC, MC, V. **Map** p309 G3.

This seafood restaurant made quite a splash when it opened in 1997. With an interior that looks like an underwater fantasy world (think Jules Verne meets Walt Disney), diners have much to peruse in addition to the menu. Good thing, too, because the menu is long on ideas but short of execution. Preparations tend to be elaborate and beautiful, but are typically underwhelming to taste. The raw bar items – oysters, tuna tartare – are more reliable. Despite the lukewarm reviews and exorbitant prices, the place remains wildly popular. A good way to wade in without getting soaked is to try the better-priced bistro menu offered in the bar area.

The Financial District

American

Cypress Club

500 Jackson Street, between Montgomery Street & Columbus Avenue (296 8555/www.cypressclub.com). Bus 12, 15, 41, 83. **Open** 5.30-10pm Mon-Thur, Sun; 5.30-11pm Fri, Sat. **Main courses** $23-$29. **Credit** AmEx, DC, MC, V. **Map** p309 H3.

Clubby, but with a touch of whimsy, the Cypress Club is as popular for its eye-popping design (outsize Doric-like columns and brassy, sculptural wall mouldings) as for its cuisine. The menu changes frequently, but typically features such luxuries as seared dayboat scallops, tandoori-roasted lamb loin and filet mignon. Although it tends to move in and out of fashion with the locals, the live jazz, dramatic room and busy bar scene give this place undeniable sex appeal. If you're looking for a place to splash out, this is a good choice.

Asian

Harbor Village

4 Embarcadero Center, between Sacramento & Clay Streets (781 8833/www.harborvillage.net). BART Embarcadero/Muni Metro F, J, K, L, M, N/bus 1, 15, 41, 42/cable car California. **Open** 11am-2.30pm, 5.30-9.30pm Mon-Fri; 10.30am-2.30pm, 5.30-9.30pm Sat, Sun. **Main courses** dim sum $3-$6; dinner $14-$25. **Credit** AmEx, DC, Disc, MC, V. **Map** p309 H3.

This place built a strong reputation in Hong Kong before opening this spacious downtown location. Locals love the dim sum, and many say it's the best in town. Come midday, the place is packed with patrons pointing out their favourite steamed dumplings to the smiling waitresses as they wheel delicacies by on a cart. The evening dinners are not bad either; a gourmet take on Cantonese cuisine, heavy on seafood specialities.

European

Kokkari Estiatorio

200 Jackson Street, at Front Street (981 0983/www.kokkari.com). Bus 1, 12, 42, 83. **Open** 11.30am-10pm Mon-Thur; 11.30am-11pm Fri; 5-11pm Sat. **Main courses** $14-$33. **Credit** AmEx, DC, MC, V. **Map** p309 H2.

Kokkari came on to the scene promising true 'Hellenic' cuisine. What it delivered was traditional Greek food. That's just fine, though, as it turns out they're one and the same. The striking dining room looks like it might be the home of your hip uncle from Mykonos. The pikilia (appetiser plate) is a good place to start, featuring three traditional Greek dips with fresh pita bread. Mains like swordfish, lamb chops and moussaka are standouts, although we like everything here.

The best Restaurants

For waterfront dining

Lapis and **A Sabella's** (for both, *see p130*) in Fisherman's Wharf and vegetarian **Greens** (*see p139*) in Fort Mason all offer great views of San Francisco Bay.

For old-fashioned class

San Francisco institutions for decades include seafood counter **Swan Oyster Depot** (*see p132*) and steakhouses **Harris'** (*see p137*) in Pacific Heights and **Alfred's** (*see p126*) in Chinatown.

For sushi lovers

Newcomer **Ozumo** (*see p119*) and hip **Sushi Groove** (*see p130*) have their fans, but for the best sushi in town you'll have to head to **Ebisu** (*see p141*) in the Sunset and **Kabuto** (*see p140*) in the Richmond.

For a special occasion

Whether it's your birthday or your last night in town, make it even more special at fantastical **Farallon** (*see p117*), award-winning **Gary Danko** (*see p130; pictured*), sexy **Cypress Club** (*see p117*), romantic **Fifth Floor** (*see p115*) or hipper-than-thou newcomer **Asia de Cuba** (*see p114*).

For ethnic eats

You're spoiled for choice, but you can't go wrong with **Yank Sing** (*see p119*) for dim sum; **Thep Phanom** for Thai (*see p137*); **Slanted Door** (*see p134*) for Vietnamese; **Terra Brazilis** (*see p137*) for Latin American; and the **Helmand** for Afghani (*see p130*).

For late-night dining

Asia de Cuba (*see p114*), **Globe** (*see p119*) and **Bacar** (*see p122*) are all open to 1am, but if you really need to eat in the wee hours, head to **El Farolito** or **Taqueria Cancun** (for both, *see p126* **Tasty taquerias**).

Plouf

40 Belden Place, between Bush, Pine, Kearny & Montgomery Streets (986 6491/www.plouf.com). Bus 2, 3, 4, 15. **Open** 11.30am-3pm, 5.30-10.30pm Mon-Fri; 5.30-10.30pm Sat. **Main courses** $10-$18. **Credit** AmEx, Disc, MC, V. **Map** p309 H3.

Here's a wonderful slice of European al fresco dining beneath the towering structures of the Financial District. Named after the French word for the sound a pebble makes when it's dropped into water, most of the dishes here come from the sea. Mussels are *de rigueur* starters, available in myriad varieties. Fish dishes are typically excellent, especially the signature fish and chips. If you must have turf rather than surf, try the peppery steak frites.

Seafood

Aqua

252 California Street, between Battery & Front Streets (956 9662/www.nextcenturyrestaurants.com/aquamain.htm). BART Embarcadero/bus 1, 12, 41, 42/cable car California. **Open** 11.30am-2.15pm, 5.30-10.30pm Mon-Thur; 11.30am-2.15pm, 5.30-11pm Fri; 5.30-11pm Sat. **Main courses** $14-$36. **Credit** AmEx, DC, Disc, MC, V. **Map** p309 H3.

For a time, executive chef Michael Mina's downtown restaurant typified power dining. His sleek, handsomely appointed space was wall-to-wall business execs. These days, the urgency has subsided, but the restaurant remains a popular spot among those in search of a splashy meal event. Mina has a penchant for architectural preparations. His dishes dazzle the eye, and are, in some cases, delightful, as with the miso-glazed sea bass. Mostly, though, the fare has not kept up with current tastes. If you're in the mood to indulge, go for the lobster pot pie.

The Embarcadero

American

Boulevard

1 Mission Street, at Steuart Street (543 6084/www.boulevardrestaurant.com). BART Embarcadero/Muni Metro F, J, K, L, M, N/bus 1, 2, 6, 7, 9, 14, 21, 31, 66, 71. **Open** 11.30am-2pm, 5.30-10pm Mon-Wed; 11.30am-2pm, 5.30-10.30pm Thur, Fri; 5.30-10.30pm Sat; 5.30-10pm Sun. **Main courses** lunch $9-$17; dinner $24-$32. **Credit** AmEx, DC, Disc, MC, V. **Map** p309 J3.

Many a restaurant in San Francisco would kill to know Boulevard's secret to success. The place is always packed and has been for years, attracting locals and visitors with its waterfront views. Self-taught chef Nancy Oakes's stacked, elaborate dishes are of the hearty New American variety: pork chops, steaks and risottos are the norm. Wood-roasted dishes are another strength. Service is casual although the prices are not: try the bar at lunchtime as a cheaper option.

Globe Restaurant

290 Pacific Avenue, at Battery Street (391 4132). Bus 12, 42, 83. **Open** 11.30am-1am Mon-Fri; 6pm-1am Sat; 6-11.30pm Sun. **Main courses** lunch $12-$18; dinner $16-$26. **Credit** AmEx, MC, V. **Map** p309 H2.
Chef Joseph Manzare is a New Yorker and one-time protégé of LA's Wolfgang Puck, which explains both the Globe's late opening hours and its penchant for California cuisine. An exposed-brick dining room adds a SoHo touch, as standards such as wood-oven pizzas and grilled salmon with buttery pasta and watercress are transformed by the freshness of their ingredients. Side dishes include baked tomatoes, creamed spinach and polenta.

One Market

1 Market Street, at Steuart Street (777 5577/ www.onemarket.com). BART Embarcadero/ Muni Metro F, J, K, L, M, N/bus 1, 2, 6, 7, 9, 14, 21, 31, 66, 71. **Open** 11.30am-2pm, 5.30-10pm Mon-Fri; 5.30-10pm Sat. **Main courses** lunch $14-$17; dinner $20-$36. **Credit** AmEx, DC, MC, V. **Map** p309 H3.
The most recent of many chefs here is Adrian Hoffman, who seems quite at ease with the sturdy American fare that has made One Market famous. Everything is substantial, from the big forks to the huge sidewalk windows to the giant Caesar salad to the hefty tab at meal's end. Meat and fish dishes are the speciality; the whole roasted snapper is a feast for the eyes and stomach. For a dining experience you won't forget, come in a group and request the chef's table located inside the kitchen.

Asian

Ozumo

161 Steuart Street, at Mission Street (882 1333/ www.ozumo.com). Muni Metro F/bus 1, 2, 6, 7, 9, 14, 21, 31, 66, 71. **Open** 11.30am-midnight daily. **Main courses** robata items $4-$15; box lunches $12-$20; sushi omakase from $50. **Credit** AmEx, DC, Disc, MC, V. **Map** p309 J3.
There aren't enough e's in 'sleek' to describe this new contender near the Embarcadero. Some 6,000sq ft (560sq m) of design panache surround diners at this adventurous Japanese restaurant and sushi bar. The front area holds a bar and lounge serving an exhaustive menu of sakes. Amble toward the back, past the long robata grill (available for bar seating), and you'll come to the enormous main dining room, with a sushi bar with seats on four sides, and full views of the Bay Bridge. The sushi chefs are capable, but the real attractions are the grilled meats, fish and vegetables from the robata menu.

Yank Sing

Rincon Center, 101 Spear Street, between Mission & Howard Streets (957 9300/www.yanksing.com). BART Embarcadero/Muni Metro F, J, K, L, M, N/

Enjoy sushi and noodles in a stunning setting at **Ozumo**.

backflip
601 eddy street
(at the phoenix hotel)
san francisco
415.771.FLIP (3547)
www.backflipsf.com

bus 1, 2, 6, 7, 9, 14, 21, 31, 66, 71. **Open** 11am-3pm Mon-Fri; 10am-4pm Sat, Sun. **Main courses** dim sum $3-$8. **Credit** AmEx, DC, MC, V. **Map** p309 J3.
For many San Franciscans, Yank Sing is the city's de facto official place for dim sum. Since the closing of its flagship location, the restaurant has lost a bit of its lustre, but this location, nestled in a corner of a massive office complex, still thrives. Non-English-speaking waitresses roll out an endless array of steaming dumplings, filled with everything from shrimp to pork to vegetables, and the on-the-go business crowd eagerly snaps them up.

Civic Center

American

Indigo

687 McAllister Street, at Gough Street (673 9353/ www.indigorestaurant.com). Bus 5, 42, 47, 49. **Open** 5-11pm Tue-Sun. **Main courses** $15-$20. **Credit** AmEx, MC, V. **Map** p310 F4.
'New American' cuisine is the culinary catchphrase at this restaurant, which draws its influences from both North and South America. In a comfortable, lounge-like setting with a long, open kitchen, graceful draperies and a wooden bar, the monthly changing menu might feature peppercorn-seared ahi tuna on wasabi mashed potatoes, red chilli pork chops with cranberry bean-apple pudding, or filet mignon with a purple potato gratinée. Vegetarians will find much to like. For dessert, don't miss the lavender crème brûlée, a house speciality.

Stars Bar & Dining

555 Golden Gate Avenue, between Van Ness Avenue & Polk Street (861 7827/www.stars restaurant.com). Bus 5, 19, 42, 47, 49. **Open** 11.30am-10pm Mon-Tue; 11.30am-11pm Wed-Thur; 11.30am-midnight Fri; 5pm-midnight Sat. **Main courses** lunch $8-$16; dinner $18-$32. **Credit** AmEx, DC, Disc, MC, V. **Map** p310 F4.
Once the hallowed hangout of celebs and big-shot politicos, Stars lost its lustre some years ago when its famed chef departed. Now, after an interior renewal and kitchen brush-up, it's again a bright spot in the local dining sky. The large, handsome restaurant is home to the city's longest bar, where you can get a great Martini. The staff in the exhibition kitchen make fine use of the wood-burning oven, turning out succulent roast chicken, pheasant and quail. The menu changes daily, but usually centres on rustic Mediterranean fare.

Zuni Café

1658 Market Street, between Franklin & Gough Streets (552 2522). Muni Metro F, J, K, L, M, N/ bus 6, 7, 66, 71. **Open** 11.30am-midnight Tue-Sat; 6pm-midnight Sun. **Main courses** $10-$35. **Credit** AmEx, MC, V. **Map** p310 F5.
A quintessential San Fran experience, Zuni is more than 20 years old, yet feels timeless. It serves Cal-Ital food in an art-filled setting; the choice is limited, but the use of the freshest possible ingredients makes it all memorable. For some, sourdough bread and oysters served on an iced platter is enough; others prefer more substantial dishes, such as roast chicken or delicious pizzettas cooked in a wood-fired oven. The plate-glass windows overlooking Market Street bring in light and make Zuni a great place from which to watch the world go by.

European

Carta

1772 Market Street, at Gough Street (863 3516/ www.cartasf.com). Muni Metro F, J, K, L, M, N/ bus 6, 7, 66, 71. **Open** 11.30am-3pm, 5-10.30pm Mon-Thur; 11.30am-3pm, 5pm-midnight Fri; 5pm-midnight Sat; 10am-3pm Sun. **Main courses** lunch $6-$11; dinner $7-$20. **Credit** AmEx, DC, MC, V. **Map** p310 F5.
Every other month, this small, airy restaurant features a different cuisine from around the world. You could find shrimp and coconut ceviche from Guam, or Indonesian gado gado, a vegetable dish topped with peanut sauce. From the American heartland comes cornmeal-dusted onion rings, pan-fried red trout with bacon and mint, and three-cheese macaroni. The restaurant's favourites seem to hail from Tuscany and the Mediterranean. Phone to find out what region it's currently featuring.

Jardinière

300 Grove Street, at Franklin Street (861 5555). Bus 21, 42, 47, 49. **Open** 5-10.30pm Mon-Wed, Sun; 5-11.30pm Thur-Sat. **Main courses** $25-$30. **Credit** AmEx, DC, Disc, MC, V. **Map** p310 F5.
When celebrity chef Traci des Jardin left her post at Rubicon in the late 1990s to open this namesake eatery, she single-handedly revived the city's flagging pre-opera and symphony dining scene. The whimsically shaped restaurant serves starters such a stellar ahi tuna carpaccio and a wonderful lobster and chanterelle salad. The cured pork tenderloin main is legendary; rabbit and quail are seasonally available. Start your meal with a plate of caviar-topped oysters and a fine sparkling wine.

Vegetarian

Millennium

246 McAllister Street, between Hyde & Larkin Streets (487 9800/www.millenniumrestaurant.com). BART Civic Center/Muni Metro F, J, K, L, M, N/bus 5, 19. **Open** 5-9.30pm daily. **Main courses** $12-$18. **Credit** MC, V. **Map** p310 F/G4.
An award-winning, gourmet take on vegetarian dining, upscale Millennium creates dishes that might make you decide to give up meat entirely. Salads are inventive and hearty, and the saffron risotto-stuffed pepper and grilled broccoli rabe

lasagnette are marvellous. One caveat: meat-eaters looking to find a steak replacement might do well to avoid the seitan (a meat substitute made from wheat gluten), which is definitely an acquired taste.

SoMa

American

Bacar

448 Brannan Street, between Third & Fourth Streets (904 4100/www.bacarsf.com). Bus 15, 30, 42, 45, 76. **Open** 11.30am-2.30pm, 5.30pm-1am Mon-Fri; 5.30pm-1am Sat; 4.30-11pm Sun. **Main courses** lunch $8-$14; dinner $16-$38. **Credit** AmEx, DC, MC, V. **Map** p311 H4/5.

Before it had even opened its doors in 2000, Bacar was already everybody's favourite new restaurant. A cork-dork's Valhalla, it has a bigger wine selection than most wine shops, with 1,000 varietals – 100 of them available by the glass. The bottles loom over the guests in a glass-enclosed 'wine wall', the most eye-catching aspect of this remarkable three-level, converted warehouse, which also features a stylish, basement-level lounge. Pair your wine selection with a wood-fired pizza, mesquite-grilled lamb chops or reliably good fish from its approachable mix of American and Mediterranean dishes.

Curve

747 Third Street, between Townsend & King Streets (896 2286). Muni Metro N/bus 15, 30, 42, 45, 76. **Open** 11.30am-9pm daily. **Main courses** $6-$14. **Credit** AmEx, DC, MC, V. **Map** p311 J5.

Local nightclub impresario Johnny Love resurfaced after a long absence to open this restaurant and bar near the ballpark in spring 2001. This place is more sophisticated than his unapologetic party places. The menu has a few bright spots, including the chicken scaloppini served with pancetta chive potato mash, and the seafood risotto with mussels, clams and prawns. Mostly, though, this is an unadventurous spot for burgers and salads before and after the game. Inevitably perhaps, the crowd in the bar (which is open until 2am) curves headlong into a state of sloppy drunkenness.

Paragon

701 Second Street, at Townsend Street (537 9020/www.paragonrestaurant.com). Muni Metro N/bus 15, 30, 42, 45, 76. **Open** 11.30am-2.30pm, 5.30-10pm Mon-Thur; 11.30am-2.30pm, 5.30-11pm Fri; 5.30-11pm Sat. **Main courses** $12-$19. **Credit** AmEx, DC, Disc, MC, V. **Map** p311 J4.

Before baseball games, Paragon is ground zero for fans looking to 'warm up'. They eagerly queue up shoulder to shoulder at the huge bar, and the good-looking dining room is similarly energy-charged (it's quieter on non-game days). The classic American brasserie fare is reliable, but woefully overpriced. Expect steaks and seafood dishes to be served with hearty side orders, such as mashed potatoes and vegetable gratin. There are no home runs on the menu, but there are plenty of base hits.

Choose from 1,000 wines at **Bacar**.

Thirsty Bear Brewing Company

661 Howard Street, between Second & Third Streets (974 0905/www.thirstybear.com). Bus 12, 14, 15, 30, 45, 76. **Open** 11.30am-10.30pm Mon-Thur; 11.30am-midnight Fri; noon-midnight Sat; 5-10pm Sun. **Main courses** lunch $8-$13; dinner $14-$17. **Credit** AmEx, DC, MC, V. **Map** p311 H4.

Gamers, bar flies and diners all enjoy this place, known for its pool tables and dartboards, micro-brewed beers and a rotating selection of good Spanish tapas. The sautéed shrimp and roasted scallops are two standouts. Patrons are often corporate clones from the Financial District out for an after-work beer and a quick meal, but don't let that put you off. This is a casual place where everybody feels at home, and the beers are outstanding.

21st Amendment

563 Second Street, between Bryant & Brannan Streets (369 0900/www.21stamendment.com). Bus 15, 30, 42, 45, 76. **Open** 11.30am-9pm Mon, Tue; 11.30am-10pm Wed-Fri; noon-10pm Sat; noon-9pm Sun. **Main courses** $7-$17. **Credit** AmEx, Disc, MC, V. **Map** p311 H4.

Having a microbrewery this close to the ballpark is, of course, a brilliant idea. But to also make it as good as this one is better still. A big, industrial, open space, with dining on two levels and a large social bar, it's always packed before games and can be difficult to get into. Once you squeeze in, though, you'll happily quaff the excellent house-made brews (the Amendment Pale Ale and Shot Tower Stout are recommended) and find above-average pub grub, such as the savoury Niman Ranch pork chop and pizzas from wood-fired ovens.

Twenty Four

Pacific Bell Park, 24 Willie Mays Plaza, at Third Street (644 0240). Muni Metro N/bus 15, 30, 42, 45, 76. **Open** 5.30-10pm daily; lunch on day games. **Main courses** lunch $7-$15; dinner $15-$28. **Credit** AmEx, MC, V. **Map** p311 J5.

The place is named after the jersey number worn by the Hall-of-Fame Giants player Willie Mays and is located inside the baseball stadium. But if you're dreading a sports bar, you're in for a nice surprise; this large, handsome brasserie serves anything but typical ballpark food. Ambitious starters include baked clams with bacon and an iced shellfish platter that includes oysters, clams and huge prawns. Mains are heavy on steaks and chops, but everything is done with proficiency. Pasta is another peciality; the butternut squash ravioli is a standout. The predominance of customers in ballcaps leads to a relaxed, fine dining experience.

Asian

AsiaSF

201 Ninth Street, at Howard Street (255 2742/ www.asiasf.com). Bus 12, 27, 42, 47. **Open** 5-10pm daily. **Main courses** $10-$18. **Credit** AmEx, DC, Disc, MC, V. **Map** p310 G5.

We'll do you the favour of answering the inevitable question: no, they're not. Not drag queens, that is. Those sexy creatures who bring food to your table and then dance seductively atop the long red bar prefer to be called 'gender illusionists'. Another thing they're not is women, so tread carefully when you're feeling flirty at this fun and novel restaurant. Despite the visual and aural competition, the kitchen produces an inventive and remarkably tasty menu of Cal-Asian cuisine (try the blackened tuna sashimi and the tamarind chicken satay). A restaurant, nightclub and lounge all in one, the crowd here is a compelling mix of local party-goers and wide-eyed businessmen away from the family for a few days.

Azie

826 Folsom Street, at Fourth Street (538 0918/ http://azie.citysearch.com). Bus 12, 30, 45, 76. **Open** 5.30-10.30pm Mon-Wed, Sun; 5.30-11.30pm Thur, Fri; 5-11.30pm Sat. **Main courses** $15-$25. **Credit** AmEx, DC, Disc, MC, V. **Map** p311 H4.

With its lofty ceiling, flowing red drapery, swanky lighting fixtures (always turned to 'dim') and a DJ spinning deep grooves (on Fridays), the mood is always set for a glamorous night. After an ambitious but poorly received start, Azie has settled into a comfort zone serving French-inspired Asian dishes. Specials include grilled breast of duck and leg confit, foie gras-topped Thai snapper with

It's those 'gender illusionists' again at **AsiaSF**.

Calzone's

Distinctive, contemporary Italian Cuisine.
430 Columbus Avenue
415/ 397-3600
www.calzonesf.com

Crab House

AT PIER 39 · SAN FRANCISCO

A mecca for crab lovers.
415/ 434-2722
www.crabhouse39.com

THE STINKING ROSE

A GARLIC RESTAURANT

World famous for tasty dishes even vampires love.
325 Columbus Avenue
415/781-7673
www.thestinkingrose.com

black bean sauce, and tamarind-glazed pork loin. It's one of the best looking restaurants in town, and the food continues to improve.

European

Fringale

570 Fourth Street, between Bryant & Brannan Streets (543 0573/http://fringale.citysearch.com). Bus 15, 30, 42, 45, 76. **Open** 11.30am-3pm, 5.30-10.30pm Mon-Fri; 5.30-10.30pm Sat. **Main courses** lunch $8-$17; dinner $13-$21. **Credit** AmEx, MC, V. **Map** p311 H4/5.

Literally translated, this restaurant's name means 'the urge to eat', and you'll find that desire here. The menu reads classic French, but preparations are informed by chef Gerald Hirigoyen's Basque heritage. Frisée salads, beef carpaccio, lamb sweetbread fricassee; the flavours are definitely French, but with a rural air that cuts their elaborateness and their richness. You'll need to book well in advance and come prepared to sit shoulder to shoulder, but every noisy bite will be worth the trouble. Fringale's sister restaurant, Pastis (1015 Battery Street; 391 2555), is also excellent.

Le Charm

315 Fifth Street, at Folsom Street (546 6128/ www.lecharm.com). Bus 12, 27, 30, 45, 76. **Open** 11.30am-2.30pm, 6-9.30pm Mon-Thur; 11.30am-2.30pm, 6-10pm Fri; 5.30-10pm Sat. **Main courses** lunch $7-$10; dinner $13-$16. **Credit** AmEx, MC, V. **Map** p311 H4.

This rather nondescript little restaurant is actually, as its name suggests, quite charming once you get inside, with its modest decor and friendly staff. It's one of the few places in town where you can enjoy true French bistro fare without going broke doing it. The three-course prix fixe menu ($25) can include such main courses as grilled tuna Provençal, chicken chasseur with pomme fondant and tarragon sauce, or grilled beef brochettes. Try the tarte tatin for dessert. The wine list is tiny, but well chosen.

LuLu

816 Folsom Street, between Fourth & Fifth Streets (495 5775/http://lulu.citysearch.com). Bus 12, 27, 30, 45, 76. **Open** 11.30am-10.30pm Mon-Thur, Sun; 11.30am-11.30pm Fri, Sat. **Main courses** $7-$23. **Credit** AmEx, DC, MC, V. **Map** p311 H4.

Executive chef Jody Denton turns out consistently delicious, rustic, Italian-influenced fare, including wood-fired oven, rôtisserie and grilled specialities, pizzas, pasta and shellfish. Dishes come on large platters that are meant to be shared. The industrial-looking space is usually filled to capacity, so book a table in advance, or take your chance at the bar. But be warned: conversation is difficult in the noisy and crowded room. LuLu's wine bar next door is a more intimate and quieter alternative, with some 70 wines available by the glass. Denton also owns stylish Azie (*see p123*), a couple of doors down the street.

Schnitzelhaus

294 Ninth Street, at Folsom Street (864 4038/ www.schnitzelhaus.net). Bus 12, 27, 42. **Open** 11.30am-2.30pm, 5-10pm Tue-Fri; 5-10pm Sat, Sun. **Main courses** $6-$15. **Credit** MC, V. **Map** p310 G5.

Bring a big appetite and a healthy thirst to this rustic slice of Deutchland by the Bay. The giant steins full of pilsners and lagers that dot the long pinewood tables are the first indication that you probably should be wearing lederhosen. But at least you won't have to yodel to get good service from the lively staff, who happily ply you with enormous portions of bratwurst, wiener schnitzel and a gargantuan Black Forest venison stew.

South Park Café

108 South Park Avenue, between Second, Third, Bryant & Brannan Streets (495 7275). Muni Metro N/bus 15, 30, 42, 45, 76. **Open** 7.30am-10pm Mon-Fri; 6-10pm Sat. **Main courses** lunch $5-$16; dinner $12-$18. **Credit** AmEx, DC, Disc, MC, V. **Map** p311 H/J4.

This ever-popular bistro overlooking South Park is as first-rate as ever. The service is unrushed and attentive, and the light French food satisfies both the local yups and those who arrive from far and wide. The brandade (salt cod) and potato cakes is good, as is the fillet of salmon poached in lemon and coriander broth, and roast chicken with french fries. Classic desserts include crème brûlée and the best profiteroles in town. An excellent spot for a long, relaxed dinner.

XYZ

W Hotel, 181 Third Street, at Howard Street (817 7836). Bus 12, 14, 15, 30, 45, 76. **Open** 6.30am-10.30pm Mon-Thur; 6.30am-11pm Fri; 8am-10.30pm Sat; 8am-2.30pm Sun. **Main courses** lunch $12-$16; dinner $20-$30. **Credit** AmEx, DC, Disc, MC, V. **Map** p311 H4.

Adjacent to the lobby of the swanky W Hotel (*see p42*), XYZ exemplifies trendy dining in San Francisco – this week. The minimalist decor nicely complements chef Jeffrey Amber's inspired seasonal Cal-French cooking. He's skilled at presentation, and although the dishes are too highly priced, they are memorable. The wine list is similarly overpriced, but it offers fine selections by the glass. Have starters and a half-bottle of wine and skip the rest, and you won't feel taken advantage of.

Chinatown

A culinary contradiction is that the best Chinese food in San Francisco is generally found outside Chinatown – in the Richmond District. That said, in addition to the places listed below, several low-profile spots offer good selections of dim sum, potstickers or healthy soups. The almost entirely Chinese crowd at **Dol Ho's** (808 Pacific Avenue; 392 2828) speaks volumes about the food's

Tasty taquerias

You can't swing a piñata stick in the Mission District without hitting a taqueria. These cheap and cheerful places are typically simple and unassuming, with a basic Latin American decor, tiled floors and open-grill kitchens flanked by a counter and a cash register. Order at the counter and carry your burrito or taco to a table, where you'll usually find a variety of hot sauces. While everyone has got their own favourite spot for a big, bursting burrito, here are the places that seem to be on every list. All offer the same basic menu, ranging from tacos at $1.50-$2 each to carne asada plates at $8.

El Farolito

2779 Mission Street, at 24th Street (824 7877). BART 24th Street/bus 14, 26, 48, 49, 67. **Open** 11am-1am Mon-Thur, Sun; 11am-3am Fri, Sat. **No credit cards**. **Map** p314 Y2.

Perhaps the least attractive of the outstanding taquerias, El Farolito is wildly popular for its complimentary crisp warm tortilla chips and fresh salsa. The burritos are mouth-watering, and the quesadillas are worth a look, too. Open into the wee morning hours, this is a popular draw for the dazed, post-clubbing set.

El Toro Taqueria

598 Valencia Street, at 17th Street (431 3351). BART 16th Street/bus 14, 22, 26, 33, 53. **Open** 10am-10pm daily. **Credit** MC, V. **Map** p314 Y1.

El Toro is frequented on weekends by truly devoted fans, who file in for the menudo (tasty, but don't ask the ingredients), an eye-opening traditional soup served with fresh tortillas. The rest of the menu – tacos, tamales and seafood specialities – is equally good. El Toro sets itself apart from the crowd by using fresh ingredients, and eschewing conventional recipes for those that use no lard.

La Taqueria

2889 Mission Street, at 25th Street (285 7117). BART 24th Street/bus 12, 14, 26, 27, 49, 67. **Open** 11am-9pm Mon-Sat; 11am-8pm Sun. **No credit cards**. **Map** p314 Y2.

Widely regarded as the best in town (*pictured*). It's a standard-bearer for the made-to-order burrito, stuffed with fresh carne asada (beef) or carnitas (pork). Try the aguas frescas, refreshing fruit beverages.

Pancho Villa Taqueria

3071 16th Street, at Valencia Street (864 8840). BART 16th Street/bus 14, 22, 26, 33, 53. **Open** 10am-midnight daily. **Credit** AmEx, MC, V. **Map** p314 Y1.

This is one of the more fully fledged taquerias, with a large, modern-looking dining room, an orderly ordering system and an extensive menu that includes such burrito fillings as shrimp and an amazingly good green chilli chicken. The tortillas are also varied, including spinach, tomato and whole wheat versions.

authenticity; **House of Nanking** (919 Kearny Street; 421 1429) is avoided by locals for being too touristy, but the food never disappoints; and **Kowloon** (909 Grant Street; 362 9888) features a good all-vegetarian menu and an ice-cream counter.

American

Alfred's Steak House

659 Merchant Street, between Kearny & Montgomery Streets (781 7058/www.alfredssteakhouse.com). Bus 1, 15, 41, 42. **Open** 5.30-9.30pm Mon, Sun; 11.30am-9.30pm Tue-Thur; 11.30am-9pm Fri; 5.30-9pm Sat. **Main courses** lunch $7-$16; dinner $10-$31. **Credit** AmEx, MC, V. **Map** p309 H3.

After decades in a location that featured its trademark sign above the Broadway tunnel, a few years ago Alfred's pulled up steaks (sorry), and moved to a new location near the Chinese Cultural Center. Loyal patrons eagerly followed, proving that this is still quite possibly the best steakhouse in town. It's a meat-lover's paradise, offering Chicago rib-eyes, tender T-bones and porterhouses that cover the plate. The fish and pasta dishes are also excellent, played close to the traditional vest. The bar prepares one of the best Martinis in town and stocks more than 100 single malts.

Asian

R&G Lounge

631 Kearny Street, at Clay Street (982 7877). Bus 1, 15, 41. **Open** 11am-9.30pm Mon-Thur, Sun; 11am-10pm Fri-Sat. **Main courses** lunch $6-$15; dinner $9-$28. **Credit** AmEx, DC, MC, V. **Map** p309 3H.

Recently completely remodelled and expanded, this two-level restaurant presents authentic Hong Kong-

Taqueria Cancun

2288 Mission Street, at 19th Street (252 9560). Bus 14, 33, 49. **Open** 10am-1am Mon-Thur, Sun; 10am-2am Fri, Sat. **No credit cards**. **Map** p314 Y1.
This place is so popular they've got three locations to satisfy the citywide demand. Grilled chicken, spicy carne asada and a dangerously delicious mojado (with red and green sauces and sour cream) are among the many temptations.
Branches: 1003 Market Street, at Sixth Street, Tenderloin (864 6773); 3211 Mission Street, at Fair Street, Outer Mission (550 1414).

Taqueria La Cumbre

515 Valencia Street, at 16th Street (863 8205). BART 16th Street/bus 14, 22, 26, 33, 53. **Open** 11am-10pm Mon-Sat; noon-9pm Sun. **No credit cards**. **Map** p314 Y1.
La Cumbre has been in the neighbourhood forever, and is jealously defended by Valencia Street hipsters as offering the city's best burrito. The long queue leads to an assembly-line kitchen, where your burrito is created by committee according to your specifications. The *carne asada* is the signature order: tender, flavourful and huge, weighing in at around 3lb (1.5kg).

style food. The emphasis is on seafood, most of which comes direct from in-house tanks, but many other menu items are worth a look, too. All the Cantonese standards are served in big, family-size portions. There's typically a wait for tables, but it seldom lasts long.

Yuet Lee

1300 Stockton Street, at Broadway (982 6020). Bus 12, 15, 30, 39, 41, 45, 83. **Open** 11am-3am Mon, Wed-Sun. **Main courses** $5-$12. **No credit cards**. **Map** p309 G2.
Chefs and restaurant folk are often spotted at this tiny, bright green Chinese eatery, probably because the seafood is excellent and the place stays open until 3am. Worth trying are the roasted squab with fresh cilantro (coriander) and lemon, sautéed clams with black bean sauce and 'eight precious noodle soup', made with eight kinds of meat. The lighting is glaringly unflattering and service matter of fact.

North Beach

American

Cobalt Tavern

1707 Powell Street, at Union Street (982 8123/ www.cobalttavern.com). Bus 15, 30, 41, 45/cable car Powell-Mason. **Open** 5.30-11pm Mon-Fri; 11.30am-11pm Sat, Sun. **Main courses** $16-$22. **Credit** AmEx, MC, V. **Map** p308 G2.
Amid the unwelcome pressure of filling the void left by the demise of the legendary Washington Square Bar & Grill, Cobalt has managed to garner a following all its own by staying the traditional course set by its previous tenant. Drenched in namesake blue, the place can seem sombre, or (depending, perhaps, on how much wine you drink) can be quite romantic; occasional live jazz spruces up the atmosphere. The kitchen plays it safe with hearty pork chops, roast

★NOW MORE THAN 3,000 REVIEWS BY OUR CRITICS★

Time Out
New York
2002 GUIDE

Eating & Drinking

Your complete annual guide to the city's best restaurants and bars

Available now

for only $11.95

For information, check out timeoutny.com

chicken and leg of lamb. It's done solidly and without pretence; locals wouldn't have it any other way. Visit for Sunday brunch.

Jianna

1548 Stockton Street, between Union and Green Streets (398 0442/www.jinna.com). Bus 15, 30, 39, 41, 45. **Open** 5.30-11.30pm Mon-Sat; 5.30-11pm Sun. **Main courses** $17-$23. **Credit** AmEx, DC, Disc, MC, V. **Map** p309 G2.

An overwhelming success since it opened a couple of years ago, Jianna serves what executive chef Marc Valiani calls 'evolving American' cuisine. It seems a fair description, as the dishes on his menu are rooted in the American tradition – pork chops, seared duck breast, New York steak with blue cheese – and all come with unexpected touches (the duck is served with Chinese broccoli and fried rice, for example). Fresh oysters, mussels and chilled prawns are typical starters. The dining room strikes a nice balance between a casual ambience and the sort of sophistication that comes with knowing you have more than 150 wines on your list.

Moose's

1652 Stockton Street, between Union & Filbert Streets (989 7800/www.mooses.com). Bus 15, 30, 39, 41, 45. **Open** 11.30am-10pm Mon-Thur; 11.30am-11pm Fri, Sat; 10am-10pm Sun. **Main courses** $11-$27. **Credit** AmEx, DC, MC, V. **Map** p308/309 G2.

Long-time restaurateurs Ed and Mary Etta Moose create environments that are uniquely San Franciscan. A full bar, an open kitchen serving consistently good California cuisine and an extensive wine list are the draws here; and, regardless of changes to the menu over time, the storeyed Mooseburger persists, as does the excellent Sunday brunch. This place is a popular stomping ground for local celebs, high-profile business types and big-ego politicos. Unfortunately, unless you're famous, the service can be uneven.

Asian

House

1230 Grant Avenue, at Columbus Avenue & Vallejo Street (986 8612/www.thehse.com). Bus 15, 30, 41, 45. **Open** 11.30am-10pm Tue-Thur; 11.30am-11pm Fri, Sat. **Main courses** lunch $8-$14; dinner $13-$21. **Credit** AmEx, DC, MC, V. **Map** p309 G2.

A welcome respite from the sometimes overwhelming number of Italian spots in the area, this no-frills (though often loud and clangy) Chinese fusion dining room works wonders with fresh, seasonal produce and East-meets-West preparations. The Chinese chicken salad with sesame-soy illustrates the menu; light and tangy and big enough to be a meal all on its own. The menu changes frequently, but happily resists fickle trends. And, like most things on the menu, wines are rock-bottom priced. There's a branch in the Sunset District (*see p140*).

European

Enrico's

504 Broadway, at Kearny Street (982 6223/www.enricossidewalkcafe.com). Bus 12, 15, 30, 41, 83. **Open** 11.30am-11pm Mon-Thur, Sun; 11.30am-12.30am Fri, Sat. **Main courses** lunch $9-$12; dinner $14-$23. **Credit** AmEx, Disc, MC, V. **Map** p309 G2.

Enrico's is a quintessential North Beach hangout. The outdoor patio has prime people-watching and live jazz bands playing most nights. Pizzas baked in wood-fired ovens are among the top draws, but the kitchen also ably cranks out savoury pasta, meat and fish. It's all served up in a noisy, friendly environment with a long wooden bar at one end.

L'Osteria del Forno

519 Columbus Avenue, at Union Street (982 1124/www.bstudio.com/osteria). Bus 15, 30, 41, 45/cable car Powell-Mason. **Open** 11.30am-10pm Mon, Wed, Thur, Sun; 11.30am-10.30pm Fri, Sat. **Main courses** $5-$17. **No credit cards**. **Map** p308 G2.

With just 30 seats, this is one of the great little secrets of North Beach, and usually very busy. The tables are jumbled in next to one another and the staff are welcoming – and quite aware of their restaurant's romantic European sensibility. The able kitchen serves treats from a wood-fired brick-oven; the trademark thin-crust pizzas with fresh toppings are notable. The daily made pasta and fresh fish dishes are typically wonderful and well priced.

Tommaso's Ristorante Italiano

1042 Kearny Street, at Broadway (398 9696). Bus 12, 15, 30, 41, 45, 83. **Open** 5-11pm Tue-Sun. **Main courses** $8-$20. **Credit** AmEx, DC, MC, V. **Map** p309 G2.

San Francisco's beloved Mayor Willie Brown walked in without fanfare recently and sat alone for a late-night lasagne dinner. It's that kind of place: no affectation, no frills, just good, family-style Italian food in a tiny, boisterous dining room. The wood-fired pizzas and calzones are among the best in town. The surprisingly good house red wine is served in ceramic jugs. If you're looking for a break from trendy Italian eateries, this is the place. Reservations are not accepted, so join the queue – and keep your eyes peeled: you never know who might walk in.

US Restaurant

515 Columbus Avenue, at Green Street (397 5200/www.originalusrestaurant.com). Bus 15, 30, 41, 45. **Open** 11am-9pm Tue-Thur, Sun; 11am-10pm, Fri-Sat. **Main courses** $8-$14. **Credit** AmEx, DC, Disc, MC, V. **Map** p308/309 G2.

Rising from the ashes of a temporary closure in 1997, this is once again one of the few places where you can find a true slice of historic North Beach. Named after the Unione Sportiva, an Italian sports club active on this block when the restaurant originally opened in 1919, it is rich with that sort of custom. The menu features rib-sticking fare from

Northern Italy, such as bollito (boiled beef) and rib-eye steak. The portions are huge, and the service is downright familial.

Middle Eastern

The Helmand

430 Broadway, between Kearny & Montgomery Streets (362 0641). Bus 12, 15, 30, 41, 83. **Open** 5.30-10pm Mon-Thur, Sun; 5.30-11pm Fri, Sat. **Main courses** $11-$16. **Credit** AmEx, MC, V. **Map** p309 G/H2.

The Helmand consistently appears on lists of recommended eateries, partly because the city has so few Afghani restaurants, but also because the food is inexpensive and deliciously aromatic. The recipes are influenced by the flavours of India, Asia and the Middle East; marinades and fragrant spices give each dish a unique character. The pumpkin ravioli with leek sauce (when available) is exquisite, as is koufta challow, a dish of tender lamb meatballs in a cinnamon-spiked tomato sauce. The formal dining room belies the reasonable prices on the menu.

Fisherman's Wharf

European

Gary Danko

800 North Point Street, at Hyde Street (749 2060/ www.garydanko.com). Bus 19, 30, 42/cable car Powell-Hyde. **Open** 5.30-9.30pm Mon-Wed, Sun; 5.30-10pm Thur-Sat. **Prix fixe menus** $55-$74. **Credit** AmEx, DC, Disc, MC, V. **Map** p308 F1.

Critics lined up to hand out stars to Gary Danko even before he opened his self-named, 75-seat restaurant, and it turns out praise was in order. Danko (whose credentials include a James Beard award for Best Chef in California) has created a fabulous – and fabulously understated – spot for fine dining. The best way to experience Danko's dexterity and genius is via the tasting menus, which might include such delicacies as duck prosciutto and foie gras *au torchon* starter, with Moroccan-spiced squab or pan-steamed pheasant breast with leg confit as a main. If you don't want to go all in, a more casual adventure can be found at the bar.

Lapis

Pier 33, Embarcadero, at Bay Street (982 0203). Muni Metro F/bus 15, 42. **Open** 11.30am-2.30pm, 5.30-10pm Mon-Thur; 11.30am-2.30pm, 5.30-11pm Fri; 5.30-11pm Sat. **Main courses** lunch $7-$17; dinner $17-$29. **Credit** AmEx, DC, MC, V. **Map** p309 G1.

Lapis is one of the few places in town that takes the descriptive term 'Mediterranean' literally. With a menu swayed by the techniques and flavours of Spain, Italy, Greece, Turkey, France and northern Africa, it's like a culinary circle tour of that great European sea. Most of the dishes are made with equal skill, although the Greek items (spicy lamb kebab, filo-wrapped artichokes) are the strongest. The restaurant has caught on as much for its setting as for its fare. The smooth-looking, modernist interior brings in a hip crowd, but the waterfront location, with the edge of the bay lapping at the floor-to-ceiling windows, is the central attraction.

Seafood

Alioto's

8 Fisherman's Wharf, at Taylor & Jefferson Streets (673 0183 /http://aliotos.citysearch.com). Muni Metro F/bus 39, 42. **Open** 11am-11pm daily. **Main courses** lunch $7-$19; dinner $15-$34. **Credit** AmEx, DC, Disc, MC, V. **Map** p308 F1.

Alioto's began as a sidewalk stand offering crab and shrimp cocktails served in a paper cup. Now, 70 years later, it is a hugely popular restaurant owned by a prominent San Francisco family. It offers an amazing view of the bay – and of the hordes of tourists fighting their way in. The kitchen turns out fine, though expensive, seafood prepared any way you desire, as well as fish-centred Sicilian specialities. The wine list is outstanding.

A Sabella's

Third floor, 2766 Taylor Street, at Jefferson Street (771 6775/www.asabella.com). Muni Metro F/bus 39, 42. **Open** 5.30-10.30pm daily. **Main courses** $14-$34. **Credit** AmEx, DC, MC, V. **Map** p308 F/G1.

Fisherman's Wharf has its share of pirates, but Sabella's remains one of those fighting for what's good and right in the sea of culinary tricksters. Family-owned for four generations, the restaurant takes great pride in its food and attentive service. The huge dining room, with great bay views, is comfortable for kids and adults. All the seafood is impossibly fresh and prepared with the Sicilian flair the family brought to San Francisco in 1887. Wait while fresh local Dungeness crab and lobster are cooked for you, or try the *cioppino* for a real taste of local cuisine. Although the menu is not restricted to just seafood (pasta and steak are worthwhile as well), it would be a shame to pass it up when it's done this well.

Russian Hill, Nob Hill & Polk Gulch

Asian

Sushi Groove

1916 Hyde Street, between Union & Green Streets, Russian Hill (440 1905/www.sfstation.com/ sushigroove). Bus 41, 45/cable car Powell-Hyde. **Open** 5.30-10pm Mon-Thur, Sun; 5.30-10.30pm Fri, Sat. **Main courses** sushi $3-$8; plates $13-$16. **Credit** AmEx, DC, Disc, MC, V. **Map** p308 F2.

An inventive, techno-flavoured sushi restaurant, with a rich, postmodern decor, Sushi Groove's

Enjoy wood-fired pizzas at **Tommaso's** in North Beach. *See p129.*

booming drum 'n' bass mood music and original rolls and salads attract a stylishly dressed clientele, who don't seem to mind the elbow-to-elbow seating in the postage stamp-sized dining room. Fresh crab, sea urchin and eel join traditional favourites such as mackerel, tuna and salmon; most of it's very good, although some misses the mark. The impressive sake selection is itself worth a trip up Hyde Street.

European

Acquerello

1722 Sacramento Street, between Van Ness Avenue & Polk Street, Polk Gulch (567 5432/www.acquerello.com). Bus 1, 42, 49, 76/cable car California. **Open** 5.30-10.30pm Tue-Sat. **Main courses** $27-$31. **Credit** AmEx, Disc, MC, V. **Map** p308 F3.

Blink and you might miss this unassuming, off-the-beaten-path restaurant. But once you do find it, it could very well become your favourite – especially if you're a hopeless romantic. The dining room, with its big bold floral arrangements and rustic, exposed-beam pitched ceiling, has a secluded charm. But there's nothing covert about chef and co-owner Suzette Gresham's vital, contemporary Italian food. Salads and pastas are light, but never wimpy. The lamb chops, served with risotto, are delightful, and the wine list has earned numerous awards.

Antica Trattoria

2400 Polk Street, at Union Street, Polk Gulch (928 5797). Bus 19, 41, 45, 49, 76. **Open** 5.30-11pm Tue-Sun. **Main courses** $8-$18. **Credit** DC, MC, V. **Map** p308 F2.

While Italian restaurants are a dime a dozen in San Francisco, this wood-floored gem stands out for its gorgeous simplicity and commitment to culinary quality. Antica is Italian-owned, its surroundings are casual, the mood is unpretentious, its food is great and the wine list is long. Rustic grilled meat and fish dishes set the tone, while the frequently changing pasta creations are hard to resist.

The Dining Room

Ritz-Carlton Hotel, 600 Stockton Street, at California Street, Nob Hill (773 6198). Bus 1, 30, 45/cable car California. **Open** 6-9.30pm Mon-Sat. **Prix fixe menus** $43-$69. **Credit** AmEx, DC, Disc, MC, V. **Map** p308 G3.

The place that puts the 'fine' in fine dining, the Ritz-Carlton's Dining Room is San Francisco's most honoured restaurant. Its reputation is known the world over, and eating here is nothing short of an event; the waiting-staff-to-diner ratio is close to 1:1. Opulent, but not over the top, the room is refined if a bit too serious. More elegance is found in Sylvain Portay's modern French food, all inventively imagined and artfully executed. His prix fixe menus thankfully steer clear (mostly) of lobster-and-caviar obviousness. Master sommelier Stephane Lacroix will ably guide you through appropriate libations.

La Folie

2316 Polk Street, between Union & Green Streets, Polk Gulch (776 5577/www.lafolie.com). Bus 19, 41, 42, 45, 47, 49, 76. **Open** 5.30-10pm Mon-Sat. **Main courses** $30-$45. **Credit** AmEx, DC, Disc, MC, V. **Map** p308 F2.

Bay Area dining

The greater Bay Area's dining scene is as good as San Francisco's, with a plethora of culinary options a hop, skip and a jump away across either the Bay Bridge or the Golden Gate Bridge.

In Berkeley, **Chez Panisse** – where chef/owner Alice Waters created California cuisine way back in the 1970s – continues to reign supreme, serving a formal prix fixe menu downstairs in the restaurant and a more casual, à la carte menu in the upstairs café. Ingredients are fresh, local, organic and of the very best quality, and the excellent wine list is French and Californian. Also in Berkeley, **Rivoli** is a small, French-inspired restaurant run by talented chef Wendy Brucker. The menu changes every three weeks, but three dishes always remain: portabello mushroom fritters (the Rivoli's signature dish), Caesar salad and a great hot fudge sundae.

In Oakland, chef Paul Bertoli, formerly of Chez Panisse, has brought its savvy reputation to **Oliveto**, his traditional northern Italian restaurant; the house speciality is house-cured, grilled and rotisseried meats. Also in Oakland, the **Bay Wolf**, opened by Michael Wild in 1975, serves a blend of

California and Mediterranean food using the freshest produce available. Try a Liberty Ranch duck with parsnip pancake and ginger-pear compote, followed by poached quince and pistachio gallette with Riesling sabayon.

Further afield, the wine country also has some outstanding restaurants. In the tiny town of Yountville in Napa Valley, about an hour's drive from San Francisco, you'll find one of the best restaurants in the whole of the US: the **French Laundry**, run by chef/owner Thomas Keller. A prix fixe meal for two will set you back a couple of hundred dollars, with wine, but it's worth it – every bite is nothing short of sensational. Book ahead two

Chef Roland Passot enjoys a passionate following at his delightful French-Californian eatery. The prices are steep, but the cooking is exquisite. Opt for the five-course discovery menu ($75, includes soup, appetiser, sorbet, entrée and dessert), which allows you to sample such dishes as lobster and albacore salad, roti of quail and squab or a trio of rabbit (loin, rack and braised). The Provençal decor and attentive staff add to La Folie's charm. The extensive wine list remains under the aegis of Passot's brother, Georges.

Zarzuela

2000 Hyde Street, at Union Street, Russian Hill (346 0800). Bus 41, 45/cable car Powell-Hyde. **Open** 5.30-11pm Tue-Sat. **Main courses** $7-$13. **Credit** MC, V. **Map** p308 F2.

Zarzuela features authentic Spanish cuisine in a cosy restaurant filled with posters of bull fights and maps of Spain. The tapas are always a treat, but old stand-bys, such as grilled aubergine (eggplant) filled with goat's cheese, sautéed shrimps in garlic and olive oil, and fried potatoes with garlic and sherry vinegar, never disappoint. When all else fails to inspire, go with the paella, done here as well as any place in town. Parking is impossible; take a cab or walk over Russian Hill.

Seafood

Pesce

2227 Polk Street, between Green & Vallejo Streets, Polk Gulch (928 8025). Bus 19, 41, 42, 45, 47. **Open** 5-11pm Mon-Thur; 5pm-midnight Fri, Sat. **Main courses** $7-$15. **Credit** AmEx, MC, V. **Map** p308 F2.

This simple seafood restaurant and bar is wildly popular with locals, who love the fact that they have a place nearby that proves seafood does not have to be fancy or expensive to taste fab. Starters include excellent mussels, cod cakes and calamari. Fish mains tend to have an Italian-inspired preparation. The room is modest and comfy, so you won't feel insecure about making a mess with your *cioppino*.

Swan Oyster Depot

1517 Polk Street, between California & Sacramento Streets, Polk Gulch (673 1101). Bus 1, 19, 42, 47, 49, 76/cable car California. **Open** 8am-5.30pm Mon-Sat. **Main courses** $5-$15. **No credit cards**. **Map** p308 F3.

A San Francisco institution since 1912, the Depot is half fish market and half counter-service hole in the wall. The best time of year to visit is between November and June, when the local Dungeness months to the day you want to eat, and call early. If you can't get a table there, try pretty **Tra Vigne** (*pictured*), set behind ivy-covered walls in nearby St Helena, for traditional Italian cuisine with a spicy Californian flair.

Bay Wolf

3853 Piedmont Avenue, at Rio Vista Avenue, Oakland (1-510 655 6004/ www.baywolf.com). BART MacArthur, then AC Transit bus 57. **Open** 11.30am-2pm, 6-9.30pm Mon-Fri; 5.30-9.30pm Sat, Sun. **Main courses** lunch $11-$16; dinner $16-$21. **Credit** AmEx, MC, V.

Chez Panisse

1517 Shattuck Avenue, between Cedar & Vine Streets, Berkeley (1-510 548 5525/ www.chezpanisse.com). BART Berkeley, then AC Transit bus 7, 9. **Open** 11.30am-10.30pm Mon-Thur; 11.30am-11.30pm Fri, Sat. **Main courses** $13-$22; prix fixe menus $45 Mon, $65 Tue-Thur, $75 Fri, Sat. **Credit** AmEx, DC, Disc, MC, V. **Map** p315 L2.

French Laundry

6640 Washington Street, Yountville (1-707 944 2380/www.sterba.com/ yountville/frenchlaundry). **Open** 5.30-9.30pm Mon-Thur; 11am-1pm, 5.30-9.30pm Fri-Sun. **Prix fixe menus** lunch $50; vegetarian $80; dinner $105; chef's menu $120. **Credit** Amex, MC, V.

Oliveto Café & Restaurant

5655 College Avenue, at Shafter Avenue, Oakland (1-510 547 5356/www.oliveto.com). BART Rockridge. **Open** *Café* 7am-10pm Mon-Fri; 8am-10pm Sat; 8am-9pm Sun. *Restaurant* 11.30am-2.30pm, 5.30-9pm Mon; 11.30am-2.30pm, 5.30-9.30pm Tue; 11.30am-2.30pm, 5.30-10pm Wed-Fri; 5.30-10pm Sat; 5-9pm Sun. **Main courses** lunch $5-$15; dinner $10-$28. **Credit** AmEx, DC, MC, V.

Rivoli

1539 Solano Avenue, between Neilson Street & Peralta Avenue, Berkeley (1-510 526 2542/www.rivolirestaurant.com). BART El Cerrito, then AC Transit bus 67. **Open** 5.30-9.30pm Mon-Thur; 5.30-10pm Fri; 5-10pm Sat; 5-9pm Sun. **Main courses** $15-$18. **Credit** AmEx, Disc, MC, V.

Tra Vigne

1050 Charter Oak Avenue, St Helena (1-707 963 4444/www.travignerestaurant.com). **Open** 11.30am-10.30pm daily. **Main courses** $12-$32. **Credit** DC, Disc, MC, V.

crab is in season. But at any time of year you'll find the selections are straight-from-the-water fresh. Specialities include classic clam chowder, the smoked salmon plate and an obscenely large variety of oysters. You can also buy shellfish to take away – a good option if the place is too crowded. The staff are boisterous and friendly.

The Mission

American

Delfina

3621 18th Street, between Dolores & Guerrero Streets (552 4055). Muni Metro J/bus 33. **Open** 5.30-10pm Mon-Thur, Sun; 5.30-11pm Fri, Sat. **Main courses** $12-$19. **Credit** MC, V. **Map** p314 Y1.

Chef Craig Stoll was all over the local press after the opening of his charming little restaurant a few years ago. Which explain why this is now a charming big restaurant. In an era of fusion-food madness, and rarefied recipes, Stoll keeps it simple. But don't confuse simple with ordinary; his fresh-made pasta, fish and braised meats are bursting with flavour. This is one place where you actually want to order the chicken. The menu changes daily, reflecting Stoll's desire to stay on his toes. Unfortunately, the staff doesn't always possess the same ambition.

Gordon's House of Fine Eats

500 Florida Street, at Mariposa Street (861 8900/ www.gordons.com). Bus 27. **Open** 11.30am-10pm Mon, Sun; 11.30am-11pm Tue-Thur; 11.30am-midnight Fri; 5.30pm-midnight Sat. **Main courses** $9-$28. **Credit** Disc, MC, V. **Map** p314 Z1.

A modern outpost in the nether regions of the Mission/Potrero Hill, Gordon's nonetheless has little trouble attracting customers. The menu is divided into categories such as Healthful, Comfort and Local Favourites. There's something to like in each section, but the cornflake fried chicken, pan-fried sand dabs and the lamb T-bone steak are standouts. Service is genial, if a bit impatient. The dessert menu is hard to resist; when was the last time you had a plate piled high with freshly made doughnuts?

Luna Park

694 Valencia Street, at 18th Street (553 8584/ www.lunaparksf.com). BART 16th Street/bus 14, 26, 33, 49. **Open** 11.30am-2.30pm, 5.30-11.30pm Mon-Thur; 11.30am-2.30pm, 5.30pm-midnight Fri-Sat; 11.30am-2.30pm, 5.30-10.30pm Sun. **Main courses** $9-$14. **Credit** AmEx, MC, V. **Map** p314 Y1.

Swan Oyster Depot: serving the freshest oysters and shellfish since 1912. *See p132.*

This modish little room on Valencia Street, built into the site of a former butcher's shop, has been a hit since day one. The concept is obvious: no-nonsense fare at good prices in an environment that makes people want to linger. Its diminutive size – just 50 seats – doesn't deter locals from queuing; the bar catches the spillover, becoming a highly charged lounge scene. Once you get a table, expect swift, courteous service and an accessible selection of hearty dishes, including such favourites as flatiron steak and french fries, braised lamb shank and grilled sea bass with asparagus.

Pauline's Pizza

260 Valencia Street, between Duboce Avenue & 14th Street (552 2050). Bus 14, 26, 49. **Open** 5-10pm Tue-Sat. **Main courses** $12-$21. **Credit** MC,V. **Map** p310 F6.

Unassuming Pauline's specialises in inventive, thin-crust pizzas made with top-quality produce. This is gourmet pie, with ingredients like roasted peppers, goat's cheese, edible flowers and exotic vegetables. Complement your main course with an organic salad or home-made soup. The original headquarters of Levi Strauss occupies the yellow, saloon-type building next door.

Slow Club

2501 Mariposa Street, at Hampshire Street (241 9390/www.slowclub.com). Bus 9, 22, 27, 33, 53. **Open** 11.30am-2.30pm, 6.30-10pm Mon-Thur; 11.30am-2.30pm, 6.30-11pm Fri; 10am-2.30pm, 6.30-11pm Sat; 10am-2.30pm Sun. **Main courses** lunch $7-$10; dinner $9-$17. **Credit** MC, V. **Map** p311 G6.

This is a true local spot, in part because of its remote locale, but also because people just love to hang out here. Slow Club's laid-back atmosphere and understated charm make it seem one of the coolest restaurant/bars in town. The dinner menu changes nightly. Typical mains include marinated steamed mussels, roasted chicken breast, grilled ahi and flatiron steak. They don't accept reservations, but your wait is made tolerable by the cosy bar area.

Universal Café

2814 19th Street, between Bryant & Florida Streets (821 4608). Bus 27. **Open** 5.30-10pm Mon-Thur; 5.30-11pm Fri; 9am-2.30pm, 5.30-11pm Sat; 9am-2.30pm Sun. **Main courses** lunch $7-$10; dinner $14-$24. **Credit** AmEx, DC, MC, V. **Map** p314 Z1.

The Universal Café was one of the first upmarket spots to open in this area, near what became the epicentre of the Mission's techno-based gentrification. It has held its own with an understated, industrial-look dining room and fresh, interesting food. It's a great spot for a weekend breakfast, when you can enjoy potato pancakes at an outside table; lunch features focaccia sandwiches, salads and tiny pizzas. Dinner brings higher prices, but a decent menu, too, with the likes of fresh pasta, oven-roasted meat and grilled fish. If you're in the area, don't miss it.

Asian

Slanted Door

584 Valencia Street, at 17th Street (861 8032). BART 16th Street/bus 14, 22, 26, 49, 53. **Open** 11.30am-10pm Tue-Sun. **Main courses** lunch $7-$15; dinner $12-$27. **Credit** MC, V. **Map** p310 F6.

Two words: shaking beef. Order it, and you'll be hooked. If you love Vietnamese food, this place could spoil you for all others. Chef Charles Phan lets his California location influence his otherwise authentic preparations. The aforementioned dish has earned popular accolades, but it is by no means the only trick up Phan's sleeve. Such dishes as the spicy short ribs, the shrimp-and-crab spring rolls and the tangy papaya salad are equally notable, and Phan's crêpes are loved the city over. The coolly modern room is usually crowded; be prepared to shout over the din to talk with your dining companions.

European

Fina Estampa

2374 Mission Street, between 19th & 20th Streets (824 4437). BART 16th Street/bus 14, 22, 33, 49, 53. **Open** 11.30am-3.30pm, 5-9pm Tue-Sun. **Main courses** $4-$10. **Credit** MC, V. **Map** p314 Y1.

There's not much to this little Mission eatery – just some faux wood panelling and tattered tablecloths. But that doesn't seem to bother the legion of fans who queue to get in. The menu is heavily Spanish with excellent tapas, but the house speciality is *antichucos*, the Peruvian national dish made with marinated beef hearts served in a zesty chilli sauce (surprise: it's very good). The paella and the fried calamari are other reliable favourites.

Branch: 1100 Van Ness Avenue, at Geary Street, Western Addition (440 6343).

Foreign Cinema

2534 Mission Street, between 21st & 22nd Streets (648 7600). Bus 14, 49. **Open** 6-11pm Tue-Sat; 5.30-10pm Sun. **Main courses** $18-$37. **Credit** AmEx, MC, V. **Map** p314 Y2.

After opening to the kind of fanfare usually reserved for a visit by the Pope, Foreign Cinema has settled in as one of San Francisco's fave dining destinations. The decor is dominated by films screened on a bare wall on one side of the outdoor dining room. Drive-in movie-style speakers are on each table for those who want to listen. Still, the food is the star of the show here. Specialities include pancetta-wrapped chicken breast, Provençal stew of prawns, halibut and scallops, and a tender rack of lamb that simply falls from the bone. Everything works here.

Ti Couz Crêperie

3108 16th Street, at Valencia Street (252 7373/ www.ticouz16.com). BART 16th Street /bus 14, 22, 26, 33, 49, 53. **Open** 11am-11pm Mon-Wed; 11am-midnight Thur, Fri; 10am-midnight Sat; 10am-11pm Sun. **Main courses** $2-$10. **Credit** MC, V. **Map** p310 F6.

You'll find all walks of urban life at this modest crêperie, along with the best crêpes in town. Made captivatingly before your eyes in the classic Breton tradition, the crêpes are either buckwheat or sweet. From there, you select fillings and flavours to your heart's content. They offer more than 100 varieties, from smoked salmon to ham to lemon and brown sugar. Ti Couz Two is next door, an expansion that also offers seafood and has a full bar.

Latin American

El Nuevo Frutilandia

3077 24th Street, between Folsom & Treat Streets (648 2958). BART 24th Street/bus 12, 48, 67. **Open** 11.30am-3pm, 5-9pm Tue-Thur; 11.30am-3pm, 5-10pm Fri; noon-10pm Sat; noon-9pm Sun. **Main courses** $6-$13. **Credit** MC, V. **Map** p314 Z2.

Specialising in Cuban and Puerto Rican food, this tiny, noisy eatery near Balmy Alley dishes up appetisers such as dumplings stuffed with chicken, meat-filled plantain and yucca fritters, as well as *higado a la Frutilandia*, a succulent concoction of calf's liver cooked with green peppers and onions in a spicy sauce. Vegetarian dishes include yucca with garlic, black beans and rice.

The Castro & Noe Valley

American

Chow

215 Church Street, at Market Street (552 2469). Muni Metro F, J, K, L, M/bus 22, 37. **Open** 11am-11pm Mon-Thur, Sun; 11am-midnight Fri, Sat. **Main courses** $6-$9. **Credit** MC, V. **Map** p310 E6.

As the name suggests, this is a simple, no-gimmick spot for good food. Its location in the heart of the Castro ensures the clientele is fun and vivacious, but who wouldn't be happy with food this good, at prices this low? Unadorned American fare such as roast chicken, burger and fries and short ribs share the menu with more 'exotic' selections such as Asian bok-choy noodles. Portions are enormous.

Branch: Park Chow, 1240 Ninth Avenue, at Lincoln Way, Sunset District (664 3664).

John Frank

2100 Market Street, at Church Street (503 0333/ www.johnfrankrestaurant.com). Muni Metro F, J, K, L, M/bus 22, 37. **Open** 6-10pm Mon-Thur, Sun; 6-11pm Fri, Sat. **Main courses** $16-$24. **Credit** AmEx, MC, V. **Map** p310 E6.

If you're looking for a little more atmosphere, try this stylish corner restaurant named after its two owners. With its sleek lines, low ceiling, stainless-steel bar and thoughtful lighting, the place has big-city sophistication without the fussiness. But the best part is the Modern American cuisine, which is consistently excellent – even inspired. Specialities include pan-roasted salmon with ham and corn succotash, and the very comforting, slow simmered Niman Ranch pot roast, full of English peas and baby carrots. A daily, three-course prix fixe menu is available for the bargain price of $25.

Mecca

2029 Market Street, at Dolores & 14th Streets (621 7000/www.sfmecca.com). Muni Metro F, J, K, L, M/ bus 37. **Open** 6-11pm Mon-Thur, Sun; 6.30pm-midnight Fri, Sat. **Main courses** $12-$32. **Credit** AmEx, DC, MC, V. **Map** p310 E6.

Big, bustling and utterly fashionable, this restaurant has become the de facto headquarters of the Castro cuisine scene – and not undeservedly. The food strikes a harmonious accord with its surroundings: modern, well-conceived and reliably tasty. Chef Mike Fennelly's whims range from straightahead pork chops to an unexpected (yet forgettable) portobello tempura with spicy tofu, cabbage and Chinese vegetable salad. Meanwhile, back at the bar, the mood becomes ever looser as the evening progresses and the stylised cocktails flow.

Asian

Alice's

1599 Sanchez Street, at 29th Street (282 8999/ http://alicesrestaurant.citysearch.com). Muni Metro J/ bus 24, 26. **Open** 11am-9.15pm Mon-Thur; 11am-10pm Fri, Sat; noon-9.15pm Sun. **Main courses** $7-$9. **Credit** MC, V.

Off the beaten track in Noe Valley, but worth the trek, Alice's serves spicy Hunan and Mandarin cooking in a clean, airy setting. Asparagus salmon in a black bean sauce or the delicate orange beef are favourite main courses; a plate of spicy fried string beans will sear you in the best possible way. Reasonable prices and punctual (if a little dull) service complete the experience. You'll probably have to wait a while before you're seated.

The Haight & around

Asian

Eos Restaurant

901 Cole Street, at Carl Street, Haight-Ashbury (566 3063/www.eossf.com). Muni Metro N/bus 37, 43. **Open** 5.30-9.30pm Mon-Thur; 5.30-10pm Fri, Sat; 5-9pm Sun. **Main courses** $17-$28. **Credit** AmEx, MC, V. **Map** p313 C6.

This comfortably spare, highly designed restaurant presents the best of East-West fusion by classically trained chef/owner Arnold Eric Wong. Dishes such as trumpet mushrooms on a chow mein noodle cake in a velvety, heirloom tomato sauce, and lamb garnished with cherry chutney are backed up by one of the best wine lists in the Bay Area. The same menu – as well as the restaurant's delightful dessert platter – is served in the small wine bar next door.

Mifune

Japan Center, 1737 Post Street, between Webster & Buchanan Streets, Japantown (922 0337). Bus 2, 3, 4, 22, 38. **Open** 11am-9.30pm Mon-Thur, Sun; 11am-10pm Fri, Sat. **Main courses** $8-$12. **Credit** AmEx, DC, Disc, MC, V. **Map** p310 E4.

Fun for all at **Mecca**.

Mifune's speciality is the lowly noodle, prepared in at least 30 different ways. Orders come quickly, inexpensively and deliciously to your table. It's a good place to take kids, and also great for vegetarians who can get their protein from seaweed, egg or miso. Mifune's motto is: 'It's okay to slurp your noodles', so be as noisy as you like.

Sanppo

1702 Post Street, at Buchanan Street, Japantown (346 3486). Bus 2, 3, 4, 22, 38. **Open** 11.30am-midnight daily. **Main courses** $5-$9. **Credit** MC, V. **Map** p310 E4.

For nearly 25 years, this small, casual restaurant opposite the Japan Center has been turning out consistently good, rustic Japanese food – soups, lightly battered tempura, fresh fish and East-West salads – all at just the right price. The service is charming, and so is the restaurant.

Seoul Garden

22 Peace Plaza, Geary Boulevard, at Buchanan Street, Japantown (563 7664/www.seoulgarden bbq.com). Bus 2, 3, 4, 22, 38. **Open** 11am-midnight daily. **Main courses** $6-$20. **Credit** AmEx, MC, V. **Map** p310 E4.

At Seoul Garden, grill the marinated beef at your table and try the myriad little dishes that typically make up Korean cuisine. A good place to consider when all the Japanese restaurants in the neighbourhood are too crowded for comfort.

Thep Phanom

400 Waller Street, at Fillmore Street, Lower Haight (431 2526). Bus 6, 7, 22, 66, 71. **Open** 5.30-10.30pm daily. **Main courses** $5-$9. **Credit** AmEx, DC, Disc, MC, V. **Map** p310 E5.

Possibly the best Thai restaurant in San Francisco, Thep Phanom draws rave reviews from around the country, all of which contribute to the inevitable evening queue. If you're smart, you'll make reservations; if you're brilliant, you'll order the *tom ka gai* (coconut chicken soup) as a starter. The 'angel wings' – fried chicken wings stuffed with glass noodles – are universally popular.

European

Absinthe

398 Hayes Street, at Gough Street, Hayes Valley (551 1590/www.absinthe.com). Bus 21, 42, 47, 49. **Open** 11.30am-1am Tue-Fri; 10.30am-1am Sat; 10.30am-10.30pm Sun. **Main courses** lunch $9-$22; dinner $15-$25. **Credit** AmEx, DC, MC, V. **Map** p310 F5.

In turn-of-the-20th-century France, absinthe was outlawed as a poisonous libation. In turn-of-the-following-century San Francisco, it has been reborn as a popular brasserie. The restaurant has a grand feel that is maybe just a little bit forced, but there is little coerciveness in chef Ross Browne's mostly French menu. His are among the best coq au vin and cassoulet in town. Try the veal sweetbreads or the seafood platter to start. And while you still can't get absinthe here, you can find 'Death in the Afternoon', a head-spinning combo of Pernod and champagne.

Suppenküche

601 Hayes Street, at Laguna Street, Western Addition (252 9289/ www.suppenkuche.com). Bus 21. **Open** 5-10pm Mon-Sat; 10am-2.30pm Sun. **Main courses** brunch $7-$10; dinner $9-$16. **Credit** AmEx, MC, V. **Map** p310 F5.

If you're craving the polar opposite of California cuisine, Suppenküche is a good choice. Its menu (including spätzle, schnitzels and dense, dark breads) is authentically German. The fresh ingredients can seduce a person into a love affair with sauerkraut and then draw them to commit to a relationship with sweetbreads, hearty salads and soups. German beers are served in tall steins, and the seating is on benches at bare pine tables.

Latin American

Terra Brazilis

602 Hayes Street, at Laguna Street, Western Addition (241 1900). Bus 21. **Open** 5.30-10pm Tue-Thur; 5.30-11pm Fri, Sat; 5.30-10pm Sun. **Main courses** $8-$10. **Credit** AmEx, DC, Disc, MC, V. **Map** p310 F5.

This splendid restaurant on Hayes Streets, with its large picture windows and local art on the walls, opened with one of the city's only all-Brazilian menus, but now offers dishes from Ecuador, Guatemala, Venezuela and Mexico, too. The rich, savoury (and highly calorific) menu includes Bahian chicken and rock shrimp sautée; churrasco (annatto paste-marinated steak) with yucca, collard greens and chimchurri sauce; and *moqueca de mariscos*, a hearty shellfish stew. The traditional Brazilian flan is out of this world.

The Marina & around

American

Elite Café

2049 Fillmore Street, at California Street, Pacific Heights (346 8668). Bus 1, 3, 22. **Open** 5-11pm Mon-Sat; 10am-3pm, 5-10pm Sun. **Main courses** $17-$28. **Credit** AmEx, DC, Disc, MC, V. **Map** p307 E3.

This handsome Fillmore Street stalwart has withstood every cuisine trend and restaurant fashion that the neighbourhood – and, indeed, the city – could throw at it. The locals still queue up for the marvellous Creole- and Cajun-inspired seafood, served by smiling, white-aproned staff. It offers authentic gumbo, the New Orleans stew made with celery, carrots, onions, sausage and crawfish. Other specialities include Cajun-style filet mignon and seafood chowder. All dishes have a pronounced Louisiana accent, except the sourdough bread and those from the icy oyster bar. There's a great Cajun brunch on Sunday mornings, complete with one of the best Bloody Marys in town.

Harris'

2100 Van Ness Avenue, at Pacific Avenue, Pacific Heights (673 1888/www.harrisrestaurant.com). Bus 12, 42, 47, 49, 83. **Open** 5.30-9.30pm Mon-Fri; 5-10pm Sat; 5-9pm Sun. **Main courses** $17-$38. **Credit** AmEx, DC, Disc, MC, V. **Map** p308 F3.

Unchanged for decades, Harris' offers the kind of old-style dining your great-uncle would have loved. Sink into your booth, start with a strong cocktail, then proceed with a Caesar salad (made at your table), steak and a baked potato with all the trimmings and, of course, a hefty dessert. The beef is dry-aged for 21 days. If red meat from the West Coast isn't your style, go east: try an Atlantic salmon, grilled or poached with champagne sauce or a steamed whole Maine lobster with clams.

Sadly, they don't serve absinthe at **Absinthe**. *See p137.*

PlumpJack Café

3127 Fillmore Street, between Greenwich & Filbert Streets, Cow Hollow (563 4755/www.plumpjack.com). Bus 22, 28, 41, 43, 45, 76. **Open** 11.30am-2pm, 5.30-10.30pm Mon-Fri; 5.30-10.30pm Sat. **Main courses** lunch $7-$15; dinner $14-$28. **Credit** AmEx, DC, MC, V. **Map** p307 E2.

Following the success of PlumpJack Wines down the street, this high-profile restaurant opened in 1994 as a testament to the blending of new ideas and old money. Dashing owner Gavin Newsom is on the Board of Supervisors, his partner is the son of magnate Gordon Getty, and their special-occasion eatery is a centrepiece for outstanding California cuisine. Chef James Ormsby has a penchant for doing interesting things with seafood and Mediterranean recipes. An extensive, inexpensive wine list culls the best from the wine shop.

Asian

Betelnut

2030 Union Street, between Webster & Buchanan Streets, Cow Hollow (929 8855/www.betelnut.com). Bus 22, 41, 45. **Open** 11.30am-11pm Mon-Thur, Sun; 11am-midnight Fri, Sat. **Main courses** $5-$18. **Credit** MC, V. **Map** p307 E2.

Despite the generally fickle attitude of its neighbourhood, this cool-looking restaurant has managed to retain its popularity. Probably, it's due to its relatively exotic South Pacific concept and consistent execution. Once you get past the brusque greeting up front, you can squeeze into the crowd of beautiful people at the bar. When you reach your table, you'll find that the menu is made for grazing. Order lots of small plates, such as tea-smoked duck, braised short ribs, papaya salad and spicy minced chicken and pine nuts served in lettuce cups.

European

Baker Street Bistro

2953 Baker Street, between Lombard & Greenwich Streets, Cow Hollow (931 1475/www.bakerstbistro.citysearch.com). Bus 28, 41, 43, 45, 76. **Open** 7am-2pm, 5.30-10.30pm Tue-Fri; 10am-2.30pm, 5.30-10.30pm Sat; 10am-2.30pm Sun. **Main courses** lunch $6-$11; dinner $10-$13. **Credit** AmEx, Disc, MC, V. **Map** p307 D2.

Tucked away on a out-of-sight stretch of Baker Street near the Palace of Fine Arts, this little gem oozes French charm. With wooden floors, lots of sunlight and a temperate outdoor patio, the restaurant has a loyal clientele as much for its looks as for its great food and unbelievable prices. The three-course prix fixe menu is $14.50. Appetisers include warm goat's cheese salad, and escargot and scallop mousseline. Recommended mains are Sonoma rabbit in Dijon mustard sauce, and a fabulous lamb stew.

Chez Nous

1911 Fillmore Street, at Pine Street, Pacific Heights (441 8044). Bus 1, 3, 22. **Open** 11.30am-3pm, 5.30-10pm Tue-Sun. **Main courses** $3-$9. **Credit** MC, V. **Map** p307 E3.

This small neighbourhood eatery is seemingly always crowded, sometimes frustratingly so. But take that as a recommendation, because the people are here for the delicious, small, tapas-like plates of Mediterranean food. The monthly changing menu is typified by options such as Moroccan spiced duck confit, mussels with *pommes frites*, and luscious salad Niçoise. Breads are unbelievably fresh, imported from the owner's bakery around the corner. If a table takes too long, ask to sit at the bar.

Florio

1915 Fillmore Street, between Bush & Pine Streets, Pacific Heights (775 4300). Bus 1, 3, 22. **Open** 5.30-10pm Mon-Fri; 5.30-11pm Fri, Sat. **Main courses** $18-$37. **Credit** AmEx, MC, V. **Map** p307 E4.

A quintessential neighbourhood bistro, Florio is warm and welcoming, with just the right degree of refinement. Dark wood and white tablecloths set the tone for the classic food influenced by French rural cooking. The steak frites and the roast chicken and fries are the best choices, always soul-warming on a foggy evening. The lobster bisque is also rich and reliable. The full menu is also available at the small bar at the front.

Jackson Fillmore

2506 Fillmore Street, at Jackson Street, Pacific Heights (346 5288). Bus 1, 3, 22. **Open** 5.30-10pm Mon-Sat; 5-10pm Sun. **Main courses** $10-$17. **Credit** AmEx, MC, V. **Map** p307 E3.

Perched at the top of a Pacific Heights hill, this always-packed neighbourhood fave has a formula so successful it's a wonder more places don't imitate it. A plain, kitchen-like dining room with vinyl checked tablecloths, the attention here is not on aesthetics, but on the food. The rustic Italian dishes are consistently good, especially the garlic-roasted chicken and the daily changing risotto. There's not much imagination from the kitchen, just good old-fashioned flavour and great value. Meals begin with (free) warm, delicious bruschetta and usually end a few bottles of well-priced wine later.

Restaurant Isa

3324 Steiner Street, between Chestnut & Lombard Streets,. Marina (567 9588). Bus 22, 28, 30, 43, 76. **Open** 5-10pm Tue-Thur, Sun; 5-10.30pm Fri, Sat. **Main courses** $5-$16. **Credit** AmEx, DC, MC, V. **Map** p307 D2.

At this Marina district discovery, French-meets-Spanish with a tapas-like menu. The interesting kitchen turns out ragout of veal sweetbreads and potato galette, roast mussels with shallots and white wine, and hanger steak with tarragon mustard and roast garlic potatoes. The place is charmingly cosy and devoid of the prevailing neighbourhood affectation. Make your way to the back patio for a truly secluded dining experience.

Vegetarian

Greens

Building A, Fort Mason Center, Marina Boulevard, at Buchanan Street, Marina (771 6222). Bus 28. **Open** 5.30-9.30pm Mon, Fri; 11.30am-2pm, 5.30-

Taste the South Pacific at **Betelnut**. *See p138.*

9.30pm Tue-Thur, Sat; 10am-2pm Sun. **Main courses** lunch $8-$12; dinner $14-$19. **Credit** Disc, MC, V. **Map** p307 E1.
Located in Fort Mason, and with a great view of the Golden Gate Bridge and an award-winning, all-vegetarian menu, Greens, despite its occasionally spacey service, keeps its reputation sterling. Fresh produce and an extensive wine list complement mesquite-grilled vegetables and wood-fired pizzas topped with wild mushrooms. Take advantage of the takeaway counter for sandwiches and soups if you don't want to queue for a table.

The Richmond District

American

Q Restaurant

225 Clement Street, at Second Avenue (752 2298). Bus 1, 2, 33, 38. **Open** 11.30am-3pm, 5-11pm Mon-Fri; 10am-3pm, 5-11pm Sat; 5-10pm Sun. **Main courses** lunch $7-$11; dinner $7-$14. **Credit** MC, V. **Map** p312 B4.
Squeezed into a tiny storefront along a nondescript section of Clement Street, this friendly, delightful restaurant serves up some of the best comfort food in town. The name comes from its early ambition as a barbecue joint, but the kitchen expanded its repertoire to include grilled steaks and seafood, pasta and quite possibly the best fried chicken in the city. The ribs are always a nice option, and the daily specials are worth a look, too. A good wine list and the funky, eclectic decor round out this outstanding find.

Asian

Kabuto

5116 Geary Boulevard, between 15th & 16th Avenues (752 5652). Bus 2, 28, 38. **Open** 5.30-11pm Tue-Sat; 5.30-10pm Sun. **Main courses** $9-$15; sushi $2.50-$10. **Credit** MC, V. **Map** p312 A4.
Out on Geary Boulevard, miles from the restaurants of Japantown, Kabuto's nondescript exterior disguises the excellent raw fish that is sold within. San Francisco restaurateurs have been spotted at this tiny sushi bar, so you know that the fish is fresh. Eschew the few tables and grab a seat at the sushi bar, where the chefs will give you a show – and a meal – you won't forget.

Khan Toke

5937 Geary Boulevard, between 23rd & 24th Avenues (668 6654). Bus 2, 29, 38. **Open** 5-10.30pm daily. **Main courses** $8-$12. **Credit** AmEx, DC, MC, V.
Slip off your shoes and choose a seat on the floor – on a low chair with a padded back support – in one of the city's most attractive (and overlooked) Thai restaurants. Fiery and colourful curries and excellent noodle dishes can be accompanied by a good selection of Sauvignon Blancs.

Mayflower

6255 Geary Boulevard, at 27th Avenue (387 8338). Bus 2, 29, 38. **Open** 11am-2.30pm, 5-9.30pm Mon-Fri; 10am-2.30pm, 5-9.30pm Sat, Sun. **Main courses** lunch $5-$8; dinner $8-$12. **Credit** MC, V.
This large, noisy and family-oriented Cantonese restaurant on Geary Boulevard is consistently good. Seafood is the house speciality, but the kitchen never disappoints, with several clay pot dishes as well as roast chicken or duck. Mongolian beef is another perennial favourite. Arrive after 8pm if you want to avoid the hordes of families.

Ton Kiang

5821 Geary Boulevard, between 22nd & 23rd Avenues (387 8273/http://tonkiang.citysearch.com). Bus 2, 29, 38. **Open** 10.30am-10pm Mon-Thur; 10.30am-10.30pm Fri; 10am-10.30pm Sat; 9am-10.30pm Sun. **Main courses** $7-$24. **Credit** AmEx, DC, MC, V.
This restaurant serves the traditional Chinese gypsy cuisine *hakka*. Among the authentic items are salt-baked chicken served with a paste made of ground garlic and ginger, and fresh cod fillets sautéed with black bean sauce. Around Chinese New Year (usually February), the restaurant features a delicious special menu of seasonal delicacies.

European

Chapeau!

1408 Clement Street, at 15th Avenue (750 9787/http://bistrochapeau.citysearch.com). Bus 1, 2, 28, 38. **Open** 5-10pm Tue-Thur, Sun; 5-10.30pm Fri, Sat. **Main courses** $14-$19. **Credit** AmEx, DC, Disc, MC, V. **Map** p312 A4.
If you're wondering why they'd call a restaurant 'Hat!', the owners say the exclamation point gives the French word a meaning more akin to 'Wow!' It makes sense, as you're likely to be quite taken by this charmer, where the modest bistro decor and friendly staff create a homely ambience. The Provençal French fare is equally comforting, with excellent coq au vin, onion soup and duck a l'orange. They serve a fine Sunday brunch – a good time to explore the extensive bubbly list.

The Sunset District

American

House

1269 Ninth Avenue, between Irving Street & Lincoln Way (682 3898/www.thehse.com). Muni Metro N/bus 6, 43, 44, 66. **Open** 11.30am-10pm Tue-Thur; 11.30am-11pm Fri; 5-11pm Sat; 5-10pm Sun. **Main courses** lunch $8-$14; dinner $13-$21. **Credit** AmEx, DC, MC, V. **Map** p312 B6.
Chef Larry Tse is a graduate of the California Culinary Academy and runs two restaurants, each showcasing exemplary fusion food at fantastic prices. Inside a cool, high-ceilinged room, diners

enjoy dishes such as fillet of grilled sea bass with miso soy sauce accompanied by mashed potato, or buttermilk calamari with chives, served with a side order of bean sprout salad. Soft-shell crabs arrive tempura style. Desserts run the gamut from exotic sorbets to flourless chocolate cake. The branch in North Beach (*see p129*) is worth a visit, too.

PJ's Oyster Bed

737 Irving Street, between Eighth & Ninth Avenues (566 7775). Muni Metro N/bus 6, 43, 44, 66.
Open 5-10pm Mon-Thur, Sun; 5-11pm Fri, Sat. **Main courses** $12-$20. **Credit** AmEx, DC, MC, V. **Map** p312 B6.
A noisy, friendly neighbourhood seafood restaurant, PJ's dishes out some of the freshest and most authentic Cajun food in San Francisco. Seafood selections are displayed on ice (the place used to be a fish-market) and oysters are shucked to order. Portions are generous and the restaurant is always packed. The jovial chef, sporting Mardi Gras beads, eventually slips out from the kitchen to jaw with his customers. If you're looking for dinner on a budget, enjoy a bowl of PJ's clam chowder and a salad.

Asian

Ebisu

1283 Ninth Avenue, between Irving Street & Lincoln Way (566 1770/http://ebisu.citysearch.com). Muni Metro N/bus 6, 43 44, 66. **Open** 11.30am-2pm, 5-10pm Mon-Thur; 11.30am-2pm, 5pm-midnight Fri; 11.30am-midnight Sat; 11.30am-10pm Sun. **Main courses** lunch $7-$15; dinner $10-$19; sushi $3-$6. **Credit** AmEx, DC, MC, V. **Map** p312 B6.
Considered by many to be the best sushi bar in town, Ebisu might as well be Japanese for 'long wait'. As soon as you arrive, register your name on the list and have a drink in the bar while you await your table. Once seated, try the selection of house specialties – 'pink Cadillac' (salmon sushi roll), albacore tatake, seafood salad, '49er roll – none will let you down. The more conservative can opt for salmon, tuna or cooked eel. As good as Ebisu's sushi is, their traditional Japanese food – tempura, sesame chicken and so on – is worth forgoing the raw stuff for.

Cafés

San Franciscans have no trouble whiling away a morning or afternoon over giant lattes or power-packed espressos. So populated are the city's numerous cafés, it's a wonder any work ever gets done here at all. Avoid ubiquitous Starbucks and head for the city's unique, one-off establishments. North Beach is ground zero for cafés, thanks to its Italian and beatnik heritage, but in this city of distinct neighbourhoods, you'll find a coffee-house on nearly every corner. Everybody's got their favourite, and asking the advice of locals on which to choose will yield as many different answers as people you ask.

The definition of the word 'café' is a hazy one. It can mean anything from a place serving just coffee and pastries to somewhere you can have a full meal and a bottle of wine.

Café Claude: they shipped it all the way from Paris. *See p142.*

Union Square & around

Arabi

Rincon Center, 101 Spear Street, at Mission Street, Embarcadero (243 8575). BART Embarcadero/Muni Metro F, J, K, L, M, N/bus 2, 7, 9, 14. **Open** 7am-2.30pm Mon-Fri. **No credit cards**. **Map** p309 J3.
Rincon Center is a riot of activity in the day, with office workers milling about in search of sustenance. Lately, many have discovered this marvellous little notch at the bottom of a skyscraper. Serving such specialities as shawerma (pita bread sandwich with a meat filling) and tabouleh, as well as salads and small plates, you can take a culinary trip to the Middle East in 20 minutes.

Café Claude

7 Claude Lane, between Sutter & Bush Streets, Kearny Street & Grant Avenue, Union Square (392 3515/www.cafeclaude.com). BART Montgomery Street/Muni Metro F, J, K, L, M, N/bus 2, 3, 4, 15, 30, 45, 76. **Open** 11.30am-10.30pm Mon-Sat. **Credit** AmEx, Disc, MC, V. **Map** p309 H3.
The story is now legendary: owner Stephen Decker purchased Le Barbizon café in Paris and shipped it over one piece at a time. The result is a real slice of France, from setting and service to its little alleyway locale. Signature dishes such as cassoulet and *mousse au chocolat* maintain the delightful illusion.

Café de la Presse

352 Grant Avenue, at Bush Street, Union Square (398 2680/www.cafedelapresse.com). Bus 2, 3, 4, 15, 30, 45, 76. **Open** 7am-11pm daily. **Credit** AmEx, DC, Disc, MC, V. **Map** p309 G3.
This place near the Chinatown gateway exemplifies San Francisco's cosmopolitan temperament. Catering to the many nationalities that stream through its door, it stocks a variety of foreign newspapers and magazines. Celebs filming in San Francisco tend to find their way here, as do fashion industry mavens staying at the swanky Hotel Triton (*see p34*) next door.

Café De Stijl

1 Union Street, at Front Street, Embarcadero (291 0808). Muni Metro F/bus 42. **Open** 6.30am-5pm Mon-Fri; 8.30am-2.30pm Sat. **No credit cards**. **Map** p309 H2.
Named after the early 20th-century Dutch art movement, De Stijl is a rarity: it offers easy parking, pavement seating and hearty food with a Middle Eastern flair. Try the chicken sandwich with tahini or a mixed platter complete with baba ganoush, tabouleh and kibbeh (ground lamb patty).

Caffè Kuleto

Villa Florence Hotel, 221 Powell Street, at Geary Street, Union Square (397 7720). BART Powell Street/Muni Metro F, J, K, L, M, N/bus 5, 6, 7, 21, 30, 31, 38, 45, 66, 71/cable car Powell-Hyde or Powell-Mason. **Open** 7am-11pm Mon-Fri; 8am-11pm Sat, Sun. **Credit** AmEx, DC, Disc, MC, V. **Map** p311 G4.
A great choice for refuelling while shopping around Union Square. This humble annexe of the popular Kuleto restaurant offers eye-opening coffee drinks, as well as fresh juices and house-made Italian pastries. For lunch, you'll find pizza by the slice, panini sandwiches, antipasto salads and desserts such as tiramisu, brownies and gelato.

Cheesecake Factory

Eighth floor, Macy's, 251 Geary Street, at Stockton Street, Union Square (391 4444/www.thecheesecakefactory.com). BART Powell Street/Muni Metro F, J, K, L, M, N/bus 2, 3, 4, 15, 30, 38, 45, 76/cable car Powell-Hyde or Powell-Mason. **Open** 11am-11pm Mon-Fri; 11am-12.30am Sat; 10am-11pm Sun. **Credit** AmEx, DC, Disc, MC, V. **Map** p311 G4.
Inside Macy's department store, this place is big enough to be a factory, while its menu is long enough to be considered for novel status. It's got everything from cheeseburgers to cappuccino, turkey sandwiches to tiramisu. There are more than 30 varieties of the namesake dessert, including such quirky flavours as Oreo cookie and carrot cake.

Saigon Sandwich Café

560 Larkin Street, between Turk & Eddy Streets, Civic Center (474 5698). Bus 5, 19, 31. **Open** 7am-4.30pm Mon-Sat; 7.30am-4.30pm Sun. **No credit cards**. **Map** p310 F4.
This Civic Center lunch spot is popular with workers in the many nearby government buildings, who file in for huge sandwiches at rock-bottom prices. The

Buds and suds at **Brainwash**. *See p143.*

bare-bones menu features Vietnamese-influenced sandwiches, such as five-spice chicken or roast pork topped with a sweet-and-sour sauce of chillis and coriander. The meatball sandwich is great – and big enough for two.

SoMa

There's also a decent café at **SFMOMA** (*see p107*), which is a good place for lunch after you've exhausted yourself looking at art.

Brainwash

1122 Folsom Street, at Seventh Street (861 3663/www.brainwash.com). Bus 12, 19, 27, 42. **Open** 8am-midnight Mon-Thur; 8am-1am Fri; 7.30am-1am Sat; 7.30am-midnight Sun. **Credit** MC, V. **Map** p311 G5.

It's a launderette. It's a bar. It's a café. It's a performance space. Brainwash is all of the above, located in a quirky industrial structure in the middle of the SoMa youth hostel area. The simple menu includes soups, salads and burgers. Live bands play, spoken-word artists and comedians take their stand and DJs spin (all ages, no cover) along with the laundry most nights of the week. It's also a great pick-up spot.

The Butler & the Chef Café

155A South Park, at Third Street (896 2075). Bus 15, 30, 45, 76. **Open** 7.30am-6pm Mon-Fri; 10am-4pm Sat. **Credit** MC, V. **Map** p311 H4.

This oh-so-Gallic pavement café on sunny South Park always has a tempting mound of toothsome sandwiches made with Boulangerie Bay Bread (*see p176*) – ideal for munching in the park. Breakfast on pain au chocolat or sip a Pernod while chatting with Pierre, the amiable owner. And everything's for sale, from the sweet little Calvados glasses to the old bistro chairs on which you're parked. The Butler & the Chef also has a warehouse crammed full of French antiques and collectibles (*see p163*).

Caffè Centro

102 South Park, at Jack London Place, between Bryant & Brannan Streets (882 1500). Bus 15, 30, 42, 45, 76. **Open** 7am-5pm Mon-Fri; 9am-4pm Sat. **Credit** MC, V. **Map** p311 H/J4.

Now that the queues of earnest dotcommoners no longer snake out the door of this long-time favourite South Park haunt, the mix of friendly service, fresh soups, salads and sandwiches (much of it made with organic produce) once again attracts a quirky mix of local residents, creative types and other workers. Large windows open on to the park, and the proximity of interesting shops (Jeremy's, Interieur Perdu, William Stout) is an added attraction.

Town's End Restaurant & Bakery

2 Townsend Street, at Embarcadero (512 0749). Muni Metro N/bus 15, 42. **Open** 7.30am-9pm Tue-Sat; 8am-2.30pm Sun. **Credit** AmEx, DC, MC, V. **Map** p311 J4.

This modern-looking place near the ballpark is one of the area's few breakfast spots. Most of the patrons live nearby or are picking up sandwiches for the game. The baked goods are the highlight, but weekend breakfasts have been picking up steam of late.

Chinatown

Imperial Tea Court

1411 Powell Street, at Broadway (788 6080/ www.imperialtea.com). Bus 15, 30, 39, 41, 45/ cable car Powell-Mason. **Open** 11am-6.30pm Mon, Wed-Sun. **Credit** AmEx, MC, V. **Map** p308 J2.

There is no better place in the city for tea. This serene, wood-panelled, bird-chirping, tea house seemingly offers all the tea in China. The endless assortment of rare and fine teas – brought to your table in beautiful, ornate pots – includes tikuanyin, fancy dragon well, silver needles and snow water. Teas are available to take away, too.

North Beach & Polk Gulch

Bob's Donut Shop

1621 Polk Street, at Sacramento Street, Polk Gulch (776 3141). Bus 1, 19, 42, 47, 49/cable car California. **Open** 24hrs daily. **No credit cards**. **Map** p308 F3.

This no-frills, round-the-clock joint has been the salvation of many a Polk Street nightclubber. But the amazing and consistently good doughnuts are not just for midnight snacks; they make great pick-me-ups in the morning as well. Good coffee, too.

Caffè Puccini

411 Columbus Avenue, at Vallejo Street, North Beach (989 7033). Bus 12, 15, 30, 41. **Open** 6am-12.30am daily. **No credit cards**. **Map** p309 G2.

Be prepared to listen to opera at Graziano Lucchese's place. He's from the same town as the composer after whom he named his intimate North Beach café. The sandwiches, stuffed with prosciutto, mortadella and salami, are outstanding, while the antipasto plate is ample enough for two.

Caffè Trieste

601 Vallejo Street, at Grant Avenue, North Beach (392 6739/http://caffetrieste.citysearch.com). Bus 12, 15, 30, 41, 45, 83/cable car Powell-Mason. **Open** 6.30am-11pm Mon-Thur, Sun; 6.30am-midnight Fri, Sat. **No credit cards**. **Map** p309 G2.

One of the city's great cafés. A Beat-era landmark, it was the espresso bar of choice for Jack Kerouac and Allen Ginsberg. Within walking distance of City Lights bookshop (*see p165*), its dark walls are plastered with photos of opera singers and other famous regulars. There are muffins, pastries, sandwiches and wonderfully potent lattes. Don't miss the opera sessions on Saturday afternoons.

La Boulange de Polk

2310 Polk Street, at Green Street, Polk Gulch (345 1107). Bus 19, 42, 47, 49. **Open** 7am-7pm Tue-Sun. **No credit cards**. **Map** p308 F2.

Best brunches

Brunch in San Francisco is not so much a weekend activity as a ritual. Legions file from their homes on Saturday or Sunday morning, comfy clothes on, newspaper tucked beneath the arm, in search of a plate full of pancakes, a hearty omelette, eggs Benedict or just a stiff Bloody Mary. There are numerous options for brunch – some places serve during the week, too – but the following are the tried and true of the local brunch bunch.

Dottie's True Blue Café

522 Jones Street, at O'Farrell Street, Tenderloin (885 2767). Bus 27, 38. **Open** 7.30am-3pm Mon, Thur-Sun. **Main courses** $4-$7. **Credit** Disc, MC, V. **Map** p310 G4.
This tiny and always busy breakfast spot near Union Square is a quaint slice of Americana, complete with checked tablecloths and a Formica counter-top. Arrive early to avoid the inevitable queue (you can't book), especially at the weekends. All the standards are here, including French toast, giant pancakes and eggs any way you want them. Everything comes with flour tortillas and home fries. The lunch short list features sandwiches and burgers that will last all afternoon.

Ella's

500 Presidio Avenue, at California Street, Presidio Heights (441 5669/ www.ellassanfrancisco.com). Bus 1, 3, 4, 43. **Open** 7am-9pm Mon-Fri; 9am-2pm Sat, Sun. **Main courses** breakfast & lunch $3-£10; dinner $6-$17. **Credit** AmEx, MC, V. **Map** p313 D4.
On weekends, an endless line of patient yuppies marks this stylish and comfy Presidio Heights institution (*pictured*). Brunch is a classic American affair with a gourmet twist. The chicken hash with eggs and toast is a favourite, as is the potato scramble with pea sprouts, mushrooms, roasted garlic and manchego cheese. The huge pancakes are arguably the best in town. A recent expansion has done little to diminish the length of the queue.

Kate's Kitchen

471 Haight Street, between Fillmore & Webster Streets, Lower Haight (626 3984). Bus 6, 7, 22, 66, 71. **Open** 8am-3pm Mon-Fri; 9am-4pm Sat, Sun. **Main courses** $4-$8. **No credit cards**. **Map** p310 E5.

The unofficial brunch spot for the denizens of the Lower Haight. A recent change in ownership has thankfully done little to diminish either quality or, more important, quantity. Portions are huge, whether it's a big bowl of granola or an omelette that must contain a dozen eggs. Hush puppies are a signature dish. The long line moves quickly.

Mama's on Washington Square

1701 Stockton Street, at Filbert Street, North Beach (362 6421). Bus 15, 30, 39, 41, 45. **Open** 8am-3pm Tue-Sun. **Main courses** $5-$9. **No credit cards**. **Map** p308 G2.

The weekend wait is part of the fun at this North Beach fixture, with its mix of locals and tourists milling about perusing newspapers and the menu. Once seated, you'll be faced with such tempting choices as the delicious Monte Cristo sandwich or a giant made-to-order omelette.

Miss Millie's

4123 24th Street, between Diamond & Castro Streets, Noe Valley (285 5598). Bus 24, 35, 48. **Open** 6-10pm Tue-Sun; 9am-2pm Sat, Sun. **Main courses** $4-$8. **Credit** MC, V. **Map** p314 X2.

Famed for its lemon ricotta pancakes and hearty brunch fare, this quaint Noe Valley favourite seems to hail from a bygone era. They serve consistently great French toast, omelettes and classic American fare; vegetarians will delight in the curried tofu scramble. Typically crowded, the best seats for brunch are at the outdoor patio tables.

Sears Fine Foods

439 Powell Street, between Sutter & Post Streets, Union Square (986 1160). Bus 2, 3, 4, 30, 38, 45, 76/cable car Powell-Hyde or Powell-Mason. **Open** 7am-2.30pm daily. **Main courses** $4-$10. **No credit cards**. **Map** p309 G3.

Pancakes come in 18 different varieties at this archetypal American diner. And service comes with a smile from the seasoned staff, who are used to greeting the crowd of mostly tourists. If pancakes don't tempt, try a Denver omelette or a big stack of sourdough French toast topped with fresh preserves.

Few places in town so thoroughly evoke the feel of a Parisian boulangerie as this little place on Polk Street. The pavement tables are highly coveted, which is understandable: they're a great place to enjoy a fresh brioche, croissant or quiche while watching the locals amble by.

Mario's Bohemian Cigar Store

566 Columbus Avenue, at Union Street, North Beach (362 0536/www.bsfweb.com/mariosin northbeach. htm). Bus 15, 30, 39, 41, 45/ cable car Powell-Mason. **Open** 10am-midnight Mon-Sat; 10am-11pm Sun. **No credit cards**. **Map** p308 G2.

Located on the edge of Washington Square Park, Mario's offers a light menu of focaccia sandwiches and salads, beer and coffee drinks. It's always packed and lunch may be slow in coming, but you'll find no more essential North Beach café. Despite its name, you won't find a cigar in sight, nor will you be allowed to smoke one.

Branch: 2209 Polk Street, between Vallejo & Green Streets, Polk Gulch (776 8226).

Steps of Rome

348 Columbus Avenue, between Green & Vallejo Streets, North Beach (397 0435). Bus 12, 15, 30, 41, 45, 83/cable car Powell-Mason. **Open** 8.30am-2am daily. **Credit** (dinner only) MC, V. **Map** p309 G2.

Steps of Rome's huge windows are usually open, providing excellent seats for people-watching. Open till 2am, it's often filled with party-goers staving off the next day's hangover or making a pit stop before heading to an after-hours club in SoMa. It's ideal for a caffeine break and a quick dessert.

XOX Truffles

754 Columbus Avenue, between Greenwich & Filbert Streets, North Beach (421 4814/www. xoxtruffles.com). Bus 12, 15, 30, 39, 41/cable car Powell-Mason. **Open** 8am-8pm Mon-Sat. **Credit** AmEx, Disc, MC, V. **Map** p308 G2.

It's all truffles all the time at Jean-Marc Gorce's North Beach shop. Honoured as one of the top ten chocolate-makers in the US, his tiny, colourful shop has a devoted following. He makes his truffles fresh every day – including white chocolate, hazelnut-coated, coconut-coated and vegan soy versions – with a wild variety of fillings. Grab a coffee and sit inside or at the pavment tables.

Zero Degrees

490 Pacific Avenue, at Montgomery Street, North Beach (788 9376). Bus 12, 15, 30, 42, 83. **Open** 7am-7pm Mon-Thur; 7am-1am Fri, Sat. **Credit** AmEx, DC, Disc, MC, V. **Map** p309 H2.

Probably the most stylish place in town for a cup of coffee, this is a snack and aperitif-only offshoot of the nearby MC2 restaurant. You'll find soups, light sandwiches and house-made ice-cream, as well as an impressive assortment of high-end tequilas and single malts. An enormous flatscreen plasma TV provides an ambient glow.

Grab an outside table at **Caffè Centro** in sunny South Park. *See p143.*

Fisherman's Wharf

Boudin Sourdough Bakery & Café

156 Jefferson Street, between Mason & Taylor Streets, Fisherman's Wharf (928 1849/ www.boudinbakery.com). Muni Metro F/bus 39, 42/cable car Powell-Mason. **Open** 7.30am-8pm Mon-Fri; 7.30am-9pm Sat, Sun. **Credit** AmEx, MC, V. **Map** p308 G1.

Legend has it that sourdough bread was invented in San Francisco. The Boudin family has been making it here since 1849; they have numerous outlets in the Bay Area, and even a few in Chicago. This bakery-cum-café is a relaxing alternative to the many frenetic crab and seafood stands in Fisherman's Wharf's. Try the sourdough pizzas, or the clam chowder, which is served in a fresh-baked, hollowed-out, sourdough bowl, as are the salads. **Branches**: throughout the Bay Area.

The Mission & the Casto

There's a host of good cafés and restaurants in the Castro, many popular with a queer clientele. For details, *see p235.*

Atlas Café

3049 20th Street, at Alabama Street, Mission (648 1047). Bus 27. **Open** 7am-10pm Mon-Fri; 8am-10pm Sat; 8am-8pm Sun. **No credit cards**. **Map** p314 Z1.

The comfy funk of this unassuming café represents the Mission at its best. A daily list of grilled sandwiches – including many vegetarian specialities – along with fresh soups and salads is chalked on the wall; order yours and grab a sunny seat in the patio at the back (where dogs are allowed).

Café Commons

3161 Mission Street, at Precita Avenue, Mission (282 2928). BART 24th Street/bus 12, 14, 26, 27, 67. **Open** 6am-5pm Mon-Fri; 8am-5pm Sat, Sun. **No credit cards**.

Located in a limbo area between the Mission and Bernal Heights, this comfy café is worth finding for its home-made soups and sandwiches. It has a decidedly relaxed, neighbourhood feel. Grab something from the stack of magazines (almost always current) and head for the sun-drenched deck.

Chloe's Café

1399 Church Street, at 26th Street, Noe Valley (648 4116). Muni Metro J. **Open** 8am-3pm Mon-Fri; 8am-4pm Sat, Sun. **No credit cards**.

Long known only to Noe Valley residents, Chloe's serves a great brunch on Saturdays and Sundays and is always packed. The outdoor tables are the most popular, but inside is a friendly hubbub of community and great food.

Just For You Bakery & Café

1453 18th Street, at Connecticut Street, Potrero Hill (647 3033). Bus 22, 48, 53. **Open** 7am-2pm Mon-Fri; 8.30am-3pm Sat, Sun. **No credit cards**.

This stylish, postage stamp-sized eatery is big on taste, serving the best grits and huevos rancheros on Potrero Hill. If you're in before 8.30am, you can get a full eggs-and-toast breakfast for about $3. They also do a decent burger.

The Haight & around

Café Abir

1300 Fulton Street, at Divisadero Street, Western Addition (567 7654). Bus 5, 24. **Open** 6am-midnight daily. **No credit cards**. **Map** p313 D5.

Abir has grown wildly since its modest opening, and now comprises a large café, organic grocery store, coffee roastery, international newsstand and bar. Choose from freshly made sandwiches, deli salads and mountains of bagels, and complete your meal with a latte and a copy of *The Times* (London or New York). Its friendly staff and well-chosen house music make for a great atmosphere. These days, it's got as much night life as morning life.

Citizen Cake

399 Grove Street, at Gough Street, Hayes Valley (861 2228/www.citizencake.com). Bus 21, 42, 47, 49. **Open** 8am-10pm Tue-Fri; 10am-10pm Sat; 10am-9pm Sun. **Credit** AmEx, MC, V. **Map** p310 F5.
Only in San Francisco: a bakery with a high hipness quotient. This swanky eatery in the thick of Hayes Valley sells some of the best-looking desserts you'll ever see to some of the best-looking people you'll ever see. There are non-dessert offerings, too (sandwiches and so on), but nobody seems to care.

Grind Café

783 Haight Street, at Scott Street, Lower Haight (864 0955). Bus 6, 7, 66, 71. **Open** 7am-9pm daily. **No credit cards**. **Map** p313 E5.
Casual but classic, the Grind is populated with hip and ratty denizens of the Lower Haight, who are as likely to be spending the morning leafing through Sartre as sweating off a hangover. The café's open-air patio hosts smokers and dog lovers. Don't miss the vegetable-packed omelettes and tall stacks of pancakes. Wash it all down with a chai tea.

Truly Mediterranean

1724 Haight Street, between Cole & Schrader Streets, Haight-Ashbury (751 7482). Bus, 6, 7, 33, 43, 66, 71. **Open** 11am-midnight Mon-Sat, 11am-10pm Sun. **Credit** MC, V. **Map** p313 C6.
One of two locations in the city (the original's in the Mission) the Haight version has beer on tap and much better people-watching. The menu is heavy on falafel, houmous, baba ganoush and the like. Whether you order to stay or take away, this is some of the best fast food you'll ever have.
Branch: 3109 16th Street, at Valencia Street, Mission (252 7482).

The Marina & Pacific Heights

Food Inc Trattoria

2800 California Street, at Divisadero Street, Pacific Heights (928 3728/www.foodincusa.com). Bus 1, 24. **Open** 9am-9pm Mon-Sat. **Credit** AmEx, MC, V. **Map** p307 D3.
More like a deli with a few seats, this is an outpost for good-quality food at the edge of Pacific Heights. The neo BLT is composed of bacon, mixed greens and tomato on toasted onion focaccia. Join the nannies and double-parked urbanites in the queue, then carry your lunch to nearby Alta Plaza park.

Galette

2043 Fillmore Street, between Pine & California Streets, Pacific Heights (928 1300). Bus 1, 3, 22. **Open** 11am-10pm daily. **Credit** MC, V. **Map** p307 E3.
A chic, unassuming getaway among the hustle and bustle of Fillmore Street. So authentically Gallic is Galette that most of the staff have French accents. Crêpes are the star attraction, made fresh to order and crisped to perfection. Grab one of the few outdoor seats for prime people-watching action.

The Grove

2250 Chestnut Street, at Avila Street, Marina (474 4843). Bus 28, 30, 43, 76. **Open** 7am-11pm Mon, Tue, Sun; 7am-midnight Wed-Sat. **Credit** MC, V. **Map** p307 D2.
This corner café could pass for a fraternity house, but it's the most happening spot in the Marina, albeit with more people talking on mobile phones than to each other. As well as coffee, beer, wine and comfort entrées (chicken pot pie, lasagne), it also has chess, draughts (checkers) and backgammon tables for its patrons. It's so popular that a time limit is imposed on occupying tables during peak hours.

The Richmond District

Blue Danube Coffee House

306 Clement Street, at Fourth Avenue (221 9041). Bus 2, 4, 38, 44. **Open** 7am-9.30pm daily. **No credit cards**. **Map** p312 B4.
If everyone's wearing *Simpsons* T-shirts and reciting lines along with the TV show, it must be Sunday at Blue Danube. But Simpsons Night is not the only reason to visit this cosy coffee-house. The large streetside window is opened to the sidewalk on warmer days, and locals gather around sipping lattes and nibbling cake as the hours slip by.

The Sunset District

Java Beach Café

1396 La Playa Boulevard, at Judah Street (665 5282). Muni Metro N/bus 18. **Open** 6am-9.30pm Mon-Fri; 7am-9.30pm Sat, Sun. **No credit cards**.
A hangout for surfers, cyclists and passers-by on their way to the oceanfront. With a basic sandwich, soup and pastry menu, it's both funky, civilised and – because of its wetsuit-wearing clientele and its view of the Pacific – feels rather like a café at LA's Hermosa Beach.

Tart to Tart

641 Irving Street, between Seventh & Eighth Avenues (504 7068). Muni N/bus 6, 43, 44, 66. **Open** 6am-2am Mon-Sat; 6.30am-1am Sun. **Credit** MC, V. **Map** p312 B6.
There are surprisingly few late-night options in the Inner Sunset, one of the city's best unsung neighbourhoods. Standard fare ranges from freshly made cookies and cakes to above-average salads and sandwiches. The tarts aren't bad, either.

Bars

Whatever your taste in tipples, San Francisco has a bar to match.

San Francisco has fantastic bars. No matter what your taste or mood, you'll have little trouble finding half a dozen spots that suit you perfectly. Elegant cocktail lounges, cool DJ bars, friendly pubs, neo-speakeasys, colourful dives, historic saloons – the list is endless and grows daily. All this despite the fact that San Francisco isn't in general a big drinking town; healthy, hard-working lifestyles and a 2am closing time keep people from really living it up. Two-fisted towns like New York and New Orleans could easily drink San Francisco under the table and out into the street.

However, the bar scene is currently hopping. Some owners of bar-restaurant combinations report that their restaurant receipts are down owing to the dotcom crunch, but their bar business is booming. It seems that those suddenly unable to drop a couple of hundred dollars for dinner are using bars to make the scene while drowning their money woes.

The straight young bar scene in San Francisco is an odd and frustrating cat-and-mouse game between the yuppie masses on the one hand and the boho hipsters and beautiful-people scenesters on the other. The trendsetters create cool bars and scenes only to watch in disgust as they go mainstream, killing what made the bar appealing in the first place. The cool kids move on, the yuppies follow, and so on in an ever-accelerating cycle.

The Mission still has, and likely will continue to have, the biggest and most active straight bar scene in the city. The effects of gentrification are obvious on any Friday or Saturday night, when Valencia Street and parts of Mission Street become bar-hopping highways – so you just have to look harder to find unspoiled places. The Upper Market area on the edge of the Castro has a variety of unusual and popular spots, as does the Haight, especially the less-touristy Lower Haight.

The Tenderloin is increasingly the place for unusual, very hip and highly entertaining bars and clubs, despite – or perhaps because of – its seedy, soft-underbelly surroundings. North Beach has some good spots among the tourist traps, strip joints and frenzied pick-up bars – including new, off-the-drinking-path places and older haunts infused with quirky history. Other interesting places are scattered in areas far from the tourists centres; some are destinations in themselves and justify the cab ride.

The biggest yuppie scene is still found in the Marina, a part of the city the average non-Marina-dwelling San Franciscan avoids as religiously as Fisherman's Wharf. If you want to witness the mating habits of the young SF professional in his native habitat, this is the place. The Balboa Café is the apex of a trio of bars known not so affectionately in the pre-AIDS era as 'the Herpes Triangle'. On a recent Friday night we spotted a group of researchers outside conducting a study of promiscuous sex among bar patrons. Other notorious pick-up bars include Gordon Biersch in SoMa and, on some nights, Blondie's Bar and No Grill in the Mission. They're all in the phone book.

Many of the places listed in the **Nightlife** and **Restaurants & Cafés** chapters have bars that are busy and appealing scenes in themselves. For bars aimed at the queer crowd, *see chapter* **Queer San Francisco**.

Downtown & around

For funky launderette-bar-café **Brainwash**, *see chapter* **Restaurants & Cafés**.

Annie's Cocktail Lounge

15 Boardman Place, off Bryant Street, between Sixth & Seventh Streets, SoMa (703 0865/www.annies cocktails.com). Bus 12, 27, 42. **Open** 4pm-2am Mon-Fri; 8pm-2am Sat. **Credit** MC, V. **Map** p311 H5.
The sign outside this terrific little hideaway depicts a half-devil, half-angel vixen bathing in a cocktail glass: it's the perfect symbol for such a playfully sinful place. The area looks uninviting, but is actually pretty tame, and the crowd is friendly. There's a pool table, a much-loved jukebox and a karaoke corner. Punk and hair-metal tunes are particularly popular.

Bix

56 Gold Street, between Montgomery & Sansome Streets, Financial District (433 6300/www.bix restaurant.com). Bus 12, 15, 41, 42, 83.
Open 11.30am-10pm Mon, Tue; 11.30am-11pm Wed, Thur; 11.30am-midnight Fri, Sat; 6-10pm Sun. **Credit** AmEx, DC, Disc, MC, V. **Map** p309 H2.
With its three-storey high ceilings, secretive locale and supper-club menu, Bix is the kind of place where James Bond would take one of his double-agent lady friends for more than just a little information. It combines the glamour of Harlem's 1930s Cotton Club

Wow! It's **Pow! A Cocktail Lounge**, with cartoons on the walls and real live snakes.

with the splendour of a cruise liner's dining room. It's packed with suits on weekday evenings, so go during off-hours if you don't want money talk spoiling your Martini-soaked cinematic fantasy.

Bubble Lounge

714 Montgomery Street, between Washington & Jackson Streets, Financial District (434 4204/ www.bubbleloungesf.citysearch.com). Bus 15, 41, 83. **Open** 4.30pm-1am Mon; 4.30pm-2am Tue-Fri; 5.30pm-2am Sat. **Credit** AmEx, DC, MC, V. **Map** p309 H3.

After the market closes, stockbrokers and short-skirted execs tickle their noses with an incredible selection of sparkling wines and champagnes. These are paired with pâtés, salads and caviar for a top-drawer taste of the Wall Street of the West. Dress is conservative, label-heavy and cut on the bias. Credit cards with an open limit are *de rigueur*.

Butter

354 11th Street, between Folsom & Harrison Streets, SoMa (863 5964/www.smoothasbutter.com). Bus 9, 12, 19, 27, 42. **Open** 5pm-2am Wed-Sat. **Credit** AmEx, DC, Disc, MC, V. **Map** p310 G5.

A 'white-trash bistro' is a terrific concept, and Butter does a good job of realising it. With the motto 'two turntables and a microwave', it combines a chill-room vibe, complete with DJ spinning at the bar, with trailer-trash kitsch and food. The only problem is that Butter is a bit 'over' – the hipsters have moved on, leaving a somewhat older, semi-suburban crowd – but it's still worth a visit.

C Bobby's Owl Tree

601 Post Street, at Taylor Street, Tenderloin (776 9344). Bus 2, 3, 4, 27, 38, 76. **Open** 5pm-1am Wed-Sat. **No credit cards**. **Map** p308 G3/4.

The Owl Tree isn't coyly kitsch and retro: it's genuinely weird and frozen in time. It has the dark, Naugahyde-bound feel of an Elk's Lodge bar c1950. Every available perch features a mildly tacky homage to the bar's namesake: stuffed owls, carved owls, owl paintings, you name it. The diverse crowd ranges from scenesters to bewildered, middle-aged tourists. David Lynch would love this place.

Edinburgh Castle

950 Geary Street, between Larkin & Polk Streets, Tenderloin (885 4074). Bus 2, 3, 4, 19, 38. **Open** 5pm-2am daily. **Credit** Disc, MC, V. **Map** p310 F4.

This Korean-owned, Scottish-operated pub is not to be missed, despite the dodgy neighbourhood. Upstairs is a venue for local bands, DJ nights and original plays (the stage version of Irvine Welsh's *Trainspotting* made its world debut here), and the patrons are an unpretentious mix of expats, mods and hipsters. Fish and chips are hand-delivered in rolled-up newspaper from a shop around the corner.

Pow! A Cocktail Lounge

101 Sixth Street, at Mission Street, SoMa (278 0940). Muni Metro F, J, K, L, M, N/bus 5, 6, 9, 12, 14, 26, 27. **Open** 5pm-2am daily. **No credit cards**. **Map** p311 G4.

Pow is in a downright scary area, but it's worth the risk if you taxi to and from the bar. Its theme is anime (Japanese animation); the walls are covered with giant stills of scantily clad, Bambi-eyed, super-hero babes. The cocktails are nice and strong, DJs play trip-hop, drum 'n' bass, jungle and break beat, and there are free Playstations and big jars of candy to appeal to the inner child.

The Ramp

855 China Basin Street, at Mariposa Street, China Basin (621 2378/www.theramp.citysearch.com). Bus 15, 22. **Open** 11am-10pm Mon-Fri; 9am-8.30pm Sat, Sun. **Credit** AmEx, MC, V. **Map** p311 J6.

The bay laps right up to the edge of the Ramp, almost hidden among the waterfront warehouses of China Basin. The name is apt: the bar's concrete patio is a boat-landing ramp. It's mainly a hide-away to have a drink and a bite and watch the ships rust on a sunny afternoon. In summer, salsa and 'tropical' bands perform on weekend evenings.

Red Room

Commodore International Hotel, 827 Sutter Street, between Jones & Leavenworth Streets, Tenderloin (346 7666). Bus 2, 3, 4, 27. **Open** 5pm-2am daily. **Credit** MC, V. **Map** p308 G3.

The vampire Lestat would feel right at home in this trendy bar inside the Commodore hotel (*see p45*). It's dimly lit and just about everything is blood red: the walls, the tables, the semi-circular bar, even one of the many speciality Martinis. It's wildly popular but tiny, an uncomfortable combo at the weekend, when the queue is out the door. Try to come during the week when it's cosier.

Redwood Room

Clift Hotel, 495 Geary Street, at Taylor Street, Tenderloin (775 4700). Bus 2, 3, 4, 27, 38, 76. **Open** 5pm-2am daily. **Credit** AmEx, DC, Disc, MC, V. **Map** p310 G4.

San Franciscans adore the Redwood Room, a landmark bar built in 1933. They love it so much that when celebrity hotelier Ian Schrager announced that he and designer Philippe Starck were renovating and modernising it along with the rest of the Clift Hotel (*see p37*), preservationists held a candlelight vigil to 'save' the Redwood. But the essence of this magnificent bar is unchanged. Its towering walls are still panelled in lustrous redwood rumoured to have come from a single giant tree. The decor has shifted from art deco to pomo, but it's not tacky or too flamboyant. The biggest change is the bar itself (which the renovators said was too rotten to save); it's now a cut-glass bar illuminated from within. Flat-screen TV screens project digital sculptures that slowly morph, and a DJ spins four nights a week. The bar opens on to the similarly decorated Asia de Cuba restaurant.

Tunnel Top

601 Bush Street, at Stockton Street, Union Square (986 8900/ http://tunneltop.micronpcweb.com/). Bus 30, 45/cable car Powell-Hyde or Powell-Mason. **Open** 4pm-2am Mon-Sat. **No credit cards**. **Map** p309 G3.

The two-storey Tunnel Top is perched above the Stockton Tunnel, on the border between Chinatown and Union Square. It looks like the dodgiest of dives from the outside; inside, however, the decor is urban-decay cool. Films are projected against rust-coloured walls, there's a bulky chandelier made from wine bottles, and a DJ spins from the balcony. (Literary note: outside is the spot where Sam Spade surveys the scene of his partner's murder at the beginning of *The Maltese Falcon*.)

W Hotel

181 Third Street, at Howard Street, SoMa (817 7836). Bus 12, 15, 30, 45, 76. **Open** 5pm-1.15am Mon-Sat. **Credit** AmEx, DC, Disc, MC, V. **Map** p311 H4.

The Beats live on at **Vesuvio** in North Beach. *See p152.*

There are two bars at this ultra-trendy SoMa hotel (*see p42*) filled with the beautiful people. The first is a circular affair in the ground-floor lobby, while the main bar, attached to the XYZ restaurant, is behind a beaded metal curtain on the first floor. Some find the atmosphere a bit competitive, but the scene shifts nightly (it's a hotel, after all) and the low banquettes in the upstairs bar encourage a relaxed, intimate vibe.

North Beach & around

Bohemia

1624 California Street, at Polk Street, Polk Gulch (474 6968/ www.bohemiasf.com). Bus 1, 19, 42, 47, 49/cable car California. **Open** 4pm-2am daily. **Credit** AmEx, MC, V. **Map** p308 F3.

Bohemia is a large, airy bar with a dancefloor, three jukeboxes and cosy nooks decorated like living rooms. On busy weekend nights, staff open the upstairs room, which has skylights, sofas and windows looking over California Street. DJs spin house, funk and 1970s and '80s tunes several nights a week. The vibe is more after-work rec room than trendy dance palace, though; there's ping-pong, pool, foosball and arcade games. It's 'Bohemian' in the original sense: the owner's from the Czech Republic.

15 Romolo

Basque Hotel, 15 Romolo Place, off Broadway, between Grant Avenue & Kearny Street, North Beach (398 1359). Bus 12, 15, 41, 83. **Open** 5.30pm-2am Mon-Fri, Sun; 7pm-2am Sat. **Credit** MC, V. **Map** p309 G2.

Known to most simply as 'Romolo', the only hint of this dark and sleek little bar's existence is a neon sign for the Basque Hotel. It turns into an icky singles scene at the weekend – come on a Sunday evening or in the week to enjoy its lovingly rendered touches: the candlelit café tables, the blue-tiled columns, the tiny glass light fixtures above the bar.

Li Po

916 Grant Avenue, between Washington & Jackson Streets, Chinatown (982 0072). Bus 12, 15, 30, 45, 83. **Open** 2pm-2am daily. **No credit cards**. **Map** p309 G3.

A fun spot for a pick-me-up when you've had enough of the junk shops on Grant Avenue. Li Po is basically a dive, but the cave façade and giant, tattered Chinese lantern inside set it apart from its seedy neighbours. It'll take you back to a rougher, Barbary Coast-era San Francisco.

Rosewood

732 Broadway, between Stockton & Powell Streets, North Beach (951 4886). Bus 12, 15, 30, 41, 83. **Open** 5.30pm-2am Mon-Fri; 7pm-2am Sat, Sun. **Credit** MC, V. **Map** p308 G2.

This stylish bar was opened in early 2001 by the owners of 15 Romolo (*see above*). Panelled in rosewood and furnished with low, black leather benches, it's the kind of retro-modern room that might grace the cover of *Wallpaper** magazine. DJs spin mellow hip-hop and electronica. The bar is on a neglected commercial strip at the edge of North Beach and Chinatown, and there's no sign outside – so it's not yet overrun. For now, it's one of the best places in San Francisco to sip a cocktail.

Booze, smoking & the law

You have to be aged 21 or over to buy and consume alcohol (take ID even if you look older) and it can be sold only between 6am and 2am. Last orders vary between 1.15am and 1.30am and, technically, staff are obliged to confiscate unconsumed alcoholic drinks after 2am.

Citing the health of those employed in bars, taverns and restaurants, California state law has prohibited smoking in all – and we mean all – public indoor places. An exception is made only for bars that are staffed exclusively by their owners, since they're not risking the health of employees other than themselves. Though some proprietors and bartenders may look the other way, most comply with the new regulations and will not be happy if you light up. If the SFPD drop by, they'll fine the smoker as well as the venue.

San Francisco Brewing Company

155 Columbus Avenue, at Pacific Avenue, North Beach (434 3344/www.sfbrewing.com). Bus 12, 15, 41, 83. **Open** 11.30am-1am Mon-Fri; noon-1.30am Sat, Sun. **Credit** AmEx, MC, V. **Map** p309 G2.

Housed in a restored 1907 saloon with a mahogany bar and belt-driven ceiling fans, this brew pub offers several house-made microbrews, pub grub and free tours of the brewery. The scene is a bit staid, but it's hard to pass up the $1.75 brews offered from 4pm to 6pm and midnight to 1am.

Spec's

William Saroyan Place, off Columbus Avenue, at Broadway, North Beach (421 4112). Bus 15, 30, 41, 83. **Open** 4.30pm-2am Mon-Fri; 5pm-2am Sat, Sun. **No credit cards**. **Map** p309 G2.

Spec's is the quintessential old-school San Francisco bar – one part North Beach bohemian, one part Wild West saloon, with a dash of weirdness for extra flavour. Tucked away in an alley next to Tosca (*see p152*) nearly every inch is covered with dusty detritus dating back to the 19th century. These range from a ship's wheel and an 1865 newspaper clipping about a San Francisco earthquake to a stuffed mongoose fighting a stuffed cobra.

Tonga Room

Fairmont Hotel, 950 Mason Street, at California Street, Nob Hill (772 5278/www.tongaroom.com). Bus 1/cable car California, Powell-Hyde or Powell-Mason. **Open** 5pm-midnight Mon-Thur, Sun; 6pm-1am Fri, Sat. **Credit** AmEx, Disc, MC, V. **Map** p308 G3.

This kitschy Polynesian bar comes complete with happy-hour dim sum, waitresses in sarongs and huge, exotic cocktails (Bora Bora Horror, anyone?). The real attraction, however, is the spectacle of house musicians performing off-key covers of cheesy pop songs while afloat a raft on the Tonga's indoor 'lake'. Don't miss the manmade thunderstorms that punctuate the beginning and end of each set. The Tonga Room is super-touristy, but a must for tiki worshippers and a laugh for everyone else.

Top of the Mark

Mark Hopkins Hotel, 1 Nob Hill, between California & Mason Streets, Nob Hill (392 3434/www.topofthemark.com). Bus 1/cable car California, Powell-Hyde or Powell-Mason. **Open** 5pm-midnight Mon-Thur, Sun; 5pm-1am Fri, Sat. **Admission** $8-$10 after 8.30pm Mon-Thur, Sun; after 9pm Fri, Sat. **Credit** AmEx, DC, Disc, MC, V. **Map** p308 G3.

Opened in 1939, the Top of the Mark was a favourite spot for servicemen shipping out to the Pacific in World War II. It occupies the 19th floor of the Mark Hopkins Hotel, which is in turn at the top of Nob Hill; this gives it a spectacular panoramic view that tends to attract Midwestern tourists and staid older couples. There's music and dancing seven nights a week. It's worth a quick visit just to check the view and sip a Martini, but arrive early in the evening to avoid the cover charge and dress code.

Tosca Café

242 Columbus Avenue, at Broadway, North Beach (986 9651). Bus 12, 15, 30, 41, 83. **Open** 5pm-1.45am daily. **No credit cards**. **Map** p309 G2.

San Francisco nightspots seldom boast a high concentration of celebrities. Tosca is an exception. Its old-fashioned, Italian-decadent ambience and Hollywood-connected owner Jeannette Etheridge draw visiting and local celebs, including Bono, Francis Ford Coppola, Tom Waits and Sam Shepard. It's also a hangout for politicians, including flamboyant San Francisco mayor Willie Brown. It's one of the city's oldest bars, with faded sepia oil paintings, Formica-topped café tables, deep red vinyl booths and Caruso warbling from an ancient jukebox. Try the popular house 'cappuccino', a concoction involving steamed milk and brandy.

Vesuvio

255 Columbus Avenue, between Broadway & Pacific Avenue, North Beach (362 3370/www.vesuvio.com). Bus 12, 15, 30, 41, 83. **Open** 6am-2am daily. **No credit cards**. **Map** p309 G2.

A funky old saloon with a stained-glass façade, Vesuvio does a decent job of preserving the flavour of an earlier era without feeling like a museum. It's next to the famous City Lights bookshop, across Jack Kerouac Alley (the writer was a bar regular), and its walls are covered with Beat and North Beach memorabilia. Sit on the narrow balcony, where you can check out the scene downstairs and on the street.

Don't miss Bars

Edinburgh Castle
An eternally hip Scottish pub-cum-dive in the Tenderloin. *See p149.*

Lucky 13
Head to the Castro to experience a punk/biker bar vibe without the punks/bikers. *See p154.*

Noc Noc
A Lower Haight institution that combines the worlds of Dr Seuss and Nine Inch Nails. *See p157.*

Persian Aub Zam Zam
An Arabian Nights fantasy and a San Francisco legend. *See p157.*

Pow! A Cocktail Lounge
DJs, Playstations, candy and Japanese animation. *See p149.*

Red Room
Dress in blood-red to have cocktails with the vampire set. *See p150.*

Redwood Room
Postmodern rebirth of a swanky classic, inside the ultra-hip Clift Hotel. *See p150.*

Zeitgeist
Bike messengers, bikers, burgers and a beer garden, on the edge of the Mission. *See p154.*

The Mission & the Castro

The **Orbit Room** (*see p231*) is a pleasant place to begin or end an evening of bar-hopping in the Castro, while the mainly lesbian **Wild Side West** (*see p233*) is a friendly spot if you're in Bernal Heights.

The Argus Lounge

3187 Mission Street, between Cesar Chavez (Army) & Valencia Streets, Mission (824 1447/www.argus lounge.com). Bus 12, 14, 26, 27, 49, 67. **Open** 4pm-2am daily. **No credit cards**.

Known by some as the Peacock because of the illuminated peacock feather out front (there's no other sign), the Argus is far enough down Mission Street to escape the gentrifying masses – so far. A clean, simple hangout, it draws an unpretentiously cool and happy crowd, including some local indie-rock heroes. Among the quirky touches are a stuffed peacock, cow skulls and a working version of one of those 1950s exercise belts. Shake it up, baby.

The Attic

3336 24th Street, at Mission Street, Mission (643 3376). BART 24th Street/bus 14, 48, 49, 67. **Open** 5pm-2am Mon-Fri; 6.30pm-2am Sat, Sun. **Credit** AmEx, MC, V. **Map** p314 Y2.

The Attic, as its name suggests, is decorated with cast-offs that usually end up stored and forgotten, including an old tricycle, mannequins and a sledge. Located several blocks from the main Mission boozing avenues, it draws a crowd that is neither self-consciously bohemian nor annoyingly yuppie.

Beauty Bar San Francisco

2299 Mission Street, at 19th Street, Mission (285 0323/www.beautybar.com). Bus 14, 33, 49. **Open** 5pm-2am Mon-Fri; 7pm-2am Sat, Sun. **No credit cards**. **Map** p314 Y1.

This little cocktail bar, modelled after its sister bar in New York, is decorated with bric-a-brac salvaged from a Long Island hair salon. Instead of a couch, curl up on a Naugahyde salon chair with hairdryer still attached. On Wednesday to Saturday evenings, buy a $10 cocktail and get a free manicure. It's a cool place, but absolutely overrun at the weekend.

Dalva

3121 16th Street, between Guerrero & Valencia Streets, Mission (252 7740). BART 16th Street/bus 14, 22, 26, 33, 49, 53. **Open** 4pm-2am daily. **No credit cards**. **Map** p314 Y1.

An unspoiled oasis of cool in the middle of the manic Mission bar scene, Dalva worships good music so much that management even named the jukebox (it's called Orpheus). Voted best jukebox by the readers of an alternative weekly in 2000, it carries a wonderfully eclectic array of sounds, from Cuban music to tiki kitsch. DJs spin drum 'n' bass, jazz, soul, funk, salsa and more on most nights.

Emmy's Spaghetti Shack

18 Virginia Avenue, off Mission Street, between 29th & 30th Streets, Mission (206 2086). Muni Metro J/bus 14, 24, 26, 67. **Open** 6pm-midnight Mon-Thur, Sun; 6pm-2am Fri, Sat. **No credit cards**.

To be honest, this is really a restaurant. There are only five bar stools at the tiny bar, tucked into this little Italian eatery. But if you have any kind of bohemian bent, you need to know about Emmy's, located deep in the Mission where cool kids and the Latino community still outnumber the gentrifiers. It has a corrugated aluminium roof, a bright mural painted on the old wooden façade and a string of aprons as decoration. Food is of the spaghetti-and-meatballs variety (nothing over $10), there's a decent wine selection, or you can really go downmarket and order one of several 40oz beers. A DJ spins some evenings. The whole effect is indescribably cool. Best of all, the kitchen's open late. This is a great place to begin or end an evening at the nearby Argus Lounge (*see p152*), Odeon (*see p154*) or El Rio (*see p215*). Note: it shares the building with a strictly Latino bar; go around the corner to find Emmy's.

Hush Hush Lounge

496 14th Street, at Guerrero Street, Mission (241 9944). Muni Metro F, J, K, L, M/bus 26. **Open** 6pm-2am Mon, Tue, Sun; 4pm-2am Wed-Sat. **No credit cards**. **Map** p310 F6.

The **Beauty Bar** is in the eye of the beholder, they say.

Owner Kimberly Jordan wanted to create a bar that felt illicit yet cosy, and she's done it – right down to the flickering blue candles that send shadows skittering across the cement floor. The masses are starting to discover the place, but it's still got hipster cachet. There's a pool table and a jukebox filled with early jazz and blues, old country, lounge and cabaret. From Wednesdays to Saturday nights, DJs spin mainly 1970s soul, funk and disco. Try the White Russian made with soya milk. The neighbourhood is dodgy, so be careful on the street.

Kilowatt

3160 16th Street, between Valencia & Guerrero Streets, Mission (861 2595). BART 16th Street/ bus 14, 22, 26, 33, 49, 53. **Open** 4pm-2am Mon-Fri; 1pm-2am Sat, Sun. **No credit cards**. **Map** p314 Y1.
Sadly, the beloved Kilowatt no longer hosts live music. But you'd never know it from the heavily tattooed and pierced alterna-rocker crowd that still pack this very happening shoe box of a bar.

Latin American Club

3286 22nd Street, at Valencia Street, Mission (647 2732). Bus 14, 26, 49. **Open** 6pm-2am Mon-Thur, Sun; 5pm-2am Fri; 4pm-2am Sat. **No credit cards**. **Map** p314 Y2.
There's nothing particularly Latin American about this place other than the piñata hanging from the rafters. It's just part of the funky, jumble-sale decor of this popular hipster/yupster hangout. There's a busy pool table and strong drinks.

The Liberties

998 Guerrero Street, at 22nd Street, Mission (282 6789). Muni Metro J/bus 14, 26, 49. **Open** 10am-2am daily. **Credit** AmEx, Disc, MC, V. **Map** p314 Y2.
Everything shines at this upmarket spot: the brass on the bar, the new hardwood floors, the glass in the big new windows. The Irish undercurrent keeps the place real, with ballads on the soundtrack and Irish lads pulling Guinness behind the bar. The food is a mix of classic Celtic and trendy Californian. The Lone Palm (3394 22nd Street; 648 0109) across the street is also worth a look.

Lucky 13

2140 Market Street, at Church Street, Castro (487 1313). Muni Metro F, J, K, L, M/bus 22, 37. **Open** 4pm-2am Mon-Thur; 2pm-2am Fri-Sun. **No credit cards**. **Map** p310 E6.
Dark, spacious and always busy, Lucky 13 has long been a favourite with hipsters and wannabes who crave the aura of a punk/biker bar without the real risk of getting a pool cue broken over their heads. There's pinball, pool and foosball for diversion, but the main entertainment is people-watching.

Mecca

2029 Market Street, at Duboce Avenue, Upper Market (621 7000/www.sfmecca.com). Muni Metro F, J, K, L, M, N/bus 22. **Open** 5pm-midnight Mon-Thur; 5pm-1am Fri, Sat; 4pm-11pm Sun. **Credit** AmEx, DC, MC, V. **Map** p310 E/F6.
Armani's best customers hold holy congregation at Mecca. Inside frosted-glass doors, the urban warehouse look is melded successfully with baroque red velvet and chiffon drapery. The lounge area is an excellent place to get used to the finery. It's a favourite with svelte, immaculately dressed guppies and the odd drag queen, but draws a mixed crowd, too. Soul and jazz singers perform on Mondays (8pm and 10pm; no cover) and sometimes on other nights.

Odeon Bar

3223 Mission Street, between Valencia & 29th Streets, Mission (550 6994/www.odeonbar.com). Bus 14, 26, 49, 67. **Open** 5pm-2am Mon-Sat; 7pm-2am Sun. **Credit** AmEx, Disc, MC, V.
To confirm your stereotype of San Francisco as the land of lunatics, check out this dive bar in the outer reaches of the Mission. It was recently bought by Chicken John – locally notorious as the ringmaster of Circus Redickuless, a kind of punk circus (no actual talent required) – who has turned the bar into a gathering spot for 'geeks, freaks, squids'. On most nights something strange and hard to describe is going on, delivered with a warped sense of humour. Possible events include the Mongoloid Lounge (a lounge night featuring a Devo cover band) and Porn-E-Okie (karaoke set to dirty movies). The Odeon is popular with the Burning Man crowd.

Skylark

3089 16th Street, at Valencia Street, Mission (621 9294). BART 16th Street/bus 14, 22, 26, 49. **Open** 4pm-2am Mon-Fri; 7pm-2am Sat, Sun. **No credit cards**. **Map** p314 Y1.
With low lighting and some class, the Skylark continues to bridge the gap between dance club and bar, with a DJ spinning most nights. Yuppie scenesters have more or less taken over the place, but it's one of the few bar-club hybrids where you'll actually see people dancing.

Treat Street Cocktails

3050 24th Street, at Treat Avenue, Mission (824 5954). BART 24th Street/bus 12, 48, 67. **Open** 5pm-2am daily. **No credit cards**. **Map** p314 Z2.
If you've ever watched cult TV hit *Northern Exposure*, you'll appreciate Treat Street's sense of style. Decorative effects include stuffed deer heads, fish trophies, a pool table and poor lighting – all quite an anomaly for a venue located on the most Hispanic corner of the city. Maybe that's why the erudite-looking thirtysomethings come here: Treat Street is a fluke, a groovy hideaway several blocks from the Mission's gentrifying heart.

Zeitgeist

199 Valencia Street, at Duboce Avenue, Mission (255 7505/www.sonic.net/~wwpints/zeitgeist). Muni Metro F, J, K, L, M/bus 26. **Open** 9am-2am daily. **No credit cards**. **Map** p310 F5/6.
Zeitgeist, on the unofficial border between SoMa and the Mission, is one of the hippest and least pretentious bars in town. It's popular with bikers

The weird and wonderful world of **Noc Noc**. *See p157.*

(Hondas rather than Harleys), bike messengers and people from every alternative walk of life. On sunny early evenings, it's hard to move, let alone sit at the dozens of benches and tables in the giant beer-garden-meets-junkyard back patio. The eclectic jukebox has a special emphasis on underground punk.

Zodiac Club

718 14th Street, at Market Street, Castro (626 7827/ http://zodiacclub.citysearch.com/1.html). Muni Metro F, J, K, L, M/bus 22, 37. **Open** 5pm-2am daily. **Credit** MC, V. **Map** p310 E6.

The Zodiac Club is the creation of the same minds behind the Red Room (*see p150*). Inspired by the 1958 witchcraft comedy *Bell, Book and Candle*, the walls are painted night-sky blue, galaxies swirl on a mural behind the bar and purple drapes flow from the ceiling. The room is divided between the bar, which serves 12 speciality cocktails, one for each astrological sign, and a quite good restaurant serving Mediterranean-influenced California cuisine.

The Haight & around

An Bodhrán

668 Haight Street, between Pierce & Steiner Streets, Lower Haight (431 4724/www.anbodhran.com). Bus 6, 7, 22, 66, 71. **Open** 4pm-2am Mon-Fri, Sun; 6pm-2am Sat. **Credit** MC, V. **Map** p313 E5.

This dark, low-ceilinged Irish bar seems to fly beneath the radar of both the scenesters and the yuppies in the Lower Haight. It's a friendly, low-key place to lift a pint or have a game of darts. Trad Irish music sessions are held on Sunday afternoons.

Fly

762 Divisadero Street, between Grove & Fulton Streets, Western Addition (931 4359). Bus 5, 21, 24. **Open** 4.30pm-2am Mon-Fri, Sun; 5.30pm-2am Sat. **Credit** AmEx, DC, Disc, MC, V. **Map** p313 D5.

A friendly, unpretentious bar-restaurant that attracts a casually cool, twentysomething crowd. Fly serves only beer and wine, a restriction that has made it creative with sake: it offers five different kinds, served neat or in a dozen cocktails. The Justice League (*see p211*) is just down the street.

Gold Cane Cocktail Lounge

1569 Haight Street, between Clayton & Ashbury Streets, Haight-Ashbury (626 1112). Bus 6, 7, 33, 37, 43, 66, 71. **Open** noon-2am daily. **No credit cards**. **Map** p313 D5/6.

A simple neighbourhood bar: a moosehead on the wall, a pool table, a small back patio for the rare sunny day – and that's about it. Attracting a low-key mix of hipsters, yuppies and regular working joes, it's worth a visit if you're tired of the crowded scene in other Haight bars.

Hayes & Vine

377 Hayes Street, between Franklin & Gough Streets, Hayes Valley (626 5301/www.hayesandvine.com). Bus 21, 42, 47, 49. **Open** 5pm-midnight Mon-Thur; 5pm-1am Fri, Sat; 3-9pm Sun. **Credit** DC, MC, V. **Map** p310 F5.

This elegant wine bar caters to symphony patrons, shoppers and anyone in the mood for good vino in comfortable surroundings. But don't worry about stuffy wine snobs: the staff are friendly and the vibe casual. Do ask for suggestions from the huge list (1,000 wines by the bottle, 40-plus by the glass).

Lord of Balls Lounge

Miyako Hotel, 1611 Post Street, at Laguna Street, Western Addition (922 7788/www.dotrestaurant.com/lord.html). Bus 2, 3, 4, 38. **Open** 7pm-2am Wed-Sat; 6-10pm Sun. **Credit** AmEx, Disc, MC, V. **Map** p310 E4.

This new Japantown lounge looks like a cartoonish version of an English gentlemen's club: plastic deer heads, a fake fireplace, wing-back chairs. It's the creation of Nicholas Graham, 'Chief Underpants Officer' of Joe Boxer Corp. It's very popular and might be entertaining in a tacky kind of way, if it weren't for the unpleasant crowd. If you must visit, do so during the week, preferably early in the evening.

Mad Dog in the Fog

530 Haight Street, between Fillmore & Steiner Streets, Lower Haight (626 7279/http://maddog.citysearch.com). Bus 6, 7, 22, 66, 71. **Open** 11.30am-2am Mon-Fri; 10am-2am Sat, Sun. **No credit cards**. **Map** p310 E5.

A congenial spot for anyone fancying a live broadcast of real football (aka soccer), the Mad Dog offers 20 beers on tap and another 30 in bottles. DJs spin on Fridays and Sundays and bands play everything from punk to Scottish folk on Saturdays. Traditional English breakfasts (the 'Greedy Bastard' is $7) are served mid-morning, followed by pub grub in the afternoon and evening.

East Bay drinking

So many bars beckon in San Francisco that there's no need to look elsewhere. But if you want a different pace and scene, or if you happen to be sightseeing in the East Bay, there are plenty of appealing places to check out.

The Alley

*3325 Grand Avenue, between Elwood Avenue & Lake Park Avenue, Oakland (1-510 444 8505). BART 19th Steeet, then bus 12/AC Transit bus K, N, V.***Open** 4pm-2am Tue-Sat. **No credit cards**.

The Alley is designed to look like a shanty-town alleyway, complete with knickers strung between building façades and jagged fences separating the booths. At the end of the bar is a piano surrounded by bar stools. At each stool is a microphone, and anyone is free to take a seat and join the singalong that takes place every Thursday through Saturday night. Participants are from every age group and walk of life. If you decide to join in, it will be the strangest group you'll ever experience. Don't worry if you're not quite sure of the words – neither is the piano player.

Barclays Pub & Restaurant

5940 College Avenue, at Harwood Avenue, Oakland (1-510 654 1650/www.barclayspub.com). BART Rockridge, then bus 7, 17, 51/AC Transit bus E. **Open** 11am-11.30pm daily. **Credit** AmEx, MC, V.

This below-street-level pub in Rockridge, one of Oakland's most charming districts, is known for its vast beer selection (30 kinds on tap) and its beer-tasting club. The crowd is a bit on the frat-boy side, but it's a good place to watch rugby or football (either kind), and the food is not bad. Another Oakland branch is opening soon.

First & Last Chance Saloon

Jack London Square, at Webster Street, Oakland (1-510 839 6761/www.firstandlastchance.com). BART Oakland City Center, then bus 58, 72L, 301. **Open** noon-midnight Mon-Thur; noon-1am Fri, Sat; 11am-10pm Sun. **No credit cards**.

This historic monument – a tiny building made from wood salvaged from an old whaling ship – is a must-see. Jack London used to drink here, and his memory is lovingly preserved. And it's not just the drink going to your head – the floor and bar really are tilted at an extreme angle, and have been ever since the 1906 earthquake.

Jupiter

2181 Shattuck Avenue, at Center Street, Berkeley (1-510 843 8277/www.jupiterbeer.com). BART Berkeley. **Open** 11.30am-1am Mon-Thur; 11.30am-1.30am Fri; noon-1.30am Sat. **Credit** MC, V. **Map** p315 L3.

This microbrewery is popular with UC Berkeley students, mainly for its pitchers of beer and its fire-grilled pizzas. The back patio (*pictured*) is multi-level and sprawling, and when the weather is warm there are DJs and dancing. Bands sometimes perform upstairs. It's a very chill crowd, except at the weekend, when, big as the bar is, it gets packed to capacity with students blowing off steam.

Movida Lounge

200 Fillmore Street, at Waller Street, Lower Haight (934 8637). Bus 6, 7, 22, 66, 71. **Open** 4pm-midnight/2am daily. **No credit cards**. **Map** p310 E5.

A great place to start the evening (it gets packed and horrid later on). The decor is Spanish in a Don Quixote and flamenco kind of way, and dim red lighting bathes the room in the evening. Curl up at tables and banquettes along the plate-glass windows or mingle in the middle as a DJ spins background music. The closing time depends on the crowd.

Noc Noc

557 Haight Street, between Fillmore & Steiner Streets, Lower Haight (861 5811). Bus 6, 7, 22, 66, 71. **Open** 5pm-2am daily. **Credit** MC, V. **Map** p310 E5.

An eternally hip institution. If Dr Seuss and Trent Reznor had gone into the bar business together, this is what they'd have come up with. The decor might best be described as 'post-apocalyptic industrial', and the whole place has an oddly organic Gaudian feel, as if the bar and tables had sprouted from the ground because of too much radiation. Always plunged in near darkness and with a mellow chill-room vibe, Noc Noc attracts a multi-ethnic crowd.

Persian Aub Zam Zam

1633 Haight Street, between Clayton & Belvedere Streets, Haight-Ashbury (861 2545). Bus 6, 7, 33, 37, 43, 66, 71. **Open** 3pm-2am daily. **No credit cards**. **Map** p313 C6.

This tiny bar was a legend thanks to its notoriously cantankerous owner, Bruno Mooshei; he inherited the bar from his father and waged a one-man battle

Pyramid Brewery & Alehouse

901 Gilman Street, between Seventh & Eighth Streets, Berkeley (1-510 528 9880/www. pyramidbrew.com). BART North Berkeley, then bus 9/AC Transit bus Z. **Open** 11.30am-10pm Mon-Thur, Sun; 11.30am-midnight Fri, Sat. **Credit** AmEx, DC, MC, V.

This brewpub is part of a chain started in Washington state in the mid 1980s. It has 20-plus beers, daily tours of the brewery and an outdoor cinema, which shows popular classics from *Dr No* to *The Shining* during the warmer months. It's right across from punk club 924 Gilman Street (*see p214*) – it's hard to think of two more disparate crowds.

Ruby Room

132 14th Street, between Madison Street & Lakeside Drive, Oakland (1-510 444 7224). BART 12th Street, then bus 13, 59, 82. **Open** 5pm-2am Mon-Fri; 8pm-2am Sat, Sun. **Credit** AmEx, MC, V.

A dim, smoky, womb-like bar with red walls and black ceilings, the Ruby Room is the East Bay's answer to Zeitgeist (*see p154*). Neither the fantastic jukebox nor the new-wave DJs seem able to entice people to get on to the tiny dancefloor, but everyone hums or sings along. The crowd is young, hip, tattooed and pierced.

Spats

1974 Shattuck Avenue, between Berkeley Way & University Avenue, Berkeley (1-510 841 7225/www.spats.citysearch.com/1. html). BART Berkeley. **Open** 4pm-1am Mon-Thur; 4pm-2am Fri, Sat. **Credit** AmEx, DC, MC, V. **Map** p315 L3.

Modelled on a gents' club, this is a plush bar full of lovely deep chairs. The giant novelty drinks are quite a production: the Borneo Fogcutter, for instance, comes trailing dry-ice smoke from its base. Spats is pricey and a bit too full at the weekend, but it's a nice place for a fancy cocktail early in the night.

Triple Rock Brewery

1920 Shattuck Avenue, between Berkeley Way & Hearst Avenue, Berkeley (1-510 843 2739/www.triplerock.com). BART Berkeley. **Open** 11am-1am daily. **Credit** MC, V. **Map** p315 L3.

Triple Rock is owned by brothers John and Reid Martin, who claim it is 'America's oldest original brewpub'. They're responsible for several brewpubs in the Bay Area, including nearby Jupiter (*see above*) and the now-defunct Twenty Tank in San Francisco. The crowd is mostly UC Berkeley students partying after classes.

to keep it exactly as it must have been circa World War II. This meant inexpensive drinks and old-school bar etiquette (only ladies got cocktail napkins). It also meant you stood an excellent chance of getting tossed out if you ordered the 'wrong' drink (a Martini was the safest choice), the bar was crowded or he just didn't like your looks (bland suburbanites were more likely to get the boot than odd-looking bohemians). Bruno died in 2000, but long-time patrons bought the place and are devoted to keeping its *Casablanca* aura intact. Thankfully, the most obnoxious yuppies still prefer 'the bar down the street', the purgatory to which Bruno always banished the unwelcome.

Place Pigalle

520 Hayes Street, between Laguna & Octavia Streets, Hayes Valley (552 2671/www.place-pigalle.com). Bus 21. **Open** 4pm-midnight Mon-Wed, Sun; 4pm-2am Thur-Sat. **Credit** AmEx, MC, V. **Map** p310 F5.

How very San Fran to pair an upmarket wine bar with thrift store couches and a furiously spinning DJ. The crowd is eclectic: gay and straight, bohemian and yuppie, young and not so young. The back room (with pool table) doubles as an art gallery.

Someplace Else

1795 Geary Boulevard, at Fillmore Street, Western Addition (440 2180/www.someplaceelse.citysearch.com). Bus 2, 3, 4, 22, 38. **Open** 4pm-2am Mon-Sat; 1pm-midnight Sun. **No credit cards**. **Map** p310 E4.

This small, smoky, dimly lit beer and wine bar attracts a youngish crowd that come to hang out on the thrift store sofas, bus benches and beauty parlour chairs. There are dozens of board games to play, and a good sound system. It's just a block from the Fillmore Auditorium (*see p210*) and a great place to stop before or after a gig. The bar may be moving down the street; call or check the website for details.

The Marina & around

G Bar

Laurel Inn, 444 Presidio Avenue, between Sacramento & California Streets, Presidio Heights (409 4227). Bus 1, 3, 4, 43. **Open** 5.30pm-2am daily. **Credit** AmEx, MC, V. **Map** p307 D3/4.

If you're surprised and saddened that San Francisco doesn't look like Los Angeles, head to G. The Laurel Inn was a nondescript motel until the same folks behind the Commodore (home to the Red Room – *see p150*) and the Phoenix (home to Backflip – *see p217*) got hold of it. It now has a neo-1950s look, with hep-cat light fixtures and a bachelor-pad atmosphere.

Liverpool Lil's

2942 Lyon Street, between Lombard & Greenwich Streets, Marina (921 6664). Bus 28, 41, 43, 45, 76. **Open** 11am-2am Mon-Fri; 10am-2am Sat, Sun. **Credit** MC, V. **Map** p307 D2.

This is the sole bar we recommend in the Marina area, precisely because it's the opposite of the typical Marina meat market. The façade looks like it's made from driftwood, and the main decorative touch inside is a wall covered in old sports photos. A considerable pub grub menu is served, and there's also an adjoining restaurant. The crowd ranges from square and older to young and hip.

Ocean Beach & around

The **Cliff House** and the **Beach Chalet** (for both, *see p101*) are both worth a visit.

Canvas Café Gallery

1200 Ninth Avenue, at Lincoln Way, Sunset District (504 0060). Muni Metro N/bus 6, 7, 44, 66, 71. **Open** 7am-11pm Mon-Wed, Sun; 7am-midnight Thur-Sat. **Credit** AmEx, MC, V. **Map** p312 B6.

This is one of those hybrids so popular in San Francisco: a combination beer and wine bar, café, art gallery and live performance space. The decor is Scandinavian modern, with high ceilings and plate-glass windows overlooking Golden Gate Park. There's live music – usually folk, rock and jazz or the occasional DJ – from Wednesday to Saturday.

The Other Place

408 Clement Street, at Fifth Avenue, Richmond District (831 7522). Bus 2, 4, 38, 44. **Open** 5pm-2am Mon-Sat; 2pm-2am Sun. **No credit cards**. **Map** p314 B4.

While drunken yuppies and spacy hippies groove to jam bands at the Last Day Saloon next door, the aptly named the Other Place quietly goes about its business as the coolest dive in the neighbourhood. The jukebox is killer, and there's also a pool table and a pinball machine.

The Plough & Stars

116 Clement Street, at Second Avenue, Richmond District (751 1122/ www.whatwasit.com/plough). Bus 2, 33, 38. **Open** 4pm-2am Mon-Fri; 2pm-2am Sat, Sun. **Credit** AmEx, Disc, MC, V. **Map** p312 B4.

San Francisco's Irish community is concentrated most visibly in the Inner Richmond, and it doesn't get much more Irish than the Plough & Stars. Live traditional Irish music fills this hall-like space almost every night (and has done for more than 25 years), while Irish expats and Celtophiles hoist Guinness after Guinness. Also try the Pig & Whistle (2801 Geary Boulevard; 885 4779).

Trad'r Sam's

6150 Geary Boulevard, at 26th Avenue, Richmond District (221 0773). Bus 29, 38. **Open** 10am-2am daily. **No credit cards**.

A San Francisco fave since 1939, this unabashedly traditional tiki bar serves the kind of cocktails that can only be described as dangerous. Planter's Punch, Mai Tais, Singapore Slings: there's a guaranteed hangover lurking beneath the cheesy umbrellas spinning in Sam's drinks. However, it is in the Outer Richmond, far removed from any nightlife hub and best visited if you're a tiki fan or already in the area.

Shops & Services

This is shopping heaven; from couture to street funk, San Francisco has it all.

While San Francisco may not be a shopping mecca like New York or Los Angeles, many material girls and boys prefer to hunt for loot within its friendlier, less hysterical size and pace. Here, even fashion addicts rarely take their Prada, Gucci or Helmut straight up – preferring to funk it up, dress it down and make it their own. Part of the reason is the weather – without a distinct winter or summer, it's harder to get into a lather over each new season's sartorial seductions (which makes the designer clearance sales a bonanza). And then there's the city's traditional boho sensibility, which places a higher premium on personal expression than on replicating cloned looks.

San Francisco's puzzle of intersecting neighbourhoods (like nation states, each bearing a unique flavour, character and ethnicity), means that your quest for goods has the happy result of guiding you into the very heart and soul of the city. For, while San Francisco is endowed with all the requisite designer boutiques, chainshops and department stores, our advice is to head off the beaten path to score the cool stuff you can't find back home. After all, isn't that why you came?

SHOPPING AREAS

Some shoppers never make it out of **Union Square**, a galaxy of department stores and chains as well as the deities of ready-to-wear. This is also the place to head in case of a make-up crisis, as premium brands are sold only in department stores and that secular shrine to beauty, **Sephora** (*see p180*). Some destination boutiques have real character – **Metier** (*see p170*) for women and **MAC** (*see p170*) for men are two of the most brilliant.

From Union Square, a short stroll up Grant Avenue takes you into another world. Not just a tourist magnet but a thriving community, the streets of **Chinatown** are thronged with locals who make daily expeditions to colourful and overflowing vegetable markets, fish shops and herbal apothecaries. A haven for knick-knacks, porcelain, paper lanterns, embroidered jackets and other types of Chinoiserie, there are many hidden gems to be found here, such as the **Sam Bo Trading Co** (*see p164*).

Keep walking along Grant Avenue and you'll end up at **North Beach**; ground zero for the West Coast Beat movement of the 1960s and home to a clutch of European cafés and Italian groceries. Now a fashionably quirky shopping destination, **Upper Grant** has evolved into a sort of paradise regained for hipsters with a few dollars to drop, while on **Columbus Avenue** is the legendary **City Lights** bookshop (*see p165*) which draws serious readers, poets and dreamers – as well as the requisite poseurs.

Across the city to the south is the sunny **Mission** district, where it seems as if there is a new or antiquarian bookshop and second-hand furniture shop on almost every block. A product of the truly mixed blessing of gentrification, the Mission overflows with upmarket eateries and quirky boutiques that do not necessarily speak to the neighbourhood's original mixture of immigrants and starving artists. However the best such places, such as **Paxton Gate** (*see p179*), feel comfortably integrated into the ever-evolving milieu, even now rising from the ashes of the recent dotcom crash and burn.

Light years away from the Mission is the squeaky-clean **Marina**, where the young and coiffed roam in pursuit of their decaf, non-fat lattes and protein smoothies, mostly unimpeded by urban riff-raff. The area's main arteries – **Union Street** and **Chestnut Street** – offer myriad retail opportunities, albeit with a sanitised sense of adventure.

Running off Union Street up and over a sizeable hill, **Fillmore Street** in **Pacific Heights** (sometimes sardonically dubbed 'Pacific Whites'), has managed to retain a bit more of its neighbourhood feel and offers a grab bag of shops filled with clothing, housewares and vintage threads. Continuing down Fillmore Street leads you to the **Japan Center**, a mall housing Japanese-language bookshops, sushi bars, noodle joints, housewares shops and the **Kabuki Springs & Spa** (*see p181*) – an ancient antidote for shopper's fatigue.

Continuing south, **Hayes Valley**, three blocks of Hayes Street running between Laguna Street and the Civic Center, was once a magnet for the pierced-and-tattooed crowd, although rising property prices may have taken some of the shine off of its original alternative lustre. Strolling the street (*see p175* **The city on foot: Hayes Valley crawl**) yields up treasures as diverse as vintage cowboy boots and a bespoke corset. Those in the know start with a stroll down Gough Street to **Market Street** to wander through the droves of funky antique

Find sexy clothes for women and men, and Maude the sexy dog, at **MAC**. *See p170.*

stores in droves, then cross Market to peruse the shops on and around tiny **Brady Street**, where they can find everything from imported ribbons to valuable Eames chairs.

Elsewhere in town are more varied shopping options that will attract those with particular interests. Combining sightseeing with shopping is particularly easy on **Haight Street** in the **Haight-Ashbury**. More than 30 years after its heyday, this area of town pays homage to the Summer of Love while courting a newer, more well-heeled following. Second-hand clothing shops, record shops and tattoo parlours now sit cheek by jowl with *recherché* clothing boutiques and skateboard shops. Similarly, every day is Gay Pride in the **Castro** district, marked by rainbow flags wafting in the breeze. The area also outfits the young, the hip and the fit with club-worthy threads from stores such as **Rolo** (*see p170*) and **Citizen** (*see p169*).

TAX & DUTY

Most shops accept travellers' cheques, but don't forget that local sales tax (currently 8.5 per cent) will be added to all purchases. You can avoid paying this if you live out of state and arrange for the shop to ship your purchase; or arrange shipment yourself via the US mail or a courier. If you are taking goods out of the country, remember that you will be liable for duty and tax on goods worth more than a certain amount (£145 in the UK).

Department stores

All the following are located in the Union Square area. Most have extended opening hours between Thanksgiving and Christmas.

Gumps

135 Post Street, between Grant Avenue & Kearny Street (984 9439/www.gumps.com). BART Montgomery Street/Muni Metro F, J, K, L, M, N/ bus 2, 3, 4, 15, 30, 38, 45, 76/cable car Powell-Hyde or Powell-Mason. **Open** 10am-6pm Mon-Sat. **Credit** AmEx, MC, V. **Map** p309 H3.

Presided over by a large Golden Buddha, this is where monied San Franciscans shop for wedding presents and precious baubles – including oriental wares, jade, antiques and pearls, pearls, pearls.

Macy's

170 O'Farrell Street, between Powell & Stockton Streets (397 3333/www.macys.com). BART Powell Street/Muni Metro F, J, K, L, M, N/bus 2, 3, 4, 15, 30, 38, 45, 76/cable car Powell-Hyde or Powell-Mason. **Open** 10am-8pm Mon-Thur; 10am-9pm Fri, Sat; 11am-7pm Sun. **Credit** AmEx, MC, V. **Map** p311 G4.

This mother of all department stores (actually three stores, including a men's shop across the street and a home furnishings outpost on Market Street) offers miles of aisles and racks crammed with goods at all price points in an ambience frequently devoid of charm or personal service.

Branch: Stonestown Galleria, Winston Drive, at 19th Avenue, Park Merced (753 4000).

Neiman Marcus

150 Stockton Street, at Geary Street (362 3900/www.neimanmarcus.com). BART Powell Street/Muni Metro F, J, K, L, M, N/bus 2, 3, 4, 15, 30, 38, 45, 76/cable car Powell-Hyde or Powell-Mason. **Open** 10am-7pm Mon-Wed, Fri, Sat; 10am-8pm Thur; noon-6pm Sun. **Credit** AmEx. **Map** p311 G3/4.

Completely unnecessary luxury of the mink-covered coat hangar variety, is yours, at least for as long as you can find an excuse to hang out here. The well edited selection of clothing and shoes includes many designer and diffusion labels (from Prada to Blahnik) and helpful sales staff. There's an outpost of Kiehl's, the beloved New York skincare apothecary, at the cosmetics counter (*see also p179*).

Nordstrom

San Francisco Shopping Center, 865 Market Street, at Fifth Street (243 8500/www.nordstrom.com). BART Powell Street/Muni Metro F, J, K, L, M, N/bus 5, 21, 27, 30, 31, 38, 45/cable car Powell-Hyde or Powell-Mason. **Open** 9.30am-9pm Mon-Sat; 10am-7pm Sun. **Credit** AmEx, DC, Disc, MC, V. **Map** p311 G4.

Known for offering exemplary customer service, Nordstrom's five-floor attractions include a shoe department the size of the Ritz and live piano music. It also offers a free shuttle throughout a limited area within the Financial District and Union Square. **Branch**: Stonestown Galleria, Winston Drive, at 19th Avenue, Park Merced (759 2626).

Saks Fifth Avenue

384 Post Street, at Powell Street (986 4300/www.saksfifthavenue.com). BART Powell Street/Muni Metro F, J, K, L, M, N/bus 2, 3, 4, 15, 30, 38, 45, 76/cable car Powell-Hyde or Powell-Mason. **Open** 10am-7pm Mon-Wed, Fri, Sat; 10am-8pm Thur; noon-6pm Sun. **Credit** AmEx, Disc, MC, V. **Map** p309 G3.

The San Francisco branch of this upmarket store is airier and less claustrophobic than most of its ilk. Second-floor designers include Dries Van Noten, Ann Demeulemeester, Gucci and Moschino. Two floors up, the less pricey (but just as trendy) lines by Katayone, Miu Miu and Tocca beckon. Men get their own store one block down Post Street, with the more cutting-edge creators stashed on the fifth floor (ask for the marvellous Scott to assist).

Shopping centres

The Cannery

2801 Leavenworth Street, between Beach & Jefferson Streets, Fisherman's Wharf (771 3112/www.thecannery.com). Muni Metro F/bus 10, 30, 47/cable car Powell-Hyde or Powell-Mason. **Open** *June-Aug, Dec* 10am-8pm Mon-Sat; 11am-6pm Sun. *Jan-May, Sept-Nov* 10am-6pm Mon-Sat; 11am-6pm Sun. **Map** p308 F1.

Formerly the site of the Del Monte fruit-canning factory, the upper levels are a warren of uninspiring stores, with more of the same to be found at the Anchorage across the street.

Crocker Galleria

50 Post Street, at Kearny Street, Union Square (393 1505/www.shopatgalleria.com). BART Montgomery Street/Muni Metro F, J, K, L, M, N/bus 2, 3, 4, 15, 30, 38, 45, 76/cable car Powell-Hyde or Powell-Mason. **Open** 10am-6pm Mon-Sat. **Map** p309 H3.

In this open-ended arcade a couple of blocks off Union Square, the shops of European and US designers (such as Ralph Lauren) mix with individually owned shops and eateries.

Embarcadero Center

Sacramento Street, between Battery & Drumm Streets, Financial District (772 0550/www.embarcaderocenter.com). BART Embarcadero/Muni Metro F, J, K, L, M, N/bus 1, 2, 7, 14, 21, 31, 41, 66, 71. **Open** 7am-6pm daily. **Map** p309 H3.

The shopping areas on the ground and first floors of these four downtown office towers represent most of the major chains – Banana Republic, Gap, The Limited, Pottery Barn, Williams Sonoma, Nine West et al. There's also a well stocked international newsstand and excellent multiscreen cinema.

Fisherman's Wharf

Jefferson Street, between Hyde & Powell Streets, Fisherman's Wharf (626 7070/www.fishermanswharf.org). Muni Metro F/bus 10, 15, 30, 39, 47/cable car Powell-Hyde or Powell-Mason. **Open** times vary. **Map** p308 F1.

With scarcely a fisherman – nor a local – in sight, the mystery is why so many tourists continue to flock here. Don't they sell T-shirts back home?

Ghirardelli Square

900 North Point Street, at Beach, Larkin & Polk Streets, Fisherman's Wharf (775 5500/www.ghirardellisq.com). Muni Metro F/bus 10, 15, 30, 39, 47/cable car Powell-Hyde or Powell-Mason. **Open** *mid May-Aug* 10am-9pm Mon-Sat; 10am-6pm Sun. *Sept-mid May* hours vary. **Map** p308 F1/2.

At this home of the Ghirardelli chocolate factory, you can still watch the stuff being made and consume it as you wander through the mostly souvenir-themed shops designed to lighten tourists' wallets.

Metreon

221 Fourth Street, at Mission Street, SoMa (369 6000/www.metreon.com). BART Powell Street/Muni Metro F, J, K, L, M, N/bus 9, 14, 30, 45/cable car Powell-Hyde or Powell-Mason. **Open** 10am-10pm daily. **Map** p311 H4.

Sony's sensory-overloaded addition to SF's downtown includes the interactive Discovery Channel Store; Sony Style, a fetish shop for technophiles; the Hear Music CD store; a Microsoft shop; and a host of activities for kids. No less than 15 cinemas include a monolithic Sony IMAX screen. It's all a bit overwhelming and represents a sort of soulless benchmark for 21st-century consumerism.

Pier 39

Beach Street & Embarcadero, Fisherman's Wharf (705 5500/www.pier39.com). Muni Metro F/bus 10, 15, 30, 39, 47/cable car Powell-Hyde or Powell-

The smart traveler's essential accessory:

Good Vibrations

•sex toys •books •videos •sex info • women-owned •friendly staff

call our 800# for a FREE CATALOG!

1210 Valencia, SF • 2504 San Pablo, Berkeley

1-800-BUY-VIBE • goodvibes.com

Central Park SummerStage

CATCH A WORLD OF PERFORMERS AMERICAN MUSIC WORLD MUSIC INTERNATIONAL CABARET DJS ELECTRONIC MUSIC PERFORMANCE ROCK'N ROLL AFRICAN MUSIC COUNTRY REGGAE HIP HOP POETRY

presented by Heineken & Lipton Iced Tea

NEW YORK CITY'S FAVORITE FREE PERFORMING ARTS FESTIVAL

CELTIC TRADITIONAL DANCE TRIP-HOP R&B BHANGRA SOUL GYPSY MUSIC BLUEGRASS SALSA SOUL COMPAS MERENGUE SKA SAMBA BLUES LATIN ROCK AFRO-BEAT RAI JAZZ HOUSE MUSIC BEAT BOX SOCA ZYDECO QWAALI POPULAR MUSIC CLASSICAL MANGUE BEAT AND MUCH, MUCH MORE

CONCERTS DANCE SPOKEN WORD OPERA FAMILY EVENTS

MID JUNE - MID AUGUST www.SummerStage.org

All shows at Rumsey Playfield,
72nd Street, Mid Park
INFO/VOLUNTEER HOTLINE: 212.360.2777
Pick up a summer issue of *Time Out New York* magazine for listings of Central Park SummerStage events.

Central Park SummerStage is a program of the City Parks Foundation in cooperation with the City of New York/Parks and Recreation

Time Out New York

They emptied France to fill the **Butler & the Chef**.

Mason. **Open** *Mar-mid May, mid Sept-mid Oct* 10am-8pm daily. *Mid May-mid Sept* 10am-9pm daily. *Mid Oct-Feb* 11am-7pm daily. **Map** p308 G1.
A tourist magnet with a handful of individually owned shops and the added attractions of wonderful views and noisy (sometimes smelly) seals.

San Francisco Centre

865 Market Street, at Fifth Street, Union Square (495 5656/www.sanfranciscocentre.com). BART Powell Street/Muni Metro F, J, K, L, M, N/bus 5, 21, 27, 30, 31, 38, 45/cable car Powell-Hyde or Powell-Mason. **Open** 9.30am-8pm Mon-Sat; 11am-6pm Sun. **Map** p311 G4.
Like lifeboats bobbing around the mother ship, a flotilla of mid-range chains loop around Nordstrom, including the Body Shop, J Crew, Abercrombie & Fitch, Z-Gallerie, Ann Taylor and Express.

Antiques & collectibles

For all its fascination with the next big thing, San Francisco is relatively well stocked with relics of the past. In the streets surrounding the **Design Center** in Potrero Hill (Kansas, Henry Adams, 16th and Brannan), you'll find upmarket places that cater to interior designers and decorators. Several such shops are also clustered in the narrow lanes in the **Jackson Square Historical District** (call 296 8150 for the Jackson Square Art & Antique Dealers Association). Many of the antique and novelty shops skirting the **Hayes Valley** intersection of Gough and Market Streets are a haven for the city's stylists and photographers, and the revitalised stretch of Polk Street (between Pacific and Green) in **Russian Hill** is rich with furniture and quirky collectibles.

Aria

1522 Grant Avenue, at Union Street, North Beach (433 0219). Bus 15, 30, 39, 41. **Open** 11am-7pm Mon-Sat; noon-5pm Sun. **No credit cards**. **Map** p309 G2.
The ultimate curiosity shop, where everything is coated with just the right amount of dust. Proprietor Bill Haskell's treasure trove includes a little bit of everything from everywhere in the world: old brass trophies, vintage circus and Tour de France photos, old architectural tools, Mexican *santos* shrines, paintings and ornaments imported from Italy – all illuminated by original Nelson lamps.

The Butler & the Chef

1011 25th Street, at Third Street, Potrero Hill (642 6440/www.thebutlerandthechef.com). Bus 15. **Open** 10am-6pm Mon-Fri; 11am-5pm Sat. **Credit** MC, V.
It's hard to believe there's anything left in France when you visit this warehouse, stuffed as it is with 18th- to 20th-century bar tops, ceramics, glassware, copper pots, pétanque balls, bistro tables, architectural details, advertising posters and *beaucoup plus* at *bonmarché* prices. If you're in South Park, head for the pleasant pavement café.

Dishes Delmar

558 8882/www.dishesdelmar.com. **Open** by appointment.
Inside a Haight-Ashbury Victorian, Burt Tessler and his partner have assembled a pristine collection of mid 20th-century American dishware: Fiesta,

Harlequin, Lu-Ray, Metlox, Starburst, Wright and the like. Although visits are only by appointment, it is often possible to stop by the same day.

One-Eyed Jacks

1645 Market Street, at Gough Street, Hayes Valley (621 4390/www.propcity.com). Muni Metro F, J, K, L, M, N/bus 6, 7, 9, 26, 47, 49, 66, 71. **Open** 11am-6pm Mon-Sat; noon-5pm Sun. **Credit** AmEx, Disc, MC, V. **Map** p310 F5.

Sporting Americana with a country-and-western twang, Jack's is just the place to round up that set of dishes decorated with steer heads and branding motifs you've been dying for.

Flea markets

Alemany Flea Market

100 Alemany Boulevard, at intersection of US 101 & I-280, Bernal Heights (647 2043). Bus 9, 23, 44. **Open** 8am-3pm Sun. **Credit** varies. **Map** p314 Y1.

A favourite Sunday ritual is to roam this open-air flea in the fringes of Bernal Heights, and then head for brunch with treasures (and a newspaper) in tow. A good selection of old photos and magazines can often be found among the mélange of world-weary goods and eight-track tapes.

Arts & crafts

Also check out **Studio 24** in the Mission. Part of **Galeria de la Raza** (*see p203*), it embraces everything from kitsch to crafts, with Latin American folk art and gifts as well as more serious works by contemporary artists – though prices are often wildly inflated.

The African Outlet

524 Octavia Street, between Hayes & Grove Streets, Hayes Valley (864 3576). Bus 21. **Open** 10am-7pm daily. **Credit** AmEx, MC, V. **Map** p310 F5.

A gorgeous jumble of authentic tribal artefacts and antiques – brilliantly coloured textiles, beads and jewellery, sculpture, fetishes, ceremonial masks – is culled by a Nigerian expat and his wife, who delight in explaining the meanings behind the pieces.

Polonco

393 Hayes Street, at Gough Street, Hayes Valley (252 5753). Bus 21, 47, 49. **Open** noon-7pm Tue-Sat. **Credit** MC, V. **Map** p310 F5.

Even on a grey San Francisco day, this fine and folk art gallery emotes warmth and colour. The work of new and emerging Mexican artists shares space with a refined collection of antique and contemporary crafts – including *retablos*, *santos* figures and handmade silver jewellery.

Sam Bo Trading Co

51 Ross Alley, off Washington Street, between Stockton Avenue & Grant Avenue, Chinatown (397 2998). Bus 12, 15, 30, 45, 83. **Open** 10.30am-5pm daily. **No credit cards**. **Map** p309 G3.

The best things in Chinatown are found down the sidestreets. Removed from the bric-a-brac of Grant Avenue, this tiny shop filled with Buddhist and Taoist religious items is like a secret shrine. You'll find buddhas, ceremonial candles, incense and intriguing paper goods used for burning in honour of ancestors or to ask a favour of the gods.

Tibet Shop

4100 19th Street, at Castro Street, Castro (982 0326/www.tibetshopsf.com). Muni Metro F, K, L, M/ bus 24, 33, 35, 37. **Open** 10am-6pm Mon-Sat; noon-5pm Sun. **Credit** AmEx, MC, V. **Map** p314 X1.

Bells, incense, singing bowls, carved skulls, prayer beads, lapis lazuli, turquoise, silver, coral necklaces and the clothing and crafts of Tibet come together in a shop run by a disciple of the Dalai Lama.

Bookshops

San Francisco is a literary town, where every other waiter is a writer and reading groups rival yoga as the most popular post-work activity. But here, as elsewhere, the independent bookshops are under threat from the behemoth chains. With long-time stores disappearing faster than dotcom IPOs, it's time to use them or lose them. Serious antiquarian booksellers also abound, with many conveniently clustered at **49 Geary Street** in Union Square. If you're

Top five Bookshops

A Clean Well-Lighted Place for Books
Nooks, crannies and frequent author readings make this a prime spot for cruising fellow bibliophiles. *See p165.*

City Lights
Now a historic landmark and still the best place to buy your copy of *Howl*. *See p165.*

Green Apple
Some have entered this cavern of previously read books and never been heard from since. *See p165.*

Kayo Books
Pulp fiction with fabulous cover art and titles to make a grown gal blush. *See p166.*

William Stout Architectural Books
Two floors of pornography for architects, designers, landscapers – and the people who love them. *See p166.*

Kerouac hung out at **City Lights** bookshop.

looking for good used bookshops that keep a few rare editions tucked among the workaday stock, your best bet is to head to the Mission.

Acorn Books

1436 Polk Street, at California Street, Polk Gulch (563 1736/www.acornbook.com). Bus 1, 19, 47, 49, 76/cable car California. **Open** 10.30am-8pm Mon-Sat; noon-7pm Sun. **Credit** AmEx, Disc, MC, V. **Map** p308 F3.

With a large selection of rare books in all genres (and prices to match), Acorn also offers a stellar collection of vintage science fiction magazines.

The Booksmith

1644 Haight Street, between Clayton & Cole Streets, Haight-Ashbury (863 8688/www.booksmith.com). Bus 7, 33, 37, 43, 66, 71. **Open** 10am-9pm Mon-Sat; 10am-6pm Sun. **Credit** AmEx, Disc, MC, V. **Map** p313 C6.

The Haight's best-stocked bookshop hosts many authors' readings and events (Mr Amis recently showed off his teeth here), and stocks a decent selection of literary and other magazines.

Borders Books & Music

400 Post Street, at Powell Street, Union Square (399 1633). BART Powell Street/Muni Metro F, J, K, L, M, N/bus 2, 3, 4, 15, 30, 38, 45, 76/cable car Powell-Hyde or Powell-Mason. **Open** 9am-11pm Mon-Thur; 9am-midnight Fri, Sat; 9am-9pm Sun. **Credit** AmEx, Disc, MC, V. **Map** p309 G3.

As befits a megastore, the four-floor selection of books, magazines and CDs at Borders on Union Square is vast, and some bestsellers are offered at a discount. However, the staff is not inclined to break a sweat to aid in your pursuit of less mainstream literary works.

Branches: throughout the Bay Area.

City Lights

261 Columbus Avenue, between Broadway & Pacific Avenue, North Beach (362 8193/www.citylights.com). Bus 12, 15, 30, 41, 45. **Open** 10am-midnight daily. **Credit** AmEx, Disc, MC, V. **Map** p309 G2.

The legacy of anti-authoritarian and insurgent thinking lives on in this publishing company and bookshop founded by poet Lawrence Ferlinghetti in the days when the Beats roamed North Beach. Now a bona fide historic landmark, it doesn't dwell on the past. The American and European literature selection is especially strong, and the occasional readings (such as one by the staggering and heartbreaking Dave Eggers) are real events. *See also p28.*

A Clean Well-Lighted Place for Books

Opera Plaza, 601 Van Ness Avenue, between Golden Gate Avenue & Turk Street, Civic Center (441 6670/www.bookstore.com). Bus 5, 31, 42, 47, 49. **Open** 10am-11pm Mon-Sat; 10am-9pm Sun. **Credit** AmEx, MC, V. **Map** p310 F4.

Centrally located, this well stocked, general interest bookshop hosts frequent and popular readings and events (bad boys Will Self and David Foster Wallace both recently made appearances). The employee recommendations are often worth following up.

A Different Light

489 Castro Street, at 18th Street, Castro (431 0891/www.adlbooks.com). Muni Metro F, K, L, M/bus 24, 33, 35, 37. **Open** 10am-10pm daily. **Credit** AmEx, Disc, MC, V. **Map** p314 X1.

Located in the heart of the Castro, this place has an extensive and impressive stock of books and magazines for and about the gay community, as well as gay, lesbian and transgender literature.

Get Lost Travel Book, Maps & Gear

1825 Market Street, at Guerrero Street, Upper Market (437 0529/www.getlostbooks.com). Muni Metro F, K, L, M/bus 26. **Open** 10am-7pm Mon-Fri; 10am-6pm Sat; noon-5pm Sun. **Credit** AmEx, DC, Disc, MC, V. **Map** p310 F5.

The central theme at this postage-stamp-sized shop is travel and so there's a compelling assortment of hands-on guides and literature, plus a variety of other things you might need to get on your way: maps, travel accessories, slide shows and readings.

Green Apple Books & Music

506 Clement Street, at Sixth Avenue, Richmond District (387 2272/www.greenapplebooks.com). Bus 2, 4, 44. **Open** 10am-10.30pm Mon-Thur, Sun; 10am-11.30pm Fri, Sat. **Credit** Disc, MC, V. **Map** p312 B4.

A destination for bibliophiles from all over, Green Apple offers a staggering mix of new and second-hand titles. It's nirvana for the dedicated browser who thrives on a bit of disarray.

Kayo Books

814 Post Street, between Hyde & Leavenworth Streets, Tenderloin (749 0554/www.kayobooks.com). Bus 2, 3, 4, 27, 38. **Open** 11am-6pm Wed-Sun. **Credit** Disc, MC, V. **Map** p310 F/G4.

This emporium of pulp specialises in vintage paperbacks and dime store novels with fabulous cover art from the 1940s to the 1970s. Many rare and out-of-print books – from Ed Wood to Raymond Chandler – as well as delicious exploitation ephemera. With lots of titles in the $5 range, Kayo paperbacks make great gifts for the folks back home.

Limelight Film & Theater Bookstore

1803 Market Street, at Octavia Street, Hayes Valley (864 2265). Muni Metro F, J, K, L, M, N/bus 6, 7, 26, 66, 71. **Open** 10am-7pm Mon, Tue; 11am-6pm Wed-Sat; 11am-2pm Sun. **Credit** AmEx, Disc, MC, V. **Map** p310 F5.

As you might gather from the name, this shop is dedicated to the thespian arts. Books, plays, books about plays, and so forth, line the shelves.

Marcus Book Stores

1712 Fillmore Street, between Post & Sutter Streets, Western Addition (346 4222/www.marcusbooks.com). Bus 2, 3, 4, 22, 38. **Open** 10am-7pm Mon-Sat; noon-5pm Sun. **Credit** MC, V. **Map** p310 E4.

Marcus specialises in books by African and African-American writers, and about both African and African-American culture. Great reading series. **Branch**: 3900 Martin L King Jr Way, at 39th Street, Oakland (1-510 652 2344).

Modern Times Bookstore

888 Valencia Street, between 19th & 20th Streets, Mission (282 9246/www.mtbs.com). Bus 14, 26, 33, 49. **Open** 10am-9pm Mon-Sat; 11am-6pm Sun. **Credit** AmEx, MC, V. **Map** p314 Y1.

Originally a source of left-wing political tracts, this is now a community centre for the Mission District, where political readings and forums take place amid the good selection of new and used literature, non-fiction, alternative 'zines and scholarly journals.

Rand McNally Map & Travel Store

595 Market Street, at Second Street, Union Square (777 3131/www.randmcnally.com). BART Montgomery Street/Metro Muni F, J, K, L, M, N/bus 2, 3, 4, 6, 7, 9, 21, 31, 66, 71. **Open** 9am-7pm Mon-Fri; 10am-6pm Sat; 11am-5pm Sun. **Credit** AmEx, Disc, MC, V. **Map** p309 H3.

If you're hitting the road, stop in here first. This is downtown San Francisco's source for domestic and international guidebooks, globes, folded and wall maps, and all kinds of essential travel accessories.

Richard Hilkert Bookseller

333 Hayes Street, between Franklin & Gough Streets, Hayes Valley (863 3339). Bus 21, 47, 49. **Open** 9am-5pm Mon-Fri; 11am-5pm Sat. **Credit** AmEx, MC, V. **Map** p310 F5.

A labour of love in this age of mega-chains, this independently owned little jewel of a shop is overseen by an eccentric who maintains a carefully culled selection of new and second-hand books on interior design and architecture, plus fiction, *belles lettres*, travel and children's books.

San Francisco Mystery Bookstore

4175 24th Street, between Castro & Diamond Streets, Noe Valley (282 7444/http://members.aol.com/sfmybooks). Muni Metro J/bus 24, 35, 48. **Open** 11.30am-5.30pm Tue-Sun. **Credit** Disc, MC, V. **Map** p314 X2.

With shelves stacked with mystery and detective fiction (in and out of print) and a large selection of Sherlockiana, this Noe Valley novelty is a mystery lover's tonic.

Stacey's

581 Market Street, between First & Second Streets, Financial District (421 4687/www.staceys.com). BART Montgomery Street/Metro Muni F, J, K, L, M, N/bus 2, 3, 4, 6, 7, 9, 21, 31, 66, 71. **Open** 8.30am-7pm Mon-Fri; 10.30am-7pm Sat; 10.30am-6pm Sun. **Credit** AmEx, Disc, MC, V. **Map** p311 H3.

The city's oldest and largest independent bookshop, Stacey's offers a viable alternative to the marauding chainstores, as well as frequent lunchtime author events in the heart of downtown.

William Stout Architectural Books

804 Montgomery Street, between Jackson Street & Pacific Avenue, North Beach (391 6757/www.stoutbooks.com). Bus 12, 15, 30, 41, 83. **Open** 10am-6.30pm Mon-Fri; 10am-5.30pm Sat. **Credit** MC, V. **Map** p309 H2.

Architect and publisher William Stout's two shops (this is the larger) stock every type of architectural tome, plus books on urban planning, landscaping, interior and industrial design, furniture, graphics, art and photography. Rare and out-of-print editions – such as Le Corbusier's *Radiant City* – are plentiful. **Branch**: **William Stout Design Books** 3A Gallery, 27A South Park, at Third Street, SoMa (495 6757).

Foreign-language bookshops

This is a good town for finding books in myriad languages. San Francisco is one of the country's most multi-cultural. On Valencia Street in the Mission, the following bookshops sell Spanish-language newspapers and *libros en Español*: **Dog Eared Books** (900 Valencia Street, at 19th Street; 282 1901); **Books On Wings** (La Casa de Libros, 973 Valencia Street, at 19th Street; 285 1145) and **Modern Times Bookstore** (*see above*). The magnificent **Kinokuniya** in Japantown (1581 Webster Street, between Post and Geary Streets; 567 7625) is the city's largest Japanese-language bookshop. For their part, Italians can pick up the latest instalment of *Diabolik* at **Cavalli Italian Bookstore** (1441 Stockton Street, at Columbus Avenue, North Beach; 421 4219). The **European Book Company** in the Tenderloin (925 Larkin Street, at Geary Street;

474 0626) stocks publications in various languages and has a small branch at **Café de la Presse**, which also imports magazines.

Computers & electronics

The geographical proximity of Silicon Valley means that new computer technologies are often available in the Bay Area three or four months before they're seen in other parts of the world. What's more, laptop or notebook computers often cost half European prices. Whatever you buy, make sure that your item will work in the country in which you want to use it. Beware: many of the downtown stores that advertise cheap cameras and electronics are fly-by-night. If a deal seems too good to be true, it probably is. Most locals buy their consumer electronics at **The Good Guys** (1400 Van Ness Avenue, at Bush Street; 775 9323) or **Circuit City** (1200 Van Ness Avenue, at Post Street; 441 1300). Both have low prices, and offer installation services and delivery.

Franklin Covey

50 California Street, at Davis Street, Financial District (397 1776/www.franklincovey.com). BART Embarcadero/Muni Metro F, J, K, L, M, N/bus 2, 3, 4, 6, 7, 8, 9, 15, 21, 30, 31, 45, 66, 71/cable car California. **Open** 9am-7pm Mon-Fri; 10am-5pm Sat. **Credit** AmEx, DC, Disc, MC, V. **Map** p309 H3.
All the latest Palm Pilots, Handsprings and accessories – as well as modems, cables, stylus writers – and assorted cases for schlepping it all around.

International Electronics

1163 Mission Street, between Seventh & Eighth Streets, SoMa (1-800 962 4715/626 6382/ www.msmart.com). BART Civic Center/Muni Metro F, J, K, L, M, N/bus 12, 14, 26. **Open** 10am-6pm Mon-Sat. **Credit** AmEx, Disc, MC, V. **Map** p310 G5.
IE sells Walkmans, mini-stereos that work in the UK, portable CD players and voltage converters and transformers ($50-$400) for computers.

MacAdam Computers

1062 Folsom Street, between Sixth & Seventh Streets, SoMa (863 6222). Bus 12. **Open** 9am-6pm Mon-Wed; 9am-5pm Thur; 10am-5pm Sat; 11am-4pm Sun. **Credit** AmEx, Disc, MC, V. **Map** p311 G5.
When their G4s and iMACs start to grumble or give up the ghost, Apple aficionados high-tail it to MacAdam in the SoMa district.

Duty-free

Duty-Free Shops (DFS)

233 Geary Street, at Stockton Street, Union Square (296 3620). BART Powell Street/Metro Muni F, J, K, L, M, N/bus 2, 3, 4, 6, 7, 9, 14, 15, 21, 30, 31, 45, 66, 71/cable car Powell-Hyde or Powell-Mason. **Open** 10am-8pm Mon-Sat; 10am-7pm Sun. **Credit** AmEx, Disc, DC, MC, V. **Map** p311 G3/4.
Cosmetics, perfume, clothing, liquor, tobacco, food and a small selection of cameras are on sale here. At the airport branch, you will have to show your airline ticket to the sales staff; at the downtown shop they will check your ticket and give you a shopping pass. Whatever you purchase will be waiting for you at the boarding gate of your return flight home. **Branch**: San Francisco International Airport (1-650 827 3700).

Fashion

If it's the monoliths you're looking for (Banana Republicans get almost a full city block; Gap and Old Navy addicts are similarly sated), you'll find the flagships on Union Square and will also stumble across branches most anywhere you go, including the big shopping centres (*see p161*). Chains such as Express, BCBG, Bebe, Guess, Club Monaco, Laundry Industry and the like also have a foothold (check the phonebook for listings), with a French Connection promised soon. Union Square is also ground zero for those with wheelbarrows of disposable income and a hankering for labels – Chanel, Prada, Gucci, Armani, Hermes, Ralph Lauren and Versace, among others, are all here. What we tend to prefer are the places that offer a lot of attitude for a tad less cash – here are the highlights.

AB Fits

1519 Grant Avenue, between Union & Filbert Streets, North Beach (982 5726/www.abfits.sfstation.com). **Open** 11am-7pm Tue-Sat; noon-5pm Sun. **Credit** AmEx, Disc, MC, V. **Map** p309 G2.
Jean genies Howard Gee and Christopher Louie carry a barge-load of brands. Some have familiar names (Earl, Dope, Levi's Red, Seven), others are more rarefied (hand-loomed inky jeans with silver buttons by Japan's Hollywood Ranch Market) and some are just plain fabulous (Blueline from Rome). Plus separates and accessories by forward-gazing designers, from Fresh Hype to Rebecca Taylor.

Agnès B

33 Grant Avenue, at O'Farrell Street, Union Square (772 9995/www.agnesb.fr/vr_us/index.html). BART Powell Street/Metro Muni F, J, K, L, M, N/bus 2, 3, 4, 6, 7, 9, 14, 15, 21, 30, 31, 45, 66, 71/cable car Powell-Hyde or Powell-Mason. **Open** 11am-7pm Mon-Sat; noon-5pm Sun. **Credit** AmEx, MC, V. **Map** p311 H4.
This downtown satellite of the French chain bears mention for the relentlessly pretty pieces for women (cropped cardigans, leather jackets that defy trendiness) and the upstairs boutique of stretchy, stripy tops and hipster pants for men.

American Rag

1305 Van Ness Avenue, between Bush & Sutter Streets, Pacific Heights (474 5214/www.amrag.com). Bus 2, 3, 4, 47, 49, 76/cable car California. **Open** 10am-9pm Mon-Sat; noon-8pm Sun. **Credit** AmEx, MC, V. **Map** p310 F3/4.

Don't miss Fashion

AB Fits

These doyens of denim have assembled the coolest damn jeans in the world all under one roof in North Beach. *See p167.*

Alla Prima

Hot flashes: knickers, camis, garters and all manner of featherweight unmentionables. *See p172.*

Gimme Shoes

Whether your thang is spiky heels or intellectual Belgian boots, a trip to Gimme (*pictured*) is a foot fetishist's field day. *See p174.*

MAC

A hip haberdashery that caters to all your multiple personalities, from professional to café dweller to irrepressible club kid. *See p170.*

Metier

What your wardrobe would look like if you could start over, from floaty neo-bohemian numbers to street-smart, hip-chick separates. *See p170.*

Utopia Planita

Otherworldly designs that look airlifted from the East Village, via Tokyo. *See p171.*

The ultra-hip mix of new and recycled clothing includes beaded cardigans, argyle-patterned pullovers and previously worn jeans with holes in all the right places. The once-killer shoe selection has taken a tumble, but the collection of ready-to-wearables (Diesel, William B) has its finger on the trend pulse.

Anthropologie

880 Market Street, between Powell & Stockton Streets, Union Square (434 2210/www.anthropologie.com). BART Powell Street/Metro Muni F, J, K, L, M, N/bus 2, 3, 4, 6, 7, 9, 14, 15, 21, 30, 31, 45, 66, 71/cable car Powell-Hyde or Powell-Mason. **Open** 10am-8pm Mon-Sat; 10am-7pm Sun. **Credit** AmEx, Disc, MC, V. **Map** p309 G3/4.

A bazaar-like gathering of clothing, jewellery and home furnishings, Anthropologie is like the Gap and Pottery Barn's slightly hipper cousin – the one who wore kohl, burned incense and got henna tattoos before it was cool to do so. This is the upmarket sister company of Urban Outfitters (*see p171*), with long sweeping gypsy skirts, velvet tops and bright, dangling earrings, at relatively affordable prices.

The Bar

340 Presidio Avenue, between Sacramento & Clay Streets, Presidio Heights (409 4901). Bus 1, 3, 4, 43. **Open** 10am-6pm Mon-Sat; 10am-5pm Sun. **Credit** AmEx, MC, V. **Map** p307 D3.

The owners of this boutique hope to save the well-heeled locals from making the trek downtown. Wouldn't want them wearing themselves out, now. The clothing is a mix of slightly edgy up-and-comers (William Reid, 38th Parallel), old favourites (Cashmere Studio) and grande dames (Alberata Ferretti) mixed with the odd vintage find. A year-round selection of grand swimsuits, accessories and a coffee bar turn lookers into loungers.

Behind the Post Office

1510 Haight Street, at Ashbury Street, Haight-Ashbury (861 2507). Bus 6, 7, 33, 43, 66, 71. **Open** 11am-7pm daily. **Credit** AmEx, Disc, DC, MC, V. **Map** p313 D5/6.

Glam meets grunge in this perky little Haight Street shop with the helpful-if-you're-looking-for-it name. It's well stocked with low-slung pants, tanks and tees in electric Kool-Aid acid colours, tiny cardigans, and a small cache of shoes – all priced to impart attitude without pinching the wallet.

Betsey Johnson

2031 Fillmore Street, between California & Pine Streets, Pacific Heights (567 2726/www.betseyjohnson.com). Bus 1, 3, 22. **Open** 11am-7pm Mon-Sat; noon-6pm Sun. **Credit** AmEx, MC, V. **Map** p307 E3.

When you need a fix of something fresh, girly or frankly vampy, Betsey is there for you with slip dresses, stretchy velvets, feathered boas and floaty skirts – all at digestible prices. And the neo-bordello sex 'n' roses decor is simply delicious.

Branch: 160 Geary Street, between Stockton Street & Grant Avenue, Union Square (398 2516).

Sexy, stretchy *Dolce Vita* clothes rule the day at **Metier**. *See p170.*

Citizen Clothing

536 Castro Street, between 18th & 19th Streets, Castro (558 9429/www.bodyclothing.com). Muni Metro F, K, L, M/bus 24, 33, 35, 37. **Open** 10am-8pm Mon-Sat; 10am-7pm Sun. **Credit** AmEx, Disc, MC, V. **Map** p314 X1.

Citizen's London-born proprietor outfits gays and straights alike in his own brand of utilitarian chic – streetwear, suits and shoes by DKNY, French Connection, Kenneth Cole, Calvin Klein, BCBG and Giraudon. At Body (4071 18th Street; 861 6111), its brother shop around the corner, guys get clad in all the latest garb for whatever it is they're about to do: at the gym, beach and boudoir.

Dema

1038 Valencia Street, between 21st & 22nd Streets, Mission (206 0500). Bus 14, 26, 49. **Open** 11am-7pm Mon-Sat; noon-6pm Sun. **Credit** MC, V. **Map** p314 Y2.

Instant karma's gonna get you here. Dema Grim is an unabashed mod and her clothing – with its geometric shapes, groovy prints and Audrey-in-*Breakfast-at-Tiffany* flair – define the line. Easy on the wallet, her cropped capris, cocktail dresses and flowing skirts (which she's happy to whip up in another size or colour) are supplemented with little T-shirts, cardigans and accessories by designers such as Custo and Easel.

Diana Slavin

3 Claude Lane, off Bush Street, at Kearny Street, Union Square (677 9939/www.dianaslavin.com). BART Montgomery Street/Muni Metro F, J, K, L, M, N/bus 2, 3, 4, 15, 30, 38, 45, 76/cable car Powell-Hyde or Powell-Mason. **Open** 11am-6pm Tue-Fri; noon-5pm Sat. **Credit** AmEx, MC, V. **Map** p309 H3.

In her haberdashery for women, Diana Slavin designs and displays her trademark fashions: menswear-inspired clothing in rich, subtle colours and lush fabrics. Cutler & Gross sunglasses and Clergerie shoes complete the look.

Diesel

101 Post Street, at Kearny Street, Union Square (982 7077/www.diesel.com). BART Montgomery Street/Muni Metro F, J, K, L, M, N/bus 2, 3, 4, 15, 30, 38, 45, 76/cable car Powell-Hyde or Powell-Mason. **Open** 10am-8pm Mon-Sat; noon-6pm Sun. **Credit** AmEx, Disc, MC, V. **Map** p309 H3.

Three tragically hip floors of Italian street fashion, dishing up a zillion styles of jeans and edgy separates with a sense of humour. Those looking to star in their own rock video should check out the StyleLab line upstairs, with its futuristic fabrics and lots of cropped everything.

Fishbowl

3253 16th Street, at Guerrero Street, Mission (934 1726). Bus 22, 26. **Open** noon-6pm Wed-Sat. **Credit** AmEx, MC, V. **Map** p314 Y1.

Adrian Leong divides his time between teaching at the local art college, designing and minding his little shop of delights. Fishbowl offers a sweet-and-sexy mix of street- and club-worthy wear for both genders: Blue Dot's cropped baggies in everything from black to lime, jeans and tops by Mooks, sassy T-shirts, and simply pretty little skirts.

Heather

2408 Fillmore Street, at Washington Street, Pacific Heights (409 4410). Bus 3, 12, 22, 24. **Open** 10.30am-6.30pm Mon-Fri; 10.30am-6pm Sat; noon-5pm Sun. **Credit** AmEx, Disc, MC, V. **Map** p307 E3.

The friendliest shop on Fillmore Street has a fresh approach to dressing up or down (think NoLita) with soft separates from folks like John Smedley, Ginka, and Nuala (the casual collection from model Christy Turlington in partnership with Puma). There are tiny treasures – such as precious little cameo earrings and amulets – in the display case.

Levi's Jean Store

300 Post Street, at Stockton Street, Union Square (501 0100/www.levi.com). BART Powell Street/ Muni Metro F, J, K, L, M, N/bus 2, 3, 4, 15, 30, 38, 45, 76/cable car Powell-Hyde or Powell-Mason. **Open** 10am-8pm Mon-Sat; 11am-6pm Sun. **Credit** AmEx, Disc, MC, V. **Map** p309 G3.

The flagship store of the venerable old SF-based jeans company (which outfitted gold prospectors in days of yore) manages to be big and thumpingly loud without being completely obnoxious. There's a seriously trendy collection of hip-hopped separates here, all woven around the classic line of jeans, cords and vintage reissues, successfully giving the brand cross-generational appeal. Of course, when it gets right down to it, this is a jeans store.

MAC

1543 Grant Avenue, at Union Street, North Beach (837 1604). Bus 15, 30, 39, 41, 45. **Open** 11am-6pm Mon-Sat; noon-5pm Sun. **Credit** AmEx, MC, V. **Map** p309 H3.

Cosy, intimate MAC (Modern Appealing Clothing) for women has the ecleticism of a really good closet you might peek into during a party: Yoshi Kondo's tweaked British designs (off-register argyle mohairs); Miller et Bertaux's clean-cut separates from Paris; and Dema's mod-squad dresses and capris. The men's shop in downtown offers laid-back streetwear, edgy sportswear by William Reid, John Bartlett and Paul Smith and a wall of natty suits by the likes of Armand Basi and Antwerp modernist Christoph Broich. You'll also find the best tie selection in the city. Oh, and a friendly dog named Maude. **Branch**: 5 Claude Lane, off Bush Street, at Kearny Street, Union Square (837 0615).

Metier

355 Sutter Street, between Stockton Street & Grant Avenue, Union Square (989 5395). BART Powell Street/Muni Metro F, J, K, L, M, N/bus 2, 3, 4, 15, 30, 38, 45, 76/cable car Powell-Hyde or Powell-Mason. **Open** 10am-6pm Mon-Sat. **Credit** AmEx, MC, V. **Map** p309 G3.

Sheri Evans' sun-drenched shop assumes control of your disposable income so pleasantly, you never feel the pain. Creative professionals and neo-bohemians lap up Anna Molinari's sexy, stretchy *Dolce Vita* sweaters and dresses, Rozae Nichols' gossamer separates, Katayone's street-smart slacks and Souchi's cloud-weight knits in sorbet colours. Not to mention Cosabella lingerie and a stellar collection of contemporary and vintage jewellery. Best of all, they never tell you it looks 'fabulous' when it doesn't.

Rolo

450 Castro Street, between Market & 18th Streets, Castro (626 7171/www.rolo.com). Muni Metro F, K, L, M/bus 24, 33, 35, 37. **Open** 10am-8pm Mon-Sat; 11am-7pm Sun. **Credit** AmEx, DC, Disc, MC, V. **Map** p314 X1.

Each shop in the Rolo armada caters to a slightly different crowd, but the common denominator is trendy and fashion forward. On Castro Street, the focus is on T-shirts, jeans (Lucky, Stussy) and men's shoes. Market Street has more label-conscious and edgy menswear (Helmut Lang, G-Star). Stockton Street offers streetwear, with a separate shop catering to hip working gals and club grrrls. And the Howard Street Garage marks it all down when it's time to move those tired threads out the door. **Branches**: **Rolo She** 21 Stockton Street, at Ellis Street, Union Square (421 7529); **Rolo Downtown** 25 Stockton Street, at Ellis Street, Union Square (989 7656); **Rolo on Market** 2351 Market Street, between

All funked up at **Utopia Planitia**. *See p171.*

16th & 17th Streets, Castro (431 4545); **Rolo Garage** 1301 Howard Street, at Ninth Street, SoMa (861 1999); **Undercover** 545 Castro Street, between 18th & 19th Streets, Castro (864 0505).

Susan

3685 Sacramento Street, between Locust & Spruce Streets, Presidio Heights (922 3685). Bus 1, 4. **Open** 10.30am-6.30pm Mon-Fri; 10.30am-6pm Sat. **Credit** AmEx, MC, V. **Map** p306 B3.
A splurgefest in the heart of Laurel Heights: Yohji, Comme des Garçons, Dolce & Gabbana, Helmut Lang, Marni, Margiela and Prada – all at stratospheric prices, but no higher than the department stores. Check out Grocery Store, the nearby sister shop (3615 Sacramento; 928 3615), for diffusion lines and play clothes for adults.

Urban Outfitters

80 Powell Street, at Ellis Street, Union Square (989 1515/www.urbanoutfitters.com). BART Powell Street/Muni Metro F, J, K, L, M, N/bus 2, 3, 4, 15, 30, 38, 45, 76/cable car Powell-Hyde or Powell-Mason. **Open** 9.30am-9.30pm Mon-Sat; 10.30am-9pm Sun. **Credit** AmEx, Disc, MC, V. **Map** p311 G4.
Where the young and budget-minded score the latest looks interpreted at ultra-easy prices, from rave-wear to baggy cords, sexy knee-scraping capris, clingy baby Ts, fuzzy, fake-fur jackets and adorable little embroidered bags. There is also a bevy of expressive housewares, including creative and unusual lamps, scented candles, exotic bedspreads, imported picture frames and pillows, and an excellent collection of sounds.
Branch: 2590 Bancroft Way, at Bowditch Street, Berkeley (1-510 486 1300).

Utopia Planitia

624 Bush Street, between Stockton & Powell Streets, Union Square (362 1277/www.uplanitia.com). Bus 2, 3, 4, 30, 45/cable car Powell-Hyde or Powell-Mason. **Open** noon-6.30pm Mon-Thur; 11am-7pm Fri, Sat. **Credit** AmEx, Disc, MC, V. **Map** p309 G3.
How many shops are named after both a crater on Mars and a *Star Trek* space station? At this earthly outpost, transplanted Brit Charles Burrows and his wife Minnie Yeh offer clothing imbued with an East Village sensibility, which is why it translates so well to boutiques in Tokyo and New York, too. There are few places in San Francisco with such a funked-up combination of jackets graced with fake-fur ruffs, slinky mod tops and skirts, chunky sweaters and home accessories.

Villains

1672 Haight Street, between Clayton & Cole Streets, Haight-Ashbury (626 5939). Bus 7, 33, 37, 43, 66, 71. **Open** *June-Aug* 11am-8pm Mon-Sat; 11am-7pm Sun. *Sept-May* 11am-7pm daily. **Credit** AmEx, Disc, MC, V. **Map** p313 C6.
If you're getting outfitted for Burning Man, a rave or just a roam around the 'hood, here are racks of cropped pants, cargo pockets, space-age fabrics and tiny T-shirts, plus a vast selection of trainers right next door. At Villains Vault across the street (1653 Haight Street; 864 7727), the looks and prices of the clothing and footwear are more yupscale.

Children

Kids Only

1608 Haight Street, at Clayton Street, Haight-Ashbury (552 5445). Bus 7, 33, 37, 43, 66, 71. **Open** 10.30am-6.30pm Mon-Sat; 11am-5pm Sun. **Credit** AmEx, DC, Disc, MC, V. **Map** p313 C/D5/6.
Black clothing for baby goths, leopard-print blankets and hats, handmade grape and strawberry caps and tie-dye duds for tiny Deadheads.

Laku

1069 Valencia Street, at 22nd Street, Mission (695 1462). Bus 14, 26, 49. **Open** 11.30am-6.30pm Tue-Sun. **Credit** AmEx, DC, Disc, MC, V. **Map** p314 Y2.
While many of the objects in this fanciful shop (named after the owner's son) are geared towards adults, most beguiling are the Lilliputian slippers wrought from velvet and shantung silk, and topped with confectionery-like velvet roses.

Mudpie

1694 Union Street, at Gough Street, Cow Hollow (771 9262). Bus 41, 45. **Open** 10am-6pm Mon-Sat; 11am-5pm Sun. **Credit** AmEx, MC, V. **Map** p308 E2.
A charming shop for clothes and toys, unique accessories and pricey gifts for privileged tots.

Peek-a-Boutique

1306 Castro Street, at 24th Street, Noe Valley (641 6192). Bus 24, 48. **Open** 10.30am-6pm Mon-Sat; noon-5pm Sun. **Credit** MC, V. **Map** p314 X2.
Previously worn children's clothing lives on at this second-hand shop, perfect for those whose sizes are in almost constant flux.

Discount

As is always the case, all sizeable outlet malls are well outside town. About an hour north on Highway 101 are some of the best. **Petaluma Village Premium Outlets** (2200 Petaluma Boulevard North; 1-707 778 9300), has 60 shops including Donna Karan, Gap Outlet, Nine West shoes, Puma and Bose. At the **Napa Premium Outlets** (Highway 29 to First Street exit; 629 Factory Stores Drive; 1-707 226 9876), about 90 minutes from the city, there's a Barneys New York outlet, as well as J Crew, Timberland, BCBG, Kenneth Cole and more. There are many more outlet stores in these malls, for a complete list, check www.premiumoutlets.com.

Esprit Factory Outlet

499 Illinois Street, at 16th Street, Potrero Hill (957 2540/www.esprit.com). Bus 15, 22. **Open** 10am-8pm Mon-Fri; 10am-7pm Sat; 11am-6pm Sun. **Credit** AmEx, Disc, JCB, MC, V. **Map** p311 J6.

The apex of adolescent fashion at rock-bottom prices: 30-70% off department store prices. For super bargains, head for the back.

Jeremy's

2 South Park, at Second Street, between Bryant & Brannan Streets, South Beach (882 4929). Bus 10, 15. **Open** 11am-7pm Mon-Fri; 11am-6pm Sat; 11am-5pm Sun. **Credit** AmEx, MC, V. **Map** p311 J4.

Shhhhh. This pretty, wood-panelled shop likes to stay under the radar, so as not to offend the full-price places that ship them their wares. And what wares! This is where women and men hit Dolce and Marni gold at costume jewellery prices, not to mention Armani, Demeulemeester and Tse, and shoes by Sigerson Morrison and Miu Miu. The bath products and shaving brushes make excellent gifts.

Loehmann's

222 Sutter Street, at Kearny Street, Union Square (982 3215/www.loehmanns.com). BART Montgomery Street/Muni Metro F, J, K, L, M, N/bus 2, 3, 4, 15, 30, 38, 45, 76/cable car Powell-Hyde or Powell-Mason. **Open** 9am-8pm Mon-Fri; 9.30am-8pm Sat; 11am-6pm Sun. **Credit** Disc, MC, V. **Map** p309 H3.

Women who would rather be caught in flagrante than pay full retail for cut-price fashions head here, a New York institution now found nationwide.

Lingerie

Alla Prima

1420 Grant Avenue, at Green Street, North Beach (397 4077). Bus 15, 30, 39, 41, 45. **Open** 11am-7pm Tue-Sat; noon-5pm Sun. **Credit** AmEx, MC, V. **Map** p309 G2.

From slinky, ribbed chemises by local designers Underwriters to high-concept panty-pushers La Perla and Leigh Bontivoglio, Alla Prima stocks it all – in sizes ranging from gamine to well-rounded and in colours and patterns to rival a confectionery shop. The bras, bustiers and knickers are so hot, don't be put off if the staff can be cool.

Branch: 539 Hayes Street, between Octavia & Laguna Streets, Hayes Valley (864 8180).

Dark Garden

321 Linden Street, at Gough Street, Hayes Valley (431 7684/www.darkgarden.com). Bus 21. **Open** 10am-6pm Mon-Fri; 11am-5pm Sat; noon-4pm Sun. **Credit** MC, V. **Map** p310 F5.

Autumn Carey-Adamme has a calling, and it's corsets. While the off-the-rack models are more than seductive, her real *métier* is in measuring and making the custom jobs. You select the style, fabric and colour, and 12 individual measurements (kept on file) create a bespoke garment that laces or hooks you into delightful submission.

Workshop

2254 Union Street, between Fillmore & Steiner Streets, Cow Hollow (561 9551). Bus 22, 41, 45. **Open** 10am-6pm Mon-Sat; noon-5pm Sun. **Credit** AmEx, MC, V. **Map** p307 E2/3.

Laku: for well-dressed tots. *See p171.*

The clothing in the main shop is pleasant, but can't hold a candle to the underthings arrayed in the Lingerie Cottage out back. These sophisticated confections by Laura Urbinati, Capucine Puerari, Colette Dinnegan and others are about as far as one can get from Victoria's Secret, and the small, year-round selection of swimsuits is brilliant.

Vintage & second-hand

The most fertile hunting grounds for previously worn clothing are on **Haight Street**, **Fillmore Street** and in the **Mission**.

Aardvark's Odd Ark

1501 Haight Street, at Ashbury Street, Haight-Ashbury (621 3141). Bus 6, 7, 33, 37, 43, 66, 71. **Open** 11am-7pm daily. **Credit** AmEx, Disc, MC, V. **Map** p313 D5/6.

You can pass happy hours hunting for diamonds in the rough at this packed-to-the-rafters shop.

Buffalo Exchange

1555 Haight Street, between Clayton & Ashbury Streets, Haight-Ashbury (431 7733/www.buffaloexchange.com). Bus 7, 33, 37, 43, 66, 71. **Open** 11am-7pm Mon-Fri; 11am-8pm Sat; noon-8pm Sun. **Credit** MC, V. **Map** p313 D6.

Don't know what to do with that hideous Marks & Sparks Christmas sweater that's taking up closet space? Trade it in for cash or clothing at this well-known second-hand recycler, one of the city's best.

Branch: 1800 Polk Street, at Washington Street, Polk Gulch (346 5726)

Clothes Contact

473 Valencia Street, at 16th Street, Mission (621 3212). BART 16th Street/bus 14, 22, 26, 33, 49, 53. **Open** 11am-7pm daily. **Credit** Disc, MC, V. **Map** p314 Y1.

Clothing by the pound – still only $8 per lb as we went to press – is hard to beat, unless you're looking for a lead suit. The fake furs are quite a bargain.

Crossroads Trading Company

2231 Market Street, between Sanchez & Noe Streets, Castro (626 8989). Muni Metro F, K, L, M/bus 24, 35, 37. **Open** 11am-7pm Mon-Thur; 11am-8pm Fri, Sat; noon-7pm Sun. **Credit** MC, V. **Map** p313 E6.
The Market and Haight Street branches of this favourite local trading shop house mostly 1980s wear, while the Fillmore Street shop is better for jeans, dresses and classic vintage wear.
Branches: 1901 Fillmore Street, at Bush Street, Pacific Heights (775 8885); 1519 Haight Street, at Ashbury Street, Haight-Ashbury (355 0554).

Das Pussycat

3162 16th Street, between Valencia & Guerrero Streets, Mission (255 4883). BART 16th Street/bus 14, 22, 26, 33, 49, 53. **Open** 11am-8pm Mon-Thur, Sun; 11am-9pm Fri, Sat. **Credit** MC, V. **Map** p314 Y1.
Goods from many eras and of varying levels of kitsch are carefully organised for easy browsing at this well-priced Mission fave, named in honour of a chain of 1950s strip clubs.

Departures – From the Past

2028 Fillmore Street, between Pine & California Streets, Pacific Heights (885 3377). Bus 1, 3, 22. **Open** 11am-7pm Mon-Sat; noon-6pm Sun. **Credit** AmEx, MC, V. **Map** p307 E3.
The theme here is theatrical, with a focus on costumes and formal attire from the era before global warming. And, like most of the vintage haunts on Fillmore, the pickings here are much richer than at shops in less upmarket districts. There's a good reason for that: just consider the donation pool.

GoodByes

3483 Sacramento Street, at Locust Street, Presidio Heights (674 0151). Bus 1, 4. **Open** 10am-6pm Mon-Wed, Fri, Sat; 10am-8pm Thur; 11am-5pm Sun. **Credit** Disc, MC, V. **Map** p313 C4.
Light years from the Haight/Mission scene in pristine Laurel Heights, GoodByes is a consignment shop where you might stumble across a barely worn Miu Miu sweater, last season's Prada coat or a little Chanel number some socialite decided just didn't agree with her. The menswear shop is just down the road at 3464 Sacramento (346 6388).

Martini Mercantile

1435 Grant Avenue, at Green Street, North Beach (362 1944). Bus 15, 30, 39, 41. **Open** noon-6pm daily. **Credit** AmEx, MC, V. **Map** p309 G2.
A magnet for the swing set, with vintage and vintage-looking clothing mixed together, plus lots of pretty, glittery barrettes, retro ties and accessories to go with the skirts, frocks and suits.

Schauplatz

791 Valencia Street, at 19th Street, Mission (864 5665). Bus 14, 33, 49. **Open** noon-7pm Wed-Sun. **Credit** DC, MC, V. **Map** p314 Y1.
German for 'happening place', Schauplatz's offerings are a little more curated than at other Mission haunts, which makes it easier to spot the Italian Riviera sunglass frames, intricately beaded Moroccan mules and Swedish policeman's leather jacket (with special map pocket).

Ver Unica

148 Noe Street, at Henry Street, Castro (431 0688/ www.ver-unica.com). Muni Metro F, K, L, M/bus 24, 33, 37. **Open** noon-7pm Mon-Sat; noon-6pm Sun. **Credit** AmEx, DC, Disc, MC, V. **Map** p313 E6.
Vintage vultures graduate to Ver Unica when they get a few dollars and grow weary of pawing through crammed-together cast-offs. These retro finds are unique, a bit expensive and a cut above the norm. You'll find things here are suitable for work or play, and no lingering scent of mothballs.

Wasteland

1660 Haight Street, at Belvedere Street, Haight-Ashbury (863 3150). Bus 7, 33, 37, 43, 66, 71. **Open** 11am-7pm Mon-Fri; 11am-8pm Sat, Sun. **Credit** AmEx, MC, V. Map p313 C6.
Wasteland sells trendy and sometimes outrageous second-hand clothing with history. It's possibly the most popular used clothier in town, with a good supply of vintage costume jewellery and fancy gowns.

Fashion accessories

Handbags

Whether you're after a chic little clutch or a bowling-ball scaled tote, shoe shops (especially **Gimme Shoes** – *see p174*), clothing boutiques (such as **Susan** – *see p171*) and department stores (*see p160*) also merit a look.

Kate Spade

227 Grant Avenue, between Post & Sutter Streets, Union Square (216 0880/www.katespade.com). BART Montgomery Street/Muni Metro F, J, K, L, M, N/bus 2, 3, 4, 15, 30, 38, 45, 76/cable car Powell-Mason or Powell-Hyde. **Open** 11am-7pm Mon-Sat; noon-5pm Sun. **Credit** AmEx, Disc, MC, V. **Map** p309 G/H3.
The high-priestess of handbags (nylon, leather, silk) now flogs those and more – shoes, sunglasses, day planners and pyjamas – many bearing her signature palette of bold colours and mod graphics. There are also some groovy first-edition books here (à la Paul Smith), and everything is somewhat overpriced. Most sought-after: the baby-changing bag and the laptop computer tote, cushioned for your protection.

Shine

808 Sutter Street, between Jones & Leavenworth Streets, Tenderloin (409 0991). Bus 2, 3, 4, 27. **Open** 1-7pm Tue-Fri; 11am-6pm Sat, Sun. **Credit** AmEx, MC, V. **Map** p308 G3.
The bags, shoes, and jewellery by more than 20 designers – from Cynthia Rowley to Jules & Jim Paris – you'll find here offer a high funk factor along with relatively low price tags. Purses range from one-off velvet confections to leather, straw and gold lamé, for nurturing the diva within.

True

1415 Haight Street, at Masonic Avenue, Haight-Ashbury (626 2882). Bus 6, 7, 33, 37, 43, 66, 71. **Open** 11am-7pm daily. **Credit** Disc, MC, V. **Map** p313 D5.

Top-notch messenger bags in every conceivable shape and style.

Jewellery

Also check out the superb jewellery selection at **Metier** (*see p170*).

De Vera

29 Maiden Lane, between Grant Avenue & Kearny Street, Union Square (788 0828/www.deveraobjects.com). BART Powell Street/Muni Metro F, J, K, L, M, N/bus 5, 6, 7, 9, 21, 27, 30, 31, 45, 66/cable car Powell-Hyde or Powell-Mason. **Open** 10am-6pm Tue-Sat. **Credit** AmEx, MC, V. **Map** p309 H3.

At Federico de Vera's jewel box of a shop on Maiden Lane, necklaces, bracelets, rings and earrings – many a rarefied mix of old and new elements – catch the light and ignite desire. Intricate beadwork unites precious gemstones, rosecut diamonds and Indian gold beads. And don't miss the stunning, exotic collection of beautiful *objets d'art*, both ancient and modern, at the sister shop on nearby Sutter Street. **Branch**: 580 Sutter Street, between Powell & Mason Streets, Union Square (989 0988).

Lang

323 Sutter Street, between Stockton Street & Grant Avenue, Union Square (982 2213/www.langantiques.com). BART Powell Street/Muni Metro F, J, K, L, M, N/bus 2, 3, 4, 15, 30, 38, 45, 76/cable car Powell-Hyde or Powell-Mason. **Open** 10.30am-5.30pm Mon-Sat. **Credit** AmEx, Disc, DC, MC, V. **Map** p309 G3.

A large inventory of antique and estate jewellery and timepieces, including plenty of silver flatware.

Zeitgeist

437B Hayes Street, between Gough & Octavia Streets, Hayes Valley (864 0185). Bus 21. **Open** noon-6pm Tue-Sat. **Credit** AmEx, MC, V. **Map** p310 F5.

The city's best source for vintage wrist and pocket watches, from quite reasonable lesser-known names to major players such as Philippe Patek and Rolex. They also do repairs on the premises.

Leather goods & luggage

Edward's Luggage

3 Embarcadero Center, between Davis & Drumm Streets, Financial District (981 7047/www.edwardsluggage.com). BART Embarcadero/Muni Metro F, J, K, L, M, N/bus 2, 3, 4, 6, 7, 8, 9, 15, 21, 30, 31, 45, 66, 71/cable car California. **Open** 10am-7pm Mon-Fri; noon-6pm Sat; noon-5pm Sun. **Credit** AmEx, Disc, MC, V. **Map** p309 H3.

Edward's offers everything you need to hit the road, including easy-to-roll, ultra-sturdy Tumi luggage. **Branches**: throughout the Bay Area.

Johnson Leather Corporation

1833 Polk Street, between Jackson & Washington Streets, Polk Gulch (775 7392). Bus 1, 12, 19, 27, 47, 49, 76. **Open** 10.30am-6.30pm Mon-Sat; noon-5pm Sun. **Credit** AmEx, Disc, MC, V. **Map** p308 F3.

A favourite with local motorcyclists, Johnson's is both a factory and a shop, which means good buys on lambskin unisex jackets and alterations done while you wait. You'll also find custom-made jackets at laughably low prices. It's everything you need to get your motor running.

Kenneth Cole

166 Grant Avenue, between Post & Geary Streets, Union Square (981 2653/www.kennethcole.com). BART Powell or Montgomery Streets/Muni Metro F, J, K, L, M, N/bus 2, 3, 4, 15, 30, 38, 45, 76/cable car Powell-Hyde or Powell-Mason. **Open** 10am-8pm Mon-Sat; noon-6pm Sat. **Credit** AmEx, MC, V. **Map** p309 G/H3.

The socially conscious national shoe tsar flogs more than footwear. There's also a tasty selection of men's and women's leather outerwear, sportswear, briefcases, wallets and purses at quite decent prices. **Branches**: 865 Market Street, at Grant Avenue, Union Square (227 4536); 2078 Union Street, between Webster & Buchanan Streets, Cow Hollow (346 2161).

Lava 9

542 Hayes Street, between Laguna & Octavia Streets, Hayes Valley (552 6468). Bus 21. **Open** noon-7pm Mon-Sat; noon-5pm Sun. **Credit** AmEx, MC, V. **Map** p310 F5.

A leatherfest in the heart of hipster-magnet Hayes Valley. You can buy off the rack, or have owner Heidi Werner take your measurements, spread out some skins and get that customised jacket you've always dreamed about (just don't forget to remove it for PETA meetings).

Shoes

Fetish

344 Presidio Avenue, between Clay & Sacramento Streets, Presidio Heights (409 7429). Bus 1, 3, 43. **Open** 10am-6pm Mon-Sat; noon-5pm Sun. **Credit** AmEx, MC, V. **Map** p307 D3.

If you get seized with shoe envy every time you watch the gals cavorting on *Sex and the City*, head to this ultra-femme shop for plain and bejewelled party heels by Jimmy Choo, Patrick Cox, Emma Hope and others.

Gimme Shoes

50 Grant Avenue, between O'Farrell & Geary Streets, Union Square (434 9242). BART Powell or Montgomery Streets/Muni Metro F, J, K, L, M, N/bus 5, 6, 7, 9, 21, 27, 30, 31, 45, 66. **Open** 11am-7pm Mon-Sat; noon-6pm Sun. **Credit** AmEx, Disc, MC, V. **Map** p309 H4.

Every season, shoe-mad San Franciscans flock to Gimme Shoes to check out the most coveted looks. Richer fare includes Demeulemeester, Miu Miu, Kelian, Costume National and Martine Sitbon. Momo and Clone are among the many moderate but

The city on foot: Hayes Valley crawl

Sexy corsets at **Dark Garden**.

As you stroll this three-block stretch of Hayes Street, from Franklin to Laguna Streets, pondering everything from antique French cake plates to Prada mules, it's hard to believe that, not so long ago, drug dealers, prostitutes and their clients called this street home. More than a decade after the Loma Prieta quake felled the freeway overpass that once cast the area in gloom, Hayes Valley is now a haven of hipsters and high-end shops and restaurants.

On the block between Franklin and Gough Streets, you'll find **Champ de Mars** (No.347; 252 9434), a kind of transplanted French flea market that offers everything from dog oil portraits to antique toys. Several degrees south is **Polonco** (*see p164*), a gallery-cum-shrine devoted to the fine and folk art of Mexico. Nearby, the delightful and eccentric bookseller **Richard Hilkert** (*see p166*) sells all that catches his fancy, from architecture to *belles lettres* and children's books.

On the next block, up to Octavia Street, you can get shod in everything from Miu Miu to Puma at **Gimme Shoes** (*see p174*) and pick up a vintage timepiece from the era of your choice across the street at **Zeitgeist** (*see p174*). **The African Outlet** (*see p164*) on Octavia Street imports gorgeous textiles, carvings and jewellery. And tops, bottoms and everything in-between find happiness at **Dark Garden** (*see p172*) on Linden Street, where corsets are custom-made to fit your own tastes and curves.

From Octavia to Laguna, it's a girly fest at **Haseena** (No.526 Hayes; 252 1104), with embroidered dresses, flowery sweaters and Chinese jackets, while men get their edgy separates at **Nomads** (No.556; 864 5692) and both sexes have a field day among the recycled cocktail dresses, cowboy boots and shagalicious leather jackets at **560 Hayes** (No.560; 861 7993). Former Michael Kors associate **Deborah Hampton** (No.555; 701 8682) balances the area's funk factor with high-end, tailored pieces in muted urban tones. **Lava 9** (*see p174*) will make you a leather jacket to order in record time, while at **Zonal** (No.568; 255 9307), you can find a fabulously rusted finial or a brand new club chair in which to curl up.

Alabaster (*see p178*) mingles vintage (mother-of-pearl caviar spoons) with fresh (lilac-scented bath salts). **Alla Prima** (*see p172*) stocks sweet nothings to wear underneath, and round the corner at **Mapuche** (500 Laguna Street; 551 0725), fashion stylists and club kids snatch up hand-tooled leather bags and cuffs. Fans of science fiction and fantasy score first editions at **Borderlands** (534 Laguna; 558 8978). And if the latest dance vinyl makes your heart race, duck into **BPM Music Factory** (573 Hayes; *see p182*).

If you look up now, you'll see the sign of the french fry, which means you're at **Frjtz** (579 Hayes; 864 7654) – just the place to stop and tuck into a pile of hot, crisp Belgian fries washed down with a cold beer.

forward-looking lines, and there's also an impressive cache of trainers and casual shoes from labels like Adidas, Puma and Prada.
Branches: 416 Hayes Street, at Gough Street, Hayes Valley (864 0691); 2358 Fillmore Street, at Washington Street, Pacific Heights (441 3040).

Luichiny

1529 Haight Street, between Ashbury & Clayton Streets, Haight-Ashbury (252 7065). Bus 6, 7, 33, 37, 43, 66, 71. **Open** 11am-6pm Mon-Sat; noon-5pm Sun. **Credit** AmEx, MC, V. **Map** p313 D5/6.
Where the club kids head for Italian-made, sky-high platforms and Olive Oyl-style Mary-Jane shoes fit for a friendly porn film.

Shoe Biz

1446 Haight Street, between Ashbury Street & Masonic Avenue, Haight-Ashbury (864 0990). Bus 6, 7, 33, 37, 43, 66, 71. **Open** 11am-7pm daily. **Credit** AmEx, MC, V. **Map** p313 D5.
Towering, pointy, chunky, clunky – the emphasis is on trendy and fun for men and women. Trainers are stocked at Shoe Biz II, a block away.
Branch: **Shoe Biz II** 1553 Haight Street, between Ashbury & Clayton Streets, Haight-Ashbury (861 3933).

Subterranean Shoe Room

877 Valencia Street, at 20th Street, Mission (401 9504/http://subshoeroom.com). Bus 14, 33, 49. **Open** noon-7pm daily. **Credit** AmEx, DC, Disc, MC, V. **Map** p314 Y1.
Fashion-savvy Japanese and Europeans have already sniffed out this new shop in the Mission, owned by two friendly brothers from Oklahoma. Hard-to-find gems include Redwing, Frye Boots, Blundstone from Australia, molto-trendy Italian lines Holler and Fornarina, vintage cowboy boots, and trainers by Puma and Fly London.

Shoe repair

Anthony's Shoe Service

30 Geary Street, between Grant Avenue & Kearny Street, Union Square (781 1338). BART Montgomery Street/Muni Metro F, J, K, L, M, N/bus 2, 3, 4, 15, 30, 38, 45, 76/cable car Powell-Hyde or Powell-Mason. **Open** 8am-5.30pm Mon-Fri; 9am-5pm Sat. **Credit** AmEx, DC, Disc, MC, V. **Map** p311 G/H3.
A well-known cobbler, and handy for downtown (if a tad pricey). You name it, they'll mend it – they'll even put new taps on your old tap shoes.

Food & drink

Bi-Rite Market

3639 18th Street, at Dolores Street, Mission (241 9773). Muni Metro J/bus 22, 33. **Open** 10am-9pm Mon-Fri; 9am-8pm Sat, Sun. **Credit** MC, V. **Map** p314 Y1.
First opened in 1940 and now restored to its original pre-war lustre, this speciality grocery store sells house-smoked salmon, home-made sausages, cakes, salads, Middle Eastern dips and pasta sauces. It also has an olive bar and more than 100 cheeses. Fresh Gus pickles are flown in from New York.

Bombay Ice Creamery

522 Valencia Street, at 18th Street, Mission (431 1103). BART 16th Street/bus 14, 33, 49. **Open** noon-10pm Tue-Fri; 12.30pm-11pm Sat, Sun. **Credit** AmEx, Disc, MC, V. **Map** p314 Y1.
Vanilla seems so… vanilla – when you could be lapping up flavours such as chai, ginger, rose, saffron, pistachio and cardamom.

Boulangerie Bay Bread

2325 Pine Street, at Fillmore Street, Pacific Heights (440 0356). Bus 1, 2, 3, 4, 22. **Open** 8am-6pm Tue-Sat; 8am-4pm Sun. **No credit cards**. **Map** p307 E3.
The crusty breads are all baked from organic flour in Pavailler ovens imported from France; tarts and eclairs are meltingly sweet, without being cloying. You'll also find fresh sandwiches wrapped and ready to go, in flavours like smoked turkey and cranberry, and French ham.
Branch: 2310 Polk Street, at Green Street, Polk Gulch (345 1107).

Ferry Plaza Farmer's Market

Embarcadero, at Green Street, Embarcadero (www.saturdaymarket.com). Muni Metro F/bus 10, 12. **Open** 8am-1.30pm Sat. **Credit** MC, V. **Map** p309 H2/3.
This Saturday market is where foodies flock to find all-organic fruit and veg, local goat's cheeses, fresh bread and pasta, gourmet sausages and exotic jams; sampling is encouraged. There are fresh flower stalls, and a clutch of local restaurants have stands selling top-notch fare to ravenous shoppers (don't miss the huevos rancheros).

Liguria Bakery

1700 Stockton Street, between Greenwich & Lombard Streets, North Beach (421 3786). Bus 15, 30, 39, 41, 45/cable car Powell-Mason. **Open** 8am-around 3pm Mon-Fri; 7am-around 3pm Sat, Sun. **No credit cards**. **Map** p308/309 G3.
In 1911, three brothers from Genoa had the foresight to set up this tiny North Beach *foccacceria*, which sells their famous flatbreads from morning until whenever they sell out.

Molinari Delicatessen

373 Columbus Avenue, at Vallejo Street, North Beach (421 2337). Bus 12, 15, 30, 39, 41, 45. **Open** 8am-6pm Mon-Fri; 7.30am-5.30pm Sat. **Credit** MC, V. **Map** p309 G2.
Molinari was dishing out home-made gnocchi and pesto *alla genovese* long before the yupsters ever heard of the stuff. It's still a great place to gather together an al fresco repast.

Whole Foods

1765 California Street, at Franklin Street, Pacific Heights (674 0500/www.wholefoodsmarket.com). Bus 1, 42, 47, 49, 76. **Open** 8am-10pm daily. **Credit** AmEx, Disc, MC, V. **Map** p308 F3.

You can find anything organic and health-oriented that you want here; the challenge is to leave Whole Foods with anything left in your wallet. There's a very good reason why locals call this place 'Whole Paycheck'. However, if you're feeling flush, its bakery, gourmet deli and outstanding cheese, fish, sushi and meat counters are all worth a visit. Most of the food here is organic (things that are not are marked), and there are lots of vegetarian options.

Food delivery

You don't have to leave your room to have a good meal in San Francisco. Upmarket food delivery specialists include **Ez2get** (1-800 239 2438/www.ez2get.com), which specialises in ethnic eateries, and **Waiters on Wheels** (452 6500/www.waiters onwheels.com). Many of the city's smaller restaurants offer delivery services for a minimum food order; it's worth checking those near your hotel.

Tea & coffee

Graffeo Coffee Roasting Company

735 Columbus Avenue, at Filbert Street, North Beach (1-800 222 6250/986 2429). Bus 15, 30, 39, 41, 45/ cable car Powell-Mason. **Open** 9am-6pm Mon-Fri; 9am-5pm Sat. **Credit** MC, V. **Map** p308 G2.

This long-standing North Beach shop is stocked with fresh coffees from around the world, and is a San Francisco institution.

Ten Ren Tea Company of San Francisco

949 Grant Avenue, between Washington & Jackson Streets, Chinatown (362 0656). Bus 1, 9, 15, 30, 41, 45. **Open** 9am-9pm daily. **Credit** AmEx, Disc, MC, V. **Map** p309 G3.

Ten Ren stocks 40 different types of Chinese tea, from the ordinary cuppa to expensive infusions for special occasions. Taste before you buy.

Wine

For information on exploring the wine country near San Francisco, *see p256.*

Jug Shop

1567 Pacific Avenue, at Polk Street, Polk Gulch (885 2922/www.wineshopsanfrancisco.com). Bus 12, 19, 27, 42, 47, 49, 76. **Open** 9am-9pm Mon-Sat; 9.30am-7pm Sun. **Credit** AmEx, DC, MC, V. **Map** p308 F3.

The knowledgeable staff here will help you select from vintages from around the world.

Napa Valley Winery Exchange

415 Taylor Street, between Geary & O'Farrell Streets, Tenderloin (1-800 653 9463/771 2887). Bus 27, 38. **Open** 10am-7pm Mon-Sat; 10am-5pm Sun. **Credit** AmEx, Disc, MC, V. **Map** p310 G4.

It's Martha Stewart meets David Lynch at **Paxton Gate**. *See p179.*

Eye-catching accessories for pets at **George**.

Specialising in California wines, including unusual and hard-to-find varieties, this shop has 500 wine brands in stock and will ship anywhere in the world.

The Wine Club

953 Harrison Street, between Fifth & Sixth Streets, SoMa (1-800 966 7835/512 9086/www.thewineclub.com). Bus 12, 27, 47. **Open** 9am-7pm Mon-Sat; 11am-6pm Sun. **Credit** AmEx, MC, V. **Map** p309 H5.
Some of the best wine bargains around are found in this warehouse of a shop, with prices on very drinkable varietals starting at $5 and going as high as you like. The enthusiastic staff will guide you through the 1,200 options. Tastings are held each month.

Gifts

Alabaster

597 Hayes Street, at Laguna Street, Hayes Valley (558 0482/www.alabastersf.com). Bus 21. **Open** 11am-6pm Tue-Sat; noon-5pm Sun. **Credit** AmEx, Disc, MC, V. **Map** p310 F5.
Nelson Bloncourt's homage to all things pale (alabaster lamps that glow from within, French ivory boxes, Burmese buddhas) is also sparked by objects of colour, from vintage globes to vivid, framed African butterflies. In this shop, you might discover old Venetian wine glasses shaped like the windows of a palazzo on the Grand Canal or a rare, refurbished Belgian art deco dresser. Should you be feeling romantic, you'll also find a rare cache of glorious platinum and 24-carat gold wedding rings from the Menichini Gioiellieri in Rome that could perfectly suit the moment.

Dandelion

55 Potrero Avenue, at 15th Street, Mission (436 9500/www.tampopo.com). Bus 33. **Open** 10am-6pm Tue-Sat. **Credit** AmEx, MC, V. **Map** p311 G6.
Brave the seedy underbelly of the Mission/Potrero underpass to find this enchanting gift shop, which carries exquisite gifts for every recipient imaginable, from children to cat-lovers to executives. You'll find Japanese sake and tea sets, kitchenware, bath products, books, sweets, jams and holiday offerings, all in a warm, upscale setting. Prices are startlingly reasonable; you may need to look twice at the $10 tag on that perfectly charming picnic basket.

George

2411 California Street, at Fillmore Street, Pacific Heights (441 0564/www.georgesf.com). Bus 1, 3, 22. **Open** 11am-6pm Mon-Fri; 10am-6pm Sat; noon-6pm Sun. **Credit** AmEx, MC, V. **Map** p307 E3.
Founded by a pair of fox terrier owners from Texas, George sells eye-catching accessories for pets to wear, eat, play with and sleep on. Treats, organic catnip, 'Good Dog' bath towels, 'Good Trip' catnip toys, natty jackets and sweaters, lucky charms and patterned ceramic bowls complement an enticing array of T-shirts and sweatshirts for hipster bipeds. **Branch**: 1829 Fourth Street, between Virginia Street & Hearst Avenue, Berkeley (1-510 644 1033).

Nest

2300 Fillmore Street, at Clay Street, Pacific Heights (292 6199). Bus 1, 3, 12, 22, 24. **Open** 10.30am-6.30pm Mon-Sat; noon-6pm Sun. **Credit** AmEx, MC, V. **Map** p307 E3.

Like the flea market of your dreams, Nest sells gauzy Chinese lanterns in rose garden colours, shabby chic bed linens, beaded hoop earrings, tin motorcycle wind-up toys, Moroccan glassware, Mariage Frère teapots, quirky ceramics – and all kinds of other things you can't live without.

Branch: 2340 Polk Street, between Union & Green Streets, Polk Gulch (292 6198).

Paxton Gate

824 Valencia Street, at 20th Street, Mission (824 1872/www.paxton-gate.com). Bus 14, 26, 33, 49. **Open** 11am-7pm Mon-Thur, Sun; noon-8pm Fri; 11am-8pm Sat. **Credit** AmEx, MC, V. **Map** p314 Y1.

Martha Stewart meets David Lynch at Paxton Gate, which is dedicated to 'treasures and oddities inspired by the garden'. Owner/curator Sean Quigley has everything from bulbs and flower-arranging tools to hand-painted glass eyes used for taxidermy and silver necklaces cast from the bones of rats' and pelicans' feet. It's completely bizarre, and completely unique. Don't miss it.

Quantity Postcards

1441 Grant Avenue, at Vallejo Street, North Beach (788 4455). Bus 12, 15, 30, 41. **Open** 11am-11pm daily. **Credit** AmEx, MC, V. **Map** p309 G2.

A veritable postcard museum with a funhouse atmosphere, the walls here are crammed with new and vintage examples of the art: quaint Victorian flowery tributes, old snapshots of San Francisco, tinted landscapes of faraway places, and a selection of Frank Kozik's psychedelic music posters.

Rayon Vert

3187 16th Street, at Guerrero Street, Mission (861 3516). BART 16th Street/bus 14, 22, 26, 49. **Open** noon-6pm Wed-Sat. **Credit** MC, V. **Map** p314 Y1.

Florist Kelly Kornegay's shop seduces with buckets of real blooms, which she transforms into classy arrangements. Among the flora is anything that happens to catch her eye, from refurbished stainless steel medical furniture to new and vintage housewares, vases, funky Japanese lunch boxes, old silver julep cups and striped sake bowls.

SFMOMA MuseumStore

SFMOMA, 151 Third Street, between Mission & Howard Streets, SoMa (357 4035/www.sfmoma.org). BART Powell or Montgomery Streets/Muni Metro F, J, K, L, M, N/bus 9, 15, 30, 45, 76. **Open** 10.30am-6.30pm Mon-Wed, Fri-Sun; 10.30am-9.30pm Thur. **Credit** AmEx, MC, V. **Map** p311 H4.

A lot of people never make it past the gift shop to the galleries. You'll find art and photography books, monographs and catalogues, a vast selection of cards, posters, videos, jewellery and children's toys.

Branch: San Francisco International Airport (1-650 553 8040).

SwallowTail

2217 Polk Street, between Vallejo & Green Streets, Polk Gulch (567 1555). Bus 19, 41, 45, 47, 49, 76. **Open** noon-6pm daily. **Credit** AmEx, MC, V. **Map** p308 F2.

New items are sprinkled in among the vintage home decor, which includes a wonderful collection of old clocks, aged flower paintings and unusual pieces you're unlikely to find elsewhere, like weathered, enamelled gas station numbers.

Health & beauty

Complementary & alternative medicine

Scarlet Sage Herb Co

1173 Valencia Street, between 22nd & 23rd Streets, Mission (821 0997/www.scarletsageherb.com). BART 24th Street/bus 14, 26, 48, 49. **Open** 11am-6.30pm daily. **Credit** AmEx, Disc, MC, V. **Map** p314 Y2.

The owners of this herbal apothecary stock more than 300 organic herbs, essential oils, tinctures and plant essences to soothe whatever ails you, with a substantial section dedicated specifically to homoeopathic remedies. It also offers a variety of teas, sweet-smelling soaps and plenty of books.

Vinh Khang Herbs & Ginsengs

512 Clement Street, between Sixth & Seventh Avenues, Richmond District (752 8336). Bus 1, 2, 4, 44. **Open** 9.30am-7pm Mon, Wed-Sun. **No credit cards**. **Map** p312 B4.

Thanks to the city's large Asian population, Chinese herbalism has always thrived in San Francisco. Inspect this Richmond District shop's splendid array of roots and remedies while herbal specialists create a customised concoction for you.

Cosmetics & skincare

Kiehl's

2360 Fillmore Street, between Washington & Clay Streets, Pacific Heights (359 9260). Bus 1, 3, 12, 22, 24. **Open** 11am-7pm Mon-Sat; noon-5pm Sun. **Credit** AmEx, DC, MC, V. **Map** p307 E3.

The first Kiehl's apothecary set up shop in New York's East Village in 1851; 150 years later, their second shop opened in Pacific Heights. Gentle, affordable and justifiably beloved, these products are a fave with models and Hollywood types. The 300 botanically based concoctions run the gamut from grapefruit body wash and lavender lotion to honey almond face scrub. An added bonus: they ply you with masses of free samples.

MAC Cosmetics

1833 Union Street, between Laguna & Octavia Streets, Cow Hollow (771 6113/www.maccosmetics.com). Bus 41, 45. **Open** 11am-7pm Mon-Fri; 10am-7pm Sat; 11am-6pm Sun. **Credit** AmEx, Disc, MC, V. **Map** p308 E2.

Everything is pure and simple at **Kiehl's** apothecary. *See p179.*

This is the brand embraced by the world's supermodels, including the irrepressible RuPaul, and it offers everything you could ever want in foundation, powder, eye makeup. There are more shades of MAC lipstick than colours in a Crayon box. It has a stand-alone shop near the Marina, where you can make the transformation from virgin to vamp in no time at all.

Sephora

1 Stockton Street, at Ellis Street, Union Square (392 1545/www.sephora.com/index.jhtm). BART Powell Street/Muni Metro F, J, K, L, M, N/bus 5, 6, 7, 9, 21, 27, 30, 31, 45, 66/cable car Powell-Hyde or Powell-Mason. **Open** 10am-8pm Mon-Sat; 11am-7pm Sun. **Credit** AmEx, Disc, MC, V. **Map** p311 H4.

France's largest cosmetics retailer has created an interactive shop where you can touch, smell and try on most of the premier perfumes and make-up brands to your heart's delight, without a hard-sell from the staff. In fact, finding help here can be as elusive as finding a friendly face in central Paris. This is a good place to go when you want to be alone.

Hair salons

Architects & Heroes

2239 Fillmore Street, at Clay Street, Pacific Heights (921 8383/www.architectsandheroes.com). Bus 1, 3, 12, 22, 24. **Open** 10am-7pm Mon; 9am-7pm Tue; 9am-9pm Wed-Fri; 9am-6pm Sat; 10am-6pm Sun. **Credit** AmEx, MC, V. **Map** p307 E3.

This Pacific Heights salon can usually work you in on short notice for a polished cut and dry at upper-middle prices. It also sells the delicious Bumble & Bumble line of haircare products.

Branch: 580 Bush Street, Union Square (391 8833).

Elevation Salon & Café

451 Bush Street, between Kearny Street & Grant Avenue, Union Square (392 2969). BART Powell Street/Muni Metro F, J, K, L, M, N/bus 5, 6, 7, 9, 21, 27, 30, 31, 45, 66. **Open** 9am-5pm Mon-Wed, Sat; 9am-6pm Thur, Fri. **Credit** MC, V. **Map** p309 G/H3.

Master colourist Atis Zulgis works his magic in this airy Union Square salon. Interestingly, he does his work at extremely affordable prices. A painter of fine finishes in his spare time, he'll treat your head with the same level of artistry, whether you're going goth, blonde, fiery red or somewhere in between.

Vidal Sassoon

359 Sutter Street, between Stockton Street & Grant Avenue, Union Square (397 5105/www.vssassoon.com). BART Powell Street/Muni Metro F, J, K, L, M, N/bus 5, 6, 7, 9, 21, 27, 30, 31, 45, 66/cable car Powell-Hyde or Powell-Mason. **Open** 9am-5pm Mon-Fri; 8am-5pm Sat. **Credit** AmEx, MC, V. **Map** p309 G3.

This is where to go when price is immaterial and a polished, precision cut is your goal. If top stylist Elizabeth Hartley happens to have an appointment free while you're in town (this is unlikely, but you never know), hang the cost and go for it anyway – it could quite possibly change your life.

Zip Zap

245 Fillmore Street, at Haight Street, Lower Haight (621 1671). Bus 6, 7, 22, 66, 71. **Open** 11am-7pm daily. **Credit** MC, V. **Map** p313 E5.

Drop in to this trendy haircare shop in the Lower Haight and improve your look for about $35.

Pharmacies

Walgreens Drugstore

3201 Divisadero Street, at Lombard Street, Marina (931 6417/www.walgreens.com). Bus 28, 30, 43, 76. **Open** 24hrs daily. **Credit** AmEx, Disc, MC, V. **Map** p307 D2.

Prescriptions and general drugstore purchases are available here around the clock.

Branches (24hr): 498 Castro Street, at 18th Street, Castro (861 6276); 25 Point Lobos Avenue, at 43rd Avenue, Richmond District (387 0706).

Spas, saunas & bathhouses

For spas and saunas outside San Francisco, *see p260* **Mud, mud, glorious mud**.

Kabuki Springs & Spa

Japan Center, 1750 Geary Boulevard, at Fillmore Street, Western Addition (922 6000). Bus 22, 38. **Open** 10am-10pm daily. **Admission** *Day pass* $15. *Day pass with 25-min massage* $50. *Evening pass* $18. **Credit** AmEx, MC, V. **Map** p313 E4.

This traditional Japanese bathhouse has deep ceramic communal tubs, a steam room, saunas, a cold plunge pool and a restful tatami room. Shiatsu, Swedish and deep tissue massages, body scrubs and a host of other soothing services are available by appointment. Women-only days are Wed, Fri, Sun. Men-only days are Thur, Sat, Mon.

Le Sanctuaire

Suite 224, 699 Mississippi Street, at 22nd Street, Potrero Hill (401 6930). Bus 48. **Open** Tue-Sat; call for exact hours. **Credit** AmEx, MC, V.

Seeking a natural cure for traveller's fatigue? Rebecca Whitworth's aromatherapeutic facials help to banish jetlag and restore your skin to its former radiant glow, while the foot massage leaves you ready to hit the streets with renewed vigour.

Osento

955 Valencia Street, at 21st Street, Mission (282 6333/www.osento.com). BART 24th Street/ bus 14, 26, 49. **Open** 1pm-1am daily (last admission midnight). **Admission** $10-$15. **No credit cards**. **Map** p314 Y2.

A bathhouse for women only. Walk into the peaceful surroundings, leave your clothes in a locker and relax in the whirlpool. After a cold plunge, you can choose between wet and dry saunas. An outdoor deck offers the chance to enjoy the weather on a sunny day. Massages available by appointment.

77 Maiden Lane Salon & Spa

Second floor, 77 Maiden Lane, between Grant Avenue & Kearny Street, Union Square (391 7777/391 0877). BART Powell Street/Muni Metro F, J, K, L, M, N/bus 5, 6, 7, 9, 21, 27, 30, 31, 45, 66. **Open** 9am-6pm Mon, Sat; 9am-7pm Tue-Wed, Fri; 9am-8pm Thur; 10am-6pm Sun. **Credit** MC, V. **Map** p309 H3.

This full-service salon off Union Square is a good place to head for an emergency waxing or a luxurious (and long-lasting) manicure or pedicure.

Tattoos & body piercing

Body Manipulations

3234 16th Street, between Guerrero & Dolores Streets, Mission (621 0408/www.bodym.com). BART 16th Street/Muni Metro J/bus 22, 26, 53. **Open** noon-7pm daily. **Credit** AmEx, Disc, MC, V. **Map** p310 F6.

Custom body piercing, scarring, branding and just about anything else that can be done to the human figure – except tattooing.

Lyle Tuttle Tattooing

841 Columbus Avenue, at Lombard Street, North Beach (775 4991). Bus 15, 30/cable car Powell-Mason. **Open** noon-9pm daily. **Admission** free. **Map** p308 G2.

Tuttle is one of the world's most respected tattoo artists and, for those in the know, this parlour is an essential stop-off point. If you're really interested, there's a tattoo museum next door (*see p110*).

Launderettes

Don't miss **Brainwash** (*see chapter* **Restaurants & Cafés**), San Francisco's original café/bar/ launderette in SoMa, which continues to succeed as a trendy neighbourhood gathering spot.

Star Wash

392 Dolores Street, at 17th Street, Mission (431 2443). Muni Metro J/bus 22, 33. **Open** 7am-9pm daily. **No credit cards**. **Map** p314 Y1.

A hip gathering place for cinephiles, Star Wash shows old and new movies as you sort your socks under the watchful eyes of Fred, Ginger, Bogey and Bacall, whose images stare down from the walls.

Music

CDs, tapes & records

Amoeba Music

1855 Haight Street, between Shrader & Stanyan Streets, Haight-Ashbury (831 1200/www.amoebamusic.com). Muni Metro N/bus 7, 33, 66, 71. **Open** 10.30am-10pm Mon-Sat; 11am-9pm Sun. **Credit** Disc, MC, V. **Map** p313 C6.

In a converted bowling alley in the Haight-Ashbury, a community of music lovers converges daily to sell, buy, trade and just bask in the vibe. The huge collection here includes hard-to-find releases and tons of recycled music and videos, dirt cheap. There is no musical specialty as you'll find indie rock, electronica, DJ mixes, jazz and classical in every format.

Branch: 2455 Telegraph Avenue, at Haste Street, Berkeley (1-510 549 1125).

Aquarius Records

1055 Valencia Street, at 21st Street, Mission (647 2272/647 3447/www.aquariusrecordssf.com). Bus 14, 26, 49. **Open** 10am-9pm Mon-Wed; 10am-10pm Thur-Sun. **Credit** AmEx, DC, Disc, MC, V. **Map** p314 Y2.

Aquarius sells alternative and underground music in a surprisingly friendly setting. In fact, staff often contribute helpful and highly personal descriptions of their favourites to help you decide.

BPM Music Factory

573 Hayes Street, at Laguna Street, Hayes Valley (487 8680). Bus 21. **Open** 10am-8pm Mon-Sat; 10am-7pm Sun. **Credit** AmEx, MC, V. **Map** p310 E/F5.
BPM is where local DJs gather to gossip and shop for 12-inch house, techno and acid jazz sounds, and where the rest of us go for friendly advice on what to feed our ears.

Grooves Vinyl Attractions

1797 Market Street, between Guerrero & Valencia Streets, SoMa (436 9933). Muni Metro F/bus 6, 7, 26, 66, 71. **Open** 11am-7pm daily. **Credit** AmEx, Disc, MC, V. **Map** p310 F5.
Dive into Grooves' $1 bin for 1970s crooners (remember Dan Fogelberg?) and vintage vinyl. An excellent source for out-of-print soundtracks.

Jack's Record Cellar

254 Scott Street, between Haight & Page Streets, Lower Haight (431 3047). Bus 6, 7, 24, 66, 71. **Open** noon-7pm Wed-Sun. **Credit** MC, V. **Map** p313 E5.
Think *High Fidelity* in the Lower Haight, with hard-to-find jazz, R&B, pop and country, mostly on vinyl.

Jazz Quarter

1267 20th Avenue, at Irving Street, Sunset District (661 2331). Muni Metro N/bus 28, 29, 71. **Open** 1-6pm Tue-Sat. **No credit cards**. **Map** p312 A6.
Cool cats come here to score Mingus, Miles, Chet and Charlie; Coltrane, too.

Medium Rare Records

2310 Market Street, at 16th Street, Castro (255 7273/www.neucast.com/mediumrare). Muni Metro F, K, L, M/bus 24, 33, 35, 37. **Open** 11am-7.30pm Mon-Thur; 11am-9.30pm Fri, Sat; noon-7.30pm Sun. **Credit** AmEx, Disc, MC, V. **Map** p314 X1.
This tiny shop packs a lot of sonic punch. Owner Arnold Conrad has lovingly assembled a collection that meanders across decades and genres: mega-mixes from Ibiza and other hedonistic hotspots; old Italian movie soundtracks; crooners such as Peggy Lee; and imports from Berlin, Paris and Tokyo.

Reggae Runnins Village Store

505 Divisadero Street, at Fell Street, Western Addition (922 2442). Bus 21, 24. **Open** noon-7pm daily. **Credit** AmEx, Disc, MC, V. **Map** p313 D/E5.
If reggae is your jive, this is your hive. There's also a juice bar, Jamaican food and other delights.

Ritmo Latino

2401 Mission Street, at 20th Street, Mission (824 8556). Bus 14, 26, 33, 49. **Open** 10am-9.30pm daily. **Credit** MC, V. **Map** p314 Y1.
Indulge your Latin fantasies with ranchera, mariachi, salsa, Tex-Mex, merengue and more.

Tower Records

2525 Jones Street, at Columbus Avenue, North Beach (885 0500/www.towerrecords.com). Bus 10, 30, 47/ cable car Powell-Mason. **Open** 9am-midnight daily. **Credit** AmEx, Disc, MC, V. **Map** p308 F2.

Tiny but powerful: **Medium Rare Records.**

Although the service is erratic, this is a browser's delight, especially with the addition of wall-to-wall listening stations. The Classical Annex (2568 Jones Street; 441 4880) is an oasis of calm and offers a comprehensive selection and conversant staff.
Branches: 2280 Market Street, between Noe & 16th Streets, Castro (621 0588); 660 Third Street, at Brannan Street, SoMa (957 9660); Stonestown Galleria, Winston Drive, at 19th Avenue, Park Merced (681 2001).

Virgin Megastore

2 Stockton Street, at Market Street, Union Square (397 4525/http://virginmega.com). BART Powell Street/Muni Metro F, J, K, L, M, N/bus 5, 6, 7, 9, 21, 27, 30, 31, 45, 66/cable car Powell-Hyde or Powell-Mason. **Open** 9am-11pm Mon-Thur; 9am-midnight Fri, Sat; 10am-10pm Sun. **Credit** AmEx, DC, Disc, MC, V. **Map** p311 G4.
This place is monolithic, with 60 listening stations an in-house DJ, in a sterile downtown setting.

Instruments & sheet music

Byron Hoyt

360 Florida Street, at 16th Street, Mission (431 8055). Bus 22, 27, 33, 53. **Open** 11am-5.30pm Tue-Fri; 9.30am-5.30pm Sat. **Credit** AmEx, Disc, MC, V. **Map** p314 Z1.
At this venerable sheet music and instrument shop, you'll find a stunning view, helpful, solicitous and

knowledgeable staff and copies of every possible score from Bach to Irving Berlin. It's also a good place for information on the city's musical events.

Clarion Music

816 Sacramento Street, at Waverly Place, Chinatown (1-888 343 5374/391 1317/www.clarionmusic.com). Bus 1, 30, 45/cable car California. **Open** 11am-6pm Mon-Fri; 9am-5pm Sat. **Credit** AmEx, Disc, MC, V. **Map** p309 G3.

World music central: didgeridoos, sitars, Tibetan singing bowls, African drums, Native American flutes, Chinese stringed instruments and other non-Western noisemakers are all stocked. Concerts are held at 8pm on the first Friday of the month.

Haight-Ashbury Music Center

1540 Haight Street, at Ashbury Street, Haight-Ashbury (863 7327/www.haight-ashbury-music.com). Muni Metro N/bus 6, 7, 33, 37, 43, 66, 71. **Open** 11am-7pm Mon-Fri; 10am-6pm Sat; noon-6pm Sun. **Credit** AmEx, DC, Disc, MC, V. **Map** p313 D5/6.

A stop-off point for local musicians and rockers in town for a gig. Recently expanded after a fire, it sells new and second-hand instruments, microphones, mixers, amps and sheet music, along with hundreds of acoustic and electric guitars. If you're a musician in search of a band, check out the posted notices.

Opticians

City Optix

2154 Chestnut Street, between Pierce & Steiner Streets, Marina (921 1188/ www.cityoptix.com). Bus 22, 28, 30, 43, 76. **Open** 10am-6pm Mon-Sat; 10am-8pm Thur; noon-5pm Sun. **Credit** AmEx, MC, V. **Map** p307 D2.

The most comprehensive collection of great frames in most price ranges, sold by friendly staff. Look for Matsuda, Oliver Peoples, LA Eyeworks and more. They'll also cheerfully adjust glasses you clearly didn't purchase there.

Branch: 1685 Haight Street, between Belevedere & Cole Streets, Haight-Ashbury (626 1188).

Invision Optometry

1907 Fillmore Street, between Pine & Bush Streets, Pacific Heights (563 9003). Bus 1, 2, 3, 4. **Open** 10am-6.30pm Mon-Sat; noon-4pm Sun. **Credit** AmEx, MC, V. **Map** p307 E4.

Four eyes are definitely better than two, as you will quickly learn while browsing through this spacious shop, which is filled with more than 600 frame styles as well as exhibits by local artists.

Photography

Adolph Gasser

181 Second Street, between Mission & Howard Streets, SoMa (495 3852/www.gassers.com). BART Montgomery Street/Metro Muni F, J, K, L, M, N/bus 2, 3, 4, 6, 7, 9, 12, 14, 15, 21, 31, 66, 71, 76. **Open** 9am-6pm Mon-Sat. **Credit** AmEx, Disc, MC, V. **Map** p311 H4.

This justly famous photographic shop has the largest inventory of photo and video equipment in Northern California. It stocks SLR cameras by Canon and Nikon, priced far cheaper than in the UK; all sorts of lenses; point-and-shoot cameras; and, according to one staff member, 'every kind of photographic doohickey you can imagine'.

Discount Camera

33 Kearny Street, between Post & Market Streets, Union Square (392 1100/www.discountcamera.com). BART Montgomery Street/Metro Muni F, J, K, L, M, N/bus 2, 3, 4, 6, 7, 9, 14, 15, 21, 30, 31, 45, 66, 71/cable car Powell-Hyde or Powell-Mason. **Open** 8.30am-6.30pm Mon-Sat; 9.30am-6pm Sun. **Credit** AmEx, Disc, MC, V. **Map** p309 H3.

Concierges at major downtown hotels direct their guests here in the hope that they'll avoid the unscrupulous tourist traps that lie in wait by the Powell Street cable car turnaround. Carries all major brands and has an on-site photo lab.

Photoworks

277 Market Street, at Church Street, Castro (626 6800). Muni Metro F, J, K, L, M/bus 24, 33, 35, 37. **Open** 9am-8pm Mon-Fri; 10am-8pm Sat; 10am-6pm Sun. **Credit** AmEx, Disc, MC, V. **Map** p310 E6.

Located on the fringes of the Castro district, this favourite photo processor of amateurs and pros is staffed by photographers who take unusual care with your film – even those off-centre snaps of the Golden Gate Bridge. Turnaround is two to three days; a roll of 24 pics averages $13.40.

Sex shops

Good Vibrations

1210 Valencia Street, at 23rd Street, Mission (550 7399/www.goodvibes.com). BART 24th Street/bus 14, 26, 48, 49. **Open** 11am-7pm Mon, Tue; 11am-8pm Wed-Sun. **Credit** AmEx, Disc, MC, V. **Map** p314 Y1.

At this woman-owned and operated co-operative, the art of self- and mutual lovin' is celebrated loudly and proudly. The staff are happy to walk you through the huge collqection of sex toys, reading matter and videos (many available to rent). You can even, um, try before you buy.

Branch: 2504 San Pablo Avenue, at Dwight Street, Berkeley (1-510 841 8987).

Stormy Leather

1158 Howard Street, at Seventh Street, SoMa (626 1672/www.stormyleather.com). Bus 12, 14, 19, 26. **Open** noon-7pm Mon, Wed-Sun. **Credit** AmEx, Disc, MC, V. **Map** p310 G5.

The less clinical atmosphere makes Stormy Leather more titillating than Good Vibrations (*see above*). You can buy a rubber nurse or French maid outfit and leather and latex bustiers, and peruse the edgier collection of books and magazines for as long as you like – and when you have a question about whips, say, the friendly female staff are right there for you.

Branch: 582C Castro Street, at 19th Street, Castro (671 1295).

Smoking

Ashbury Tobacco Center

1524 Haight Street, at Ashbury Street, Haight-Ashbury (552 5556). Bus 6, 7, 33, 43, 66, 71. **Open** 10am-9.30pm daily. **Credit** AmEx, DC, Disc, MC, V. **Map** p313 D5/6.

Hearkening back to the days when the area was known as the 'Hashbury', the Ashbury Tobacco Center offers a full array of psychedelic sundries (while still maintaining that the products are all intended for legal substances). In addition to the hookahs and honeybear bongs there is a vast offering of tobacco products.

Grant's Tobacconists

562 Market Street, between Sansome & Montgomery Streets, Financial District (981 1000). BART Montgomery Street/Muni Metro F, J, K, L, M, N/ bus 1, 2, 3, 4, 15, 76. **Open** 9am-5.30pm Mon-Fri; 10am-5.30pm Sat. **Credit** AmEx, Disc, MC, V. **Map** p309 H3.

Grant's sells pipes, cigars, humidors, tobacco and posh accessories. The walk-in humidor is reportedly stocked with 100,000 cigars (no Cuban brands, though – they're illegal in the US).

Smoke Signals

2223 Polk Street, between Green & Vallejo Streets, Polk Gulch (292 6025). Bus 19, 41, 42, 45, 47, 49, 76. **Open** 8am-8pm Mon-Sat; 8am-7pm Sun. **Credit** AmEx, Disc, MC, V. **Map** p308 F2.

Part of the bustling Russian Hill warren of cafés and shops, Smoke Signals has a staggering range of tobacco products, as well as more than 1,500 periodicals from around the world. Famously, they also once sold a $88-million-winning lottery ticket.

Sport

For other shops selling and renting skis, snowboards, rollerblades and other sporting equipment, *see chapter* **Sport & Fitness**.

Lombardi Sports

1600 Jackson Street, at Polk Street, Polk Gulch (771 0600/www.lombardisports.com). Bus 12, 19, 27, 47, 49, 76. **Open** 10am-7pm Mon-Wed; 10am-8pm Thur, Fri; 10am-6pm Sat; 11am-6pm Sun. **Credit** AmEx, Disc, MC, V. **Map** p308 F3.

A good, big, all-purpose sporting goods shop, where you can find everything from tents to trainers, drinking bottles to mountain bikes.

See Jane Run Sports

3870 24th Street, at Sanchez Street, Noe Valley (401 8338/www.seejanerunsports.com). Muni Metro J/ bus 48. **Open** 11am-7pm Mon-Fri; 10am-6pm Sat; 11am-5pm Sun. **Credit** AmEx, MC, V. **Map** p314 X2.

A well edited selection of gear for women who run, cycle, swim, hike or do yoga. The staff are more than willing to spend a lot of time helping you match the right shoe for the sport, and the clothing selection doesn't shun the more ample-sized athlete.

Sports Basement

1301 Sixth Street, at Channel Street, SoMa (437 1011/www.sportsbasement.com). Bus 10, 15. **Open** 10am-6pm Mon-Wed, Fri; 10am-8pm Thur; 10am-6pm Sat, Sun. **Credit** AmEx, MC, V.

This huge SoMa warehouse gathers end-of-line goods from top-tier brands such as North Face, Teva, Speedo, Pearl Izumi, Cannondale and more, and offers them at savings of 30-60%. Sizes and colours can be odd, but great buys are frequently

What size, ma'am? Small, medium or... **Good Vibrations**. *See p183.*

Buying Berkeley

More shopping opportunities abound just over the Bay Bridge. To see a lot of stuff in a walkable space, head straight to **Fourth Street** in Berkeley, which has evolved into something of an outdoor shopping mall, attracting Bay Area denizens en masse on sunny weekends. Among the highlights are **Erica Tanov** (No.1827, at Hearst Street; 1-510 849 3331) for pretty hand-knitted sweaters, stretchy Italian jeans and girly frocks; a branch of **George** (No.1829; 1-510 644 1033), simply the best pet products store in the world; **Hear Music** (suite B, No.1809; 1-510 204 9595), where the eclectic collection of folk, blues, ambient, country and classical music can be heard on multiple listening stations; and **Rabat Shoes** (No.1825; 1-510 549 9195), which brings together Kelian, Camper, Clergerie and more.

The Gardener is a collection of books, ceramics, furniture, bulbs and botanicals (No.1836; 1-510 548 4545, while **Builder's Booksource** (No.1871; 1-510 845 6874) is a valuable resource for architects, interior designers and landscapers. There is also a **Crate & Barrel Outlet** (1785 Fourth Street, at Virginia Street; 1-510 528 5500) for discounted glassware and other household items, as well as a branch of the stellar bookshop **Cody's** (No.1730;1-510 559 9500). A few streets away, **Urban Ore** (1333 Sixth Street, at Gilman Street; 1-510 559 4450) attracts second-hand junkies for the vast collection of architectural salvage and recycled oddities.

Also in Berkeley, **Telegraph Avenue** is a classic university main drag mix of cafés, fast food and shops. For new books, there's another **Cody's Bookstore** (No.2454, at Haste Street; 1-510 845 7852). For rare or used tomes, immerse yourself in multi-level **Moe's Books** (No.2476; 1-510 849 2087). For CDs and vinyl, the original **Amoeba Music** (No.2455; 1-510 549 1125) and **Rasputin's** (No.2350, at Channing Street; 1-510 848 9004) are still going strong.

Closer to Oakland, collectors of pretty ephemera and vintage jewellery make a pilgrimage to **Tail of the Yak** (2632 Ashby Avenue, at College Avenue; 1-510 841 9891), and fashion-minded folks head to **Dish** (2981 College Avenue, at Ashby Avenue; 1-510 540 4784). Finally, close to the Berkeley border in Oakland, you'll find dozens of boutiques and antique shops clustered in Rockridge on Piedmont and College Avenues.

found here. It's worth noting that the shop can be tricky to find; their website recommends visitors call ahead or use mapquest.com for directions.

Toys

There's a giant branch of the celebrated New York play palace **FAO Schwarz** near Union Square (48 Stockton Street; 394 8700).

Chinatown Kite Shop

717 Grant Avenue, at Sacramento Street, Chinatown (989 5182). Bus 1, 15, 30, 45/cable car California. **Open** 9.30am-10pm daily. **Credit** AmEx, Disc, MC, V. **Map** p309 G3.

In a breezy city like San Francisco, this shop is a child's – and an adult's – dream. Hundreds of different kites in every imaginable shape and colour, for flying or just for decoration.

Imaginarium

Laurel Shopping Center, 3535 California Street, at Spruce Street, Presidio Heights (387 9885). Bus 1, 3, 4, 33. **Open** 9.30am-7pm Mon-Fri; 9.30am-6pm Sat; 11am-6pm Sun. **Credit** AmEx, Disc, MC, V. **Map** p313 C4.

Imaginarium selects toys for their ability to stimulate developing minds rather than numb them. Many hard-to-find European imports are stocked and playful weapons of destruction are noticeably absent.

kar'ikter

418 Sutter Street, between Stockton & Powell Streets, Union Square (434 1120/www.karikter.com). BART Powell Street/Muni Metro F, J, K, L, M, N/bus 5, 6, 7, 9, 21, 27, 30, 31, 45, 66/cable car Powell-Hyde or Powell-Mason. **Open** 10am-6pm Mon-Sat; 11am-5pm Sun. **Credit** AmEx, MC, V. **Map** p309 G3.

A friendly antidote to the nearby Disney and Warner Bros megastores, kar'ikter's books and nicely designed products are based on such old, familiar Eurocentric literary favourites as Tintin, Babar, Asterix and the Little Prince.

Sanrio

39 Stockton Street, between Ellis & O'Farrell Streets, Union Square (981 5568/www.sanrio.com). BART Powell Street/Muni Metro F, J, K, L, M, N/bus 5, 6, 7, 9, 21, 27, 30, 31, 45, 66/cable car Powell-Hyde or Powell-Mason. **Open** 10am-8pm Mon-Sat; 11am-6pm Sun. **Credit** AmEx, Disc, MC, V. **Map** p311 G4.

Irresistible toys from the creative folks behind Hello Kitty, whose image now seems to mark everything.

Shopping by area

Union Square & around

Agnès B (Fashion, p167); **Anthropologie** (Fashion, p168); **Borders** (Bookshops, p165); **A Clean Well-Lighted Place** (Bookshops, p165); **De Vera** (Jewellery, p174); **Diana Slavin** (Fashion, p169); **Diesel** (Fashion, p169); **Elevation** (Hair salons, p180); **Gimme Shoes** (Shoes, p174); **Kate Spade** (Handbags, p173); **kar'ikter** (Toys, p185); **Kayo** (Bookshops, p166); **Kenneth Cole** (Leather, p174); **Lang** (Jewellery, p174); **Levi's** (Fashion, p170); **Loehmann's** (Discount fashion, p172); **Metier** (Fashion, p170); **Napa Vallery Winery** (p176); **Rand McNally** (Bookshops, p166); **Sanrio** (Toys, p185); **Sephora** (Cosmetics, p180); **77 Maiden Lane** (Spas, p181); **Shine** (Handbags, p173); **Stacey's** (Bookshops, p166); **Urban Outfitters** (Fashion, p171); **Utopia Planita** (Fashion, p171); **Virgin** (Music, p182).

SoMa

Grooves (Music, p182); **Jeremy's** (Discount fashion, p172); **SFMOMA** (Gifts, p179); **Stormy Leather** (Sex shops, p183); **Sports Basement** (p184); **Wine Club** (p177).

North Beach & around

AB Fits (Fashion, p167); **Acorn Books** (Bookshops, p165); **Alla Prima** (Lingerie, p172); **Aria** (Antiques, p163); **Chinatown Kite** (Toys, p185); **City Lights** (Bookshops, p165); **Clarion** (Music, p183); **Graffeo Coffee** (Tea & coffee, p177); **Johnson** (Leather, p174); **Jug Shop** (Wine, p176); **Liguria** (Food, p176); **Lombardi** (Sport, p184); **Lyle Tuttle** (Tattoos, p181); **MAC** (Fashion, p170); **Martini** (Vintage fashion, p173); **Molinari** (Food, p176); **Quantity Postcards** (Gifts, p179); **Sam Bo** (Arts & crafts, p164); **SwallowTail** (Gifts, p179); **Ten Ren** (Tea & coffee, p176); **Tower Records** (p182); **William Stout** (Books, p166).

The Haight & around

Aardvark's (Vintage fashion, p172); **Amoeba** (Music, p181); **Behind the Post Office** (Fashion, p168); **Booksmith** (Bookshops, p165); **Buffalo Exchange** (Vintage fashion, p172); **Dishes Delmar** (Antiques, p163); **Haight-Ashbury Music** (Music, p183); **Jack's** (Music, p182); **Kabuki** (Spas, p181); **Kids Only** (Children's fashion, p171); **Luichiny** (Shoes, p176); **Marcus Book Stores** (Bookshops, p166); **Reggae Runnins** (Music, p182); **Shoe Biz** (Shoes, p176); **True** (Handbags, p174); **Villains** (Fashion, p171); **Wasteland** (Vintage fashion, p173); **Zip Zap** (Hair salons, p180).

Hayes Valley

African Outlet (Arts & crafts, p164); **Alabaster** (Gifts, p178); **BPM** (Music, p182); **Dark Garden** (Lingerie, p172); **Limelight** (Bookshops, p166); **One-Eyed Jacks** (Antiques, p164); **Polonco** (Arts & crafts, p164); **Richard Hilkert** (Bookshops, p166); **Zeitgeist** (Jewellery, p174).

The Mission & Potrero Hill

Aquarius (Music, p181); **Bi-Rite Market** (Food, p176); **Body Manipulations** (Piercing, p181); **Bombay Ice Creamery** (Food, p176); **The Butler & the Chef** (Antiques, p163); **Byron Hoyt** (Music, p182); **Clothes Contact** (Vintage fashion, p172); **Dandelion** (Gifts, p178); **Das Pussycat** (Vintage fashion, p173); **Dema** (Fashion, p169); **Esprit** (Discount fashion, p171); **Fishbowl** (Fashion, p169); **Good Vibrations** (Sex shops, p183); **Laku** (Children's fashion, p171); **Le Sanctuaire** (Spas, p181); **Modern Times** (Bookshops, p166); **Osento** (Spas, p181); **Paxton Gate** (Gifts, p179); **Rayon Vert** (Gifts, p179); **Ritmo Latino** (Music, p182); **Scarlet Sage** (Complementary medicine, p179); **Schauplatz** (Vintage fashion, p173); **Subterranean** (Shoes, p176).

The Castro & Noe Valley

Citizen Clothing (Fashion, p169); **Crossroads** (Vintage fashion, p173); **A Different Light** (Bookshops, p165); **Get Lost** (Bookshops, p165); **Medium Rare** (Music, p182); **Peek-a-Boutique** (Children's fashion, p171); **Rolo** (Fashion, p170); **See Jane** (Sport, p184); **SF Mystery Bookstore** (p166); **Tibet Shop** (Arts & crafts, p164); **Ver Unica** (Vintage fashion, p173).

The Marina & around

American Rag (Fashion, p167); **Architects & Heroes** (Hair salons, p180); **The Bar** (Fashion, p168); **Betsey Johnson** (Fashion, p168); **Boulangerie** (Food, p176); **Departures** (Vintage fashion, p173); **Fetish** (Shoes, p174); **George** (Gifts, p178); **GoodByes** (Vintage fashion, p173); **Heather** (Fashion, p170); **Imaginarium** (Toys, p185); **Kiehl's** (Cosmetics, p179); **MAC Cosmetics** (p179); **Mudpie** (Children's fashion, p171); **Nest** (Gifts, p179); **Susan** (Fashion, p171); **Whole Foods** (p176); **Workshop** (Lingerie, p172).

Arts & Entertainment

By Season 188
Children 195
Film 199
Galleries 203
Nightlife 209
Performing Arts 221
Queer San Francisco 228
Sport & Fitness 238

Features

Day of the Dead 190
Burn, baby, burn 193
Going up 196
Out of town 198
The city on foot: Murals 204
Support local music 213
East Bay sounds 214
Don't miss dance clubs 219
Tender is the theatre district 223
Take Pride 232
Trans San Fran 236
Home run 241
On your bike 244
Escape from Alcatraz 247

By Season

Enjoy a non-stop round of parties, parades and perambulations.

More than any other city in California (possibly the whole US), San Francisco knows how to throw a party. Free events, street fairs and festivals litter the city's annual calendar. During the region's cool springs and foggy summers, neighbourhood fests are plentiful, as are parades and theatre in the parks. In the rainy autumn and winter months, frequent showers nudge happenings indoors to local performance spaces and artists' studios. No matter what season you choose to explore San Franciso, chances are good that you'll have your pick of entertainment options. And, unlike some other popular tourist destinations, where special events are primarily magnets for out-of-towners, San Francisco's happenings cater to the locals first and visitors second. So it's no surprise that residents respond in kind by coming out in droves year after year for their favourite get-togethers. So, expect crowds, arrive early, wear layers and take public transport when possible.

The dates listed below are approximate. For the most up-to-date information on events, contact the **San Francisco Visitor Information Center** (*see p287*) or consult local weekly alternative rags and the city's more mainstream daily newspapers. For a list of annual public holidays, *see p288*.

Spring

St Patrick's Day Parade

391 2000. Parade goes from Fifth & Market Streets to the Embarcadero, Downtown. BART Powell Street/Muni Metro F, J, K, L, M, N/ bus 5, 9, 14, 26, 27, 31, 66, 71. **Map** p311 G4.
Date Sun before 17 Mar.

San Francisco has a large Irish population, so this parade is one of the city's biggest. Most pubs celebrate long into the night.

St Stupid's Day Parade

www.saintstupid.com. Parade usually starts at Transamerica Pyramid, 600 Montgomery Street, between Clay & Washington Streets, Financial District. Bus 1, 12, 15, 41, 42. **Map** p309 H3.
Date 1 Apr.

On April Fools' Day for the past two decades, Bishop Joey of the First Church of the Last Laugh has led the St Stupid's Day Parade, a zany, parodic assembly that snakes through San Francisco's Financial District. The parade concludes on the steps of the Pacific Stock Exchange, where sermons are given and everyone removes a sock for the 'Pacific Sock Exchange'. It should come as no surprise to learn that many go home sockless, as the event usually degenerates into a sock fight. The starting point varies, so check the website or the local papers for the latest information.

Japantown comes alive for the **Cherry Blossom Festival**. *See p189.*

Cherry Blossom Festival

563 2313. Japan Center, Geary Boulevard, between Fillmore & Laguna Streets, Japantown. Bus 2, 3, 4, 22, 38. **Map** p310 E4. **Date** Apr.

For two consecutive weekends in April, the Cherry Blossom Festival transforms the ordinarily sleepy Japantown into a bustling whirlwind of Japanese culture. The celebration pays tribute to the delights of Japanese cuisine as well as traditional arts and crafts, including dance, drumming and martial arts demonstrations. Parking is scarce, so public transport is your best bet.

San Francisco International Film Festival

931 3456/www.sfiff.org. **Date** mid Apr-early May.

Featuring two weeks of events, the SFIFF may not be the largest, but it definitely screens enough films to make a run at being the world's most eclectic cinematic experience. It is particularly strong on independent documentaries and Third World films rarely shown at other US festivals. Tickets sell out quickly, so book in advance. *See also p202.*

Cinco de Mayo

826 1401. Civic Center Plaza, between McAllister, Grove, Franklin & Hyde Streets, Civic Center. BART Civic Center/Muni Metro F, J, K, L, M, N/ bus 5, 19, 21, 42, 47, 49. **Map** p310 F4. **Date** Sun before 5 May.

Join San Francisco's Latino residents and their friends in this annual springtime celebration of General Ignacio Zaragoza's defeat of the French army at Puebla in 1862. This raucous weekend of parades, fireworks and music is one of the best parties of the year.

Aids Candlelight Memorial March & Vigil

863 4676/www.actupgg.org. March starts at Castro & Market Streets, Castro. Muni Metro F, J, K, L, M/ bus 24. **Map** p314 X1. **Date** late May.

This annual candlelit vigil begins with a solemn procession from the Castro district, down Market Street, ending at the United Nations Plaza at the Civic Center, where crowds gather to hear an evening of speeches, awards, celebrations and remembrances.

Examiner Bay to Breakers Foot Race

808 5000 ext 2222/www.baytobreakers.com. Race starts at Howard & Spear Streets, SoMa. BART Embarcadero/Muni Metro F, J, K, L, M, N/bus 14, 41. **Map** p309 J3. **Date** 3rd Sun in May.

The *San Francisco Examiner* and other corporate sponsors encourage 70,000 athletes, weekend warriors, jog-walkers, joggers-for-a-day and fleet-footed zanies to run to Ocean Beach. The course is about 12km (7½ miles), a perfect length for most to make it without much training. The race is famous for its costumes, party atmosphere, nudity (there are always a few running free and bouncy), and a school of runners dressed as salmon who attempt to run the course 'upstream'. On the subject of futility, don't attempt to cross the city from north to south on the morning of the race.

Carnaval

826 1401. Parade starts at Mission & 24th Streets. BART 24th Street/bus 14, 48, 49. **Map** p314 Y2. *Festival at Civic Center Plaza, between McAllister, Grove, Franklin & Hyde Streets. BART Civic Center/Muni Metro F, J, K, L, M, N/bus 5, 19, 21, 42, 47, 49.* **Admission** $5. **No credit cards**. **Map** p310 F4. **Date** Memorial Day weekend.

This South American festival features a dazzling parade along Mission Street, excellent cuisine and music that will get even the most staid souls up and dancing. In 2001, organisers moved the party from its home in the Mission to the Civic Center and began charging admission; it's still too early to tell whether or not the event will lose steam as a result.

Summer

Haight Street Fair

666 9952/www.haightstreetfair.org. Haight Street, between Masonic Avenue & Stanyan Street, Haight-Ashbury. Muni Metro N/bus 6, 7, 33, 43, 66, 71. **Map** p313 C/D6. **Date** early June.

Compare and contrast: the weekend Haight Street Fair, as opposed to its North Beach counterpart (*see below*), is a sardine-fest with more than 200 booths of greasy food, hippy crafts and drug paraphernalia, plus live music stages and plenty of folks tripping on acid, both real and imaginary. Go early to beat the crowds.

North Beach Festival

989 2220/www.sfnorthbeach.com. Grant Avenue, Green Street, Stockton Street & Washington Square, North Beach. Bus 15, 30, 39, 41/cable car Powell-Mason. **Map** p308/309 G2. **Date** June.

San Francisco's oldest street shindig, the North Beach festival is heavy on art, home-made crafts and authentic Italian food from neighbourhood eateries. And it's not overcrowded, unlike many other San Francisco street fests.

San Francisco Lesbian/Gay/ Bisexual/Transgender Pride Celebration Parade

864 3733/www.sfpride.org. Parade goes along Market Street, between Embarcadero & Eighth Street, Downtown. BART Embarcadero, Montgomery Street, Powell Street or Civic Center/ Muni Metro F, J, K, L, M, N/bus 5, 6, 7, 9, 21, 31, 66, 71. **Map** starts at p309 J3. **Date** late June.

A San Francisco rite of passage, the Pride Parade (held on a Sunday) and the celebration that follows are every bit as wonderful and outlandish as you'd expect. Local pols cruising for votes share the route with drag queens, leather daddies, Harley-revving dykes, stroller-pushing parents and gay marching bands. It's the wildest, friendliest parade you'll witness, and possibly the longest (often lasting three to four hours). Arrive at least an hour early to nab a kerbside seat. *See also p232* **Take Pride**.

Summer Solstice

431 9962. **Date** 21 June.

On this longest day of the year, pagans and their sympathisers meet on the city's hills and beaches to drum, dance and celebrate. At sunset, pound along with a drum circle in Justin Herman Plaza at the Embarcadero, or join bonfires on Baker Beach.

Fourth of July Waterfront Festival

San Francisco Visitor Information Center (391 2000). Between Aquatic Park & Pier 39, Fisherman's Wharf. Bus 15, 19, 30, 42/cable car Powell-Hyde, Powell-Mason. **Map** p308 F/G1. **Date** 4 July.

On Independence Day, even San Franciscans swell with patriotic pride. Spend the day on the waterfront, where you'll find live entertainment and food stalls. Stay for the spectacular (and often foggy) firework display, held shortly after sunset.

Fillmore Street Jazz Festival

1-510 232 5030. Fillmore Street, between Jackson & Eddy Streets, Western Addition. Bus 1, 2, 3, 4, 12, 22, 31, 38. **Map** p307 E3. **Date** early July.

Politicians and local merchants are struggling to breathe new life back into Fillmore Street by capitalising on its legacy as a jazz district. This steadily growing festival pays tribute to the genre and its SF heritage, especially among local African Americans. The usual crafts and handiwork are mixed with booths selling original art, and live music stages.

Chronicle Marathon: San Francisco

284 9294/www.chroniclemarathon.com. **Date** July.

It may not be as well known as the London or New York version yet, but the San Francisco marathon has grown larger every year since its inception in 1999. The 26.2-mile (42km) course starts in the heart of Golden Gate Park and crosses the entire city, taking participants through some of San Fran's most colourful neighbourhoods, including the Mission, the Haight, Fisherman's Wharf and the Marina.

Day of the Dead

The Mission District is home to a flourishing Latino community, so it comes as no surprise that the biggest celebrations on the Latino calendar – **Carnaval**, **Cinco de Mayo** (for both, *see p189*) and **Día de los Muertos** – all take place in the community's backyard. The first two are lavish productions complete with parades, dancers, food stalls and bands, but it's the latter that offers an experience you won't find in other US cities.

The premise of Día de los Muertos is that the spirits of the dead return once a year to visit families and loved ones. It originated with the Aztecs, who celebrated the entire month of August; with the arrival of the Spaniards came Christianity, and the pagan holiday was moved to coincide with All Saints' Day (1 November) and All Souls' Day (2 November).

It's a reflective and celebratory time during which families honour their spirit guests by building altars. Depending on how much space a family has to spare, an altar can fill a shoebox or a room. Aromatic offerings, such as marigolds, incense and scented candles, guide lost souls home via smell, while a plateful of tamales, mole or a jigger of tequila tempts a hungry spirit's taste buds. Other common altar embellishments include photos of the deceased or items of their jewellery and clothing.

The month of October preceding the big event is chockfull of Dead activities. Owners of Latino-themed boutiques – including **Art Beat Gallery** (3266 21st Street, between Mission and Valencia Streets; 643 8721) and **Encantada** (904 Valencia Street, at 20th Street; 642 3939) – sell traditional items such as sugar skulls and skeleton masks, and invite local artists to erect elaborate altars inside their shops. Also check out the **Mission Cultural Center** (2868 Mission Street; 821 1155) and **Galeria de la Raza** (*see p203*).

On the night of 2 November, hundreds of marchers gather at the intersection of 24th and Bryant Streets. As people mill about lighting candles and burning sage sticks,

Books by the Bay

927 3937/www.booksbythebay.com. Yerba Buena Gardens, Mission Street, between Third & Fourth Streets, SoMa. BART Powell Street/Muni Metro F, J, K, L, M, N/bus 12, 14, 15, 30, 45, 76. **Map** p311 H4. **Date** July.

San Francisco's reputation as the most literary city in the US is well deserved this weekend. At this open-air festival you can browse bookseller booths, attend author signings and participate in book panel discussions. A plethora of children's activities makes this a great stop for those with kids.

Stern Grove Festival

252 6252/www.sterngrove.org. Stern Grove, 19th Avenue, between Sloat Boulevard & Wawona Street, Sunset District. Muni Metro K, M/bus 23, 28. **Date** early June-late Aug.

A summer favourite among locals, this free concert series includes jazz, classical and world music. The amphitheatre, set in a 33-acre grove of eucalyptus trees in the Sunset District, is an idyllic setting – as long as the fog doesn't roll in. Go early to claim a patch of grass, and bring snacks, a picnic blanket and an extra sweater just in case. Parking is limited; use public transport.

Gilroy Garlic Festival

1-408 842 1625/www.gilroygarlicfestival.com. Gilroy, south of San Jose on US 101. **Date** last weekend in July.

For 16 years, this food and wine fest has featured the 'stinking rose' of Gilroy – the lowly garlic clove, made into every edible concoction you can imagine, from ice-cream to jelly. More than 100 craft booths and three stages of entertainers, including puppetry, magicians and live music, round out the event.

Mime Troupe in the Park

285 1717/www.sfmt.org. First show held at Mission Dolores Park, 18th & Dolores Streets, Mission. Muni Metro J/bus 33. **Map** p314 Y1. **Date** early July-early Sept.

Only in San Francisco does the local mime troupe perform leftist, political musicals with themes such as the evils of genetic engineering and dotcom gentrification. Rotating through the Bay Area's parks each summer, the 42-year-old Troupe puts on a side-splitting, thought-provoking show that caters to both adults and children.

Comedy Celebration Day

339 8050/www.comedyday.com. Sharon Meadow, between Kezar & John F Kennedy Drives, Golden Gate Park. Muni Metro N/bus 5, 7, 21, 33, 66, 71. **Map** p312 C6. **Date** mid-late Aug.

A free funny-bone frenzy, Comedy Celebration Day is the perfect way to round out the summer. Lie on a blanket in the park, drink, nosh and laugh at local and national stand-up comedians. Watch out for cameos by famous figures from San Francisco's early days as a comedy launching ground.

A La Carte, A La Park

458 1988. Kezar & John F Kennedy Drives, Golden Gate Park. Muni Metro N/bus 5, 7, 21, 33, 66, 71. **Tickets** $10; $8 concessions; free under-12s. **No credit cards**. **Map** p312 C6. **Date** early Sept.

Sample culinary creations from the Bay Area's best restaurants during this popular Labor Day event. More than 40 eateries are represented, as well as dozens of Californian wineries and local microbrews.

Autumn

Renaissance Pleasure Faire

1-800 523 2473/www.renfair.com/NorthernCA. Vacaville. **Tickets** $17.50. **Credit** Disc, MC, V. **Date** Sat, Sun late Aug-early Oct.

For 20 years, the Renaissance Faire was held in the incomparable Black Point Forest near Novato, transforming the ancient grove into an Elizabethan festival complete with jousting, jesting and plenty of meat and mead. After a long battle, development won over, and the medieval lords and ladies have moved across the bay to Vacaville. Huzzah!

the mood is both sombre and celebratory. A traditional blessing of the four points of the compass by a community elder starts the procession. Then a truck carrying loudspeakers lurches into gear, providing musical accompaniment for a troupe of young Aztec dancers. Behind them come hippie musicians beating old drums and tambourines, women in antique wedding dresses clutching bouquets of dead flowers, and sleepy children in papier-mâché skeleton masks.The slow-moving throng processes up 25th Street and down the neighbourhood's main artery, Mission Street, before winding back to Garfield Square, a small park at the foot of Balmy Alley. There, people leave their candles and other offerings at a huge community altar before heading for home.

Taking part is always more fun that gawking, and visitors are welcome to get involved as long as they are respectful of the culture's traditions. To keep from looking like a tourist, wear dark, sombre clothes (the dressier the better) and keep your camera tucked away. If you want to look like a local, paint your face a ghoulish white and bring a noisemaker.

Día de los Muertos

826 8009. Procession starts at 24th & Bryant Streets, Mission. Bus 27, 33, 48. **Map** p314 Z2. **Date** 2 Nov.

Ghirardelli Square Chocolate Festival

775 5500/www.ghirardellisq.com. Ghirardelli Square, between North Point, Beach, Larkin & Polk Streets, Fisherman's Wharf. Muni Metro F/bus 19, 30, 42/ cable car Powell-Hyde. **Map** p308 F1. **Date** early Sept.
A chocolate lover's dream come true. Get to sample a variety of luscious treats, including chocolate-covered strawberries, brownies, chocolate cheesecake and more. Good news: the proceeds go to a local charity. Bad news: the calories go to your hips.

San Francisco Fringe Festival

673 3847/www.sffringe.org. **Tickets** up to $8.
No credit cards. **Date** early Sept.
This dramatic, non-juried, non-censored marathon features 260 performances by some 50 local, national and international theatre companies – a broad spectrum of comedy, classic theatre and performance art. Performances are held at various locations.

San Francisco Shakespeare Festival

422 2222/www.sfshakes.org. Golden Gate Park. Muni Metro N/bus 5, 7, 21, 28, 29, 44, 71.
Map p312. **Date** Sept.
The Bard knows no chronological or geographical limits, especially in Northern California. No less than five Bay Area theatre companies produce Shakespeare plays during the summer, but the event closest to home is the San Francisco Shakespeare Festival, performed free to the public on outdoor stages in Golden Gate Park throughout September. Shows begin at 1.30pm, but locals arrive by noon to get a seat and have a picnic.

San Francisco Blues Festival

979 5588/tickets from BASS 478 2277/ www.sfblues.com). Great Meadow, Fort Mason Center, Marina Boulevard, at Buchanan Street, Marina. Bus 28, 30, 47, 49. **Tickets** from $25.
Credit AmEx, DC, Disc, MC, V. **Map** p308 E1/2.
Date 3rd or 4th weekend in Sept.
The oldest blues festival in America, this weekend-long shindig blurs into one eternal afternoon. Hear set after set of broken-hearted chords from some of the best blues musicians in the world. Don't come without your shades, a blanket and a cooler packed with refreshments.

Folsom Street Fair

861 3247/www.folsomstreetfair.com. Folsom & Harrison Streets, between Seventh & 12th Streets, SoMa. Bus 9, 12, 14, 26, 42. **Map** p310/311 G5.
Date last Sun in Sept.
The Queen Mother of all leather street fairs, the Folsom Fair is an out-of-towner's gawkfest. But don't worry, it's still as fun and kinky as ever. Be prepared for hairy butts and bone-crushing crowds.

ArtSpan Open Studios

861 9838/www.artspan.org. **Date** Oct.
Get a behind-the-scenes peak at San Fran's creative visionaries each weekend in October. More than 700 artists' studios are open to the public, showing paintings, sculpture, ceramics, glass, jewellery and more. A free map and the *Directory of San Francisco Artists* ($12.95) are available from bookshops; a map is also published in the *San Francisco Chronicle* on the last Sunday in September.

San Francisco International Art Exposition

391 2000/www.sfiae.com. Fort Mason Center, Marina Boulevard, at Buchanan Street, Marina. Bus 28, 30, 47, 49. **Tickets** $12; $9 concessions; free under-10s. **Credit** AmEx, MC, V. **Map** p308 E1.
Date late Sept-early Oct.
This highbrow event includes work from some 100 art galleries representing more than 2,000 artists from 12 countries. Prices are considerably higher than those at the Artspan Open Studios (*see above*). Bring your credit card.

Castro Street Fair

467 3354/www.castrostreetfair.org. Market & Castro Streets, from 16th to 19th Streets, Castro. Muni Metro F, K, L, M/bus 24, 35, 37. **Date** early Oct.
Map p314 X1.
Presenting the softer side of gay life in SF, the one-day Castro Fair – started in 1974 by Harvey Milk – features food and crafts stalls, community activists and the full spectrum of rainbow merchandise.

Reggae in the Park

458 1988/eventswest@aol.com. Sharon Meadow, between Kezar & John F Kennedy Drives, Golden Gate Park. Muni Metro N/bus 5, 7, 21, 33, 66, 71.
Tickets from $17. **Credit** (in advance only) AmEx, Disc, MC, V. **Map** p312 C6.
Date early Oct.
You'll hear it from blocks away and smell the smoke long before you get there: RITP is quickly becoming one of the city's best-attended music festivals, mainly because it always seems to take place during the best autumn weather. A two-day event, it attracts artists and fans from all over the world.

Fleet Week

705 5500/www.fleetweek.com. Fisherman's Wharf & Piers 30-32, Embarcadero. Muni Metro F/bus 15, 39, 42. **Map** p308 F1. **Date** Oct.
Frightening pets and setting off car alarms throughout the city, the US Navy's Blue Angels tear up the heavens on Columbus Day weekend in a *Top Gun* display of speed, daring and taxpayer-baiting – though to watch them fly *beneath* the Golden Gate Bridge is an undeniable thrill. The fleet sails in on Saturday morning (the best viewpoint is from the Golden Gate Bridge), and there are free tours of various US and international ships.

San Francisco Jazz Festival

788 7353/www.sfjazzfest.com. **Tickets** $3-$50.
Credit DC, Disc, MC, V. **Date** 3rd & 4th weeks in Oct.
In competition with the well-known festival in Monterey each summer, the San Francisco Jazz Festival has angled itself to attract some of the biggest names in the jazz biz. More than 30 swinging

Burn, baby, burn

Every year in the first week of September, over 25,000 people gather in Nevada's harsh Black Rock Desert to build a temporary city. The physical, spiritual and symbolic centre of the city is a 50-foot (15-metre) monstrous wooden man, laced with neon and packed with fireworks, and surrounded by outrageous art installations. At the end of the week-long event, when the man is burned, his flaming, exploding skeleton marks the climax of one of the most mind-boggling celebrations anywhere on earth.

Trying to explain what Burning Man is to someone who has never been is a bit like trying to explain what a particular colour looks like to someone who is blind. It's about as close as you'll ever get to passing time on a different planet. The Black Rock Desert is an ancient lake bed, a vast expanse of cracked clay where absolutely nothing grows. Above you is a giant dome of the purest blue sky; at night, it pulses with the cool fire of millions of stars.

In the middle of this rugged, surreal setting, artists, engineers, hipsters, tripsters, cosmic comedians and even some ordinary people build the most unabashed and unflinchingly psychedelic city that ever existed. Black Rock City, which has two newspapers, a post office, at least two dozen radio stations, and an airstrip, exists to astonish, to expose, to make sacred, to make fun, to unsettle and to undress (it's perfectly acceptable to be naked).

Participants are expected to stay for a minimum of four days, and to bring with them everything (including water and food)

they might need to remain comfortable in awesome thunderstorms, tent-ruffling winds and temperatures ranging from 0°C-43°C (32°F-110°F). The impact of the Burning Man experience has been so profound that a culture has formed around it, with events and parties throughout the year in the Bay Area.

For more information, your first stop should be the festival website. Click straight through to the Survival Guide, which drives home the absolute necessity of proper preparation. And get your tickets ($150-$200) well in advance.

Burning Man

863 5263/www.burningman.com. Black Rock Desert, Nevada. **Date** Labor Day weekend.

and singing festival events take place in venues around San Francisco and Oakland. Buy tickets early for the best choice.

Exotic Erotic Ball

1-888 396 8426/www.exoticerotic.com. Cow Palace, 2600 Geneva Avenue, at Santos Street, Daly City. Bus 9, 9AX. **Tickets** $50-$125. **Credit** MC, V. **Date** late Oct.

It's obnoxious! It's exploitative! It's 22 years old now and is the bridge-and-tunnel crowd's annual excuse to pull on the latex and fishnets and party with other sex kittens at the world's largest indoor masquerade ball. Strippers, sideshows and a costume competition are among the tamer perks.

Halloween San Francisco

San Francisco Visitor Information Center (391 2000/www.sfvisitor.org). **Date** 31 Oct.

All attempts by city leaders to divert Halloween revellers from the traditional, if claustrophobic fray in the Castro to the staid Civic Center have been a monumental flop. Forget what the SFPD says and head for the Castro, where crazy costumes, drag queens and half-naked pagans still offer the best show in town. If you're going to gawk, return the favour and wear something outlandish.

Holiday Tree Lighting Festivities

705 5500. Union Square, Powell & Geary Streets. Bus 2, 3, 4, 30, 38/cable car Powell-Hyde, Powell-Mason. **Map** p309 G3/4. *Ghirardelli Square, 900 North Point Street, at Polk Street, Fisherman's Wharf. Bus 19, 30, 42/cable car Powell-Hyde.* **Map** p308 F1. **Date** late Nov.

Kick off the holiday season with entertainment, food and ice-skating, leading up to the lighting of an 80ft (24m) California white fir at Union Square, with

Put on your glad rags for **Halloween**. *See p193.*

12,000 lights and 1,000 gold ornaments, and a 50ft (15m) tree in Ghirardelli Square. Check the local press for precise starting times and places.

Run to the Far Side

759 2690/www.calacademy.org. Music Concourse, Ninth Avenue & JFK Drive, Golden Gate Park. Muni Metro N/bus 5, 7, 21, 28, 29, 44, 71. **Map** p312 B5. **Date** weekend after Thanksgiving.
Dress as your fave character from Gary Larson's cartoons for this annual footrace. A fund-raiser for the California Academy of Sciences, participants can walk or run 5km (3 miles) or run 10km (6 miles) through Golden Gate Park. Entrance fee is $18-$30.

Winter

The Nutcracker

War Memorial Opera House, 301 Van Ness Avenue, at Grove Street, Civic Center (865 2000/www.sfballet.org). BART Civic Center/Muni Metro F, J, K, L, M, N/bus 6, 7, 21, 42, 47, 49, 66, 71. **Tickets** $9-$120. **Credit** AmEx, MC, V. **Map** p310 F5. **Date** Dec.
The San Francisco Ballet (*see p225*), America's oldest ballet company, presents Tchaikovsky's beloved classic ballet every holiday season. The company puts on dozens of performances, so you have no excuse not to see it.

New Year

San Francisco Visitor Information Center (391 2000/www.sfvisitor.org). **Date** 31 Dec.
Traditionally, people see in the New Year in Union Square, where (taking its cue from New York's Times Square midnight ball drop), a huge, illuminated olive drops seven storeys into the world's largest Martini glass. In recent years, the city fathers have been discouraging street celebration, so it's best to check local papers of the Visitor Center before heading for the square. Other traditional festivities include a cavalcade of bands performing in tents along the Embarcadero.

Martin Luther King Jr Birthday Celebration

771 6300. Parade ends with rally at Yerba Buena Gardens, Mission Street, between Third & Fourth Streets, SoMa. BART Powell Street/Muni Metro F, J, K, L, M, N/bus 12, 14, 15, 30, 45, 76. **Map** p311 H4. **Date** Mon after 15 Jan (King's birthday).
In honour of the great civil rights leader, the United States takes a day off and holds birthday parades. The start of the route varies.

Tet Festival

885 2743. **Date** Jan-Feb.
San Francisco has a sizeable population of Vietnamese-Americans who, together with Cambodian, Latino- and African-American families, transform the Civic Center and Tenderloin areas into a multicultural carnival.

San Francisco Tribal, Folk & Textile Arts Show

1-310 455 2886. Fort Mason Center, Marina Boulevard, at Buchanan Street, Marina. Bus 28, 30, 47, 49. **Admission** $10; free under-16s. **No credit cards**. **Map** p308 E1. **Date** early Feb.
More than 100 folk and ethnic art dealers converge at Fort Mason in the Marina to sell pottery baskets, textiles, jewellery and the like.

Chinese New Year

982 3071/www.chineseparade.com. Parade starts at Market Street, at Second Street. BART Montgomery Street/Muni Metro F, J, K, L, M, N/bus 5, 6, 7, 9, 21, 31, 66, 71. **Map** p309 H3. **Date** Feb.
San Francisco's Chinese New Year is the biggest event of its kind outside Asia, and the best parade in the city. With beauty pageants, drumming, martial-arts displays, mountains of food, endless strings of fireworks and a huge parade through Chinatown, complete with dancing dragons, acrobats and stilt-walkers, the party turns the city jubilant and upside-down. If you're in town, don't miss it.

Children

Don't panic, there's plenty to keep the kids amused.

It's not hard to have fun in San Francisco, no matter what your age. From an exhilarating walk across the Golden Gate Bridge to a stomach-lurching ride on another of its famous symbols, the cable car, you'll find plenty to do to keep the family entertained. Below we've listed the most family-friendly attractions in and around town, but there are numerous other sights – see the **Sightseeing** chapters for more details.

For special seasonal events, check the pink 'Datebook' section of the Sunday *San Francisco Chronicle* under 'Children's Events'. You can hone your stilt-walking skills during the **Make-A-Circus Free Summer Festival Days**; the professional circus troupe performs throughout California from June through August, with several dates in San Francisco (details on 242 1414). Outlandish Canadian circus outfit **Cirque du Soleil** performs in the city every second summer.

Babysitting & childcare

American Child Care Service

285 2300/www.americanchildcare.com. **Rates** (minimum 4hrs) $15.50 per hr per family; $5-$10 transport fee. **Credit** AmEx, Disc, MC, V.

An upmarket childcare agency serving the downtown hotels, which will also take children on excursions to the Zoo, Exploratorium and other places.

Bay Area Childcare Agency

1-650 991 7474. **Rates** (minimum 4hrs) $10 per hr for up to 4 children, depending on age; $8 transport fee. **Credit** AmEx, MC, V.

In business for more than 50 years, this independent agency serves all the major hotels, screens sitters and won't employ anyone aged under 40. Expect to pay at least $50 for a child-free evening.

Aquariums & zoos

For details of the **Oakland Zoo**, *see p198* **Out of town**. If you're heading up or down the coast, don't miss the the **Marine Mammal Center** (*see p251*) in Marin or the world-class **Monterey Bay Aquarium** (*see p265*).

Aquarium of the Bay

Pier 39, Embarcadero, at Beach Street, Fisherman's Wharf (1-888 732 3483/www.aquariumofthebay.com). Muni Metro F/bus 10, 15, 39, 47. **Open** *Summer* 9am-8pm daily. *Winter* 10am-6pm Mon-Fri; 10am-7pm Sat, Sun. **Admission** $12.95; $6.50 3-11s, concessions. **Credit** MC, V. **Map** p308 G1.

Renovated in 2001, this aquatic theme park in Fisherman's Wharf gives you a diver's-eye view of the bay through clear plastic underwater tunnels. Though admission prices are a bit steep, it's an amazing place to spy on crabs and sharks, stare in wonderment at the benign-looking jellyfish and watch the slow, gentle combat of giant octopuses.

Have fun learning about science at the **Exploratorium**. *See p196.*

Randall Museum

199 Museum Street, off Roosevelt Way, Buena Vista (554 9600/www.randallmuseum.org). Bus 24, 37. **Open** 10am-5pm Tue-Sat. **Admission** free. **Map** p313 E6.

This small, friendly museum is located above the city in Corona Heights Park, south of the Haight, and features a petting zoo with lambs, raccoons, hawks and a lovely pair of garter snakes. There are art workshops, storytellers and a model railway that enthusiasts run occasionally. Perfect for small children.

San Francisco Zoo

Sloat Boulevard, at 45th Avenue, Sunset District (753 7080/www.sfzoo.org). Muni Metro L/bus 18, 23. **Open** *Main zoo* 10am-5pm daily. *Children's zoo Mid June-Labor Day* 10.30am-4.30pm daily. *Labor Day-mid June* 11am-4pm Mon-Fri; 10.30am-4.30pm Sat, Sun. **Admission** $10; $7 12-17s, concessions; $4 3-11s. **Credit** AmEx, MC, V.

Located in the far south-west of the city, the zoo contains more than 1,000 species of mammals and birds. Kids will love Koala Crossing (this is one of the few zoos in the US that has koalas), Musk Ox Meadows, Wolf Woods and Gorilla World (inhabited by three families of gorillas). New is the Family Farm, where children can pet a draught horse named Coulter, stroke a Scottish Highland cow and feed Ginger the goat. Recent zoo babies include alpacas, gorillas, snow leopards and rhinos. Child-oriented features include feeding times (2pm daily; 3pm for penguins) and a wonderfully creepy Insect Zoo.

Steinhart Aquarium

California Academy of Sciences, 55 Concourse Drive, Golden Gate Park (recorded information 750 7145/ www.calacademy.org). Bus 5, 21, 44, 71. **Open** *Summer* 9am-6pm daily; 9am-8.45pm 1st Wed of the month. *Winter* 10am-5pm daily; 10am-8.45pm 1st Wed of the month. **Admission** $8.50; $5.50 concessions, 12-17s; $2 4-11s; free under-4s. Free 1st Wed of the month. **Credit** (museum only) MC, V. **Map** p312 B6.

Part of the California Academy of Sciences (*see p106*) in Golden Gate Park, the Steinhart's dark confines are loved by kids. As well as snakes and reptiles, it's got more than 14,000 sea creatures from all over the globe – check out the grumpy eels, fluorescent-gilled sailfish and scary-looking piranhas. The recently remodelled Fish Roundabout is a delightfully disorienting spiral; try to arrive at feeding time for the most active panorama. Children can touch slimy creatures in the Tidal Pool. It's best to go in the week, when the aquarium is less crowded.

Going up

The best things in life are free, the old saying goes, and while that's only so true, children can be easily amused. For fast, free fun, try entertaining lifts. The fastest elevator ride in the city can be found in the five glass lifts that cling vertically to the 32-storey tower of the **Westin St Francisco Hotel** on Powell Street in Union Square. At a speed of 1,000 feet (305 metres) per minute, the elevators whoosh you from the ground to the 32nd floor in 30 seconds. The kids will love the ride, while grown-ups marvel at the stunning view of bay. Or try the **Hyatt Regency San Francisco** in the Embarcadero Center. Its four brass and glass lifts aren't as fast as the Westin's (a mere 750 feet/229 metres per minute), but offer a breathtaking view of the hotel's glistening 17-storey atrium.

Libraries

San Francisco's gorgeous **Main Library** (*see p68*) boasts half a floor just for children, with a circular storytelling room and more than a dozen computer and Internet terminals; videos, audio tapes and books in 40 languages; a kids' multimedia and electronic discovery computer unit; a fairytale and folk collection; a creative centre for live performances and crafts; and a teenagers' drop-in section. Children's art exhibitions change periodically.

Many local libraries offer story hours – especially recommended are the multilingual branches in the **Mission** (300 Bartlett Street, between Mission and Valencia Streets; 695 5090) and **Chinatown** (1135 Powell Street, near Jackson Street; 274 0275).

Museums

At the **Museum of the City of San Francisco** (*see p110*), there's a special earthquake display and regular storytelling sessions. Curator Gladys Hansen is usually on hand to show you her great-aunt's sewing machine (saved from the flames of the Great Fire) and to tell tales about the survivors. Other museums that kids enjoy include the **Cable Car Museum** (*see p109*), the **National Maritime Museum** (*see p111*) and the **Musée Mécanique** (*see p110*).

Exploratorium

3601 Lyon Street, at Marina Boulevard, Presidio (563 7337/www.exploratorium.edu). Bus 22, 28, 30, 41, 45. **Open** *Memorial Day-Labor Day* 10am-6pm Mon, Tue, Thur-Sun; 10am-9pm Wed. *Labor Day-Memorial Day* 10am-5pm Tue, Thur-Sun; 10am-9pm Wed. **Admission** $9; $7.50 concessions; $6 5-17s; free under-5s. **Credit** AmEx, MC, V. **Map** p307 C2.

If you and your kids are looking for something uniquely San Franciscan, put the Exploratorium at the top of your list. This science museum is perfect

Plenty of fun, indoors and out, at **Zeum**.

for kids: everything is designed to be touched. With more than 700 hands-on experiments, your family can learn about sensory perceptions, weather, botany, mechanics, health issues and the physics of sound and light. The favourite attraction is the Tactile Dome, a geodesic hemisphere of total blackness where you fumble around in the dark touching different objects (it's very popular and often crowded, so book in advance). The gift shop is full of educational and scientific toys.

Mission Science Workshop

City College of San Francisco, Mission Campus, 106 Bartlett Street, at 22nd Street, Mission (550 4419). BART 24th Street/bus 14, 49, 67. **Open** 3-5.30pm Mon-Thur. **Admission** free. **Map** p314 Y2.

This workshop for kids aged eight upwards is the antidote to the super-tech Zeum (*see above*), with a collection of gadgets and geegaws – microscopes, electronic parts, magnets and more – all designed for children. Summer hours differ from those during the school year, so phone first to check details. Wednesdays are for girls only.

Zeum

221 Fourth Street, at Howard Street, SoMa (777 2800/www.zeum.org). BART Powell or Montgomery Streets/Muni Metro F, J, K, L, M, N/bus 9, 15, 30, 45, 76. **Open** *Summer & school holidays* 11am-5pm Wed-Sun. *Winter* 11am-5pm Sat, Sun. **Admission** $7; $6 concessions; $5 5-18s. **Credit** AmEx, MC, V. **Map** p311 H4.

San Francisco's newest art and technology centre (aimed at 8-18s) is the kind of place that threatens adults with a headache, so, of course, kids love it. Exhibits are interactive: kids can direct their own video production, create sculptures or experiment with computer-aided design. Nearby is a bowling alley (with gutter bumpers, so that no one strikes out), a garden, a child-sized labyrinth, an ice-skating rink and a lovely, old-fashioned carousel.

Outdoors

San Francisco can be cool and foggy in summer, but that shouldn't keep you from spending a day outside. You should certainly spend some time in **Golden Gate Park** (*see p90*). There's tons to see and do – cycling, rollerskating, horse-riding, buffalos and museums. At the south-eastern corner, opposite Kezar Stadium, you'll find an old-fashioned carousel, a tree house and swings in the children's playground, and Punch and Judy shows in summer. At Stow Lake you can hire rowing boats and paddle boats.

For a walk on the wilder side, at least as far as the weather goes, head out to the western edge of the city to **Ocean Beach** (*see p100* **On the beach**), a wide, four-mile sandy stretch. To warm up, have a hot chocolate in the Cliff House at the north end of the beach and watch seals sunning on the Seal Rocks below and at nearby Point Lobos. The ones with little ears are California seals; the shiny graceful ones are Harbour seals.

Overpriced kitsch may predominate at **Fisherman's Wharf** (*see p76*), but for free entertainment there are dozens of street performers and, at Pier 39, you can see and hear – and certainly smell – a crowd of gallumphing sea lions, who've taken up residence at one of the docks. Other child-friendly attractions here include the historic ships at **Hyde Street Pier**, the World War II submarine **USS Pampanito** and the **Jeremiah O'Brien Liberty Ship** (*see p198*) moored on Pier 45. Fisherman's Wharf is also the departure point for trips around the bay.Visit the prison on **Alcatraz Island** or take a ferry to **Angel Island** (for both, *see p74* **Fantasy islands**).

Organised tours include **Fire Engine Tours & Adventures** (*see p53*), which kids love: they get to ride an old-fashioned, open-air fire engine across the Golden Gate Bridge. Cable cars may be too much of an adventure for very

All aboard the **Fire Engine Tour**. *See p197.*

young children, but they don't have to miss out on the fun: the **Cow Hollow Playground** near Union Street has a tot-sized replica of a cable car. The tiny park is easy to miss: it's hidden at the end of Miley Street, a half-block alley between Greenwich and Filbert Streets.

Jeremiah O'Brien Liberty Ship

Pier 45, Embarcadero, at Taylor Street, Fisherman's Wharf (441 3101/www.ssjeremiahobrien.com/). Bus 19, 30, 32/cable car Powell-Hyde. **Open** 9am-5pm daily. **Admission** $6; $5 concessions; $3 6-14s; free under-6s. **No credit cards**. **Map** p308 F1.
Kids can explore the faithfully restored ship's engine room and officers' bunk rooms, and operate the foghorn – but not the three-inch 50-calibre gun. The ship occasionally leaves the dock for cruises or other events, so call ahead to be sure it's there.

Out of town

Bay Area Discovery Museum

557 McReynolds Road, Fort Baker (487 4398/www.badm.org). **Open** *Summer* 10am-5pm Tue-Sun. *Winter* 9am-4pm Tue-Thur; 10am-5pm Fri-Sun. **Admission** $7. **No credit cards**.
Just under the north tower of the Golden Gate Bridge, this collection of historic army barracks has been imaginatively transformed into a place for kids aged up to ten. There's an art room, a pleasant café and a shop. There is no public transport to the museum.

Chabot Space & Science Museum

10000 Skyline Boulevard, at the edge of Joaquin Miller Park, Oakland (1-510 336 7373/www.chabotspace.org). BART Fruitvale, then AC Transit bus 53. **Open** 10am-5pm Tue-Sun. **Admission** $8 general; $8.75 Planetarium; $8.75 MegaDome Theatre; $14.75 two venues; $19.75 three venues; concessions available. **Credit** MC, V.
This 13-acre centre high in the Oakland Hills is the next best thing to space travel. Gaze at the night sky through one of two giant telescopes or experience a total solar eclipse in the large domed theatre. Kids will love the hands-on exhibit called Planetary Landscapes: Sculpting the Solar System, where they can wave their hands through a cauldron of billowing fog. Afterwards, let them cool off with some astronaut ice-cream.

Children's Fairyland

699 Bellevue Avenue, Oakland (1-510 452 2259/www.fairyland.org). **Open** hours vary; call for details. **Admission** $6. **Credit** MC, V.
Legend has is that Walt Disney was so taken with this whimsical storybook theme park when he visited it in 1950 that he decided to build his own. The 50-year-old playland on Oakland's Lake Merritt recently got a facelift, but retains its uncommon charm. Kids can follow Alice down the rabbit hole, ride a tiny Ferris wheel and catch one of the daily puppet shows.

Lawrence Hall of Science

Centennial Drive, near Grizzly Park Boulevard, Berkeley (1-510 642 5132/ www.lhs.berkeley. edu). BART Berkeley, then AC Transit bus 8, 65. **Open** 10am-5pm daily. **Admission** $7; $5 5-18s, concessions; $3 3-4s; free under-3s. **Credit** Disc, MC, V.
Perched on the hills facing San Francisco and the bay, this science museum in Berkeley has computers to explore the inside of your brain, a Young Explorers Area and a huge DNA model to scramble over. Check out the giant telescope and the wind-driven organ pipes at the back.

Oakland Zoo

9777 Golf Links Road, off I-580, Oakland (1-510 632 9525/www.oaklandzoo.org). AC Transit bus 56. **Open** 10am-4pm daily. **Admission** $7.50; $4.50 2-14s, concessions; free under-2s. **Credit** AmEx, Disc, MC, V.
Oakland Zoo has more than 1,000 species of mammals and birds. Most are not caged. Kids can visit Emma, the baby wart-hog piglet, and ride the new CP Huntington miniature train, a tiny replica of the Civil War-era locomotive.

Film

A popular movie location, SF also has a thriving independent filmmaking scene.

San Francisco prides itself on a strong, savvy cinematic spirit. Film-goers here tend to be sophisticated and discriminating, while still enthusiastic over new discoveries. And it's not just a hotspot of film appreciation – it's also a nexus for filmmaking. Movies like *Vertigo*, *Bullitt*, *Dirty Harry* and *Mrs Doubtfire* have made the best of the city's magnificent scenery, while its location not too far – but just far enough – away from Hollywood makes it an attractive base for dozens of directors. Francis Ford Coppola has an office in North Beach, for instance, and George Lucas (whose LucasFilm studio is just over the Golden Gate Bridge in Marin County) has recently relocated some of his operations to the Presidio. Sharon Stone, Robin Williams and Nicolas Cage are among the many stars with homes here.

Still, this isn't just a Hollywood suburb. San Francisco's film scene is vibrantly avant-garde and independent. Local documentarians include Terry Zwigoff (*Crumb*, *Ghost World*) and duo Rob Epstein and Jeffrey Friedman (the Oscar-winning *The Life and Times of Harvey Milk*), while a never-ending parade of film festivals throughout the year spotlights lesser-known talents from near and far.

TICKETS & INFORMATION

You can usually purchase tickets direct from cinema box offices immediately before any showing. Check local newspapers for listings and film times (the *Chronicle*, *Examiner* and *Bay Guardian* have up-to-date listings and reviews). Expect opening nights to be popular. Most cinemas run bargain-price matinées – check each venue for its policy. Showtimes, cinema locations and ticket purchases for many theatres and festivals are also available from the national, all-in-one **Moviefone** (777 3456/www.moviefone.com), but there's a $1 service charge per ticket.

Cinemas

Mainstream

In days of old, San Franciscans had more than a dozen grand movie palaces to choose from; armed with popcorn and a sweating soda, movie-goers would settle down as the lights dimmed inside a beautifully decorated, regal cinema. These days, all those architectural lovelies are nothing more than memories,

San Francisco movie classics include Hitchcock's 1958 masterpiece *Vertigo*.

except for a few that still cling to life. Among them are the colossal **United Artists Coronet** in the Richmond District (3575 Geary Boulevard, at Arguello Street; 752 4400), the recently restored **United Artists Metro** (Union Street, at Webster Street, Cow Hollow; 931 1685) and the palatial **Castro** (*see below*).

Part of the reason the old movie palaces faded was the growth of the massive and excessively modern multiplexes. Gleaming escalators and superlong hallways at **AMC Kabuki 8** in Japantown (1181 Post Street, at Fillmore Street; 931 9800), AMC's 14-screen **1000 Van Ness** on the western edge of the Tenderloin (1000 Van Ness Avenue, at O'Farrell Street; 931 9800) and the 15-screen **Sony Metreon** in SoMa (221 Fourth Street, at Mission Street; 369 6000) have all the calm of shopping malls and airport waiting rooms. To their credit, the screens are state-of-the-art, the seats high-backed and comfortable and the sound systems excellent. The Kabuki 8 is also the main venue for the prestigious **International Film Festival** (*see p202*).

Other good, centrally located houses are the **United Artists Galaxy** on the edge of the Tenderloin (1285 Sutter Street, at Van Ness Avenue; 474 8700) and funky **Presidio** in the Marina (2340 Chestnut Street, at Scott Street; 921 6720).

Tickets at all cost around $9 and AmEx, MasterCard and Visa credit cards are accepted.

Lumière

1572 California Street, between Polk & Larkin Streets, Polk Gulch (352 0810/www.landmark theater.com). Bus 1, 19/cable car California. **Tickets** $8.75; $5.75 concessions. **Credit** AmEx, MC, V. **Map** p308 F3.

New releases and underground hits often pop up at the Lumière – and the other four cinemas in the Landmark Theatres chain. Admission prices are the same at all cinemas, and you can get listings for all from the same phone number (or the website). **Branches**: **Bridge** 3010 Geary Boulevard, at Blake Street, Richmond District; **Opera Plaza** 601 Van Ness Avenue, between Turk Street & Golden Gate Avenue, Civic Center; **Clay** 2261 Fillmore Street, at Clay Street, Pacific Heights; **Embarcadero Center** 1 Embarcadero Center, Battery Street, between Sacramento & Clay Streets, Financial District.

Repertory

Most interesting are the independently owned cinemas housed in unique buildings, such as the **Castro**, **Roxie** and **Red Vic**, while the **San Francisco Cinematheque** (*see p201*) provides a prime venue for avant-garde screenings. Across the bay, a repertory-film scene thrives at a handful of unique venues. Sadly, Berkeley's beloved UC Theater, which helped launch the cinematic rep movement in the US, closed its doors in 2001 because of the prohibitive cost of seismic retrofitting.

Castro Theatre

429 Castro Street, between 17th & 18th Streets, Castro (621 6120/www.thecastrotheatre.com). Muni Metro F, K, L, M/bus 24, 33, 35, 37. **Tickets** $7.50; $4.50 concessions. **No credit cards**. **Map** p314 X1.

Go on a weekend night for the full experience. The popcorn-munching audience is entertained before the screening by an organist playing a battery of favourites on a Wurlitzer; painted murals line the art deco walls and ceilings. The film might be anything from an old Bette Davis picture (where everyone knows and recites the best lines) or a *Sound of Music* sing-along to a world première by an independent queer filmmaker.

Fine Arts Cinema

2451 Shattuck Avenue, at Haste Street, Berkeley (1-510 848 1143/www.finearts cinema.com). BART Berkeley, then AC Transit bus 43, 65/AC Transit bus F. **Tickets** $7; $4-$5 concessions. **No credit cards**. **Map** p315 M4.

A truly eclectic calendar of art flicks, foreign films and seldom-seen documentaries.

Pacific Film Archive

2575 Bancroft Way, at Bowditch Street, Berkeley (1-510 642 1124/www.sirius.com/~sstark/org/pfa/pfa.html). BART Berkeley, then AC Transit bus 7, 40, 51, 64/AC Transit bus F. **Tickets** $7; concessions $4.50. **Credit** Disc, MC, V. **Map** p315 N4.

On the edge of the University of California campus, the PFA screens some 650 films and videos a year from its world-renowned collection of more than 7,000 titles, including Soviet, US avant-garde and Japanese cinema, with an intellectual crowd dissecting every camera angle.

Paramount Theatre

2025 Broadway, between 20th & 21st Streets, Oakland (1-510 465 6400/www.paramounttheater.com). BART 19th Street. **Tickets** $5. **Credit** AmEx, Disc, MC, V.

An art deco masterpiece outside and in – thus a tourist attraction in its own right – the Paramount shows old classics on Friday evenings.

Parkway Theater

1834 Park Boulevard, at E 18th Street, Oakland (1-510 814 2400/www.picturepubpizza.com). BART 12th Street/City Center, then AC Transit bus 13, 14, 15/AC Transit bus K. **Tickets** $5. **No credit cards**.

This folksy movie house doubles as a casual restaurant; munch pizza and throw back beer while watching new releases and independent productions.

Red Vic

1727 Haight Street, at Cole Street, Haight-Ashbury (668 3994/www.redvicmoviehouse.com). Bus 7, 33,

Roxie: top rep house.

43, 66, 77. **Tickets** $6.50; $3 concessions. **No credit cards. Map** p313 C6.
Where else can you sprawl on an old sofa, eat popcorn (with butter and brewer's yeast) out of wooden bowls and watch revivals or a current funky flick with a wildly eclectic crowd? The Red Vic is worker-owned and operated, so the price of your ticket supports a good cause.

Roxie

3117 16th Street, at Valencia Street, Mission (863 1087/www.roxie.com). BART 16th Street/ bus 14, 22, 26, 33, 49, 53. **Tickets** $7; $3 concessions. **No credit cards. Map** p310 F6.
Revivals of film noir classics, Fassbinder festivals and horror movies only begin to touch on the range of the Roxie's roster. The seats are hard and the sound system is not great, but the atmosphere makes up for such shortcomings.

Experimental & foreign

SFMOMA (*see p107*) has a large 278-seat cinema, which usually hosts screenings in the spring and autumn (mostly on Thursdays and Sundays), often in conjunction with exhibitions. The 96-seat media screening room at **Yerba Buena Center for the Arts** (*see p107*), located on the second floor, is often used for contemporary and experimental offerings connected with the Center's exhibitions.

For orginal-language European fare, try the **Alliance Française** in Polk Gulch (1345 Bush Street; 775 7755/www.afsf.com), **Goethe Institute** near Union Square (530 Bush Street; 263 8760/www.goethe.de/uk/saf/enindex.htm) and the **Instituto Italiano di Cultura** in the Financial District (425 Washington Street; 788 7142/www.sfiic.org), all of which have occasional screenings.

Artists' Television Access

992 Valencia Street, at 21st Street, Mission (824 3890/www.atasite.org). BART 24th Street/ bus 14, 26, 49. **Open** 10am-10pm daily. **Tickets** from $5. **No credit cards. Map** p314 Y2.
Artists' Television Access has experimental and unusual programming, including open screenings, usually from Thursday to Sunday.

San Francisco Cinematheque

822 2885/www.sfcinematheque.org. **Tickets** $7. **No credit cards.**
Cinematheque is at the centre of avant-garde film in the Bay Area, offering programmes twice weekly from late September until July. From documentaries to features and animated films, this is where to see stuff you can't see anywhere else. Venues vary, but include Yerba Buena Center for the Arts and the San Francisco Art Institute.

Festivals

That the Bay Area loves a good flick is obvious: almost every month there's a film festival of some sort, many drawing directors from around the world. The works of local movie-makers feature prominently in every San Francisco festival, where films can vary from extremely high quality to dire 'difficult viewing' experiences. Along with the major fests listed below, many tiny festivals come and go. Notable among them is the New York-based **RESFEST** (1-212 217 1154/www.resfest.com), an international touring celebration of cutting-edge digital video experiments, which makes a stop in San Francisco.

Black Filmworks Festival of Film & Video

1-510 465 0804/www.blackfilmmakershall.org. Venues: Paramount Theatre, Parkway Theater, Laney College, Oakland Museum, all in Oakland. **Date** late Sept-early Oct.
Presented by the Black Filmmakers Hall of Fame, this ten-day competitive fest features films by, for and about Africans and African-Americans. It has included tributes to US director Spike Lee and the late Marlon Riggs, whose groundbreaking experimental documentary *Tongues Untied* explored the experiences of African-American gay men.

Festival ¡Cine Latino!

553 8140/www.cineaccion.com. Venues vary; phone for details. **Date** mid Sept.
Over the past decade, Cine Acción's festival has come into its own as the premier showcase for films from Latin America and by Latino-American filmmakers. As well as screenings of films and videos, events include appearances by filmmakers, plus great food and music at the opening ceremonies. The festival lasts for ten days.

Film Arts Festival of Independent Cinema

552 8760/www.filmarts.org. Venues: Castro Theatre, Castro; Zeum, SoMa; Fine Arts Cinema, Berkeley; and others. **Date** early Nov.
This six-day festival provides the essential venue for a real snapshot of inventive filmmaking in Northern California. All programming is drawn from Bay Area independent work and features documentary, experimental and traditional narrative pieces. Many artists who debuted here went on to illustrious careers.

Jewish Film Festival

621 0556/www.sfjff.org. Venues: Castro Theatre, Castro; Wheeler Auditorium, Berkeley; Fox Theatre, Redwood City. **Date** late July-early Aug.
Launched in 1981, this two-week event presents contemporary films from around the world on Jewish subjects and in celebratation of Jewish secular culture. There is also some retrospective and archival work.

MadCat Women's International Film Festival

436 9523/www.somaglow.com/madcat/. Venues vary; phone for details. **Date** Sept.
The alternative alternative women's film festival, tiny MadCat features short films, panel discussions and pioneering features that range from earnest feminist polemics to raunchy sexploitation. Events take place over a three-week period.

Mill Valley Film Festival & Videofest

383 5256/www.finc.org. Venues: Sequoia Twin Theater, Mill Valley; Rafael Film Center, San Rafael. **Date** early Oct.
New American and international independent films and videos are the focus of this ten-day Marin County festival, which screens dozens of different works and also includes a six-day 'Videofest', interactive media exhibitions, seminars, special events and children's programmes. It has grown to become one of the most well-known and influential film events in the state.

San Francisco International Asian American Film Festival

255 4299/www.naatanet.org/festival/. Venues: Kabuki 8 Cinema, Japantown; Pacific Film Archive, Berkeley. **Date** mid Mar.
Now 20 years old, the hip and prestigious AAFF draws huge audiences for its screenings of about 100 films and videos by and about Asians and Asian Americans – it's the largest event of its kind in North America. The festival runs for ten days.

San Francisco International Film Festival

931 3456/www.sfiff.org. Venues: Kabuki 8 cinema, Japantown; and others in the Bay Area.
Date mid Apr-early May.
Produced by the San Francisco Film Society, this nearly 50-year-old festival is North America's longest-running and considered one of the best in the United States. Over the course of a few weeks, more than 200 films and videos from dozens of countries are screened, and it's rare to find a clunker in the bunch. Glitterati attend – director Wim Wenders, Clint Eastwood and Wayne Wang all showed up in recent years – and more than 80,000 tickets sell like hot cakes. Most films are screened at the Kabuki 8 in Japantown, and tickets go on sale at the Kabuki a few weeks before the festival opens. Not quite Cannes, but a must for film fans.

San Francisco International Lesbian & Gay Film Festival

703 8650/www.frameline.org. Venues: Castro Theatre, Castro; Victoria, Mission; Roxie, Mission: and others. **Date** late June.
This two-week festival, which celebrated its 25th anniversary in 2001, is a crucial part of the month-long Gay Pride celebration. It's the world's oldest and largest event of its kind. Mainstream, gay-themed films are part of a selection that runs the gamut from independent shorts and features with a queer sensibility to avant-garde experiments. Programmes are available a month in advance from bookshops and cafés and in the *Bay Guardian*.

San Francisco Silent Film Festival

777 4908/www.silentfilm.org. Venue: Castro Theatre, Castro. **Date** early July.
This one-day festival focuses exclusively on silent-era masterpieces that have not been screened in 70 or 80 years. Performances are accompanied by the Castro's wonderful organist.

Spike & Mike's Festival of Animation

1-800 457 7453/www.spikeandmike.com. Venues: Castro Theatre, Castro; Palace of Fine Arts, Presidio; and cinemas in Berkeley, San Jose and other cities. **Date** late Apr-early May & Nov.
The kings of the cartoon carnival are Spike and Mike, whose biannual, two-week, 50-city fest has reigned supreme in Bay Area movie houses for almost a quarter of a century. Both the spring and autumn festivals have become launching pads for local artists including Pixar producer John Lasseter (*Toy Story*). The 'Sick and Twisted' special, added ten years ago, is a must-see for non-fragile minds.

Schools & classes

San Francisco State University, UC Berkeley, the San Francisco Art Institute and City College all have thriving film study or filmmaking programmes, each encouraging and developing new and established film and video artists. In addition, two San Francisco institutions – the **Film Arts Foundation** (which runs the annual Independent Cinema festival – *see p201*) and the **Bay Area Video Coalition** (861 3282/www.bavc.org) – provide services and continuing education and networking for filmmakers and videographers in the area.

To find out casting and production details of films currently being made in the Bay Area, contact the **San Francisco Film Commission** (554 6244/www.ci.sf.ca.us/film).

Film Arts Foundation

Second floor, 346 Ninth Street, at Folsom Street, SoMa (552 8760/www.filmarts.org). BART Civic Center/Muni Metro F, J, K, L, M, N/bus 12, 19, 27, 42. **Map** p310 G5.

Galleries

Where San Francisco stops apologising, and gets down to art.

There's a joke out here on the Left Coast: where can you find all the best San Francisco artists? Answer: in New York. OK, so it's not that funny, and it's more a reflection of San Francisco's inferiority complex when it comes to the bigger, more famous East Coast city than of San Fran's impressive arts scene. It is true that local artists seeking a breakthrough in their careers do tend to go east in search of greater visibility and better sales. But, dammit, it's time for California to stop apologising. The arts are something for which San Francisco is best known, and what makes the scene extraordinary is the way it reflects its location on the edge – literally and figuratively – of the continent.

The region has been ground zero for a number of significant art movements over the years – from the *plein air* Impressionists of the Society of Six, established in 1918 (who were inspired by the extraordinary Pacific Ocean light) to the post-war Bay Area figuratives and the 'happenings' of the 1960s, which led to a rich vein of performance art. Home to a multicultural stew since the Gold Rush days, San Francisco embraces the visual expression of its ethnic history, whether the references are to hundreds of years of Mexican-American presence or to Asian-American perspectives that barely span a generation.

As you might expect from its proximity to Silicon Valley and the influence of Hollywood, interactive video, computer-assisted art and sculpture made of high-tech cast-offs are quite ubiquitous in the landscape. Recently, though, the high-tech connection has shaken the art community as profoundly as the earthquakes rippling along the famous San Andreas fault rattle houses. In the early 1990s, many dotcom businesses gobbled up space, forcing galleries to close or move. The Internet market crash in early 2001 actually helped, in a way, by stabilising the exodus, and allowing spaces to remain in long-established neighbourhoods, thus keeping it relatively easy to visit galleries on foot.

Many commercial galleries are clustered within a few blocks of Union Square, and some are stacked within single buildings like a club sandwich. For edgier work, head for non-profit galleries in the formerly low-rent SoMa and Mission districts. A good time to visit is during **First Thursdays**, a tradition whereby many galleries schedule exhibition openings and stay open late on the first Thursday of every month, plying visitors with wine and cheese. In July, there's a chance to see new work by young and emerging artists at **Introductions** and **Summer ArtWalk**, presented by the San Francisco Art Dealers Association (626 7498/ www.sfada.com), a non-profit organisation composed of 35 Bay Area galleries. Also look out for **ArtSpan Open Studios** and the **San Francisco International Art Exposition**, both held in the autumn (for both, *see p192*).

Keep your eyes open for the wealth of mural art on the city's streets (*see p204* **The city on foot: Murals**).

ART SCHOOLS

Don't forget the three major art schools – the **San Francisco Art Institute** in Russian Hill; the **Academy of Art College**, with campuses in SoMa and on Nob Hill; and the **California College of Arts and Crafts** near Potrero Hill – each offering student and faculty shows as well as independently curated exhibitions. Out near Lake Merced you'll find **San Francisco State University**, which has also opened a new gallery for exhibiting work. For all, *see chapter* **Directory: Study**.

INFORMATION

For the best of the city's art scene, pick up a copy of the *San Francisco Bay Area Gallery Guide*, published bi-monthly and available at virtually every gallery in town. The handy brochure is a bible for addresses, individual shows and out-of-town museum listings; it also mentions special events such as art walks, emerging artists' tours and auctions. If you'd like a copy before you arrive in town, write to 1369 Fulton Street, San Francisco, CA 94117, or phone 921 1600. Admission is free to all the galleries listed below.

Non-profit galleries

Galeria de la Raza/Studio 24

2857 24th Street, at Bryant Street, Mission (826 8009/www.galeriadelaraza.org). BART 24th Street/ bus 9, 27, 33, 48. **Open** noon-6pm Tue-Sat. **Credit** MC, V. **Map** p314 Z2.

Since 1970, this tiny shopfront gallery in the heart of the Mission District has celebrated contemporary Mexican-American culture with bi-monthly exhibitions. From cartoonists and performance artists to

You'll be bug-eyed at **111 Minna Street**. *See p208.*

muralists and cyber-installations, the diversity of artistic talent is superb. With an archive of protest and political art, it leans toward the left. One of its most noted projects is (Re)generation, which helps develop the careers of emerging Latin American artists via training and mentorships.

Intersection for the Arts

446 Valencia Street, between 15th & 16th Streets, Mission (626 2787/www.theintersection.org). BART 16th Street/bus 14, 22, 26, 33, 49. **Open** by appointment Tue; noon-5pm Wed-Sat. **Credit** MC, V. **Map** p314 Y1.

This is a venerable local institution where many up-and-coming artists make their debut in well-chosen group shows, solo exhibitions and performances. The gallery's nondescript shopfront is at the centre of a new arts community that has begun to assemble around the Mission/16th Street area. It also hosts artists' talks and events outside the gallery.

The Lab

2948 16th Street, between Mission Street & S Van Ness Avenue, Mission (864 8855/www.thelab.org). BART 16th Street/bus 14, 22, 26, 33, 49. **Open** 1-6pm Wed-Sat. **No credit cards**. **Map** p314 Y1.

A ground-floor space on a slightly seedy corner, the Lab favours often political, subversive or controversial punk photography, painting and multimedia displays. It holds art auctions several times a year, and can always be counted on as a resource for edgy pieces at decent prices.

The Luggage Store

1007 Market Street, between Sixth & Seventh Streets, Tenderloin (255 5971). BART Powell Street/

The city on foot: Murals

The Mission District is renowned for its vibrant mural art; dozens of schools, shops, houses – almost every available wall, it seems – are emblazoned with explosively colourful paintings celebrating the area's Latino heritage and designed to encourage pride and community activism. They uphold the traditions of public art with a political message – in the vein of Mexican muralists Diego Rivera, José Clemente Orozco and David Alfaro Siquieros. The best-known mural street is **Balmy Alley** (which runs from 24th to 25th Streets, between Harrison Street and Treat Avenue). You'll also find many murals near **24th Street**, between Mission and Potrero Streets, and in SoMa, between **Third** and **Tenth Streets**.

The Mission District was just a sleepy Irish neighbourhood when Rivera arrived in San Francisco in 1930 to paint the first large-scale frescos. One was installed – ironically, for a Communist activist – inside the **Pacific Coast Stock Exchange** (*see p61*). Another, *The Making of a Fresco*, is inside what is now the **San Francisco Art Institute** (*see p81*). A third work, completed for the 1941 Golden Gate International Exposition, is now on the Phelan campus of **City College of San Francisco** (*see p285*) in the Outer Mission. It's a huge and fantastical creation, incorporating everything from Aztec Indians to the Golden Gate Bridge, Abe Lincoln, Rivera's artist wife Frida Kahlo and scenes from Charlie Chaplin's *The Great Dictator*. It's open to the public while school is in session (noon-5pm Mon, Wed; 2-5pm Tue, Thur). Also visit www.riveramural.com.

The Mexican muralist touched off a citywide fresco fervour. For an outstanding example, head to **Coit Tower** (*see p82*) on Telegraph

Muni Metro F, J, K, L, M, N/bus 5, 6, 9, 19, 21, 27, 66, 71. **Open** noon-5pm Wed-Sat. **Credit** MC, V. **Map** p314 Y1.

You won't find any luggage at the top of the grungy flight of stairs that leads to this gallery in a low-rent area of downtown, but you will find an earnest, innovative space that takes most of its cues from its surroundings. In addition to modern and minimalist art by both emerging and established artists, who like the gallery's political, *arte povera* stance, you'll find open-mike readings on Tuesdays at 8pm – underscoring a commitment to the junction of art and community. A satellite space in the Tenderloin 509 Cultural Center (509 Ellis Street) offers art classes, street photography workshops and internships for neighbourhood youth.

New Langton Arts/San Francisco Camerawork

1246 Folsom Street, between Eighth & Ninth Streets, SoMa (New Langton Arts 626 5416/www.newlangtonarts.org; San Francisco Camerawork 863 1001/www.sfcamerawork.org). Bus 9, 12, 19, 27. **Open** noon-5pm Tue-Sat. **Credit** MC, V. **Map** p310 G5.

In the forefront of the alternative arts scene, this first-floor loft is as unprepossessing as its obscure black façade. The choice of exhibitions is eclectic, to say the least, although the gallery is best known for its installations and performance pieces. It hosts the annual Bay Area Awards show in summer, presenting top regional talent in literature, music and the arts. When the artist-run San Francisco Camerawork, which specialises in contemporary photography, lost its own space in 2001, New Langton Arts offered to share its own space, so the two now alternate exhibitions, which usually run for about five weeks.

San Francisco Art Commission Gallery

Veterans' Memorial Building, 401 Van Ness Avenue, at McAllister Street, Civic Center (554 6080/http://sfac.sfsu.edu/gallery/). Muni Metro F, J, K, L, M, N/bus 5, 21, 42, 47, 49. **Open** 11am-5.30pm Wed-Sat. **No credit cards**. **Map** p310 F4.

This tidy exhibition space in the Civic Center draws from local and national artists, and exhibits all kinds of media in many contexts. The SFAC also maintains Grove Street Windows (155 Grove Street, between Van Ness and Polk Streets), two blocks from the gallery, where you can watch video projections, soundworks and other site-specific installations through shopfront windows. City Site, a third exhibition programme set up in a vacant lot next door, is temporarily inactive, but that doesn't stop the occasional 'plop art' left under cover of darkness by guerrilla artists.

SoMarts Gallery

934 Brannan Street, between Eighth & Ninth Streets, SoMa (552 2131/www.somarts.org). Bus 19, 27, 42. **Open** noon-4pm Tue-Sat. **No credit cards**. **Map** p310 G5.

Tucked under the freeway, this gallery can be easy to miss. But don't overlook it, as it's one of the city's long-lived art traditions, housed in an ancient warehouse with a cavern-like series of rooms. Besides being headquarters for ArtSpan, the organisation that runs Open Studios each October (*see p192*),

Balmy Alley.

The city on foot: Murals (continued)

Hill. In 1933, 26 painters were hired by the federal government as part of the WPA (Works Progress Administration) project to beautify public buildings. The frescos on the ground floor of the tower are a snapshot of the times, depicting bucolic farm scenes and workaday chaos on Market Street, complete with businessmen and armed thieves, muscled labourers, fat union bosses and Dust Bowl migrants. The political content caused an uproar, and for decades the murals were covered and neglected. Other politically radical works include the frescos depicting the history of Northern California in the **Rincon Center** (*see p63*), created in 1941 by Moscow-born artist Anton Refrigier.

Elsewhere in the city, look for more recent examples of the muralists' art. Head to the Fillmore District to find a mural by Dewey Crumpler on the wall of the **Center for African & African-American Art & Culture** (762 Fulton Street, between Buchanan and Webster; 928 8546). Images of Billy Holliday, Duke Ellington and Charlie Parker are a reminder of the Fillmore's past as a centre for jazz and blues. In SoMa, keep an eye out for huge faux street signs by Rigo 99, including his two-part artwork **SKY/GROUND** at Third and Mission Streets (although a new hotel currently under construction may soon obliterate it). His **Interstate Home** can be seen from the Highway 280 exit at Sixth Street; another ironic comment is the **One Tree** arrow near the I-280 on-ramp at Eighth Street.

One of the city's oldest murals, now somewhat faded, is John Wehrle's dreamy seascape **Reflections** on Fifth Street at Bryant Street. One of the newest is the stunning **Bikeway Mural** on the back of the Safeway building on Duboce Avenue between Church and Market Streets, which is a celebration of two-wheeled travel.

SoMarts hosts its own group and solo shows, as well as live music performances. It's also the new home for Kearny Street Workshop (503 0520), the oldest Asian-American arts organisation in the country, which hosts exhibitions and readings.

Southern Exposure

401 Alabama Street, at 17th Street, Mission (863 2141/www.soex.org/). Bus 12, 22, 27, 33, 53. **Open** 11am-5pm Tue-Sat. **Credit** MC, V. **Map** p314 Z1.

Much like Intersection for the Arts (*see p204*), Southern Exposure has made its reputation as the place for emerging artists to show – and to be discovered shortly thereafter. There the comparison ends, because where Intersection is small and focused, SoEx is large and inclusive, with a bright, sunny space on the west side of Theater Artaud (*see p224*). SoEx's group shows and parties are legendary, and their juried art shows have drawn nationally respected curators. If you visit just one non-profit gallery, make it this one.

Commercial galleries

Bomani Gallery

296 8677. Muni Metro N/bus 6, 37, 43, 66. **Open** by appointment only. **Credit** AmEx, MC, V. **Map** p314 Z1.

Located in a two-storey Victorian house in the Haight-Ashbury, the Bomani (owned by the wife of actor Danny Glover) was one of many galleries forced out of downtown by sky-rocketing rents. Visiting takes an effort – you'll need to call first to make an appointment and get the address – but it's the only gallery in the city that represents the masters of African-American art as well as emerging Third World artists. Look for works on paper by Elizabeth Catlett, Jacob Lawrence and Romare Bearden, as well as local artists such as Sandria Hu and Ethiopian abstractionist Wosense.

Catharine Clark Gallery

49 Geary Street, between Kearny Street & Grant Avenue, Union Square (399 1439/www.cclarkgallery.com). BART Montgomery Street/Muni Metro F, J, K, L, M, N/bus 9, 15, 30, 38, 45. **Open** 10.30am-5.30pm Tue-Fri; 11am-5.30pm Sat; 5.30-7.30pm 1st Thur of the month. **Credit** AmEx, MC, V. **Map** p309 H3.

Director Catharine Clark has a keen eye for modern art with legs – many of the works by her sculptors, painters and mixed-media artists walk their way into regional museums. The gallery's three rooms display art ranging from dangerous-looking kinetic sculptures to figurative paintings. Recently, Clark showed an amazing, poignant piece by Yoram Wollberger of household furnishings (a coffee table, armoire and refrigerator) sliced into slivers. The gallery is located in the Geary Street 'art mall' – along with the Stephen Wirtz Gallery, Fraenkel Gallery and Robert Koch Gallery (for all, *see p208*).

City Art

828 Valencia Street, at 19th Street, Mission (970 9900/www.cityartgallery.org). Bus 14, 26, 33, 49. **Open** noon-9pm Wed-Sun. **Credit** AmEx, MC, V. **Map** p314 Y1.

A quirky, collective enterprise that's commercial in intent, but has the panache of a non-profit space, this no-frills venue is filled from floor to ceiling with art by co-op members. The members also staff the

Perhaps the best resource for information about the city's murals is **Precita Eyes**, which was established by Susan Cervantes. Dedicated to preserving the Mission District's murals, the centre specialises in guided tours; many of the murals visited were painted by Cervantes and her followers.

Precita Eyes Mural Arts & Visitors Center

2981 24th Street, at Harrison Street, Mission (285 2287/www.precitaeyes.org). BART 24th Street/bus 12, 27, 48. **Open** 10am-5pm Mon-Fri; 10am-4pm Sat, Sun. **Credit** MC, V. **Map** p314 Z2.
Tours include Mission Mural Walks ($10), at 1.30pm on Saturdays and Sundays; BART Mural Walks ($7), at 1.30pm on Saturdays; BART Mural Tours ($5), at 11am on Saturdays; Bike Mural Tours ($10), at 11am on the second Sunday of every month; and Mexican Bus Mural Tours ($16), at 12.30pm on the third Sunday of every month.

Section of **Dewey Crumpler**'s mural.

gallery during the month-long exhibitions, so expect to be greeted by personalities as varied as the works on the walls. Prices are affordable ($100-$500) and there are some gems hidden among the predictably odd, and even downright awful, art. This aura of unpredictability, in fact, is a large measure of the gallery's overall charm.

Crown Point Press

20 Hawthorne Street, between Howard & Folsom Streets, SoMa (974 6273/www.crownpoint.com). BART Montgomery Street/Muni Metro F, J, K, L, M, N/bus 9, 12, 14, 15, 30, 45, 76. **Open** 10am-6pm Tue-Sat. **Credit** MC, V. **Map** p311 H4.
Opened as a print workshop in 1962, the Press invites noted artists such as Ed Ruscha, Nathan Oliveira, Wayne Thiebaud and April Gornick to create editions of prints, which are exhibited and sold in the large, airy space upstairs from the underground Refusalon gallery (*see p208*). In addition to an exhibition programme, it holds a summer workshop open to all artists. Tucked into a corner of the space is Califia (284 0314), an outlet for all manner of exquisite artist-made books.

Dolby Chadwick

Third floor, 266 Sutter Street, between Kearny Street & Grant Avenue, Union Square (956 3560/www.dolbychadwickgallery.com). BART Montgomery Street/Muni Metro F, J, K, L, M, N/bus 9, 15, 30, 38, 45. **Open** 10am-6pm Tue-Sat; 5.30-8.30pm 1st Thur of the month. **Credit** AmEx, MC, V. **Map** p309 3H.
Don't be intimidated by the creaky ride up in a dingy old lift: it takes you directly into the gallery, which couldn't be a friendlier place. Tall windows frame a view as compelling as the clean-lined still-life paintings on the walls. The gallery offers paintings, drawings and monotypes by emerging and mid-career artists, mainly interiors, figures and a few abstract works. Many are priced at under $1,000. In addition, it can be a funky place to hang out: during First Thursday openings, you're likely to find a saxophonist wailing on the fire escape and Cosmopolitans served at the bar.

Hackett-Freedman Gallery

250 Sutter Street, between Kearny Street & Grant Avenue, Union Square (362 7152/www.realart.com). BART Montgomery Street/Muni Metro F, J, K, L, M, N/bus 9, 15, 30, 38, 45. **Open** 10.30am-5.30pm Tue-Fri; 11am-5pm Sat. **Credit** MC, V. **Map** p309 3H.
This is one of the city's 'art towers' – a building filled with galleries. Hackett-Freedman contains a comprehensive stable of California artists of the major West Coast schools. Bay Area figurative paintings by Elmer Bischoff, Joan Brown and Kyle Staver, realist works by Guy Diehl and Marc Trujillo, California colourist Terry St John and San Francisco expressionists Clyfford Still and Charles Strong are all represented here. With detailed colour catalogues to accompany most shows, this place is a one-stop visual art tour of the state.

Modernism

685 Market Street, between Third & New Montgomery Streets, Financial District (541 0461/www.artnet.com/modernism.html). BART Montgomery Street/Muni Metro F, J, K, L, M, N/bus 9, 15, 30, 38, 45. **Open** 10am-5.30pm Tue-Sat. **Credit** MC, V. **Map** p309 H3.

This place grapples with the ages-old contradiction of how to meld fine art that attracts a high price with a hospitable atmosphere. And loses. If you're not rich, and relatively conservatively dressed (DKNY rather than Prada), you simply might not feel comfortable here. Don't let that stop you, however. The art on display is amazing, ranging from moody figures by Mark Stock and Sheldon Greenberg to Cesar Santander's wacky tin-toy portraits.

111 Minna Street Gallery

111 Minna Street, at Second Street, SoMa (974 1719/www.111annex.com). BART Montgomery Street/Muni Metro F, J, K, L, K, M, N/bus 9, 12, 14, 15, 30, 45, 76. **Open** 1-7pm Tue-Fri; noon-5pm Sat. **Credit** AmEx, MC, V. **Map** p309 H3/4.

This shop combines contemporary painting and sculpture with a bar and dancefloor (*see p218*). The formula has proved so successful that the space doubled in size in 2001. Ostensibly, the idea is to make connections between all forms of media; locals approved by voting it the city's best gallery in the *San Francisco Bay Guardian*. If you like the exhibition, stay for happy hour on Wednesdays and Fridays (5-10pm) – and if you're already inside, you're in luck, because the queue on those nights can stretch around the block.

Refusalon

20 Hawthorne Street, between Howard & Folsom Streets, SoMa (546 0158/www.refusalon.com). BART Montgomery Street/Muni Metro F, J, K, L, M, N/bus 9, 12, 14, 15, 30, 45, 76. **Open** noon-6pm Tue-Sat; noon-8pm 1st Thur of the month. **Credit** AmEx, DC, MC, V. **Map** p311 H4.

Though its artists might not yet be household names, this charming, austere gallery in the shadow of SFMOMA (*see p107*) houses some of the most interesting art in the city. Specialising in so-called 'peripheral' works, Refusalon has hosted shows by Eric Saks, Patrick Tierney, Pip Culbert and her sons Rae and Clay, as well as edge-surfers such as Gay Outlaw. For yet another perspective, you can climb the stairs to Crown Point Press (*see p207*), the city's premier print studio/gallery.

Stephen Wirtz Gallery

49 Geary Street, between Kearny Street & Grant Avenue, Union Square (433 6879/www.wirtzgallery.com). BART Montgomery Street/Muni Metro F, J, K, L, M, N/bus 9, 15, 30, 38, 45. **Open** 10.30am-5.30pm Tue-Sat; 10.30am-7.30pm 1st Thur of the month. **No credit cards**. **Map** p311 H4.

All is hushed here except for the clicking of expensive heels on the highly polished wood floors. There's a sophistication and restraint to the work as well as the atmosphere; on view are contemporary, conceptual paintings and sculpture that prompt discussion, and launch young artists to major museum shows. The stable includes Katheryn Spence, Todd Hido, Deborah Oropallo, Lewis Baltz, Raymond Saunders and Lucy Puls. If Hackett-Freedman (*see p207*) is the place to see California's art history, this is a place to see the present unfold.

Walls of photos at the **Fraenkel Gallery**.

Photography galleries

Fraenkel Gallery

49 Geary Street, between Kearny Street & Grant Avenue, Union Square (981 2661/www.fraenkelgallery.com). BART Montgomery Street/Muni Metro F, J, K, L, M, N/bus 9, 15, 30, 38, 45. **Open** 10.30am-5.30pm Tue-Fri; 11am-5pm Sat; 10.30am-7.30pm 1st Thur of the month. **No credit cards**. **Map** p309 H3.

This gallery has shown most of the major figures including Chuck Close, Richard Misrach, Diane Arbus, Nan Goldin, Garry Winogrand and other modernists. In addition, the curators use photography as a nexus of interchange between media, showing sculpture or film alongside works on paper.

Robert Koch Gallery

49 Geary Street, between Kearny Street & Grant Avenue, Union Square (421 0122/www.kochgallery.com). BART Montgomery Street/Muni Metro F, J, K, L, M, N/bus 9, 15, 30, 38, 45. **Open** 10.30am-5.30pm Tue-Sat; 10.30am-7.30pm 1st Thur of the month. **Credit** MC, V. **Map** p309 H3.

This gallery has established itself as one of the city's most reliable vendors of photographic art. The curators seem to have honed an environmental edge, favouring such international photographers as Ed Burtynsky and Josef Koudelka alongside experimental works by Shimon Attie, Lynn Hershman Leeson and Robert Parke Harrison. There's also a good selection of 19th-century artists.

Shapiro Gallery

760 Market Street, at Grant Avenue, Union Square (398 6655). BART Powell Street/Muni Metro F, J, K, L, M, N/bus 9, 15, 30, 38, 45. **Open** 11am-5.30pm Tue-Fri; 11am-5pm Sat; 10.30am-7.30pm 1st Thur of the month. **Credit** MC, V. **Map** p309 H3.

The Shapiro deals in primarily 20th-century black and white photography, and some vintage pieces. It's housed in yet another art mall, which also contains tribal art dealer Gallery de Roche (989 0300/www.galleryderoche.com) and the small, quirky Quotidian Gallery (788 0445/www.quotidiangallery.com), which specialises in local emerging artists.

Nightlife

Folk music fan or hardcore clubber? There's something for all musical tastes.

San Francisco has been known as an exciting spot for music and dance since its wild Barbary Coast days. It remains best known for the so-called 'San Francisco sound' of the 1960s, the psychedelic rock movement that produced the Grateful Dead, Jefferson Airplane, and Big Brother and the Holding Company. But Bay Area musicians have made many other distinctive contributions before and since that era, in every conceivable popular-music form. The city and its suburbs have been especially noted for innovative fusions of genres, including pop-punk, funk-metal and acid jazz.

Marquee names from the Bay Area or with strong San Francisco ties include Metallica, Green Day, the Dead Kennedys, John Lee Hooker, Creedence Clearwater Revival, Tupac Shakur, Charlie Hunter, Tracy Chapman, Chris Isaak, Joe Henderson, Primus, Charles Brown, Neurosis, Faith No More and Rancid.

The Bay Area, especially Oakland to the east and Vallejo to the north, has also been a potent source for all kinds of hip hop, from gangsta rap to progressive hip hop to Funkadelic-style goofiness. Important figures include E-40, Too $hort, Digital Underground, Michael Franti, Del the Funky Homosapien, the Marginal Prophets, DJ Shadow, Blackalicious and Latyrx. The recently retired Invisibl Skratch Piklz, arguably the greatest practitioners of turntabling, have produced celebrated alumni, including DJ Q-Bert and Beastie Boys associate Mix Master Mike. Tireless house innovator Mark Farina, who seems to spin just about nightly somewhere in San Francisco, is a rising international star.

The Bay Area also keeps producing vibrant jazz musicians. A single high-school programme, the Berkeley High Jazz Ensemble, has given rise to some of the brightest stars in jazz today, including Joshua Redman, Dave Ellis, Will Bernard, Craig Handy, Jessica Jones, David Murray and Miles Perkins.

A NIGHTLIFE RECESSION

All that said, San Francisco nightlife is in trouble as the new millennium kicks into gear. The city finds itself in danger of becoming a musical theme park: a great place to hear the best touring acts in the world, but a tough place to catch local talent. The problem is usually traced to 1988, when a change in zoning laws turned previously industrial areas into residential ones. Noise complaints inevitably followed, forcing long-established clubs to turn down the volume or, in many cases, to close altogether.

This means there are fewer places for bands to play. Especially hard hit are bottom-rung clubs where fledgling acts hone their craft and build an audience. To make matters worse, the city's absurdly high cost of living was already making it difficult for musicians to find places to live and rehearse, but the dotcom boom of the late 1990s made it nearly impossible. In 2000 alone, more than 700 bands lost their rehearsal spaces while property owners made fortunes selling to developers or dotcoms. The closing of Downtown Rehearsal Studios, near the 3 Com Park sports stadium, left an estimated 500 acts studio-less, including such big names as Chris Isaak. Activists estimate that San Francisco has less than half the commercial rehearsal space it had just a couple of years ago.

Many musicians have finally given up and moved to LA or out of California altogether. Ironically, the dotcom collapse of 2000-2001 appears, if anything, to have made matters worse; many musicians supported themselves with dotcom day jobs and are now unemployed as well as gigless. So the exodus continues.

Musicians also complain that Bay Area residents just don't go out to hear music as much as they used to. Rock bands now find themselves in the same predicament as local jazz musicians, who have long had the same complaint. In the 1990s, there was a brief surge of interest in 'acid jazz' – a jazz-funk fusion with Bay Area roots. But the fading of that scene means there are few places in San Francisco to hear anything but mild, cocktail-lounge jazz.

Musicians have reacted by organising to save some semblance of a scene. Groups such as the Popular Noise Foundation, the San Francisco Late Night Coalition and Save Local Music have emerged. But musicians must also compete for a shrinking number of gigs. Rock bands may be in a losing battle against DJs, who are replacing them as the musical entertainment of choice. It sometimes seems as though every club, restaurant, bar, café, boutique and doughnut shop in the city now comes equipped with a pair of turntables. That's good news for DJ culture, which has never been so active above ground in San Francisco (even if the art form is not nearly as dominant a force in the US as it is in the UK) – though many complain that the scene is dominated by unimaginative trance and progressive house music meant to appeal to the suburban masses rather than dance-music connoisseurs.

Despite the bad news, San Francisco has more nightlife options that most visitors could ever experience in just one trip. Only New York and Los Angeles attract more bands, and you can find a different place to dance or listen to live music every night of the week.

INFORMATION

The best overall sources are the *San Francisco Bay Guardian* (www.sfbg.com) and *SF Weekly* (www.sfweekly.com), both of which have extensive listings of live music, dance clubs and special events. For the latest dance club info, the venerable **Be-At Line** (626 4087) lists daily details of where to be and when; call after 2pm. The best of the dance websites is **SF Raves** – www.sfraves.org – which carries an exhaustive list of dance events, including some underground parties. (Don't confuse it with the less comprehensive www.sfraves.com.) Or try **SF Station** – www.sfstation.com – which assumes less insider knowledge and gives some background on the events and venues it lists.

Record shops where you can get tips on dance parties as well as fliers and free, CD-sized dance-culture magazines with detailed listings include **Zebra Records** (475 Haight Street, at Fillmore Street; 626 9145), **Spundae Records** (678 Haight Street, between Steiner and Pierce Streets; 575 1580) and **BPM Music** (*see p182*).

TICKETS AND ADMISSION

Where possible, buy tickets to concerts from the box offices of the major venues (most of which accept credit cards), where you won't have to pay the mark-up charged by **Ticketmaster** (421 8497). Admission prices for the clubs listed below depend on the night, but usually vary between free entry and $25.

Although many dance clubs remain open well past last orders, by law they cannot serve alcohol between 2am and 6am, nor to anyone under 21. Some clubs are strictly 21 and over; if you're under 21, ask about the club's policy before you go – otherwise you may get turned away at the door.

LATE-NIGHT TRANSPORT

The **Muni Owl Service** operates on the Muni Metro L and N lines and on the 5, 14, 22, 24, 38, 90 and 91 bus lines from 1am until 5am. All other lines stop at 12.30am. BART runs roughly until midnight, although it's always best to check the time of the last train to your destination. For a list of taxi companies, *see p275*.

Live Music

Large venues

San Francisco's two sports stadiums, **Pac Bell Park**, not far from downtown, and **3Com Park**, on the southern edge of San Francisco, host the occasional massive rave and monster rock show. Several other huge Bay Area venues are outside San Francisco, including the **Greek Theater** in Berkeley and the **Oakland Coliseum** in Oakland.

Bill Graham Civic Auditorium

99 Grove Street, between Polk & Larkin Streets, Civic Center (974 4000/www.billgrahamcivic.com). BART Civic Center/Muni Metro F, J, K, L, M, N/bus 9, 19, 21, 26. **Open** *Box office* 1hr before shows. **Admission** varies. **Credit** MC, V. **Map** p310 F5.

The San Francisco Opera was born in this 5,000-seat auditorium on 26 September 1923. Later renamed after the city's famous rock impresario, it now hosts a variety of events, from not-quite-arena-sized rock shows to conferences. The acoustics are poor and the place is cavernous, but it's centrally located and hosts many well regarded rock acts. It's only open when it's holding an event.

Bimbo's 365 Club

1025 Columbus Avenue, at Chestnut Street, North Beach (474 0365/www.bimbos365club.com). Bus 30/ cable car Powell-Mason. **Open** *Box office* 10am-4pm Mon-Fri. **Admission** $15-$25. **Credit** MC, V. **Map** p308 G2.

Bimbo's began its glamorous life in 1931 as a Market Street speakeasy before taking up residence in North Beach in 1951. It's still owned by the descendants of one of its original owners, Agostino 'Bimbo' Giuntoli, who have lovingly preserved this jewel from a more elegant time. It's a regular stop on the touring circuit of world-class musicians, including many UK acts (Roni Size, Spiritualized, Blur, Pulp), and shows happen four or five nights a week. A mermaid theme runs throughout, from statues to ornate murals; on some nights you can spot 'Dolfina', a naked woman who, through the magic of mirrors, seems to swim in a fishbowl behind the bar.

Fillmore Auditorium

1805 Geary Boulevard, at Fillmore Street, Fillmore District (24hr hotline 346 0600/www.thefillmore.com). Bus 22, 38. **Open** *Box office* 10am-4pm Sun; 7.30-10pm on show nights. **Admission** $15-$30. **Credit** AmEx, MC, V. **Map** p313 E4.

The Fillmore began life in 1912 as a dance hall, but is better known as the place where the late Bill Graham launched his rock-promotion empire in the 1960s with the likes of the Grateful Dead and Jefferson Airplane. It remains a favourite venue for all kinds of big-name musicians and their fans. With a capacity of 1,200, it's relatively intimate and quite relaxed. The Fillmore is also a shrine to San

Rock on at the venerable **Fillmore Auditorium**. *See p210.*

Francisco musical history: check out the photos in the lobby and the amazing array of vintage posters lining the walls of the upstairs lounge and hall.

Great American Music Hall

859 O'Farrell Street, between Polk & Larkin Streets, Tenderloin (885 0750/www.musichallsf.com). Bus 19, 38, 42, 47, 49. **Open** *Box office* 10am-4pm Mon, Sun; noon-6pm Tue-Sat; until 9.30pm on show nights. **Admission** $8-$22. **Credit** MC, V. **Map** p310 F4.

The Great American Music Hall is the grande dame of the city's smaller venues and well worth a visit. Originally a bordello, its lavish decor remains intact, with huge mirrors, rococo woodwork and gold leaf trim. It presents a cutting-edge playbill that includes highly regarded local and touring musicians, especially of the indie-rock variety. Snag a coveted seat in the upper balcony, where you'll get a bird's-eye view of the band and the crowd below.

The Justice League

628 Divisadero Street, between Grove & Hayes Streets, Western Addition (440 0409). Bus 21, 24. **Open** varies; phone for details. **Admission** free-$20. **Credit** MC, V. **Map** p313 D5.

The ultimate place to dance to local hip hop, dance hall, dub and world beat DJs. It regularly hosts big-name international acts such as Fatboy Slim, Roni Size, DJ Spooky and Kid Koala. The space is huge with a large round bar in the middle of the floor and a stage at the far back. Check out the graffiti-inspired artwork by the renowned Twist while you groove to the incredible sound system.

Maritime Hall

451 Harrison Street, between Fremont & First Streets, SoMa (974 0634/www.maritimehall.com). Bus 12, 42, 76. **Open** varies; phone for details. **Admission** $15-$40. **Credit** MC, V. **Map** p311 J4.

This impressive streamlined moderne building began life in 1950 as the home for the Sailors' Union of the Pacific. It regularly books shows most other venues won't touch, from hip hop and reggae to hardcore punk and death metal. Don't be alarmed if a goth band is booked the same night as a Senegalese singer: the club has two venues, with the smaller one downstairs. Unfortunately, the acoustics are murky and the seating awkward.

Slim's

333 11th Street, between Folsom & Harrison Streets, SoMa (255 0333/www.slims-sf.com). Bus 9, 12, 27, 42. **Open** *Shows* 8pm or 9pm. **Admission** free-$25. **Credit** AmEx, MC, V. **Map** p310 G5.

One of San Francisco's most important venues, offering two or more bands four or five nights a week. Holding about 550, it attracts mainly rock acts and post-punk singer/songwriters (local, cult and national headliners on the way up or down). It's not the most comfortable place to hear music: most patrons have to stand, the sightlines are compromised by floor-to-ceiling pillars and it can get pretty steamy on a busy night. Slim's – which is owned by '70s musician Boz Scaggs, a local, though he's not very involved in the club's daily operations – also hosts smaller acoustic shows at the Cellar at Johnny Foley's (*see p212*).

Warfield Theater

982 Market Street, at Mason Street, Union Square (775 7722/www.thefillmore.com/warfield.asp). BART Powell Street/Muni Metro F, J, K, L, M, N/ bus 7, 27, 31, 66, 71. **Open** *Box office* 10am-4pm Sun; 7.30-10.30pm on show nights. **Admission** usually $25-$35. **Credit** AmEx, MC, V. **Map** p310 G4.

The Warfield is an ornate 1922 theatre converted into a 2,100-seat venue for popular music, especially rock. Major national and international acts play here, sometimes as the last step before vaulting to arena-sized venues. It's designed so that even the back balcony seats have a good view of the stage.

Smaller venues

Downtown & around

Biscuits & Blues

401 Mason Street, at Geary Street, Union Square (292 2583/www.biscuitandblue.citysearch.com). Bus 2, 3, 4, 38, 76/cable car Powell-Hyde or Powell-Mason. **Open** 5pm-1am Mon-Fri; 6pm-1am Sat, Sun. **Admission** $5-$20. **Credit** AmEx, DC, MC, V. **Map** p310 G4.

This subterranean nightclub/restaurant is, like any good blues joint, a pretty basic affair. It attracts mainly middle-aged tourists and suburbanites and can get stuffy when crowded, but it's one of the few places in San Francisco where you can regularly see blues legends and national up-and-comers. It's also refreshing to see a genuinely excited crowd, unlike the jaded scenesters at so many cooler clubs. The 'award-winning' southern cooking is mediocre, but portions are huge; best to book and come early – the kitchen has been known to run out of food.

Cellar At Johnny Foley's

Johnny Foley's Irish House, 243 O'Farrell Street, between Mason & Powell Streets, Union Square (954 0777/www.johnnyfoleys.com). **Open** 10.30am-2am daily. **Admission** $8-$20. **Credit** AmEx, MC, V. **Map** p310/311 G4.

On the ground floor is a large, rather touristy Irish pub and restaurant that often features traditional Irish music. Downstairs is altogether different. Designed to resemble an intimate speakeasy, it hosts modern singer/songwriters and solo acoustic shows by rock musicians – such as John Frusciante (Red Hot Chili Peppers), Frank Black (Pixies), Kristin Hersh (Throwing Muses) and cult faves Marshall Crenshaw, Vic Chestnutt and Mary Lou Lord.

Covered Wagon Saloon

917 Folsom Street, at Fifth Street, SoMa (974 1585). Bus 12, 27. **Open** 4.30pm-2am Mon-Fri; 7.30pm-2am Sat. **Admission** free-$10. **No credit cards**. **Map** p311 H4.

With two rooms and a bar that can feel cramped, the CW is no place to go if you can't stand to sweat. The place is a bit grungy and the music runs towards hard rock and metal. Stinky's Peep Show features bands and a rotating line-up of chubby go-go dancers.

Hotel Utah Saloon

500 Fourth Street, at Bryant Street, SoMa (546 6300/www.hotelutahsaloon.com). Bus 30, 45, 76. **Open** noon-2am daily. **Admission** free-$7. **Credit** MC, V. **Map** p311 H4.

This place has a Barbary Coast saloon feel, and has long been the kind of place where musicians go to hear other musicians. Though its star has faded in recent years, it's still a good place for a low-key evening of experimental rock or acoustic singer/songwriter fare. The performance area is microscopic, but the bar next to it is comfortable, serves food and allows you to escape if you don't care for what's coming from the stage.

Great American Music Hall. *See p211.*

Paradise Lounge

1515 Folsom Street, at 11th Street, SoMa (621 1912). Bus 9, 12, 42. **Open** 6pm-2am daily. **Admission** $5-$12. **Credit** MC, V. **Map** p310 G5.

The Paradise's three stages cater for a variety of musical tastes: local bands, touring rockers, singer/songwriters and novelty acts. The intimate upstairs lounge, Above Paradise, is reserved for acoustic and folk music or spoken-word events. Once the premier showcase for local bands, the Paradise has faded along with the scene in recent years. Put up for sale in 2001, its future was uncertain at press time.

North Beach

The Saloon

1232 Grant Avenue, at Vallejo Street & Columbus Avenue (989 7666). Bus 15, 30, 41, 45. **Open** noon-2am daily. **Admission** free-$5. **No credit cards**. **Map** p309 G2.

Built in 1861 as a beer hall that scandalised the neighbourhood, the Saloon has survived earthquakes and shifting musical tastes to remain a no-nonsense, rough-edged joint with a busy calendar of blues and blues-rock. Psychedelic-era rockers you might see include former members of Jefferson Airplane, Big Brother and the Holding Company, and Country Joe and the Fish.

The Mission & the Castro

Bottom of the Hill

1233 17th Street, at Missouri Street, Potrero Hill (box office 621 4455/tickets 1-510 601 8932/ www.bottomofthehill.com). Bus 22, 53. **Open** 3pm-2am Mon-Thur; 2pm-2am Fri; 8pm-2am Sat; 3-10pm Sun. **Admission** $5-$12. **Credit** MC, V. **Map** p311 H6.

Support local music

If San Francisco is to hold on to its musicians, bands need places to play and people to play for. Both are in short supply these days. Many of the clubs listed elsewhere in this chapter do promote local bands, but if you really want to get to the heart of the local music scene, you've got to head to the below-the-radar spots. The clubs listed below are widely deemed entry-level or uncool and often get snubbed by local music snobs. But these are precisely the kind of venues that have been known to create vital scenes and exciting bands. Maybe you'll leave after three notes. Maybe you'll discover the next big thing. You won't know unless you go.

Blue Lamp

561 Geary Street, between Taylor & Jones Streets, Tenderloin (885 1464/www.bluelamp.com). Bus 2, 3, 4, 27, 38, 76. **Open** 3pm-2am daily. **Admission** free-$5. **No credit cards**. **Map** p310 G4.

A comfy Tenderloin dive bar with live music seven nights a week, mostly local blues, roots rock and funk acts. You can sometimes catch a rising star here. If you're staying near Union Square, the Blue Lamp is an easy, safe walk away.

Kimo's

1351 Polk Street, between Bush & Pine Streets, Polk Gulch (885 4535). Bus 19, 42, 47, 49, 76/cable car California. **Open** 8am-2am daily. **Admission** free-$5. **Credit** MC, V. **Map** p308 F3.

Kimo's is a Tenderloin gay bar with live music upstairs that attracts a mixed crowd. Sounds tend towards the harder edge – punk, industrial, goth, metal – as well as some mod and pop bands and offbeat experimentalists.

Last Day Saloon

406 Clement Street, at Fifth Avenue, Richmond District (387 6343/www.lastdaysaloon.com). Bus 2, 4, 38, 44. **Open** 2pm-2am daily. **Admission** free-$10. **No credit cards**. **Map** p312 B4.

Swarms of hippies and yuppies come to check out the jam bands and funk acts playing upstairs at this prefab-looking sports bar. Cover bands are also popular, especially those devoted to the 1980s. If all that sounds ghastly, there's also a hip hop showcase every Tuesday.

Red Devil Lounge

1695 Polk Street, at Clay Street, Polk Gulch (921 1695/www.reddevillounge.com). Bus 1, 19, 27, 42, 47, 49. **Open** 9pm-2am Tue-Sat. **Admission** $3-$8. **Credit** AmEx, MC, V. **Map** p308 F3.

This roomy and pleasantly wicked-looking funk and funk-rock club (*pictured*) has a decent dance space and an upstairs area, where you can retreat from the music and commune in a dark corner.

Tempest

431 Natoma Street, at Mary Street, SoMa (495 1863). Bus 12, 14, 26, 27. **Open** 7am-11pm Mon-Thur; 7am-2am Fri; 9am-2am Sat. **Admission** free-$10. **Credit** AmEx, MC, V. **Map** p311 G4.

This place is beyond divey – it's a true hole-in-the-wall, buried in an alley just south of Market Street. In fact, it's so hidden away that even local music fans barely realise it exists. Who knows what you'll find lurking here?

Tongue & Groove

2513 Van Ness Avenue, at Union Street, Cow Hollow (928 0404). Bus 41, 42, 45, 49, 76. **Open** 6pm-2am daily. **Admission** free-$15. **Credit** AmEx, MC, V. **Map** p308 F2.

This club is hidden among cheap motels near the edge of the Marina and the end of Van Ness Avenue. It's so far removed from the scene that it has to create its own. Expect a mix of rock bands (original and retro-cover), DJs, funk and the occasional hip hop crew.

East Bay sounds

The East Bay in general and Oakland in particular has long been the cool, if sometimes grungy, alternative to the glam and glitz of San Francisco. The rising cost of living in the city has driven many artists and musicians east, which has given a boost to an already burgeoning music scene. And it all begins less than 20 minutes away by BART.

Blake's

2367 Telegraph Avenue, at Durant Avenue, Berkeley (1-510 848 0886/www.blakesbar.com). BART Berkeley, then bus 51, 64. **Open** 11.30am-2am Mon-Fri; noon-midnight Sat. **Admission** free-$6. **Credit** AmEx, Disc, MC, V. **Map** p315 N4.

A 50-year-old Berkeley institution. There's a studenty restaurant with fare such as burgers and pizza. The music is downstairs, in the dingy basement. The favoured genres are classic Berkeley sounds (jam bands, funk) mixed in with some newer ones (live hip hop, DJs).

Club Ibiza

Hotel Ibiza, 10 Hegenberger Way, at Doolittle Drive, Oakland (1-510 383 9888/www.hotelibiza.com). BART Coliseum, then bus 49, 58/AC Transit bus A. **Open** phone for details. **Admission** $20-$30; free for guests. **Credit** AmEx, MC, V.

Opened in 2001, this huge nightclub is in the deliberately 'outrageous' party playground of Hotel Ibiza (formerly the Edgewater Hotel and infamous for wife-swapping and poolside orgies) near Oakland Airport. It's being compared to Club MTV and the spring-break ethos that implies. If you get tired of dancing, there's a massive hot tub and Olympic-sized pool. Be sure to practise safe dancing.

924 Gilman Street

924 Gilman Street, at Eighth Street, North Berkeley (1-510 525 9926/www.924gilman.com). BART North Berkeley, then bus 9/AC Transit bus Z. **Open** *Shows* 8pm. **Admission** $5. **No credit cards**.

An East Bay institution and world-famous among punks, Gilman is an all-ages, alcohol-free nightclub run by an idealistic collective. It's the most important venue for the East Bay punk scene and attracts a deeply committed crowd. Green Day started here and still attend shows, though they're no longer allowed to play: major-label acts are banned from the stage.

Starry Plough

3101 Shattuck Avenue, between Prince & Woolsey Streets, Berkeley (1-510 841 2082). BART Ashby. **Open** 11am-2am Mon-Sat; 4pm-2am Sun. **Admission** free-$6. **Credit** MC, V.

This pub serves up truly talented local bands and nationally famous cult figures such as Victoria Williams, Vic Chestnutt and the Loud Family. The music favours modern folk and folk-rock, singer/songwriters and indie and roots rock. The crowd and staff are friendly and the atmosphere is relaxed.

The Stork Club

2330 Telegraph Avenue, between 23rd & 24th Streets, Oakland (1-510 444 6174/www. daniland.com/stork). BART 19th Street, then bus 40/AC Transit bus B, K. **Open** daily; phone for details.

This funky, two-room bar is *the* place in the East Bay to hear local avant-garde bands, and its busy roster (multiple bands play each show night) includes the best local punk, hard-core and indie rock bands around. It's worth going if only to see its slightly bizarre decor: hundreds of Barbie dolls share wall space with cowboy-and-indian art. The owners are incredibly sweet and drinks are strong and reasonably priced.

Yoshi's at Jack London Square

510 Embarcadero West, at Jack London Square, Oakland (1-510 238 9200/www.yoshis.com). BART Oakland City Center, then bus 58, 72L, 301. **Open** *Club* 6pm-12.30am Mon-Sat; noon-12.30am Sun. *Shows* 8pm, 10pm daily; matinées Sun. **Admission** $10-$30. **Credit** AmEx, DC, Disc, MC, V.

Yoshi's (*pictured*) offers the kind of refined setting that makes for a splendid occasion. Its separate dining room does good business on the strength of its Japanese food, but come for the music. It's the Bay Area's premier jazz house and one of the finest you'll find anywhere. Book in advance.

Real mermaids at **Bimbo's**. *See p210.*

This aptly named little club, wedged among warehouses at the bottom of Potrero Hill, has long been a favourite with the indie-rock crowd. Underground bands that play here this year may well become cult sensations or major stars the next. It features a mix of local and touring acts almost every night, as well as the occasional big star from abroad trying to get a toehold in the US (Oasis played in 1994). The decor is classic dive with quirky, surrealistic touches.

Bruno's

2389 Mission Street, between 19th & 20th Streets, Mission (648 7701/www.brunoslive.com). Bus 14, 26, 49. **Open** 7pm-2am daily. **Admission** varies. **Credit** MC, V. **Map** p314 Y1.

For such an attractive and popular place, Bruno's can't hold on to an owner for long: it's been bought and sold four times since 1994. First opened in the late 1930s, it retains an old supper club feel, with a sleek modern edge. There's a smart dining room and a long bar that ends in a seating area with a huge salt water aquarium. Music is in the Cork Room, a narrow lounge that was gaining a reputation as a place for experimental jazz when the club was sold again in mid 2001. Early indications are that the jazz will compete with DJ nights, funk, rock and the kind of post-punk singer/songwriters that the club used to attract.

Café Du Nord

2170 Market Street, between Church & Sanchez Streets, Castro (861 5016/www.cafedunord.com). Muni Metro F, K, L, M/bus 22, 37. **Open** 6pm-2am Mon, Tue; 4pm-2am Wed-Sun. **Admission** varies. **Credit** AmEx, MC, V. **Map** p310 E6.

There are several SF nightspots with the feel of a Prohibition-era speakeasy, but none captures that spirit quite so well as the always popular Café Du Nord. Perhaps that's because it really was one during its nearly 100-year existence. A subterranean place, the front room has red velvet walls and a 40ft (12m) mahogany bar, and is bustling with scenesters. There's a second room in the back, where dinner is served and jazz, swing, salsa, R&B, cabaret, electronic music and rock (especially theatrical, experimental rock) fill the place nearly every night. Eating is a good way to score a table.

Elbo Room

647 Valencia Street, between 17th & 18th Streets, Mission (552 7788/www.elbo.com). BART 16th Street/bus 26, 33. **Open** 5pm-2am daily. **Admission** $4-$8. **Credit** MC, V. **Map** p314 Y1.

Although the Elbo has been commandeered by yuppies of late, it continues to be a place to hear good music, usually performed in the open-raftered space upstairs. You're likely to hear jazz (usually with a funk edge), pure funk, soul, Latin jazz, hip hop or the occasional whacked-out experimentalist. The Dub Mission DJ nights on Sundays are legendary.

El Rio

3158 Mission Street, at Precita Street, Mission (282 3325/www.elriosf.com). Bus 12, 14, 27, 49. **Open** 3pm-midnight Mon; 3pm-2am Tue-Sun. **Admission** free-$10. **No credit cards**.

You owe it to yourself to take part in a San Francisco tradition – head to El Rio early on a sunny Sunday afternoon and squeeze past the shuffleboard and pool tables to the back garden, where you'll find the city's most diverse and lively Latin jazz party. There's an outdoor barbecue, decent Margaritas and a friendly crowd of straights and gays. Come before 4pm for a dance lesson. On other nights, you're likely to encounter experimental rock bands, DJ dance parties and, in the summer, an outdoor film series.

Make-Out Room

3225 22nd Street, between Mission & Valencia Streets, Mission (647 2888/www.makeoutroom.com). BART 24th Street/bus 14, 26, 49. **Open** 6pm-2am daily. **Admission** free-$10. **No credit cards**. **Map** p314 Y2.

One of the best places to see a good band, but one of the worst for encountering yuppies. The key is to go only when there's live music, when you're likely to see a laid-back, alternative and young crowd. The decor lives up to the name: there's a bearskin rug on one wall and a stag's head on another, with a rainbow of bras strung from the antlers. The lighting's dim enough to have a snog, if you're so inclined.

Voodoo Lounge

2937 Mission Street, between 25th & 26th Streets, Mission (285 3369/www.voodoolounge-sf.com). BART 24th Street/bus 14, 26, 49. **Open** 5.30pm-2am daily. **Admission** free-$5. **Credit** MC, V.

The Voodoo Lounge holds only about 200 people, but manages to pack a lot into a small space. The

Don't miss the Sunday afternoon Latin jazz party at **El Rio**. *See p215.*

main room – its walls painted with towering flames – is in the back, and filled with booths, tables, a small stage and a pool table. A small sushi restaurant is in the front; staff separate the rooms during shows by drawing a curtain across the bar corridor. Some nights (especially at the weekend) are given over to DJ parties; others offer local and touring rock, funk and folk acts. The Hells Angels meet here on the first Wednesday of every month.

The Haight & around

Boom Boom Room

1601 Fillmore Street, at Geary Boulevard, Fillmore District (673 8000/www.boomboomblues.com). Bus 2, 3, 4, 22, 38. **Open** 2pm-2am daily. **Admission** $5-$12. **No credit cards**. **Map** p313 E4.

Located opposite the Fillmore (*see p210*), the Boom Boom Room stands on the site of what was once Jack's Bar, a blues dive and SF nightlife fixture for more than 50 years. It's been remade as a classy version of a traditional blues joint. Until his death in 2001, blues legend John Lee Hooker held court at his personal booth up front. The club attracts solid blues acts, and rock stars occasionally put in surprise appearances, but the crowd can be obnoxious.

Club Deluxe

1511 Haight Street, at Ashbury Street, Haight-Ashbury (552 6949/www.clubdeluxe.com). Bus 6, 7, 33, 37, 43, 66, 71. **Open** 4pm-2am Mon-Fri; 3pm-2am Sat; 2pm-2am Sun. **Admission** $3-$5. **No credit cards**. **Map** p313 D5/6.

Deluxe, designed to recall a hep-cat New York jazz house, was a breeding ground for the swing revival that swept San Francisco in the 1990s. With the fading of that scene – its dancefloor was too tiny for swing dancing anyway – it's now searching for an identity. It still attracts the vintage-wear crowd, but features a grab-bag of roots music, DJ nights, retro jazz and even a comedy night, with the occasional big-name headliner. Come on a Tuesday, when the Church of Sinatra hosts a cocktail party (6-9pm) with DJs spinning lounge and classic soundtracks.

Rasselas on Fillmore Jazz Club & Restaurant

1534 Fillmore Street, at Geary Boulevard, Fillmore District (346 8696). Bus 1, 22, 24, 38. **Open** 5pm-midnight Mon-Thur, Sun; 5pm-1am Fri, Sat. **Admission** $10-$15. **Credit** MC, V. **Map** p313 E4.

The new Rasselas, like the Fillmore Historic Jazz District it's meant to anchor, has yet to live up to its potential. With its two-storey ceilings, bachelor-pad furniture and fireplace crackling behind the band, it suggests the kind of den Hugh Hefner might have had at the Playboy Mansion back in the 1960s. But the music tends towards cocktail jazz, the cover charges are high and the crowd is yuppified. The original Rasselas in Pacific Heights has an older and cosier atmosphere, and attracts a diverse mix, including suburban families with kids. The cuisine at both branches is Ethiopian.

Branch: 2801 California Street, at Divisadero Street, Pacific Heights (567 5010).

Other neighbourhoods

Pound SF

Pier 96, 100 Cargo Way, near Third Street, Hunter's Point (826 9202/www.poundsf.com). Bus 15. **Open** *Shows* 7pm or 8pm. **Admission** varies. **No credit cards**.

San Francisco's newest rock club is hidden in the furthest reaches of sketchy Hunter's Point (though it's quite a quick cab ride from downtown), on a pier with a view of giant cranes and San Francisco Bay. The club itself is your basic squat black box, but the management has invested in a decent light and sound system. When it opened in February 2001, it booked mainly local and touring hard rock, punk, and metal bands. Since then it has branched out into everything from indie pop to funk. Plans are afoot to build an outdoor stage next to the club. Shows happen five or six nights a week, and the club is also open in the week for lunch (11am-3pm).

Dance Clubs

Downtown & around

An-Sibin DJ Bar

1176 Sutter Street, at Polk Street, Polk Gulch (929 1992/www.sfstation.com/clubs/ansibin.htm). Bus 2, 3, 4, 19, 76. **Open** 6pm-2am. **Admission** free before 10pm; $3-$5 after 10pm. **Credit** AmEx, MC, V. **Map** p310 F4.

Along with Light (*see below*), An-Sibin is making the Polk Gulch an increasingly popular spot for serious devotees of DJ culture. The bar itself is fairly nondescript, but the scene is happening, with a weekly or monthly club party every night, a small dancefloor and cheap admission. Music tends towards drum 'n' bass, house and techno. Hardcore clubbers love Step, a Friday garage night.

Backflip

Phoenix Hotel, 601 Eddy Street, at Larkin Street, Tenderloin (771 3547/www.backflipsf.com). Bus 19, 31. **Open** 9pm-2am Tue; 5pm-2am Wed-Fri; 7pm-2am Sat; occasional parties Sun. **Admission** free-$5. **Credit** AmEx, DC, MC, V. **Map** p310 F4.

This bar-restaurant-nightclub is part of the Phoenix Hotel, a retro-fitted motor inn that attracts slumming rock stars to the mean streets of the Tenderloin. Exquisitely decorated with chrome and aqua fixtures and furnishings, Backflip's motif is best described as 1950s space-age bachelor pad; it's the work of the same team who decorated the Red Room (*see p150*), Sno-Drift (*see p219*) and several other popular nightspots. Check out the tiki courtyard and cabana-style pool while you sip gorgeous (if pricey) drinks. Not renowned for its food.

Harry Denton's Starlight Room

Sir Francis Drake Hotel, 450 Powell Street, between Post & Sutter Streets, Union Square (395 8595/ www.harrydenton. com). Bus 2, 3, 4, 30, 45, 76/cable car Powell-Hyde or Powell-Mason. **Open** 4.30pm-12.30am Mon; 4.30pm-1.30am Tue-Sat. **Admission** $5-$10. **Credit** AmEx, MC, V. **Map** p309 G3.

Harry Denton and his places are a love 'em or leave 'em affair. This one has a stunning 21st-floor view over Union Square, lots of mirrors, floral carpets and booths filled with social and financial climbers. The music tends to be cocktail jazz and R&B covers; don't come if you can't stand 'Mustang Sally' or don't feel like playing dress-up.

Branch: **Harry Denton's Rouge** 1500 Broadway, at Polk Street, Polk Gulch (346 7683).

Light

839 Geary Street, between Hyde & Larkin Streets, Tenderloin (474 3216). Bus 19, 38. **Open** 6pm-2am daily. **Admisson** free-$3. **No credit cards**. **Map** p310 F4.

To find this little gem of a DJ bar, look for a bright yellow façade and a small sign depicting an illuminated bulb. Light is an ironic moniker for this place, since its sleek interior is perpetually plunged in darkness. But it's certainly a beacon for the cool kids. They show up nearly every night to dance to progressive house, trance, hip hop or the sound of the moment on the handkerchief-sized dancefloor or to drink at the stainless steel bar.

Polly Esther's

181 Eddy Street, at Taylor Street, Tenderloin (885 1977/www.pollyesthers.com). BART Powell Street/Muni Metro F, J, K, L, M, N/bus 27, 31. **Open** 8pm-2am Thur; 8pm-4am Fri, Sat. **Admission** $5-$15. **Credit** AmEx, MC, V. **Map** p310 G4.

The Hard Rock Café of the dance world, the Polly Esther's chain celebrates a kitschy, cartoonish version of 1970s and '80s pop culture. This branch has a replica of the *Partridge Family* bus, a psychedelic Volkswagen Bug, a stylised Twister game – you get the idea. It's cheesy, but wildly popular, has lots of room to dance and stays open late. Warning: this is one of the seediest stretches of the Tenderloin, so be alert on the street.

Ruby Skye

420 Mason Street, between Geary & Post Streets, Union Square (693 0777/www.rubyskye.com). Bus 2, 3, 4, 38, 76/ cable car Powell-Hyde or Powell-Mason. **Open** 7pm-3am Wed-Sat. **Admission** varies. **Credit** AmEx, Disc, MC, V. **Map** p308 G3/4.

The newish Ruby Skye is an attractive place, with a huge dancefloor. Converted from an elegant 1890s theatre, the designers retained plenty of ornate Victorian touches while installing a thoroughly modern sound and light system. But the whole scene feels imported from LA – this is one of the few San Francisco clubs where you'll see young women proudly parading their breast implants.

SoMa

Mainly gay venue **Club Townsend** (*see p234* **Club Q**) also hosts Club Universe on Saturdays, a good option for both gays and straights. Decorated around a different theme each week – A Night in Paris one week, A Midsummer Night's Dream the next – it pumps out house music all night long. However, the club is set to close in June 2002.

Cat Club

1190 Folsom Street, at Eighth Street (431 3332). Bus 12, 19. **Open** 6pm-2am daily. **Admission** free-$10. **Credit** AmEx, MC, V. **Map** p310 G5.

A smallish, black-walled space, with a dancefloor in front, followed by a narrow passage with a bar, then another room and dancefloor in the back. Aimed mainly at rockers, it has a different theme each night. Especially popular are Bondage a Go Go on Wednesdays (industrial and alternative music, lots of leather) and 1984 on Thursdays ('80s all night'). Saturdays are drum 'n' bass nights.

Club NV

525 Howard Street, at Second Street (538 7977/ www.sfclubs.com). Bus 12, 15, 76. **Open** 9.30pm-3.30am Fri, Sat. **Admission** $20. **Credit** V. **Map** p311 H4.

The younger sibling in a family of huge dance clubs, NV attracts young suburbanites, especially gold-chain-sporting fellas on the make and hoochie-mamas with Spandex stretched tightly across their ample booties. In its favour, it's the swankiest and most attractive family member, and has roulette and blackjack tables where you can win such prizes as a ride in a limo or free club passes. The security guys are courteous (unlike the prison guards with metal detectors that patrol many other clubs) and it's not ridiculously crowded. On the other hand, the cover is high and the masses are beginning to line up around the block to get in.

DNA Lounge

375 11th Street, at Harrison Street, SoMa (626 1409/www.dnalounge.com). Bus 9, 12, 27, 42. **Open** 9am-4am Tue-Sat. **Admission** $5-$20. **No credit cards**. **Map** p310 G5.

The DNA is a long-time fixture of the local music scene, and like the scene itself, has had trouble staying alive recently. Traditionally a hard-rocking place, it reopened in mid 2001 with a full schedule of DJ nights. It has a largish dancefloor below the stage, flanked by stairs that lead to a mezzanine with corner booths for drinking and necking. No matter who's spinning, it still looks like a cavish rock club.

Kelly's Mission Rock

817 China Basin, at Mission Rock Street (626 5355/ www.kellysmissionrock.com). Bus 15. **Open** 9pm-4am Fri, Sat. **Admission** $10-$20. **Credit** AmEx, DC, MC, V. **Map** p311 J5.

To come all the way out to this sprawling glass-and-steel structure in China Basin – not far from the Ramp (*see p150*) and Sno-Drift (*see p219*) – you really have to care about what's on the turntables. DJs spin downstairs, where there's a winding, tiki-torch-lit back patio overlooking the bay, but the main action is upstairs. The long-running Come-Unity is held on the first Friday of every month.

King Street Garage

174 King Street, between Second & Third Streets (974 6020). Muni Metro N/bus 30, 42, 45. **Open** 9pm-4am Fri, Sat; 6-11pm Sun. **Admission** $10-$20. **No credit cards**. **Map** p311 J4/5.

King Street Garage is essentially a two-storey, black-walled warehouse, but its features – a circular dancefloor ringed by a balcony with dimly lit tables – keep it from feeling cold and impersonal. Nearby Club Townsend books special events here, and every night is different: call ahead if you're unlikely to be interested in, say, a gay line-dancing party. New Wave City, a 1980s dance night, currently takes over the place on the first Saturday of every month.

Backflip: definitely not a dive. *See p217.*

111 Minna

111 Minna Street, at Second Street (974 1719/ www.111annex.com). BART Montgomery Street/ Muni Metro F, J, K, L, M, N/bus 9, 12, 14, 15, 30, 45, 76. **Open** 7pm-2am Tue-Sat. **Admission** $3-$10. **No credit cards**. **Map** p311 H4.

This nondescript, concrete box of a place down an alley just south of Market Street is an art gallery (*see p208*) by day, but by night it's a truly happening dance club. It draws an unusual hybrid – serious rave yuppies – but is popular with all kinds of dance-music freaks due to its innovative offerings, which range from garage to Afrobeat to South Asian sounds. Check out long-running Qoöl, a techno party from 5-9pm on Wednesdays.

Six

60 Sixth Street, between Market & Mission Streets (863 1221/www.clubsix1.com). BART Powell Street/ Muni Metro F, J, K, L, M, N/bus 14, 26. **Open** 10pm-2am Thur-Sat. **Admission** $5-$10. **No credit cards**. **Map** p310 G4.

A fairly new club, Six sits on one of the scariest blocks in the city – although south of Market Street, it's considered part of the Tenderloin; it's best to go in a group and avoid looking rich or touristy. If you make it inside without incident, you'll find a high-ceilinged chill room/bar, below which is the 'Bassment', the low-ceilinged dancefloor. Created by the same guy responsible for Liquid (*see p220*), Six offers house, dub, trance, breaks and whatever else may be filling dancefloors at the moment.

Sno-Drift

1830 Third Street, at 16th Street (431 4766/ www.sno-drift.com). Bus 15. **Open** 9pm-4.30am Mon, Wed-Sun. **Admission** $5-$20. **Credit** AmEx, MC, V. **Map** p311 J6.

This place is a beauty. Located on a barren commercial strip near the light-industrial waterfront of China Basin, it's easy to spot from the road: foreign movies are beamed on to its plate-glass windows. Inside, the cocktail lounge has the feel of a swinging sixties ski lodge, with a circular fireplace, a deer statue and a long, curved bar behind which mountains of crushed ice chill cocktail glasses. Sno-Drift is a fairly small club, so if you don't like crowds, come early or during the week. And it's wise to call first, as its days of operation shift constantly.

Ten 15 Folsom

1015 Folsom Street, between Sixth & Seventh Streets (431 7444/recorded information 431 1200/ www.1015.com). Bus 12, 27, 42. **Open** 10pm-6am Thur, Fri; 10pm-9am Sat. **Admission** free-$20. **No credit cards**. **Map** p311 G5.

San Francisco's meat-and-potatoes dance club: it's always a safe bet for dancing, before, during or after hours. With three rooms, each with its own vibe, you can move through space and time without changing venues. While it draws the same suburban crowd of sad pick-up artists and bimbos that you'll find in any big club, they don't overwhelm the place.

Don't miss Dance clubs

Backflip

A space-age bachelor pad with a dancefloor and a pool. *See p217.*

Light

Hipster hideaway in the heart of the Tenderloin. *See p217.*

Six

A popular new playland on a dodgy old street. *See p218.*

Sno-Drift

Swinging sixties' ski lodge meets tomorrow's dance music. *See above.*

Ten 15 Folsom

The giant mainstay of the San Francisco dance scene. *See above.*

330 Ritch

330 Ritch Street, between Brannan & Townsend Streets (541 9574/522 9558/www.sfstation.com/ bars/330ritch). Bus 15, 30, 42, 45, 76.

Open 5pm-2am Wed, Thur; 8pm-2am Fri; 9pm-2am Sat. **Admission** varies. **Credit** AmEx, MC, V. **Map** p311 H/J4/5.

The young crowd seems right at home in this spacious yet intimate spot hidden down an alley among the SoMa warehouses. Sounds include hip hop, classic soul and 'urban grooves'. Thursdays belong to the long-running Popscene, a Britpop night that also features indie rock, mod music (spot the scooters out front), electronica and 1960s soul. If you have a British accent, you'll make friends easily that night.

North Beach

Blind Tiger

787 Broadway, at Powell Street (788 4020/www. blindtigersf.com). Bus 12, 83/cable car Powell-Mason. **Open** 8pm-2am daily. **Admission** free before 10pm; $5 after 10pm. **No credit cards**. **Map** p308 G2.

Although DJs spin eclectic, innovative sounds nearly every night (midweek is especially experimental), the crowd varies enormously: you can go on a Friday and find nothing but a handful of geeky single men, then go back late on a Sunday and find it crawling with hipsters. The space is attractive, though the dancefloor is small and near the toilets. One of the club's best features is its location on a quiet stretch of Broadway at the very edge of North Beach. If nothing's happening, just go across the street to the ultra-cool Rosewood bar (*see p151*).

Club 238

238 Columbus Avenue, between Broadway & Kearny Street (402 0000/www.clubvibes.com). Bus 12, 15, 30, 41, 83. **Open** 9pm-4am Thur-Sat; 9pm-2am Sun. **Admission** $10-$20. **Credit** AmEx, MC, V. **Map** p309 G2.

Club 238 stands on the site of the old Palladium (aka the 'Get-laid-eum'), a late-night San Francisco dancing institution. Club nights – house, hip hop, trance – usually go on until 4am, sometimes later. The set-up resembles an upscale ice-skating rink, with a medium-sized dancefloor ringed by a ramp designed for maximum people-watching.

The Mission & around

Amnesia

853 Valencia Street, between 19th & 20th Streets, Mission (970 8336). Bus 14, 26, 49. **Open** 6pm-2am daily. **Admission** free-$10. **No credit cards**. **Map** p314 Y1.

Amnesia seems to be resisting the party-hearty armies that take over this stretch of the Mission at the weekend. Instead, it draws a diverse, friendly, multi-ethnic crowd. DJs spin eclectic sounds most nights, with drum 'n' bass and international beats particularly popular. Equally exotic is the interna-

Chill out at **Sno-drift**. *See p219.*

tional beer collection. There are two dozen beers on tap and another two dozen by the bottle, with Belgian brews predominating.

Liquid

2925 16th Street, between South Van Ness Avenue & Mission Street, Mission (431 8889). BART 16th Street/bus 14, 22, 26, 53. **Open** 9pm-2am Mon-Sat. **Admission** free-$5. **No credit cards**. **Map** p310 F6.

A favourite spot for fans of DJ culture, Liquid is a narrow bar with a small dancefloor. There's no sign out front, but that hasn't kept the Marina masses from discovering the place. Uncomfortably crowded at the weekend, if anything it gets more packed on Tuesdays for Taboo, when resident DJ David Harness spins garage and house to a cool mix of straights and gays. There's a different club every night of the week, and the cover is always low.

Metronome Ballroom

1830 17th Street, at De Haro Street, Potrero Hill (252 9000/www.metronomeballroom.com). Bus 19, 22. **Open** 7.30pm-midnight Fri, Sat; 5-11pm Sun. **Admission** free-$15. **Credit** AmEx, MC, V. **Map** p311 H6.

If you love to dance, but clubs aren't your thing, the spacious, airy Metronome Ballroom is for you. Set at the base of Potrero Hill, the long-established venue offers dance lessons and a friendly place to shake your thang seven days a week. Lessons are offered in lindy hop, tango, swing, foxtrot, waltz, cha cha, salsa, merengue, West Coast swing and hip hop.

26 Mix

3024 Mission Street, at 26th Street, Mission (248 1319/ www.26mix.com). BART 24th Street/ bus 14, 26, 49. **Open** 9pm-2am daily. **Admission** free before 10pm; $5 after 10pm. **No credit cards**.

A couple of years ago, 26 Mix spearheaded the San Francisco trend of combining the vibe of a friendly neighbourhood bar with the cool intimacy of a small DJ club. Now, though, it's been all but annexed by bellowing frat boys trying to score with aerobicised, blonde-ponytailed clones. 26 Mix isn't giving up without a fight, though. A variety of music is offered seven nights a week, and there are still some intriguing parties – but it's best avoided at the weekends. Some nights are women-only.

The Haight & around

Galaxy Club

1840 Haight Street, at Stanyan Street, Haight-Ashbury (387 2996/www.sfstation.com/clubs/galaxy). Bus 6, 7, 33, 66, 71. **Open** 2pm-2am daily. **Admission** $3-$10. **No credit cards**. **Map** p313 C6.

The Galaxy replaces the Boomerang, a dive bar that was the starting point (or last resort) for local bands trying to gain an audience. That's yet another blow for Bay Area musicians, and leaves the Haight, a place once practically synonymous with the 'sound of San Francisco', almost devoid of spots to hear rock. However, the Galaxy is a cool new place to enjoy the art of the DJ, with a busy roster of club nights, a spiffy modern decor and a decent-sized dancefloor.

Nickie's BBQ

460 Haight Street, between Webster & Fillmore Streets, Lower Haight (621 6508/www.nickies.com). Bus 6, 7, 22, 66, 71. **Open** 9pm-2am daily. **Admission** $3-$5. **No credit cards**. **Map** p310 E5.

At the weekend, this small, divey DJ bar can get absurdly overcrowded with drunken louts and the women who tolerate them. Come on a Thursday, when DJ Motion Potion spins lesser-known classic and contemporary funk. On Mondays, there's a long-running Deadhead dance party; the music comes from concert bootlegs. On other nights, you may encounter world music, house, reggae, funk or disco.

Storyville

1751 Fulton Street, between Masonic & Central Avenues, Western Addition (441 1751/www.storyvillesf.com). Bus 5, 43. **Open** 9.30pm-2am Tue-Sat. **Admission** $5-$10. **Credit** AmEx, MC, V. **Map** p313 D5.

Storyville is an odd club in an odd location, in a residential section of the Western Addition. Originally opened as a jazz house/supperclub, it retains the trappings (red velvet walls, dimly lit cocktail tables, Cajun dinners), but these days you're more likely to hear hip hop, soul, funk, reggae and dancehall. In fact, it's one of the best places in the city to catch good hip hop; especially popular are the Friday night performances sponsored by True Skool.

The Top

424 Haight Street, between Fillmore & Webster Streets, Lower Haight (864 7386). Bus 6, 7, 22, 66, 71. **Open** 7pm-2am daily. **Admission** $5-$10. **No credit cards**. **Map** p310 E5.

Just down the street from Nickie's (*see above*), on the edge of a somewhat sketchy part of the Lower Haight, this place is nothing special – it's essentially a converted dive bar with a smallish dancefloor. But it's got a good reputation as a centre for turntable culture, with DJs spinning house, dub, hip hop, funk, breaks and more most nights of the week.

Performing Arts

Enjoy a thriving theatre scene and world-class ballet and opera companies.

From the days of the Barbary Coast, which catered to those looking for excitement in San Francisco in the years following the Gold Rush, this port city has always had an active and varied performing arts scene. In the early days, it was the likes of Lola Montez, Gilbert and Sullivan and Jenny Lind, the 'Swedish Nightingale'. San Francisco has always been an appealing city, and many producers and playwrights are drawn here by both the theatre scene and the city's beauty. Playwright Tony Kushner launched his award-winning *Angels in America* here, and, more recently, Sam Shepard, who cut his playwriting teeth at the city's Magic Theatre, returned with the premiere of his play *The Late Henry Moss*.

More commercial efforts are attracted to San Francisco as a launching pad for national tours. The Abba musical, *Mama Mia*, made its American debut here, and the Pulitzer Prize-winning *Contact* was restaged for proscenium theatres in San Francisco, where it opened its American tour. Festivals, readings and the first productions of lesser-known works abound, and the city is filled with experimental works.

Similar situations can be found in music and dance. The world-class San Francisco Ballet draws audiences from the same crowds that frequent Mission District ethnic and experimental dance groups. Classical music and opera ranges from grand operas and symphonies at the War Memorial Opera House to small, edgy works in venues around the city.

Edward II at **ACT**. *See p222.*

INFORMATION

For up-to-date information, the *San Francisco Chronicle*'s Sunday 'Datebook' section has extensive listings, as do many of the smaller, free weekly tabloids available at newsstands around the city. Good websites include www.citysearch7.com, www.artsmonthlysf.org and www.bayinsider.com. For Broadway touring shows, check out www.bestofbroadway-sf.com.

TICKETS

Ticket prices range from $5 for an experimental show to more than $80 for a Broadway-style extravaganza. Theatre box offices are usually the cheapest bet for tickets (bear in mind there's often a fee for telephone bookings). Or you can try one of several ticket sales outfits. **TIX Bay Area** (433 7827), is located in the Union Square Garage on the Geary Street side of Union Square while the square is being remodelled. It sells half-price tickets for theatre, dance and opera events on the day of the show (cash only), as well as full-price tickets in advance (for which you can pay by credit card).

Tickets.com (776 1999/www.tickets.com) sells tickets by phone and email, as well as from outlets all over the city – expect to pay a hefty surcharge of $2-$6 per ticket . You can also try the **St Francis Theater Ticket Service** (362 3500), **Mr Ticket** (292 7328/1-800 424 7328/1-888 722 5737/www.mrticket.com) or **City Box Office** (392 4400/www.citybox office.com). You can buy tickets for some venues through **Ticketmaster** (512 7770/ www.ticketmaster.com).

► For information on annual **theatre festivals**, *see chapter* **By Season**.

Theatre

The variety of theatres is immense: there are mainstream theatres that attract national touring acts and Broadway shows; regional theatres that draw performers from throughout California; other significant theatres that offer a mix of ethnic, new and established works; and a host of small and experimental theatres.

Mainstream theatres

Curran Theater

445 Geary Street, between Mason & Taylor Streets, Tenderloin (551 2000). BART Powell Street/Muni Metro F, J, K, L, M, N/bus 27, 38/cable car Powell-Hyde or Powell-Mason. **Tickets** $20-$70. **Credit** AmEx, MC, V. **Map** p310 G4.

Opened in 1922, the Curran has enough gilt and gewgaws – carved wood in the lobby, two-storey murals, an enormous chandelier – to make audiences feel they have been transported to a fantasy castle. Seating about 1,600, it is often used for non-musical Broadway-type shows – although *Phantom of the Opera* ran here for five years.

Golden Gate Theater

1 Taylor Street, at Golden Gate Avenue, Tenderloin (551 2000). BART Civic Center/Muni Metro F, J, K, L, M, N/bus 5, 6, 7, 9, 21, 26, 66, 71. **Tickets** $16-$68. **Credit** AmEx, MC, V. **Map** p310 G4.

This rather down-at-heel theatre, a former movie and vaudeville house, may be the next big house due for major renovation. A large space, seating 2,300, the Golden Gate often hosts travelling musicals for a longer-than-average run. *Rent* played here for several months.

Herbst Theatre

Veterans' Memorial Building, 401 Van Ness Avenue, between Grove & McAllister Streets, Civic Center (621 6600/www.sfperf.org/theaters/herbst.asp). Muni Metro F, J, K, L, M, N/bus 5, 21, 42, 47, 49. **Tickets** $20-$50. **Credit** MC, V. **Map** p310 F4.

A bit like a stuffy old aunt, the Herbst – located inside the Veterans' Memorial Building – is the smallest of the mainstream houses, seating just over 900. With poor acoustics in the balcony, it plays host to smaller touring shows, concerts, comedy and cabaret. It's a beautiful building – with eight huge Beaux Arts murals first painted for the 1915 Panama-Pacific Exposition and a glorious blue and gold ceiling – but it's not the best place to see a show.

Orpheum

1192 Market Street, at Hyde Street, Civic Center (551 2000). BART Civic Center/Muni Metro F, J, K, L, M, N/bus 6, 5, 7, 9, 21, 31, 66, 71. **Tickets** $22-$70. **Credit** AmEx, MC, V. **Map** p310 G5.

The most recently renovated of the big theatres in the city, the 2,200-seat Orpheum has a spacious lobby and Moorish design, and is a delightful place to see a show. Once a vaudeville house and later a movie theatre, it was where *Hair* was first performed more than 30 years ago.

Regional theatres

For **Brava! for Women in the Arts**, based in the Mission, *see p235*.

American Conservatory Theater (ACT)

Geary Theater, 415 Geary Street, between Mason & Taylor Streets, Tenderloin (834 3200/box office 749 2228/www.act-sfbay.org). BART Powell Street/Muni Metro F, J, K, L, M, N/bus 27, 38/cable car Powell-Hyde or Powell-Mason. **Tickets** $11-$70. **Credit** AmEx, MC, V. **Map** p310 G4.

This is the company that brought the concept of regional repertory theatre to San Francisco in the late 1960s. Economics have changed all that, but ACT seems to be returning, at least somewhat, to the repertory format, using several actors who will appear in a number of plays per season. It presents new works by both new and established writers, such as Tom Stoppard and David Mamet, as well as ancient and modern classics. Former students of the conservatory include Winona Ryder, Danny Glover and Denzel Washington.

Lamplighters Musical Theater

978 2787/www.lamplighters.org. **Tickets** $20-$34. **Credit** MC, V.

Best known for its award-winning productions of Gilbert and Sullivan operettas, this group is now nearing its 50th anniversary, making it one of the oldest theatre companies in San Francisco. It has a considerable following not only for its Gilbert and Sullivan works, but also contemporary musical comedies from Sondheim to Lerner and Loewe. The company's annual gala, usually staged in the autumn or winter, is a G&S-style parody aimed at local targets. In San Francisco, it performs at the Yerba Buena Center for the Arts (*see p224*) in SoMa and the Ira & Leonore S Gershwin Theater in the Western Addition.

Magic Theatre

Building D, Fort Mason Center, Marina Boulevard, at Buchanan Street, Marina (441 8822/www.magictheatre.org). Bus 28. **Tickets** $8-$30. **Credit** AmEx, MC, V. **Map** p308 E1.

With material often newer and more cutting-edge than the other regional theatres, the three-decade-old Magic Theatre represents a happy medium between new, mainstream plays and more experimental work. In the past couple of years, it has introduced San Francisco to shows that have gone on to considerable success, most notably *Stones in His Pocket*, which became a hit in New York and London, and the world premiere of Sam Shepard's *The Late Henry Moss*. The group also offers 'raw play' readings of new works. It has two spaces, Northside and Southside, each seating 150.

Tender is the theatre district

Within a five- or six-block area in the Tenderloin – the area bounded by Powell, O'Farrell, Leavenworth and Sutter Streets – you'll find San Francisco's theatre district. There are more than a dozen venues (though only two look like 'real' theatres) offering cultural fare ranging from experimental and ethnic shows to Broadway spectaculars.

The **Curran Theater** (*see p222*) on Geary Street hosts best-of-Broadway extravaganzas, while around the corner on Post Street, the **Theatre on the Square** (*see below*), an ex-lodge hall, specialises in smaller Broadway and off-Broadway shows, as well as shows heading for New York. The **American Conservatory Theater** (*see p222*) – San Francisco's major theatre company – is on Geary Street in the **Geary Theater**. Further up Geary toward Leavenworth, you'll find the **Alcazar Theatre** (*pictured*), another converted lodge hall. Up on Sutter Street, two blocks from Geary, the **Lorraine Hansberry Theatre** (*see p224*) hosts a season of African-American plays. Directly across the street from the Lorraine (which is housed in a former YMCA) is the **Marine's Memorial Theatre** (in a military club and hotel), where *Stomp*! is currently on a lengthy run. Other smaller theatres are scattered throughout the area, and often show new or experimental works.

Oh, and the only two that look like theatres – that's the Curran and the Geary.

Theatre on the Square

450 Post Street, between Powell & Mason Streets, Union Square (433 9500/www.theatreonthesquare.com). BART Powell Street/Muni Metro F, J, K, L, M, N/bus 2, 3, 4, 15, 30, 38, 45, 76/cable car Powell-Hyde or Powell-Mason. **Tickets** $30-$50. **Credit** AmEx, MC, V. **Map** p308 G3.

Housed in a remodelled Elks Lodge auditorium, the 700-seat Theatre on the Square has built a reputation for bringing in shows fresh from Broadway runs and launching shows headed for bigger things. Tony award-winning producer Jonathan Reinis is always on the lookout for interesting projects, and some of the most exciting commercial theatre offered in San Francisco can be seen here.

Other theatres of note

The **Asian American Theater Company** (440 5545/www.asianamericantheater.org), focuses on plays by and about Americans of Asian and Pacific Island descent.

Climate Theatre

252 Ninth Street, between Folsom & Howard Streets, SoMa (626 6422/www.well.com/user/tcircus/Climate). Bus 12, 19, 26. **Tickets** $12-$15. **No credit cards. Map** p310 G5.

The Climate nurtures new work by solo performers who have often gone on to achieve wider acclaim. It runs the annual Solo Mio festival, a puppet festival and also produces readings and works in progress.

Eureka Theatre Company

215 Jackson Street, between Front & Battery Streets, Embarcadero (788 7469/www.eurekatheatre.org). Bus 12, 42, 83. **Tickets** $15-$25. **Credit** AmEx, MC, V. **Map** p309 H2.

This group moved into new digs a couple of seasons ago, but has had trouble building the sort of momentum it saw when introducing such shows as Tony Kushner's *Angels In America*. It does, however, rent its space to other troupes, most notably 42nd Street Moon (255 8207/www.42ndstmoon.com), a group devoted to rediscovering lost musicals and staging them in delightful script-in-hand concerts.

EXITheater

156 Eddy Street, between Mason & Taylor Streets, Tenderloin (931 1094/festival information 673 3847/www.sffringe.org). BART Powell Street/Muni Metro F, J, K, L, M, N/bus 27, 31. **Tickets** $5-$20. **No credit cards**. **Map** p310 G4.

The central complex for San Francisco's Fringe Festival (*see p192*), this three-theatre group offers a lively assortment of shows ranging from new one-acts to works by established authors. It's one of the city's most eclectic theatres, and almost always has something interesting or provocative playing.

Lorraine Hansberry Theatre

620 Sutter Street, between Mason & Taylor Streets, Nob Hill (474 8800/www.lorrainehansberrytheatre.com). Bus 2, 3, 4, 76/cable car Powell-Hyde or Powell-Mason. **Tickets** $15-$30. **Credit** AmEx, MC, V. **Map** p308 G3.

This is the Bay Area's best-known African-American theatre group. It produces plays by black playwrights or plays that deal with issues affecting the black community. The group stages a four- or five-play season, usually with a musical Christmas season offering the likes of Langston Hughes' *Black Nativity*. The theatre seats 300.

New Conservatory Theatre

25 Van Ness Avenue, between Fell & Oak Streets, Hayes Valley (861 8972/www.nctcsf.org). Muni Metro F, J, K, L, M, N/bus 42, 47, 49. **Tickets** $20-$35. **Credit** AmEx, Disc, MC, V. **Map** p310 F5.

This well designed performing arts complex in Hayes Valley houses three fully equipped theatres ranging in size from 50 to 132 seats, a video studio, art gallery and classroom studios. The resident company produces an annual Pride Season, featuring works by and about the gay community, along with a series of musicals.

Theater Artaud

450 Florida Street, between 17th & Mariposa Streets, Mission (621 7797/www.theaterartaud.org). Bus 22, 27, 33, 53. **Tickets** $18-$25. **Credit** MC, V. **Map** p310 G6.

Located in a former warehouse bordered by 17th, Florida, Alabama and Mariposa Streets, this large live-work space in the Mission District houses several theatres (Traveling Jewish Theatre, Theater of Yugen) that make their facilities available to many groups. This gives the building a richness of offerings, with plays ranging from traditional to experimental, ethnic shows and performance art. It's worth checking out, if for no other reason than to see what can happen when artists take charge of an enormous old commercial building.

Yerba Buena Center for the Arts

701 Mission Street, at Third Street, SoMa (978 2787/www.yerbabuenaarts.org). BART Powell or Montgomery Streets/Muni Metro F, J, K, L, M, N/ bus 9, 15, 30, 45, 76. **Tickets** $5-$100. **Credit** AmEx, MC, V. **Map** p311 H4.

Inside this angled, blue-tiled box, built in the 1990s, is the city's most striking new performance space. It boasts a wide variety of events, ranging from the Afro Solo Festival in August to the Lamplighters' Gilbert and Sullivan season to touring plays and musicals. The theatre entrance is at the intersection of Third and Howard Streets.

Experimental theatres

Audium

1616 Bush Street, at Franklin Street, Pacific Heights (771 1616/www.audium.org). Bus 2, 3, 4, 42, 47, 49, 76. **Shows** 8.30pm Fri, Sat. **Tickets** $12. **No credit cards**. **Map** p308 F3.

Behind its bland streetside façade in Pacific Heights, the 25-year-old Audium's tiny theatre is wired with 169 speakers. Composer/sound manipulator Stan Shaff creates multi-dimensional audio sculptures – chirps and burps that ping-pong around the room; atonal passages of synthesiser music that transmogrify into oppressive industrial static; an invisible marching band. A whimsical sculpture lobby and Shaff's post-performance pontification make this one of the city's best entertainment deals.

Beach Blanket Babylon

Club Fugazi, 678 Green Street, between Columbus Avenue & Powell Street, North Beach (421 4222/ www.beachblanketbabylon.com). Bus 15, 30, 41, 45. **Tickets** $25-$62. **Credit** MC, V. **Map** p308 G2.

This long-running musical revue (it's been around for more than 25 years) features a constantly changing array of characters drawn from US popular culture, local legend and the politics of the day. The slapstick humour places heavy emphasis on the formulaic and the visual – notably the use of huge, elaborate headgear. Beach Blanket Babylon is a San Francisco original, and worth seeing.

George Coates PerformanceWorks

110 McAllister Street, at Leavenworth Street, Civic Center (863 8520/www.georgecoates.org). BART Civic Center/Muni Metro F, J, K, L, M, N/bus 5, 19. **Tickets** $27-$42. **Credit** AmEx, V. **Map** p310 G4.

Techno wizard George Coates is a pioneer in 'virtual' theatre, working actors and musicians into dazzling computer-generated environments. There's usually only one show a year, which runs from November to March and then goes on tour.

The Marsh

1062 Valencia Street, at 22nd Street, Mission (826 5750/www.themarsh.org). BART 24th Street/ bus 14, 26, 49. **Tickets** $7-$15. **Credit** MC, V. **Map** p314 Y2.

This has become one of the most exciting venues in the city. Located in a lively nightlife section of the Mission District, it seems to work hard at presenting new works that often move on to larger venues in the Bay Area or across the country. It prides itself on being a breeding ground for new performance, and allows performers to take risks.

East Bay

Head to Berkeley for two of the Bay Area's finest theatre offerings.

Berkeley Repertory Theater

2025 Addison Street, between Shattuck Avenue & Milvia Street, Berkeley (1-510 845 4700/ www.berkeleyrep.org). BART Berkeley/AC Transit bus F. **Tickets** $16-$51. **Credit** MC, V. **Map** p315 L3.

Now a two-theatre complex – the original, 400-seat thrust-stage auditorium and a new, 600-seat proscenium space, which opened in March 2001 – Berkeley Rep accommodates smaller, more unusual touring shows. A typical season might include a classic drama, several new works and plays by contemporary writers such as Pulitzer Prize-winning Donald Margulies and historian-turned-playwright Charles Mee. Productions enjoy long runs – a month or two is not uncommon – but the spaces are small and tickets are sometimes difficult to find, particularly if a show draws rave reviews.

Cal Performances

Zellerbach Hall, UC Berkeley campus, Berkeley (1-510 642 9988/www.calperfs.berkeley.edu). BART Berkeley/AC Transit bus F. **Tickets** $18-$94. **Credit** MC, V. **Map** p315 M3/4.

As an adjunct of UC Berkeley, Cal Performances offers a smattering of everything – dance, music and drama – along with ethnic presentations you'll probably not see elsewhere in the Bay Area. It presents nationally regarded dance companies, such as Alvin Ailey and the Mark Morris Dance Group, plays by Brecht and performances by the likes of the Kronos Quartet, the American Ballet Theatre and the National Acrobats of Taiwan.

Dance

Dance groups & venues

The leading dance group in the Bay Area is the **San Francisco Ballet** (865 2000/www.sfballet.org). Founded in 1933, it's the oldest professional ballet company in the United States; it presented the first full-length production of *Coppélia*, followed in 1940 by the country's first production of the complete *Swan Lake* and the first full-length *Nutcracker* in 1944. It faced its lowest point in the 1970s when it came close to bankruptcy, but has long since recovered. The company is based in the **War Memorial Opera House** (*see p226*), along with the San Francisco Opera. The ballet's annual season (February to May) is typically an even-handed blend of traditional pieces and new works. There is a also *Nutcracker* season in December. Tickets range from $10 to $120.

San Francisco Ballet: dancing since 1933.

ODC Performance Gallery

3153 17th Street, between South Van Ness Avenue & Shotwell Street, Mission (box office 863 9834/ administration 626 6745). BART 16th Street/bus 12, 14, 22, 33, 49, 53. **Tickets** $10-$40. **Credit** AmEx, MC, V. **Map** p310 F6.

With its own dance company, and works by other artists in dance, theatre and music, ODC is active in creating new and innovative works in the world of modern dance. The group also operates its own school and a gallery.

SF Performances

Suite 710, 500 Sutter Street, at Powell Street, Union Square (398 6449/www.sfperformances.org). Bus 2, 3, 4, 30, 45, 76/cable car Powell-Hyde or Powell-Mason. **Tickets** $24-$60. **Credit** AmEx, MC, V. **Map** p309 G3.

As well as being a music venue, SF Performances attracts some of the biggest national and international names in dance. Its dance series runs from November to April, and groups have included Bill T Jones and the Netherlands Dance Theatre. Tickets are available from City Box Office.

Smaller dance groups

Alonzo King's **LINES Ballet** (863 1248/ www.linesballet.org) travels throughout the country performing primarily new ballet works. The company performs locally at the Yerba Buena Center (*see p224*) and has produced a home season since 1982. **Smuin Ballets/SF** (665 2222/www.smuinballets.com) was founded in 1994 by choreographer Michael Smuin, former director of the San Francisco Ballet. In 2001, its original programme *Dancin' with Gershwin* was one of the hottest tickets on the local dance scene. **Dandelion Dance**

Theater (1-510 444 2820) is winning considerable recognition for its postmodern dance style; athletic and theatrical, the group performs at various locations. Oakland-based **Savage Jazz Dance Company** (1-510 496 6068/www. savagejazz.org), under the direction of Reginald Ray-Savage, produces dance inspired by jazz and performs throughout the Bay Area. **TRANSIT** (273 5890/www. transitdance.com), a multi-ethnic company formed in 1995, consists of five dancers whose artistic heritage is rooted in German Expressionist dance.

Classical Music & Opera

The two main companies in the city – both with a world-class reputation – are the **San Francisco Opera** and the **San Francisco Symphony Orchestra**. Since its founding in 1923, the SF Opera has presented numerous world premières of major operatic works; it performs in the historic War Memorial Opera House (*see below*) in the Civic Center. The SF Symphony Orchestra, another grande dame of local music, is one of the oldest performing arts groups in the city. Formed shortly after the 1906 earthquake and fire, it performed its first concert in 1911. Today, under the direction of Michael Tilson Thomas, the symphony is recognised worldwide as a leading innovator in classical music. It's based at the Louise M Davies Symphony Hall (*see below*).

Other smaller groups include the ten-year-old **New Century Chamber Orchestra** (433 6226/www.ncco.org), which specialises in new ways of performing and interpreting chamber music. A 16-member, conductorless orchestra, it's led by music director Krista Bennion Feeney and performs throughout the Bay Area; in San Francisco you're most likely to find it at the Herbst Theatre (*see p222*). Donald Pippin's **Pocket Opera** (575 1100/ www.pocketopera.org) is a professional group that presents operatic works (in English) in an intimate setting, with an emphasis on clarity. The company performs at the Palace of the Legion of Honor in Lincoln Park and several other Bay Area locations.

Two well known music groups are based in San Francisco, but often on tour around the world. Widely respected for its ability to combine old and new techniques in classical music, the **Kronos Quartet** (731 3533/ www.kronosquartet.org), founded in 1973, returns to the city and the Bay Area for frequent performances. **Chanticleer** (252 8589/ www.chanticleer.org) bills itself as an orchestra of voices. An all-male a cappella group that performs an eclectic variety of vocal music, it also performs locally.

Also look out for the **Bach Choir** (441 4942/ www.sfbach.org). Small but widely respected, it's one of the oldest choral groups in the western US – it's been around for six decades. Despite the name, the choir isn't limited to Bach, but performs works from the 16th to the 18th centuries.

Venues

Louise M Davies Symphony Hall

201 Van Ness Avenue, at Hayes Street, Civic Center (864 6000/www.sfsymphony.org). BART Civic Center/Muni Metro F, J, K, L, M, N/bus 21, 42, 47, 49. **Tickets** $15-$88. **Credit** MC, V. **Map** p310 F5.

A multi-tiered, curved glass edifice with good sightlines, the Louise M Davies Symphony Hall, the home of the San Francisco Symphony Orchestra, opened in 1980 – to disappointing aural effect. Renovated in the early 1990s, Davies now flaunts expensively improved, hear-every-pin-drop acoustics. Even from the top row of the back balcony, you can hear everything – and see it all, too. Often, generous discounts are available to those interested in watching rehearsals (usually held in the daytime), a fascinating way to hear a concert at minimal expense.

Masonic Auditorium

1111 California Street, at Taylor Street, Nob Hill (776 4702/www.masonicauditorium.com). Bus 1/ cable car California. **Tickets** $25-$75. **Credit** MC, V. **Map** p308 G3.

A classic example of late 1950s design, which still manages to seem contemporary, this auditorium has a wonderfully warm feeling and tremendous acoustics. Dark walls and excellent sightlines make it a fine venue for concerts, readings, music and other events. It seats 3,100.

War Memorial Opera House

301 Van Ness Avenue, at Grove Street, Civic Center (864 3330/www.sfopera.com). BART Civic Center/ Muni Metro F, J, K, L, M, N/bus 21, 42, 47, 49. **Tickets** $23-$165. **Credit** AmEx, MC, V. **Map** p308 F5.

This grand Beaux Arts building, designed by Arthur Brown (who was also the architect of nearby City Hall), was built in 1932 as a memorial to the soldiers who fought in World War I. The 3,176-seat auditorium is modelled on European opera houses, with a vaulted ceiling, a huge, silver art deco chandelier and a marble foyer. In 1997, a $84.5-million revamp not only restored the elegant building, but installed up-to-date electronics and stage gear. The United Nations charter was signed here in 1945. The opera season runs from the first Friday in September to late January, with a summer season in June. The San Francisco Ballet is also based here.

Enjoy superb acoustics at the **Davies Symphony Hall** in the Civic Center. *See p226.*

Churches & other venues

Recitals and concerts – often free – are performed in many of San Francisco's churches. They include the **Old First Presbyterian Church** on the edge of Pacific Heights (1751 Sacramento Street, at Van Ness Avenue; 776 5552/www.oldfirst.org) where Chanticleer often performs; the **First Unitarian Universalist Church** near the Civic Center (1187 Franklin Street, at Geary Boulevard; 776 4580); and **Grace Cathedral** on Nob Hill (749 6355/www.gracecathedral.org – *see p82*). **St Patrick's**, a beautifully restored Catholic church just across the street from Yerba Buena Gardens, hosts noontime concerts every Wednesday (details on 777 3211). A great venue for organ recitals or performances by the San Francisco Bach Choir is **St Mary's Cathedral** (*see p89*) in the Fillmore District.

One of the most visible of the city's churches is the **Glide Memorial United Methodist Church** (*see p63*) in the heart of the Tenderloin. Offering programmes ranging from social activism to blues and jazz, Glide ministers to an eclectic audience, and is often a prime spot for visiting celebrities, especially those from music and entertainment. You never know, you might run into Bono here. It's happened before. Also in the Tenderloin, the **Luggage Store** (*see p204*) is an art gallery most of the week, but also offers a Thursday night creative/experimental music series with unusual programmes curated by composer/improviser Ernesto Diaz-Infante.

Out of town

Nip across the San Francisco Bay to find some of the more interesting classical music in the region. Zellerbach Hall on the UC Berkeley campus is used by the **Berkeley Symphony Orchestra** (1-510 841 2800/www.berkeley symphony.org), which attracts a roster of distinguished stars under music director Kent Nagano. It is also the venue for concerts, recitals and solo shows organised by **Cal Performances** (*see p225*); **Berkeley Opera** (1-510 841 1903/www.berkeleyopera.com) also puts on three productions a year there.

Other East Bay venues worth investigating include the **First Congregational Church** in Berkeley (1-510 848 3696/www.fccb.org) and the **Paramount Theater** in Oakland, where the **Oakland East Bay Symphony** (1-510 444 0801/www.oebs.org) and the **Oakland Symphony Chorus** (1-510 465 4199/www.oakland-sym-chorus.org) regularly perform.

Over the Golden Gate Bridge, the **West Marin Music Festival** (663 9650) presents concerts throughout the year, most of which take place at St Columba's Church in Inverness, a delightful village near Point Reyes. It's about an hour north of San Francisco by car.

Queer San Francisco

Every day is gay day in San Francisco.

For decades, San Francisco's gay, lesbian, bisexual and transgender community has been a vital part of the city's character. Along with cable cars, pastel-coloured Victorian houses and hippies, the gay population largely defines this city. For gays in the US, and, to a lesser extent, worldwide, a visit to San Francisco has taken on the feel of a pilgrimage.

At the heart of it all is the Castro district. At one time, this neighbourhood was home to little more than dairy farms and dirt roads. Early homesteaders, including Irish, German and Scandinavian immigrants, built rambling, hillside Victorian houses for their large broods. What would those prudish (if prolific) folks think if they knew that almost all those houses now belong to monied gay men who needed a place into which to pour their extensive disposable income and Martha Stewart decorating skills? Once a working-class area, in the 1960s and '70s the neighbourhood's predominant collar colour switched from blue to pink. In those days, queers could snap up a huge Victorian for chump change ($20,000 to $40,000 was not unusual). Today, these queenly mansions sell for a cool $1 million.

Of course, not all San Francisco's queers are so wealthy, and not all the city's gays embrace the Castro queen scene. Throughout the city you'll find queers from all walks of life. You can connect with lesbian mums at PTA meetings or make new gay friends at church suppers just as easily as you can flirt with a boytoy at a trendy nightclub. If you're queer and you're into the scene, plan a trip to coincide with the Pride celebrations in June. The month-long festival culminates in a massive party commemorating the 1969 Stonewall Riots in New York (the birth of the modern American gay liberation movement); *see p232* **Take Pride** for details.

Although the AIDS epidemic cast a pall over the world's queerest neighbourhood in the 1980s and early '90s, the success of new drug therapies in counteracting the disease has since renewed the community's spirit. The question now is: has the optimism gone too far? Coinciding with the mood boost is an increasingly lax attitude toward the dangers of unprotected sex; in 2000, the number of San Franciscans with HIV rose after many years of steady decline. Local agencies are countering the tide with a variety of potent, educational campaigns aimed at young gay men.

For an in-depth look at San Francisco's gay life – past and present – explore the **Gay & Lesbian Center** at the Main Library (*see p68*), or join a walking tour – either one organised by the Gay, Lesbian, Bisexual, Transgendered Historical Society of Northern California (777 5455) or Trevor Hailey's Cruisin' the Castro (*see p54* **The city on foot: Walking tours**).

NEIGHBOURHOODS

In large part, the **Castro** lives up to its reputation as the centre of the known queer universe, even if it is a bit boy-heavy. But gay life in San Francisco extends beyond the Castro to lesser-known but equally interesting neighbourhoods. **Polk Street** is poorer, rougher and draggier. **SoMa** has bars, trendy restaurants, sex clubs and dance venues packed with hot, muscled men. It's also the setting of the infamous leather **Folsom Street Fair** (*see p192*). **Hayes Valley** is more artsy, low-key and mixed. Although women patronise the Castro and Hayes Valley bars, cafés and restaurants, the more affordable **Mission** district – particularly **Valencia Street** from 16th to 22nd Streets – provides a scene for many lesbians, especially younger ones. A perennial favourite is **Osento** (*see p181*), a women-only spa where you can soak in a hot tub or eucalyptus-scented sauna, and then lie outside on the deck beneath the stars. And don't leave the city without discovering the charms of **Bernal Heights**, a quietly romantic neighbourhood way off the tourist map that's become a hub for gay and lesbian home-owners. Walk up its winding streets past cottages covered in flowering vines to the top of Bernal Hill. On a sunny day you'll be rewarded with a spectacular view of the bay, and of beautiful Bernal residents walking their dogs.

INFORMATION

The best sources for up-to-date information on new clubs, shows, films, events and general gay news are the free newspapers – notably the *Bay Times* and the *Bay Area Reporter* (*BAR*) – which can be found in almost every café or in boxes on street corners. You can also find information, to a lesser extent, in the free *San Francisco Bay Guardian* and *SF Weekly*.

Enjoy a room with a garden at the **Parker House**. *See p230.*

The newly renovated **Women's Building** (*see p84*) in the Mission shelters various women's organisations and is also a central place to find newspapers, bulletin board postings and information. The rich colours of the murals that cover the outside of the building have made the centre a landmark.

Accommodation

Most San Francisco hoteliers either openly welcome same-gender couples or are utterly indifferent to their guests' sexuality. However, a few establishments do cater specifically to queer clients. (For a complete list of lodgings, *see chapter* **Accommodation**.)

The Castro

Beck's Motor Lodge

2222 Market Street, CA 94114, at 15th Street (621 8212/fax 421 0435). Muni Metro F, J, K, L, M/bus 22, 37. **Rates** single $99; double $109-$139. **Credit** AmEx, MC, V. **Map** p310 E6.

A quintessential American motel, down to its tacky carpets and glasses sealed in plastic. The relatively cheap rates and prime Castro location keep it popular, however. The management frowns on cruising from the balconies overlooking the parking lot, so behave yourself. Free parking.

Inn on Castro

321 Castro Street, CA 94114, at Market Street (861 0321/www.innoncastro2.com). Muni Metro F, K, L, M/bus 24, 33, 35, 37. **Rates** single $135; double $160; suite $135-$175. **Credit** AmEx, MC, V. **Map** p314 X1.

This beautifully restored Edwardian has served as San Francisco's premier gay and lesbian hotel for more than two decades. Its eight rooms are decorated with original modern art and elaborate flower arrangements. The highlight of the stay is the breakfast, including home-made muffins and piles of fresh fruit. The hotel is non-smoking (it's allowed on the back patio) and there are rooms for disabled visitors.

Nancy's Bed

In Twin Peaks, near the Castro; phone for exact address (239 5692). **Rates** single $25-$35. **No credit cards**.

Nancy and her partner rent a room in their home to women travellers who seek a respite from the city's many cookie-cutter hotels. Allergy sufferers, take note: the cosy household includes cats.

► For more information on what the **Castro** has to offer, *see chapter* **The Mission & the Castro**.
► For **AIDS helplines**, **gay counselling** and **medical services**, *see chapter* **Directory**.

The Parker House

520 Church Street, CA 94114, at 18th Street, Castro (1-888 520 7275/621 3222/fax 621 4139/ www.parkerguesthouse.com). Muni Metro J/bus 22, 33. **Rates** $119-$189. **Credit** AmEx, MC, V. **Map** p314 Y1.

This 1909 Edwardian mini-mansion was completely renovated a few years ago. All ten rooms (two with shared baths) have 21st-century touches, including voicemail and dataports. Guests have access to the garden, deck, library and sauna/steam room. The owners, Bob and Bill, just bought the house next door, so look for them to expand soon.

24 Henry Guesthouse & Village House

24 Henry Street, CA 94114, between Sanchez & Noe Streets (1-800 900 5686/864 5686/fax 864 0406/www.24henry.com). Muni Metro F, K, L, M/ bus 24, 37. **Rates** single $66-$109; double $80-$119; apartment suite from $119. **Credit** AmEx, MC, V. **Map** p313 E6.

Gay-owned and operated, this refurbished Victorian caters to queer vacationers, although everyone with an open mind is welcome (as long as they don't try to smoke in their rooms). Conveniently located only steps away from Castro Street, each of the five rooms has a phone, voicemail and a shared or private bath.

The Willows Inn

710 14th Street, CA 94114, between Sanchez & Church Streets (431 4770/fax 431 5295). Muni Metro F, K, L, M/bus 22, 24, 37. **Rates** single $90-$110; double $100-$130. **Credit** AmEx, Disc, MC, V. **Map** p310 E6.

Located a few blocks from the Castro's crazy core, this is a converted 1903 Edwardian home, with 12 comfy rooms decked out in antique furnishings. Guests are served breakfast and cocktails daily. All rooms have sinks, but baths are shared. Limited parking is available for $10 per night.

Other neighbourhoods

Alamo Square Inn

719 Scott Street, CA 94117, at Fulton Street, Western Addition (922 2055/fax 931 1304/ www.alamoinn.com). Bus 5, 21, 24. **Rates** single $90-$130; suite $195-$305. **Credit** AmEx, MC, V. **Map** p313 E5.

An immaculately restored Victorian, this is one of the most charming and comfortable guesthouses in the city. Its prime location, on Alamo Square directly across from the famous row of painted Victorians, makes it an ideal San Francisco experience. All rooms are non-smoking, breakfast is included and there is free parking – a rarity in the area.

Hayes Valley Inn

417 Gough Street, CA 94102, at Hayes Street, Hayes Valley (431 9131/www.hayesvalleyinn.com). Bus 21. **Rates** single $58; double $79. **Credit** AmEx, MC, V. **Map** p310 F5.

With its fine restaurants, expensive boutiques and pricey art galleries, Hayes Valley has become the new neighbourhood in which to see and be seen. This pleasant, gay-run pension sits on the edge of the trendy 'hood not far from the newly refurbished City Hall. There's a friendly bar downstairs and parking is available nearby for $12 a day.

Ruth's House

641 8898; call for exact address. **Rates** single/ double $50. **No credit cards**.

A bit off the beaten path, this place consists of one room rented out – to women only – in the owner's Bernal Heights residence. Although far removed from the Castro, Bernal Heights is a lesbian-friendly neighbourhood with a laid-back charm. It borders the Outer Mission, a dyke haven. You'll find that there are plenty of restaurants, coffeeshops and eclectic bars within easy reach.

The **Metro**: a buzzing bar with a great balcony. *See p231.*

Bars

The Castro

Badlands

4121 18th Street, at Castro Street (626 9320). Muni Metro F, K, L, M/bus 24, 33, 35, 37. **Open** 2pm-2am daily. **No credit cards**. **Map** p314 X1.

The ever-popular Badlands used to be a real dive, but since remodelling has turned out to be one of the hottest hangouts in the heart of the Castro. Pop in to check out its plethora of video screens, especially during the weekend rush, when boy-watching is at its peak.

Detour

2348 Market Street, at Noe Street (861 6053). Muni Metro F, K, L, M/bus 24, 37. **Open** 2pm-2am daily. **No credit cards**. **Map** p313 E6.

If you haven't found Mr Right, this is the place to pick up Mr Right Now. Progressive music, a daunting chainlink fence and angst-ridden twenty- and thirtysomething guys with piercings galore make this the place to look rougher than you are, and get away with it. Pool and pinball are sidelines to the ferocious cruising.

Harvey's

500 Castro Street, at 18th Street (431 4278). Muni Metro F, K, L, M/bus 24, 33, 35, 37. **Open** 11am-2am Mon-Fri; 9.30am-2am Sat, Sun. **Credit** AmEx, MC, V. **Map** p314 X1.

Named after slain San Francisco supervisor Harvey Milk, this friendly neighbourhood bar and restaurant also serves as an ersatz community centre for the neighbourhood. If you're around on a Monday night, stop in for the popular trivia contest.

The Metro

3600 16th Street, at Market Street (703 9750). Muni Metro F, K, L, M/bus 24, 37. **Open** 4pm-2am Mon-Thur; 3pm-2am Fri; 1pm-2am Sat, Sun. **No credit cards**. **Map** p310 E6.

Perched above the busy intersection at 16th and Market, the Metro's balcony is a great place to have a drink and watch the crowds heading out for the night. It has friendly bartenders, great Margaritas and a karaoke machine. It can get very crowded on weekend nights; the weekday happy hour (5-7pm) is a more sedate affair.

The Midnight Sun

4067 18th Street, between Castro & Noe Streets (861 4186). Muni Metro F, K, L, M/bus 24, 33, 35, 37. **Open** noon-2am daily. **No credit cards**. **Map** p314 X1.

Guys who like to multi-task will like this place. They can cruise for hours while pretending to watch the music videos and comedy skits playing on the bar's walls. Go for the generous two-for-one cocktail hour (2-7pm weekdays) and come back at the weekend for the wall-to-wall boy fest.

Moby Dick's

4049 18th Street, at Hartford Street (no phone). Muni Metro F, K, L, M/bus 24, 33, 35, 37. **Open** noon-2am daily. **No credit cards**. **Map** p314 X1.

A cross between a neighbourhood pub and a gay bar, Moby Dick's is popular with pool players (although there's only one table) and pinball addicts (four machines at the back). Big windows and a prime Castro location make street cruising easy.

Orbit Room

1900 Market Street, at Laguna Street (252 9525) Muni Metro F, J, K, L, M/bus 6, 7, 66, 71. **Open** 3pm-1am Mon-Thur; 3pm-2am Fri, Sat; noon-midnight Sun. **No credit cards**. **Map** p310 F5.

This high-ceilinged deco retreat is a coffee bar by day and a cocktail bar by night. Its location on the edge of the Castro attracts both straight and queer patrons. If you aren't into the hardcore drinking and dancing scene, the Orbit Room's mellow crowd and tasty cocktails make it a relaxing place to spend an evening out of the fray.

The Mission

Though not strictly a gay bar, **El Rio** (*see p215*) hosts one-of-a-kind salsa parties on Sunday afternoons. The mostly lesbian crowd heads to the back garden, blooming with bougainvillaea and beautiful women.

Esta Noche

3079 16th Street, at Mission Street (861 5757). BART 16th Street/bus 14, 22, 26, 33, 49, 53. **Open** 2pm-2am daily. **No credit cards**. **Map** p310 F6.

The only gay Latino drag bar in the Mission, this is a unique experience, even for San Francisco. In business more than 20 years, the club hosts a lip-synching drag show every night at 11.30pm and three shows on Sundays (7pm, 10pm and midnight). On weekends, the divas spill out on to 16th Street to smoke their cigarettes and cat-fight with the neighbourhood drug pushers.

Lexington Club

3464 19th Street, at Lexington Street (863 2052). Bus 14, 26, 33, 49. **Open** 3pm-2am daily. **No credit cards**. **Map** p314 Y1.

San Francisco's sole grrrl bar, the Lexington is a funky, mellow spot tucked into a corner of the women-friendly Mission. Blood-red walls and wooden church pews give the place a cosily devilish feel. Grab a bar stool and flirt with the cute dyke bartender or put some coins in the jukebox and settle into a corner table to suck face with your sweetie.

SoMa

Hole in the Wall

289 Eighth Street, between Howard & Folsom Streets (431 4695). Bus 12, 19. **Open** noon-2am Mon-Fri; 6am-2am Sat, Sun. **No credit cards**. **Map** p310 G5.

Take Pride

San Francisco is queer any time of year, but to catch the city at its rainbow best, visit in June. You'll know you've come at the right time because, on 1 June, city workers hang hundreds of rainbow flags from lampposts up and down Market Street to signal that the entire month belongs to queers; it's enough to bring a tear to the eye of even the most jaded gay resident. The entire month is spent celebrating the city's gay, lesbian, bisexual and transgendered residents, with hundreds of queer events, from film festivals to art exhibitions.

If you're itching to flaunt your pride, but feeling the pinch of limited holiday time, visit during the last full week of June when things reach fever pitch. The Castro, in particular, is filled with revellers. If you can squeeze only a short fling into your busy travel calendar, make it the last full weekend of the month, when thousands of queers from all over the world swarm the city during this two-day extravaganza.

The Saturday belongs to the women. In 1992, Bay Area dykes decided they needed an oestrogen-only parade, but were unable to cough up the thousands of dollars required for an official city permit. In true radical, feminist form, they marched anyway, keeping the gathering hush-hush. Today, the time and date is advertised several weeks in advance, and the SFPD happily escort thousands of marchers, a handful of whom always go topless, through the congested streets.

Take the morning to sleep in (you'll need it), then don your cutest chick-magnet outfit, grab a picnic blanket and amble to Mission Dolores Park for an afternoon of

This is rapidly becoming one of the most popular hangouts of the Gen-X queers who are turning their backs on the Castro's clone scene. Drop in to compare tattoos with hot boys in torn clothing.

Loading Dock

1525 Mission Street, between 11th Street & South Van Ness Avenue (864 1525/www.loadingdocksf.com). Muni Metro F, J, K, L, M, N/bus 14, 26, 42, 47. **Open** 8pm-2am daily. **No credit cards. Map** p310 F5.

With the taming of the San Francisco Eagle (*see p233*), this is the only true leather/fetish bar left in the city. Its dress policy (leather, latex, Levi's with boots, uniforms) and serious attitude are sure to weed out the fairies and drag queens. A minimum of Levi 501s and black boots is needed to get in.

Lone Star Saloon

1354 Harrison Street, between Ninth & Tenth Streets (863 9999). Bus 19, 27, 42. **Open** noon-2am Mon-Fri; 9am-2am Sat, Sun. **No credit cards. Map** p310 G5.

entertainment, including DJs, comedy, dancers, T-shirt contests and picnicking. Watch the women roll in with the fog. (Don't forget your sweater!) By late afternoon, the park is pulsating with the combined energy of thousands of revved-up grrrl watchers. Eventually, everyone stops cruising and floods into Dolores Street for the half-mile march through the Mission. The final destination is the intersection of Market and Castro, where there's music and dancing till the wee hours of the morning.

Sunday's main event is the morning Pride Parade along Market Street. It's cleaned up its image considerably in the past few years. Sure, a couple of local S&M bars sponsor flogging floats, but they are nearly lost among the stroller-pushing, same-sex parents, docile waves of the Lavender Senior group and handshaking politicians. Luckily, some nudity (mostly bare bums) still pops up, but not enough to shock any TV viewer.

Even toned down, it's not unusual for the Pride Parade to attract up to a million onlookers, so arrive at least two hours early to secure a seat. Otherwise, you won't be able to see the rollerskating drag queens, the dykes on bikes or the flying fairies of the San Francisco cheerleading team. Be forewarned, the parade often lasts a bum-numbing four hours. Afterwards, follow the boisterous crowd to the street party at the Civic Center, where you can buy a rainbow sweater for your dog, nosh on carnival fare and jive to numerous bands. If you still have an ounce of energy left by the end of the day, all the usual queer watering holes host Pride parties.

For more information, call 864 3733 or check www.sfpride.org. *See also p189.*

A biker bear bar, Lone Star is an important centre for San Francisco's leather scene. Country music is prevalent, as the name suggests, but it's interspersed with other styles. If your taste runs toward large men with facial hair, this is the place to come.

Powerhouse

1347 Folsom Street, between Ninth & Tenth Streets (552 8689). Bus 12, 19, 27, 42. **Open** 4pm-2am daily. **No credit cards**. **Map** p310 G5.

Hard and hot, this is one of the most popular (male) gay bars in the city. Underwear night, leather night, uniform and boot night… you get the idea. Complete with sexy bartenders and sexy customers.

San Francisco Eagle

398 12th Street, at Harrison Street (626 0880). Bus 9, 12, 27, 42. **Open** noon-2am daily. **No credit cards**. **Map** p310 G5.

The row of motorcycles parked outside signifies that the Eagle was once the centre of San Francisco's leather community. It's tamed a bit, but the Sunday afternoon beer bash is still legendary for consumption levels and for blatant cruising. On Thursday nights, there are free performances by local bands.

Other neighbourhoods

The Lion Pub

2062 Divisadero Street, at Sacramento Street, Pacific Heights (567 6565). Bus 1, 24. **Open** 3pm-2am daily. **No credit cards**. **Map** p307 D3.

The Lion Pub is not just the only chi-chi (or is it she-she?) gay bar in Pacific Heights, but also the oldest continuously operating gay bar in the city. It's location on the first floor of a renovated Victorian makes it easy to miss. Queers with an eye for moneyed honeys and an appreciation for a Martha Stewart-style ambience should be sure to drop by.

Martuni's

4 Valencia Street, at Market Street, SoMa (241 0205/http://martunis.citysearch.com). Muni F, J, K, L, M, N/bus 6, 7, 26, 66, 71. **Open** 2pm-2am daily. **Credit** MC, V. **Map** p310 F5.

Don't be fooled by the tacky exterior. Inside, Martuni's is classy in a 1980s way, with lots of glass and chrome. And its location is perfect – near but not in the Castro, Hayes Valley and Mission districts – and the ambience warm and welcoming. Great drinks and a phalanx of friendly staff make it worth a visit; the piano jazz (and an occasional drunken torch song) make it worth returning often.

Wild Side West

424 Cortland Avenue, at Wool Street, Bernal Heights (647 3099). Muni Metro J/bus 24. **Open** 1pm-2am daily. **No credit cards**.

This place has been around forever (although it used to be located in North Beach), and it is said that Janis Joplin used to pick up girls at the same wooden bar that now graces its Bernal Heights location. The walls are a shifting art installation, the pool table is cherry red and the clientele mixed. There's also a fabulous jukebox of classics – count on hearing Joplin, Patsy Cline and, of course, Lou Reed's *Walk on the Wild Side*.

Dance clubs

The dance scene is always morphing as new clubs appear and old ones fade away like ageing drag queens. The places listed below are likely to be around for some time, but it's smart to check first: pick up a copy of *Odyssey*, the club scene magazine, to find out the latest on what's in and who's wearing what to go where. Most clubs are restricted to those aged 21 and over, so don't leave your photo ID in your hotel room.

The Castro

The Café

2367 Market Street, at Castro Street (861 3846). Muni Metro F, K, L, M/bus 24, 33, 35, 37. **Open** 2pm-2am Mon-Fri; 12.30pm-2am Sat, Sun. **Admission** free. **No credit cards**. **Map** p314 X1.

Once bitchily dubbed the 'lesbian airport lounge', the Café is now the Castro's most popular dance club – maybe because it's free. It has two bars, a dancefloor, patio, pool table and pinball machine – plus some of the hottest young things (male and female) in town. Expect to queue on Friday and Saturday, and wear something lightweight (and revealing): the temperature soars as the night gets going.

Hip diner **Blue**, in the Castro. *See p235.*

SoMa

Sadly, Club Townsend (*see p217*) – where **Club Universe**, **Club Q** and **Pleasuredome** happen – is due to close in June 2002, so this may mean the end of these club nights, too.

Club Q

Club Townsend, 77 Townsend Street, at Third Street (974 6020/www.clubtownsend.com). Muni Metro N/bus 30, 42, 45, 76. **Open** 9pm-3am 1st Fri of the month. **Admission** $10. **No credit cards**. **Map** p311 J5.

If you've ever dreamed of being surrounded by thousands of gyrating women, this place is for you. One of San Fran's longest-running women's clubs, everyone comes to Club Q to dance, flirt and gawk. Too bad it happens only once a month.

Club Universe

Club Townsend, 177 Townsend Street, at Third Street (974 6020/www.clubuniverse.com). Muni Metro N/bus 30, 42, 45, 76. **Open** 9.30pm-7am Sat. **Admission** $14. **No credit cards**. **Map** p311 J5.

One of SoMa's most popular club nights, Club Universe takes place every Saturday night. The cavernous warehouse is quick to fill with a mixed crowd (queer and straight) dancing to house sounds.

The Endup

401 Sixth Street, at Harrison Street (357 0827/ www.theendup.com). Bus 12, 27, 42. **Open** 10pm-4.30am Thur; 10pm-6am Fri; 6am-4pm, 10pm-4am Sat; 6am-8pm, 8pm-2am Sun. **Admission** $6-$12. **No credit cards**. **Map** p311 H5.

If Saturday night has turned into Sunday morning and you're still going strong, the party continues here, with the T-Dance starting at 6am. Fag Friday is popular, too. If you don't visit the Endup, you can't really say you've seen gay San Francisco.

Kandy Bar

The Endup, 401 Sixth Street, at Harrison Street (357 0827). Bus 12, 27, 42. **Open** 9pm-6am Sat. **Admission** $10. **No credit cards**. **Map** p311 H5.

A new women's dance club, the Kandy Bar is trying to fill the void left when the CoCo Club closed. If you're in town on a Saturday night, join hundreds of other women as they dance and sway to house and hip hop.

Pleasuredome

Club Townsend, 177 Townsend Street, at Third Street (974 6020/www.pleasuredomesf.com). Muni Metro N/bus 30, 42, 45, 76. **Open** 9pm-3.30am Sun. **Admission** $10. **No credit cards**. **Map** p311 J5.

On Sundays you can dance to progressive and hard house till the wee hours at the Pleasuredome, the longest-running men's club in the city. You'll see more bare pecs than you can shake a stick at.

Rawhide II

280 Seventh Street, at Folsom Street (621 1197). Bus 12. **Open** 4pm-2am Mon-Thur; noon-2am Fri-Sun. **Admission** free-$15. **No credit cards**. **Map** p311 G5.

During the week, this SoMa spot is an authentic country and western bar full of almost authentic cowboys and cowgirls. There is western dancing (free) on Tuesdays and Wednesdays from 10.30pm to 2am. On weekends, various clubs play everything from hip hop to techno – call for details.

The Stud

399 Ninth Street, at Harrison Street (863 6623). Bus 19, 27, 42. **Open** 5pm-2am daily. **Admission** free-$15. **No credit cards**. **Map** p310 G5.

A San Francisco institution buried in SoMa (take a cab both ways), the Stud has one of the most varied crowds – from college students out for an exploratory evening to hardcore muscle boys posing in the corners. Trannyshack (Tuesdays, 10pm-3am, $4), is a gender-bender's delight. Every first and third Sunday of the month is Death Rock Booty Call, while every second and fourth Sunday is Planet Big, a club for chubby chasers. If you just want to drop in, Wednesday night is the time to go.

Entertainment

Although the community is still mourning the loss of two queer theatrical institutions – Josie's Cabaret & Juice Joint and the drag show at the Finocchio Club – there is still plenty of fun to be had. Check local alternative weeklies for information on upcoming performances. For other venues, *see chapters* **Film** and **Performing Arts**.

The Castro

Castro Theatre

429 Castro Street, between 17th & 18th Streets (621 6120/www.thecastrotheatre.com). Muni Metro F, K, L, M/bus 24, 33, 35, 37. **Tickets** $7.50; $4.50 concessions. **No credit cards**. **Map** p314 X1.

A true movie palace, the Castro is one of the city's finest rep houses – with a mighty Wurlitzer organ that is played before all features. It really comes into its own for gay and camp classics; until you've seen *Mommie Dearest*, *Valley of the Dolls* or *All About Eve* in a queer-packed theatre with full audience participation, you haven't really lived. *See also p200.*

The Mission

Brava! for Women in the Arts

Theatre Center, 2781 24th Street, between York & Hampshire Streets (641 7657/www.brava.org). Bus 9, 27, 33. **Tickets** free-$50. **Credit** MC, V. **Map** p314 Z2.

Brava specialises in presenting new work by women of colour and lesbians. Founded in 1986, the group has put on more than 1,000 performances for 150,000 people. Its home is in a former vaudeville house.

LunaSea Women's Performance Project

2940 16th Street, between Capp Street & South Van Ness Avenue (863 2989/www.lunasea.org). BART 16th Street/bus 14, 22, 33, 49, 53. **Tickets** $11-$14. **No credit cards**. **Map** p310 F6.

LunaSea came uncomfortably close to losing its home during the Mission's gentrification battle. Luckily, the quirky lesbian performance space pulled through and is back hosting local talent, including an annual Dyke Drama Festival, which runs from late July through mid-August. Shows are usually held every Friday and Saturday.

Theatre Rhinoceros

2926 16th Street, between Mission Street & South Van Ness Avenue (861 5079/www.therhino.org). BART 16th Street/bus 14, 22, 33, 49, 53. **Tickets** $10-$30. **Credit** MC, V. **Map** p310 F6.

This place bills itself as the nation's longest-running gay, lesbian, bisexual and transgendered theatre company. To find out what kinky queer performance is on stage this week, check the website or listings in any of the free weeklies.

Restaurants & cafés

San Francisco doesn't have queer restaurants per se: gay, lesbian and transgendered diners are welcome everywhere. That said, if you're looking to snuggle with your same-sex sweetie, you'll have the best opportunity in the Castro, Mission, Bernal Heights and SoMa. It's common to have a beer in one venue, dinner in another and dessert down the street. *See also chapter* **Restaurants & Cafés**.

The Castro

Bagdad Café

2295 Market Street, at Noe Street (621 4434). Muni Metro F, K, L, M/bus 24, 35, 37. **Open** 24hrs daily. **Main courses** $4-$10. **No credit cards**. **Map** p310 E6.

The Bagdad owes its popularity to its central location and the fact that it's one of very few 24-hour restaurants in the Castro. Comfort food and generous portions make up for the fact that the food is only so-so. Lots of window tables make the restaurant an excellent place to scope out cute guys and gals strutting through the Castro.

Blue

2337 Market Street, at 16th Street (863 2583). Muni Metro F, K, L, M/bus 24, 37. **Open** 11.30am-11pm Mon-Thur; 11.30am-11.30pm Fri; 11am-11.30pm Sat; 11am-10.30pm Sun. **Main courses** $6.50-$18. **Credit** AmEx, MC, V. **Map** p310 E6.

Down-home cooking in a hip diner atmosphere is Blue's attraction. A recent addition to the Castro's culinary scene, it invites you to slide into a smooth, black booth, stare at the beautiful people passing by, and nosh on a plate of gourmet macaroni and cheese, home-made meatloaf, or pork chops. The food's a bit pricey, but you're paying for the atmosphere. Oh, and skip the dinky sidewalk tables – it's a busy street, you don't want to eat on it.

Café Flore

2298 Market Street, at Noe Street (621 8579). Muni F, K, L, M/bus 24, 37. **Open** 7am-11.30pm daily. **Main courses** $5-$12. **No credit cards**. **Map** p310 E6.

Yet another Castro eatery where patrons spend more time studying one another than their plates. It's always crowded with beefcake men (thanks in

Trans San Fran

The States' growing acceptance of gays and lesbians is making it easier than ever to settle down outside the Bay Area with your same-sex sweetie. But for trannies, San Francisco is still one of the few places where support networks, such as healthcare and job protection, are readily available. The City by the Bay is ground zero for trans tolerance. In 1995, the San Francisco Board of Supervisors extended civil rights protections to sexual minorities, including transgendered residents. In 2001, in a groundbreaking move, the City became the first in the country to offer its workers healthcare coverage for hormone treatments and sex-reassignment surgery.

In response to San Francisco's highly sophisticated queer scene, an equally sophisticated – and politically charged – vocabulary has evolved. So if you want to keep your foot out of your mouth, it helps to know the terminology. Here are some common terms:

- **Transgender** An all-encompassing word for people whose outward expression of gender doesn't necessarily match their birth gender. Includes drag queens, drag kings, crossdressers and transsexuals.
- **Transsexual** A person whose birth gender is incongruent with his/her identity. Not all transsexuals have sexual reassignment surgery (SRS). Those who don't are considered 'non-op'; those who do often refer to themselves as 'post-op'.
- **Crossdresser/transvestite** People who regularly wear or eroticise clothing considered inappropriate for their gender.
- **Genderqueer/Polygender/Multigendered/Thirdgendered** Often synonymous, these identities are used by a person who rejects the binary gender system of male and female, preferring instead to create a new, individualised expression of gender, which is often androgynous in appearance.
- **GLBT** An umbrella acronym for the gay, lesbian, bisexual and transgendered community.
- **Intersexed** People born with sex chromosomes, reproductive organs or genitals that aren't considered 'standard' for either men or women.

Trans Action (775 5500 ext 315) is a direct action group that seeks empowerment through political action. If you want to join in the trannie scene, check out **Divas** (1081 Post Street; 928 6006) a three-tier trannie bar in the Tenderloin, with nightly shows, dancing and carousing. Or visit **Trannyshack**, a weekly, gender-bending cabaret at the Stud (*see p234*) and **Pink Pony**, held at the Paradise Lounge (*see p212*) at 9pm on the second Thursday of every month.

part to the gym across the street), and cruising is a serious sport here, so be prepared. The food (salads and burgers) is basic, but the coffee is excellent. Outside tables offer prime viewing, but you'll have to be quick to get one. Dykes tend to steer clear due to the excessive boy energy, so women travellers may want to opt out, too.

Chow

215 Church Street, at Market Street (552 2469). Muni F, J, K, L, M/bus 22. **Open** 11am-11pm Mon-Thur, Sun; 11am-midnight Fri, Sat. **Main courses** $6-$11. **Credit** MC, V. **Map** p310 E6.

Chow is a noisy, friendly place with a menu that ranges from basic pasta to heartier dishes such as grilled fish and roast meat. Arrive early to get a table for dinner, especially on weekends, or you may have to wait up to an hour to be seated.

Firewood Café

4248 18th Street, between Collingwood & Diamond Streets (252 0999). Muni Metro F, K, L, M/ bus 24, 33, 35, 37. **Open** 11am-11pm Mon-Sat; 11am-10pm Sun. **Main courses** $6.50-$13.50. **Credit** MC, V. **Map** p314 X1.

This hip, high-ceilinged bistro has a queue most nights – but don't let that put you off. Order before you sit down from the large overhead menu and your food will be brought to your table shortly. The roast chicken is moist and succulent and the pizzas consistently delicious. Head elsewhere for coffee and dessert, so that someone else can have your table.

Fuzio

469 Castro Street, between Market & 18th Streets (863 1400). Muni Metro F, K, L, M/bus 24, 33, 35, 37. **Open** 11.30am-10pm Mon-Thur, Sun; 11.30am-11pm Fri, Sat. **Main courses** $6.50-$9.50. **Credit** AmEx, Disc, MC, V. **Map** p314 X1.

A loud, energetic eatery smack dab in the middle of the Castro, Fuzio can be a little overwhelming. It's a good thing the food is so good. Asian, Italian and American styles all influence the diverse menu.

Sparky's

242 Church Street, at Market Street (626 8666). Muni Metro F, J, K, L, M/bus 22, 37. **Open** 24hrs daily. **Main courses** $5.50-$10.25. **Credit** DC, Disc, MC, V. **Map** p310 E6.

Sparky's is open 24 hours – head here if you're craving hash browns at 4am. The menu is long and prices relatively low; the food is poorish, but after a long night of drinking and dancing, who cares?

Tin Pan

2251 Market Street, at 16th Street (565 0733). Muni Metro F, K, L, M/bus 24, 37. **Open** 11am-11pm Mon-Thur; 11am-midnight Fri, Sat; 10am-3pm Sun. **Main courses** $9-$10.50. **Credit** MC, V. **Map** p310 E6.
A popular noodle bar. Start off with the fire cracker ahi tuna roll and work your way up to the blazing beef noodle dish. There are also plenty of options for herbivores, including the very veggie noodles, crispy golden tofu and sweet Asian greens.

Yokoso Nippon

314 Church Street, at 15th Street (no phone). Muni Metro F, J, K, L, M/bus 22, 37. **Open** noon-10pm Mon-Sat. **Main courses** $2-$10. **No credit cards**. **Map** p310 E6.
Yokoso Nippon has no sign, no phone and no liquor licence, and business couldn't be better – the place is packed every night of the week. Dubbed 'no name sushi' by locals because of its anonymous façade, this tiny restaurant serves up the tastiest, cheapest sushi in the Castro. Act like a regular and buy a beer at the cornershop, then queue up on the pavement (rickety chairs provided) and prepare to wait.

The Mission

Red Dora's Bearded Lady

485 14th Street, at Guerrero Street (626 2805). Muni Metro F, J, K, L, M/bus 26. **Open** 7am-7pm Mon-Thur, Sun; 7am-10pm Fri, Sat. **Main courses** $2-$6. **No credit cards**. **Map** p310 F6.

Tattoos for you, too, at **Black & Blue**.

The newly remodelled Bearded Lady is a local dyke institution, a café by day and performance space by night. Visit early for an espresso drink and one of the cheapest scrambled egg breakfasts in town. Come back later to see spoken word performances or concerts by local musicians. If the weather's nice, squeeze down the hall and into the tiny garden. If you want to look the part, pop in next door to woman-run tattoo parlour **Black & Blue Tattoo** (626 0770/www.black-n-blue-tattoo.com).

Other neighbourhoods

Da Flora

701 Columbus Avenue, at Filbert Street, North Beach (981 4664). Bus 15, 30, 39/cable car Powell-Mason. **Open** 6.30-9.30pm Tue-Sat. **Main courses** $16-$19. **Credit** MC, V. **Map** p308 G2.
This delightful osteria marks a first for San Francisco: a decent, lesbian- and gay-friendly Italian restaurant in North Beach. The place is tiny, with kitsch decor and excellent food. Try the baccala on fresh polenta, the sardines with balsalmic onions or any number of fresh, seasonal pasta dishes cooked to order. There's great vegetarian fare, too.

Just for You

1453 18th Street, at Connecticut Street, Potrero Hill (647 3033). Bus 22, 53. **Open** 7am-2pm Mon-Fri; 8.30am-3pm Sat, Sun. **Main courses** $3-$9.25. **No credit cards**. **Map** p311 H6.
Its Potrero Hill location is a bit out of the way, but this 15-seat dyke-run restaurant is worth the trip. The house speciality is a New Orleans-style breakfast, complete with superb grits and fluffy pancakes.

Working out

Building muscle and keeping a sleek physique is an art form for queer San Franciscans. The presence of several well equipped gyms in the Castro means that it's not unusual to see throngs of buff boys in tiny shorts and tight tank tops walking to and from their daily workouts. All the neighbourhood gyms are queer-friendly, but the recent influx of straight people seems to have cut down on cruising. Note that Muscle System is for men only.
See also chapter **Sport & Fitness**.

Gold's Gym Castro

2301 Market Street, at Noe Street, Castro (626 4488). Muni Metro F, K, L, M/bus 24, 37. **Open** 5am-midnight Mon-Thur; 7am-9pm Sat; 7am-8pm Sun. **Admission** $15 per day. **Credit** AmEx, MC, V. **Map** p310 E6.

Muscle System

2275 Market Street, between Sanchez & Noe Streets, Castro (863 4700). Muni Metro F, K, L, M/bus 24, 37. **Open** 5am-midnight Mon-Fri; 7am-10pm Sat; 8am-8pm Sun. **Admission** $8 per day; $27 per week. **Credit** MC, V. **Map** p310 E6.

Sport & Fitness

San Franciscans love their sporting life. You can, too.

Spectator sports

On the surface, San Francisco might seem more intellectual than athletic, its citizens apparently more interested in cafés than contests, in shopping than sporting. But come the weekend, many a business person trades in the suit for a sweaty T-shirt, a pair of running shoes or a mountain bike.

Big-money spectator sports are hugely popular, not least because the city's two major teams – the 49ers (football) and the Giants (baseball) – have both proved particularly successful in the past decade. The recent success of the Oakland Raiders (football) and A's (baseball) has also created a great Bay Bridge rivalry. Further afield, the San Jose Sharks hockey team draws large, raucous crowds to the South Bay, while the always struggling Golden State Warriors basketball team continues to attract its own loyal fan base. Also, college athletics can produce as much excitement as pro sports, and spectators keep a watchful eye on their favourite collegiate team.

The biggest news has been the opening of Pacific Bell Park, the new Giants stadium in China Basin. It's part of a trend among US cities trying to revitalise downtrodden districts by injecting them with sports money. In fact, the stadium has given a facelift to Giants baseball. The chill of the old and dilapidated Candlestick Park has been replaced with a vibrant, charming ballpark that's walking distance from downtown San Francisco (*see p241* **Home run**).

INFORMATION

The 'Sporting Green' section of the *San Francisco Chronicle* has a calendar of local pro team engagements and broadcasts. The *Chronicle* maintains a free sports information line (808 5000 ext 6000), as does KRON-TV (837 5000 ext 1710). Sports talk radio on KNBR (680 AM) and KCBS (740 AM) remains a popular, if inefficient, source of information and hyperbole. Newsstands satisfy the nation's passion for sport with weekly and monthly publications; *Sports Illustrated* is one of the best-written. On the web, the Gate's sporting section – www.sfgate.com/sports – is a good bet. For special events or printed schedules, try the Visitor Information Center on Market Street (*see p287*).

TICKETS, BROKERS & SCALPERS

The best place to buy tickets is at the box office of the team you want to see. This direct approach may save effort and, even if you do end up going to a ticket broker, will give you a better idea of prices. You can find ticket brokers in the Yellow Pages under 'Ticket Sales: Entertainment & Sports'. **Tickets.com** (1-510 762 2277/www.tickets.com), has several offices and a telephone switchboard, but expect to be asked to pay 'convenience fees' of $3 and more. If you're stuck with a ticket you can't use, you could sell it for some quick cash. Try **Premier Tickets** (346 7222/www.selltickets.com), or others like **Entertainment Ticketfinder** (1-800 523 1515 ext 3/www.ticketfinder.com), and **Mr Ticket** (1-800 424 7328/www.mrtix.com), any one of which might be able to help you.

Avoid buying tickets via a scalper (tout) – you might end up with a fake ticket or one for the following evening's game, or find yourself with a seat in the third deck where you need binoculars to see the action.

Auto racing

Sears Point Raceway

At the intersection of Highways 37 & 121, Sonoma (1-707 938 8448/www.searspoint.com). US 101 north to Highway 37 exit, then ten miles (16km) to Highway 121. **Open** *Box office* 9am-5pm Mon-Fri & race days. **Tickets** $5-$85. **Credit** Disc, MC, V. Hosting just about every kind of motorised race on land, from nostalgic cars to monster truck derbies, this is a loud slice of Americana. It's only an hour away from San Francisco, but there's no public transport, so you'll need a car.

Baseball

The Bay Area supports two major league baseball teams: the **San Francisco Giants** and the **Oakland Athletics**. As with many West Coast clubs, both have a prior East Coast history (the Giants in New York and the As in Philadelphia). But they're well loved local franchises: the As won three World Series in a row in the 1970s, and the Giants currently have Barry Bonds on their roster, three-time winner of the Most Valuable Player award. The two teams rarely play each other (the Giants are in the National League and the As are in the American); though there was a moment when they might have: they were to play one another during the 1989 World Series, but were rudely interrupted by the Loma Prieta earthquake.

The Giants' new stadium, Pacific Bell Park, is a great success and a fab place to watch a game, but bring a jacket to combat the chilly wind. The baseball season runs from April to September. Tickets are usually available at the ballparks on the day of the game.

Oakland Athletics

Oakland-Alameda County Coliseum Complex/ Network Associates Coliseum, 7000 Coliseum Way, Nimitz Freeway, at Hegenberger Road, Oakland (1-510 568 5600/www.oaklandathletics.com). BART Coliseum. **Open** *Box office* 9am-6pm Mon-Fri; 10am-4pm Sat. **Tickets** $6-$28. **Credit** AmEx, Disc, MC, V.

San Francisco Giants

Pacific Bell Park, 24 Willie Mays Plaza, at Third & King Streets, South Beach (972 2000/www.sfgiants.com). Muni N/bus 15, 30, 42, 45. **Open** *Box office* 8.30am-5.30pm Mon-Fri; 2hrs before game time on weekends. **Tickets** $9-$38. **Credit** Disc, MC, V. **Map** p311 J5.

Basketball

From fast, trash-talking pick-up games in the panhandle of Golden Gate Park to college and professional squads, you'll have plenty of good company if you want to watch roundball while in San Francisco. The **Golden State Warriors** represent the area in the National Basketball Association (NBA), and play from November to May, while the **Sacramento Monarchs**, a new Women's National Basketball Association (WNBA) team, play from June to September.

As for college basketball, Stanford women's Cardinal basketball team is impressive, while the men's team has also been a hot ticket item recently (for details, check www.gostanford.com or call 1-800 782 6367). The Bears from the University of California at Berkeley (1-800 462 3277/www.calbears.com) are inconsistent, but still have a strong fan base and draw large and rowdy crowds. The college ball season runs from December to March.

Aspiring to NBA heights yourself? If you're up to it, there's no shortage of options: in addition to Golden Gate Park action, pick-up games at James Lick Middle School, at the corner of Clipper and Castro Streets in Noe Valley, can be highly competitive. Of course, you might want to practice first.

Golden State Warriors

The Arena in Oakland, 7000 Coliseum Way, just behind the Coliseum, Oakland (1-510 986 2222/ www.warriors.com). BART Coliseum. **Open** *Box office* 10am-6pm Mon-Fri; 10am-4pm Sat. **Tickets** from $13.75. **Credit** AmEx, Disc, MC, V.

Sacramento Monarchs

Arco Arena, 1 Sports Parkway, at Arco Arena Boulevard, Sacramento (1-916 928 3650/ www.wnba.com/monarchs). **Open** *Box office* 10am-6pm Mon-Sat. **Tickets** $8-$27.50. **Credit** AmEx, Disc, MC, V.
No public transport from San Francisco.

Football

Autumn Sunday and Monday nights in the Bay Area could leave any visitor convinced that football is the new religion. The return of the **Oakland Raiders** in 1995 brought the league's most notorious winners of yesteryear back into the fold, while the **San Francisco 49ers** continue among the National Football League's elite. The season runs through the winter, from September to January, but be warned: it gets very cold and getting tickets is almost impossible.

At the college level, there's even more football action for fans of collegiate gridiron. Despite being consistently inconsistent, the Bears football team (www.calbears.com/ 1-800 462 3277) from the UC Berkeley gets tremendous support. Huge rivalry at the annual Cal-Stanford intercollegiate 'big game' football contest generates enormous press interest, though the Stanford Cardinal

The **San Francisco 49ers**. *See p240.*

(1-800 782 6367www.gostanford. com) have given the Bears a pounding for most of the past decade. The season runs from Labor Day to Thanksgiving.

Oh, did you mean soccer? It's not very big in the Bay Area (or the US, in general), although that may change thanks to the new, popular local women's pro soccer team, the San Jose-based **CyberRays**, which includes many of the players who helped the US win the women's World Cup in 1999. They've also just won the first-ever Women's United Soccer Association championship. They play from April to August; check www.bayareacyber rays.com or call 1-408 260 3900 for tickets and more information.

Oakland Raiders

Oakland-Alameda County Coliseum Complex/ Network Associates Coliseum, 7000 Coliseum Way, Nimitz Freeway, at Hegenberger Road, Oakland (1-510 762 2277/www.raiders.com). BART Coliseum. **Open** *Box office* 9am-6pm Mon-Fri; 10am-4pm Sat; 2hrs before game time on Sun. **Tickets** from $51. **Credit** AmEx, Disc, MC, V.

San Francisco 49ers

3Com Park, Giants Drive, at Gilman Avenue, Bayview (656 4900/www.sf49ers.com). Special event Muni bus 47X at Van Ness Avenue & California Street, 28X at Funston & California Streets. **Open** *Box office* 9am-5pm Mon-Fri & for weekend games. **Tickets** from $50. **Credit** V.
Buy tickets in person at the stadium (cash or Visa only), or by phone from TicketMaster (421 8497) from the second-to-last week in July. Bring warm clothing.

Horse-racing

Bay Meadows Racecourse

2600 S Delaware Street, San Mateo (1-650 574 7223/www.baymeadows.com). CalTrain to Bay Meadows or Hillsdale. **Open** *Box office* 9.30am-7pm Wed-Sat. **Tickets** $3-$15. **Credit** AmEx, Disc, MC, V.

Golden Gate Fields

1100 Eastshore Highway, Albany (1-510 559 7300/ www.ggfields.com). BART North Berkeley, then AC Transit shuttle bus on race days. **Open** *Box office* 9.30am-7pm Mon-Fri; 9am-5pm Sat. **Tickets** $2.50-$15. **Credit** MC, V.

Ice hockey

Spectacularly fast-paced and still known for its violence, ice hockey has nevertheless found broad support in the Bay Area. The **San Jose Sharks** may not be the most accomplished team in the National Hockey League, but they are one of the leading merchandisers – their teal and black colours are worn all over. And their fans are rabid: Sharks games come complete with *Jaws* music and a signature cheer, the 'Shark bite'. The season runs from October to May.

San Jose Sharks

Compaq Center at San Jose, West Santa Clara & Autumn Streets, San Jose (tickets 1-800 888 2736/ www.sjsharks.com). CalTrain to San Jose Diridon/ Cahill Street. **Open** *Box office* 9.30am-5.30pm Mon-Fri; 9.30am-1pm Sat. **Tickets** $16-$85. **Credit** AmEx, MC, V.

Active sports/fitness

To claim that many people enjoy the Bay Area's easy access to outdoor adventures is an understatement comparable to 'San Francisco sees its share of fog'. Like arcane healing arts and body piercing, participatory sports come with the territory.

For runners, excellent paths traverse the Marina, Golden Gate Park and the perimeter of Lake Merced, and if you're into aerobics or cross-training, there's a health club on nearly every corner. The city also has numerous superb bike and skate shops, as well as many more shops that sell surfing, camping and rollerblading equipment. New bike paths and a gloriously car-free Golden Gate Park on Sundays are further draws.

Some aquatic sports are better served by other parts of the region: the best resources for kayaking and scuba diving can be found in nearby Bay Area cities, and for skiing and snowboarding, head to the Sierras.

When hiring equipment, photo ID or a credit card is usually required for a deposit.

INFORMATION

The *San Francisco Chronicle* has listings and information on outdoor activities. Every Thursday, it publishes 'Outdoors', a mini-section within the 'Sporting Green' pages devoted to athletic activity. Also useful is *CitySports*, a free national magazine available in many gyms and sports shops.

Bowling

Virtual Bowling at Sony Metreon Center

101 Fourth Street, at Mission Street, SoMa (369 6000/www.metreon.com). BART Powell/ Muni Metro J, K, L, M, N/bus 7, 14, 30, 31, 38, 45, 76. **Open** 10am-10pm daily. **Credit** AmEx, DC, Disc, MC, V. **Map** p311 H4.
A virtual bowling game in the Sony Metreon arcade. Silly as it may sound, it's actually a lot of fun. Ten bucks buys 1,300 credits; 600 credits buys one game.

Presidio Bowling Center

Building 93, Montgomery Street & Moraga Avenue, Presidio (561 2695/www.hwm64.tripod.com/ presidiobowl). Bus 29. **Open** 9am-1am Mon-Thur, Sun; 9am-2am Fri, Sat. **Rates** $2.50-$3.75 per game; $2.50 shoe rental. **No credit cards**. **Map** p306 B2.

Home run

If baseball stadiums were ranked on the Richter scale, San Francisco would have barely registered a quiver before the new millennium. The sun never seemed to shine on the Giants' former home at Candlestick Park (now called 3Com), infamous for its freezing foggy weather and no-frills seating. Thankfully, that's all in the past now, after the privately financed Pacific Bell Park opened to eager Giants fans just in time for the 2000 season.

At a price tag of $357 million, the China Basin stadium didn't come cheap; in comparison, the 1960 'Stick cost a mere $24.6 million. But now slugger Barry Bonds can hit his endless stream of home runs in a setting worthy of his talents, and a deep homer to right field just might make a splash in the bay. Devoted fans, in turn, have been rewarded with a brand-new park that is old-fashioned in style and somehow manages to feel intimate while making room for more than 40,000 spectators (Candlestick has a capacity of 63,000). It's also in a much more convenient location, near downtown.

The setting is stunning – the stadium is perched on the very edge of the bay – seating and sightlines are good, there's a play area for kids, good public transport connections (Muni Metro N runs past the front door) and plenty of parking. In a nod to tradition, a bronze statue of Giants legend Willie Mays greets visitors at the park's entrance. Inside, however, the pungent smell of garlic fries replaces the traditional ballpark aroma of sizzling hot dogs. Next door is top-notch American restaurant Twenty-Four.

So even if you don't know Barry Bonds from Barry Manilow, an evening at Pac Bell Park is a lovely way to experience America's favourite pastime. If you can't get to a game, tours of the stadium ($10; $8 concessions; $5 under-13s) are held daily from 10am to 2pm, baseball schedule permitting. For more details, call 972 2000 or check the team's website, www.sfgiants.com.

Yerba Buena Bowling Center

750 Folsom Street, between Third & Fourth Streets, SoMa (820 3541/www.yerbabuena.org). Bus 12, 15, 30, 45, 76. **Open** 10am-10pm Mon-Thur, Sun; 10am-midnight Fri, Sat. **Rates** $4 per game; $2.50 concessions; $2.50 shoe rental. **Credit** MC, V. **Map** p311 H4.

Golf

Golden Gate Park Course

John F Kennedy Drive, at 47th Avenue, Golden Gate Park (751 8987). Bus 5, 18, 31, 38. **Open** 6am-8pm daily. **Rates** $10 Mon-Fri; $13 Sat, Sun. **No credit cards**.
A nine-hole course sits at the far west end of the park, with a pro shop, café and cart rental.

Harding Park & Golf Course

Harding Road & Skyline Boulevard, Lake Merced (664 4690). Bus 18, 29. **Open** 6.30am-7pm daily. **Rates** $26 Mon-Fri; $31 Sat, Sun. **No credit cards**.
City-owned and operated, the 18-hole Harding course lies by Lake Merced, below the Sunset District, and has a shop and a small bar and café.

Lincoln Park Golf Course

34th Avenue & Clement Street, Lincoln Park (221 9911). Bus 1, 2, 18, 38. **Open** sunrise-sunset daily. **Rates** $9-$23 Mon-Fri; $10-$27 Sat, Sun. **Credit** MC, V.
Lincoln Park, above the Outer Richmond District, is one of the most photographed courses in the States, with a famous 17th-hole view of the Golden Gate Bridge. There's also a practice area, putting green, rental shop, pro shop, bar and refreshments. Prices drop as the light fades.

Mission Bay Golf Center

1200 Sixth Street, at Channel Street, China Basin (431 7888). Bus 15. **Open** 7am-11pm daily. **Rates** $8 for a basket of balls. **Credit** MC, V. **Map** p310 H5.
With a unique view of the freeway, East Bay and the South San Francisco hills, Mission Bay Golf Center offers a 300-yard, two-tiered driving range, as well as a restaurant and discount golf shop. There is no golf course.

Presidio Golf Course

300 Finley Road, at Arguello Gate, Presidio (561 4653/www.presidiogolf.com). Bus 28. **Open** 6am-dusk daily. **Rates** $57-$87. **Credit** AmEx, MC. **Map** p306 B3.
Built in 1885, former presidents Teddy Roosevelt and Dwight D Eisenhower played this 18-hole course when it was strictly military only; it opened to the public in 1995.

Gyms

Just as San Franciscans savour their corner cafés and bars, they love their corner gyms; every neighbourhood seems to have at least one, some have many. Just a few are listed here.

Embarcadero YMCA

169 Steuart Street, at Mission Street, SoMa (957 9622/www.ymcasf.org). BART Embarcadero/Muni Metro F, J, K, L, M, N/bus 2, 6, 7, 9, 14, 21, 31, 32, 66, 71. **Open** 5.30am-10pm Mon-Fri; 8am-8pm Sat; 9am-6pm Sun. **Rates** $15 day pass. **Credit** AmEx, MC, V. **Map** p309 J3.
One of several YMCAs in the city, the Embarcadero serves downtown San Francisco from a waterfront location. A day pass covers aerobics classes, free weights, Cybex and Nautilus machines, racquetball and basketball courts and the 25m pool.

Koret Health & Recreation Center

2130 Fulton Street, at Parker Street, USF, Richmond District (422 6821/www.usfca.edu/koret). Bus 31. **Open** (to non-USF students) 6am-2pm Mon-Fri; 8am-2pm Sat, Sun. **Rates** $10 day pass; $5 with any student ID. **Credit** MC, V. **Map** p313 C5.
This health club is part of the University of San Francisco, but non-students can use the facilities until 2pm. There's an Olympic-sized pool, a gym and six racquetball courts (bring your own equipment).

24 Hour Fitness Center

1200 Van Ness Avenue, at Post Street, Tenderloin (776 2200/www.24hourfitness.com). Bus 2, 3, 4, 38, 42, 47, 49. **Open** 24hrs daily. **Rates** $15 day pass. **Credit** AmEx, MC, V. **Map** p308 F3.
You'll find free weights, plus cardiovascular and weight machines. Most aerobics and fitness classes are held around the workday schedule: in the early morning, at lunchtime or in the early evening. This place has several branches around San Francisco; most are open 24 hours.
Branches: call 1-800 249 6756 for details.

Hiking

Trails with rewarding views and long paths through spectacular redwood groves await your wandering feet just 30 minutes from downtown San Francisco. For a short, introductory hike, try the **Morning Sun Trail**, which climbs from a parking lot at the Spencer Avenue exit off US 101 north, just above the Golden Gate Bridge. Look east over the Bay, Angel Island and the urban sprawl or west to the Pacific. A good day-long hike is found on the **Dipsea Trail** from Mill Valley to Stinson Beach; you can reach Mill Valley on Golden Gate Transit bus 10. The **Bootjack Trail**, which leads to the summit of Mount Tamalpais, is also popular. You can get trail information for Mount Tam from the Pan Toll Ranger Station (388 2070).

For more information, contact the Bay Area **Sierra Club** (1-510 848 0800/www.sanfranciscobay.sierraclub.org), located in Berkeley, to find out about upcoming hikes and walks. The city's hills should take care of all your quadriceptic exercise needs.

Horse riding

Unless you're a mounted police officer, horse riding in San Francisco is limited to Golden Gate Park. Out of town, horses and tours are available from the **Sea Horse & Friendly Acres Ranch** (1-650 726 8550) near Half Moon Bay or the **Chanslor Guest Ranch & Stables** (1-707 875 2721) next to Bodega Bay.

Golden Gate Park Stables

John F Kennedy Drive, at 36th Avenue, Golden Gate Park (668 7360/www.extendinc.com/ggps). Bus 5. **Open** 9am-5pm daily. **Rates** private lesson $33-$50; trail ride $30. **Credit** MC, V.

Golden Gate Park Stables, at the west end of the park, offers everything from pony rides for small kids to advanced equestrian courses for experienced cowboys and girls.

Paragliding

Not to be confused with parasailing, paragliding involves no boat and allows you to fly after less than a day's instruction. The equipment itself weighs only 10lb (4.5kg) and can do just about anything a hang-glider does, except turn upside-down. Still, those with a fear of heights probably need not apply.

Glidell Paragliding

555 Bryant Street, between University & Hamilton Avenues, Palo Alto (1-650 799 8812/www.glidell.com). CalTrain to Palo Alto. **Open** weekends by appointment. **Rates** tandem flight $150; full training packages from $1,500. **Credit** MC, V.

Since 1990, this outfit has offered novice, intermediate and advanced programmes to would-be flyers who long to float in the great blue yonder. Palo Alto is 32 miles (51km) from San Francisco.

Pool & billards

Pool tables are as common in bars as sofas are in living rooms, but the city also has several purpose-designed pool halls specifically for the experts among us, who are satisfied with nothing less. These are just a few of them.

Chalkers

1 Rincon Center, at Spear & Mission Streets, SoMa (512 0450/www.chalkers.com). BART Embarcadero/Muni Metro F, J, K, L, M, N/bus 2, 6, 7, 9, 14, 21, 31, 32, 66, 71. **Open** 11.30am-1am Mon-Wed; 11.30am-2am Thur-Sat; 3-11pm Sun. **Rates** $5-$14 per hr Mon-Thur, Sun; $7-$15 per hr Fri, Sat. **Credit** AmEx, DC, MC, V. **Map** p309 J3.

Chalkers has 30 cherrywood tables, a bar and restaurant, and occasionally invites trick-shot experts and pros to dazzle the lunch crowd. Families are allowed from 2-7pm at the weekend. If you prefer it busy, Friday night happy hour is definitely the time to go.

The Great Entertainer

975 Bryant Street, between Seventh & Eighth Streets, SoMa (861 8833/http://tge.com). Bus 19, 27, 42. **Open** 11am-2am daily. **Rates** $8-$11 per hr. **Credit** MC, V. **Map** p311 G5.

San Francisco's largest indoor gaming facility, with masses of entertainment options, including 40 billiard tables, shuffleboard, snooker, table tennis, darts, foosball and a video arcade.

Hollywood Billiards

61 Golden Gate Avenue, at Market Street, Tenderloin (252 9643). BART Powell/Muni Metro F, J, K, L, M, N/bus 5, 6, 7, 9, 14, 21, 66, 71. **Open** 3pm-2am Mon-Thur, Sun; 3pm-3am Fri, Sat. **Rates** $4-$12 per hr. **Credit** AmEx, Disc, MC, V. **Map** p310 G4.

A dodgy neighbourhood and infamous 'ladies' nights' make Hollywood Billiards a pool room of note. The rates are decent, but the equipment isn't of the highest calibre.

Rock climbing

Devoted Bay Area climbers travel to Lake Tahoe and Mount Shasta for extreme fun, but **Yosemite** (*see p269*) is the California climbing mecca; beginners and intermediates can get lessons year-round. Alternatively, you can try this indoor climbing centre.

Mission Cliffs

2295 Harrison Street, at 19th Street, Mission (550 0515/www.mission-cliffs.com). Bus 12, 27. **Open** 6.30am-10pm Mon-Fri; 10am-6pm Sat, Sun. **Rates** $10-$20 per day. **Credit** AmEx, Disc, MC, V. **Map** p314 Z1.

To enter Mission Cliffs is to penetrate a 12,000sq ft (3,800sq m) kingdom that melts the boundary of 'urban' and 'wilderness' and distills it into a highly polished jungle gym. An X sports HQ. Lessons for beginners start at noon on weekdays and run every 90 minutes until 7.30pm.

Rollerblading

These days, Rollerblading (aka inline skating) is a mainstream pursuit. For either the novice or veteran, Sunday skating in Golden Gate Park is hard to beat: the beach at one end, plenty of sunny meadows along the way, and no auto traffic. A mix of rollerblading and break dancing provides entertainment near Sixth Avenue on John F Kennedy Drive. You can rent equipment at **Golden Gate Park Skate & Bike** (*see p244* **On your bike**) or the place listed below.

Skates on Haight

1818 Haight Street, at Stanyan Street, Haight-Ashbury (752 8375/www.skates.com). Bus 7, 33, 37, 66, 71. **Open** 11am-7pm Mon-Fri; 10am-6pm Sat, Sun. **Rates** $6 per hr; $24 per day. **Credit** AmEx, Disc, MC, V. **Map** p313 C6.

On your bike

Despite the daunting hills, which require mega-legs, you can go just about anywhere in San Francisco by bicycle. It's a great way to explore Golden Gate Park, especially on Sundays when auto traffic is banned, while day trips to Angel Island, over the Golden Gate Bridge to Marin, or to Tilden Park in Berkeley offer an excellent combination of exercise and sightseeing. And, of course, the mountain bike was born on Mount Tamalpais, an hour (by bike) north of San Francisco. Popular trails include Bolinas Ridge and Railroad Grade; for specific trail information, call the Golden Gate National Recreation Area Visitor Center (331 1540) or the Pan Toll Ranger Station (388 2070). Cycle route maps (which helpfully show the gradient of streets) are available in most bike shops and some bookshops, and Ray Hosler's book Bay Area Bike Rides ($12.95) is a good investment.

This being San Francisco, there's a counter-culture element, too. Riders use bikes as a way to advocate a reduction in traffic and smog in a crowded city. In 1992, Critical Mass rides took off, with hordes of cyclists taking to the streets during rush hour on the last Friday of every month. The rides snowballed into a major event, and later a political issue when more than 5,000 bikers clogged city streets during a July 1997 ride. Although Critical Mass has been fairly quiet since then, the bikers haven't disappeared from the city's consciousness: a recent protest against dog-leash laws was named Critical Mutt.

Thanks to such Bay Area bike activism, you can take bikes on BART free of charge, except during commuter hours (7am-9am, 4pm-6pm weekdays). CalTrain has limited bike space in designated cars on a first come, first served basis, and some Muni buses should be able to handle bikes by the time you read this. Currently, however, the best way to travel with a bike on public transport is by ferry.

If you want to rent a bicycle, try the places below. For more on getting around the city by bike, *see p276*.

Golden Gate Park Skate & Bike

3038 Fulton Street, between Sixth & Seventh Avenues, Richmond District (668 1117). Bus 5, 21, 44. **Open** 10am-6pm Mon Fri; 10am-7pm Sat; 9am-7pm Sun. **Rates** $5 per hr; $25 per day. **Credit** MC, V. **Map** p312 B5.
This shop on the northern edge of Golden Gate Park rents bikes for all budgets.

This place was at least partly responsible for inspiring the worldwide skateboard craze back in the 1970s, and it now rents and sells inline skates, rollerskates and snowboards. Worth a visit.
Branch: 1219 Polk Street, at Sutter Street, Tenderloin (1-800 554 1235).

Running

After an extensive three-year restoration, Crissy Field has become the destination *du jour* for local runners. One of the most popular routes starts at Fort Mason and follows the path past the Marina Green along the Golden Gate Promenade; the stunning route extends all the way to Fort Point, beneath the Golden Gate Bridge (*see also p94* **The city on foot: Along the waterfront**). With the recent expansion of the Embarcadero, though, many runners prefer the lovely view it offers of the Bay Bridge and piers. Of course, Golden Gate Park remains one of the best places to run, bike or rollerblade, and the track at Kezar Stadium, on the eastern edge of the park, is a perfect spot for running sprints.

You can also rent rollerskates and rollerblades; rates include a helmet and knee and elbow pads.

New World Sports

1365 Columbus Avenue, at Beach Street, Fisherman's Wharf (776 7801). Muni Metro F/bus 30, 32/cable car Powell-Hyde. **Open** 8am-9pm daily. **Rates** $5 per hr; $25 per day. **Credit** MC, V. **Map** p308 F1.
From here you can cycle across the Golden Gate Bridge to Sausalito and then return by ferry. A helmet and lock are included in the price; bring a passport or credit card for a deposit. Electric and tandem bikes are also available. You can also rent bikes from nearby Blazing Saddles (1095 Columbus Avenue, at Francisco Street; 202 8888/www.blazingsaddles.com).

Solano Avenue Cyclery

1554 Solano Avenue, at Peralta Avenue, Albany (1-510 524 1094/www.solanoavenuecyclery.com). BART El Cerrito Plaza, then AC Transit bus 43/AC Transit bus G. **Open** 11am-7pm Mon-Fri; 10am-6pm Sat; noon-5pm Sun. **Rates** $25 per day. **Credit** Disc, MC, V.
If you want to ride the East Bay trails, pop into this shop near Berkeley for mountain bike rentals and knowledgeable advice on gear and routes. Ask about the Nimitz Bike Path.

Surrey Bikes & Blades

50 Stow Lake Drive, at John F Kennedy & Crossover Drives, Golden Gate Park (668 6699/www.bikeroute.com). Bus 5, 28, 29. **Open** 9am-7pm daily. **Rates** $8 per hr; $25 per day. **No credit cards**. **Map** p312 A5.
An unbeatable location makes this the rental shop of choice for a day of bicycling in Golden Gate Park.

If you want to some company on your run, the **San Francisco Dolphin South End Runners**, founded in 1966, have almost weekly group runs at 9.30am every Sunday at various locations. Non-members pay $5. Check out the club's online schedule (www.dserunners.com) for event details or call the hotline (978 0837).

Annual races include the **Bay to Breakers Foot Race** (*see p189*), a 12-kilometre (7½-mile) run from downtown to Ocean Beach, which is held at the end of May, and the **San Francisco Marathon** (*see p190*) in mid-July.

Sailing, kayaking & rowing

The Bay Area and Pacific coastline features numerous boating, sailing and kayaking outfits that offer equipment, lessons and trips. Rowing opportunities range from single sculls to whale boat racing: for details, call **Open Water Rowing** (332 1091/www.owrc.com) in Sausalito or **South End Rowing Club** (776 7372/www.south-end.org) in San Francisco.
If that all sounds a bit ambitious, head to Stow Lake in Golden Gate Park, where you can rent a paddleboat or rowing boat.

Cal Adventures

UC Aquatic Center, Berkeley Marina, Berkeley (1-510 642 4000/www.strawberry.org/caladv). BART Berkeley, then AC Transit bus 51. **Open** 10am-6pm Mon-Fri. **Rates** kayaks $13 per hr; sailboats $15 per hr. **Credit** Disc, MC, V.
Berkeley's Cal Adventures hires out Coronado 15-footers for sporty sailing on the South Sailing Basin. To lease one without recognised certification, you must spend $60 to sail with an instructor who will confirm your ability.

California Canoe & Kayak

409 Water Street, Jack London Square, at Franklin Street, Oakland (1-510 893 7833/www.calkayak.com). BART 12th Street. **Open** 10am-7pm Mon-Thur, Sun; 9am-8pm Fri, Sat. **Credit** AmEx, MC, V.
Oakland is home to one of the best shops for hiring and buying kayaks and sea-going gear of all sorts. A sea canoe costs $25 for one hour; lessons and day trips are available on the nearby Oakland Estuary.

Sailing Education Adventures

Fort Mason Center, Laguna & Buchanan Streets, Marina (775 8779/www.sailsea.org). Bus 28. **Open** 8am-10pm daily. **No credit cards**. **Map** p308 E2.
This non-profit charity based in the Marina offers instruction for all levels of sailing skill, and a summer sailing camp for children. You must be a SEA member before you can rent boats.

Sea Trek

Schoonmaker Point Marina, at Libertyship Way, Sausalito (488 1000/www.seatrekkayak.com). Blue & Gold Fleet ferry from Pier 41, Fisherman's Wharf or Golden Gate ferry from Ferry Building, Embarcadero/bus Golden Gate Transit 10, 50. **Open** 8.30am-5pm daily. **Credit** AmEx, Disc, MC, V.
On the Sausalito waterfront, Sea Trek runs summer camps for kids, books expeditions to Alaska and Baja and joins forces with environmentalists to preserve waterways. Beginners' classes in bay kayaking, guided tours ($65 for three hours) and moonlight paddles are also available.

Spinnaker Sailing

Pier 40, Embarcadero, at Townsend Street, South Beach (543 7333/www.spinnaker-sailing.com). Muni Metro N/bus 42. **Open** 9am-5.30pm daily. **Credit** AmEx, MC, V. **Map** p311 J4.

Professional instruction, 22-80ft (7-24m) boats and a great location off the Embarcadero. Boat rental costs $100-$420 per day.

Scuba diving

Divers should be warned that the closest diving locale is **Monterey Bay** (*see p265*), several hours south of San Francisco.

Bamboo Reef Scuba Diving

584 Fourth Street, at Brannan Street, SoMa (362 6694/www.bambooreef.com). Bus 15, 30, 42, 45, 76. **Open** 10am-7pm Mon-Fri; 9am-5.30pm Sat. **Rates** scuba rental $60 per day. **Credit** AmEx, Disc, MC, V. **Map** p311 H5.
In addition to organising trips to Monterey Bay, this shop sells all the necessary gear, and offers rentals, repairs and training.
Branch: 614 Lighthouse Avenue, at Hoffman Avenue, Monterey (1-831 372 1685).

Cal Dive & Travel

1750 Sixth Street, between Delaware & Virginia Streets, Berkeley (1-510 524 3248/www.caldive.net). BART North Berkeley. **Open** noon-6pm Tue-Fri; 10am-2pm Sat. **Rates** scuba rental $60 per day. **Credit** AmEx, MC, V.
This Berkeley-based outfit arranges trips to Monterey Bay for the best scuba diving on the California coast. It also offers beginners' classes.

Skateboarding

No one needs to tell a skate rat where to go. If you're one, you'll find Justin Herman Plaza, a Safeway parking lot or any of a number of downtown concrete ramps on your own. If you're a wannabe skate rat, spend time and trouble to protect yourself against sprains and scrapes by investing in a helmet, knee and elbow pads and gloves, then you're ready for a little learning and a lot of fun.

DLX

1831 Market Street, between Guerrero & Pearl Streets, Mission (626 5588/www.dlxsf.com). Muni Metro F, J, K, L, M, N/bus 26. **Open** noon-8pm Mon-Sat; noon-7pm Sun. **Credit** AmEx, MC, V. **Map** p310 F5.
The skateboard merchandiser formerly known as 'Deluxe' is the mother of them all. Make the trip for a complete line of clothes, boards, accessories and stickers. For an idea of what's on offer, check out the shop's slick website. No rentals.

FTC Skateboarding

622 Shrader Street, between Haight & Waller Streets, Haight-Ashbury (386 6693/www.ftcskate.com). Bus 7, 33, 37, 43, 66, 71. **Open** 10am-6pm Tue-Sun. **Credit** AmEx, Disc, MC, V. **Map** p313 C6.
Located on the western edge of the Haight-Ashbury, FTC is one of many small shops in the area dedicated to baiting your riskier senses. Leave your fear at the door and bring your credit card. No rentals.

Skiing & snowboarding

Although a day trip is possible, it would surely be better to give yourself at least a weekend for skiing in the Sierras. For leading resorts around **Lake Tahoe** (which is about 3½ hours from San Francisco by car), *see p267*. During the season (usually the end of November to early April), most ski shops will have calendars of events and ads for package deals. **Skates on Haight** (*see p243*) also rents snowboards. Check www.goski.com/ for listings of all the major Californian resorts.

FTC Ski & Sports

1360 Bush Street, between Polk & Larkin Streets, Nob Hill (673 8363). Bus 2, 3, 4. **Open** 10am-7pm Mon-Fri; 10am-5pm Sat, Sun. **Rates** ski/snowboard rental from $35 per weekend. **Credit** AmEx, MC, V. **Map** p308 F3.
Extensive selection of skis, snowboards and all the accoutrements. If you're interested in buying, they have great deals on used equipment.

SFO Snowboarding

618 Shrader Street, at Haight Street, Haight-Ashbury (386 1666/www.sfosnow.com). Bus 7, 33, 37, 43, 66, 71. **Open** 10am-6pm Tue-Sun. **Rates** full gear rental $25 per day. **Credit** AmEx, Disc, MC, V. **Map** p313 C6.
Boards, boots, bindings and more for rent, plus an array of cold-weather clothes and gear for sale.

Sullivan's Ski World

5323 Geary Boulevard, between 17th & 18th Avenues, Richmond District (751 3515). Bus 38. **Open** 10am-6.30pm Mon-Fri; 10am-6pm Sat; 10am-5pm Sun. **Credit** AmEx, Disc, MC, V. **Map** p312 A4.
This Richmond District shop, in business for more than 50 years, has competitive prices on everything you'll need for a ski trip to Tahoe. No rentals as yet, but there are plans for them in the near future.

Surfing

Right. Here's the facts: you have to be an experienced surfer to tackle the waves around San Francisco. Do not choose to learn out there on your own. Currents are strong, sharks are frequently spotted and temperatures are icy enough to put an amateur in the hospital. So, whether you're a pro headed to Ocean Beach or Fort Point, or a newbie boogie-boarding the black sand beaches in Marin County, you'll need the appropriate gear. For most surfers, a wetsuit is a must (in fact, lifeguards will haul you out of the water at Ocean Beach if you haven't got one). About an hour north of San Francisco on Highway 1, **Stinson Beach** (*see p254*) has gentler waves and fewer surfers, while the real pros head to Steamer Lane in **Santa Cruz** (*see p263*), two hours south.

Wise Surfboards

800 Great Highway, between Fulton & Balboa Streets, Ocean Beach (750 9473). Bus 5, 18, 31, 38. **Open** 9am-6pm Mon-Fri; 9am-5pm Sat, Sun. **Credit** AmEx, MC, V.

This new shop right on Ocean Beach (just south of the Cliff House) is sure to put Wise at the top of local surfboard outlets. The shop sells boards, wetsuits and accessories, and maintains a 24-hour information line (273 1618) for surf conditions. Mermen, San Francisco's favourite psychedelic-surf band, live just down the street. No rentals.

Swimming

The ocean is usually too chilly and turbulent for a proper swim, but don't despair: there are plenty of swimming pools in San Francisco, including ones at the **Embarcadero YMCA** and the **Koret Center** (*for both, see p242*). The City of San Francisco maintains eight municipal pools, each with separate times for open swimming. The most central swimming pools can be found at **Hamilton Recreation Center** (Geary Boulevard and Steiner Street; 292 2001) and the **North Beach Pool** (Lombard and Mason Streets; 274 0200); adult admission is $3. For your nearest pool, check the White Pages under 'City Government Offices: Recreation and Parks'. Some health and fitness clubs also have pools. For information on the best beaches in the city, *see p100* **On the beach**.

Tennis

Indoor tennis in San Francisco is almost exclusively a members-only affair, but that's just fine, because this is California, so much of the best play can be found outdoors in the sunshine. **Golden Gate Park** has several courts (at the Stanyan Street entrance; 753 7101), and **Dolores Park** in the Mission is always busy. Both are open from sunrise to sunset and both are free. For a complete list of tennis (and other public recreation) facilities, see the 'Neighbourhood Parks' section of the Pacific Bell Yellow Pages.

Volleyball

Although it is more popular in Southern California, volleyball is also played in San Francisco. Experienced players can get in contact with the **San Francisco Volleyball Association** (931 6385), which organises leagues. Otherwise, look for pick-up action at the north end of Marina Green on weekend mornings. Games at Lindley Meadow in Golden Gate Park are usually private. For further details, check www.volleyball.org/bay_area.

Whale watching

Whale watching happens during the migration season, between November and April, and occurs primarily just north and south of San Francisco (in Mendocino or Monterey, for example). On occasion, however, it can be as easy as taking a pair of binoculars to the shore and having a look. One recommended location is the tip of **Point Reyes** (*see p255*), an hour's drive north of San Francisco. What you might see are glorious humpback and blue whales, as well as other wildlife like sea lions.

Oceanic Society Expeditions

Fort Mason Center, Laguna & Beach Streets, Marina (474 3385/www.oceanic-society.org). Bus 22, 28, 42, 47, 49. **Open** 9am-5pm Mon-Fri. **Rates** $28-$67. **Credit** AmEx, MC, V. **Map** p308 E1.

This is a cut above most tourist trips as the staff are experts in natural history and marine life. On weekends between June and November, a full-day trip heads 26 miles (42km) west to the Farallon Islands, home of the largest sea bird rookery in the continental US, searching along the way for humpback

Escape from Alcatraz

Al Capone, Machine Gun Kelly and other dangerous criminals all dreamed of swimming away from Alcatraz, but the icy waters and strong currents, not to mention a maximum-security prison, would have stopped them cold. These days, you still have to be a bit crazy to take the plunge, but if you sign up with the thousand-plus athletes who sign up for the gruelling Escape from Alcatraz triathlon in June, you'll have your chance.

However, you need to understand what you're getting yourself into: a 12-mile (2.4-kilometre) swim from the island across San Francisco Bay; an 18-mile (29-kilometre) bike ride out to the Great Highway and through Golden Gate Park; and a hilly 8-mile (13-kilometre) run, which ends at the Marina Green. Competitors have been as old as 66, so don't try to use that recent birthday as an excuse to join the spectators at the Marina Green finish line. You can also watch wetsuit-clad swimmers at Aquatic Park as they drag themselves out of the water after the first leg of the event. For more information, check out www.tricalifornia.com.

Have a good stretch at **Mindful Body**.

and blue whales, seals and sea lions. Between December and mid-May, there are 6½-hour gray whale cruises, leaving from San Francisco.

Windsurfing

This is a windsurfing centre: the Bay Area boasts no less than 32 launch sites for windsurfing (aka sailboarding), including Coyote Point, 3Com Park and local favourite Crissy Field – the site of several international competitions, including windsurfing's World Cup. If you do give it a shot, be sure to wear a wetsuit. If you're not eager to battle the cold water, Crissy Field and Fort Point are scenic spots to observe braver souls in action.

City Front Boardsports

2936 Lyon Street, between Lombard & Greenwich Streets, Cow Hollow (929 7873/www.boardsports.com). Bus 28, 41, 43, 45. **Open** 11am-7pm Mon-Fri; 10am-6pm Sat, Sun. **Credit** AmEx, Disc, MC, V. **Map** p307 D2.

With shops in Berkeley and Marin, City Front is the place to go if you're already a seasoned windsurfer with your own wetsuit and harness. You can rent a complete sailing rig for $40-$70.

Branches: **Berkeley Boardsports** 1601 University Avenue, at California Street, Berkeley (1-510 527 7873); **Boardsports Marin** 446 West Francisco Boulevard, near Rice Drive, San Rafael (1-800 262-7379).

SF School of Windsurfing

Candlestick State Recreation Area, 100-199 Candlestick Park, Bayview (1-707 265 8819/www.sfwindsurf.com). Bus 29. **Open** 9am-3pm Sat, Sun. **Credit** MC, V.

Offers lessons for all levels on Candlestick Beach, one of the premier training grounds in the US. A 3-hour beginners' course costs $100. Gear rental costs $10-$30 per hour or $40-$70 per day.

Yoga

Yoga is now so mainstream that every local gym has a yoga class on its schedule. But in San Francisco, where yoga has a huge following, there's no need to suffer through a mediocre lesson when countless yoga schools offer a wonderful variety of styles for students of all levels. For more information about Bay Area yoga, call ahead to the **Yoga Society of SF** (285 5537).

BKS Iyengar Yoga School of San Francisco

321 Divisadero Street, between Oak & Page Streets, Haight-Ashbury (626 8441/www.yogaschool.com). Bus 6, 7, 24, 66, 71. **Open** 9am-8pm Mon-Fri; 8am-3pm Sat; 8am-6.30pm Sun. **Rates** $10-$17 per class. **No credit cards**. **Map** p313 D/E5.

Located upstairs in a landmark building, this school is rigorous and serious. Offerings include classes for back care and a number of classes for beginners, as well as other levels.

Mindful Body

2876 California Street, between Divisadero & Broderick Streets, Pacific Heights (931 2639/www.themindfulbody.com). Bus 1, 24. **Open** 9am-9pm Mon-Fri; 9am-7pm Sat, Sun. **Rates** $12 per class. **Credit** MC, V. **Map** p313 D4.

Popular classes here include Astanga, which builds endurance, strength and flexibility, and power yoga, which is a more athletic yoga for greater strength and stamina building.

Yoga College of India

Second floor, 910 Columbus Avenue, at Lombard Street, Russian Hill (346 5400). Bus 15, 30, 39/cable car Powell-Mason. **Open** classes for visitors 9am, 4.30pm, 6.30pm Mon-Fri; 9am, 10.45am, 4.30pm Sat; 9am, 5pm Sun. **Rates** $10 per class. **Credit** MC, V. **Map** p308 G2.

The San Francisco branch of the Yoga College of India teaches the techniques of Bikram Choudhury, a yogi who brought his brand of the practice to the US in 1971. A popular new trend is 'hot yoga', practised in a sweltering, heated room. Bring a towel.

Yoga Tree

780 Stanyan Street, at Waller Street, Haight-Ashbury (387 4707/www.yogatreesf.com). Bus 7, 33, 37, 43, 66, 71. **Open** 7am-9pm Mon-Fri; 9am-8pm Sat, Sun. **Rates** $12 per class. **Credit** AmEx, MC, V. **Map** p313 C6.

You'll find numerous classes and styles here, including Iyengar. The room is heated, but it's not nearly as hot as a Bikram yoga class.

Branch: 1234 Valencia Street, at 23rd Street, Mission (647 9707).

Trips Out of Town

Introduction 250
Heading North 251
Wine Country 256
Heading South 262
Heading East 267

Features

The best day trips 250
Gentle giants 252
Buying wine 259
Mud, mud, glorious mud 260

Introduction

California is packed with natural and man-made wonders. Off you go.

If you're planning to explore the countryside around San Francisco, you're faced with an enormous number of choices. On even a short visit to the greater Bay Area, most people leave at least a bit of their heart behind, and for good reason. The region holds an embarrassment of travel riches, including empty beaches, windswept islands, craggy mountains, vast parks, gourmet restaurants and gorgeous wineries. All those options, though, often mean that the biggest problem faced is simply finding a way to fit it all in. Whether you head north or south along the Pacific coast or east inland, each area has its own unique identity and array of offerings.

Close to San Francisco are sleepy fishing villages, wildlife refuges, towering redwood forests and picturesque vineyards and spas. Further afield lie the dramatic slopes of the Sierra Nevada mountain range, the celebrated golf courses of the Monterey peninsula, Lake Tahoe's exhilarating ski slopes and the soaring peaks of Yosemite National Park.

For more information, or to plan your trip in advance, contact the relevant local tourist information centres listed in this chapter; they're generally very well organised, have good websites and will send out a visitor pack on request. All phone numbers are listed as if dialled from San Francisco. For a map of the Bay Area and surrounding coast, *see p302*.

TRANSPORT

Most destinations listed in this chapter are within easy reach of San Francisco and can be covered as a day trip or overnight stay. However, many of the areas are ill-served by public transport. If you can't hire a car, try the BART rail service, which connects San Francisco with the East Bay (through an underground tunnel) or Golden Gate Transit, which has a regular schedule of bus services to and from many Marin County destinations. It also has less frequent services to Sonoma County. You can also use Greyhound buses, Amtrak (although the nearest train station is in Oakland), a charter tour or one of the ferries that run frequently to the North Bay during the day. But if your budget permits it, rent a car; it's the best way to explore the area and, after all, driving is the California way. For more information on public transport providers and car rental, *see p272* **Getting Around**.

The best Day trips

In less than a couple of hours from San Francisco you can be lying on a beach, climbing a mountain, playing golf, soaking in a spa, skiing or wine tasting in the grape capital of California. The following are our recommended day trips from the city.

Feeling romantic

Take your time meandering through **Napa Valley** or **Sonoma Valley** and then stop off at one of the spas for a couple treatment. *See p256.*

Feeling adventurous

Drive to **Lake Tahoe** (*see p267*) for a half-day on the slopes in winter or a boat trip in summer.

Feeling energetic

Park at **Stinson Beach** (*see p254*) and hike up until you're tired. Finish off with a dip in the cold Pacific before returning home.

Feeling lazy

Pack a picnic and drive south down **Highway 1**, stopping off at one of the many beaches and simply vegging out. *See p262.*

Feeling urban overload

Take a ferry trip across the bay for lunch in **Sausalito** or **Larkspur** (*see p251*), or refresh yourself with a walk among the coastal redwoods in **Muir Woods** (*pictured; see p254*).

Heading North

Coastal villages and wildlife refuges await across the Golden Gate Bridge.

Marin County extends from the Golden Gate Bridge north, along the coast to Bodega Bay and inland to Petaluma. With some of the most gorgeous scenery in Northern California and a warm climate all year round, it lends itself to outdoor life. It's one of the state's richest counties – with the most SUVs per capita – as well as one of the most laid-back, embodying a uniquely Californian combination of yuppie wealth and hippie ideals.

The county is bisected north to south by US 101, which runs the length of California. It's the most popular (and fastest) route, but not very scenic. The other main road is Highway 1 (also known as the Coast or Shoreline Highway), which is much prettier. To see the lie of the land from above, try an excursion with **San Francisco Seaplane Tours** (*see p53*), which offers a unique view of the bridges, islands, peninsulas and waterfronts of the Bay Area. All the places listed below are within an hour's journey – by car or ferry – from San Francisco, so make an ideal day trip.

Sausalito, Tiburon, Mill Valley & Larkspur

Stop at **Vista Point**, the first exit north of the Golden Gate Bridge, for a spectacular view (if there's no fog) of San Francisco. Just under the northern foot of the bridge is the **Bay Area Discovery Museum,** an imaginative museum for kids (*see p198* **Out of town**). Further north, the **Marin Headlands** offer some of the best hiking and biking – mountain or otherwise – in the Bay Area. You can see the city to the east and the wide-open ocean to the west – it's all strangely familiar to most Americans from the innumerable car ads that use San Francisco and the Golden Gate as a backdrop. World War II battlements can still be seen dotted about the hilltops. The **Marine Mammal Center** (289 7325/www.tmmc.org) is a sanctuary where sick or injured seals and sea lions are fed and nursed back to health by young volunteers.

Sailing boats docked along the **Sausalito** waterfront.

Gentle giants

The tallest known tree in the world, the California coastal redwood (Sequoia sempervirens) can grow as tall as 360 feet (110 metres) – the height of a 35-storey building. Its trunk can be as wide as 22 feet (seven metres). And the average age of the trees in a redwood forest is 500-700 years old, though many are much older. These are no more just trees than a dinosaur was just an animal.

In order to grow, the coastal redwood requires a perfect environment: 60-140 inches (152-355mm) of rain each year, regular fog to create an atmosphere of constant damp, and a moderate climate. Such a climate was once very common in the US and Canada, as the distribution of fossilised redwoods show. The trees live for as long as they do in part because they have unusually thick bark (which shields them from forest fires) and a high tannin content (which protects them from insects).

Still, the trees are vulnerable to man. The changing environment, along with massive logging, mean that only a small percentage of redwoods still exist. The US National Park Service estimates that 96 per cent of the original old-growth coastal redwoods have been logged. Now, they grow only in a narrow strip along the Pacific Coast, from just below San Francisco into southern Oregon. (The coastal redwood's fatter and shorter cousin, Sequoiadendron gigantea, grows inland in California, in the Sierra Nevada mountains.)

Near San Francisco, the best places to see redwoods for yourself is at Muir Woods (see p254) just over the Golden Gate Bridge, or Big Basin State Park and Henry Cowell Redwoods State Park (see p264) down the coast near Santa Cruz

Sausalito, the southernmost Marin County town, may not be as quaint as its reputation suggests, but it is undeniably picturesque, with a maze of tiny streets stretching from the shoreline up to US 101 far above. The best way to get to Sausalito is by ferry; it takes about 30 minutes to cross the bay from San Francisco and it's one of the best cheap thrills in the Bay Area. If the weather is good, sit on the top deck for unsurpassed views of the San Francisco waterfront, the Golden Gate Bridge and Alcatraz. The boat docks in downtown Sausalito, close to shops and restaurants. Originally a fishing village, Sausalito has a population of artists and writers that helps support the coffee-shops, waterfront restaurants and galleries for which it is best known. Along North Bridgeway, opposite Spring Street, is the turn-off for the town's only true sight: the **Bay Model Visitor Center** (*see p111*), a scale model of the San Francisco and San Pablo Bays. Charming bungalows, well-kept gardens and bougainvillaea-covered fences characterise the area, which is best appreciated on foot. Most visitors come here for a relaxing afternoon of shopping, or for dinner.

If you didn't come over by ferry, you can always explore the bay from the deck of the **Hawaiian Chieftain** (331 3214/www.hawaiianchieftain.com), which is docked in Sausalito. A replica of a late 18th-century sailing ship, it offers brunch, sunset and adventure sails. On some trips you get to help with the sails; great fun, if exhausting.

Across Richardson Bay from Sausalito – and also accessible by ferry from San Francisco – **Tiburon** has a tiny, old-fashioned downtown. As with Sausalito, there are no real sights; it's simply a lovely place to wander and the views of the city skyline are postcard-perfect. The best thing to do is to have brunch/lunch (which often turns into dinner) at one of the restaurants on Ark Row, which all have enormous sundecks that overlook the harbour. If you're driving, park your car in any one of the parking lots on Tiburon Boulevard and continue the rest of the way on foot; if you're biking, the bike path brings you directly into town.

Marin lacks a real centre: **San Rafael** is its biggest town, but it's also the least interesting unless you're shopping for a BMW or a hot tub. If you have the time, it's worth making a short detour to see 'Big Pink', the grand **Marin Civic Center** designed by Frank Lloyd Wright (North San Pedro Road, at US 101, San Rafael, 499 6646/www.marincenter.org).

For a little diversity, head to **Mill Valley**, the quintessential Marin town, home to dozens of charming boutiques, antique shops and restaurants. **Larkspur** is also charming but less visited (even though it's also on a ferry route). As well as the **Larkspur Landing** shopping centre and a first-rate pub, the **Marin Brewing Company** (1809 Larkspur Landing Circle, 461 4677/www.marinbrewing.com), it also has an old-fashioned downtown, located on the other side of the freeway away from the ferry landing. It's got a cinema, several good restaurants (including the Lark Creek Inn) and a few small shops.

Nearby is notorious **San Quentin Prison**, which is often mistaken by out-of-towners for a holiday resort. The prison museum (454 8808; admission $2) inside the main gate is open daily except Sunday.

Where to eat

In Sausalito, you'll find plenty of places to eat on the main drag, Bridgeway. **Guernica** (No.2009, 332 1512, closed Mon, main courses $14-$21) has been serving unpretentious French-Basque cuisine for more than 25 years; some say it has the best paella in the Bay Area. The early-bird specials and set meals are a huge bargain at **Christophe** (No.1919, 332 9244, closed Mon, main courses $17-$23). **Ondine** (No.558, 331 1133, closed lunch, main courses $28-$30) was originally a yacht club, and is a dramatic space with a circular entrance and large picture windows. It offers a fusion of Eastern and Western cuisine.

In Tiburon, most people come to **Guaymas** (5 Main Street, 435 6300, main courses $10-$25) to eat lunch, drink Margaritas and take in the view. Recommended dishes include the sole ceviche, home-made tamales and seafood platters. Excellent for Sunday brunch, **Sam's Anchor Café** (27 Main Street, 435 4527, main courses $10-$18) invites you to sit on the waterfront deck, order a Bloody Mary and watch the boats go by. Locals say there's a trap door inside the place that was used to access boats bringing in whisky during Prohibition.

In Larkspur, the **Lark Creek Inn** (234 Magnolia Avenue, 924 7766/www.larkcreek.com, closed lunch Sat, main courses $17-$32) is located in a grove of redwoods, in a charming Victorian house with giant sloping skylights. Try baked flatbread with duck confit, pan-roasted halibut with chanterelle and lobster mushrooms, and home-made butterscotch pudding for dessert. **Left Bank** (507 Magnolia Avenue, 927 3331, main courses $15-$24) feels like a Parisian bistro. The polenta terrine with root vegetables is especially good, as are the grilled lamb chops with flageolet beans.

In Mill Valley, the **Buckeye Roadhouse** (15 Shoreline Highway, 331 2600/www.buckeyeroadhouse.com, main courses $15-$20) offers all-American food in a setting reminiscent of a ski lodge. Specialities include baby-back ribs, fluffy horseradish mashed potatoes and huckleberry ice-cream sundae. **La Ginestra** (127 Throckmorton Avenue, 388 0224, closed Mon, main courses $10-$16) is an old-time favourite; the linguine with clams, garlic and white wine and the home-made cheese and spinach ravioli are recommended.

Getting there

By car

Take US 101 across the Golden Gate Bridge. For Sausalito (8 miles/13km from San Francisco), take the Alexander Avenue or Spencer Avenue exit. For Mill Valley (10 miles/16km) and Larkspur, take the East Blithedale exit; you can also reach Larkspur by the Paradise Drive or Lucky Drive exits. For Tiburon, turn off at the same point as to Mill Valley, but to the right, on Highway 131.

By bus

Golden Gate Transit buses link San Francisco to Marin County. For Sausalito, take bus 20 or 50. For Tiburon or Mill Valley, take bus 10. For Larkspur, take bus 20. Buses leave from the Transbay Terminal at Mission and First Streets.

By ferry

Golden Gate Transit ferries run from the Ferry Building on the Embarcadero to Sausalito and Larkspur (on separate schedules) daily. There are more ferries during the week than at weekends. Blue & Gold Fleet ferries run from Pier 41 in Fisherman's Wharf to Sausalito and from the Ferry Building to Tiburon.

Tourist information

Mill Valley Chamber of Commerce

85 Throckmorton Avenue, Mill Valley (388 9700/ www.millvalley.org). **Open** 10am-4pm Mon, Tue, Thur, Fri.

Sausalito Chamber of Commerce & Visitor Center

780 Bridgeway, at Bay Street, Sausalito (332 0505/ www.sausalito.net). **Open** 11.30am-4pm Tue-Sun.

Mount Tamalpais & Muir Woods

Visible from as far away as Sonoma, Mount Tamalpais soars to nearly 2,600 feet (800 metres), but its dramatic rise is so steep that it seems far taller. It dominates and defines recreational life in southern and central Marin County. **Mount Tamalpais State Park** (388 2070) covers some 6,200 acres on the mountain's western and southern slopes. The roads that snake over Mount Tam, though steep, are great for bicycling; indeed, the mountain bike was invented here. To fully appreciate the area's majestic beauty, pack a picnic lunch and head over in the late afternoon to watch the sunset.

Within the park is **Muir Woods National Monument** (admission $2), named after 19th-century naturalist John Muir and containing majestic groves of towering coastal redwoods, many between 500 and 800 years old. Their shade creates an excellent environment for hiking on several miles of trails; there is also a short path that is accessible to the disabled. Redwood Creek is lined with oak, madrone and buckeye trees, wild flowers (even in winter), ferns and mushrooms. Deer, chipmunks and a variety of birds wander peacefully in the verdant spaces beneath the redwoods. The visitor centre at the entrance has a gift shop and toilets, and also offers walks led by park rangers. Muir Woods gets very crowded at the weekend; visit on a weekday morning or late afternoon to discover it at its most peaceful.

While in the area, take a spin on the **Panoramic Highway**, a beautiful two-lane spur with lots of hairpin bends that leads through sun-dappled forests to the coast at **Stinson Beach**. Popular with surfers and sun worshippers, this is the closest you'll get in these parts to the Californian beach life of legend. If you want to ride the waves, you can rent open-top kayaks at **Off the Beach Boats** (868 9445).

Just over three miles north of Stinson Beach – just before you reach Point Reyes National Seashore – is the **Audubon Canyon Ranch** (4900 Highway 1, 868 9244/www.egret.org), a large preserve on the shore of the Bolinas Lagoon. Headquartered in a 19th-century white frame house, the ranch houses environmental displays and, in an old milking barn at the back, a natural history bookshop. The Alice Kent Trail leads to an observation point for viewing egrets and great blue herons nesting in the vicinity. The ranch is open at weekends from mid-March to mid-July.

Where to eat

The delightful, Elizabethan-style **Pelican Inn** (10 Pacific Way, at Highway 1, 383 6000/ www.pelicaninn.com, closed dinner Mon Nov-Apr, main courses $14-$26) could have been transplanted straight from Surrey. The food's not fantastic, but if you decide to stay for dinner, ask for a table near the fire. The rooms (from $184) are quaint, with canopied beds, balconies and private bathrooms.

Tourist information

Muir Woods Visitor Center

388 2595/www.visitmuirwoods.com. **Open** *Summer* 9am-6pm daily. *Winter* 9am-4.30pm daily.

Waterfall on **Mount Tam**.

On the edge: the lighthouse at **Point Reyes**.

Point Reyes National Seashore

Thanks to state and federal legislation, a large percentage of Marin County is open space. North of Stinson Beach along Highway 1 at Olema is the turn-off for the most famous parcel of land in these parts: the **Point Reyes National Seashore**, 72,000 acres of wilderness, beach and ranchland from which one can still see San Francisco. This vast, protected peninsula is an unforgettable wildlife refuge with sea mammals and waterfowl, miles of unspoiled beaches, waterfalls and campsites. At Olema, turn off to the **Bear Valley Visitor Center**, then head west along Sir Francis Drake Boulevard to Drakes Beach. The road ends at the Point Reyes Lighthouse, located at the tip of the peninsula and the perfect spot for whale-watching (the season is December to late March/early April). A number of trails start here, including the popular Chimney Rock.

The small, picturesque town of **Inverness** is the last settlement before entering the mass of Point Reyes. Many of the homes are still owned by the families that built them, and over the years the town has drawn its share of artists and academics. It's a good option for restaurants and accommodation.

Swimmers should bypass the beaches of this windswept coast and head along Highway 1 to **Tamales Bay**. Tiny beaches such as Heart's Desire offer mild tides and water that locals swear is 'really not *that* cold'. If you want to get to grips with the natural history of the area, **Blue Waters Kayaking** (on Sir Francis Drake Boulevard, beyond Inverness; 669 2600) offers half- or full-day paddle trips, and full-moonlight tours on Saturday nights, as well as basic kayak hire. Prices start at $25 and the company provides all the gear (including wetsuits); all you need are the biceps.

Outside Point Reyes on the other side of Highway 1, hikers flock to **Mount Wittenberg**, criss-crossed by miles of hiking and riding trails. Here chaparral, wildlife and fog are all facts of life. There are excellent vantage points throughout for sighting migrating Pacific gray whales during winter, as they pass on their round trip from Alaska to Mexico. The **Miwok Indian Village** is nearby.

Where to eat

Vladimir's Czech Restaurant in Inverness (12785 Sir Francis Drake Boulevard, 669 1021, closed lunch & Mon, main courses around $20) is one of a kind. Try the roast duckling, wiener schnitzel and the delicious apple strudel. Also on Sir Francis Drake Boulevard, **Johnson's Oyster Company** (No.17171, 669 1149, closed Mon) hasn't changed after almost 50 years in business: same location, same family, same buildings, even the same Japanese method of farming oysters in clusters. If you plan to buy oysters, bring a cooler.

Manka's Inverness Lodge (30 Calendar Way, 669 1034/www.mankas.com, closed lunch, closed dinner Tue & Wed, prix fixe $32-$68) was built as a hunting and fishing lodge. It's a small compound of eight rooms, one suite, two cabins and a dramatic 1911 boat-house built over the water, with intimate boatman's quarters above. Rooms cost $185-$515. The food is the best in Inverness; owner/chef Margaret Grade is known for her fresh seasonal cuisine and her fire-roasted local game.

Tourist information

Bear Valley Visitor Center

Point Reyes National Seashore (464 5100/ www.nps.gov/pore). **Open** 9am-5pm Mon-Fri; 8am-5pm Sat, Sun.

Getting there

By car

Take US 101 across the Golden Gate Bridge, then turn on to to Highway 1. Muir Woods is 15 miles (24km) from San Francisco. It's another 17 miles (27km) to Point Reyes.

By bus

There is no direct public transport to Muir Woods or Point Reyes. Bus 63 (Sat & Sun only) takes you to the trailheads at the weekend and also stops at Stinson Beach and Audobon Canyon Ranch.

Wine Country

An hour's drive from San Francisco lie the lush vineyards of Napa and Sonoma.

For all of its own undeniable urban appeal, some would argue that San Francisco's best feature is its proximity to wine country (the general region encompassing Napa and Sonoma Counties). It's an easy trip, as the wine regions are almost a suburb: jump in your car in San Fran, and you can be lounging in a tasting room sipping some of the region's best vintages in an hour. The area is understandably popular for romantic weekend retreats, but avoid, if you can, going during the height of the summer when temperatures soar and tourists arrive in droves. October is also very busy. Off-season discounts are available in lush autumn and floral spring, when the area is more peaceful.

This hilly region is essentially divided by the Napa and Sonoma Valleys. Of the two, Napa is the largest and most famous, and subsequently the most popular. Sonoma is smaller and slower and retains much of its bucolic charm. Most settlers in the area originally came from France, Italy or Germany, bringing with them their family traditions, foodstuffs and wine-making methods. A European sensibility still predominates. Most wineries are open daily and charge a nominal amount (a few are free) for tastings of several different wines and often a tour, too. For hints on what to take home with you, *see p259* **Buying wine**. Several San Francisco operators run wine country tours: for more information, contact the **San Francisco Visitor Information Center** (*see p287*) or a local tourist office. A useful online resource is www.winecountryguide.com.

Whether or not you're a wine buff, this is beautiful countryside. A lovely way to see it is from above in a hot-air balloon, a thrilling pre-dawn experience that demands several rolls of film and a mastery of any fear of heights. Numerous companies offer balloon flights, among them **Above the Wine Country Ballooning** (1-888 238 6359/1-707 829 9850/www.balloontours.com), **Bonaventura Balloon Company** (1-800 359 6272/www.bonaventuraballoons.com) and **Balloon Aviation** (1-800 367 6272/www.nvaloft.com).

Sonoma Valley

The Sonoma Valley runs about 23 miles (37 kilometres) north from San Pablo Bay; Highway 12 goes through the centre of the valley. Besides the wine itself, one of the principal attractions of a Sonoma wine tour is driving along winding roads with sweetly rural views of vineyards and farms. The **Sonoma County Wineries Association** (1-800 939 7666/1-707 586 3795) organises winery tours and daily tastings. It's located near US 101 in Rohnert Park.

The small town of Sonoma was founded in 1823 as the Mission San Francisco Solano, the last and northernmost of the Franciscan missions. It developed around a Mexican-style plaza and, in 1846, was where the Bear Flag was raised to proclaim the independent Republic of California. The plaza is now flanked by adobe and western-style, false-fronted buildings, with restaurants, bookshops and plenty of places to grab picnic supplies, including a cheese shop, a bakery and a wine tasting room offering samples and sales of the local vintages. Shady trees and picnic tables dot the square, and on Tuesdays in summer it's the site of an excellent farmer's market. Pick up a leaflet on walking tours of the downtown area from the visitor bureau.

Local landmarks include the whitewashed adobe **Sonoma Mission** on the edge of the main plaza (1-707 938 9560/www.iktome.com/svvb/mission.html), which served as a Mexican outpost in the 17th century. Now restored, it houses a variety of relics. **Sonoma State Historic Park** includes the mission building and the town hall, as well as the Toscano Hotel and the Sonoma barracks, where troops under Mexican General Mariano G Vallejo were once stationed. About a mile south of the plaza, **Sonoma Train Town** (Broadway, at Highway 12, 1-707 938 3912/www.traintown.com), is a good stop for families. Take a 20-minute ride on a miniature steam train past scale models of buildings, a petting zoo and a couple of waterfalls.

The history of Sonoma is intertwined with that of the Californian wine industry, which first began here. Hungarian count Agoston Haraszthy planted the first European grapevines in Sonoma in the 1850s at **Buena Vista Historical Winery** (18000 Old Winery Road, 1-800 926 1266/www.buenavistawinery.com). It's open 10am-5pm daily. Of the 35 wineries in the Sonoma Valley, several are near Sonoma's central plaza. One that also makes a great picnic choice is **Bartholomew Park**

Wine country: pretty as a picture – and ideal for a day trip from the city.

Winery (1000 Vineyard Lane, 1-707 935 9511/ www.bartholomewparkwinery.com, 10.30am-4pm daily, $3), which has a museum and a relief map dedicated to the appellation. Or you can head to the **Wine Exchange of Sonoma** (452 First Street East, 1-800 938 1794, open 10am-6pm Mon-Sat, 11am-6pm Sun), which offers up to 18 Californian and European wines as well as a half-dozen beers for daily tasting.

North of Sonoma are the small settlements of Glen Ellen and Kenwood. Jack London – adventurer, farmer and one of the most prolific authors of his day – made his home in Glen Ellen. A mansion full of memories and the charred remains of Wolf House make **Jack London Historic State Park** (2400 London Ranch Road, Glen Ellen, 1-707 938 5216/www.parks.sonoma.net) one of the valley's top attractions. It's a nice place to stroll in the shade among oak and madrone trees. Near the entrance to the park, the **Sonoma Cattle Company** (1-707 996 8566) leads guided tours of the area on horseback.

One of the most popular stops in Kenwood is the **Kenwood Winery** (9592 Sonoma Highway, 1-707 833 5891/www.kenwood vineyards.com, open 10am-4.30pm daily). This friendly, classic Sonoma winery is known for making wine with grapes grown on Jack London's former ranch. The original barn, now the tasting room and shop, dates from the pre-Prohibition days of the early 20th century. Tastings are free.

The **Carneros** region, straddling southern Sonoma and Napa, is the area's only true appellation. Wineries here take advantage of the cooler climate to produce excellent Pinot Noirs and sparkling wines. The **Gloria Ferrer Champagne Caves** (23555 Highway 121, 1-707 996 7256/www.gloriaferrer.com) are worth a visit to glimpse the intricacies of the age-old process of making sparkling wine. They're open 10.30am-5.30pm daily; tastings cost $4-$7. The area is also home to the **Viansa Winery & Italian Marketplace** (25200 Arnold Road, on Highway 121, Sonoma, 1-800 995 4740/1-707 935 4700). Sam Sebastiani, a scion of one of the state's oldest wine families, and his wife Vicki have built a Tuscan-style winery on a knoll facing the Sonoma Valley. Their tasting room (open 9.30am-5.30pm daily) also sells Italian foods, and the trellis-topped picnic tables outside overlook the valley.

Where to eat

The **General's Daughter** (400 West Spain Street, 1-707 938 4004, main courses $15-$26, closed first two weeks of Jan) is based in a beautifully restored Victorian building, and is an excellent place for brunch. **The Girl & the Fig** (1-707 938 3634, main courses $16-$21) was an institution in Glen Ellen before it moved to a corner of Sonoma Plaza, bringing with it its delightful French-style country menu. For a spicy change of pace, try **Maya** (1-707 935 3500, main courses $12-$20, closed lunch Mon & Sun) a casual spot on the square serving great Mexican fare and as many kinds of tequila as there are wines in the area. If you're in the mood for a picnic, pick up cheese and crackers at the **Sonoma Cheese Factory** (1-707 996 1000), also located on the central plaza.

Where to stay

Two good options on Sonoma Plaza are the **Sonoma Hotel** (1-707 996 2996, rates $95-$245) and the luxurious **El Dorado Inn** (1-707 996 3030, rates $205-$245). Just a few blocks

Napa wineries include **Niebaum-Coppola**...

south is the recently opened **Lodge at Sonoma** (1325 Broadway Avenue, 1-707 935 6600) with comfy, cottage-style rooms ($199-$279) and the latest in spa amenities. If you're looking for peace and quiet, the **Gaige House Inn** in Glen Ellen (13540 Arnold Drive, 1-707 935 0237) is worth the extra drive (and cash – rooms cost $250-$550): sit outside by the pool, where the creek gurgles, the sun shines and time seems to stop.

Tourist information

Sonoma Valley Visitor Bureau

453 First Street East, Sonoma (1-707 996 1090/ www.sonomavalley.com). **Open** 9am-5pm daily.

Napa Valley

The 25-mile (40-kilometre) long Napa Valley, running almost parallel to the Sonoma Valley on the other side of the Mayacamas Mountains, forms the backbone of the Napa wine industry. Napa was originally populated by the Nappa Indian tribe; after Europeans settled here, Charles Krug introduced grapes into the valley in 1861. Highway 29 (also called the St Helena Highway) runs up the centre of the valley and is usually crowded with traffic because the largest wineries are found on it. Boutique wineries are mostly to be found on the **Silverado Trail** (parallel to Highway 29 to the east) or on one of the lanes that criss-cross the valley or lead up one of the many hillsides.

The town of Napa itself, at the bottom end of the valley, has traditionally had little to offer the traveller other than a heap of outlet stores. Lately, however, there's been a bit of rejuvenation, especially in the historic downtown area where a restoration of the Gold Rush-era Opera House has been indicative of renewed civic pride. In autumn 2001, Napa opened **Copia: The American Center for Wine, Food & The Arts** (1700 Soscol Avenue, 1-707 257 3606/www.copia.org), an elaborate $50-million facility dedicated to exploring food and wine and its influence on American culture. Spearheaded by Robert Mondavi, it offers everything from art shows and cooking demonstrations to live music.

Wine-tasting is the number one attraction here, with dining a close second – some of the Bay Area's best restaurants are in the wine country. For a complete list of wineries, pick up a map at any one of the vineyards en route. **Robert Mondavi Winery** in Oakville (7801 St Helena Highway, 1-888 766 6328/1-707 226 1335/www.robertmondaviwinery.com) is a good bet for first-time wine tasters. It's open 10am to 5pm daily; tastings cost $4-$8. Also worth investigation is the historic German mansion of the **Beringer Vineyards** in St Helena (2000 Main Street, 1-707 963 7115/www.beringer.com, open 9.30am-6pm, $5) and the sparkling wines bottled at **Domaine Chandon** in Yountville (1 California Drive, 1-707 944 2280/www.dchandon.com). It offers one of the best tours (11am-5pm, $5), including a stellar Californian interpretation of *méthode champenoise*.

For a winery with a difference, visit film director Francis Ford Coppola's **Niebaum-Coppola Winery** in Rutherford (1991 St Helena Way, 1-707 963 9099, www.niebaum-coppola.com, open 10am-5pm daily), where you can see memorabilia from Coppola's movies, including a vintage Tucker automobile. In addition to producing award-winning wines, the **Hess Collection**, six miles from Napa (4411 Redwood Road, 1-707 255 1144/www.hesscollection.com, open 10am-4pm daily, $4-$6),

... and postmodern **Clos Pegase**.

has a museum-quality selection of art in its gallery, including sculptures by Frank Stella and Robert Rauschenberg.

At the northern end of Napa Valley is Calistoga, home of the hot springs and bottled water. More than any other town in the wine country, it looks Western: it's got saloons and a wide main street (Lincoln Avenue) often festooned with banners promoting beer tastings, mustard festivals or other celebrations of the California good life. Calistoga is famous for its numerous spas; don't leave without spending a few hours soaking in a mud bath or relaxing with a massage – *see p260* **Mud, mud, glorious mud**.

Several wineries are located in and around Calistoga. Take the tram ride to **Sterling Vineyards** (1111 Dunaweal Lane, 1-707 942 3344/www.sterlingvineyards.com). Famous for its Cabernet Sauvignon as well as its white wines, this hilltop winery (open 10.30am-4.30pm daily, $4) has commanding views of the countryside and an excellent self-guided tour. **Château Montelena** (1429 Tubbs Lane, 1-707 942 5105/www.montelena.com, open 10am-4pm daily, $10) is an 1882 house overlooking a Chinese garden complete with a lake, tea houses, bridges and a Chinese junk. **Clos Pegase** (1060 Dunaweal Lane, 1-707 942 4981/ www.clospegase.com, open 10.30am-5pm daily, $5-7.50) is a large winery in a stunning structure designed by postmodern architect Michael Graves. The grounds contain a bewitching sculpture garden.

One of the best tours in the area is at sparkling wine specialist **Schramsberg** (1400 Schramsberg Road, 1-707 942 2414/www.schramsberg.com, open 9am-4pm daily, $4-$6). The tour takes visitors through a maze of caves dug at the turn of the 20th century by Chinese labourers. And a charming example of a small, family-owned winery is **Wermuth** (3942 Silverado Trail, 1-707 942 5924/www.wines.com/wermuth.html). It's open 11am-5pm daily.

If you're bored of wineries, there are other things to do in and around Calistoga. Dioramas depicting 19th-century Calistoga life, along with photos and other artefacts, are displayed in the **Sharpsteen Museum** (1311 Washington Street, 1-707 942 5911/www.sharpsteen-museum.org), while a mile north of town, on Tubbs Lane, little **Old Faithful** geyser erupts about every 15 minutes. Water comes from an underground river and heats to around 177°C (350°F) before spewing high into the air. Another quirk of nature is the **Petrified Forest**, a few miles west on Petrified Forest Road. Seven miles (11 kilometres) north on Highway 29 is **Robert Louis Stevenson State Park** (1-707 942 4575), named after the writer who honeymooned in the area in 1880. The **Robert Louis Stevenson Museum** (1490 Library Lane, 1-707 963 3757) in St Helena contains memorabilia related to the author.

Of course, there is more to enjoy in Napa than just wine. There's fishing and boating on remote Lake Berryessa, cycling, hiking and horse-riding. If you'd prefer to cycle from winery to winery, a few companies arrange special tours. Outfits include **Napa Valley Bike Tours** in Napa (1-800 707 2453/ www.napavalleybiketours.com) and **Getaway Adventures in Calistoga** (1-800 499 2453/ http://getawayadventures.com). Alternatively, the **Napa Valley Wine Train** (1-707 253 2111/www.winetrain.com) runs daily lunch and dinner trips ($35-$105) up and down the valley. Cheesy it may be, but at least you don't have to fight the summer traffic, and the food, paired with local wines, is actually quite good.

Buying wine

Not all Californian wines are widely available outside the state, so here are some hints on what to buy while you're in wine country. The huge volume of fruit and flavour is the hallmark of today's Californian wines; the most common varieties include crisp Chardonnays, big Cabernet Sauvignons, soft Merlots, Sauvignon Blancs, Pinot Noirs, Rieslings and the versatile Zinfandel.

Sonoma labels

Cline (Zinfandel); **Dry Creek** (Chardonnay); **Field Stone** (Cabernet, Petite Syrah); **Foppiano** (Petite Syrah, Zinfandel); **Geyser Peak** (Chardonnay); **Gundlach Bundschu** (Merlot, Pinot Noir, Chardonnay, Cabernet, Zinfandel); **Lambert Bridge** (Fumé Blanc, Pinot Noir, Zinfandel); **Matanzas Creek** (Chardonnay); **Pezzi King** (Pinot Noir, Zinfandel, Cabernet); **Roche** (Chardonnay, Pinot Noir).

Napa labels

Carneros Creek (Pinot Noir); **Chimney Rock** (Chardonnay, Cabernet); **Clos Pegase** (Cabernet, Chardonnay, Merlot, Petite Syrah port); **Cuvaison** (Cabernet, Chardonnay); **Joseph Phelps** (Chardonnay); **Opus One** (Cabernet); **Pine Ridge** (Chardonnay, Cabernet, Merlot); **Robert Sinskey** (Pinot Noir); **Silver Oak** (Cabernet); **Stag's Leap** (Cabernet, Chardonnay, Sauvignon Blanc).

Mud, mud, glorious mud

If you're exploring the wine country, take time to indulge yourself at one of the many spas in the vicinity. Calistoga – at the top end of Napa Valley – has a spa on almost every corner, and specialises in mud baths, using volcanic ash from neighbouring St Helena Mountain superheated with water from Calistoga's underground hot springs. The town got its name in the mid-1800s, when San Franciscan Sam Brannan created the resort. Instead of saying the spa would be 'the Saratoga of California' (referring to the New York resort), a purportedly drunk Brannan slurred that it would be 'the Calistoga of Sariforna'. Other spas dot the surrounding area, including Sonoma Valley. It's best to make an appointment, especially at weekends.

Dr Wilkinson's Hot Springs

1507 Lincoln Avenue, Calistoga (1-707 942 4102/6257/www.drwilkinson.com). **Open** 8.30am-4.45pm daily.
Bang in the centre of town, Dr Wilkinson's is sweet, old-fashioned and good value. For $99, you get a mud bath, mineral bath, steam, blanket wrap and a half-hour massage – about two hours in total. The mud is a mix of peat, volcanic ash and mineral water, and feels distinctly bog-like, but afterwards you'll feel rejuvenated and renewed.

Harbin Hot Springs

18424 Harbin Springs Road, Middletown (1-800 622 2477/1-707 987 2477/ www.harbin.org). **Open** 24hrs daily.
A 30-minute drive north of Calistoga, this spiritual retreat offers spa treatments and yoga and meditation workshops. Discard your inhibitions about public nudity, then discard your clothes and enjoy a water Shiatsu massage: rates start at $40 for 30 minutes.

Indian Springs Spa

1712 Lincoln Avenue, Calistoga (1-707 942 4913/www.indianspringscalistoga.com). **Open** 9am-8pm Mon-Fri; 8.30am-9pm Sat, Sun.
Also in Calistoga, and very sumptuous, with pretty white cottages surrounded by lawns, and the most enormous mineral water swimming pool (*pictured*). Try a mud bath or mineral bath followed by a massage – packages start at $110.

The Kenwood Inn & Spa

10400 Highway 12, Kenwood (1-800 353 6966/www.sterba.com/kenwood/inn/spa). **Open** 9am-9pm daily.
A refuge for the likes of Bruce Willis, Sharon Stone and Christy Turlington. The grounds are shaded by olive trees, and the five treatment rooms are bathed in candlelight. There's a huge range of massages (aromatherapy, stone, Ayurvedic), facials and spa packages.

Mount View Spa

Mount View Hotel, 1457 Lincoln Avenue, Calistoga (spa 1-707 942 5789/www. mountviewspa.com). **Open** 9am-9pm daily.
This upscale spa inside the Mount View Hotel offers mud baths and all kinds of water treatments, as well as body wraps, facials,

Where to eat

The top-rated **French Laundry** in Yountville (6640 Washington Street, 1-707 944 2380, closed lunch Mon-Thur) prepares what may be the best meal you'll ever eat for an average of around $70 a head, but make your dinner reservation well ahead – it's booked up at least three months in advance. In central Napa, try **Celadon** (1040 Main Street, 1-707 254 9690, main courses $16-$23, closed Sat & first two weeks of Jan), a comfortable neighbourhood-style restaurant. Its sister establishment just across the road, **Cole's Chop House** (1122 Main Street, 1-707 224 6328, main courses $16-$36, closed lunch & first week of Jan) takes its steaks and chops very seriously. Also in Napa, **Mustards Grill** (7399 St Helena Highway, 1-707 944 2424, main courses $15-$25) is a popular upmarket diner.

St Helena has a number of excellent restaurants, including newcomer **Pinot Blanc** (641 Main Street, 1-707 963 6191, main courses $16-$24, closed Mon) and local favourite **Terra** (1345 Railroad Avenue, 1-707 963 8931, main courses $15-$22, closed Tue). **Miramonte** (1327 Railroad Avenue, 1-707 963 1200, main courses $14-$19) is under the same ownership as Mustards in Napa. For a picnic, the West Coast installation of New York deli **Dean & Deluca** (607 South St Helena Highway, 1-707 967 9980) offers gourmet delicacies from around the world. Both St Helena's **Cantinetta Tra Vigne** (1050 Charter Oak Avenue, 1-707 963 8888) and the **Oakville Grocery** in Oakville (7845 St Helena Highway, 1-707 944 8802) will pack you a picnic hamper if you phone the day before. The **Bale Grist Mill State Historic**

aromatherapy and reflexology massage. Rates start at $100. If you really feel like splashing out, try the three-hour Head to Toe ($220), which includes a bath of your choice, massage, facial and pedicure.

Sonoma Mission Inn & Spa

18140 Highway 12, Boyes Hot Springs (1-800 862 4945/www.sonomamission inn.com). **Open** spa 6am-9pm daily; bath house 7.30am-9pm daily.
Located in Sonoma Valley, and considered by some to be the best spa in the Bay Area. Try the 100-minute Couples Wine and Roses Kur: relax in a bubble bath with a glass of wine, followed by a side-by-side massage with grapeseed oil and lotion for $200 each. Ideal for romantic couples.

Park on Highway 29, between St Helena and Calistoga, is a good place for a picnic.

In Calistoga, the **Catahoula Restaurant & Saloon** inside the Mount View Hotel (1457 Lincoln Avenue, 1-707 942 2275, main courses $13-$24, closed lunch Mon-Fri) offers part Cajun, part Californian, but mostly American cooking for about $20 for three courses. Try the cornmeal fried catfish, seafood gumbo or Mardi Gras slaw, but save room for dessert. The **Wappo Bar & Bistro** (1226 Washington Street, 1-707 942 4712, main courses $12-$20) is a long-time favourite that serves a surprising array of cuisine types – from Asian to Italian – all of them very well. For snacks, the quintessentially Californian **Calistoga Natural** healthfood store and café on the main street serves fabulous sandwiches, smoothies and vegetable and fruit juices.

Where to stay

For information on places to stay in Napa, contact **Napa Valley Reservations Unlimited** (1-800 251 6272/1-707 252 1985/ www.napavalleyreservations.com) – bear in mind that rooms are often booked up and most options are expensive.

A deluxe option is the **Vintage Inn** in Yountville (6541 Washington Street, 1-800 351 1133/1-707 944 1112/www.vintageinn.com, from $225), which is close to shops and restaurants. Even more expensive is the **Auberge du Soleil** in Rutherford (180 Rutherford Hill Road; 1-707 963 1211; rooms from $350), which is worth booking for very special occasions. The **Harvest Inn** in St Helena (1 Main Street, 1-800 950 8466/www. coastalhotel.com/california/ st_helena/harvest.html) offers a series of Tudor-style cottages (all named after knights or romantic figures) set in pretty gardens and overlooking a vineyard. Rates start at $200.

In Calistoga, try the historic **Mount View Hotel** on the main street (1457 Lincoln Avenue, 1-707 942 6877/www.mountview hotel.com, rates from $145); it's also got a first-class spa. The **Pink Mansion** (1415 Foothill Boulevard, at Main Street, 1-707 942 0558/www.pink mansion.com, rates $145-$325) is an elegant restored building with in-house wine tastings, while the **Mountain Home Ranch** (3400 Mountain Home Ranch Road, 1-707 942 6616/ www.mtnhomeranch.com) is a secluded resort with swimming pools, tennis and volleyball courts, fishing and hiking trails. Rooms cost $49-$139.

Tourist information

Calistoga Chamber of Commerce & Visitors Center

1458 Lincoln Avenue, Calistoga (1-707 942 6333/ www.calistogafun.com). **Open** 10am-5pm Mon-Fri; 10am-4pm Sat; 11am-3pm Sun.

Napa Valley Conference & Visitor Center

1310 Napa Town Center, Napa (1-707 226 7459/ www.napavalley.com). **Open** 9am-5pm daily.

Getting there

By car

The wine country is roughly an hour by car from San Francisco (44 miles/71km) over the Golden Gate Bridge along US 101. Turn east at Ignacio to Highway 37 and take Highway 121 north. From here, Highway 12 takes you along Sonoma Valley; Highway 29 along Napa Valley. Traffic can be hellish, especially over the Golden Gate Bridge, but driving is still the best way to see the wine country.

Heading South

Discover the rural romance of Half Moon Bay, Santa Cruz and Carmel.

The San Francisco peninsula stretches 42 miles (68 kilometres) south until it merges with the mainland near San Jose. On the bay side, there's little of interest to the tourist, with the suburbs melting together into a single blur. On the Pacific side, you'll notice a change of scenery as well as a change of pace: from the bustling city to rolling hills full of artichokes, miles of beautiful rugged beaches full of surfers and beachcombers, and dozens of sleepy towns full of ramshackle barns and country stores. The flat bay shores contrast with the steep terrain of the Santa Cruz Hills. Agriculture has been the economic mainstay of the area since World War II, until the booming 1980s gave way to the technological explosion of Silicon Valley. You'll pass strawberry fields, pumpkin patches, Christmas tree farms, fruit orchards and flower nurseries. Inland, instead of orchards of apple trees, there are grids of concrete business parks many of which are lined with high-tech giants like Hewlett-Packard, Intel, Apple and Oracle.

From San Francisco, weave your way down I-280 – it's far more picturesque and much less congested than Highway 101, which hugs the bay and is the main artery for Silicon Valley commuters. Then look out for signs directing you to the lovely Pacific Coast Highway (aka Highway 1), where the peninsula's rural charms can still be found. Bear in mind that the weather can be mixed along the coast: that means fog in summer and the surprise of Indian summers in late September and early October.

Half Moon Bay

Half Moon Bay (just off Highway 1 and about a 45-minute drive from San Francisco) is a small, easygoing seaside town with a rural feel. It's perhaps most famous for growing Halloween pumpkins and Christmas trees. It's also got a couple of golf courses, riding stables, bike paths and beaches. The quaint Main Street is filled with bookshops, boutiques, health food stores, flower gardens and antiques shops. Worth a visit is the **San Georgio General Store**, eight miles (13 kilometres) south of Half Moon Bay on Highway 84. This funky store has been serving the local farming community since 1889, and lives up to its name by selling just about everything: from cast-iron pots and pans to second-hand books, antiques and music.

A string of beaches stretches down the coast from Half Moon Bay, including the popular **Half Moon Bay State Beach**. Probably the best of the lot is **San Gregorio State Beach**, a strip of white sand distinguished by sedimentary cliffs and its proximity to a nude beach further north. If you feel like taking a horse ride for an hour-long trip along the coast, call the **Sea Horse & Friendly Acres Ranch** (at Half Moon Bay and Highway 1; 1-650 726 9903/www.horserentals.com), which offers beach rides for all levels of experience.

Another 15 miles (25 kilometres) down the coast, the town of **Pescadero** is a step back in time. Its historic buildings surround hundreds of rolling acres of farmland. As you drive into town, the scenes of farm workers out in the open fields of artichokes, Brussels sprouts and strawberries conjure a feeling of the past.

Where to eat

In Half Moon Bay, **Pasta Moon** (315 Main Street, 1-650 726 5125, main courses $14-$18) serves elegant Italian cuisine in a cosy setting and has been a popular spot for ten years. Most of the produce comes fresh each day from nearby farms, and the pasta is home-made. Alternatively, there's pasta and local fish at **San Benito House** (356 Main Street, 1-650 726 3425, closed lunch and Mon-Wed, main courses $15-$19), an old-fashioned saloon gleaming with polished wood and brass chandeliers. Save room for dessert; the warm fruit tart with local berries is more than worth seconds.

In Pescadero, enjoy a beer at **Duarte's Tavern** (202 Stage Road, 1-650 879 0464, main courses $14-$26), the town's most celebrated saloon for over a century. The crab sandwiches are legendary and the cream of artichoke soup is created from locally grown crops.

Where to stay

There's no shortage of places to stay (motels, B&Bs, cottages, luxury hotels) in and around Half Moon Bay. The newest and probably the grandest as well is the 261-room **Ritz-Carlton** (1 Miramontes Point Road, 1-800 241-3333/1-650 712 7000, rates $300-$375). Opened in May 2001, it resembles a grand 19th-century seaside lodge, and is situated on scenic bluffs overlooking the rugged coastline. Facilities include two golf courses and a spa. Or you can try the **Cypress Inn** (407 Mirada Road, 1-800 832 3224/1-650 726 6002), a contemporary inn located along a five-mile (eight-kilometre) stretch of smooth white-sand beach. It's a rather expensive hideaway (rates $215-$345), but the atmosphere is both romantic and peaceful. Most rooms offer a private deck and ocean view. There are also 12 rooms (nine en suite) at the turn-of-the-20th-century **San Benito House** (*see p262*). Some rooms ($80-$176) are small, so make sure you request a large one. For more options, check the Chamber of Commerce's website (*see below*).

About 25 miles south from Half Moon Bay, **Costanoa Coastal Lodge & Camp** (2001 Rossi Road at Highway 1, 1-800 738 7477/ 1-650 879 1100/www.costanoa.com) is not your typical campground. It even offers room service. There are three types of accommodation to choose from – a 40-room lodge ($205-$240), individual wooden cabins ($175) and canvas cabins ($70-$130) – as well as bicycle rentals, horse-riding, a spa and a general store/café.

Getting there

By car

Half Moon Bay is 30 miles (48km) south of San Francisco on Highway 1 – about a 45-minute drive. Pescadero is 20 miles (32 km) further south, and is signposted off Highway 1.

By train & bus

From San Francisco, take a BART train to Daly City (about a 15-minute journey), from where you can catch SamTrans bus 110 to Linda Mar, where you transfer to bus 294 to Half Moon Bay. The journey from Daly City to Half Moon Bay takes around one hour; the one-way fare is $2.20. SamTrans bus 15 runs between Half Moon Bay and Pescadero.

Tourist information

Half Moon Bay Coastside Chamber of Commerce

First floor, 520 Kelly Avenue, Half Moon Bay (1-650 726 8380/www.halfmoonbaychamber.org). **Open** 9am-4pm Mon-Fri.

Santa Cruz

Originally established as a mission at the end of the 18th century, and still recovering after extensive damage from the big Loma Prieta earthquake in 1989, this quirky, quintessentially Californian beach town is well known for being easygoing and politically progressive. Home of the University of California at Santa Cruz, it has a constantly evolving population of young people who have a way of keeping things lively,

Seaside fun at the **Santa Cruz Boardwalk**.

as well as a substantial permanent population of long-time residents who are fiercely protective of the city's liberal heritage.

The popularity of Santa Cruz as a beach resort dates back to the mid-19th century. The small **Surfing Museum** (Mark Abbott Memorial Lighthouse, West Cliff Drive, 1-831 420 6289/ www.cruzio.com/arts/scva/surf.html), contains old photographs and vintage boards that tell the story of the sport that has become an entrenched part of the Santa Cruz scene. It's open noon-4pm except Tuesdays (it's also closed on Wednesdays in winter). Conveniently enough, **Steamer Lane**, considered one of the best surfing spots in California, is right outside the lighthouse.

Bang on the beach, the **Santa Cruz Beach Boardwalk** amusement park (400 Beach Street, 1-831 423 5590/www.beachboardwalk.com) is a hybrid of the tacky and the nostalgic, although mostly the tacky, really. It offers more than 30 rides (including bumper cars and the Tilt-a-Whirl) as well as a rambling arcade all the traditional games, shops and fast-food joints. The Giant Dipper, a classic wooden rollercoaster, has been declared a National Historic Landmark, along with the nearby 1911 carousel. The Boardwalk's **Cocoanut Grove Ballroom** (1-831 423 2053) is another remnant of the town's 19th-century heyday. It still comes into its own at weekends, when a mixture of big bands and local rock and pop groups play.

All that remains today of the **Misión la exaltación de la Santa Cruz** – the 12th of the 21 Californian Franciscan missions – is the current replica (Mission Plaza, 1-831 425 5849), built in the 1930s, though the nearby **Mission Adobe** is one of California's few remaining original adobe structures. Built in 1929, the **Santa Cruz Museum of Natural History** (1305 East Cliff Drive, Tyrone Park, 1-831 420 6115/6451/www.santacruzmuseums.org) contains vast information on the Ohlone Native Americans who originally populated the area.

The lovely redwood forests covering the hills surrounding Santa Cruz, are ideal for hiking and biking. A few miles north, off Highway 17, you can visit the **Mystery Spot** (465 Mystery Spot Road, 1-831 423 8897), a bizarre plot of land in the woods that apparently defies all known laws of physics – even without the aid of recreational drugs. More details about its strange abilities can be found online at www.mysteryspot.com. Fans of towering redwoods should head to **Big Basin Redwoods State Park** (1-831 338 8860) and **Henry Cowell Redwoods State Park** (1-831 335 4598), both to the north. Just south of Santa Cruz, you can visit the **Forest of Nisene Marks** (1-831 763 7063) to see the ruins of a Chinese labour camp, as well as the epicentre of the Loma Prieta earthquake.

There are two dozen wineries in the Santa Cruz area, which are open for tastings and tours, but without the crowds of Napa. They include **Boony Doon** (10 Pine Flat Road, Santa Cruz, 1-831 425 3625), which creates good, Italian-style wines, as well as the **Storrs Winery** (35 Potrero Street, Santa Cruz, 1-831 458 5030, closed Tue & Wed), run by an award-winning husband-and-wife team. **Bargetto Winery** in Soquel, a few miles from Santa Cruz (3535 North Main Street, 1-831 475 2258/http://web winery.com/bargetto/), is widely known for its fruit wines, such as olallieberry and apricot.

Where to eat

Azur (1001 Center Street, 1-831 427 3554/ www.restaurantazur.com, closed Mon, main courses $12-$20) is a light and airy place, with a high, beamed ceiling and colourful Spanish tiling. The Mediterranean menu is constantly changing but is also consistently good, with gourmet pizzas, seafood,vegetarian dishes and an impressive wine list. High above Santa Cruz Yacht Harbor, the **Crow's Nest** (2218 East Cliff Drive, 1-831 476 4560, main courses $13-$19) offers magnificent views of the Monterey Bay and specialises in seafood.

Where to stay

Frankly, most of the hotels in Santa Cruz itself are substandard motels and cheap chains, but, luckily, there are a few charming spots that could be worth your while. The **Babbling Brook Inn** (1025 Laurel Street, 1-800 866 1131/ 1-831 427 2456/www.babblingbrookinn.com) is aptly named; its setting cannot be beat, as it is surrounded by an acre of gardens filled with pine trees, redwoods and a meandering brook. It was first built in 1909, on the site of an 1870s tannery, a 1790s grist mill and a 2,000-year-old Indian fishing village. Its 13 rooms ($165-$250) are all named after artists (Cezanne, Renoir, Van Gogh, Monet and the like). Also in Santa Cruz, the **Pleasure Point Inn** (2-3665 East Cliff Drive, 1-877 557 2567/1-831 469 6161/ www.pleasurepointinn.com) is a departure from traditional, antique-laden B&Bs. Set overlooking the sea, this is a modern, upscale and well appointed house with four bedroom suites, a central living and dining area and a large rooftop deck with an eight-person jacuzzi. Rooms cost $220-$265; continental breakfast and evening hors d'oeuvres are included. The **Adobe on Green Street** (103 Green Street, 1-888 878 2789/1-831 469 9866/www.santa-cruz-california.com) is a historic adobe B&B, ideally located. Its four rooms ($135-$205) are mission-style, with antique dressers, Shaker canopy beds and Native American-influenced art.

Getting there

By car

Santa Cruz is 74 miles (119km) south of San Francisco on Highway 1 – about a two-hour drive.

By bus

Greyhound buses travel from San Francisco to Santa Cruz about four times a day. The trip takes just under three hours and costs $12.

By train & bus

From San Francisco, take CalTrain to San Jose. Trains leave from two stations in SF (Fourth and King, 22nd and Pennsylvania) about every 30 minutes; the one-way fare is $5.25. From San Jose CalTrain station, a shuttle bus (about ten a day) run by Amtrak goes to Santa Cruz. The trip takes 45 minutes and costs $6.

Tourist information

Santa Cruz Area Chamber of Commerce

1211 Ocean Street, near Washburn Avenue, Santa Cruz (1-800 833 3494/1-831 425 1234/www. santacruzchamber.org). **Open** 9am-5pm Mon-Sat; 10am-4pm Sun.

Monterey peninsula

Jutting into the Pacific between the fun-loving town of Santa Cruz and the dramatic coastline of Big Sur, the Monterey peninsula is one of the most popular places on the coast. Writers and artists have been drawn to the area for decades, among them Simone de Beauvoir, Robinson Jeffers, Jack Kerouac and Henry Miller. The **Monterey Jazz Festival** (1-831 373 3366) in September and the **Monterey Bay Blues Festival** (1-831 394 2652) at the end of June draw the top names in jazz and blues, but the area is perhaps best known for its spectacular golf courses, fishing and cycling. The three major towns on the peninsula are **Carmel**, where Clint Eastwood famously served a stint as mayor, **Monterey** and **Pacific Grove**.

When you get right down to it, **Carmel** is a love-it-or-hate-it sort of place. Once a secluded seaside village favoured by the likes of Robert Louis Stevenson and Ansel Adams, it is now an over-popular town, chock-full of mediocre (and expensive) shops. Much of it resembles a picturesque film set, with fake adobe mansions discreetly tucked away in leafy groves leading down to the ocean. Once there, the beach is a fantastic-looking white crescent of sand, but it's all for show; don't be lured into the water as it's not suitable for swimming. **Ocean Avenue** is the main shopping street, with antique shops, art galleries, boutiques and a tea shop that's straight out of *Snow White*.

World-class: the **Monterey Bay Aquarium** shouldn't be missed.

Still, some things are definitely worth a visit. **Carmel Mission** (3080 Rio Road, 1-831 624 3600/www.carmelmission.org) – the second of the Californian missions – has a baroque church first built in 1797, three museums and beautiful gardens. Father Junipéro Serra, the founder of the mission, is buried inside the church. Outside, for hikers and bikers, the **Mission Trail Park** across the street is a serious attraction, while just below the Carmel Highlands, off Highway 1, is one of the most beloved parks in California, **Point Lobos State Reserve**. It's possible to spend a whole day exploring its nooks, crannies, beaches and awesome promontories.

The capital of Alta California under Spanish, Mexican and American governments, the town of **Monterey** is one of the state's most historic communities. Popular spots include **Colton Hall** (Monterey City Hall, Pacific Street, 1-831 646 5640), where California's first constitution was written in 1849, as well as the **Monterey State Historic Park** (1-831 649 7118), which contains an extensive collection of artefacts relating to the area's architecture and history. **Jacks Peak Regional Park** (1-831 647 7795), located just ten miles (16 kilometres) to the south of town, provides an escape from the tourists and traffic of downtown Monterey.

The town's best attraction, however, is undoubtedly the world-class **Monterey Bay Aquarium** (886 Cannery Row, 1-831 648 4800/ www.mbayaq.org). Its spectacular, labyrinthine display of undersea forests, marine life, tide pools and jellyfish are a real treat. Even the gift shop deserves some serious browsing. If you can, time your visit to coincide with the regularly scheduled feeding times for the absolutely adorable sea otters. It will make your day. The aquarium is open 9.30am-6pm daily (from 10am in winter); admission costs $15.95, $7.95-$13.95 concessions.

The aquarium is located on **Cannery Row**, a neighbourhood made famous by native son John Steinbeck. Today, the canning factories are gone, abandoned in the 1940s when the commercial sardine population was fished out, to be replaced by tacky shops and mediocre restaurants that occupy the old warehouses. However, this is a wine-producing region and one well known for its Chardonnay, so you can always stock up on some bottles while you're here – try the **Bargetto Winery Tasting Room** (700 Cannery Row, 1-831 373 4053) or, in the same building, the **Cannery Row Bay View Tasting Room** (1-831 646 5446).

Just a couple of miles west of Monterey is the small and much prettier town of **Pacific Grove**, founded in 1875 as a camping retreat for the Methodist Church. If you're in the area in winter, watch out for the annual phenomenon of thousands of migrating Monarch butterflies: the **Pacific Grove Museum of Natural History** (at Forest and Central Avenues, 1-831 648 5716/www.pgmuseum.org) has extensive information on the lovely creatures. Nearby, the tiny **Point Pinos Light Station** (at the end of Lighthouse Avenue) has been working since 1855 and is the oldest continuously operating lighthouse on the coast.

The **17-Mile Drive**, from Pacific Grove through **Pebble Beach**, takes you by some of the most famous and challenging golf courses in the country – although you have to pay for the privilege of even passing through the area at strategically placed toll booths (whether you're on foot or in a car). Save your change and instead walk along the coastal path from Pacific Grove: the views are just as good and it's free.

Where to eat

There are plenty of places to eat, but many are tourist traps with staff on the street trying to lure you in with platters of the catch of the day. They're all pretty much the same and not worth writing home about. Instead, try the following.

Overlooking the ocean in Pacific Grove, the **Old Bath House Restaurant** (620 Ocean View Boulevard, 1-831 375 5195/www.oldbathhouse.com, closed lunch, main courses $23-$45) specialises in French and European dining. Each table has a view of the ocean and it's very popular, so be sure to book well ahead. Of all the restaurants on Monterey's Cannery Row, the **Sardine Factory** (701 Wave Street, 1-831 373 3775/www.sardinefactory.com, closed lunch, main courses $20-$35) is the best. The decor is a little ornate and staff can be a bit over-attentive, but the food is good – especially the seafood platter. Try the tasting menu if you can't make up your mind.

Where to stay

Most accommodation on the Monterey peninsula falls somewhere between pricey and extravagant. Some are worth it, others are overrated and overrun with tourists – so proceed with caution.

If you're looking to splash out, **Bernardus Lodge** in Carmel Valley (415 Carmel Valley Road, 1-888 648 9463/1-831 658 3550/www.bernardus.com) is an intimate retreat with 57 luxurious rooms and suites ($420-$1,690), a full-service spa, swimming pool and a winery. Each room has stone fireplaces, built-in wine grottoes and two-person tubs. Some also have sweeping views of the Santa Lucia Mountains.

In Carmel, the 34-room **Cypress Inn** (Lincoln and Seventh Streets, 1-800 443 7443/1-831 624 3871/www.cypress-inn.com) is a small, old-fashioned hotel near the centre of town. While its façade suggests a formal establishment, the Cypress feels more like a bookworm's retreat, with exposed rafters, overstuffed couches and a small library bar. All the rooms ($125-$395 including continental breakfast) come complete with a decanter of sherry and a fruit basket. For more Carmel options, try the **Carmel Area Reservation Services** (1-888 434 3891/1-831 659 7061/www.carmel-california.com).

To get away from it all in Pacific Grove, try **Andril Fireplace Cottages** (569 Asilomar Boulevard, 1-831-375 0994/www.andrilcottages.com). As the name suggests, most of the cosy and rustic bungalows ($74-$400) have wood-burning fireplaces, as well as all the comforts of modern homes including full-size kitchens, microwaves, TVs and VCRs. And all are within walking distance from Pebble Beach.

Tourist information

Carmel California Visitor & Information Center

San Carlos Street, between Fifth & Sixth Streets, Carmel (1-800 550 4333/1-831 624 2522/www.carmelcalifornia.org). **Open** 9am-5pm Mon-Fri. In summer, you can also get maps and information from a small kiosk at Carmel Plaza.

Monterey Visitors Center

Lake El Estero, at Franklin Street, Monterey (1-888 221 1010/1-831 649 1770/www.montereyinfo.org). **Open** *Apr-Oct* 9am-6pm Mon-Sat; 9am-5pm Sun. *Nov-Mar* 9am-5pm Mon-Sat; 10am-4pm Sun. The Maritime Museum Visitors Center is in town on Custom House Plaza, near Fisherman's Wharf.

Pacific Grove Information Center

Central & Forest Avenues, Pacific Grove (1-800 656 6650/1-831 373 3304/www.pacificgrove.org). **Open** 9.30am-5pm Mon-Fri; 10am-3pm Sat.

Getting there

By car

Carmel is 125 miles (200km) from San Francisco on Highway 1 – about a 2½-hour drive. It's five miles (8km) to Monterey from Carmel, and 6½ miles (10km) to Pacific Grove.

By bus

Greyhound buses travel from San Francisco to Monterey five times daily. The trip takes 4-5 hours and costs $16. There is no bus service from San Francisco direct to Carmel or Pacific Grove, but Monterey-Salinas Transit buses go from Monterey to the other two towns. For Carmel, take bus 4 or 5. For Pacific Grove, take bus 1 or 2. In both cases, the journey takes about 40 minutes and costs $1.75.

Heading East

Head inland for skiing at Lake Tahoe or the natural beauty of Yosemite.

Besides Berkeley and some enclaves in the Oakland Hills, the East Bay is really just a sprawling mass of suburban bedroom communities. If you're craving the outdoors and want an adventure, rent a car and explore the natural wonders of **Lake Tahoe** or **Yosemite National Park**. Open year round, each offers different experiences. Tahoe is a skier's haven in winter, a hiker's delight in summer, and a treasure chest for gamblers all the time. Yosemite is loved by adventure sport enthusiasts, but you don't have to be an expert hiker, backpacker or climber to enjoy its cascading waterfalls and breathtaking views.

Lake Tahoe

At the eastern border of California, beautiful Lake Tahoe draws millions of visitors each year. No one knows how deep the lake actually is; locals call it 'Big Blue'. Flanked by snow-capped peaks, it has become California's primary playground for skiing, waterskiing, fishing, hiking and gambling at casinos that line the main drag nearby in the aptly named community of Stateline, just over the border in Nevada. (The border between California and Nevada runs through the centre of the lake.)

The north end of the lake is a three-and-a-half hour drive from San Francisco (longer if there's heavy snow on I-80, in which case you'll be driving slowly and you'll need snow chains on your tyres). The other route, via US 50, leads to the south shore, where hotels are usually packed with skiers and gamblers. From March to early November, it's easy to drive the 72-mile (116-kilometre) perimeter of the lake, much of which is serviced by public transport. On the California side are attractions such as the **Sugar Pine Point State Park** (1-530 525 7982), near Meeks Bay, and the **Emerald Bay State Park** (1-530 541 3030), further south, which overlooks the bay of the same name.

There are plenty of beaches around the lake: **Sand Harbour**, **Zephyr Cove** and **Camp Richardson** are all on the water. Fed by snow and surrounded largely by mountains, the water is only warm enough for swimming during August and September, and then only barely. A better idea is to book a cruise on the **Tahoe Queen Paddlewheeler** out of South Lake Tahoe (1-530 541 3364). Daily scenic cruises are available on this and several other tour boats.

Tahoe: heaven for skiers.

Truckee, an old West town about 12 miles (19 kilometres) north of the lake, has wooden sidewalks and wood-framed shopfronts designed to make it look like the backdrop for a John Wayne film – if it weren't for all the tourists and modern bars and restaurants. **Donner Memorial State Park** (1-530 525 7232), a few miles west of Truckee off Highway 80, is named after the Donner family, the notorious, doomed group of pioneers who perished horribly while trying to cross the pass in the viciously cold winter of 1842. The visitor centre has a short movie detailing their grisly fate (they ate each other).

For a bird's-eye view of the area, a trip with **Mountain High Balloons** (locations in Truckee and Tahoe City; 1-888 462 2683/ 1-530 587 6922) will take you soaring over the Sierras and, upon landing, will treat you to a glass of champagne to celebrate your survival.

Soaring Liberty Cap and Nevada Falls in **Yosemite National Park**. *See p270.*

Skiing

The ski season varies each year, but usually starts around November and lasts until late April, sometimes later.

Two of the most popular ski areas in the West are **Squaw Valley** (1-530 583 6985/www.squaw.com), site of the 1960 Winter Olympics, and **Alpine Meadows** (1-800 441 4423/1-530 583 4232/snow conditions recorded message 1-530 581 8374/www.alpinemeadows.com). Alpine is a bit more family-oriented and has the best snowboarding, while Squaw is glitzier and has more exciting runs. Other ski areas include **Boreal** (1-530 426 3666/www.borealski.com), where the lower prices attract snowboarders; **Northstar at Tahoe** (1-530 562 1010/www.skinorthstar.com), which offers excellent beginners' slopes; and **Sugar Bowl** (1-530 426 1111/9000/www.sugarbowl.com), where there's a creaky old gondola that takes you to the base lodge. For those who are just in it for the view, **Heavenly Valley**'s ski lifts operate for sightseeing in summer (1-775 586 7000/www.skiheavenly.com).

The **Ski Club Hotline** (1-925 827 4303) has information on many Bay Area ski clubs. Ski rental is available at the resorts, but if you're driving, it's probably cheaper to rent your gear in San Francisco and avoid the queues. Lift passes tend to be expensive, but most resorts offer half-day passes for the afternoon and sometimes midweek specials. If you're not confident about your ability or haven't been on the slopes in a while, invest in a lesson (which also includes a lift pass for the day, and can work out to be a pretty good deal).

If you're driving and not tied to a particular schedule, avoid going on Friday afternoon as San Franciscans tend to leave work early to get a head start to the slopes. Likewise, Sunday evenings can be a nightmare if you're trying to get back into the city. Still, if you play your cards right, you can go skiing in a day. Leave San Francisco around 6am and you'll arrive at the slopes around 9.30am, when the lifts open – so you'll be the first to experience the day's fresh powder snow – then you can head back to the city when the lifts close down at 4pm.

Where to eat

Gourmet dining is rare in Tahoe, but you will find loads of unpretentious, family-owned restaurants with easygoing atmospheres and friendly service, and relatively cheaper compared to the city. The bigger restaurant chains are in the hotel casinos as well as the 'all you can eat' buffets, which are quite an experience if you haven't been to one before.

The **Cantina Bar & Grill** (711 Emerald Bay Road, 1-530 544 1233, www.cantinatahoe.com, closed breakfast, main courses $5-$12) is a South Lake Tahoe icon. Hit their happy hour (3-6pm Mon-Fri) for delicious Margaritas and traditional Mexican fare. Also in South Lake Tahoe, **Lakeside Beach Grill** (4081 Lakeshore Boulevard, 1-530 544 4050, closed dinner, main courses $6-$12) serves salads with grilled prawns, and calamari burgers. There's an outdoor patio in summer.

From the outside, the **Cottonwood Restaurant** in Truckee (Highway 267 & Old Brockway Road, 1-530 587 5711, closed breakfast and lunch, main courses $9-$25) appears rustic and worn, but don't be fooled – the cuisine is eclectic and the wine list adventurous. There's jazz on Saturdays. **Le Petit Pier** (7238 North Lake Boulevard, Tahoe Vista, 1-530 546 4464, closed breakfast & lunch, main courses $25-$30) is one of the most romantic restaurants in the area, with an elegant setting, an award-winning wine list and food to match. The herb-roasted rack of lamb with truffle sauce is excellent. Reservations are recommended.

Where to stay

South of Lake Tahoe, **Kirkwood Ski & Summer Resort** (1377 Kirkwood Meadows Drive, off Highway 88, 1-800 967 7500/www.skikirkwood.com, rates $139-$359) is a family-oriented resort. Guests stay in slopeside lodges; most have a fireplace, washing machine and dryer, and some have a spa, gym and massage room. Nearby, **Historic Camp Richardson Resort** (2100 Jameson Beach Road, South Lake Tahoe, 1-800 544 1801/1-530 541 1801/www.camprich.com, rates $150-$650) has lakefront cabins with incredible views. Each cabin has a wood stove or fireplace and a basic kitchen, but if you don't feel like cooking, the camp's **Beacon Bar & Grill** (1-530 541 0630, main courses $10-$25) will do the work for you. In Truckee, the **Truckee Hotel** (10007 Bridge Street, 1-800 659 6921/www.truckeehotel.com, rates $45-$135) has 37 immaculately furnished rooms decked out with antiques and clawfoot tubs.

If you want to live large, but don't have enough time to hit Las Vegas, **Caesars Tahoe** in Stateline, Nevada (55 Highway 50, 1-888 829 7630/www.caesars.com/tahoe, rates $89-$155) is the next best thing. As well as a spa and pool – and gambling, of course – there are sell-out shows by the likes of James Brown, the Temptations and Cirque du Soleil.

Getting there

By car

A car is your best means of transport for exploring Lake Tahoe, especially if you're skiing. It takes 3½ hours from San Francisco, traffic and weather permitting.

To reach the north shore, follow I-80 over the Bay Bridge all the way to Truckee; then take Highway 89 to Tahoe City. To reach the south shore, take I-80 as far as Sacramento and then turn off on to US 50 to South Tahoe.

By air

Reno Canyon International Airport, 58 miles (93km) north-east of the lake, is served by several airlines. United Airlines (1-800 241 6522/www.ual.com) has half a dozen flights a day; for a 21-day advance, booking return fares from San Francisco are around $100. The Tahoe Casino Express (1-800 446 6128/www.tahoecasinoexpress.com) offers a regular daily shuttle bus and limo service to South Lake Tahoe from the airport for around $80.

By bus

Greyhound buses stop in Truckee, South Lake Tahoe and Reno (in Nevada), about a 5-hour trip. Buses to Truckee and South Lake Tahoe run about three or four times a day and cost $25-$37 one way. Buses to Reno cost about $25 and run all day.

By train

The Amtrak train line (1-800 872 7245/www.amtrak.com) leaves once a day from San Francisco International Airport at 8.30am and arrives in Truckee at just after 3pm. Cost is $110 round trip.

Tourist information

A good online resource is **Lake Tahoe Vacation Guide** (www.tahoevacationguide.com), which provides info on where to stay and where to play.

North Lake Tahoe Chamber of Commerce

245 North Lake Boulevard, Tahoe City (1-530 581 6900). **Open** 9am-5pm Mon-Fri; 9am-4pm Sat, Sun.

South Lake Tahoe Chamber of Commerce

3066 Lake Tahoe Boulevard, South Lake Tahoe (1-530 541 5255/www.tahoeinfo.com). **Open** 8.30am-5.30pm Mon-Sat.

Truckee Chamber of Commerce
10065 Donner Pass Road, Truckee (1-530 587 2757/www.truckee.com). **Open** 8.30pm-5.30pm daily.

Yosemite

It's enchanting, intoxicating, stunning, breathtaking – the descriptions of **Yosemite National Park** are as superlative as they are numerous. The park covers some 1,200 square miles (3,108 square kilometres) of forests, alpine meadows, sheer granite cliffs, lush waterfalls, undisturbed wildlife and hiking trails. Park elevations range from 2,000 feet (609 metres) to more than 13,000 feet (3,960 metres). Highway 120 runs the entire east–west length of the park, climbing up to 9,945 feet (3,031 metres) at Tioga Pass, the highest automobile pass in California. Admission to the park costs $20 per car.

Most people head for touristy, seven-mile-(11-kilometre-) long **Yosemite Valley**, where most of the accommodation and park services are located. It's packed with traffic, especially in the summer – best to use the free shuttle buses – but the views are indisputably spectacular. For non-valley sites, head for **Crane Flat** and **Tuolumne Meadows** (via Highway 120), **Glacier Point** (near Badger Pass) and the **Hetch Hetchy Reservoir** (north of Big Oak Flat). If you can, avoid visiting Yosemite in high summer; spring finds the wildflowers in bloom and in winter the untamed majesty of the snowcapped peaks is awesome; many have been famously captured by photographer Ansel Adams – but remember that much of the park is inaccessible during the winter months.

Yosemite is all about views: as you drive into the valley, **El Capitan** is the first dramatic sight, a sheer rock wall 3,000 feet (914 metres) high. Look out for tiny, ant-like figures slowly crawling up its grey granite face; it's one of the most popular climbing spots in the US. You'll get a bird's eye view from **Glacier Point** and a spectacular view of the Sierras from **Tunnel View**.

There are numerous hiking trails throughout the park. **Mist Trail** is the most popular: it's a three-mile (five-kilometre) round-trip to Vernal Falls and a seven-mile (11-kilometre) round trip to Nevada Falls. Standing beneath the pounding water of **Yosemite Falls** is heart-stopping and an ambitious hike is the round-trip to the top (just under seven miles/ 11 kilometres) to Yosemite Point. The hike to **Glacier Point** is just as challenging, but you can also drive there. The 16-mile (26-kilometre) round-trip **Half Dome** hike is the one to do if you're hard-core, but it's not for the fainthearted as you have to cling on to cables for the last half-mile because the terrain is so steep.

Backpacking is the best way to avoid the crowds and get the most out of Yosemite, but the park has a visitor's quota depending on the season, so make sure you plan ahead. If you really want to leave your fear behind, the **Yosemite Mountaineering School** (1-209 372 8344) offers excellent classes for first-time climbers, as well as five-day climbs. You can also hire rafts to float down the Merced River, which winds through the valley, and bikes.

The bulk of the park's accommodation and eating places, plus camping supplies, grocery stores and gift shops, are in the valley. Accommodation ranges from campsites to tent cabins at Curry Village to lodges to the spectacular 1927 Ahwahnee Hotel. For more information, call **Yosemite Reservations** (1-559 22 4848) or check www.yosemitepark.com. Always heed the warnings about bears and the advice about locking away food and cosmetics in bear-safe boxes; everything you've heard about bears breaking into cars for a packet of biscuits is true.

Getting there

By car

There are three routes to Yosemite: Highway 41 from the south; Highway 140 from the west; and Highway 120 from the north-west. Highway 120 (the Tioga Road) is the only road across the park and is closed in winter (usually between November and May) due to snow. The recommended entrance to the park is Highway 140: from San Francisco, take I-580 east to I-205, and connect to Highway 120 and then Highway 140. In winter, you'll need to have snow chains for your car; allow four hours from San Francisco in summer, five hours in winter.

By bus

There is no direct public bus service to Yosemite from San Francisco. However, several companies run private tours, including Gray Line Tours (558 9400; one-day tour $139). Greyhound runs buses to Merced ($24 one-way; 4 hours). From Merced, Via Adventures (1-209 722 0366) runs buses to and from Yosemite daily ($10 one-way; 2½ hours).

By train

Each morning, Amtrak trains 712 and 714 from Oakland to Merced ($23 one way; 3 hours) connect with a VIA Adventures bus to Yosemite.

Tourist information

General information is available from the National Park Service on 1-209 372 0200 and the website www.nps.gov/yose/. The Yosemite Association is a non-profit organisation that sells Yosemite-related books and interpretive materials; contact them at 1-209 379 2646 or online at www.yosemite.org. Other useful websites include www.yosemite.com.

Directory

Getting Around	**272**
Resources A-Z	**277**
Further Reference	**289**
Index	**291**
Advertisers' Index	**298**

Features

Emergencies	278
Earthquakes	284
Tourist information	287
Average monthly climate	288

Directory

Getting Around

To & from the airports

San Francisco Airport (SFO)

SFO (1-650 821 8211/transport hotline 1-800 736 2008/ www.flysfo.com) lies 14 miles (22.5 kilometres) south of the city in South San Francisco, near US 101. The brand-new International terminal – the largest in the US – opened in December 2000. Gleaming, airy, spacious and well served with shops (including a branch of the SFMOMA Museum Store) and eating places, it's a pleasure to spend a few hours here. Artworks and exhibition cases dot the terminal, and there's a charming Aviation Museum. A new BART train station at SFO should be completed in 2002, when it will be possible to get directly to downtown San Francisco in 30 minutes. Until then, these are your options:

By bus

There are three main options for getting to and from the airport. The cheapest (and least convenient) method is via two buses; SamTrans KX and 292, which run every 30 minutes between the airport's lower level and the Transbay Terminal at First and Mission Streets in downtown San Francisco. Bus 292 runs from 5.27am to 1.19am, costs $1.10, takes an hour and has no luggage restrictions. Bus KX runs from 6.01am to 12.50am, costs $3 and takes 30 minutes, but you can take only one small carry-on bag.

There are two more complicated but cheap routes. From outside SFO's terminals 1 and 3, catch a BX bus to Colma or 193 to Daly City BART stations ($1.10) and then transfer to a BART train. You can also take the free CalTrain shuttle from SFO's terminals 3 and International to Millbrae Station and then a 24-minute train ride ($2) to the CalTrain Depot on Fourth and Townsend Streets in SoMa. Do not choose this option if you're travelling alone at night.

By passenger van/ shuttle

Passenger vans (shuttles) are a definite step up from bussing it. Rates range from $12 to $20 per person (tickets can be bought from the driver) and it's a door-to-door service. Ask about coupons or discounted rates for two or more travellers. Most passenger vans leave every 10-15 minutes from the upper level of the airport terminal at specially marked kerbs – follow the red signs that read 'passenger vans' outside the baggage claim area. Vans run throughout the night, but are few and far between in the small hours; if your plane arrives late you may be faced with a long wait or an expensive taxi ride. For your return journey to the airport, book the shuttle at least 24 hours in advance.

Companies include **Lorrie's Airport Service** (334 9000), **SuperShuttle** (558 8500), **Bay Shuttle** (564 3400), **American Airporter Shuttle** (202 0733), **Quake City Airport Shuttle** (255 4899) and **SFO Airporter** (major hotel service only; 1-650 624 0500).

By taxi or limousine

The most expensive – but most convenient – option for getting into town may be your only recourse if your plane lands in the wee hours. Expect to pay about $35 plus tip for the trip to the city; be sure to haggle for a flat rate. Taxis are found outside the baggage claim area in a zone marked with yellow columns.

For limousine service, use the toll-free white courtesy phones located in the terminal or phone **Associated Limousine** (1-888 544 5466).

> This guide went to press a few weeks after the terrorist attacks on New York and Washington on 11 September 2001. Some of the information may change as a result.

Oakland International Airport (OAK)

Many travellers (including San Franciscans) opt to fly into the tiny Oakland Airport (1-510 577 4000/ www.oaklandairport.com) across the bay. To get to San Francisco using public transport, catch the Air-BART shuttle from the airport terminal to the Coliseum/ Oakland BART station ($2; you'll need exact change for the perpetually malfunctioning ticket machines). They run every 15 minutes from the central island outside terminals 1 and 2, and the journey takes about 15 minutes. Then catch the next Daly City BART to San Francisco ($2.75; about 25 minutes to downtown); for schedule information phone 989 2278. This is not a safe option for passengers travelling alone at night.

Other options include a shuttle service (**Super-Shuttle**; 558 8500) or a very expensive taxi or limo ride.

San Jose International Airport (SJC)

Though it's 50 miles (80 kilometres) to the south, San Jose Airport (1-408 277 4759/www.sjc.org) is becoming the destination of choice for many Silicon Valley travellers. It's a tiny, efficient airport, but more than an hour from San Francisco.

To get to the city from SJC, take Santa Clara Transit bus 10 to Santa Clara CalTrain station (every 20 to 30 minutes from 5.26am to 11.21pm; $1.25), then board CalTrain to San Francisco (it runs from 4.51am to 10.30pm, takes about 1 hour 20 minutes and costs $4.75 at peak hours). Get off at the end of the line, the Fourth & Townsend station (not recommended if you're travelling alone at night).

Don't even think of taking a taxi or limo to San Francisco from San Jose unless you're a wealthy multimedia tycoon.

Major airlines

This is not an exhaustive list; for other airlines, consult the Yellow Pages.

American Airlines
1-800 433 7300/www.aa.com
British Airways
1-800 247 9297/
www.british-airways. com
Continental Airlines
1-800 525 0280/
www.continental.com
Delta Airlines
1-800 221 1212/www.delta.com
Northwest Airlines
domestic 1-800 225 2525/
international 1-800 447 4747/
www.nwa.com
Southwest Airlines
1-800 435 9792/www.iflyswa.com
TWA
domestic 1-800 221 2000/
international 1-800 892 4141/
www.twa.com
United Airlines
1-800 241 6522/www.ual.com
USAir
1-800 428 4322/www.usairways.com
Virgin Atlantic
1-800 862 8621/www.virgin.com

Public transport

Unlike many US cities, San Francisco has a comprehensive and efficient public transport network. The city's buses, streetcars and cable cars are all run by the San Francisco Municipal Railway or Muni (673 6864/hearing-impaired 923 6366/www.sfmuni.com). The best plan for finding your way around the city's transport network is to buy a Muni Street & Transit map (available online, and at most bookshops and drugstores or from the Visitor Information Center – *see p287*).

If you plan to use Muni often, purchase a one-day ($6), three-day ($10) or seven-day ($15) Passport, which is valid on all Muni vehicles. Passes are available at the Visitor Information Center; the Muni ticket booth/police kiosk at Powell and Market Streets; the Muni ticket booth at Hyde and Beach Streets; the Bay Area TIX booth at Union Square; Muni headquarters in the Western Addition (949 Presidio Avenue, at Geary Boulevard); and various other locations. The CityPass (*see p105* **CityPass**) gives you free travel on Muni as well as free admission to several museums. If you're staying for a while, buy a FastPass ($35), available at shops around town and valid from the first to the last day of the current month.

Buses

The number one mode of public transport is Muni's creaking fleet of orange and white buses. Spewing fumes or sparks as they make their perpetually off-schedule rounds, they are at least relatively cheap and can get you within a block or two of almost anywhere you might want to go.

Fares are $1 for adults (18-64-year-olds), 35¢ for seniors, disabled and kids, and travel is free for under-5s. Exact change is required (paper money is accepted). Place your change or bills in the automatic toll-taker and take your proof-of-payment ticket. This ticket also doubles as a free transfer and is valid for two changes of vehicle in any direction within 90 minutes.

Bus stops are marked by one or more of the following: a large white rectangle painted on a street with a red kerb; a yellow marking on a telephone or light pole; a glass-walled bus shelter; a brown and orange sign listing the bus or buses that serve that route.

Route numbers are posted on the front and rear of the bus (so you know which one you've just missed). Buses run 5am-1am Mon-Fri; 6am-1am Sat; 8am-1am Sun. On busy lines, they run every five to ten minutes during peak hours. Between midnight and 5am a skeleton crew operates the Owl Service – nine lines on which buses run every 30 minutes.

Outside San Francisco

Bus services that connect to the city include:

AC Transit
817 1717/www.actransit.dst.ca.us
Alameda and Contra Costa Counties and a transbay service between those counties and San Francisco. Buses numbered A to Z go across the Bay Bridge to Berkeley and Oakland.
Golden Gate Transit
923 2000/www.goldengate.org.
Marin and Sonoma Counties from Sausalito to Santa Rosa.
Greyhound Bus Line
1-800 231 2222/
www.greyhound.com.
Long-distance bus routes throughout the US.
SamTrans
1-800 660 4287/www.samtrans.com.
San Mateo County with a service to downtown San Francisco.

> **TravInfo** (817 1717/ www.transitinfo.org) is a very useful information line for all forms of public transport in the Bay Area.

Muni Metro streetcars

A cross between an electric bus and a cable car, the Muni Metro streetcar (or tram) is used surprisingly rarely by tourists. Five lines (J, K, L, M and N) run underneath Market Street in the downtown area and above ground in the outer neighbourhoods; the recently revived F line is made up of restored vintage streetcars that run along Market Street and north along the Embarcadero as far as Fisherman's Wharf. Heading from east to west on Market, Muni makes the same stops as BART, but past the Civic Center routes branch off in different directions towards outlying districts such as the Mission, Castro and Sunset. Fares are the same as on the buses and the same passes apply. Lines run between 5am and midnight daily.

Cable cars

Brought back to life in 1984 at a cost of more than $60 million, San Francisco's beloved cable cars are without question the most enjoyable ride in town, as the lengthy queues at the turnarounds will attest. There are 44 cable cars in all, 27 of them used at peak times, travelling at a steady 9½mph on three lines: **California** (along California Street from the Financial District to Van Ness Avenue), **Powell-Mason** and **Powell-Hyde** (both from Market Street in downtown to Fisherman's Wharf). The Powell-Hyde line has the most thrills, the best scenery and the most tourists.

Lines operate from 6am to 1am daily. If you don't have a Muni pass or CityPass, buy a $2 one-way ticket from the conductor on board (under-fives go free). Transfers are not issued or accepted on cable cars. Cable car stops are marked by pole-mounted brown signs with a cable car symbol; their routes are marked on all Muni bus maps. Hold on tight, or you'll get thrown about as the car lurches around a corner and down a precipitous hill.

See also p60 **Cable cars**.

BART

Looking more like a ride at Disneyland than a form of public transport, BART (Bay Area Rapid Transit – 989 2278/hearing-impaired 1-510 839 2220/www.bart.gov) is a $5-billion network of five interconnected high-speed rail lines that serve San Francisco, Daly City, Colma and the East Bay counties. It's one of the most modern, automated and efficient systems in the world, run by computers at the Lake Merritt station in Oakland. Almost everything – trains, ticket dispensers, entry and exit gates, announcements – is automated.

Passengers feed money into a vending machine, which dispenses a reusable ticket encoded with the dollar amount entered. When you reach your destination, the cost of the ride (measured by the distance travelled) is deducted from the ticket as you pass through the exit gate – so save your ticket! Any remaining value can be used towards the next trip.

Though BART is of minor use for getting around the city – it only stops at six locations within San Francisco, four of them along Market Street in downtown and two along Mission Street in the Mission – it's an excellent way to get an inexpensive tour of the Bay Area, as much of the rail is elevated above the streets. It's also the best way to get across the bay to Berkeley and Oakland. Special excursion-ride tickets allow passengers to ride all the lines for up to three hours, but they must enter and exit from the same station, and travelling during peak hours (7-9am and 4-6pm weekdays) isn't recommended.

BART stations close at around midnight and open at 4am on weekdays, 6am on Saturday and 8am on Sunday. Fares range from $1.10 to $4.70. Look out for the blue and white 'ba' signs and the escalators leading down into the station.

CalTrain

The CalTrain commuter line (1-800 660 4287/hearing-impaired 508 6448/www.caltrain.com) connects San Francisco with San Jose and ultimately Gilroy, 'the garlic capital of the world', passing through Burlingame, Redwood City, Palo Alto, Mountain View, Sunnyvale as well as through the other peninsula cities. Famously punctual, it runs from 5am to midnight.

One-way adult fares range from $1.25 to $6.75 ($5.25, for example, from San Francisco to San Jose); senior, disabled, child and off-peak discounts are available, as is a ten-ride ticket on certain trains.

Ferries

The completion of the Golden Gate Bridge in 1937 marked the end of the ferry route between San Francisco and Marin – until 1970, when the service resumed to take a load off commuter traffic. Used mainly by suits during peak commuting hours, ferries double as wonderful and inexpensive excursions across the bay to Sausalito, Tiburon or Larkspur. Ferries also go to Alcatraz and Angel Island in San Francisco Bay.

Blue & Gold Fleet

recorded information 773 1188/tickets 705 5555/www.blueandgoldfleet.com.
Runs a service to Sausalito and various cruises to Alcatraz and Angel Island, all of which leave from Pier 41 at Fisherman's Wharf. Its commuter services to Alameda, Oakland (both $5 one way), Tiburon ($6) and Vallejo ($7.50) leave from the Ferry Building on the Embarcadero, at the end of Market Street.

Golden Gate Transit Ferry Service

923 2000/www.goldengate.org.
Serves Sausalito ($5.30 one way) and Larkspur ($3.10). Ferries leave from the Ferry Building.

Taxis

Getting around San Francisco in a taxi is an interesting experience. Because the city is so small, doing so is moderately cheap – fares average $7-$10, with a base fee of $1.70 and $1.50 for each additional mile. But the trick is finding a cab to hire. If you're downtown on a weekday afternoon, you'll have little problem flagging one from a street corner. If you're in an outlying or shabbier neighbourhood, however, or if it's suppertime, or a holiday, or raining, or the commute is heavy that day, forget about it.

There just aren't enough taxis to serve the city. This aberration is created by a quirky local law limiting the number of cab licences, or medallions. In a city with 25 per cent fewer parking spaces than it has cars in business districts, cabs could easily come to San Francisco's snarled transportation rescue – but they don't: repeated attempts to deregulate the medallion monopoly have been thwarted by the cab lobby.

If you're downtown, head for the big hotels, where most have a queue of cabs lurking nearby. If you're out to dinner or shopping, ask the business to call one for you. If you're in an outlying area, phone early and often to request one and ask the dispatcher how long you'll have to wait.

Taxi companies

City Wide Dispatch 920 0700
Luxor 282 4141
www.luxorcabsf.com
National 648 4444
Veteran's 552 1300
Yellow 626 2345
www.yellowcabsf.com

Limousine companies

Pure Luxury 485 1764
Robertson's 775 6024

Driving

It's not sensible to rent a car to explore San Francisco. There's no street parking and private parking garages charge up to $12 an hour. Locals honk and curse at you for slowing them down. The steep hills fry your nerves and your clutch, and you're more than likely to get a parking ticket – the city's favourite source of revenue. The only reason for renting a car is to have wheels to explore the Bay Area and beyond.

If you must drive in the city, you should know the following. Unless otherwise posted, the speed limit within the city is 25mph and all occupants must wear seatbelts. Cable cars always have the right of way and should be given a wide berth. When parking in residential neighbourhoods, do not block driveways even slightly, or you'll get fined and towed away. When parking on hills, set the hand brake and 'kerb' your front wheels (turn them towards the kerb when facing downhill, away from the kerb when facing uphill) or you'll get ticketed. You must always park in the direction of the traffic.

Parking spaces in San Francisco are as rare as they are tightly regulated: always read the information on the meter and/or all the signs on your side of the block. One missed warning could lead to a towed car, in which case you'll have to take a taxi to the municipal garage, pay $135.50 plus your parking ticket and possibly more in storage fees.

But wait – there's more! Don't park at kerbs painted white, as that colour indicates passenger drop-off zones; blue, which are reserved for drivers or passengers with disabilities; yellow, which are for loading and unloading commercial vehicles; or red, in front of bus stops or fire hydrants. Green kerbs signify parking for ten minutes only, while some yellow and white kerbs are only patrolled during business hours. Infringement could net you a $250 ticket.

Most parking meters accept quarters only, and for long-term parking, car parks (public garages) are generally your best bet in the downtown area, particularly if you're there for more than an hour. And if you should venture across the Golden Gate or Bay Bridges, make sure you have enough cash to pay the toll on the return trip ($3 for the Golden Gate Bridge and $2 for the Bay Bridge).

CalTrans Highway Information Service

817 1717/www.dot.ca.gov/hq/roadinfo. **Open** 24hrs daily.
This automated service, which gives information on the latest highway conditions, is accessed by touchtone telephone only. Alternatively, phone 1-916 445 1534 and listen to a recorded message.

Breakdown services

AAA Emergency Road Service

1-800 222 4357/www.aaa.com.
Open 24hrs daily.
AAA members (including members of affiliated clubs, such as the British AA) receive free towing and roadside service. *See also p276*.

Golden Gate Towing Company

826 8866.
If you don't have a motorclub card, phone this outfit for roadside service. It will also recommend repair shops.

Fuel stations

Chevron

2399 Market Street, between Castro & Noe Streets, Castro (621 2570).
Open 8am-midnight daily.
Map p314 X1.

Downtown Union

390 First Street, between Folsom & Harrison Streets, SoMa (957 1754).
Open 24hrs daily. **Map** p311 H/J4.

76 19th

1401 19th Avenue, between Kirkham & Judah Streets, Sunset District (681 3860). **Open** 24hrs daily.

Shell Oil

1898 Van Ness Avenue, between Washington & Clay Streets, Pacific Heights (567 6737). **Open** 24hrs daily. **Map** p308 F3.

Parking

Although there are some low-cost garages, prices increase dramatically for long-term parking. Check the posted prices before you park and inquire about discounted (or 'validated') rates and times. If you're parking during the day, keep an eye out for a few large city lots where you can plug a parking meter by the hour (keep a pocketful of quarters handy). Here are some useful, late-opening parking garages.

Embarcadero Center Parking

Between Battery, Drumm, Clay & Sacramento Streets, Financial District (772 0670). **Open** 24hrs daily. **Map** p309 H3.

Located under the Embarcadero Center. At certain hours, having your ticket validated at an Embarcadero establishment will decrease the rate.

Fifth & Mission Yerba Buena Gardens Garage

833 Mission Street, between Fourth & Fifth Streets, SoMa (982 8522). **Open** 24hrs daily. **Map** p311 G/H4.

Japan Center Garage

1660 Geary Boulevard, between Webster & Laguna Streets, Western Addition (567 4573). **Open** 6.30am-2.30am Mon-Thur, Sun; 24hrs Fri, Sat. **Map** p310 E4.

Lombard Garage

2055 Lombard Street, between Webster & Fillmore Streets, Marina (440 1984). **Open** 7am-midnight Mon, Sun; 7am-1am Tue-Wed; 7am-2.30am Thur; 7am-3am Fri, Sat. **Map** p307 E2.

New Mission Bartlett Garage

3255 21st Street, between Bartlett & Valencia Streets, Mission (821 6715). **Open** 6.30am-midnight Mon-Thur; 6.30am-2am Fri, Sat; 8.30am-midnight Sun. **Map** p314 Y2.

St Mary's Garage

433 Kearny Street, between Pine & California Streets, Chinatown (956 8106). **Open** 24hrs daily. **Map** p309 H3.

Union Square Garage

333 Post Street (enter on Geary Street), between Stockton & Powell Streets, Union Square (397 0631). **Open** 24hrs daily. **Map** p309 G3/4.

Vallejo Street Garage

766 Vallejo Street, between Stockton & Powell Streets, North Beach (989 4490). **Open** 24hrs daily. **Map** p308 G2.

Vehicle hire

A credit card and driver's licence are required when renting a car. There are dozens of rental companies within the city as well as at San Francisco International Airport, and it definitely pays to shop around (national companies usually offer the best deals and service). Before you rent a car, make sure your own motor insurance or credit card company covers you; otherwise, you'll need to pay an additional surcharge. Most car rental companies stipulate minimum and maximum age requirements. Carrying car insurance is mandatory for all drivers in California.

National rental companies

Alamo 1-800 327 9633
www.alamo.com
Avis 1-800 831 2847
www.avis.com
Budget 1-800 527 0700
www.drivebudget.com
Dollar 1-800 800 4000
www.dollar.com
Enterprise 1-800 325 8007
www.enterprise.com
Hertz 1-800 654 3131
www.hertz.com
Rent-A-Wreck 282 6293
Thrifty 1-800 367 2277
www.thrifty.com

Local rental companies

Ace 771 7711
A-One 771 3977
City Rent-A-Car 861 1312
www.cityrentacar.com
Payless Car Rental 292 1000
www.800-payless.com

Motorbike rental

Easy riders should head for **Dubbelju Motorcycle Rentals** in SoMa (271 Clara Street, between Fifth and Sixth Streets; 495 2774), which can set you up with a Harley or BMW of your choice (from $99 a day), as long as you have a valid driver's licence, credit card deposit and plenty of dollars burning a hole in your pocket.

American Automobile Association (AAA)

150 Van Ness Avenue, CA 94102, between Fell & Hayes Streets, Civic Center (565 2012/touring info 565 2711/emergency service 1-800 222 4357). **Open** 8.30am-5pm Mon-Fri. **Map** p310 F5.
The fabulous Triple A provides excellent – and free – maps, guides, specific travel routes (TripTiks) and towing services to members of the AAA or an affiliated organisation (such as the British AA or RAC).

Cycling

Bike routes & rental

The San Francisco Department of Parking and Traffic recently designated a grid of major cycle routes across the city, indicated by oval-shaped bike-and-bridge markers. North–south routes employ odd numbers; east–west routes even; full-colour signs indicate primary crosstown routes; neighbourhood routes appear in green and white. Look in the Yellow Pages for a map or call the Bicycle Information Line on 585 2453 for more details.
In addition, two scenic cycle routes – one from Golden Gate Park south to Lake Merced, the other from the southern end of Golden Gate Bridge north to Marin County – invite cyclists to share the road with the ubiquitous automobile. For more about cycling and places that rent bikes, *see p244* **On your bike**.

Bikes on public transport

You can take bicycles on BART free of charge, except between 6.30am and 9am and 3.30pm and 6.30pm Monday to Friday, when they are banned. Bike racks on the front of certain Muni buses take up to two bikes. On CalTrain, cyclists can bring their bikes on to cars displaying yellow bike symbols and stow them in lockers at the stations at either end of their trip.

Walking

Exploring on foot isn't the fastest way to see the city, but it's the most enjoyable and certainly the most complete. Not until you've peeped in while passing a Pacific Heights window, hiked the twisting trails in the Presidio, slurped gelato while strolling through Washington Square park or window-shopped wistfully the *panaderías* of the Mission have you truly begun to experience the pleasure of pedestrian San Francisco. In a city with more than its share of frustrated drivers, surly cabbies and behind-schedule bus drivers, pedestrians – for the most part – walk unimpeded, often arriving sooner than their petrol-consuming counterparts.

To avoid the steepest hills, get a copy of the *San Francisco Bike Map & Walking Guide*, which indicates the gradient of the city's streets. The Sunday *San Francisco Chronicle*'s 'Datebook' lists more than 20 walking tour companies. *See also p54* **The city on foot: Walking tours**.

Resources A-Z

Age restrictions

In California, you have to be 16 years old to drive, 18 to smoke and have sex (not necessarily at the same time) and 21 to drink. California's drinking laws are particularly strict; a major error is having an 'open container' in your car or any public area that isn't zoned for alcohol consumption. Cops will give you a ticket on the spot for walking down the street with a beer in your hand, or even having an empty beer can on the back seat of your car. You don't want to know what happens if you're busted for drunk driving, so don't do it.

Business

There are, arguably, only a few cities in the US that can match San Francisco's simultaneous qualifications as a world-class holiday and business destination. From MacWorld conferences to the 50th Anniversary gala held for the United Nations, conventions annually draw 1.4 million participants to the city. Based on a 1999 survey, San Francisco Convention & Visitor Bureau officials say that 1.2 million of San Francisco's 17.3 million yearly visitors are on a combined business/pleasure trip.

The city and its greater Bay Area zone of influence are home to several of the country's biggest companies. Besides banking (the Pacific Stock Exchange, a Federal Reserve Bank and the California State Banking Department are all based in the city, as are Wells Fargo Bank and Charles Schwab & Co), the region's list of resident corporations covers industries such as telecommunications, bio-medical technology, law, shipping and clothes manufacturing. Another big business here, of course, is technology. Silicon Valley, the name given to the stretch of the Bay Area from Redwood City to San Jose, is where the earliest working models of personal computers were first developed more than 30 years ago. Today, Apple Computers, Sun Microsystems, Hewlett-Packard, Intel and Advanced Micro Devices are all based in Silicon Valley.

With high-tech comes the high life, hard work and long hours. It is not uncommon to see the CEO and lower ranks playing foosball in the early evening while brainstorming new ideas. Catered meals from area restaurants are the standard – and never fear, vegans and carnivores alike will enjoy what's being served. However, laid-back or not, meetings with potential investors, and luncheons with new clients, both still demand the token tie.

Convention centres

Moscone Convention Center

747 Howard Street, between Third & Fourth Streets, SoMa (974 4000/ www.moscone.com). Bus 12, 15, 30, 45, 76. **Map** p311 H4.
Moscone Center is San Francisco's meeting and exhibition facility. It is situated on two adjacent, 11-acre blocks bounded by Mission, Folsom, Third and Fourth Streets. The centre is within walking distance of nearly 20,000 hotel rooms. It is already booked through February 2003; reservations for hotels in the area should be made as early as possible. The busiest convention months are usually May and September, and mid-January, when San Francisco hosts the MacWorld Expo.

Courier services

Local messenger & delivery services

Local companies include **Quicksilver Messenger Service** (431 2500), famous for its daring bikers; **Aero Special Delivery** (1-800 443 8333/www.aerodelivery.com), which specialises in statewide message and parcel delivery; and **California Overnight** (1-877 334 2022/www.calover.com). The **US Post Office** (1-800 222 1811/ www.usps. com) can deliver overnight to most US cities and, in some neighbourhoods, delivers express parcels on Sundays. Check the Yellow Pages for more courier services.

International couriers

DHL *1-800 225 5345/www.dhl.com.* **Open** 24hrs daily. **Credit** AmEx, Disc, MC, V.

Federal Express
24hr 1-800 238 5355/www.federalexpress.com. **Open** 8.30am-8pm Mon-Sat. **Credit** AmEx, DC, MC, V.

UPS
24hr 1-800 742 5877/www.ups.com. **Open** 9am-5pm Mon-Fri. **Credit** (deliveries by air only) AmEx, MC, V.

Message services

American Voice Mail

1-800 347 2861/www.americanvoicemail.com. **Open** 5am-7pm Mon-Fri; 6.30am-4pm Sat. **Credit** (after 1st payment only) MC, V.
Confidential voicemail service for unlimited messages, 24 hours a day.

Mail Boxes Etc USA

2269 Chestnut Street, at Scott Street, Marina (922 4500/www.mbe.com). Bus 28, 30, 43, 76. **Open** 9am-6pm Mon-Fri; 10am-4pm Sat. **Credit** AmEx, DC, Disc, MC, V. **Map** p307 D2.
Passport photos, mailbox rental, mail forwarding, packing, shipping, copy and facsimile services.

Office services

Copy Central

705 Market Street, at Third Street, Financial District (882 7377/ www.copycentral.com). BART Montgomery Street/Muni Metro F, J, K, L, M, N/bus 5, 6, 7, 9, 21, 31, 66, 71. **Open** 7.30am-10pm Mon-Thur; 7.30am-7pm Fri; 10am-6pm Sat; noon-6pm Sun. **Credit** AmEx, MC, V. **Map** p311 H4.
One of seven franchised shops specialising in photocopying, printing, binding, fax and overnight mail delivery services. Copy Central

Emergencies

Ambulance, fire brigade or police
Dial 911 (toll-free from any phone booth).

Pacific, Gas and Electric Company (PG&E)
Emergency service 1-800 743 5000/information hotline 1-800 743 5002.
Open 24hrs daily.

Poison Control Center
1-800 523 2222.
Open 24hrs daily.

Water Department City & County of San Francisco
Emergency service 550 4911.
Open 24hrs daily.

is trying to compete with the omnipresent Kinko's and though they're not open 24 hours,they're nearly as successful. Many branches have attached desktop publishing centres. Staff are friendly and helpful.

Kinko's

201 Sacramento Street, at Davis Street, Financial District (834 0240/ www.kinkos.com). BART Embarcadero/Muni Metro F, J, K, L, M, N/bus 1, 41. **Open** 24hrs daily. **Credit** AmEx, Disc, MC, V. **Map** p309 H3.
Kinko's numerous outlets offer an array of services, including on-site use of computers, online facilities, printing, photocopying, fax and overnight mail delivery and collection. Be prepared to queue. **Branches**: throughout the Bay Area. Phone 1-800 254 6567 for your nearest.

Office Depot

855 Harrison Street, between Fourth & Fifth Streets, SoMa (243 9959/ www.officedepot.com). Bus 27, 30, 42, 45, 76. **Open** 8am-7pm Mon-Fri; 9am-6pm Sat; 11am-5pm Sun. **Credit** AmEx, Disc, MC, V. **Map** p311 H4.
Photocopying, printing, desktop publishing, custom stamps, engraved signs, fax devices and every office product on the planet.

Useful organisations

The **San Francisco Main Library** (*see p68*) offers access to annual reports from most major US and Bay Area corporations; Standard & Poors' evaluations of publicly owned companies; the Dunn and Bradstreet Business Database; Securities and Exchange Commission data on US businesses; US Census information; environmental compliance records; medical news and statistics. You don't need a library card for in-house print research or to read back-dated newspapers and magazines. The research desk staff are among the best in the business and information professionals – journalists, in particular – often seek their help. Phone 557 4488.

Law Library

401 Van Ness Avenue, at McAllister Street, Civic Center (554 6821/ www.ci.sf.ca.us/sfll). Bus 5, 42, 47, 49. **Open** 8.30am-5pm Mon-Fri. **Map** p310 F4.
Open to the public for research, but only San Francisco-based lawyers can borrow books and materials.

Mechanics Institute Library

57 Post Street, between Montgomery & Kearny Streets, Financial District (393 0101/www.milibrary.org). BART Montgomery Street/Muni Metro F, J, K, L, M, N/bus 2, 5, 6, 7, 9, 21, 31, 38, 66, 71. **Open** 9am-9pm Mon-Thur; 9am-6pm Fri; 10am-5pm Sat; 1-5pm Sun. **Admission** *Non-members* day pass $5; weekly pass $10. **Map** p309 H3.
This private organisation offers many of the same data sources as the Main Library, especially CD-Rom-based search tools, but in only a fraction of the space. Its true source of fame, however, lies in its chess room (421 2258/www.chessclub.org; open 11am-10.50pm daily), which has long been considered one of the best places in town for a quiet game.

Consulates

For a complete list, consult the Yellow Pages, or phone directory assistance (411).

Australia 362 6160
Britain 981 3030
www.britainusa.com
Canada 1-213 346 2700
EU Delegation (based in Washington, DC) 1-202 862 9500
www.eurounion.org
Republic of Ireland 392 4214
New Zealand 399 1255

Consumer

Better Business Bureau

243 9999/www.bbbgoldengate.org. **Open** 24hrs daily.
Provides information on the reliability of a company or service and a list of companies with good business records. The bureau also has referral listings for anything from accountants to zipper repair services, plumbers to auto repair, and is the place to call to file a complaint about a company.

California Attorney General's Office Public Inquiry Unit

1-800 952 5225/http://caag.state.ca.us/consumers. **Open** 24hrs daily.
This office reviews consumer complaints. Call to make a complaint about consumer law enforcement or any other agency.

Disabled

Despite its challenging topography, San Francisco has made its mark as a highly accommodating city for most disabled travellers. In fact, California is the national leader in providing the disabled with ready access to facilities and attractions. General privileges include unlimited free parking in designated (blue) parking stalls and free parking at most metered spaces (a visible blue and white disabled 'parking placard' is required for both); as well as special prices and arrangements for train, bus, air and sightseeing travel.

In addition, all public buildings within the city are required by law to be wheelchair accessible and have disabled-accessible toilets; most city buses can 'kneel' to make access easier and have handgrips and spaces designed for wheelchair users; most city street corners have ramped kerbs and most restaurants and hotels are either designed (or have been redesigned) to accommodate wheelchairs.

Of course, what a building is supposed to have and what it really has can be two different things, so the wheelchair-bound traveller's best bet is to contact the **Independent Living Resource Center** (543 6222/www.freed.org).

Braille Institute of San Francisco

1-800 272 4553. **Open** 9am-5pm Mon-Fri.
Volunteers connect anyone who has sight difficulties with services for the blind throughout the US.

California Relay Service

TTD to voice 1-800 735 2929/ voice to TTD 1-800 735 2922.
Relays telephone calls between TTD and voice callers. The service is available 24hrs daily.

Crisis Line for the Handicapped

1-800 426 4263. **Open** 24hrs daily.
A phoneline and referral service offering advice on topics ranging from transport to stress.

Electricity

Throughout the United States, electricity voltage is 110-120V 60-cycle AC. Except for dual-voltage, flat-pin plug shavers, any European appliances will need to be run with an adaptor, available at airport shops, some pharmacies, electronics stores (such as Radio Shack) and department stores.

Gay, lesbian & queer

For more information on all aspects of queer life in the city, *see chapter* **Queer San Francisco**.

Helplines

For HIV and AIDS helplines, *see p280*.

Community United Against Violence

333 4357. **Open** 24hrs daily.
A counselling group assisting gay, lesbian, bisexual and transgender victims of domestic violence and hate crimes.

New Leaf

626 7000.
Open 9am-9pm Mon-Fri.
A counselling service for gay men, transgenders, lesbians and bisexuals, that deals with issues ranging from substance abuse to HIV.

Parents, Families & Friends of Lesbians and Gays (P-FLAG)

921 8850.
Open 24hr answerphone.
A helpline offering support for families and friends of gay and lesbian teens and adults.

Other groups

Gay & Lesbian Medical Association

255 4547.
Open 9am-5.30pm Mon-Fri.
Nearly 2,000 gay, lesbian and bisexual physicians and medical students make up this professional organisation, which publishes guides, holds forums, advocates rights of gay and lesbian physicians and offers medical referrals.

Health & medical

For complementary and alternative medicine, *see p179*. For opticians, *see p183*. For pharmacies, *see p180*.

Accident & emergency

You will have to pay for emergency treatment. Contact the emergency number on your travel insurance before seeking treatment and you will be directed to a hospital that will deal directly with your insurance company back home. Emergency rooms are open 24hrs a day at:

Davies Medical Center

Castro Street, at Duboce Avenue, Lower Haight (565 6060). Muni Metro N/bus 24. **Map** p313 E6.

St Francis Memorial Hospital

900 Hyde Street, between Bush & Pine Streets, Nob Hill (353 6300). Bus 2, 3, 4, 27/cable car California. **Map** p308 F3.

San Francisco General Hospital

1001 Potrero Avenue, between 22nd & 23rd Streets, Potrero Hill (206 8111). Bus 9, 33, 48. **Map** p314 Z2.

UCSF Medical Center

505 Parnassus Avenue, between Third & Hillway Avenues, Sunset District (476 1037). Muni Metro N/bus 6, 43, 66. **Map** p312 B/C6.

Clinics

Haight Ashbury Free Clinic

558 Clayton Street, at Haight Street, Haight-Ashbury (487 5632). Muni Bus 7, 33, 37, 43, 66, 71. **Open** 1-9pm Mon; 9am-9pm Tue-Wed; 1-5pm Thur, Fri; 24hr answerphone. **Map** p313 C6.
Free primary health care is provided to the uninsured. Speciality clinics include podiatry, chiropractics, pediatrics and HIV testing. You will need to make an appointment.

Lyon-Martin Women's Health Services

1748 Market Street, between Octavia & Gough Streets, Upper Market (565 7667). Muni Metro F, J, K, L, M, N/bus 6, 7, 66, 71. **Open** 8.30am-5pm Mon, Tue, Thur, Fri; 11am-7pm Wed. **Credit** MC, V. **Map** p310 F5.
Named after two of the founders of the modern lesbian movement in the US, the Lyon-Martin clinic offers affordable health care for women in a lesbian-friendly environment. Phone to make an appointment.

St Anthony Free Medical Clinic

105 Golden Gate Avenue, at Jones Street, Tenderloin (241 8320/ www. stanthonysf.org). BART Civic Center/ Muni Metro J, K, L, M, N/bus 5, 6, 7, 9, 21, 66, 71. **Open** *Drop-in clinic* 8am-noon, 1-4.30pm Mon, Tue, Thur, Fri; 8am-noon Wed. **Map** p310 G4.
Free medical services for those with or without insurance. Arrive early.

Contraception & abortion

Planned Parenthood Clinics

815 Eddy Street, between Van Ness Avenue & Franklin Street, Tenderloin (1-800 967 7526). Bus 31, 42, 47, 49. **Open** 9am-5pm Mon, Wed, Fri; 8.30am-4pm Tue; noon-8pm Thur; 9am-2pm Sat. **Credit** MC, V. **Map** p310 F4.
In addition to contraception services and the morning-after pill, Planned Parenthood provides low-cost general health care services, HIV testing and gynaecological exams.

Dentists

Dental Society Referral Service

421 1435. **Open** 24hrs daily.
Referrals are made by the Society, based on geographic location and the services desired.

University of the Pacific School of Dentistry

2155 Webster Street, at Sacramento Street, Pacific Heights (929 6501). Bus 1, 3, 22. **Open** 8.30am-5pm Mon-Fri. **Map** p307 E3.
Supervised dentists-in-training provide a low-cost service. Be warned, though: you'll spend little money for a long time in the chair.

HIV & AIDS

AIDS-HIV Nightline

434 2437. **Open** 5pm-5am daily.
Crisis hotline offering emotional support. English only.

California AIDS Foundation Hotline

1-800 367 2437/863 2437. **Open** 9am-9pm Mon-Fri; 11am-6pm Sat, Sun.
A multilingual hotline that offers the most up-to-date information related to the HIV virus, as well as advice on safe sex, taken from an enormous database of Californian services.

Helplines

Alcoholics Anonymous

621 1326. **Open** 24hrs daily.

Center for Substance Abuse Treatment

1-800 662 4357. **Open** 8am-4.30pm Mon-Fri.

Drug Crisis Information

362 3400/hearing-impaired 781 2224. **Open** 24hrs daily.
Call Drug Crisis Information if you need someone to talk you through a bad drug trip or want to know the effects of a particular drug, an overdose remedy or how to get into a treatment programme.

Lawyers Committee for Civil Rights, Immigrant & Refugee Rights Project

543 9444. **Open** 9am-5.30pm Mon-Fri.
Legal services are provided on a case-by-case basis for those seeking political asylum.

Narcotics Anonymous

621 8600. **Open** 24hrs daily.

SF General Hospital

206 8125. **Open** 24hrs daily.
Those suffering from a psychiatric breakdown or looking for someone who has been taken by the police or paramedics for acting out of control should contact this hotline.

SF Rape Treatment Center

821 3222. **Open** 24hrs daily.
Call here within 72 hours of a sex crime and nurses or social workers will provide counselling and guide you through medical and legal procedures. Patients must be residents of San Francisco or victims of a crime occurring within the city.

Suicide Prevention

781 0500. **Open** 24hrs daily.
Trained community volunteers lend a sympathetic ear.

Talk Line Family Support

441 5437. **Open** 24hrs daily.
Trained volunteers counsel children suffering from abuse or parents involved in child abuse and provide follow-up services.

Victims of Crime Resource Center

1-800 842 8467. **Open** 8am-6pm Mon-Fri; 24hr answerphone Sat, Sun.
Advises victims of their rights and refers them to local resources.

Women Against Rape Crisis Hotline

647 7273. **Open** 24hrs daily.
This is the place to find counselling, support and legal service for sexual assault victims and their partners.

ID

Even if you look 30, you'll need photo ID (preferably a driver's licence with a photo, or a passport) to get into most of San Francisco's bars or nightclubs (and to buy alcohol in a restaurant or shop).

Immigration & Customs

Standard immigration regulations apply to all US visitors, which means you may have to wait (maybe an hour or more) when you arrive at Immigration. During your flight, you will be issued with two forms – an immigration and a customs declaration form – to be presented to an official when you land. You will need to explain the nature of your visit. Expect close questioning if you're planning a long visit and don't have a return ticket or much money with you. You will usually be granted an entry permit to cover the length of your stay. Work permits are hard to get, and you are not permitted to work without one (*see p288*).

US Customs rules allow foreigners to bring in $100 worth of gifts ($400 for returning Americans) before paying duty. One carton of 200 cigarettes (or 100 cigars) and one litre of liquor (spirits) is allowed. No plants, fruit, meat or fresh produce can be taken through Customs. For more detailed information, contact your nearest US embassy or consulate. If you have questions about US immigration policies, you can call the **Northern California Coalition for Immigrant Rights** (243 8215/ www.nccir.org).

Insurance

It's advisable to take out comprehensive insurance cover before arriving: it's almost impossible to arrange in the US. Make sure you have adequate health cover, since medical expenses can be high. See p279 for a list of San Francisco hospitals and emergency rooms.

Internet

As you might expect from such a high-tech city, it is relatively easy to get online in San Francisco. Almost all hotel rooms have dataports; the most expensive ones offer high-speed Internet access and laptops. Many hotels provide at least one computer for their guests' use, where you can receive and send email via a free account with Hotmail, Yahoo or similar. If you already have an account with a global Internet Service Provider (ISP), such as AOL or CompuServe, you can use it in San Francisco – all you need to do is change the dial-up access number (although you may have to pay a surcharge on top of your current plan). Alternatively, set up a temporary account with a reliable local or national provider, such as Earthlink.

If you're travelling without a computer and your hotel does not have one, the best places to log online are office services centres (*see p277*) or the Main Library (*see p68*), which has six express terminals on the first floor, available for free for 15 minutes on a first come, first-served basis.

For the best of San Francisco-related websites, *see p289*.

AOL 1-800 827 6364/national dial-up number 1-800 716 0023
www.aol.com
CompuServe 1-800 848 8990
www.compuserve.com
Earthlink 1-800 327 8454
www.earthlink.net

Left luggage

You could also contact one of the larger hotels and see if you can leave bags with them.

Airport Travel Agency

1-650 877 0421.
Open 7am-11pm daily.
Located at the International terminal of the San Francisco airport, this company will store anything from a carry-on piece of luggage to a bicycle. Prices vary depending on size and length of time.

Oakland International Airport

1-510 577 4000.
Located in terminals 1 and 2. Lockers are $4.50 per day.

San Jose International Airport

Lockers are located in terminal A across from Gates A4 and A8 and in terminal C next to Gate C7. Locker rentals are $2 for the first 24 hours; $4 each additional 24-hour period.

Legal help

Lawyer Referral Service

989 1616.
Open 8.30am-5.30pm Mon-Fri.
Legal interviewers refer callers to experienced attorneys and mediators for all legal problems, including criminal, business and immigration.

Libraries

For **San Francisco Main Library**, *see p68*. For legal and business libraries, *see p278*.

Lost property

Property Control

850 Bryant Street, between Sixth & Seventh Streets, SoMa (553 1377). Bus 27, 42. **Open** 8am-4.30pm Mon-Fri. **Map** p311 H5.
Make a police report and cross your fingers – the chance of someone returning a lost item is about as good as winning the California lottery.

Airports

For items lost during flight, contact the specific airline.

San Francisco International Airport
1-650 821 7014. **Open** 8am-8pm Mon-Fri.
Oakland International Airport
1-510 577 4095. **Open** 8.30am-noon, 1-5pm Mon-Fri.
San Jose International Airport
1-408 277 5419. **Open** 7am-6pm Mon-Fri.

Public transport

If you have left something on **Muni** transport, phone its lost-and-found office on 923 6168. For **BART**, phone 1-510 464 7090 for **AC Transit** 1-510 891 4706; **Golden Gate Transit** 257 4476; and **SamTrans** 1-800 660 4287.

Taxis

Phone the relevant cab firm:
City Wide Dispatch 920 0700
Luxor 282 1224 ext 209
National 648 4444
Veteran's 552 3116
Yellow 282 3737 ext 221

Media

San Francisco media evidently exists not only to report and reflect what's going on, but to confirm its readers' and viewers' collective belief that they're living in the most trend-setting quadrant of the globe. Oddly, media here isn't a highly competitive realm – the city supports only one major newspaper, the *San Francisco Chronicle*. Its only competitor, the *Examiner*, was shut down in a controversial buy-out by its parent company in 2000, leaving the remaining paper in the hands of new owners, who seem to have neither the resources nor the know-how to make anything of it. Possibly the only ones to benefit from the sale have been the alternative weekly tabloids, the *San Francisco Bay Guardian* and *SF Weekly*, which now command more respect and readership.

In general, though, some of the best media is based out of town. The *San Jose Mercury News* remains the best read, and Oakland's KTVU receives the best ratings for news.

Newspapers

There are a few local papers to choose from, but if you're looking for more international coverage, the regional edition of the *New York Times* ($1) or national edition of the *Los Angeles Times* (50¢) are your best bets. *The Wall Street Journal* ($1) has an excellent news brief on the front page and some of the best feature writing in the country – though its op-ed page is famously dominated by a slew of reactionary conservatives. The vapid *USA Today* (50¢) works well as fishwrap; you'll soon learn why it's distributed free in hotels.

San Francisco Chronicle

www.sfgate.com
Complaining about 'the Chron', or 'the Comical' as locals call it, has become something of a cliché. The region's largest circulation paper (50¢) is the only real choice for local news since the Hearst Corporation purchased it for $660 million in 2000 and closed down its only rival, the *Examiner*. Since the buy-out, the paper has doubled its staff, beefed up its local and international coverage and been given a new, more mature look. Still, aside from a number of good columnists who make it an entertaining Sunday read, it still lacks the punch and vigour of a big-city newspaper in the mould of those in New York or Los Angeles. The Sunday 'Datebook', or what locals call the 'pink', is a tabloid entertainment and arts supplement published on pink paper, which includes listings, concert reviews, capsule movie reviews and suchlike – remains the most compelling reason to pick up the Chron.

San Jose Mercury News

www.bayarea.com
If you're thirsting for news outside San Francisco, this paper (50¢) offers the Bay Area's best overall news reporting, business and sport; its business coverage of Silicon Valley and Internet commerce is first-rate.

San Francisco Bay Guardian

www.sfbg.com
One of a pair of free weekly arts tabloids (the other is the *SF Weekly*) that battle for supremacy in San Francisco, this is a thick, lively rag that mixes an unapologetically progressive stance with dedication to a full range of arts listings. Exhaustive and opinionated, it's definitely the better of the two weeklies. It eagerly pisses off the conservative local establishment by exposing cronyism, graft, fraud or double standards. Distributed free from newspaper boxes and in cafés and coffee-shops.

SF Weekly

www.sfweekly.com
Though light on politics and in-depth, issue-oriented pieces, the *Weekly* is an invaluable resource for keeping up with the ever-changing arts and music scene. Highlights include Seattle-based syndicated columnist Dan Savage's brutally frank sex advice column, 'Savage Love', and a personal ads section so steamy it would make an exhibitionist blush. Available in the same places that carry the *Guardian*.

San Francisco Bay Times

A free fortnightly tabloid directed at the gay and lesbian community, the *Bay Times* features events listings, social and political commentary and classified advertisements and personals. It can be found in coffee-shops and bookstores in the Castro.

BAR (Bay Area Reporter)

www.ebar.com
Similar to the *Bay Times*, free weekly *BAR* features listings and news that affects the gay community. Copies can be found in most of the same places as the *Times*.

Magazines

One of the best in town, **San Francisco Magazine** is an increasingly lively glossy monthly covering everything from local politics and policy issues to the Bay Area's ravenous restaurant scene. **Zyzzyva** is a literary publication produced three times a year, offering short stories, poetry, creative non-fiction and original art. **Speak**, a fiction-music-fashion-film quarterly is artful and interesting, while the quarterly **Juxtapoz** preaches to the alternative arts crowd.

Several business publications, a few devoted to the rapidly fading Internet economy, continue to publish in San Francisco, among them **Red Herring**, **Business 2.0** and the seminal **Wired**. Computer magazines such as **PCWorld** and **MacWorld** continue to thrive, proving that in the Bay Area geekdom will always survive.

Television

The Bay Area has affiliates of all three major networks: ABC (local station is **KGO**, found on channel 7), NBC (is about to change to **KNTV**, probably channel 3) and CBS (**KPIX**, channel 5). Long-lasting independent station **KTVU** (channel 2) is now part of the Fox TV network. Acting as an alternative to the relentless advertising of commercial stations, PBS, the Public Broadcasting Service, has stations in San Francisco (**KQED**, on channel 9), in San Jose (**KTEH**, channel 54) and in San Mateo (**KCSM**, channel 60). These stations receive a meagre subsidy from the federal government and solicit funds from viewers.

Radio

San Francisco's constantly changing radio profile reflects a number of ongoing difficulties: that of attracting elusive listeners in a competitive market and of outsmarting weather and geography, which combine to undermine reliable radio signals. But don't think for a minute that Bay Area radio isn't spectacular. The weaker, non-commercial stations lie to the left of the FM dial; the powerhouses with the loudest ads cluster on the right. AM is mostly reserved for talk, news shows and sports broadcasts, with a few foreign-language, oldie and Christian stations peppering the mix.

News & talk

For the latest news, **KGO** (810 AM), **KQED** (88.5 FM) and its competitor, **KALW** (91.7 FM), remain your best bets. Beyond that, Berkeley-based **KPFA** (94.1 FM) is also determined to give KQED a run for its money, and **KCBS** (740 AM), the local CBS affiliate, has likewise proved itself a station devoted to quality news (and priceless traffic reports, every ten minutes). **KSFO** (740 AM), meanwhile, boasts reactionary talk radio programmes in the morning and broadcasts the Oakland A's baseball games in the afternoon. **KNBR** (680 AM) is the voice for the SF Giants' baseball games and the place to tune in later for well-informed sporting debate.

Classical & jazz

KDFC (102.1 FM, 1220 AM) advertises itself as a 'radio concert hall'; however, it remains a bit on the stuffy side, and interrupts its conservative classical repertoire to run hyperactive ads for cars, wine and singles clubs.

Following the demise of KJAZ in the mid 1990s, San Francisco and the region have been hurting for a good jazz station. The adventurous **KCSM** (97.7 FM), a public radio station broadcast from a college in San Mateo, has taken up much of the slack, though its signal is relatively weak. Local **KKSF** (103.7 FM) bills itself as a 'soft jazz' station, but all too often sounds more like muzak than anything worth an extended listening – don't tune in while operating any heavy machinery.

Dance, hip hop & soul

Rarely can one find more energy than on **KMEL** (106 FM), the Bay Area's foremost station for pop and hip hop.

KYLD (94.9 FM) is something of a contender and definitely gets party-goers in the mood on weekend nights. For something different, tune in to tiny **KPOO** (89.5 FM), where innovative hip hop and hardcore rap alternate with cool blues shows on weekend nights. A Tuesday afternoon slot features music by John Coltrane.

Rock & pop

The hot station for alternative rockers is **KLLC** (97.3 FM). 'Alice', as it calls itself, seems to have stolen listeners from the weakening **KITS** ('Live 105', 105 FM), which seems to focus too often on bands that made it big in the 1980s – U2 and Depeche Mode meet Nirvana and Alanis Morissette. **KFOG** (104.5 FM) has a loyal following, providing an above-average mix of classic rock with new material and live concerts, much of it local. **KOME** (98.5 FM) has staked out the newest and youngest rock/pop territory and is a hit with teenagers. **KRQR** (97.3 FM) leans towards heavy metal; **KSAN** (107.7 FM) recently displaced 'Wild 107' and plays generic rock classics – more Steve Miller Band, anyone?

Those in search of more eclectic listening tune to college and independent stations such as **KALX** (90.7 FM), **KUSF** (90.3 FM), **KFJC** (89.7 FM) or **KPOO** (89.5 FM). On all these channels, you'll find diversity and innovative sounds, including acid jazz, Irish music, kids' shows, African and Latin music and the latest trip-hop remix. The best aural blend in the region, these indie stations represent the diverse, non-commercial musical bouillabaisse for which the Bay Area is known.

Country

Several country stations have popped up of late, most notably 'Young Country' **KYCY** (93.3 FM, 1550 AM), which plays a range from Garth Brooks and Wynona Judd to some of the genre's early innovators, such as Johnny Cash and Hank Williams.

Money

The US dollar ($) equals 100 cents (¢). Coins range from copper pennies (1¢) to silver nickels (5¢), dimes (10¢) and quarters (25¢). Half-dollar and dollar coins do exist, but are rarely used. Bills are all the same size and colour and come in $1, $5, $10, $20, $50 and $100 denominations, though the $100 bill is not universally accepted. In an attempt to clamp down on forgeries, there are new paper money designs (except the $1 bill); the old bills remain legal tender.

ATMs/cashpoints

Most ATMs accept Visa, MasterCard and American Express, among other cards. Note: almost all ATMs charge a usage fee. If you don't remember your PIN number or have somehow de-magnetised your card, most banks will dispense cash to card holders. The most omnipresent bank in the city, Wells Fargo, offers cash advances at any of its branches. Phone the following numbers for ATM locations:

Cirrus 1-800 424 7787
Plus System 1-800 843 7587
Wells Fargo 1-800 869 3557

Banks & bureaux de change

Most banks are open from 9am to 6pm Monday to Friday and on Saturday from 9am to 3pm. Photo ID is required to change travellers' cheques. Many banks do not exchange foreign currency, so arrive with some US dollars. If you're scheduled to arrive in San Francisco after 6pm, change money at the airport or, if you have US dollar travellers' cheques, buy something in order to get some change. If you want to cash travellers' cheques at a shop, ask first – some require a minimum purchase. You can also obtain cash with a credit card from certain banks, but be prepared to pay interest rates that vary daily. Most banks and shops accept travellers' cheques in US dollars.

American Express Travel Services

455 Market Street, at First Street, Financial District (536 2600/ www.americanexpress.com/travel). BART Montgomery Street or Embarcadero/Muni Metro F, J, K, L, M, N/bus 2, 5, 6, 7, 9, 21, 31, 38, 66, 71. **Open** 8.30am-5.30pm Mon-Fri; 9am-3.30pm Sat. **Map** p309 H3.

American Express will change money and travellers' cheques, and offers, for AmEx cardholders only, a poste restante service.

Thomas Cook

75 Geary Street, between Grant Avenue & Kearny Street, Union Square (1-800 287 7362/www.us.thomascook.com). Muni Metro F, J, K, L, M, N/bus 2, 3, 4, 30, 45, 76. **Open** 9am-5pm Mon-Fri; 10am-4pm Sat. **Map** p309 H3.

A complete foreign exchange service, including money transfer by wire. **Branch**: 2301 Shattuck Avenue, at Bancroft Way, Berkeley (1-510 849 8520). **Map** p315 L/M4. Closed Sat.

Western Union

1-800 325 6000/www.westernunion.com. **Open** 24hrs daily.

The old standby for bailing cash-challenged travellers out of trouble. Get advice on how to get money wired to you and where to pick it up at one of a dozen San Francisco locations. You can also wire money to anyone outside the state over the phone, using your MasterCard or Visa. Expect to pay a whopping 10% or more commission when sending money. Western Union also takes telegrams over the phone and charges them to your credit card.

Credit cards

You are strongly advised to bring at least one major credit card on your trip. They are accepted (and often required) at nearly all hotels, car rental agencies and airlines, as well as most restaurants, shops and petrol stations. The five major credit cards most accepted in the US are American Express, Diners Club, Discover, MasterCard and Visa.

Lost/stolen cards

American Express 1-800 992 3404
Diners Club 1-800 234 6377
Discover 1-800 347 2683
MasterCard 1-800 826 2181
Visa 1-800 336 8472

Lost/stolen travellers' cheques

American Express 1-800 221 7282
Visa 1-800 227 6811

Tax

In shops, sales tax of 8.5 per cent is added on to the label price within city limits, and

Earthquakes

It's unlikely that a major quake will strike during your stay, but for those who believe in being prepared, local lore has it that the safest place to be during a quake is on top of Twin Peaks – they are made of granite.

Check the United States Geological Survey's website – http://quake.wr.usgs.gov/ – for facts and figures, including hourly updated maps of recent quakes in California and Nevada.

What to do during a quake

● If indoors, stay there. Keep away from windows and, if you can, get under a sturdy piece of furniture, such as a desk. Steer clear of elevators.

● If outdoors, get into an open area away from anything that might shatter or collapse, such as windows, buildings, trees, bridges and power lines.

● If you're driving, pull over to the side of the road and stop. Avoid overpasses and power lines. Stay inside the vehicle until the shaking has stopped.

● After the earthquake, think before you act. Because gas lines may have ruptured, do not use lighters or candles or light a cigarette. Do not turn on lights or use electrical appliances.

American Red Cross

427 8000/http://www. crossnet.org/services/disaster/keepsafe/readyearth.html. **Open** 8.30am-5pm Mon-Fri. Information on earthquake and disaster preparedness.

8.25 per cent in surrounding cities. Hotels charge a 14 per cent room tax.

Police stations

Central Station

766 Vallejo Street, between Stockton & Powell Streets, North Beach (553 1532). Bus 12, 15, 41, 45/cable car Powell-Mason. **Map** p308 G2.

Southern Station

850 Bryant Street, between Sixth & Seventh Streets, SoMa (553 1373). Bus 27, 42. **Map** p311 H5.

Postal services

Most post offices are open from 9am to 5.30pm Monday to Friday, 9am to 2pm Saturday. All are closed on Sundays. Phone 1-800 275 8777 for information on your nearest branch hours and mailing facilities. Stamps can be bought at any post office and also at some hotel receptions, vending machines and ATMs. Stamps for postcards within the US cost 21¢; for Europe Australia and New Zealand 70¢. If you want to send a telegram, contact Western Union (*see p283*). For couriers and shippers, *see p277*.

Poste Restante (General Delivery)

Civic Center, 101 Hyde Street, San Francisco, CA 94102, at Golden Gate Avenue (1-800 275 8777). BART Civic Center/Muni Metro F, J, K, L, M, N/bus 5, 19. **Open** 10am-2pm Mon-Sat. **Map** p310 G4.

If you need to receive mail in SF and you're not sure where you'll be staying, have it posted to the General Post Office. Mail is kept for ten days from receipt and you must present some photo ID to retrieve it.

Religion

San Francisco is teeming with temples, whether Baptist or Buddhist, Jewish or Jehovah's Witness, Nazarene, New Age or Satanic. For more places of worship, see the Yellow Pages.

Calvary Presbyterian

2515 Fillmore Street, at Jackson Street, Pacific Heights (346 3832). Bus 3, 12, 22, 24. **Map** p307 E3.

First Congregational

Urban Life Center, 1101 O'Farrell Street, at Franklin Street, Western Addition (392 7461). Bus 38. **Map** p310 F4.

Glide Memorial

330 Ellis Street, at Taylor Street, Tenderloin (771 6300/www.glide.org). BART Powell Street/Muni Metro F, J, K, L, M, N/bus 27, 31, 38. **Map** p310 G4.

Grace Cathedral

1100 California Street, at Taylor Street, Nob Hill (749 6300/www.gracecathedral.org). Bus 1, 27/cable car California. **Map** p308 G3.

Old St Mary's Cathedral

660 California Street, at Grant Avenue, Chinatown (288 3800). Bus 1, 15, 30, 45/cable car California. **Map** p309 G/H3.

St Boniface Catholic Church

133 Golden Gate Avenue, at Leavenworth Street, Civic Center (863 7515). Bus 5. **Map** p310 G4.

St Mary's Cathedral

1111 Gough Street, at Geary Boulevard, Western Addition (567 2020). Bus 2, 3, 4, 38. **Map** p310 F4.

St Paul's Lutheran Church

930 Gough Street, between Turk & Eddy Streets, Western Addition (673 8088). Bus 31. **Map** p310 F4.

Temple Emanu-el

2 Lake Street, at Arguello Boulevard, Presidio Heights (751 2535). Bus 1, 4, 33. **Map** p306 B/C4.

Zen Center

300 Page Street, at Laguna Street, Lower Haight (863 3136/www.sfzc. org). Bus 6, 7, 66, 71. **Map** p310 F5.

Safety & security

Crime is a reality in all big cities, but San Franciscans generally feel secure in their town and follow one basic rule of thumb – use common sense. If a neighbourhood doesn't feel safe to you, it probably isn't. Only a few areas warrant caution during daylight hours and are of particular concern at night. These include the Tenderloin (north and east of Civic Center); SoMa (near the Mission/Sixth Street corner); Mission Street between 13th and 22nd Streets; and in the Hunter's Point neighbourhood near 3Com Park. Golden Gate Park and the Haight-Ashbury should be avoided at night. Many tourist areas are sprinkled with homeless people (notably the Union Square area), who beg for change but for the most part are harmless.

If you are unlucky enough to be mugged, your best bet is to give your attacker whatever he wants, then call the police from the nearest pay phone by dialling 911. (Don't forget to get the reference number on the claim report for insurance purposes and to get travellers' cheques refunds.) If you are the victim of a sexual assault and wish to make a report, call the police, who will escort you to the hospital for treatment. For helplines serving crime or rape victims, *see p280*.

Smoking

Smokers may rank as the only group of people who are not particularly welcome in San Francisco, home to some of the stiffest anti-smoking laws in the US (and possibly in the world). Smoking is banned in *all* public places, including building lobbies, banks, public buildings, sports arenas, theatres, offices, shops, restaurants, bars and any form of public transport. Many small hotels and B&Bs don't allow you to light up either (and, boy, do they get cross if you do). A select few bars cheerfully ignore the law.

Study

The California higher education system operates as a hierarchy, starting with publicly funded community colleges and city colleges at the lower end of the scale, followed by California State Universities, which cater primarily to undergraduates and do not grant doctorates, and, at the top of the pile, the University of California system, which includes formal, research-oriented universities with rigorous entry demands. There are also many private (and expensive) universities such as Stanford and the University of San Francisco.

In general, US universities are much more flexible about part-time studying than their European counterparts. Non-English-speaking students might have to pass a TOEFL (Test of English as a Foreign Language) exam and most students have to show proof of financial support.

The colleges

Academy of Art College

79 New Montgomery Street, CA 94105, between Mission & Market Streets, SoMa (274 2200/www.academyart.edu). BART Montgomery Street/Muni Metro F, J, K, L, M, N/bus 2, 3, 4, 5, 9, 30, 66, 71, 76. **Map** p309 H3.
Foreign students flock to this visual arts college, with satellite campuses all over the city, offering practical graduate and postgrad courses in fine arts, history and graphic design.

California College of Arts & Crafts

450 Irwin Street, CA 94107, between Eighth & Wisconsin Streets, Potrero Hill (703 9523/www.ccac-art.edu). Bus 19, 22. **Map** p311 H6.
With several campuses in both San Francisco and Oakland, the CCAC specialises in architecture as well as fine arts and design.

City College of San Francisco

50 Phelan Avenue, CA 94112, at Ocean Avenue, Balboa Park (main switchboard 239 3000/international students 239 3837/www.ccsf.cc.ca. us). Muni Metro J, K, M/bus 15, 29, 36, 43, 49.
The largest community college in the US, City teaches more than 80 subjects on its eight campuses and 150 satellite sites. It's the most affordable place to study in SF, and a good choice for a foreign language or computer class over the summer.

Mills College

5000 MacArthur Boulevard, Oakland, CA 94613 (undergraduate admissions 1-800 876 4557/graduate admissions 1-510 430 3309/www.mills.edu). BART Coliseum, then AC Transit bus 57, 58 to main entrance at Richards Gate/AC Transit bus N to Richards Gate.
A beautifully set, prestigious liberal women's college in Oakland, founded in 1852. Mills offers excellent MFA courses in art and creative writing.

San Francisco Art institute

800 Chestnut Street, CA 94133, between Jones & Leavenworth Streets, Russian Hill (1-800 345 7324/771 7020/www.sanfrancisco art.edu/). Bus 30/cable car Powell-Hyde or Powell-Mason. **Map** p308 F2.
A hip and prestigious art school, offering the spectrum in fine arts including painting, film, photography, sculpture and new genres. Expensive but well respected, SFAI has a good reputation for fostering one-on-one apprenticeships. Its student shows are legendary.

San Francisco Conservatory of Music

1201 Ortega Street, CA 94122, at 19th Avenue, Sunset District (564 8086/www.sfcm.edu). Bus 28.
Full- and part-time students study music at this small, independent conservatory, known for its excellent faculty and high standards.

San Francisco State University

1600 Holloway Avenue, CA 94132, at 19th Avenue, Stonestown (admissions 338 1113/www.sfsu.edu). Muni Metro M/bus 17, 18, 28, 29.
Like all publicly funded California schools, SFSU is trying desperately to do more with fewer resources. It's the largest in the city, with 27,000 students, and good for creative writing, business, ethnic studies and engineering disciplines. But be

patient: undergrad classes are always full and many potential students are turned away at the beginning of each semester. As a result, it can take five or six years to complete a degree.

Stanford University

Stanford, CA 94305. CalTrain to Palo Alto, then free Marguerite shuttle to campus (graduate admissions 1-650 723 4291/ undergraduate admissions 1-650 723 2091/www.stanford.edu).
A late 19th-century campus near Palo Alto, this private college is out of many students' league, with tuition, room and board costing about $31,500 a year. Academically highly competitive, Stanford is known for its business, law and medicine curricula.

UC Berkeley

Office of Undergraduate Admissions, 110 Sproul Hall, UC Berkeley, CA 94720 (graduate admissions 1-510 642 7404/undergraduate admissions 1-510 642 3175/ international students 1-510 642 3246/www.berkeley.edu). BART Berkeley. **Map** p315 M/N3.
The oldest in the nine-campus University of California system, Berkeley (called 'Cal' by locals) attracts some 30,000 students, including 9,000 postgrads. Famous for law and engineering, Berkeley also runs a controversial nuclear research lab in Livermore, an East Bay suburb. *See also p103.*

UC Berkeley Extension

English Language Programme, 55 Laguna Street, CA 94102, between Haight & Market Streets, Upper Market (course information & registration 1-510 642 4111/ www.unex.berkeley.edu). Muni Metro F/bus 6, 7, 66, 71. **Map** p310 F5.
Berkeley Extension in San Francisco and other Bay Area sites offers night and weekend courses in such subjects as film, the Internet, writing and women's studies. Classes are offered for working adults for college credits, but not for degrees.

University of California, San Francisco

400 Parnassus Avenue, CA 94143, at Fourth Avenue, Parnassus Heights (476 9000/www.ucsf.edu). Muni Metro N/bus 6, 43, 66. **Map** p312 B/C6.
A top-notch health and sciences university with schools of medicine, dentistry, pharmacy and nursing. UCSF also operates one of the best and least expensive clinics in the city for good health care. Admission to the school is rigorous, but it's certainly not impossible.

University of San Francisco

2130 Fulton Street, CA 94117, at Masonic Avenue, Richmond District (admissions 422 6563/financial aid 422 6303/www.usfca.edu). Bus 5, 31, 43. **Map** p313 C5.
One of 28 Jesuit universities and colleges in the US, USF has reputable business, law and communication arts. It has around 8,000 students. International students make up 10% of the student body and must show proof of financial support.

Visas & ID cards

To study in the Bay Area (or anywhere else in the US), you must apply for either an F-1 visa (for exchange students) or a J-1 visa (for full-time students enrolled in a degree programme). Both are valid for the duration of your course and a limited period afterwards. Foreign students will need to have an International Student Identity Card (ISIC) as proof of student status. This can be bought from your local travel agent or student travel office. In San Francisco, an ISIC costs $20 at Council Travel (530 Bush Street, between Grant Avenue and Stockton Street; 421 3473) or STA (36 Geary Street, between Kearny Street and Grant Avenue; 391 8407) – you need proof of studenthood, ID and a passport-size photo. Both also offer student discounts.

Telephones

Dialling & codes

The phone system in San Francisco is reliable and, at least for local calls, cheap. Long-distance, particularly overseas, calls are best paid for with a rechargeable, pre-paid phonecard ($6-$35) available from many shops and vending machines. You can also your MasterCard with AT&T (1-800 225 5288), MCI (1-800 532 8045) or Sprint (1-800 877 4646).

Direct dial calls

If you are dialling outside your area code, dial 1 + area code + phone number; on pay phones an operator or recording will tell you how much money to add.

Collect calls

For collect calls or when using a phone card, dial 0 + area code + phone number and listen for the operator or recorded instructions. If you are completely befuddled, you can always just dial 0 and plead your case with the operator.

Area codes

San Francisco and **Marin County** 415
Oakland and **Berkeley** 510
The peninsula cities 650
San Jose 408
Napa, **Sonoma** and **Mendocino Counties** 707

International calls

Dial 011 followed by the country code. If you need operator assistance with international calls, dial 00.
Australia 61
Germany 49
Japan 81
New Zealand 64
UK 44

Public phones

Public pay phones only accept nickels, dimes and quarters, but check for a dialling tone before you start feeding them your change. Local calls cost 35¢ and the price rises quickly as the distance between callers increases (an operator or recorded message will tell you how much to add).

Operator services

Operator assistance 0
Emergency (police, ambulance and fire) 911
Local and **long-distance directory enquiries** 411
Toll-free numbers generally start with 1-800 or 1-888, while pricey pay-per-call lines (usually phone-sex numbers) start with 1-900; don't confuse them.

Telephone directories

Directories are divided into Yellow Pages (classified) and White Pages (business and residential), and are available at most public phones and in hotels. They contain a wealth of travel info, including area codes, event calendars, park facilities, post office addresses and city zip codes. If you can't find one in the phone booth you're using, dial 411 (directory assistance) and ask for your listing by name.

Tourist information

For tourist centres outside San Francisco, *see chapter* **Trips Out of Town**.

San Francisco Visitor Information Center

Lower level of Hallidie Plaza, corner of Market & Powell Streets (391 2000/ www.sfvisitor.org). BART Powell Street/ Muni Metro J, K, L, M, N/bus 6, 7, 8, 9, 21, 26, 27, 31, 66, 71. **Open** 8.30am-5pm Mon-Fri; 9am-3pm Sat, Sun. **Map** p311 G4.
Located in downtown, this is the visitor centre for the very efficient and helpful San Francisco Convention & Visitor Bureau. You won't find any parking, but you will find tons of free maps, brochures, coupons and advice. For a 24-hour recorded message listing daily events and activities, or to request free information about hotels, restaurants and shopping, phone the number above. Or send a postcard with your address to PO Box 429097, San Francisco, CA 94102, USA.

Berkeley Convention & Visitors Bureau

2015 Center Street, Berkeley, CA 94704, at Shattuck Avenue (1-510 549 7040/ www.visitberkeley.com). BART Berkeley. **Open** 9am-5pm Mon-Fri. **Map** p315 L3.
A block from the downtown Berkeley BART station. Will post a visitors' guide on request.

Oakland Convention & Visitors Bureau

Suite 120, 475 14th Street, Oakland, CA 94612, between Broadway & Clay Street (1-510 839 9000/ www.oaklandcvb.com). BART 12th Street/City Center. **Open** 8.30am-5pm Mon-Fri.
Located in downtown Oakland, opposite City Hall. Call if you would like to be sent a visitors' guide to Oakland.

Mobile phones

Whereas in Europe mobile (cellular) phones work on the GSM network at either 900 or 1800mHz, the US does not have a standard mobile phone network that covers the whole country – which means that visitors from other parts of the US will have to check with their service provider that they can use their phone in San Francisco. However, the Bay Area does offer access to the GSM network at 1900mHz, so European visitors – with 'tri-band' phones that work in the US – should contact their service provider a few days before they leave to set up international roaming. (If you are taking your mobile to San Francisco, don't forget to pack your charger and any adaptor you might need.)

Also check the price of calls before you go; rates will be hefty and you will probably be charged for receiving as well as making calls. So it might be cheaper to rent a mobile phone while you're in town – try the dealer below, or check the Yellow Pages – or even buy one with a prepaid amount of time on it.

AllCell Rentals

1-800 724 2355/www.allcellrentals.com. **Open** 24hrs daily. **Credit** AmEx, DC, Disc, MC, V.
Rentals of mobile, GSM and satellite phones and pagers. There's no daily rental charge for mobiles; you pay for the airtime ($1.95 per minute including domestic long-distance). One-hour delivery in San Francisco.

Time

San Francisco is on Pacific Standard Time, which is three hours behind Eastern Standard Time (New York) and eight hours behind Greenwich Mean Time (Britain). Daylight Savings Time (which runs almost concurrent with British Summer Time) runs from the first Sunday in April, when the clocks are rolled ahead one hour, to the last Sunday in October. Going from the west to east coast, Pacific Time is one hour behind Mountain Time, two hours behind Central Time and three hours behind Eastern Time.

In the US, dates are written in the order of month, day, year: therefore 2.5.98 is the fifth of February, not the second of May.

Tipping

Unlike in Europe, tipping is a way of life in the US: many locals in service industries rely on gratuities as part of their income, so you should tip accordingly. In general, tip bellhops and baggage handlers $1-$2 a bag; cab drivers, waiters and waitresses, hairdressers and food delivery people 15-20 per cent of the total tab; valets $2-$3; and counter staff from 25¢ to 10 per cent of the order, depending on the size. In restaurants you should tip at least 15-20 per cent of the total bill; most will automatically add this to the bill for a table of six or more. If you get good service, leave a good tip; if you get bad service, leave little and tip the management with words.

Toilets/restrooms

These can be found in tourist areas such as Golden Gate Park and Fisherman's Wharf, as well as in shopping malls. Otherwise, don't hesitate to enter a restaurant or a bar and ask to use its facilities. In keeping with its cosmopolitan standing, San Francisco has installed 20 self-cleaning, French-designed, JC Decaux lavatories throughout the

Average monthly climate

	High temp	Low temp	Rainfall
Jan	56°F (13°C)	46°F (8°C)	4.5in (11.4cm)
Feb	60°F (15°C)	48°F (9°C)	2.8in (7.1cm)
Mar	61°F (16°C)	49°F (9°C)	2.6in (6.6cm)
Apr	63°F (17°C)	50°F (10°C)	1.5in (3.8cm)
May	64°F (17°C)	51°F (10°C)	0.4in (1cm)
June	66°F (19°C)	53°F (11°C)	0.2in (0.5cm)
July	66°F (19°C)	54°F (12°C)	0.1in (0.25cm)
Aug	66°F (19°C)	54°F (12°C)	0.1in (0.25cm)
Sept	70°F (21°C)	56°F (13°C)	0.2in (0.5cm)
Oct	69°F (20°C)	55°F (13°C)	1.1in (2.8cm)
Nov	64°F (18°C)	51°F (10°C)	2.5in (6.4cm)
Dec	57°F (14°C)	47°F (8°C)	3.5in (8.9cm)

high-traffic areas of the city. Keep an eye out for the forest-green commodes (they're plastered with high-profile advertising). Admission is 25¢ for 20 minutes; after that, you may be fined for indecent exposure, because the door opens automatically.

Visas

Under the Visa Waiver Scheme, citizens of the UK, Japan and all West European countries (except for Ireland, Portugal, Greece and the Vatican City) do not need a visa for stays in the United States of less than 90 days (for business or pleasure). Visitors are required to have a passport that is valid for the full 90-day period and a return or open standby ticket. Canadians and Mexicans do not need visas but must have legal proof of their citizenship. All other travellers must have visas.

Full information along with visa application forms can be obtained from your nearest US embassy or consulate. In general, it's a good idea to send in your application at least three weeks before you plan to travel. Visas required more urgently should be applied for via the travel agent booking your ticket.

For further information on visa requirements in the UK, phone the US Embassy Visa Recorded Information Line (0891 200 290).

Weights & measures

The US uses the imperial system. Here are some basic metric equivalents:

1 foot = 0.3048 metre
1 mile = 1.6093 kilometre
1 square yard = 0.836 square metre
1 acre = 0.405 hectare
1 pound (lb) = 0.4536 kilogramme
1 pint (16 fluid ounces) = 0.8327 UK pint = 0.4732 litre

When to go

Climate

San Francisco may be in California, but its climate, like its politics, is all its own. When planning a trip, don't anticipate the normal seasons, climatically, at least. Spring and autumn are relatively predictable, with warm days and cool nights. During the summer, however, the days are usually chilly and foggy, alleviated by two or three hot days that momentarily lift the city's collective spirit. Conversely – or is it perversely? – the nights are usually mild. In midwinter, what seems like months of constant rain will suddenly break for a week of brilliant sunshine. Tourists shivering in T-shirts are a never-ending source of amusement for the always well-layered locals. For information on how the weather varies in different neighbourhoods of San Francisco, *see p66* **Sun, wind and fog**.

Public holidays

New Year's Day (1 Jan); **Martin Luther King Jr Day** (3rd Mon in Jan); **President's Day** (3rd Mon in Feb); **Memorial Day** (last Mon in May); **Independence Day** (4 July); **Labor Day** (1st Mon in Sept); **Columbus Day** (2nd Mon in Oct); **Veterans' Day** (11 Nov); **Thanksgiving Day** (4th Thur in Nov); **Christmas Day** (25 Dec).

Work permits

It's difficult for foreigners to find work in the US. For you to work legally, a US company must sponsor you for an H-1 visa, which enables you to work in the country for up to five years. For the H-1 to be approved, your employer must convince the Immigration Department that no American is qualified to do the job as well as you.

Students have a much easier time. Your student union should have information on US working holidays. For information on studying over the summer, contact the **Council on International Education Exchange** (CIEE), Work Exchanges Dept, 205 East 42nd Street, New York, NY10017, USA (www.ciee.org).

Further Reference

Fiction & poetry

Jim Fadiman: *The Other Side of Haight*.
Details the early psychedelic experiments in the Haight-Ashbury neighbourhood.
Allen Ginsberg: *Howl and Other Poems*
Grab your chance to read the rant that caused all the fuss way back in the 1950s.
Dashiell Hammett: *The Maltese Falcon*
One of the greatest detective writers and one of the world's best detective novels, in a dark and dangerous San Fran.
Jack Kerouac: *On the Road; Desolation Angels; The Dharma Bums*
Famous for a reason: bittersweet tales of drugs and sex in San Francisco and around the world, from the most best Beat of them all.
Jack London: *Tales of the Fish Patrol; John Barleycorn*
Early works, set in London's native city.
Armistead Maupin: *Tales of the City* (6 volumes)
Witty soap opera following the lives and loves of a group of San Francisco friends.
Frank Norris: *McTeague*
Cult classic of the 1890s: working-class life and loss set in unromanticised Barbary Coast days.
John Steinbeck: *The Grapes of Wrath*
Grim tales of California in the Great Depression by the master of American fiction.
Amy Tan: *The Joy Luck Club*
Moving tale of the lives and loves of two generations of Chinese-American women living in San Francisco.
Alfredo Vea: *Gods Go Begging*
A San Francisco murder trial has ties to the Vietnam War.
William T Vollmann: *Whores for Gloria*
The boozy story of a middle-aged alcoholic whose fall into decrepitude occurs in the underbelly of the Tenderloin.
Tom Wolfe: *The Electric Kool-Aid Acid Test; The Pump House Gang*
Alternative lifestyles in trippy, hippy, 1960s California.

Non-fiction

Walton Bean: *California An Interpretive History.*
Anecdotal account of California's shady past.
Po Bronson: *The Nudist on the Late Shift*
Unblinking treatise on the Silicon Valley scene.
Carolyn Cassady: *Off the Road: My Years with Cassady, Kerouac and Ginsberg*
Not enlightened feminism, but an interesting alternative examination of the Beats.
Randolph Delehanty: *The Ultimate Guide: San Francisco*
Meticulously researched compendium of 13 walking tours through the city.
Joan Didion: *Slouching Towards Bethlehem; The White Album*
Brilliant essays examining California in the past couple of decades by one of America's most respected authors.
Timothy W Drescher: *San Francisco Bay Area Murals*
A well-resourced book with plenty of maps and 140 photos.
Lawrence Ferlinghetti & Nancy J Peters: *Literary San Francisco*
One of the better accounts of the city's literary pedigree.
Robert Greenfield: *Dark Star: An Oral Biography of Jerry Garcia*
The life and (high) times of the Grateful Dead's late frontman.
Malcolm Margolin: *The Ohlone Way*
A cultural history of the Bay Area's original inhabitants.
John Miller (ed): *San Francisco Stories: Great Writers on the City*
Contributions by Herb Caen, Anne Lamott, Amy Tan, Ishmael Reed and many others.
Ray Mungo: *San Francisco Confidential*
A gossipy look behind the city's closed doors.
John Plunkett & Barbara Traub (eds): *Burning Man*
Photo-heavy manual to the po-po-mo festival.
Richard Schwartz: *Berkeley 1900*
An indepth account of the early origins of complex and controversial Berkeley.
Joel Selvin: *San Francisco: The Magical History*
Tour of the sights and sounds of the city's pop music history by the *Chronicle*'s music critic.
Randy Shilts: *The Mayor of Castro Street*
On the tragedy of Harvey Milk and the development of gay politics in San Francisco.
John Snyder: *San Francisco Secrets: Fascinating Facts About the City by the Bay*
Amusing collection of city trivia, complete with facts and figures galore.
Sally Socolich: *Bargain Hunting in the Bay Area*
A must for shopaholics. A truly useful guide that is regularly updated.
Gertrude Stein: *The Making of Americans*
Autobiographical work that includes an account of her early childhood in Oakland.
Robert Louis Stevenson: *An Inland Voyage; The Silverado Squatters*
Autobiographical narratives describing the journey from Europe to western America.

Film

Bullitt (1968)
This Steve McQueen film may have the all-time greatest San Fran car chase scene.
Chan Is Missing (1982)
This mystery, in which two cab drivers search for a man who stole their life savings, gives an authentic, insider's look at Chinatown.
Dark Passage (1947)
This classic thriller starts in Marin County, where Humphrey Bogart has escaped from San Quentin Prison, and heads to 1360 Montgomery Street in San Francisco, where he hides out at Lauren Bacall's apartment.
The Graduate (1967)
Hoffman at his best; with shots of Berkeley, as well as a a cool wrong-direction shot on the Bay Bridge.
Harold and Maude (1971)
Bay Area scenery abounds in this bittersweet cult classic about an unbalanced boy who falls in love with an elderly woman.
Jimi Plays Berkeley (1970)
Documentary about a famous Jimi Hendrix concert, with stirring footage of the town during its radical days.
The Joy Luck Club (1993)
Appallingly manipulative but charming weepie traces the lives of four mah jong-playing Chinese women and their daughters in San Fran.
The Maltese Falcon (1941)
Hammett's classic features good SF street scenes, above the Stockton Street Tunnel near Chinatown.
Mrs Doubtfire (1993)
The relentlessly hammy Robin Williams as a divorced San Fran man who poses as a nanny to be near his children.
The Presidio (1988)
Set on the eponymous military base; Sean Connery involves himself in great street chases.
The Rock (1996)
Nic Cage and friends attack Alcatraz for some reason.
The Times of Harvey Milk (1984)
Oscar-winning documentary about the life (and death) of the US's first 'out' gay politician.
Vertigo (1958)
A veteran San Francisco cop becomes obssessed with a mysterious blonde in this Hitchcock classic.

Music

Big Brother and the Holding Company: *Cheap Thrills* (1968)
Janis Joplin's band wails the 1960s blues.
Chris Isaak: *Heart Shaped World* (1989)
What a 'Wicked Game' to be so good-looking, with a voice like that – and an SF boy, too.
Creedence Clearwater Revival: *Willie and the Poor Boys* (1969)
Classic southern rock with a San Francisco touch.
The Dead Kennedys: *Fresh Fruit for Rotting Vegetables* (1980)
Excellent, angry SF punk, featuring the classic song, 'California Uber Alles'.
Del the Funkee Homosapien: *I Wish My Brother George Was Here* (1991)
Ice Cube's funnier cousin raps important songs, such as 'Pissin' on your Steps'.
Digital Underground: *Sons of the P* (1991)
Seriously crazy funk.
The Disposable Heroes of Hiphopricy: *Hiphopricy is the Greatest Luxury* (1992)
This is rap with a political conscience; their hit song, 'Television: The Drug of the Nation', still spins on campuses everywhere. Right after *The Simpsons* ends, of course.
Faith No More: *Real Thing* (1989)
Has it really been more than ten years since the song 'Epic' rocked the world? Damn.
Green Day: *Dookie* (1994)
The much-beloved, street-smart revivers of the once-comatose California punk scene tell it like they see it.
The Grateful Dead: *Best of: What a Long Strange Trip It's Been* (1977)
Jerry Garcia and the boys get 'Truckin' as only they could.
John Lee Hooker: *Definitive* (2000)
The late, great Mississippi bluesman who made San Fran his home.
Jefferson Airplane: *Surrealistic Pillow* (1967)
Grace Slick and co bang on about bunnies.
Primus: *Pork Soda* (1993)
Wryly intelligent punk-funk in the Zappa tradition.
Rancid: *And Out Come the Wolves (*1994)
If you don't like this solid, California ska, you just don't know how to have fun.
Too $hort: *Life is Too $hort* (1988)
Hard-core West Coast rap.

Websites

http://sfbay.yahoo.com
An excellent online source, including restaurants, classifieds, traffic reports and an events calendar for the city and the Bay Area.
www.citysearch7.com
Exhaustive, well researched, daily updated guide to SF and the Bay Area, plus links to other North American city guides.
www.kpix.com/live
City Camera site with cameras perched atop the Fairmont Hotel and in the Presidio for breathtaking views.
www.sfbayconcerts.com
Tells who's playing where at which Bay Area music venues.
www.sfstation.com
Upcoming events, clubs, parties, film and restaurant reviews and more.
www.transaction.net/sanfran/ult/index.html
Easy-to-use general guide, with an alternative bent.

Index

Note: Page numbers in **bold** indicate key information on a topic; page numbers in *italics* indicate photographs.

a

A La Carte, A La Park 191
A's, the Oakland 238
Academy of Art College 203, **285**
Acid Tests 14
accommodation **29-50**
  best 33
  budget 39-41, 42, 43, 46, 47, 49, 50
    by area
    Castro, the 46-47
    Chinatown 42
    Civic Center 41
    Cow Hollow 48-49
    Fisherman's Wharf 43
    Haight-Ashbury, the 47
    Marina, the 49
    Mission, the 46-47
    Nob Hill 43-46
    North Beach 42-43
    Pacific Heights 48
    Richmond District, the 50
    SoMa 41-42
    Tenderloin, the 37-41
    Union Square 30-35
    Western Addition, the 47-48
  first-class 30-34, 35-37, 41-42, 43-45, 47-49
  gay & lesbian 229-230
  hostels 50
  hotel chains 43
  mid-range 34-35, 38-39, 41, 42-43, 45-47, 48, 49
  reservations agencies 38
African & African-American Art & Culture, Center for 206
African American Historical & Cultural Society 19, **109**
age restrictions 277
AIDS 15, 86, 280
AIDS Candlelight Memorial March & Vigil 189
AIDS Memorial Grove, National 90
airports, getting to and from 272-273
Alamo Square *20*, 22, 88
Alcatraz *11*, 12, 24, 53, **74**, 197, 247
alcohol and the law 151
Allende, Isabelle 28
Alta Plaza Park 93
American Conservatory Theater (ACT) 20, **222**
And the Band Played On 28
Angel Island **74-5**, 76, 197
Angels in America 221
Ansel Adams Center *see* Friends of Photography
Anza, Captain Juan Bautista de 7, 98
Applegarth, George 99
Aquarium of the Bay 195
aquariums 195-196
Aquatic Park 77
Arbuckle, Fatty 56, **59**
architecture 93, **21-24**
  walks 55
art
  events 192, 194
  museums 105, 106, 107, *107*, 110
  schools 203
  shops 164
  walk 204
  see also galleries
Artists' Television Access 201
arts & entertainment **187-248**
ArtSpan Open Studios **192**, 203, 205
Asian Art Museum 19, 23, 66, 90, **106**
Audobon Canyon Ranch 254
auto racing 238

b

babysitting & childcare 195
Bach Choir 226
Baker Beach 98, **100**
Ballet, San Francisco 194, 221, **225**, *225*
balloon flights 256, 267
Balmy Alley *205*
Bank of America 57
Bank of California 10
Bank of Canton 72
Barbary Coast 9, **12**, 55
Barbary Coast Trail **12**, 55
Barry Bridge 12
bars **148-158**
  queer 231-233
BART 19, 103, **274**
baseball **238**, 241
basketball 239
Bay Area, the 209
  restaurants 132-133
Bay Area Discovery Museum **198**, 251
Bay Meadows Racecourse 240
Beach Blanket Babylon revue 24
Beach Chalet 91, **101**
Beat Generation 13, 27, 28
Be-At Line 210
beaches 100-101
  Baker Beach 98, **100**
  China Beach 100
  Ocean Beach **100**, 102, 197
  out of town 101, 262, 267
  Stinson Beach 250, **254**
bed & breakfast *see* accommodation
Belden Place 61
Belluschi, Pietro 24, 88
Berkeley 103-104
  shopping 185
Berkeley Art Museum & Pacific Film Archive Galleries 111
Bernal Heights 228
best, the
  brunches 144-145
  hotels 33
  restaurants 118
bicycles *see* cycling
Bierce, Ambrose 25
Big Basin State Park 252
'Big Four' 10, 22, 81
Bill Graham Civic Auditorium 23, 65, **210**
billiards 243
Bimbo's 365 Club 210, *215*
Black Filmworks Festival of Film & Video 201
Black Mask 26
Black Panthers 14, 103
Black Rock Desert 193
Bloody Thursday 12
blues *see* music
Bomani Gallery 206
'Bonanza Kings' 10
book
  festivals 191
  shops 159, 164, **165-167**
Books by the Bay 191
Bootjack Trail 242
bowling 240-242
Brady Street 160
Brangwyn, Frank 24
Brannan, Sam 8, 9, 72
bridges 96-97
Broadway 76, 93
Brown, Arthur 66
brunch 144-145
Buchanan Mall 92
Burnham, Daniel 23
Burning Man 193
bus tours 52-53
buses 272, 273
business 277-278

c

Cable Car Museum 60, 82, 106, **109**, 196
cable cars 53, **60**, 273-274
Cabrillo, Juan 7
Café Niebaum-Coppola 75
cafés **141-147**
  Castro, the 146
  Chinatown 143
  Fisherman's Wharf 146
  Haight & around, the 146-147
  Marina, the 147
  Mission, the 146
  North Beach 143
  Pacific Heights 147
  Polk Gulch 143
  Richmond District, the 147
  SoMa 143
  Sunset District, the 147
  Union Square & around 142-143
Cal *see* University of California
California Academy of Sciences 90, *90*, **106**
California College of Arts & Crafts 203, **285**
California Historical Society 69
California Palace of the Legion of Honor 99, 105, *105*, **106**
California Star 8, 72
Calistoga **259**, 260
Call of the Wild, The 25
CalTrain 274
Camera Obscura 102, **109**
Cameron House 72
Cameron, Donaldina 72
Candlestick Park *see* 3Com
Cannery, the 77
Carmel 265
  Carmel Mission 265
Carnaval 189
Carnelian Room 59, 80
Carneros region 257

Cartoon Art Museum 105
Cassady, Neal 13, 27, 28
Castro, the 28, **86**, 160, 228
  accommodation 46-47
  bars 148, **153-155**
  cafés 146
  queer 229-230, 231, 234, 235
  music venues 212-216
  restaurants 135-136
  shopping 186
  walk **54**, 228
Castro Street Fair 192
Castro Theatre *85*, 86, **200**
Catharine Clark Gallery 206
Cathedral of St Mary of the Assumption 24, 88, **89**, 227
Celebrated Jumping Frog of Calaveras County, The 25
Center for African & African-American Art & Culture 206
Central Pacific Railroad 10
Chabot Space & Science Museum 198
Chanticleer 226
Cherry Blossom Festival 92, *188*, **189**
Chestnut Street 94
children **195-198**
  babysitting & childcare 195
  fashion shops 171
  outdoors 197-198
  sightseeing 195-198
  toy shops 185
  Trips Out of Town 198
Children's Fairyland 103, **198**
China Beach 100
Chinatown 10, **71-73**, *72*, 159
  accommodation 42
  cafés 143
  restaurants 125-127
  walks 54
Chinatown Gate 71
Chinese American National Museum & Learning Center 109
Chinese American Telephone Exchange 72
Chinese Culture Center 72, **73**
Chinese New Year 194
Chocolate Festival, Ghirardelli Square 192
Chronicle Marathon: San Francisco **190**, 245
Church of Saints Peter and Paul 75-76
Cinco de Mayo 189
cinemas *see* film
Cirque du Soleil 195
Cities on a Hill 28
City Art 206-207
'City Beautiful' Project 23
City College of San Francisco 204, **285**
City Guides 54
City Hall 11, 23, 53, *63*, 65, **67**, 76
City Lights bookshop 13, 28, 75, 159, **165**, *165*
city on foot, the *see* walks
CityPass 105
Civic Center 23, **65-68**
  accommodation 41
  restaurants 121-122
Civic Center Plaza 65
Civil War 10, 56
Claremont Resort & Spa 104
classical music *see* music
Claudel, Camille 99
Cleaver, Eldridge 14
Clemens, Samuel 57
Clement Street 99
Cliff House 22, **101**, 102
climate 288
coffee walk 55
Coit Tower 24, 53, 76, 80, **82**, 204
Cole Valley 88
Columbarium 23, 101, **102**
Columbus Avenue 75, 159
Columbus Tower 75
Condor Club 76
Conley, Chip 18
Conservatory of Flowers 90, *91*
consulates 278
consumer 278
Contact 221
Conversation, The 56
Conzelman Road 81
Copia: the American Center for Wine, Food & the Arts 258
Coppola, Francis Ford 56, 75, 199, 258
Comstock, Henry 9
'Comstock Lode' 9
Cortés, Hernán 7
Cow Hollow 94
  accommodation 48-49
Cow Hollow Playground 198
Craft & Folk Art, Museum of 110
Crocker, Charles 10, 22, 81
Crocker Mansion 22
Crown Point Press 207
Crumb 199
Culbra Terrace 78
Curran Theater 222
customs 280
cycling 90, **244-245**, 276

dance
  clubs 217-220
    queer 233-235
  events 194
  groups & venues 225-226
David, Elizabeth 93
Dharma Bums, The 27
Dia de los Muertos/Day of the Dead 83, **190-191**
DiMaggio, Joe 65, 76
Dipsea Trail 242
Directory **271-290**
disabled 278-279
Disneyland 13
Divakaruni, Chitra Banerjee 28
Dog Soldiers 28
Dolby Chadwick 207
don't miss
  bars 152
  dance clubs 219
  fashion shops 168
Donner Memorial State Park 267
Downtown & Around **56-70**
  bars 148-151
  dance clubs 217-219
  music venues 212
Drake, Francis 7
driving 275-276
drugs 14
Ducks, the 9
Duncombe Alley 73
Dutch Windmill 91

earthquakes *6*, 10-11, 15, 59, 62, 66, 94, 96, 102, 263, 264, 284
East Bay 97, **103-104**
  drinking 156-157
  music venues 214
  theatres 225
Eastlake, Charles 22
Eastwood, Clint 265
Electric Kool-Aid Acid Test 25, 28
electricity 279
elevators 196
Embarcadero, the 61-63, *62*
  restaurants 118-121
Embarcadero Center 62, **161**
Emerald Bay State Park 267
emergencies 278
entertainment, arts & **187-248**
  queer 235
Escape from Alcatraz triathlon 247
Esplanade Gardens 24, 69
Examiner Bay to Breakers Foot Race **189**, 245
Exotic Erotic Ball 193
Exploratorium 95, *195*, **196-197**

Farnsworth, Philo T 62
Federal Building 24
Ferlinghetti, Lawrence 13, *25*, 28
ferries 274
Ferry Building 23, **62**
Festival Cine Latino! 201
Feusier Octagon House **81**, 94
Filbert Street 79
Fillmore Auditorium 89, **210-211**, *211*
Fillmore District 89
Fillmore Street Jazz Festival 190
film **199-202**, 290
  cinemas 199-201
    experimental & foreign 201
    mainstream 199-200
    repertory 200-201
  festivals 189, **201-202**
  schools & classes 202
  tickets & information 199
Film Arts Festival of Independent Cinema 201
Film Arts Foundation 202
Financial District, the 57-61
    accommodation 35-37
    restaurants 117-118
Fine Arts Cinema 200
Fire Engine Tours & Adventures, San Francisco **53**, 197
First Thursdays 203
Fish Alley 77
Fisherman's Wharf **76-79**, 103, 197
    accommodation 43
    cafés 146
    restaurants 130
fitness *see* sport & fitness
Fleet Week 192
Flood, James C 10, 22, 81
Flood Mansion 22
Flower Power Walking Tour **54**, 87
Folk Art International 24, *24*, **57**
Folsom Street Fair **192**, 228
food
  festival 191
  shops 176-178
  walks 54
football 239-240
Forbes Island 77
Ford, President Gerald 56

Fort Funston Reservation 102
Fort Mason 95
Fort Point 77, 95, **98**
Fourth of July Waterfront Festival 190
49ers, San Francisco 18, 238, 239, **240**
49-Mile Scenic Drive 53
Fourth Street 104
Fraenkel Gallery 208, *208*
Francis 'Lefty' O'Doul Bridge 70
Franklin, Benjamin 76
Fremont, John 8, *8*
Friends of Photography/ Ansel Adams Center 69, 106, **109**
Funston, General Frederick 11
further reference 289-290

g

Galeria de la Raza/Studio 24 203-204
galleries **203-208**
  commercial 206-207
  non-profit 203-206
  photography 208
Garcia, Jerry 90
Garlic Festival, Gilroy 191
gay & lesbian **228-237**, 279
  see also queer
Gay & Lesbian Center 228
gay radicalism 14
Geary, John White 9
Ghirardelli Square 77
Ghirardelli Square Chocolate Festival 192
ghost walk 55
Ghost World 199
Giants, San Francisco 238, **239**, *239*
Gilroy Garlic Festival 191
Ginsberg, Allen 13, 14, *25*, 27, 28, 75, 93
Glass Key, The 26
Glen Ellen 257
Glide Memorial United Methodist Church **63**, 227
Godfather, The 75
Gold Rush 8, 21, 57, 71, 96
Golden Gate Bridge 12, 23, 53, 62, 77, 95, **96**, 99, 244
Golden Gate Fields 240
Golden Gate Fortune Cookie Factory 73
Golden Gate International Exposition 13
Golden Gate National Recreation Area 77, 98, 102
Golden Gate Park 22, 53, 54, 87, **90-91**, 99, 197, 244
Golden Gate Park Stables 91, **243**
Golden Gate Park walk 54
Golden Gate Promenade 77, 80, **94**, 95
Golden Gate Theater 222
Golden State Warriors 239
golf 242
Grace Cathedral 22, 53, **82**, 227
Grand View Park 80
Grant Avenue 71
Grateful Dead 14, 87, 90
Great American Music Hall 211
Great Depression 12
Great Quake, the 10-11
Guadalupe-Hidalgo Treaty 8
gyms 242
  queer 237

h

Haas-Lilienthal House 22, *23*, **93**
Hackett-Freedman Gallery 207
Haight & Around, the **87-92**, 160
  accommodation 47
  bars 155-158
  cafés 146-147
  dance clubs 220
  music venues 216
  restaurants 136-137
  shopping 186
  walk 54
Haight-Ashbury, the 14, 28, **87-88**
Haight Street 87
Haight Street Fair 189
Half Moon Bay 262-263
Hall, William Hammond 10, 90
Hallidie, Andrew 60
Halloween 86, **193**, *194*
Hammett, Dashiell 25, 26, 27, 55
Harold and Maude 101
Harte, Bret 25
Harvey Milk Plaza 86
Hayes Street 92
Hayes Valley **92**, 159, 228
  shopping 186
  walk 175
health 279-280
Hearst Castle 23
Hearst, Patty 14, *14*
Hell's Angels 103
Hellman, Lillian 26
Hendrix, Jimi 87
Henry Cowell Redwoods State Park 252
Herbst Theatre 24, 67, **222**
Herzog & de Meuron 24
Hess Collection 258
hiking 242
Hippie Hill 90
history **6-16**
  key events 16
  walks 55
Holiday Tree Lighting Festivities 193-194
Holographic Museum 102, **109**
homelessness 18
Hooker, John Lee 89
Hopkins, Mark 10, 22, 81
horse-racing 240
horse riding 243
hostels 50
hotels *see* accommodation
Hounds, the 9
House of Representatives Un-American Activities Committee (HUAC) 14
Howl 27, 28, 93
Huntingdon, Collis P 10, 22, 81
Huntington Park 81
Hutton, Bobby 14
Hyde Street Pier 77, **79**, 197

i

ice hockey 240
ID 280
immigration 280
Ina Coolbrith Park 79
insurance 280-281
International Longshoremen's Association 12
internet 281, 290
Intersection for the Arts 204
Introductions 203
Inverness 255
Irving Street 102
islands 74
Italianate style 22

j

Jack London Square 103
Jack London State Historic Park 26, **257**
Jackson Square Historical District 21, **61**
Japan Center **89**, 159
Japanese Tea Garden 91, *91*
Japantown 89, *92*
jazz *see* music
Jenkins, John 9
Jeremiah O'Brien Liberty Ship 197, **198**
Jewish Film Festival 202
Jewish Holocaust Memorial 99
Jewish Museum of San Francisco 19, 24, **109**
John's Grill 57
Jolson, Al 56, 59
Joplin, Janis 14, 87
Justice League, the 211
Justin Herman Plaza 62

k

Kabuki Springs & Spa 92, 159, **181**
kayaking 245-246
Kennedy Drive, John F 90
Kenwood 257
Kerouac, Jack 13, *25*, 27, 28, 75, 81
Kesey, Ken 28
King Jr, Martin Luther 69
Kipling, Rudyard 22
Kong Chow Temple 73
Koolhaas, Rem 24
Kronos Quartet 226
Kushner, Tony 221

l

Lab, the 204
Lafayette Park 93
Lake Berryessa 259
Lake Merced 102
Lake Merritt Park 103
Lake Tahoe 246, 250, 267-269, *269*
Lamplighters Musical Theater 222
Larkspur 250, **253**
Late Henry Moss, The 221
law, alcohol, smoking and the 151
Lawrence Hall of Science **81**, 104, **198**
left luggage 281
legal help 281
lesbian *see* queer
Libeskind, Daniel 24
libraries 196
Library, San Francisco Main 24, 65, **68**, 196
Life and Times of Harvey Milk, The 199
lifts *see* elevators
Lilienthal-Pratt House 22
limousines 272
Literary San Francisco **25-28**
Literary World of San Francisco, The 27
'Little Chile' 9
Little House on the Prairie 79
Loma Prieta earthquake 15, 62, 66, 263, 264
Lombard Street 79, *79*
London, Jack 25, 26, 103, 257
Lotta's Fountain 59
Louise M Davies Symphony Hall 66, **226**
Lower Haight 88

LSD 14
Lucas, George 199
Luggage Store, the **204-205**, 227
Lumière 200
Lyon Street Steps 78

m

MAC 159, **170**
Mackay, John 10
Macondray Lane 78
MadCat Women's International Film Festival 202
Maestrapeace 84
Magic Theatre 20, **222**
Maiden Lane 57
Main Post 98
Make-A-Circus Free Summer Festival Days 195
Maltese Falcon, The 26, 27
Manson, Charles 87
Marconi, Guglielmo 88
Marin County 251
Marin Headlands 251
Marina & Around, the **93-98**, 159
  accommodation 49
  bars 148, **158**
  cafés 147
  restaurants 137-140
  shopping 186
Marina Green 95
Marine Mammal Center 195, **251**
Maritime Hall 211
Maritime National Historical Park Museum Building, San Francisco 77, **111-112**, 196
Market Street 159-160
Marshall, James 8
Marshall Plaza 24
Martin Luther King Jr Birthday Celebration 194
Masonic Auditorium 226
Maupin, Armistead 28
Maybeck, Bernard 23
McClure, Michael 27
McLaren Lodge 90
McLaren, John 90
McMillan, Terry 28
McTeague 26
media 281-283
medical 279-280
Merchant's Exchange 59, **61**
Mermaid Fountain 77
Metier 159, *169*, **170**
Metreon 24
Mexican Museum 19, **105**
Mexican-American War 8
MH de Young Memorial Museum 19, 24, 90, **105**
Milk, Harvey 28, 65
Mill Valley 253
Mill Valley Film Festival & Videofest 202
Mime Troupe in the Park 191
Mission, the 20, **83-85**, *83*, 159, 204, 228
  accommodation 46-47
  bars 148, **153-155**
  cafés 146
  dance clubs 219-220
  music venues 212-216
  queer 231, 235, 237
  restaurants 133-135
  shopping 186
Mission Bay 17
Mission Dolores 84, **85**
Mission Dolores Park 84, *84*
Mission Science Workshop 197
Mission Street 84
Mission Trail Park 265
Mitchell Brothers O'Farrell Theatre 63, **65**
Modernism 207-208
Mondavi, Robert 258
money 283-284
Monroe, Marilyn 65, 76
Monterey 7, **265**
  Bay Blues Festival 265
  Cannery Row 265
  Colton Hall 265
  Jacks Peak Regional Park 265
  Jazz Festival 265
  Monterey Bay Aquarium 195, 265, *265*
  peninsula 265-266
  State Historic Park 265
  wineries 265
Montez, Lola 10
Morgan, Julia 23
Morrison Planetarium 90
Morrow, Irwin F 96
Moscone Convention Center 24, **69**
Moscone, Mayor George 15, 65, 69
Mount Diablo 81
Mount Tam 254, *254*
Mount Tamalpais State Park 254
Mount Wittenberg 255
Mountain Lake Park 98
Moviefone 199
mud baths 259, **260-261**
Muir Woods National Monument 250, 252, **254**
Muir, John 254
'Multimedia Gulch' 70
Muni Metro streetcars 273
Muni Owl Service 210
Municipal Pier 77
murals 83, 203, **204-207**
Musée Mécanique 102, **110**, *110*, 196
Museo ItaloAmericano 110
Museum of Craft & Folk Art 110
Museum of the City of San Francisco **110**, 196
Museum of the Money of the American West 59, **61**
museums **105-112**
  for children 196-197
music 290
  classical music & opera 226-227
  churches & other venues 227
  main venues 226
  out of town 227
  festivals 190, 191, 192-193
  live venues 210-217
  local venues 213
  shops 181-183
Mystery Spot 264

n

Napa Valley 250, 256, **258-261**
  Wine Train 259
National Park Service 98, 102
New Century Chamber Orchestra 226
New Journalism 14
New Langton Arts/ San Francisco Camerawork 205
New Year 194
Newton, Huey 14
nightlife **209-220**
Nob Hill 9, 10, 22, 60, **81-82**
  accommodation 43-46
  restaurants 130-133
  walk 54
Noe Valley 86
  restaurants 135-136
  shopping 186
Norris, Frank 26
North Beach & Around 53, **71-82**, 159
  accommodation 42-43
  bars 151-152
  cafés 143
  dance clubs 219
  Festival 189
  music venues 212
  restaurants 127-130
  shopping 186
  walk 55
Nutcracker 194

o

O'Brien, William 10
Oakland 103
Oakland Athletics 238, **239**
Oakland International Airport (OAK) 272
Oakland Museum of California 103, **111**
Oakland Raiders 238, 239, **240**
Oakland Zoo 195, **198**
Ocean Beach & Around 53, **99-102**, 158, 197
Octagon House 23, **93**
Octopus, The 26
ODC Performance Gallery 225
Ohlone Way, The 7
Old Faithful geyser 259
Old St Mary's Cathedral 72, **73**
Oldenberg, Charles 18
On the Road 13, 27
111 Minna Street *204*, 208
opera *see* music
Opera, San Francisco 20, **226**
Ord Court Feline Appreciation Walk 78
Orlovsky, Peter 28
Orpheum 222
Osbourne, Fanny 25
Osento **181**, 228
out of town *see* Trips Out of Town

p

Pacific Bell Park/PacBell Park 19, 70, *70*, 210, 238, **241**
Pacific Coast Highway 262
Pacific Coast Stock Exchange 24, 59, **61**, 204
Pacific Film Archive 200
Pacific Grove 265
Pacific Heights **93-94**, 98, 159
  accommodation 48
  cafés 147
  walk 55
Pacific Heritage Museum 59, **111**
Pacific Union Club 81
'Painted Ladies' 22
Palace Hotel 22, **41**, 59
Palace of Fine Arts 23, **95**, *95*
Panama-Pacific Exposition 11, 23
Panoramic Highway 254
paragliding 243
Paramount Theatre 200
parks
  Alamo Square park 88

Alta Plaza Park 93
Aquatic Park 77
Esplanade Gardens 69
Golden Gate Park 22, 53, 87, **90-91**, 99, 197, 244
Grand View Park 80
Huntington Park 81
Ina Coolbrith Park 79
Lafayette Park 93
Lake Merritt Park 103
Mission Dolores Park 84, *84*
Mountain Lake Park 98
Redwood Park 57
Sutro Heights Park 101
Tilden Regional Park 104
Parkway Theater 200
passenger vans (shuttles) 272
Paxton Gate 84, 159, *177*, **179**
Peace Pagoda 89
performing arts **221-227**
festivals 191, 192
museum 112
Pescadero 262
Pet Cemetery 98
Petrified Forest 259
Phelan Building 57
Phelan, Mayor James 57
photography
galleries 208
museums 106, **109**
shops 183
Pier 39 77
Pioneer Log Cabin 91
Pocket Opera 226
poetry slams 26
Point Lobos State Reserve 265
Point Pinos Light Station 266
Point Reyes National Seashore 255, *255*
police stations 284
Polk Gulch 82
cafés 143
restaurants 130-133
Polk, Willis 23, 24, 79, 81
Polo Field 91
Pony Express 10
pool 243
Pórtola, Gaspar de 7
Portsmouth Square 72
postal services 284
'Postcard Row' 88
Potrero Hill 85-86
shopping 186
Powell Street cable car turnaround 56
Precita Eyes Mural Arts & Visitors Center 207
Presidio Golf Course 98
Presidio Trust 98
Presidio, the 98
Pride, gay & lesbian 228, **232-233**
public transport 273-274
Purcell, Charles H 97

Queen Anne style 22
queer **228-237**, 279
accommodation 229-230
bars 231-233
dance clubs 233-235
entertainment 235
events 189-190, 202, 232-233
restaurants & cafés 235-237
walk **54**, 228
see also gay & lesbian

Ralston, Billy 22
Ralston, William 10
Randall Museum 196
reading 289
Red Harvest 26
Red Vic 87, **200-201**
redwood 252
Redwood Creek 254
Redwood Park 57
Refusalon 208
Reggae in the Park 192
religion 284
Renaissance Pleasure Faire 191
RESFEST 201
resources A-Z 277-288
Restaurants **114-141**
best, the 118
by area
Bay Area 132-133
Castro, the 135-136
Chinatown 125-127
Civic Center 121-122
Embercadero, the 118-121
Financial District 117-118
Fisherman's Wharf 130
Haight & around, the 136-137
Marina & around, the 137-140
Mission, the 133-135
Nob Hill 130-133
Noe Valley 135-136
North Beach 127-130
Polk Gulch 130-133
Richmond District, the 140
Russian Hill 130-133
SoMa 122-125
Sunset District, the 140-141
Tenderloin, the 114-117
Union Square 114-117
by cuisine
American 114-115, 117, 118-119, 121, 122-123, 126, 127-129, 133-134, 135-136, 137-138, 140-141
Asian 117, 119-121, 123-125, 126-127, 129, 130-131, 134-135, 136-137, 138, 140, 141
European 115-118, 121, 125, 129-130, 131-132, 135, 137, 138-139, 140
Latin American 135, 137
Middle Eastern 130
seafood 117, 118, 130, 132-133
taquerias 126-127
vegetarian 121-122, 139-140
queer 235-237
Rexroth, Kenneth 27
Richmond District, the 99-102
accommodation 50
cafés 147
restaurants 140
Rigo 99 69
Rincon Center 24, 62, **63**, 206
Ringolevio 28
Ripley's Believe It Or Not! Museum 76
Rivera, Diego 24
Robert Koch Gallery 208
Robert Louis Stevenson 25, 81, 259
museum 259
state park 25, **259**
rock climbing 243
Rodin 99
rollerblading 90, **243-244**
Rolling Stone 14
Rolph, Mayor 'Sunny Jim' 23
Rooftop at Yerba Buena Gardens 69
Rosenberg, Pamela 20
rowing 245-246
Roxie 84, **201**, *201*
Run to the Far Side 194
running 244-245
Russian Hill 60, **79-81**, 94
restaurants 130-133

Sacramento Monarchs 239
safety 285
sailing 245-246
St Boniface Catholic Church 63, **65**
St Patrick's Church 69
St Patrick's Day Parade 188
St Stupid's Day Parade 188
Sam Bo Trading Co 159, **164**
San Andreas Fault 10, 15
San Carlos 7
San Francisco Airport (SFO) 19, **272**
San Francisco Art Institute 79, *79*, **81**, 203, 204, 285
San Francisco Arts Commission Gallery 66, **205**
San Francisco Ballet 194, 221, **225**, *225*
San Francisco Bay Model Visitor Center **111**, 252
San Francisco Blues 27
San Francisco Blues Festival 192
San Francisco Cinematheque 200, **201**
San Francisco Fire Engine Tours & Adventures **53**, 197
San Francisco 49ers 18, 238, 239, **240**
San Francisco Fringe Festival 192
San Francisco Giants 238, **239**, *239*
San Francisco International Art Exposition **192**, 203
San Francisco International Asian American Film Festival 202
San Francisco International Film Festival 92, 189, 200, **202**
San Francisco International Lesbian & Gay Film Festival 202
San Francisco Jazz Festival 192-193
San Francisco Lesbian/Gay/Bisexual/Transgender Pride Celebration Parade 189-190
San Francisco Main Library 24, 65, **68**, 196
San Francisco Maritime National Historical Park Museum Building 77, **111-112**, 196
San Francisco Museum of Modern Art (SFMOMA) 24, 53, 69, 106, **107**, *107*, 201

San Francisco National Cemetery 98
San Francisco-Oakland Bay Bridge 12, 23, 62, 81, **96-97**
San Francisco Opera 20, **226**
San Francisco Peninsula 98
San Francisco Performing Arts Library & Museum 67, **112**
San Francisco Seaplane Tours **53**, 251
San Francisco
Shakespeare Festival 192
San Francisco Shopping Centre 56
San Francisco Silent Film Festival 202
'San Francisco sound' 209
San Francisco State University 203, **285-286**
San Francisco Stories 26
San Francisco Symphony Orchestra 66, **226**
San Francisco Today **17-20**
San Francisco Tribal, Folk & Textile Arts Show 194
San Francisco Visitor Information Center 56, 105, 188, 256, **287**
San Francisco Women Artists 92
San Francisco Zoo 102, **196**
San Jose International Airport (SJC) 272
San Jose Sharks 240
San Quentin Prison 253
San Rafael 253
Santa Cruz 263-264
  Beach Boardwalk 263, *263*
  Coconut Grove Ballroom 263
  Giant Dipper 263
  Misión la exaltación de la Santa Cruz 264
  Mission Adobe 264
  Museum of Natural History 264
  Steamer Lane 263
  Surfing Museum 263
  wineries 264
Saroyan, William 25
Sather Tower 104
Sausalito 250, *251*, **252-253**
Sawyer, Tom 57
Schmitz, Mayor Eugene 11
Sciences, California Academy of 90, *90*, **106**
scuba diving 246
Sea Wolf, The 25
Seale, Bobby 14
Seaplane Tours, San Francisco **53**, 251
season, by **188-194**
Sebastiani, Sam 257
security 285
Segal, George 99
Sephora 159, **180**
Sequoia sempervirens see redwood
Serra, Father Junipéro 7
services *see* shops & services
17-Mile Drive 266
Sex Pistols 89
SF Performances 225
SF Raves 210
SF Station 210
SFMOMA *see* San Francisco Museum of Modern Art
Shakespeare Festival, San Francisco 192
Shapiro Gallery 208
Sharpsteen Museum 259
Shattuck Avenue 104
Shepard, Sam 221
Shilts, Randy 15, 28
shops & services **159-186**
  antiques & collectibles 163-164
  arts & crafts 164
  bookshops 164-167
    foreign language 166-167
    top five 164
  by area 186
  computers & electronics 167
  department stores 160
  duty-free 167
  fashion 167-173
    children 171
    discount 171-172
    don't miss 168
    lingerie 172
    vintage & second-hand 172-173
  fashion accessories 173-176
    handbags 173-174
    jewellery 174
    leather goods & luggage 174
    shoes 174-176
    shoe repair 176
  flea markets 164, 175
  food & drink 176-178
    tea & coffee 177
    wine 177
  gifts 178-179
  health & beauty 179-181
    complementary & alternative medicine 179
    cosmetics & skincare 179-180
    hair salons 180
    pharmacies 180-181
    spas, saunas & bathhouses 181
    tattoos & body piercing 181
  laundrettes 181
  music 181-183
    CDs, tapes & records 181-182
    instruments & sheet music 182-183
  opticians 183
  photography 183
  sex shops 183
  shopping centres 161-163
  smoking 184
  sport 184-185
  toys 185
sightseeing **51-112**
Silicon Valley 15, 262
Silver Rush 9
Silverado Squatters, The 25
Silverado Trail 258
Simon, Carly 24
16th Street 84
skateboarding 246
skiing 246, 268
Skin Zone 86
Slim's 211
Smith, Jedediah 8
smoking 151, 285
snowboarding 246
Snyder, Gary 27
Society of Californian Pioneers 69, **70**
Society of Individual Rights (SIR) 14
Society of Six 203
SoMa 17, **68-70**, 228
  accommodation 41-42
  cafés 143
  dance clubs 217-219
  queer 231-233, 234
  restaurants 122-125
  shopping 186
SoMarts Gallery 205-206
Sonoma State Historic Park 256
Sonoma Train Town 256
Sonoma Valley 250, **256-258**
South Beach 70
South Park 70
Southern Exposure 206
Spade, Sam 26, 27
spas, out of town 260-261
Spike & Mike's Festival of Animation 202
Spinnaker Sailing 53
Spofford Alley 73
sport & fitness **238-248**
  active sports 240-248
  events 189, 190
  shops 184-185
  spectator sports 238-240
Spreckels, Adolph 23
Spreckels Lake 91
Spreckels Mansion 23, 93
Stairway Walks in San Francisco 78
stairways 78
Stanford, Leland 10, 22, 81
Stanford University 28, **286**
Stanley, Owsley 14
Steel, Danielle 23, 25, 28
Stegner, Wallace 28
Stein, Gertrude 25, 26
Steinbeck, John 14
Steinhart Aquarium 90, **196**
Stephen Wirtz Gallery 208
Stern Grove Festival 102, **191**
Stevenson, Robert Louis 25, 81, 259
Stick-Eastlake style 22
Stockton Street 72-73
Stone, Robert 28
Stow Lake 91
Strauss, Joseph 96
Strauss, Levi 10
Strawberry Hill 91
Strybing Arboretum & Botanical Gardens 90
study 285
Subterraneans, The 27
Sugar Pine Point State Park 267
Sullivan, Dennis 11
Summer Art Walk 203
Summer of Love **13**, *13*, 14, 87
Summer Solstice 190
Sunset District, the 102
  cafés 147
  restaurants 140-141
surfing 246-247
Sutro Baths 22, **101**
Sutro Heights Park 101
Sutro, Adolph 10, 22, 101
Sutter, John 8
swimming 247
Symphony Orchestra, San Francisco 66, **226**

Tales of the City 28
Tamales Bay 255
Tan, Amy 28
Tattoo Art Museum 112, *112*
taxis 272, 274-275
Teatro ZinZanni 62
Telegraph Avenue 104
Telegraph Hill 76
telephones 286-287
Tenderloin, the **63-65**, 148

accommodation 37-41
restaurants 114-117
theatres 223
tennis 247
theatre 222-225
experimental 224
mainstream 222
regional 222-223
Tet Festival 194
Theatre on the Square 223
Thin Man, The 26
3Com Park 210, 238, 241
Tiburon 253
tickets & information
film 199
nightlife 210
performing arts 221
sport 238
Tilden Regional Park 104
tipping 287
Tix Bay Area booth 56
toilets 287-288
Toklas, Alice B 26
top five museums 106
top ten sights 53
tourist information 287
tours 52-53
Towering Inferno, The 59
transgender 236
Transamerica Pyramid 24, *57*, 57, **61**, 62
transport, late-night 210
Treasure Island 75
Trips Out of Town **249-270**
best, the 250
children 198
Heading East 267-270
Heading North 251-255
Heading South 262-266
museums 111
music venues 227
wine country 256-261
Truckee 267
Twain, Mark 9, 25, 57
23 Street Urban Hike 78
Twin Peaks 80
Twin Peaks Bar 86

U

Union Square **56-57**, 159, 160, 186
accommodation 30-35
cafés 142-143
restaurants 114-117
Union Street 94
United Nations charter 13
United Nations Plaza 66
University of California, Berkeley 104, *104*, **286**
Upper Fillmore Street 93
Upper Market 148
USS Pampanito 77, **79**, 197

V

Valencia Street 84
Vallejo Street Stairway 79
Vertigo 85, 98, 199, *199*
Veterans' Memorial Building 66
Vietnam War 14
views 80-81
visas 288
Visitor Information Center, San Francisco 56, 105, 188, 256, **287**
Vista Point 251
volleyball 247

W

Wah Lee 10
Waldman, Ayelet 28
Walker, Alice 28
walks/walking 276
Along the waterfront **94**, 244
Barbary Coast Trail **12**, 55
City Guides 54
Cruisin' the Castro **54**, 228
Dashiell Hammett Walking Tour 55
Flower Power Walking Tour **54**, 87
Friends of Recreations and Parks 54
Glorious Food Culinary Walktours: Chinatown 54
Hayes Valley crawl 175
History Walkabouts 55
Hobnob Tours 54
Javawalk 55
Mangia! North Beach Tour 55
murals 83, 203, **204-207**
neighbourhood walks 54-55
Pacific Heights Walking Tour 55
San Francisco Ghost Hunt 55
San Francisco Then… and Now 55
stairways 78
themed walks 55
Victorian Home Walk 55
Wok Wiz Chinatown Tour 54
War Memorial Opera House 12, 23, 65, 66, 221, 225, **226**
Warfield Theater 211
Washington Square *73*, 75
waterfront, along the (walk) **94**, 244
Waters, Alice 104
Wave Organ 95
Waverley Place 73
Wax Museum 76
weather 66-67
websites 290
Wells Fargo History Museum 59, **112**
Wenner, Jann 14
Wentworth Alley 73
Westerfield House 88
Western Addition, the 88-92
accommodation 47-48
Westin St Francis Hotel 56
whale watching 247-248
Whalen, Philip 27
What is Remembered 26
White, Dan 15, 65
White Night Riot 15
Wilder, Laura Ingalls 79
Wilhelmina Tulip Garden 91
windsurfing 248
wine country 256-261
wineries 256-259, 264, 265
Winterland 89
Wolfe, Tom 25, 28
Woman's Building 84
Women's International Film Festival, MadCat 202
work permits 288
World War I 11
World War II 13, 70, 251
Wormser-Coleman House 22
Wrecker, The 25
Wright, Frank Lloyd 24, 57, 253

Y

Yerba Buena 8
Yerba Buena Center for the Arts 69, 106, **107**, 201
Yerba Buena Center for the Arts Theater 69, **224**
Yerba Buena Gardens Complex 68, *68*
Yerba Buena Island 75, 97
yoga 248
Yosemite National Park *268*, 270
Yosemite Valley 270
Yuppie Eradication Project 20

Z

Zeum 69, **197**, *197*
Zoo, San Francisco 102, **196**
zoos 195-196
Zwigoff, Terry 199

Advertisers' Index

Please refer to the relevant pages for addresses and telephone numbers.

Pearl Paint **IFC**

In Context

timeout.com **4**

Accommodation

Hotel Nikko San Francisco **32**
Comfort Inn by the Bay **36**
Grant Plaza Hotel **36**
First Internet Travel **40**

Sightseeing

Stomp **58**
Beach Blanket Babylon **58**
CityPass **64**
Ghirardelli Square **64**
111 Minna Street Gallery **108**

Restaurants

Harris' Restaurant **116**
Back Flip **120**
Calzone's/Crab House/The Stinking Rose **124**
TONY Eating & Drinking Guide **128**

Shops & Services

Good Vibrations **162**
SummerStage **162**

Time Out City Guides **IBC**

Points of interest .....

Hospital or college .....

Neighbourhoods ..... FILLMORE

Visitor Information Center .....

Muni Metro BART station .....

Parks .....

Cable car line ..... (PH)

0 1/4 1/2 mile

0 500 m

Maps

BART & Muni map	300
Bay Area	302
City Overview	303
San Francisco by Area	304
San Francisco street maps	306
Berkeley street map	315
Street Index	316

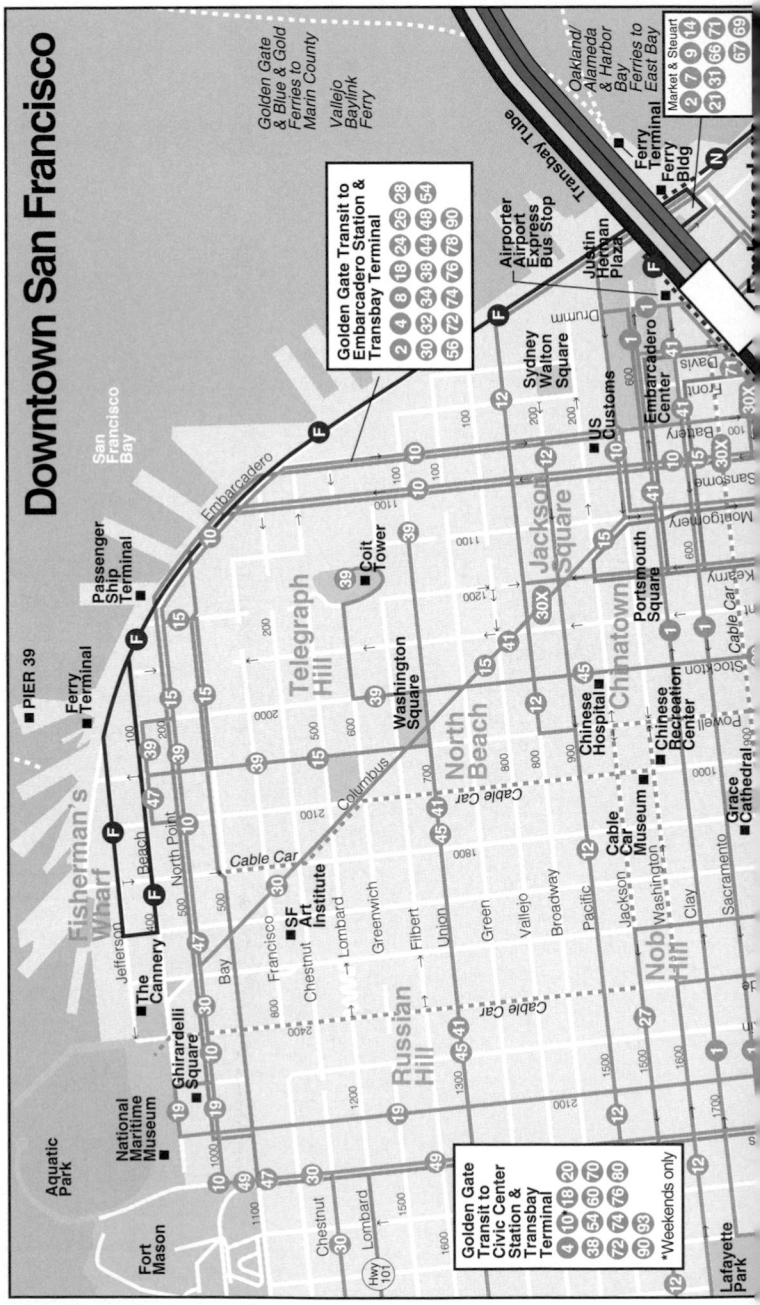
Downtown San Francisco
PIER 39
Ferry Terminal
Passenger Ship Terminal
San Francisco Bay
Fisherman's Wharf
Aquatic Park
National Maritime Museum
Fort Mason
The Cannery
Ghirardelli Square
Jefferson
Beach
North Point
Bay
Embarcadero
Cable Car
Columbus
Telegraph Hill
Coit Tower
Washington Square
North Beach
Russian Hill
Francisco
Chestnut
SF Art Institute
Lombard
Greenwich
Filbert
Union
Green
Vallejo
Broadway
Pacific
Jackson
Washington
Clay
Sacramento
Cable Car Museum
Chinese Hospital
Chinatown
Jackson Square
Portsmouth Square
Chinese Recreation Center
Grace Cathedral
Sydney Walton Square
US Customs
Embarcadero Center
Drumm
Davis
Front
Battery
Sansome
Montgomery
Kearny
Stockton
Powell
Hwy 101
Lafayette Park
Nob Hill
Golden Gate Transit to Civic Center Station & Transbay Terminal
4 10 18 20
38 54 60 70
72 74 76 80
90 93
*Weekends only
Golden Gate Transit to Embarcadero Station & Transbay Terminal
2 4 8 18 24 26 28
30 32 34 38 44 48 54
56 72 74 76 78 80
Golden Gate & Blue & Gold Ferries to Marin County
Vallejo Baylink Ferry
Transbay Tube
Airporter Airport Express Bus Stop
Justin Herman Plaza
Ferry Terminal
Ferry Bldg
Oakland/ Alameda & Harbor Bay Ferries to East Bay
Market & Steuart
2 7 9 14
21 31 66 71
67 69

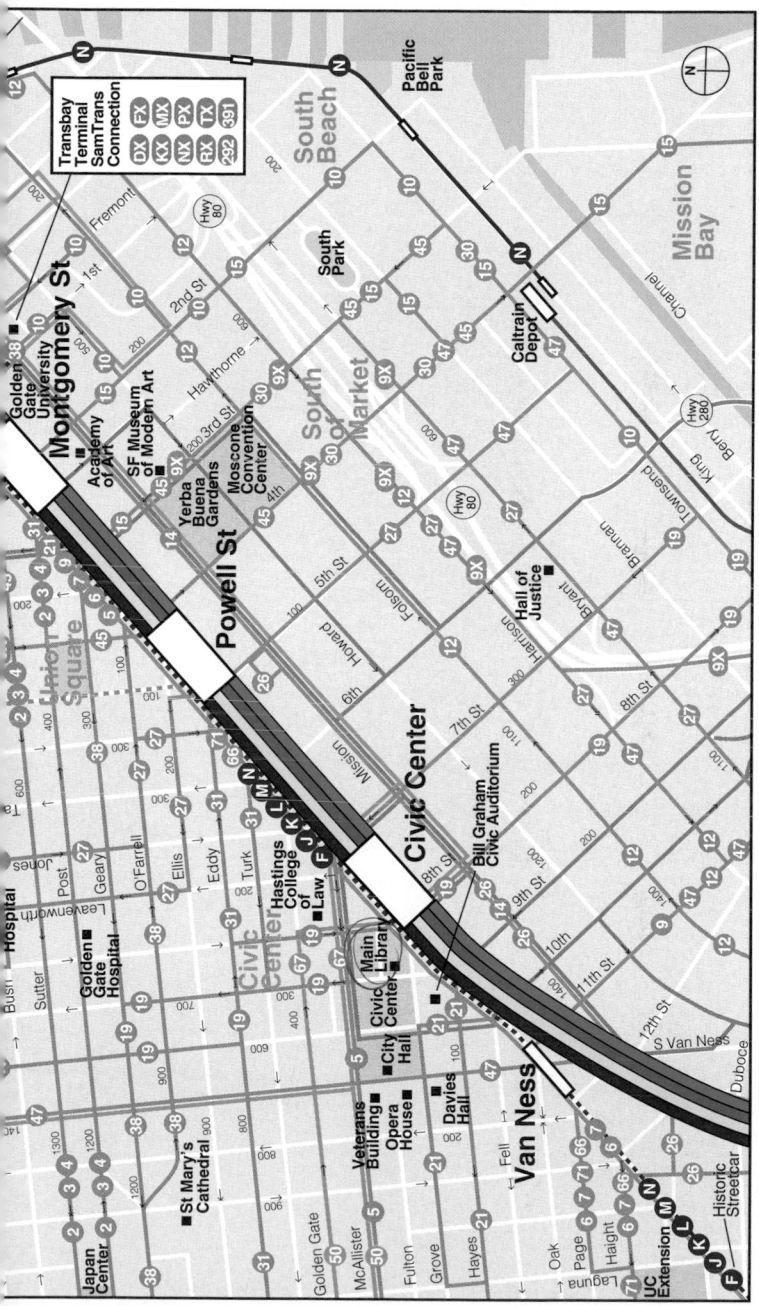

BART/reineckandreineck.com

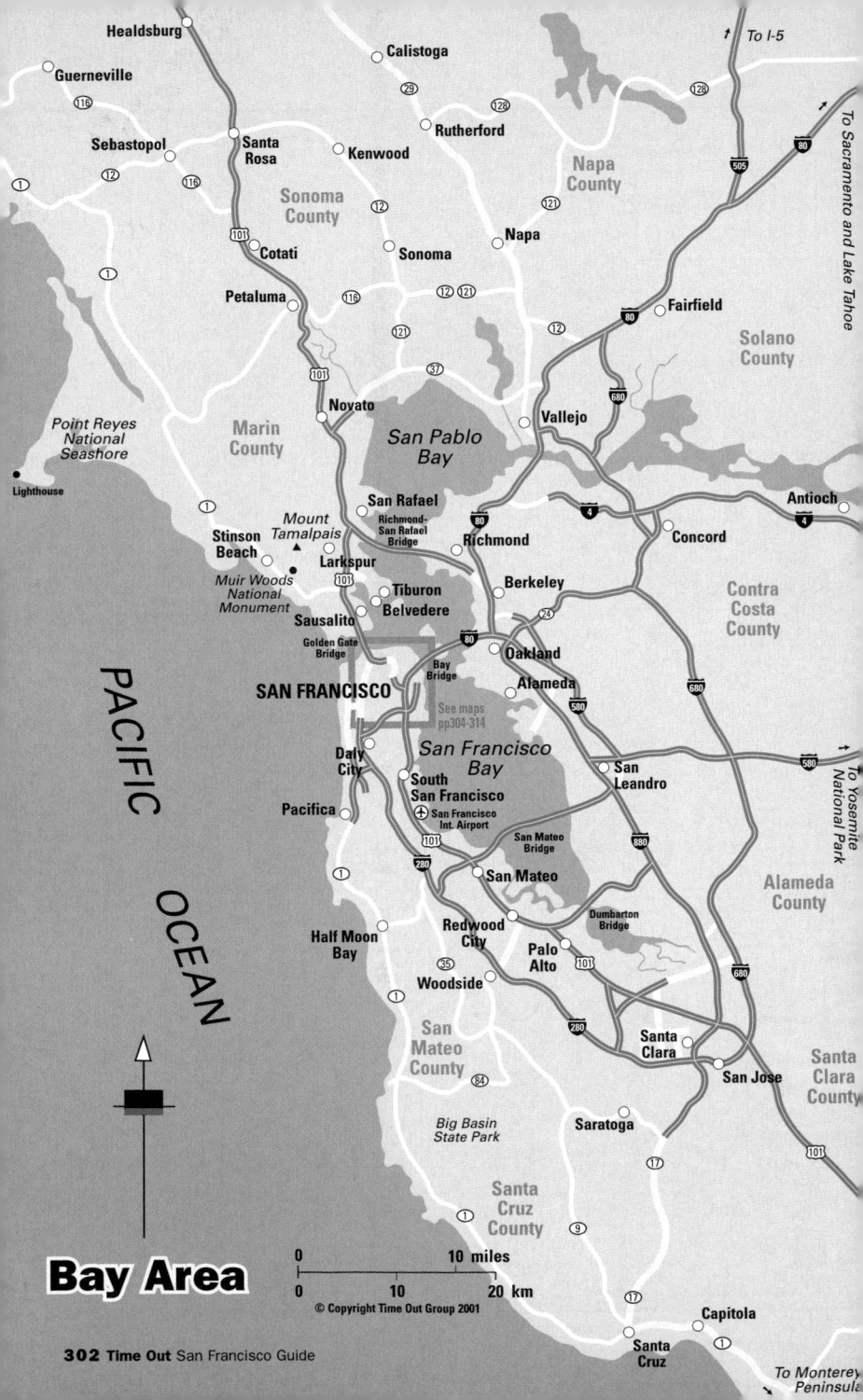
Healdsburg
Calistoga
To I-5
Guerneville
Rutherford
Sebastopol
Santa Rosa
Kenwood
Napa County
To Sacramento and Lake Tahoe
Sonoma County
Napa
Cotati
Sonoma
Petaluma
Fairfield
Solano County
Novato
Vallejo
Point Reyes National Seashore
Marin County
San Pablo Bay
Lighthouse
San Rafael
Antioch
Mount Tamalpais
Richmond-San Rafael Bridge
Richmond
Concord
Stinson Beach
Larkspur
Muir Woods National Monument
Tiburon
Berkeley
Belvedere
Contra Costa County
Sausalito
Golden Gate Bridge
Oakland
Bay Bridge
SAN FRANCISCO
Alameda
See maps pp304-314
PACIFIC
San Francisco Bay
Daly City
San Leandro
To Yosemite National Park
South San Francisco
Pacifica
San Francisco Int. Airport
San Mateo Bridge
San Mateo
Alameda County
OCEAN
Dumbarton Bridge
Half Moon Bay
Redwood City
Palo Alto
Woodside
San Mateo County
Santa Clara
San Jose
Santa Clara County
Big Basin State Park
Saratoga
Santa Cruz County
0 10 miles
0 10 20 km
© Copyright Time Out Group 2001
Capitola
Santa Cruz
To Monterey Peninsula

Bay Area

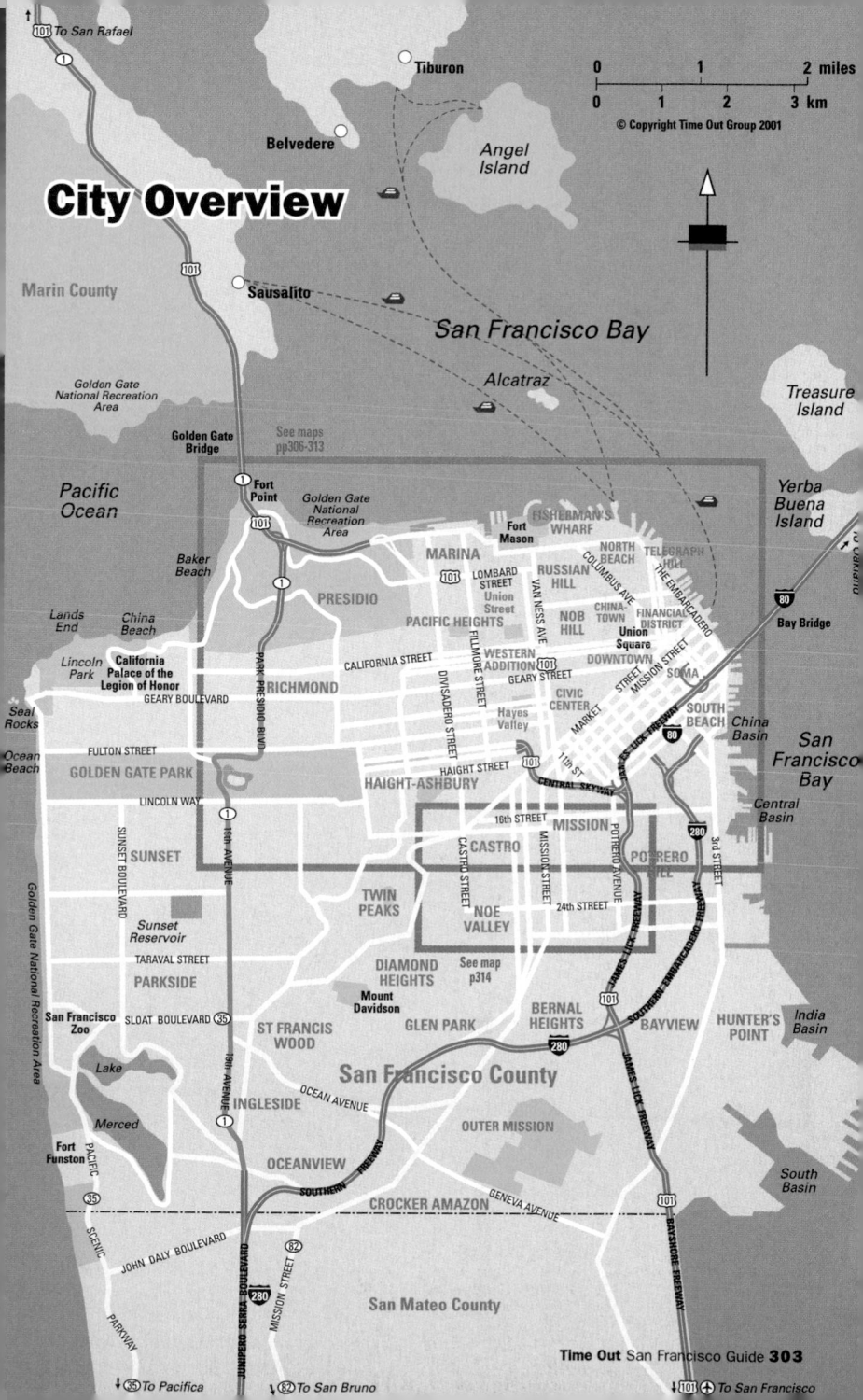
City Overview
0 1 2 miles
0 1 2 3 km
© Copyright Time Out Group 2001
To San Rafael
Tiburon
Belvedere
Angel Island
Marin County
Sausalito
San Francisco Bay
Alcatraz
Treasure Island
Golden Gate National Recreation Area
Golden Gate Bridge
See maps pp306-313
Pacific Ocean
Fort Point
Golden Gate National Recreation Area
Yerba Buena Island
Fort Mason
FISHERMAN'S WHARF
Baker Beach
MARINA
NORTH BEACH
TELEGRAPH HILL
RUSSIAN HILL
LOMBARD STREET
Union Street
PRESIDIO
PACIFIC HEIGHTS
NOB HILL
CHINA-TOWN
FINANCIAL DISTRICT
THE EMBARCADERO
Bay Bridge
To Oakland
Lands End
China Beach
Lincoln Park
California Palace of the Legion of Honor
CALIFORNIA STREET
WESTERN ADDITION
Union Square
DOWNTOWN
GEARY STREET
MISSION STREET
SOMA
RICHMOND
GEARY BOULEVARD
CIVIC CENTER
Hayes Valley
MARKET STREET
SOUTH BEACH
China Basin
Seal Rocks
Ocean Beach
FULTON STREET
GOLDEN GATE PARK
HAIGHT-ASHBURY
HAIGHT STREET
11th ST
CENTRAL SEAWAY
San Francisco Bay
Central Basin
LINCOLN WAY
16th STREET
MISSION
SUNSET
CASTRO
POTRERO HILL
3rd STREET
TWIN PEAKS
NOE VALLEY
24th STREET
Sunset Reservoir
TARAVAL STREET
PARKSIDE
DIAMOND HEIGHTS
See map p314
Mount Davidson
BERNAL HEIGHTS
BAYVIEW
HUNTER'S POINT
India Basin
San Francisco Zoo
SLOAT BOULEVARD
ST FRANCIS WOOD
GLEN PARK
Lake
San Francisco County
INGLESIDE
OCEAN AVENUE
Merced
OUTER MISSION
Fort Funston
OCEANVIEW
South Basin
CROCKER AMAZON
GENEVA AVENUE
JOHN DAILY BOULEVARD
San Mateo County
To Pacifica
To San Bruno
To San Francisco

San Francisco by Area

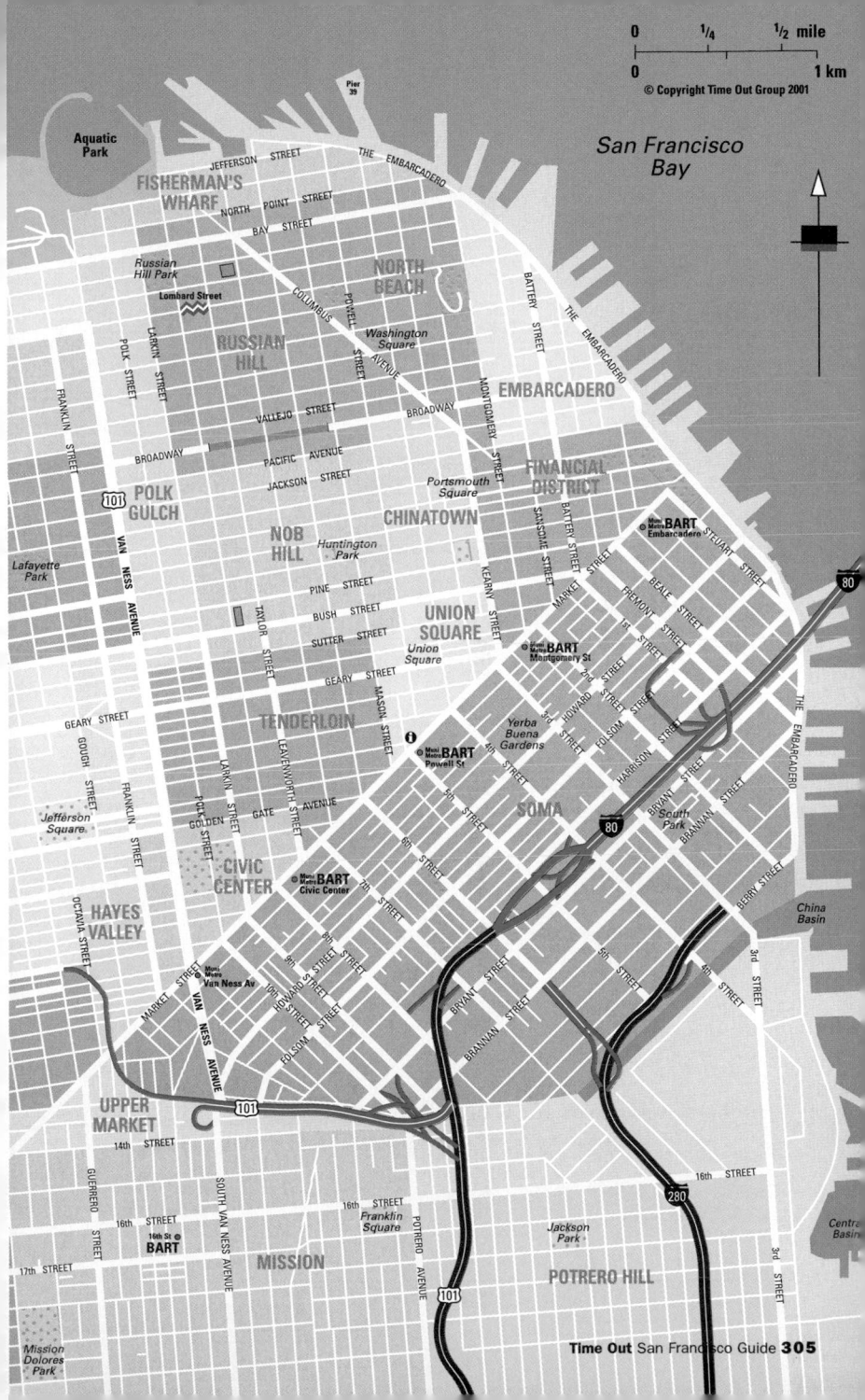
0 1/4 1/2 mile
0 1 km
© Copyright Time Out Group 2001
San Francisco Bay
Aquatic Park
Pier 39
FISHERMAN'S WHARF
JEFFERSON STREET
THE EMBARCADERO
NORTH POINT STREET
BAY STREET
Russian Hill Park
Lombard Street
NORTH BEACH
COLUMBUS AVENUE
POWELL STREET
Washington Square
RUSSIAN HILL
POLK STREET
LARKIN STREET
FRANKLIN STREET
VALLEJO STREET
BROADWAY
PACIFIC AVENUE
JACKSON STREET
BATTERY STREET
MONTGOMERY STREET
EMBARCADERO
FINANCIAL DISTRICT
Portsmouth Square
POLK GULCH
101
VAN NESS AVENUE
CHINATOWN
NOB HILL
Huntington Park
Lafayette Park
SANSOME STREET
Muni Metro BART Embarcadero
STEUART STREET
80
PINE STREET
BUSH STREET
SUTTER STREET
TAYLOR STREET
UNION SQUARE
Union Square
KEARNY STREET
Muni Metro BART Montgomery St
MARKET STREET
BEALE STREET
FREMONT STREET
1st STREET
2nd STREET
HOWARD STREET
FOLSOM STREET
HARRISON STREET
BRYANT STREET
BRANNAN STREET
THE EMBARCADERO
GEARY STREET
MASON STREET
TENDERLOIN
Yerba Buena Gardens
Muni Metro BART Powell St
4th STREET
GOUGH STREET
LARKIN STREET
LEAVENWORTH STREET
GATE AVENUE
Jefferson Square
GOLDEN GATE STREET
SOMA
South Park
5th STREET
6th STREET
7th STREET
8th STREET
9th STREET
CIVIC CENTER
Muni Metro BART Civic Center
HAYES VALLEY
OCTAVIA STREET
BERRY STREET
China Basin
3rd STREET
Muni Metro Van Ness Av
MARKET STREET
VAN NESS AVENUE
101
HOWARD STREET
FOLSOM STREET
BRYANT STREET
BRANNAN STREET
UPPER MARKET
14th STREET
16th STREET
280
GUERRERO STREET
16th St BART
SOUTH VAN NESS AVENUE
Franklin Square
POTRERO AVENUE
Jackson Park
17th STREET
MISSION
POTRERO HILL
Mission Dolores Park

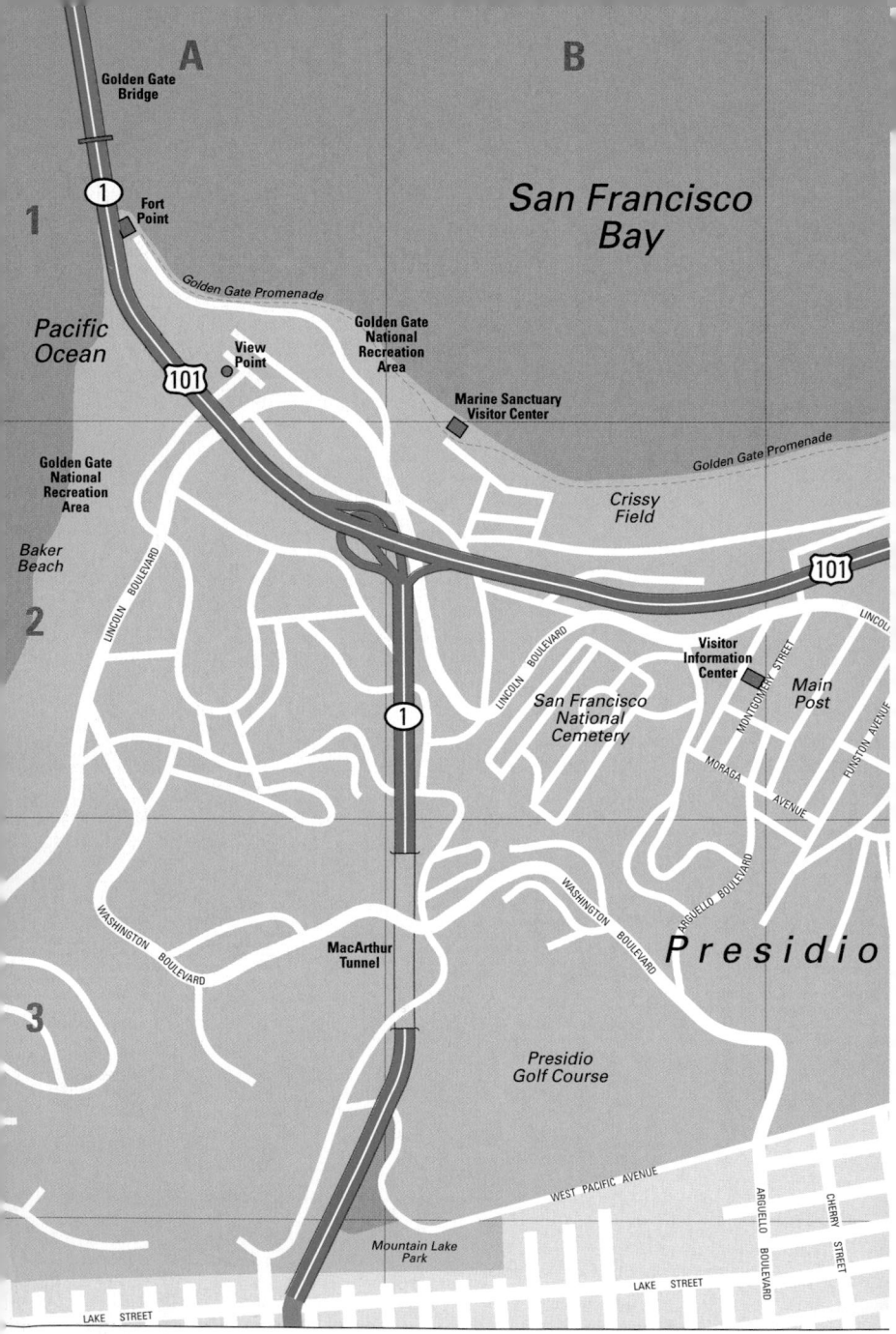

pp306-307
pp308-309
pp312-313
pp310-311

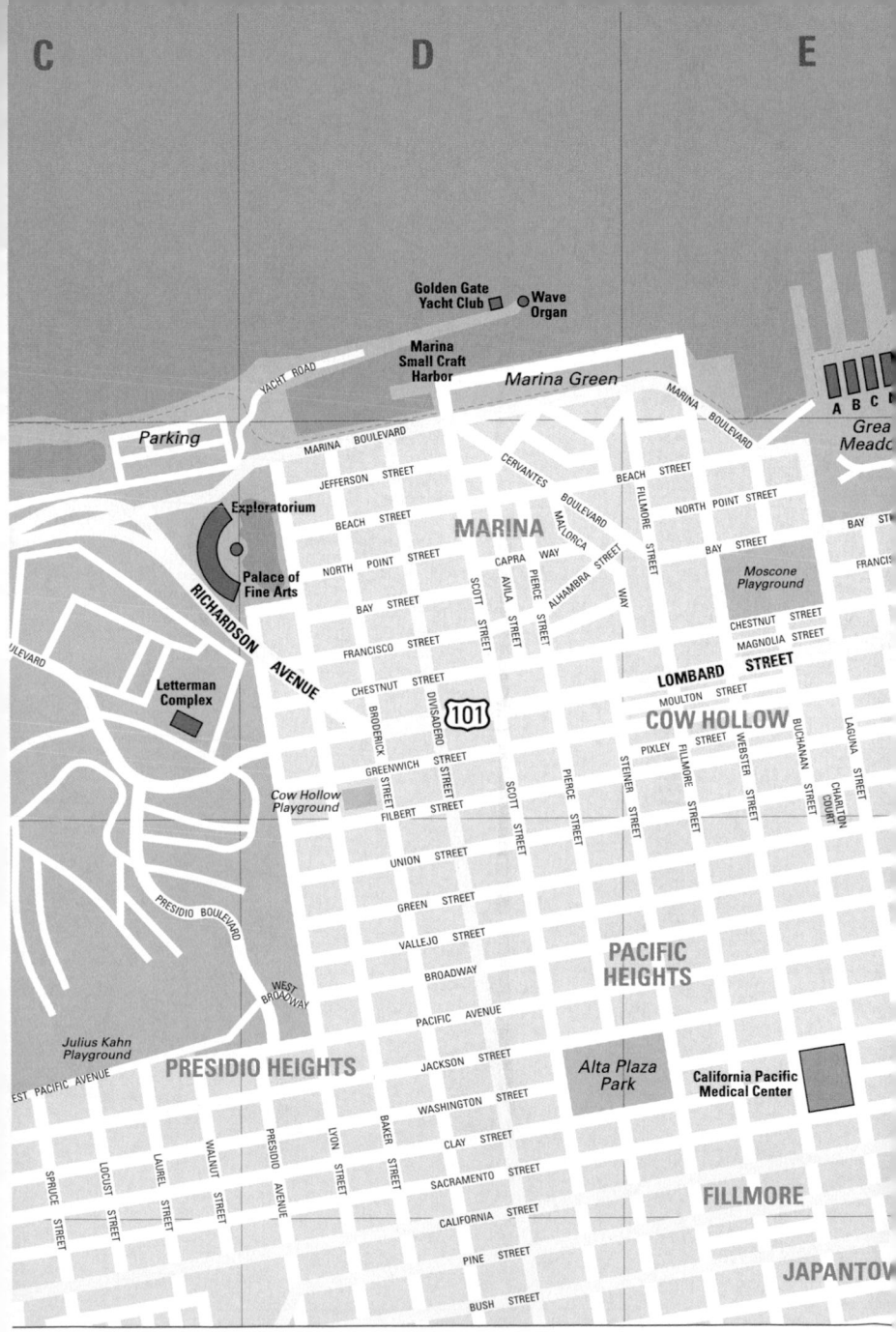

© Copyright Time Out Group 2001

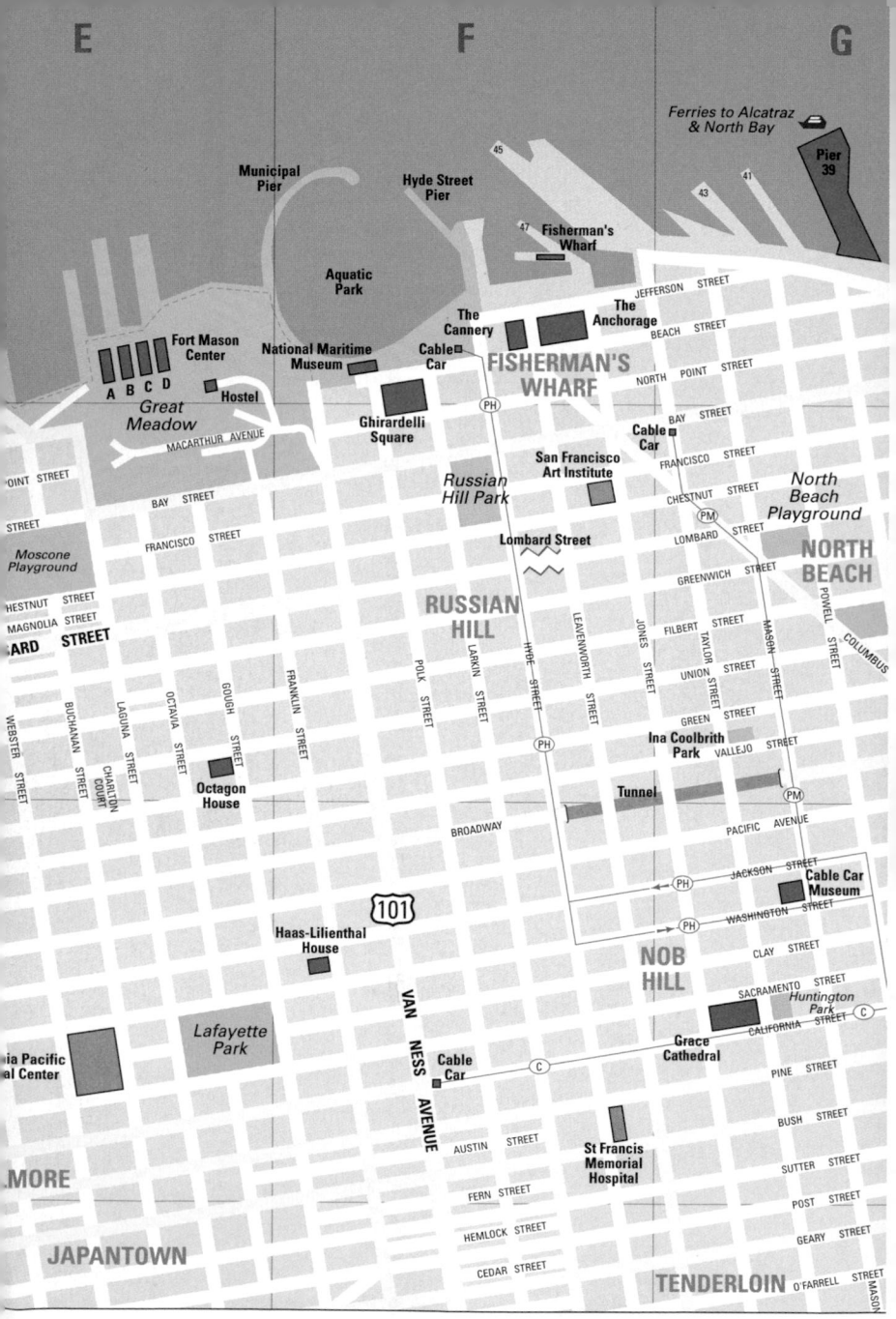

pp306-307
pp308-309
pp312-313
pp310-311

© Copyright Time Out Group 2001

pp306-307
pp308-309
pp312-313
pp310-311

0 1/4 1/2 mile

0 500 m

© Copyright Time Out Group 2001

pp306-307
pp308-309
pp312-313
pp310-311

0 ¼ ½ mile

0 500 m

© Copyright Time Out Group 2001

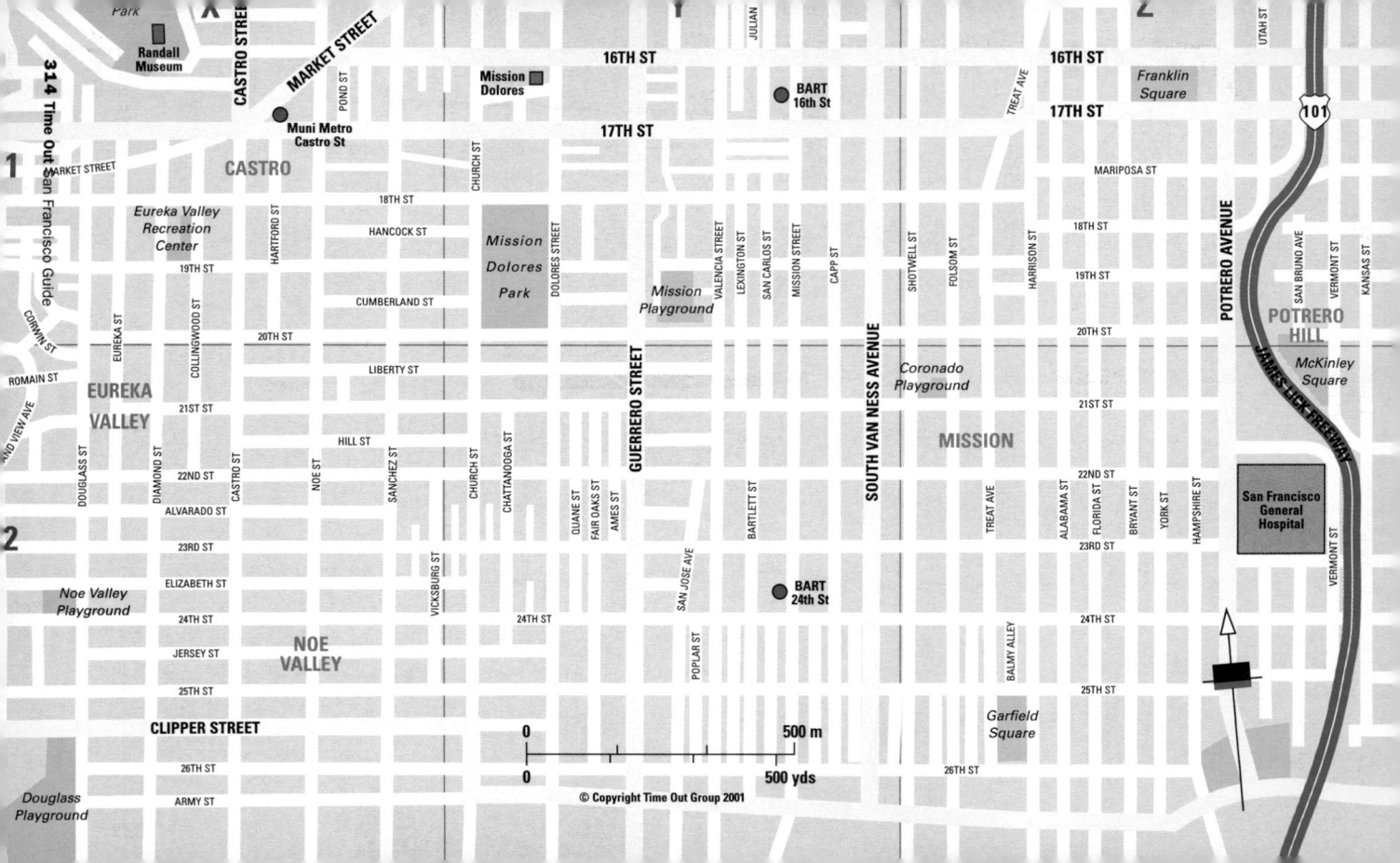
Park
Randall Museum
CASTRO STREET
MARKET STREET
POND ST
Muni Metro Castro St
Mission Dolores
16TH ST
JULIAN
BART 16th St
TREAT AVE
16TH ST
Franklin Square
UTAH ST
17TH ST
17TH ST
101
MARKET STREET
CASTRO
CHURCH ST
MARIPOSA ST
Eureka Valley Recreation Center
18TH ST
HANCOCK ST
HARTFORD ST
Mission Dolores Park
DOLORES STREET
Mission Playground
VALENCIA STREET
LEXINGTON ST
SAN CARLOS ST
MISSION STREET
CAPP ST
SHOTWELL ST
FOLSOM ST
HARRISON ST
18TH ST
POTRERO AVENUE
SAN BRUNO AVE
VERMONT ST
KANSAS ST
19TH ST
19TH ST
CUMBERLAND ST
CORWIN ST
EUREKA ST
COLLINGWOOD ST
20TH ST
20TH ST
POTRERO HILL
ROMAIN ST
LIBERTY ST
GUERRERO STREET
SOUTH VAN NESS AVENUE
Coronado Playground
McKinley Square
EUREKA VALLEY
21ST ST
21ST ST
AND VIEW AVE
HILL ST
MISSION
DOUGLASS ST
DIAMOND ST
22ND ST
CASTRO ST
NOE ST
SANCHEZ ST
CHURCH ST
CHATTANOOGA ST
QUANE ST
FAIR OAKS ST
AMES ST
BARTLETT ST
TREAT AVE
ALABAMA ST
FLORIDA ST
BRYANT ST
YORK ST
HAMPSHIRE ST
22ND ST
San Francisco General Hospital
ALVARADO ST
23RD ST
23RD ST
VERMONT ST
ELIZABETH ST
VICKSBURG ST
SAN JOSE AVE
BART 24th St
Noe Valley Playground
24TH ST
24TH ST
24TH ST
JERSEY ST
NOE VALLEY
POPLAR ST
BALMY ALLEY
25TH ST
25TH ST
CLIPPER STREET
Garfield Square
0
500 m
0
500 yds
26TH ST
26TH ST
Douglass Playground
ARMY ST
© Copyright Time Out Group 2001

© Copyright Time Out Group 2001

Street Index to San Francisco

1st Street – p309 H3, p311 H3
2nd Avenue – p312 B4/C6
2nd Street – p311 H4
3rd Avenue – p312 B5
3rd Street – p311 H4/J6
4th Avenue – p312 B4/B6
4th Street – p311 H4/J5
5th Avenue – p312 B5
5th Street – p311 G4/H5
6th Avenue – p312 B4/B6
6th Street – p311 G4/H6
7th Avenue – p312 B5
7th Street – p310 G5, p311 H6
8th Avenue – p312 B4/B
8th Street – p310 G5, p311 H5
9th Avenue – p312 B5
9th Street – p310 G5
10th Avenue – p312 B4/B6
10th Street – p310 G5
11th Avenue – p312 B5
12th Avenue – p312 A4/B6
12th Street – p310 F5
13th Avenue – p312 A5
14th Avenue – p312 A4/A6
14th Street – p310 F6, p313 E6
15th Avenue – p312 A5
15th Street – p310 F6, p311 H6, p313 D6, p314 Z1
16th Avenue – p312 A4/A6
16th Street – p310 F6/G6, p311 J6, p314 Y1/Z1
17th Avenue – p312 A5
17th Street – p310 E6, p311H6, p313 C6/D6, p314 Y1/Z1
18th Avenue – p312 A4/A6
18th Street – p310 F6, p314 X1/Z1
19th Avenue – p312 A5
19th Street – p314 X1/Z1
20th Avenue – p312 A4/A6
20th Street – p314 X1/Z1
21st Avenue – p312 A5
21st Street – p314 X2/Z2
22nd Avenue – p312 A6
22nd Street – p314 X2/Z2
23rd Street – p314 X2/Z2
24th Street – p314 X2/Z2
25th Street – p314 X2

Alabama Street – p310 G6, p314 Z2
Albion Street – p310 F6
Alhambra Street – p307 D2
Alvarado Street – p314 X2
Ames Street – p314 Y2
Anza Street – p312 A5/B5, p313 C4
Anza Vista Avenue – p313 D4
Arguello Boulevard – p306 B3, p312 B3/C5
Arkansas Street – p311 H6
Ash Street – p310 E/F5
Ashbury Street – p313 D6
Austin Street – p308 F3
Avila Street – p307 D2

Baker Street – p307 D3, p313 D3/D5
Balboa Street – p312 A5/B5
Balmy Alley – p314 Z2
Bartlett Street – p314 Y2
Battery Street – p309 H2/H3
Bay Street – p307 D2/E2, p308 E2/G2
Beach Street – p307 D2/E2, p308 G1
Beale Street – p309 H3
Belvedere Street – p313 C/D6
Berry Street – p311 H5/J5
Birch Street – p310 E/F5
Boardman Place – p311 H5
Brady Street – p310 F5
Brannan Street – p311 H5/J4
Broadway – p307 D3, p308 F3, p309 G2
Broderick Street – p307 D2
Brosnan Street – p310 F6
Bryant Street – p311 G/H5/J4, p314 Z2
Buchanan Street – p308 E2, p310 E4
Buena Vista Avenue – p313 D6
Buena Vista Avenue West – p313 D6
Buena Vista Terrace East – p313 D6
Bush Street – p309 G3, p311 G4, p313 D4

Cabrillo Street – p312 A5/B5
California Street – p308 G3, p312 A4/B4, p313 D4
Capp Street – p314 Y1
Capra Way – p307 D2
Carl Street – p313 C6
Carolina Street – p311 H6
Castro Street – p313 E6, p314 X1/X2
Cedar Street – p310 F4
Central Avenue – p313 D5
Cervantes Boulevard – p307 D2
Charlton Court – p308 E2
Chattanooga Street – p314 Y2
Cherry Street – p306 C3
Chestnut Street – p307 D2/E2, p308 E2/G2
China Basin Street – p311 J5/J6
Church Street – p310 E6, p314 Y1/Y2
Clara Street – p311 H4
Claude Lane – p309 H3
Clay Street – p307 D3, p308 G3
Clayton Street – p313 D6
Clement Street – p312 A4/B4
Clementina Street – p311 H4
Clifford Terrace – p313 D6
Clinton Street – p310 F6
Cole Street – p313 C6
Collingwood Street – p314 X1/2
Collins Street – p313 C4
Columbus Avenue – p308/309 G2
Commercial Street – p309 H3
Commonwealth Avenue – p312 C4
Connecticut Street – p311 H6
Cornwall Street – p312 B4
Corwin Street – p314 X1/2
Cumberland Street – p314 X1

Davis Street – p309 H2/H3
De Haro Street – p311 H6
Delmar Street – p313 D6
Diamond Street – p314 X2
Divisadero Street – p307 D2, p313 D/E5
Division Street – p311 H6
Dolores Street – p310 F6, p314 Y1
Dore Street – p310 G5
Douglass Street – p314 X2
Downey Street – p313 D6
Drumm Street – p309 H3
Duboce Avenue – p310 E6, p313 E6

Eddy Street – p313 D4/G4
Elizabeth Street – p314 X2
Ellis Street – p313 D4, p310 G4
Elm Street – p310 F4
Embarcadero, The – p308 G1, p309 H2, p311 J4
Eureka Street – p314 X1/2

Fair Oaks Street – p314 Y2
Fell Street – p310 E5/F5, p313 C5/E5
Fern Street – p308 F3
Filbert Street – p307 D2, p308 G2
Fillmore Street – p307 E2, p310 E4/5
Florida Street – p310 G6, p314 Z2
Folsom Street – p310 G5, p311 H4, p314 Z1
Francisco Street – p307 D2, p308 E2/G2
Franklin Street – p308 F2, p310 F4
Frederick Street – p313 C6
Freelon Street – p311 H5
Fremont Street – p309 H3
Front Street – p309 H2/H3
Fulton Street – p312 A5/B5, p313 C5/D5
Funston Avenue – p306 C2

Geary Boulevard – p312 A4/B4, p313 C4
Geary Expressway – p310 E4
Geary Street – p310 G4
Gilbert Street – p311 H5
Gold Street – p309 H2
Golden Gate Avenue – p310 F4, p313 C5/D5
Gough Street – p308 E2, p310 F4/F5
Grace Street – p310 G5
Grand View Avenue – p314 X2
Grant Avenue – p309 G2/G/H3,
Green Street – p307 D3, p308 G2
Greenwich Street – p307 D2, p308 G2
Grove Street – p310 E/F5, p313 C5/D5
Guerrero Street – p310 F6, p314 Y1

Haight Street – p310 E5, p313 C6/E5
Hampshire Street – p311 G6, p314 Z2
Hancock Street – p314 X1
Harriet Street – p311 G5/H5
Harrison Street – p310 G5, p311 H5/H4, p314 Z1
Hartford Street – p310 E6, p314 X1
Hawthorne Street – p311 H4
Hayes Street – p310 E5, p313 C5/E5
Heather Avenue – p313 C4
Hemlock Street – p310 F4
Henry Street – p313 E6
Hermann Street – p310 E5
Hickory Street – p310 E5
Hill Street – p314 X2
Homestead Street – p314 X2
Hooper Street – p311 H6
Howard Street – p309 H4, p310 G5, p311 H4
Hubbell Street – p311 H6
Hugo Street – p312 B6
Hyde Street – p308 F2, p310 G4

Illinois Street – p311 J6
Indiana Street – p311 J6
Iris Avenue – p313 C4
Irving Street – p312 A6/B6
Irwin Street – p311 H6

Jack Kerouac Alley – p309 G2
Jackson Street – p307 D3, p308 G3
James Lick Freeway – p314 Z2
Jefferson Street – p307 D2, p308 F/G1
Jersey Street – p314 X2
John F Kennedy Drive – p312 B5
Jones Street – p308 F2, p310 G4
Jordan Avenue – p312 C4
Judah Street – p312 A6/B6
Julian Street – p314 Y1

Kansas Street – p311 H6, p314 Z1
Kearny Street – p309 G2/H3
Kezar Drive – p312/313 C6
King Street – p311 H5/J4

Lafayette Street – p310 F5
Laguna Street – p308 E2, p310 E4
Lake Street – p312 A4/B4
Langton Street – p310/311 G5
Larkin Street – p308 F2, p310 F4
Laurel Street – p307 C3, p313 C4
Leavenworth Street – p308 F2, p310 G4
Lexington Street – p314 Y1
Liberty Street – p314 X2
Lily Street – p310 F5
Lincoln Boulevard – p306 A2/C2
Lincoln Way – p312 A6/B6
Linden Street – p310 E/F5
Locust Street – p307 C3
Lombard Street – p307 E2, p308 G2
Lyon Street – p307 D3, p313 D5

MacArthur Avenue – p308 E2
Magnolia Street – p307 E2
Maiden Lane – p309 G/H3
Main Street – p309 J3
Mallorca Way – p307 D2
Manzanita Avenue – p313 C4
Maple Street – p306 C3
Marina Boulevard – p307 D2/E1
Mariposa Street – p314 Z1
Market Street – p309 H3, p310 E6/F5, p311 F4, p313 D6,
Martin Luther King Jr Drive – p312 B6
Mary Street – p311 G4
Mason Street – p308 G2, p310 G4
Masonic Avenue – p313 D4/D5/D6
Maybeck Twin Drive – p315 N1
McAllister Street – p310 F4, p312 C5, p313 D5
McCoppin Street – p310 F5
Minna Street – p309 H3, p310 F5, p311 G4
Minnesota Street – p311 J6
Mission Street – p309 H3, p310 F5/F6, p311 G4, p314 Y1
Mission Rock Street – p311 J5
Mississippi Street – p311 H6
Missouri Street – p311 H6
Montgomery Street (Presidio) – p306 B2
Montgomery Street (Financial District) – p309 H2/H3
Moraga Avenue – p306 B2
Moss Street – p311 G5
Moulton Street – p307 E2
Museum Way – p313 D6
Myrtle Street – p310 F4

Natoma Street – p309 H3, p310 F5, p311 G4
New Montgomery Street – p309 H3/4, p311 H3/4
Noe Street – p310 E6, p314 X2
North Point Street – p307 D2/E2, p308 G1

Oak Street – p310 E5, p313 C5/E5
Octavia Street – p308 E2, p310 F4/5
O'Farrell Street – p308 G4, p310 G4, p313 D4
Olive Street – p310 F4
Owens Street – p311 H6

Pacific Avenue – p307 D3, p308 G3
Page Street – p310 E5, p313 C5/E5
Palm Avenue – p312 C4
Park Presidio Boulevard – p312 A4
Parker Avenue – p313 C4
Parnassus Avenue – p313 C6
Pearl Street – p310 F5
Pennsylvania Avenue – p311 J6
Pierce Street – p307 D2, p313 E4/5
Pine Street – p308 G3, p313 D4
Pixley Street – p308 E2
Polk Street – p308 F2, p310 F4
Pond Street – p313 E6, p314 X1
Poplar Street – p314 Y2
Portrero Avenue – p311 G6, p314 Z1
Post Street – p308 G3, p313 D4
Powell Street – p308 G2, p309 G3, p311 G4
Presidio Avenue – p307 D3
Presidio Boulevard – p307 C3

Quane Street – p314 Y2

Rhode Island Street – p311 H6
Richardson Avenue – p306 C2
Ritch Street – p311 H4
Romain Street – p314 X2
Romolo Place – p309 G2
Roosevelt Way – p313 D6
Rose Street – p310 F5
Rossi Avenue – p312 C5
Russ Street – p311 G5

Sacramento Street – p307 D3, p308 G3
San Bruno Avenue – p311 G6, p314 Z1
San Carlos Street – p314 Y1
San Jose Avenue – p314 Y2
Sanchez Street – p310 E6, p314 X2
Sansome Street – p309 H2/H3
Scott Street – p307 D2, p313 E4/5
Shipley Street – p311 H4
Shotwell Street – p310 F6, p314 Z1
Shrader Street – p313 C6
South Park Avenue – p311 H4/J4
South Van Ness Avenue – p310 F6
Spear Street – p309 J3
Spruce Street – p307 C3/4, p313 C4
St Joseph's Street – p313 D4
Stanyan Street – p313 C5/C6
States Street – p313 D6
Steiner Street – p307 E2, p310 E4/5, p313 E4/5
Steuart Street – p309 J3
Stevenson Street – p310 F5/G4
Stockton Street – p311 G2/G3/4, p311 G3/4
Sutter Street – p308 G3, p313 D4

Taylor Street – p308 G2, p310 G4
Tehama Street – p311 H4
Tennessee Street – p311 J6
Terra Vista Avenue – p313 D4
Texas Street – p311 H6
Townsend Street – p311 H5/J4
Treat Avenue – p310 G6, p314 Z2
Turk Street – p310 G4, p313 C5

Union Street – p307 D3, p308 G2
Upper Terrace – p313 D6
Utah Street – p311 G6, p314 Z1

Valencia Street – p310 F6, p314 Y1
Vallejo Street – p307 D3, p308 G2
Van Ness Avenue – p308 F3, p310 F5
Vermont Street – p311 H6, p314 Z1
Vicksburg Street – p314 X2

Waller Street – p310 E5, p313 C6/E5
Walnut Street – p307 C3
Washington Boulevard – p306 A3/B3
Washington Street – p307 D3
Waverly Place – p309 G3
Webster Street – p308 E2, p310 E4
Welsh Street – p311 H5
West Broadway – p307 D3
West Pacific Avenue – p306 B3, p307 C3
Willard Street North – p312 C5
Willow Street – p310 F4
Wisconsin Street – p311 H6

Yacht Road – p307 D1
York Street – p310 G6, p314 Z2